Contemporary Employment Relations

Contemporary Employment Relations

A Critical Introduction

Steve Williams and Derek Adam-Smith

OXFORD
UNIVERSITY PRESS

OXFORD

UNIVERSITY PRESS

Great Clarendon Street, Oxford OX2 6DP

Oxford University Press is a department of the University of Oxford.
It furthers the University's objective of excellence in research, scholarship,
and education by publishing worldwide in

Oxford New York

Auckland Cape Town Dar es Salaam Hong Kong Karachi
Kuala Lumpur Madrid Melbourne Mexico City Nairobi
New Delhi Shanghai Taipei Toronto

With offices in

Argentina Austria Brazil Chile Czech Republic France Greece
Guatemala Hungary Italy Japan Poland Portugal Singapore
South Korea Switzerland Thailand Turkey Ukraine Vietnam

Oxford is a registered trade mark of Oxford University Press
in the UK and in certain other countries

Published in the United States
by Oxford University Press Inc., New York

British Library Cataloguing in Publication Data
Data available

Library of Congress Cataloging in Publication Data
Data available

Typeset by Newgen Imaging Systems (P) Ltd., Chennai, India
Printed in Great Britain
on acid-free paper by
Ashford Colour Press Ltd., Gosport, Hampshire

ISBN 0–19–927243–3   978–0–19–927243–3

1 3 5 7 9 10 8 6 4 2

For Mary Williams and in memory of Roy Williams

■ ACKNOWLEDGEMENTS

We would like to thank our colleagues at the University of Portsmouth who helped with ideas, offered encouragement, and commented on some of the material in draft form: Richard Christy, Sarah Gilmore, Fiona Goss, Gill Norris, Peter Scott, and Roger Welch. Jane Stewart provided important administrative support. The university's library staff were particularly efficient at facilitating inter-library loan requests. Parts of the book benefited from discussions with postgraduate students: Rachel Suff, Mark Stevenson, Deborah Taylor, and Louise Alcott in particular. Samantha Bairstow's doctoral work on diversity and union representation was a constant source of stimulating ideas. We also thank Patrick McGovern of the London School of Economics for permission to cite his unpublished paper (co-written with Stephen Hill) on the status divide. We benefited from the exceptional support of Oxford University Press while working on the book. Patrick Brindle backed it enthusiastically at the outset. Subsequently, Angela Adams looked after the project splendidly. Her guidance was much appreciated. We received very helpful feedback on draft chapters from the publisher's reviewers: Gregor Gall, Mike Marshall, Stephen Perkins, and Karen Williams. Our thanks go to them. Finally, Steve Williams thanks his mother, Mary Williams, for her support, and also Anna, for her everlasting patience.

■ CONTENTS

LIST OF TABLES   x

LIST OF ABBREVIATIONS   xi

PART 1   Introducing Employment Relations

Introduction   **3**

The employment relationship and employment relations   3

Regulating the employment relationship   5

Employment relations as a 'field of study'   8

The approach of this book   11

1   The elements of employment relations   **17**

1.1   Introduction   17

1.2   Managing with trade unions   18

1.3   The development of trade unionism in Britain   23

1.4   The state and employment relations   30

1.5   The nature and development of collective bargaining in Britain   37

1.6   Worker participation and involvement in historical context   41

Conclusion   45

Assignment and discussion questions   46

Chapter case study: managing with unions in the Royal Mail   46

PART 2   Contemporary Employment Relations in Context

---

2   Employment relations in the contemporary economy   **51**

2.1   Introduction   51

2.2   Employment relations in the 'new' economy   52

2.3   Employment relations in a global economy I: multinationals and the management of employment relations   61

2.4   Employment relations in a global economy II: multinationals and the debate on international labour standards   71

Conclusion   80

Assignment and discussion questions   80

Chapter case study: union organization of 'atypical' workers   81

3 The politics of employment relations   **83**

3.1   Introduction   83

3.2   State policy and employment relations: a contemporary assessment   84

3.3   Employment relations and the politics of European integration   91

3.4   The politics of trade unionism I: trade unions and the Labour party in Britain   101

3.5   The politics of trade unionism II: union democracy and the internal politics of the unions   107

Conclusion   112

Assignment and discussion questions   113

Chapter case study: trade unions and the Euro   114

4 Social divisions and employment relations   **115**

4.1   Introduction   115

4.2   Workplace inequality and employment relations   116

4.3   Managing equality and diversity at work   120

4.4   Public policy, equality at work, and the work–life balance   127

4.5   Trade unions, collective bargaining, and the pursuit of workplace equality   135

Conclusion   142

Assignment and discussion questions   143

Chapter case study: employer attitudes to employees' work–life balance   144

PART 3   **Key Issues in Contemporary Employment Relations**

---

5 Managing employment relations   **147**

5.1   Introduction   147

5.2   Challenging unions   148

5.3   Human resource management and employment relations   154

5.4   Managing employment relations in non-union environments   162

5.5   Conceptualizing the management of employment relations   168

Conclusion   173

Assignment and discussion questions   174

Chapter case study: human resource management and the hotel industry   175

6 Representation at work   **177**

6.1   Introduction   177

6.2   Trade unions, worker representation, and the rise of a 'representation gap'   178

6.3   Non-union forms of employee representation   183

6.4   Partnership agreements   190

6.5   Organizing unionism   196

Conclusion   202

Assignment and discussion questions   204

Chapter case study: e-unions   204

7 Contemporary developments in pay and working time   **207**

7.1   Introduction   207

7.2   The changing pattern of pay determination in Britain   208

7.3   Pay inequality, low pay, and the National Minimum Wage   219

7.4   Developments in working time   227

Conclusion   234

Assignment and discussion questions   234

Chapter case study: the National Minimum Wage and the hairdressing industry   235

8 Experiencing employment relations   **237**

8.1   Introduction   237

8.2   Developments in employee involvement and participation   238

8.3   Discipline at work   244

8.4   Redundancy and insecurity   250

8.5   The intensification of work   257

Conclusion   263

Assignment and discussion questions   263

Chapter case study: one service, two types of worker?   264

9 Conflict and employment relations   **267**

9.1   Introduction   267

9.2   Strikes and employment relations   268

9.3   Other forms of industrial conflict   279

9.4   Resolving disputes in employment relations   287

Conclusion   296

Assignment and discussion questions   297

Chapter case study: a British Airways case   297

PART 4   **Conclusion**

Employment relations: regulating, experiencing, and contesting the employment relationship   **301**

Regulating the employment relationship   301

Experiencing the employment relationship   304

Contesting the employment relationship   305

BIBLIOGRAPHY   307

INDEX   339

■ LIST OF TABLES

1.1   Trade union membership 1892–1979   29

5.1   Percentage of workplaces with a recognized union 1980–98   148

6.1   Trade union membership and density in Great Britain 1980–2003   180

7.1   Percentage of non-managerial employees covered by particular pay-setting arrangements, by workplace sector 1998   211

7.2   National Minimum Wage rates 1999–2005   223

7.3   Number of hours usually worked each week by full-time employees in selected EU countries 2002   229

8.1   Percentage of workplaces where particular methods to communicate with employees are used   238

9.1   The level of strike activity in Britain 1946–2003   270

LIST OF ABBREVIATIONS

ACAS	Advisory, Conciliation and Arbitration Service
AEEU	Amalgamated Engineering and Electrical Union
APC&T	Administrative, Professional, Clerical and Technical
ASTMS	Association of Supervisory Technical and Managerial Staff
BA	British Airways
CAC	Central Arbitration Committee
CBI	Confederation of British Industry
CEEP	European Centre of Enterprises with Public Participation and of Enterprises of General Economic Interest
CEF	College Employers' Forum
CIPD	Chartered Institute of Personnel and Development
CRE	Commission for Racial Equality
CWU	Communication Workers' Union
DRC	Disability Rights Commission
DE	Department of Employment
DTI	Department of Trade and Industry
EC	European Community
ECA	Electrical Contractors' Association
ECB	European Central Bank
ECJ	European Court of Justice
EEC	European Economic Community
EEF	Engineering Employers' Federation
EI	employee involvement
EIF	European Industry Federation
EIRO	European Industrial Relations Observatory
EMU	Economic and Monetary Union
EO	equal opportunity
EOC	Equal Opportunities Commission
EPZ	export processing zone
ERA	Employment Relations Act (1999)
ETI	Ethical Trading Initiative
ETUC	European Trade Union Confederation
EU	European Union
EWC	European Works Council
FBI	Federal Bureau of Investigation
FBU	Fire Brigades Union
FDI	foreign direct investment
FLA	Fair Labor Association
GCHQ	Government Communications Headquarters
GMB	General, Municipal and Boilermakers' Union

GPMU   Graphical Paper and Media Union
GSP   Generalized System of Preferences
HCA   healthcare assistant
HRM   human resource management
ICFTU   International Confederation of Free Trade Unions
IDS   Incomes Data Services
ILO   International Labour Organization
IMF   International Monetary Fund
ISTC   Iron and Steel Trades Confederation
IRS   Industrial Relations Services
JCC   joint consultative committee
JI   job involvement
JIB   Joint Industry Board
JIC   Joint Industry Council
JPC   joint production committee
LPC   Low Pay Commission
MFGB   Miners' Federation of Great Britain
MNC   multinational company
MSF   Manufacturing Science and Finance Union
NAALC   North American Agreement on Labor Cooperation
NAFTA   North American Free Trade Agreement
NCB   National Coal Board
NEC   National Executive Committee
NEDC   National Economic Development Council
NHS   National Health Service
NIDL   New International Division of Labour
NMW   National Minimum Wage
NOTA   'Not on the Agenda' group
NPM   New Public Management
NUM   National Union of Mineworkers
NUT   National Union of Teachers
OECD   Organization for Economic Cooperation and Development
PFI   Private Finance Initiative
POA   Prison Officers' Association
PRP   performance-related pay
QMV   Qualified Majority Voting
RMT   Rail Maritime and Transport Union
RPA   Redundancy Payments Act (1965)
SEA   Single European Act
SEIU   Service Employees' International Union
SSP   Scottish Socialist Party
SWT   South West Trains
SWU   Service Workers' Union
TELCO   The East London Communities' Organization
TGWU   Transport and General Workers' Union

TQM	Total Quality Management
TUC	Trades Union Congress
TUPE	Transfer of Undertakings (Protection of Employment) Regulations
UDM	Union of Democratic Mineworkers
UEAPME	European Association of Craft, Small and Medium-Sized Enterprises
UNICE	Union of Industrial and Employers' Confederation of Europe
USDAW	Union of Shop Distributive and Allied Workers
WERS	Workplace Employment Relations Survey
WTO	World Trade Organization
WTR	Working Time Regulations
ZCTU	Zimbabwe Congress of Trade Unions

PART 1

Introducing Employment Relations

Introduction 3

1   **The elements of employment relations** 17

Introduction

SECTION OBJECTIVES

The main objectives of this section are to:

- examine the characteristics of the employment relationship in capitalist market economies, and how it informs an understanding of the nature of employment relations

- consider the perspectives applied to employment relations as a field of study

- provide a critically informed assessment of approaches to employment relations

- establish the distinctive contribution of this book, its structure, and major features

Employment relations affects most people in Britain. Close to 30 million are employed in some way or another; many of those who are not depend upon the income generated from a parent's or partner's job for their subsistence. Employment relations, then, is a vital topic of contemporary enquiry.

The employment relationship and employment relations

The notion of contract is ostensibly central to the employment relationship. Contractual relationships, and the capacity of the law to enforce contractual obligations and property rights, are defining features of capitalist market economies. With the development of capitalism in Britain, by the middle of the nineteenth century the system of wage labour, based on the notion of a contractual relationship between an employer and employee, had largely displaced traditional forms of work relations based on status, such as servitude (Burgess 1980). In theory, the employment contract captures the reciprocity evident in the agreement by an employer to provide workers with wages in exchange for their capacity to labour. Thus it is ostensibly characterized by the free and equal exchange of resources between the parties.

But is there such a thing, in reality, as an employment contract? The advantage of using a contractual framework to describe the employment relationship is that it captures the way in which the employment relationship is an economic transaction, something that concerns the willingness of workers to offer their capacity to labour in exchange for the promise of wages (Kahn-Freund 1977). But there are two fundamental problems with viewing the employment relationship in purely contractual terms.

First, the notion of a contract assumes that both parties to it come together in a free and equal way, without any obligation or pressure upon them to participate. However, the individual worker is in a much weaker position than the prospective employer. It is rare for workers to be in a position where they have as much freedom to choose between alternative offers of employment as employers have in selecting employees. Moreover, the consequences of refusing an offer of employment are potentially serious for the worker, since jobs, and the wages they attract, are most people's primary source of income. Employers can simply offer the job to someone else (Fox 1974).

Furthermore, by accepting an offer of employment, workers come under the authority of an employer. A purely contractual approach, then, fails to capture the way in which the employment relationship is a power relationship, characterized by the capacity of an employer to command and the obligation on the worker to obey (Kahn-Freund 1977). Thus the 'brute facts of power' (Fox 1974: 183) mean that it is inappropriate to consider the employment relationship as a contract, in the sense of a voluntary agreement between two equal parties. Indeed, British law has long recognized that the employment contract is not a purely economic relationship; it is infused by the assumption that the relationship between an employer and employee is akin to that which exists between masters and their servants. Thus the employment relationship cannot be equated with 'freedom of contract' (Wedderburn 1986).

The second reason why the employment relationship cannot be understood in pure contractual terms concerns the special nature of labour as a commodity. Employers do not buy employees in the way that a consumer purchases a tin of baked beans from a supermarket. Rather, they secure the capacity of employees to engage in productive work, their potential labour power; having hired an employee, the employer must then convert latent labour power into productive effort, through systems of control and supervision for example, or by eliciting employee commitment. Labour power, then, is an 'entirely fictitious commodity' (Polanyi 1957: 72); employers buy the capacity of workers to engage in productive effort. Therefore, 'labour differs from all other commodities in that it is enjoyed in use *and* is embodied in people' (Edwards 2003: 8).

The employment contract, then, is 'open-ended' or 'indeterminate' (Fox 1974; Marsden 1999). What this means is that when an employment contract is formed, it is impossible for the parties to specify all of the likely obligations. Neither the employer nor the employee can foresee all of the eventualities that may arise during the term of the contract.

In a commercial contract, a product or service is supplied for a price. In the labour contract, the worker sells an ability to work, which is translated into actual labour during the course of the working day. Expectations about standards of performance have to be built up during the process of production. (Edwards 2003: 14)

The result is that the characteristics of the employment relationship are the outcome of both 'market' and 'managerial' relations (Flanders 1975). Market relations determine wages, or the price of a worker's employment, whereas managerial relations are concerned with establishing how much work is to be undertaken by the employee, of what kind, how quickly, and the sanctions for non-compliance (Edwards 2003).

Rather than viewing the employment relationship as a contract, then, it is generally more accurate to consider it as an ongoing series of contracts, which are continually being re-negotiated between employers and their employees as changes in their circumstances alter the expectations of the parties (Commons 1924), and thus their behaviour. The employment relationship is a process, one in which an employer, driven by a concern to produce goods or deliver services at minimum cost, seeks greater effort from employees whose main interest, obtained in the form of wages, is the maximum return possible for their labour. It can be conceptualized, then, as a 'wage-work' or 'effort bargain' (Behrend 1957), since both the employer and the employee seek to influence and adjust its terms in ways that are beneficial to their own interest.

An important implication of conceptualizing the employment relationship as an 'effort' or 'wage-work bargain' is that the interests of employers and employees, or capital and labour, are in opposition (Baldamus 1961). Thus it is characterized by a constant struggle over its terms, over what Goodrich called 'the frontier of control' (Hyman 1975). Some perspectives characterize the employment relationship as a 'stark conflict of interests' (Hyman 1975: 27), between an employer who is concerned to extract the maximum effort from employees at minimum cost, and an employee whose concern is to secure better wages, and limit the amount of work he or she is expected to undertake. But it is overly simplistic to view the employment relationship just in terms of conflict between employers and employees; cooperation is also an essential feature (Edwards 1986, 2003). Employees share an interest with their employer in maintaining the competitiveness of their firm, for example, otherwise their jobs, and hence their livelihoods, are jeopardized (Kelly 1998). The employment relationship is, then, characterized both by conflict and cooperation. Nevertheless, the power differential in favour of the employer renders it an essentially exploitative relationship; employers use their superior power to shift the terms of the wage-work bargain in a way that is favourable to their interest. Employees react to this, often by organizing themselves collectively in trade unions, to combat the imbalance of power. Although cooperation is an important characteristic of the employment relationship, there remains a basic antagonism between employers and employees that generates an inherent potential for conflict (Edwards 1986, 2003).

Regulating the employment relationship

Traditionally, investigating the way in which the terms of the employment relationship are established has been a major concern of employment relations. Thus the subject matter of employment relations is about the rules that govern the employment relationship, or the way in which it is regulated. By this we mean understanding how the terms of the employment relationship, such as pay, working hours, holiday entitlement, and the extent to which employees are able to influence decisions that affect them at work, are generated. The systems-based approach to understanding employment relations, for example, focuses on how the activities of employment relations' actors – employers, trade unions, and the state – mediated by certain processes, such as negotiations between employers and unions, generate workplace rules in particular contexts (Dunlop 1958). This informed the development of employment relations as an area of study in Britain, where the rules-based approach, focusing on the regulation of the employment relationship, became influential. Thus employment relations became defined as 'the study of the rules governing employment, together with the ways in which the rules are made and changed, interpreted and administered. Put more briefly, it is the study of job regulation' (Clegg 1979: 1). If the regulation of the employment relationship is so important to developing an understanding of employment relations, how, then, do the rules originate?

Five main sources of rules can be identified which govern employment relationships, although it is important to recognize that the influence of each will vary according to the situation. First, managers attempt to determine the terms of the employment relationship unilaterally. Except in very small firms, the employing organization entrusts day-to-day control to salaried managers who are responsible, among other things, for managing employment relations. During the nineteenth and twentieth centuries, the development of the management function was particularly associated with the growth of large-scale enterprises and the increasing separation of ownership of the organization, shareholders in the private sector, from the control of activities within it, increasingly the province of expert managers. In a market economy their principal aim, in theory, is to manage the employment relationship efficiently in order to realize profitability, and thus maximize returns to shareholders. Thus control over employees – the terms and conditions of their employment, and their behaviour – is an essential feature of management activity.

The concept of managerial prerogative, or the 'right' to manage, is, then, integral to understanding the management of employment relations. It should be understood primarily in ideological terms since it 'reflects an area of decision-making over which management believes it has (and acts as if it does have) sole and exclusive rights of determination and upon which it strenuously resists any interference . . .' (Storey 1983: 102).

What factors influence this belief in the right of managers to exercise control over employment relations? Most obviously, managerial prerogative rests upon the role of management as the legitimate agent of the employer – the organization, and its shareholder owners. This is supported by statutory obligations that compel managers to undertake their function and operate in the interests of the shareholders. Managerial prerogative is also founded upon the belief that managers have the right to exercise control over employment relations by virtue of their abilities, expertise, and leadership skills (Storey 1983: 103–4). The right to manage, then, is important as an ideology, or set of ideas, to which many managers, especially senior ones, subscribe.

In practice, though, managerial prerogative is constrained in two important ways. First, it is necessarily influenced by the characteristics of the organizational environment, such as the state of product and labour markets. Low unemployment may oblige managers to improve pay and conditions in order to attract and retain employees. Second, the efforts of workers themselves, who, to a varying degree, challenge and contest managerial imperatives, limit the extent to which managers can exercise control in practice. Thus the nature of the employment relationship itself, as a wage-work bargain, implies that managerial prerogative, though important as an ideology that informs managers' behaviour, is never absolute.

The second source of rules concerns the ability of some workers to influence aspects of their own terms and conditions of employment by engaging in individual bargaining with employers. Given the power differential that exists in the employment relationship, few have the ability to exercise significant influence in this way, though individuals may obtain employer consent to relatively minor changes in work arrangements, such as starting and finishing times. Workers who possess particular skills for which there is high demand, in certain types of professional information technology work, for example, enjoy greater power to extract more favourable terms from employers.

Third, more commonly, though less so than used to be the case, the rules that govern the employment relationship are determined by collective bargaining between employers and trade unions, or 'joint regulation'. The unequal balance of power between the individual employee and employer in the employment relationship impels employees to combine in, and organize, trade unions, collective organizations of employees one of whose main purposes is to influence, principally through negotiations with employers, the terms of the wage-work bargain. Collective agreements are the outcome of the collective bargaining process. They may be procedural, setting out rules that govern the bargaining relationship between the employer and the union, or substantive, those that deliver concrete results to employees, in the form of pay rises or changes to working time, for example.

The fourth source of rules that govern the employment relationship emanate from the state, legislation in particular. Whereas the emphasis in Britain used to be on the desirability of joint regulation as a source of rules in employment relations (Flanders 1974), in recent years legislation has come to exercise an ever-greater influence, in order to challenge discrimination for example (see Chapter 4), or to alleviate low pay (see Chapter 7).

Fifth, rules are also generated informally, through the day-to-day experiences of, and relationships between, managers and workers. Often referred to as 'custom and practice', informal rules are tacitly understood expectations of what is, and what is not, acceptable, and are an important feature of employment relations (Edwards 2003). Numerous workplace studies demonstrate the way in which unwritten, informal, and tacit understandings influence the terms of the wage-work bargain (e.g. Brown 1973; Scott 1994). In Chapter 8, for example, we examine the way in which workplace discipline, and managerial toleration of indiscipline, is conditioned by such expectations.

These sources of rules do not exist in isolation from each other. Plenty of research studies demonstrate, for example, that the presence of robust joint regulation enhances the effectiveness of legislation designed to protect workers. Although it highlights the important role that trade unions often have in influencing managerial decision-making through joint regulation, the rules-based approach to understanding employment relations has a number of related weaknesses (Hyman 1975). First, it tends to concentrate on the formal institutions of job regulation, trade unions, and collective bargaining in particular, to a perhaps unwarranted degree. Second, following on from this, the rules-based approach implies an emphasis on stability and order in the employment relationship; the processes by which workplace rules are challenged and changed, and the dynamic nature of the wage-work bargain, influenced, as it often is, by informal expectations and understandings based on custom and practice, tends to be neglected. Third, it overlooks the way in which the employment relationship, understood as a wage-work bargain, is concerned with struggle as employees attempt to exercise control over their working lives. A proper understanding of employment relations, then, not only demands an analysis of how the employment relationship is regulated, but also how employees experience, challenge, and contest the rules.

Employment relations as a 'field of study'

Employment relations is not an academic discipline in its own right; rather it is better conceptualized as a 'field of study' (Edwards 2003). Thus it does not have its 'own conceptual and theoretical analysis', but is an area in 'which a variety of disciplinary perspectives can be applied and tested' (Hyman 1994a: 3). The origins of employment relations as a field of study can be traced to the late nineteenth century. This period saw the first major studies of the trade unions and collective bargaining, for example (Webb and Webb 1920a). It was also characterized by significant instances of labour unrest, the causes of which governments and official agencies were anxious to understand (Hyman 1989).

Early studies of employment relations were largely influenced by theoretical perspectives drawn from the discipline of economics. Writers were concerned about the way in which the demand for, and the supply of, labour determined wage rates, for example. Studies of employment relationships in specific contexts discovered that the characteristics of the external labour market could not adequately explain differences in wage levels (Brown and Nolan 1988). Hence, there was an increasing emphasis on the way in which the institutions of job regulation, the bargaining role of trade unions in particular, shaped employment relationships (Ackers and Wilkinson 2003). Perspectives in this tradition were heavily influenced by the need for a proper historical understanding of the institutions they described. They were characterized by intricately detailed historical accounts of the development of trade unions and collective bargaining arrangements in particular (see Flanders and Clegg 1964).

One of the leading writers on employment relations in Britain during the 1960s and 1970s, along with Flanders and Clegg, was Alan Fox. In 1966, he established a distinction between unitary and pluralist 'frames of reference' in employment relations. These frames of reference are perspectives that can be applied to employment relations, not theories of employment relations (Blyton and Turnbull 2004). Fox articulated them as 'ideologies of management' (Fox 1966: 10), beliefs held by managers that influence their approach to employment relations. They can be likened to lenses, tools which people use to 'perceive and define social phenomena', in this case the nature of the employment relationship, and which thus influence and shape their actions (Fox 1974: 271).

The unitary perspective is characterized by an emphasis on cooperative relations at work. It rejects the assumption that a basic antagonism exists between employers and employees; conflict is largely caused by external agitators, trade unions, whose interference disrupts the harmonious state of relations that would otherwise exist. Holders of unitary beliefs rely on the 'liberal use of team or family metaphors' (Fox 1974: 249) when conceptualizing the nature of the employment relationship. Managers, in particular, often use the team analogy to describe relations in their organizations, based on the assumption that employers and their employees share the same goals, something that renders managerial prerogative legitimate, and trade union representation unnecessary. In his evidence to the 1994 House of Commons Employment Committee investigation into the future of trade unions, for example, the then chief executive of Zurich Insurance contended that it 'is the job of the company to create an environment in which a trade union becomes irrelevant...the very nature of the unions, sitting in there in a divisive capacity, stops the employees and managers of an organization getting together as one team' (House of Commons Employment Committee 1994: 342).

The unitary perspective on employment relations is often criticized for advancing an unrealistic view of workplace life, in particular for denying the basic antagonism that characterizes the employment relationship. Yet, as a perspective on the nature of employment relations, and, moreover, one which is subscribed to by a great deal of managers (Poole and Mansfield 1993), it must be taken seriously (Edwards 2003). Most senior managers, if asked their views about the nature of the employment relationship, would articulate a unitary perspective, stressing the importance of common goals, shared objectives, and the absence of any conflict of interest between the employer and employee. These beliefs influence their behaviour, most notably the importance of upholding managerial prerogative, and of resisting what they see as trade union interference in the operation of their organizations.

There is evidence that the unitary perspective influences developments in contemporary employment relations. In a study of hotels, for example, Head and Lucas (2004) found that managers expressed hostility towards trade unions, rejected the notion that there was antagonism in the employment relationship, and emphasized the extent to which their organization was a 'happy team'. The food company studied by Wray (1996) attempted to secure the loyalty and cooperation of its employees, and thus render trade unions unnecessary, by offering relatively good benefits. There is considerable interest, as we show in Chapter 5, in how organizations can develop sophisticated human resource management (HRM) approaches in order to enhance the commitment of their staff. Interest in the 'neo-unitary' (Farnham and Pimlott 1995) character of HRM, demonstrates the extent to which perspectives drawn from the discipline of psychology, those concerning human relations at work in particular (Edwards 2003), such as the relationship between work, commitment, and performance, influence the study of employment relations.

The pluralist frame of reference is a perspective which recognizes the existence of a basic antagonism in the employment relationship, and hence the inevitable potential for conflict. The principal concern of pluralists is with ensuring that conflict is managed appropriately, and contained in a way that prevents it from causing too much disruption. Thus there is an emphasis on developing procedures that are designed to resolve conflict, in particular the establishment of bargaining relationships with trade unions, given the array, or plurality, of interests that potentially exist within the organization. Therefore, 'management has to face the fact that there are other sources of leadership, other focuses of loyalty, within the social system it governs, and that it is with these that management must share its decision-making' (Fox 1966: 8). In other words, managers cannot assume that the organization is characterized by shared interests and common goals; in particular employees will have divergent interests, and may want to express them through their own independent institutions, trade unions. Unions, then, are not external agitators to be resisted if harmonious relations are to be upheld, but are the legitimate representatives of employees' interests.

The pluralist frame of reference was enormously influential in the development of employment relations as an academic field of study (Ackers and Wilkinson 2003; Hyman 1989). The emphasis on employment relations as the 'study of the institutions of job regulation' (Flanders 1975), noted above, was informed by a belief in the legitimacy of trade unions, and accorded a special role to collective bargaining as the means by which they secured their goals, something that became the 'dominant paradigm' (Ackers and Wilkinson 2003: 7).

During the 1960s and 1970s, the pluralist orthodoxy developed in the context of the emergence of employment relations as an important public policy issue (Ackers and Wilkinson 2003; Hyman 1989). Governments were concerned that particular characteristics of Britain's system of employment relations, most notably the growth of workplace bargaining between union representatives and managers, generated unnecessary levels of disruptive industrial conflict and inflationary wage increases (see Chapter 1). From a pluralist perspective, the solution was not, as the holders of unitary views would argue, to resist the encroachment of the unions as a means of reasserting managerial authority; rather, stronger bargaining relationships between employers and unions should be encouraged, given the advantages of developing robust and effective procedures for containing, or institutionalizing, conflict through the joint regulation of the workplace. According to one leading pluralist, the 'paradox, whose truth managements have found it so difficult to accept, is that they can only regain control by sharing it' (Flanders 1975: 172). Until the 1980s, then, the pluralist perspective exercised an important influence over both public policy and even management attitudes towards employment relations, though not at the expense of the latter's fundamentally unitary beliefs.

Since the 1980s, pluralism has been eclipsed by the growing dominance of the unitary perspective in employment relations (Edwards 2003), as the importance of trade unions and collective bargaining have declined markedly. But the principal criticisms of pluralism have come from radical perspectives on employment relations. These share with pluralism a belief in the essentially antagonistic nature of the employment relationship. However, they do not accept its assumption that conflict can be resolved by the development of procedures, or even the desirability of attempting to do so. We do not deal with Marxist approaches to employment relations separately from the umbrella of radicalism (Edwards 1986). Generally, Marxism differs from other radical approaches in its emphasis on the way in which the exploitation of workers in the employment relationship generates class conflict between the working class, who produce goods and services, and the owners of capital, something that results in deepening class consciousness, and the development of a socialist political project (see Gall 2003b).

What criticisms, then, do radical approaches make of the pluralist perspective? First, it is argued that pluralism fails to address the issue of power seriously enough, assuming that, in an environment where bargaining relationships have been established, a balance of power exists between employers and unions (Fox 1974), although this has been rebutted by pluralist writers (Clegg 1975). Employers, by virtue of their ownership of, and control over, the production of goods or delivery of services, enjoy far greater power than even the most well-organized union (Fox 1974). Second, radical writers contend that pluralism is an essentially conservative ideology, concerned with upholding the existing order in society rather than challenging it (Fox 1974; Goldthorpe 1977). Thus, while pluralism ostensibly appears to advance the interests of employees, by recognizing the desirability of union organization and collective bargaining, in fact the development of procedures ensures they are kept within narrow limits, and do not challenge the economic power of employers. Joint regulation contains conflict, resolves it, and thus ameliorates its potential for disruption in a way that helps the interests of capital rather than those of labour.

Following on from this, the third main criticism of the pluralist approach is that by focusing on procedural reform, it neglects the important substantive outcomes for employees (Hyman 1989). In other words, pluralism is more concerned with the system of joint regulation than whether or not it produces anything worthwhile for employees. However, it is suggested that the radical approach places an unwarranted emphasis on conflict and disorder in employment relations (Ackers and Wilkinson 2003).

During the late 1960s and the 1970s, a number of important sociological studies of workplace employment relations were strongly influenced by a radical perspective. Huw Beynon's study of Ford's Halewood car manufacturing plant is a particularly notable example of the genre (Beynon 1973). Since the 1980s, though, the influence of both pluralist and radical perspectives has waned, largely because of the marked decline in the level of trade union membership and organization, and the dwindling extent of collective bargaining activity. The emergence of HRM, and the revival of unitary thinking noted above, challenged the position of employment relations as a field of study, given the extent to which, notwithstanding the increasing importance of radical perspectives, it was concerned with the joint regulation of the workplace. By the late 1990s, a 'discipline focused on trade unions and collective bargaining had found it increasingly difficult to conceptualize a society in which both were increasingly marginal to the world of work' (Ackers and Wilkinson 2003: 12–13). While perspectives drawn from academic disciplines such as law (e.g. Davies and Freedland 1993), geography (e.g. Herod, Peck, and Wills 2003), and politics (e.g. Ludlum and Taylor 2003) have increasingly enhanced our understanding of employment relations, its importance as an academic field of study dwindled during the 1980s and 1990s. The purpose of this book, though, is to demonstrate that employment relations is about more than just trade unions and collective bargaining. Moreover, an understanding of employment relations is essential if one is to develop a proper understanding of economic, industrial, political, and social developments in contemporary societies.

The approach of this book

One of the main aims of this book is to demonstrate the continued importance of employment relations, based on the assumption that, as a field of study, its boundaries are wide-ranging, and cannot be restricted just to the study of trade unions and collective bargaining. The changing nature of the economy, which has seen a considerable decline in employment in sectors like manufacturing where joint regulation was traditionally strong, does not imply that the study of employment relations is now unimportant. Rather, the expansion of the service sector, together with other political, economic, and social changes, have contributed to a widening of its boundaries such that it incorporates a range of issues that are of important contemporary relevance.

This is best illustrated with reference to a current area of interest. At the time of writing, one of the most pressing public policy issues concerns the extent to which people's family responsibilities can be accommodated by employers. This is an issue – it concerns the way in which people's employment is regulated and experienced, and how they seek a more equitable balance between work and family commitments – which is by any measure something that concerns employment relations. Traditional approaches, those that focus on the institutions of joint regulation, would pay little attention to the development of so-called family-friendly policies, not least because until relatively recently such topics rarely appeared on the male-dominated union bargaining agendas (see Chapter 4). We do not imply that trade unions and collective bargaining are unimportant. On the contrary, they are important features of contemporary employment relations, as we demonstrate throughout the book. Where family-friendly policies are regulated jointly, they often function more effectively than if their existence depends upon the whim of managers, as we show in Chapter 4. But employment relations cannot be restricted just to the study of joint regulation; it encompasses a much broader range of structures, processes, and activities.

Before we set out the approach of this book in more detail, it is necessary to consider why it goes under the title of 'contemporary employment relations' rather than 'contemporary industrial relations'. As other writers have noted (Blyton and Turnbull 2004), the term 'industrial relations', although still widely used, is often associated with developments in traditional industries, like manufacturing, and with an emphasis on trade unions and joint regulation; 'employment relations', however, is more appropriate to understanding greater diversity in work and employment patterns. For this reason, it is better suited to the approach adopted here even though 'industrial' and 'employment' relations can be, and often are, used interchangeably.

This book is distinguished by five main characteristics. First, it adopts an explicitly critical approach to employment relations. What do we mean by this? Rather than understanding it just as the regulation of the employment relationship, we prefer to conceptualize employment relations as the study of the way in which the employment relationship is regulated, experienced, and contested. Clearly, we need to understand the ways in which the rules that govern the employment relationship are constituted, but how do workers experience the employment relationship and how far, and in what ways, do they challenge, or contest, their employment situations? This is what distinguishes this study of employment relations from books about HRM, which, by tending to adopt an explicitly managerial focus, largely neglect the implications of management decisions for employees, and their responses.

Second, the book treats employment relations in a more thematic way than is often the case in conventional accounts. These tend to be influenced by an assumption that trade unions and collective bargaining constitute its principal subject matter. Given the diminishing significance of joint regulation, such an approach is clearly no longer tenable (Ackers and Wilkinson 2003). Rather than devote chapters to trade union organization and collective bargaining, we focus instead on the broader themes of employee representation (see Chapter 6), and developments in pay determination and working time (see Chapter 7). This more thematic approach better captures the broader conceptualization of employment relations advanced in this book.

Third, an important aim of this book is to establish the contemporary relevance of employment relations. The broader, critical approach, one that focuses on the way in which the employment relationship is regulated, experienced, and contested, allows us to consider a range of current employment relations issues. We have already referred to the implementation of family-friendly policies for example, which we examine in Chapter 4. In other chapters, we address other important contemporary topics, including the relationship between the trade unions and the Labour government (Chapter 3), and the legal regulation of working time (Chapter 7). Much of the book, but Chapters 2, 3, and 4 in particular, are informed by the need to consider employment relations in a broader context. Much of what happens at work is influenced by economic, political, and social changes. Thus there is the need to recognize that factors constituted mainly outside the workplace, such as gender for example, shape employment relations patterns and activities (Ackers 2002; Greene 2003). The contemporary focus is further informed by the inclusion of material taken from a wide range of recent and up-to-date research findings.

Fourth, our intention is to offer a relatively concise assessment of developments in employment relations. We do not aim to provide a comprehensive, encyclopaedic account of the subject, and important historical developments are treated rather cursorily. Instead, we hope this book contributes to an understanding of contemporary employment relations and helps stimulate debate and provoke arguments over what is an endlessly fascinating, often controversial, and rarely consensual area of economic, social, and political life.

Fifth, while for reasons of space we concentrate largely on developments in Britain, it is important to recognize that employment relations is of international significance. European Union (EU) policies influence employment relations in important ways. At various points in the book we include examples taken from experiences in other countries. Moreover, in Chapter 2 we consider the implications of economic globalization for employment relations, and the policies and practices of multinational companies.

The book is organized in four main sections. This chapter and the next provide an introduction to employment relations as a field of study. In Chapter 1, we are concerned, particularly, with establishing the characteristics of the main actors and processes of employment relations, and with discussing their historical development. In Part 2, we commence our thematic assessment of developments in contemporary employment relations by focusing on the important influence of contextual developments. In Chapter 2, for example, we consider the effect of changes in the labour market, such as the growth of part-time work. The effects of economic globalization, and the policies and practices of multinational companies, are also considered in this chapter. Chapter 3 is about the political dimension of employment relations. We examine contemporary public policy developments, consider the implications of European integration for employment relations, assess the relationship between trade unions and the Labour party, and analyse the political nature of the unions themselves. In Chapter 4, we consider the implications of social divisions for employment relations. Inequality is a durable feature of jobs and the labour market. Although we address other forms of disadvantage at work, we concentrate in particular on efforts to tackle gender inequality.

We continue with our thematic approach in Part 3 of the book, and examine five major issues in contemporary employment relations. Chapter 5 considers the management of employment relations, the implications of HRM, and the rise of non-unionism. Chapter 6 deals with the representation of employees' interests in contemporary employment relations. We critically assess the extent to which non-union works council arrangements, partnership agreements, and a more assertive form of union organizing can respectively provide employees with effective representation. In Chapter 7, we consider current developments in pay determination, and the organization of working time. The distinctive feature of Chapter 8 concerns the way in which it highlights the experience of employees, and how the nature of that experience often puts them at odds with their employers.

We consider four topics: employee involvement and participation; workplace discipline; redundancy and job insecurity; and work intensification. Following on from this, in Chapter 9 we assert the importance of conflict in contemporary employment relations. We discuss the various manifestations of industrial conflict, including the significance of strike activity, and explore methods of dispute resolution.

Part 4 of the book provides a brief concluding chapter in which we draw together the main themes of the book in a way that demonstrates the relevance of employment relations to contemporary societies.

Each chapter includes a number of supporting features. The chapter boxes comprise case studies, examples drawn from outside Britain, and other information, all of which are designed to illustrate aspects of, and thus be read in conjunction with, the main text. Most chapter sections come with summaries, designed to reinforce the main arguments developed in the preceding pages, and with guidance on further reading suggestions, including appropriate website links. Each chapter ends with assignment and discussion questions to reinforce learning activity, and a relevant case study exercise. See the companion website for further relevant features, including a glossary of key terms used in the book.

SECTION SUMMARY AND FURTHER READING

- The employment relationship should be conceptualized not as a contract, but as a wage-work or effort bargain. This refers to the ongoing process of struggle over the terms of the employment relationship between an employer, who wishes to convert latent labour power into productive effort, and an employee, who is concerned with increasing the return, in the form of wages and better working conditions, from his or her labour.

- Conceptualizing it as a bargain implies that the potential for conflict is an inevitable feature of the employment relationship. Not only is there is a basic antagonism between employer and the employee, but the employment relationship is also exploitative, characterized by an imbalance of power, between a powerful employer and a relatively powerless individual employee.

- The unitary perspective, which denies this basic antagonism in the employment relationship, can be criticized for being unrealistic, though its tenets influence the attitudes and behaviour of managers. Pluralism recognizes the potential for conflict, but tends to focus on how it can be contained by the development of procedures, collective bargaining in particular. Radical approaches, which developed out of a critique of pluralism, perhaps over-emphasize the degree of conflict and disorder in employment relations.

- As a field of study, employment relations was traditionally concerned with understanding the rules that govern employment relationships, in particular joint regulation, collective bargaining between trade unions and employers. This is too narrow an approach, however; it has been rendered untenable, moreover, by declining unionization and falling levels of collective bargaining. Therefore, employment relations is better defined as the study of the way in which the employment relationship is regulated, contested, and experienced.

For an extended discussion of the employment relationship and the nature of employment relations, see Edwards (2003). Ackers and Wilkinson (2003) consider the evolution of employment relations as a field of study. For an advanced conceptualization of employment relations, see Fox (1974: Chapter 6).

■ **ASSIGNMENT AND DISCUSSION QUESTIONS**

1. Which of the three perspectives – unitary, pluralist, or radical – most closely fits your own view of the world of work? Why?

2. Why is 'power' such an important concept in understanding employment relations?

■ **WEBSITE MATERIALS**

 Visit the companion web site to this book for interesting and updated material at **www.oup.com/booksites/busecon/business**

CHAPTER 1
The elements of employment relations

CHAPTER OBJECTIVES

The main objectives of this chapter are to:

- examine the development of the management role in employment relations in a context of growing unionization
- consider the evolution of trade unionism in Britain
- develop an understanding of the role of the state in employment relations
- examine the nature and evolution of collective bargaining as a means of regulating the employment relationship
- explore the nature of employee involvement and participation

---

1.1 Introduction

In the introductory chapter, we established the nature of employment relations and critically assessed the theoretical perspectives that have been used to conceptualize the employment relationship. This chapter has two main purposes. First, it considers the main features of employment relations. We discuss the management of employment relations in a unionized context, the development of the trade unions, the role of the state, the functions and evolution of collective bargaining, and the nature of employee involvement and participation respectively. By reading this chapter, you will acquire a sound knowledge and understanding of the role of the main actors in, and processes of, employment relations. This is a book that, as we established in the introductory chapter, aims to discuss and demonstrate the importance of employment relations in contemporary societies, most notably Britain. In order to do this, however, some historical perspective is necessary. Thus the second main purpose of this chapter is to assess how employment relations in Britain developed prior to the 1980s.

1.2 Managing with trade unions

As we saw in the introductory chapter, a belief in managerial prerogative, or the right to manage, underpins management behaviour in employment relations. Historically, although managements vigorously attempted to exclude trade unions from their workplaces, in practice the strength of union organization in many areas of the economy obliged them to try to sustain their prerogative by accommodating workers' demands. During the twentieth century, employers often recognized unions for collective bargaining so as to mitigate disruption, and foster order and stability (Hyman 1975). This was, however, in large part a reaction by employers to the pressure coming from workers themselves to organize unions (Clegg, Fox, and Thompson 1964). Attempts to exclude unions caused too much disruption, given the collective power that workers were able to wield. Thus employers took a pragmatic approach, recognizing unions, but doing so in a way that disturbed managerial prerogatives as little as possible (Gospel 1992).

During the 1960s and 1970s, in a context of growing union power, companies that had hitherto not recognized a union found it advantageous to do so, in order to quell workplace militancy. For example, management in the biscuit works studied by Scott (1994) were aware of a growing union presence within the factory and chose to accommodate it by means of a centralized negotiating relationship with union full-time officers, from which workplace union activists were distanced. The company embraced collective bargaining with a recognized union, but did so in a way that upheld managerial rights and secured workplace order. Although, for pragmatic reasons, employers may have chosen to recognize unions, by no means does this mean that they accepted their legitimacy and, indeed, made every effort to restrict union influence over employment relations within the workplace. For much of the twentieth century, many employers chose to try to exclude unions from their workplaces by dealing with them through employers' associations. However, the growth of workplace bargaining prompted employers to look for more sophisticated ways of managing employment relations in unionized environments.

1.2.1 The rise and fall of employers' associations

Employers tried to externalize their employment relations activity, and thus uphold managerial prerogative in the workplace, by bargaining with trade unions through employers' associations. The origins of employers' associations in Britain can be traced to the late eighteenth and early nineteenth centuries; although these early organizations were local and transient in character, employers often combined to challenge the efforts of the nascent trade unions to organize workers (Clegg 1979; McIvor 1996). The 1890s and 1900s saw the emergence of permanent national federations of employers, such as the Engineering Employers' Federation (EEF) (Wigham 1973).

The development of employers' associations during this period is ascribed to three factors (Bean 1985). First, growing state intervention in employment relations was seen to necessitate a more coordinated response by employers. Second, employers were better able to cope with increasing competitive pressures by combining for collective bargaining purposes. Multi-employer bargaining over pay meant that firms did not have to compete on wage costs, removing a potential source of destructive competition. Third, most importantly, multi-employer bargaining, through the offices of employers' associations, helped to negate the growing power of workplace trade unionism in a number of important sectors of the economy, in particular the building, engineering, and printing industries (Sisson 1983). By negotiating with unions away from the workplace, externalizing their relationship through the institution of multi-employer bargaining, employers aimed to 'neutralize' union power in the workplace. In matters that went unregulated by collective agreements, particularly those pertaining to the organization and pace of work, the assumption was that management prerogative would predominate (Sisson 1987).

Although the structure and policies of employers' associations often varied considerably, the development of permanent, national bodies between the 1890s and 1920s reflected the concern of employers that union power be accommodated and contained within the institution of collective bargaining. Many employers' associations also operated disputes procedures. These helped to resolve disputes between a union and one or more of its member firms. It is important, then, not to understate the influence of employers' associations on the development of employment relations in Britain. Although employers' associations sometimes engaged in crude anti-union activities, such as undermining strikes, their role in the joint regulation of employment relations, particularly through multi-employer collective bargaining and procedures for dispute resolution, became an important means of maintaining managerial control, and thus upholding employers' interests (McIvor 1996).

Nevertheless, during the late 1960s and the 1970s there was a major trend away from multi-employer bargaining as an increasing number of firms, especially larger ones, chose to develop organization-specific procedures (Gospel 1992). By the late 1970s, although multi-employer bargaining remained important in some parts of the private sector, particularly over matters like working hours, bargaining activity was increasingly conducted at company level (Sisson 1987). In 1980, just 30 per cent of private sector employees had their pay determined largely by multi-employer bargaining, compared to 40 per cent by single-employer bargaining (Brown, Marginson, and Walsh 1995). During the 1980s, the importance of employers' associations in employment relations declined still further following the termination of multi-employer bargaining arrangements in industries such as retail banking, supermarkets, and engineering. Only about one in twenty employees in the private sector now have their pay determined by multi-employer bargaining (Cully et al. 1999).

Given these developments, it is hardly surprising that the membership of employers' associations has diminished, although they are increasingly focusing their activities on commercial matters, and the provision of employment relations advice (IRS 1998b). Data from successive Workplace Employee Relations Surveys show that, in 1990, just 13 per cent of private sector workplaces reported that they were in organizations that were members of an employers' association. Although this figure rose to 18 per cent in 1998, because of changes in how the data were collected 'it seems unlikely that there was any increase in membership between 1990 and 1998' (Millward, Bryson, and Forth 2000: 75). Nevertheless, employers' associations remain an integral feature of public sector employment relations, as we will see in a number of instances later in this book.

1.2.2 Managerial innovation in employment relations

Attempts to bargain with unions by means of employers' associations contributed to the widespread neglect of employment relations management in many firms, or what Hyman (2003) refers to as the 'tradition of unscientific management'. The historical weakness of the personnel management function in Britain has long been acknowledged (e.g. Flanders 1975). Writers point to the history of unsophisticated managerial control systems, the lack of complex managerial hierarchies within firms, and the slow, and indeed relatively late, diffusion of scientific management techniques (Gospel 1992; Tolliday and Zeitlin 1991). Employers exhibited a preference for *ad hoc*, informal, and unsophisticated ways of managing their workforces, such as a reliance on simple payment by results techniques.

What factors contributed to managerial neglect of employment relations matters? Clearly the externalization of relations with trade unions was one influence. Three other elements were also important: first, the process of industrialization in Britain, which started earlier than in other competitor economies, delayed the emergence of the modern corporate firm; second, diverse and fluctuating product markets, and an ample labour supply were obstacles to modernization; and third, in some industries, a pre-industrial craft ethos, in which workers enjoyed a degree of control over the content of their jobs, prevailed (Gospel 1992). How realistic was it, then, to expect workplace unionism to be contained so easily, given the weakness of managerial control systems and the lack of attention given to employment relations by senior managers? Employers therefore found it increasingly hard to maintain managerial prerogatives within the workplace.

During the 1940s and 1950s, there was a marked growth in the incidence of workplace bargaining in Britain, particularly in the engineering sector (Gospel 1992). Not only did this reflect the increasing difficulty employers had in upholding managerial rights in the workplace, but the weakness of agreements reached by means of multi-employer bargaining, and a tight labour market created by full employment, which enhanced workers' bargaining power, were also contributory factors (Terry 1983). The reluctance of senior managers to take control over their own employment relations during this period in a resolute and strategic way, and to come to terms with, and accommodate the growth of, workplace unionism, rather than see it as a threat to be nullified, was seen by the pluralists as a major error, contributing to industrial disputes and workplace disorder (Flanders 1964, 1975).

Employers were encouraged to secure greater control over employment relations within the workplace by recognizing, formally, the legitimacy of shopfloor unionism rather than by trying to extinguish it, something that would only cause greater disruption. Such a prescription characterized the findings and recommendations of the 1965–68 Royal Commission on Trade Unions and Employers' Associations, established under the chairmanship of Lord Donovan. It was set up to examine the system of employment relations in Britain, and to make proposals for its reform, given the detrimental effect aspects of it were held to have on British economic performance, in particular, 'wage drift', inflationary increases in earnings caused by workplace bargaining, and the associated high level of industrial conflict. Influenced by prominent pluralist writers such as Allan Flanders, Donovan identified managerial weakness as a prime source of Britain's employment relations problems and strongly recommended that, in order to rectify them, managers should secure greater control over workplace employment relations (Royal Commission 1968).

During the 1960s and 1970s, in a context of growing union militancy, managers adopted a notably more interventionist approach in respect of workplace employment relations anyway, in order to contain and accommodate trade union power, and thus exercise greater control. Employers were increasingly the 'main instigators in reshaping the system of industrial relations in Britain' (Gospel 1992: 140). Perhaps the most significant managerial intervention during this period was the rise of 'productivity bargaining', heralded as a major managerial initiative in the reform of employment relations. The theory and practice of productivity bargaining were popularized by Allan Flanders's celebrated study of the negotiation of a path-breaking collective agreement, known as the 'Blue Book', at Esso's Fawley oil refinery, near Southampton during the early 1960s (Flanders 1964). Not only was it held to be important as a pioneering attempt to resolve some of the problems caused by unregulated workplace bargaining, but it was also deemed significant as an example of managerial initiative in employment relations (Ahlstrand 1990).

What, then, were the features of the Blue Book deal struck between management and unions at Fawley? Its major targets were the perceived 'under-utilization' of labour and excessive overtime working. The high level of overtime allowed workers to supplement low basic wages with premium payments for doing the extra work. This not only contributed to wage drift, since earnings became increasingly distant from formally negotiated pay rates, but it also encouraged workplace bargaining over overtime rates and allocation. Furthermore, the prospect of supplementing earnings through opportunities for overtime was detrimental to productivity since it gave workers an incentive to reduce their effort during their normal working time in the hope that this would make overtime necessary. The productivity agreement struck at Fawley, then, saw management 'buy out' overtime and other inefficient practices in return for higher basic earnings and a fixed working week. It was envisaged that such an approach would encourage order and stability, as well as generating productivity improvements (Flanders 1964).

Over and above the features of the agreement itself, the deal struck at Fawley was held to be significant in two important respects. First, it was an example of managerial innovation in employment relations, standing out from the hitherto *ad hoc*, unsophisticated, and reactive approach to employment relations exhibited within most British firms (Flanders 1964). Second, the agreement appeared to possess a 'higher order function', being the 'very embodiment of pluralist industrial relations' (Ahlstrand 1990: 61, 60). It represented an attempt by management to secure control of the workplace through cooperative means, by explicitly recognizing the legitimacy of the unions as the representatives of the workforce, rather than trying to marginalize or exclude them (Flanders 1964).

The Fawley experiment, then, appeared not only to be beneficial for the employer, in that it led to improved economic performance, but it also seemed to secure, and legitimize, the interests of employees through the establishment of a cooperative relationship with the unions. Ensuing productivity gains, though, were limited and largely the result of staffing cuts, rather than the more efficient utilization of labour, and overtime working remained commonplace. Managers, moreover, never eschewed their unitary beliefs; indeed, they used productivity agreements to undermine union power in the workplace, part of a long-term strategy to manage without unions altogether (Ahlstrand 1990).

During the late 1960s and early 1970s, there was a marked increase in the popularity of productivity agreements, though they varied considerably in their scope, detail, and outcomes. Perhaps their most important function, however, was to signal the growth of a more resolute and sophisticated approach to the management of employment relations within British firms (Clegg 1979), contributing to the declining incidence of multi-employer bargaining through employers' associations. In particular, employers increasingly sought to gain control of their own employment relations, encouraged by a process of corporate restructuring and rationalization which stimulated demand for greater managerial expertise and professionalism (Batstone 1988; Gospel 1992). Personnel policies were reformed. More sophisticated payment systems were introduced, for example, involving the introduction of new job evaluation techniques.

Moreover, workplace trade unionism, particularly the role of shop stewards (see below), became increasingly formalized as managers encouraged, or 'sponsored', them in an attempt to accommodate union power (Terry 1983). In the Cadbury's confectionery plant at Bourneville, for example, managers acceded to the operation of a closed shop arrangement (see Box 1.1) as part of an attempt to contain and accommodate the growing influence of the shop stewards, and to direct it in a 'responsible and realistic' direction (Smith, Child, and Rowlinson 1990: 195). During the 1970s, shop steward structures were extended into areas, such as the public sector, where the presence of formal workplace unionism had hitherto been rare (Terry 1983). One should not disregard the extent to which the development of workplace union organization derived from the efforts of workers themselves to secure change. In practice, it 'is impossible to disentangle the influence of management acquiescence from that of worker pressure' (Marchington and Parker 1990: 208). Union activity was not always amenable to management objectives. In Cadbury's, for example, the Transport and General Workers' Union (TGWU) became rather more powerful in the workplace than managers considered desirable (Smith, Child, and Rowlinson 1990).

BOX 1.1 MANAGING WITH THE CLOSED SHOP

Union membership agreements, or 'closed shops' as they are more popularly known, were a major feature of British employment relations for many years. Under closed shop arrangements, union membership was a condition of employment. The 'pre-entry' closed shop restricted particular jobs to members of a specific union. The more commonplace 'post-entry' closed shop made union membership mandatory when a worker commenced employment. While union pressure was an important factor stimulating the growth of closed shop arrangements (McCarthy 1964), they became increasingly widespread in British industry during the 1970s, largely due to management acquiescence (Dunn and Gennard 1984; Gospel 1992; Marchington and Parker 1990). This was part of the broader concern of managers to accommodate and contain workplace trade unionism, to push it in a moderate and cooperative direction.

By 1980, some five million workers may have been covered by closed shop arrangements, mostly of the post-entry type (Millward et al. 1992). Margaret Thatcher's Conservative governments, however, made reform of the closed shop a key feature of their legislative assault on the trade unions until, with the enactment of the 1990 Employment Act, the operation of one was effectively made unlawful altogether. Perhaps a more influential factor contributing to the decline of the closed shop – by 1990 only about half a million workers were still covered by such an arrangement (Millward et al. 1992) – was the decline of employment in those industries, such as printing for example, where it was prominent.

From this overview of how employment relations was managed in Britain before the 1980s, it should be clear that while employers accepted trade unionism, this reflected a pragmatic response to circumstances, notably union power, rather than a genuine belief in the virtues of a pluralist approach. If managers had to deal with trade unions, they tried to do so in such a way that it contained workplace militancy. Managers may have been obliged to respond constructively to the implications of growing union power, but their fundamentally unitary values generally remained constant.

SECTION SUMMARY AND FURTHER READING

- Employers have long played a leading role in employment relations by initiating union recognition, albeit under pressure from workers for union representation. In forming employers' associations and instituting multi-employer bargaining arrangements, employers sought to maintain managerial prerogative in the workplace by externalizing their relationship with trade unions.

- Among other things, this process of externalization contributed to a tradition of 'unscientific management', the weakness of managerial structures and systems in respect of employment relations. The growth of workplace bargaining and its effects encouraged firms to develop a more sophisticated approach to managing employment relations in the workplace, accommodating trade union power rather than attempting to repulse it.

- The reform of employment relations in the 1960s and 1970s, the conclusion of productivity agreements for example, while predominantly management led, was encouraged by the need to accommodate growing union power. There was no general shift in managerial philosophy away from unitary values, rather a pragmatic acceptance of pluralist approaches as the most effective means of ensuring stability in employment relations.

Gospel (1992) is the most authoritative study of the historical development of the management of employment relations. McIvor (1996) assesses the growth and development of employers' associations. Allan Flanders's classic 1964 account of the Fawley experiment, *The Fawley Productivity Agreements* (Flanders 1964), is seminal. It should be read in conjunction with Ahlstrand (1990).

1.3 The development of trade unionism in Britain

As we established in the introductory chapter of this book, there is an imbalance of power in the employment relationship in favour of the employer. The main way in which workers have attempted to challenge this power differential is to combine in collective organizations, trade unions, so that they can influence the terms of their employment relationships from a position of greater strength. Thus one of the earliest and most well-known definitions of a trade union, dating from the end of the nineteenth century, refers to it as 'a continuous association of wage earners for the purpose of maintaining or improving the conditions of their working lives' (Webb and Webb 1920b: 1). A more sophisticated definition should, however, be more specific about the means by which unions seek to improve the conditions of people's working lives. For our purposes, then, a trade union can be defined as a body comprised mainly of workers that, by means of collective organization and mobilization, represents and advances their interests both in the workplace and in society at large. It does so by providing workers with protection from the arbitrary exercise of managerial prerogative, bargaining with management over the terms and conditions of their employment, giving them influence over decisions that affect them at work, and by providing them with a means of effecting political changes that are favourable to their interests.

1.3.1 The origins of trade unions in Britain

While one can trace their ancestry further back in time to the trade clubs and friendly societies of the eighteenth century, in Britain the trade unions originated in the nineteenth century during a period of sustained and rapid industrialization. Although there were attempts to form workers into unions during the early nineteenth century, these were generally transient bodies that either lacked formal organizational arrangements or were local affairs. The first stable and permanent national bodies date from around the middle of the nineteenth century and were mainly combinations of local organizations in industries such as engineering, construction, and printing (Hyman 2001b: 72). Two related developments during this period, the emergence of large-scale production enterprises, or the factory system (Hobsbawm 1968; Pollard 1968), in industries like cotton manufacture, and the increasing prevalence of the capitalist system of wage labour (Burgess 1980), would, given their potentially exploitative effects, appear to have generated the necessary conditions for the emergence of trade unionism. Writing in the 1860s, Karl Marx observed that under the hitherto prevalent system of craft production, skilled workers enjoyed considerable control over how they used the available machinery to undertake their jobs. In the factory system, however, 'the machine makes use of him...we have a lifeless mechanism independent of the workman, who becomes its mere living appendage' (Marx 1996: 425).

To what extent, though, is the emphasis on the factory system, which was specific to the Lancashire cotton industry at this time, an accurate representation of the industrialization process during the nineteenth century? Samuel (1977) argues that much industrial production continued to be concentrated in small workshops. Moreover, there was a marked reluctance among the nascent industrial capitalists to abandon aspects of the tried and tested craft production system. Thus rather than subjugate all their workers to the rigours of new and more intensive production techniques, as suggested by Marx, employers came to depend upon the expertise of skilled, generally male workers who exercised considerable discretion over the production process. Indeed, in what came to be known as the process of 'internal sub-contracting' employers actually ceded a considerable amount of control over the manufacture of goods to key groups of skilled craft-workers (Hyman 2003; Lazonick 1994), many of whom employed their own helpers and assistants.

Thus the early trade unions in Britain did not represent a workforce that had been increasingly emiserated by the exploitative conditions of wage labour under capitalism. Rather, union organization developed as a means of maintaining craft control, and of regulating the terms and conditions of the trade (Clegg, Fox, and Thompson 1964). Indeed, many 'of the early British trade unions were primarily associations of internal contractors and they often used the union to develop a set of rules regulating the work done by helpers and underhands' (Littler 1982: 68). A major function of these early trade unions was to provide their skilled craft-worker members with 'friendly benefits' such as unemployment and sick pay. In 'many industries it was the oldest form of trade union activity' (Webb and Webb 1920a: 153). These workers aimed to defend and maintain their customary working practices and pay rates, and thus control, through the principle of unilateral regulation, their conditions of employment (Hyman 1975: 44).

The existence of strict apprenticeship rules, which prevented employers from recruiting outside the trade, and the provision of friendly benefits, which enabled workers to refuse jobs unless they were paid at the customary rate, helped them to do so. Increasingly, though, friendly benefits came to be used not just as a means of defending customary practices, but as a way of establishing, and then enforcing, common terms and conditions of employment, or the 'common rule' (Webb and Webb 1920a). From the 1860s onwards, moreover, trade unionism began to take root in industries such as coal mining, the railways, and steel making where craft practices, while evident, were much less deep-rooted (Hyman 2003), something that placed a greater onus on collective bargaining as a means of regulating pay and employment conditions.

1.3.2 Trade unionism in Britain (1880s–1930s): growth and decline

The period between 1880 and 1920 saw a major expansion of trade unionism in Britain. The development of 'general' unions, in industries such as the docks, transport, and gas for example, in two waves, first during the 1880s, and second, during the 1910s, demonstrates how, under the influence of prominent leaders, many of whom were imbued with a socialist outlook, increasing numbers of semi- and unskilled workers became organized (see Hyman 2001b, 2003). This has been described as 'the most radical alteration in union structure and the most explosive lasting extension of union coverage of any period of labour history' (Hyman 1975: 50).

Unlike their skilled craft counterparts, most of the workers who unionized in this period looked to secure improvements in their pay and conditions through widespread collective organization, and a readiness to use strikes and political activity, including the formation of a dedicated parliamentary party to represent the labour interest (see Chapter 3). By 1910, trade union membership had reached over 2.5 million, albeit concentrated in certain areas such as coal mining – the Miners' Federation of Great Britain (MFGB) was the largest union in the country – engineering, railways, and cotton production. These were industries in which trade unionism had secured a foothold before the 1880s (Burgess 1980). The most sizeable occupation, domestic service, was almost entirely unorganized however (Clegg 1985; Hyman 1975).

Between 1910 and 1914, there was a sustained period of major industrial unrest in Britain, particularly in the coal mining and transport industries, a function of increasing union membership and a reluctance on the part of some employers to concede moderate wage demands (Clegg 1985). In turn, the disputes stimulated further union growth which continued during the First World War (1914–18) and its immediate aftermath, a period of further industrial unrest that even included a police strike, and was in part stimulated by the quasi-revolutionary conditions that characterized the post-war years. By 1921, trade union membership in Britain had risen to more than 8 million.

Most of the inter-war period, however, saw a considerable erosion in the level of union membership and organization. By 1934, it had declined to less than 4.5 million. This happened for a number of interrelated reasons. Employment in some of the large, staple industries in which there was a robust union presence, such as cotton and coal mining for example, declined because increased international competition eroded export markets (Hatton 2004). Moreover, the government's concern with maintaining tight control over the supply of money also challenged the competitiveness of British industry and further encouraged employers to examine ways in which they could institute cost savings and roll back the influence of trade unionism. Although employers in the engineering industry won a notable victory over the main engineering union in 1922, the major arena of conflict was the coal industry. Proposals to cut miners' wages and increase their hours of work resulted in a 1926 'general strike' as workers throughout Britain stopped work to support them. Union leaderships, though, worried about the constitutionality of the strike, called it off after nine days, leaving the miners to suffer a heavy defeat (Morris 1976).

In the early 1930s, the trade unions were further weakened by the onset of a major economic recession and the resulting mass unemployment it created, especially in the major industrial regions of north-east England and South Wales (Pollard 1992). In places dominated by a single industry, such as shipbuilding in the north-eastern town of Jarrow for example, industrial closure had devastating consequences. Elsewhere, however, particularly in the Midlands, south-east England, and the areas to the north and west of London, new industries developed, such as light engineering, food processing and the mass production of consumer goods, including radios. In respect of industry, then, 'Britain was turning into two nations' (Hobsbawm 1968: 197). One of the most notable aspects of employment relations in the new factories was the attempt to introduce more sophisticated and rigorous systems of managerial control, based on scientific management techniques. Although there was some union opposition to the imposition of such practices, overall it was rather limited (Glucksmann 1990; Littler 1982). Many of the jobs in the new factories were taken by women. There is evidence that the unions, however, were reluctant to recruit such workers (Glucksmann 1990). While union membership started to recover as the economy picked up in the second half of the 1930s, it was still only three-quarters of what it had been in 1921.

1.3.3 Trade unions and employment relations in post-war Britain

Although trade union membership had started to increase again during the late 1930s, the Second World War (1939–45), and the political and economic climate of the post-war period, in which full employment predominated, were major sources of union growth. Trade union membership reached 13 million by the 1970s. The development of trade unionism in Britain during this period was marked by a number of distinctive features, including the growing significance of shop stewards, the spread of unionization beyond its manual worker origins, and the increasing influence of the Trades Union Congress (TUC).

To start with, the traditional basis of trade unionism in the old, staple industries of the nineteenth century, such as coal mining, continued to be eroded as a result of employment contraction (Hudson 1989). The post-war economic boom was predicated upon the growth of manufacturing industry, the mass production of electrical goods and other standardized products such as motor vehicles, based on a narrow division of labour. Full employment conditions, as we have already seen, encouraged greater shopfloor bargaining activity, creating the conditions that enabled trade unionism to flourish at workplace level (Terry 1983). Moreover, the rather monotonous nature of the assembly-line work in large-scale factory environments, allied with the more vigorous exercise of managerial prerogative, generated increasingly adversarial and 'low-trust' relations between managers and workers (Fox 1974).

The growth of shop stewards

Thus the role of shop stewards, unpaid union representatives based in the workplace, attracted greater attention. Although the shop steward position originated in the first two decades of the twentieth century (Hinton 1973), the growth of workplace bargaining saw a massive rise in their numbers, particularly in engineering and parts of manufacturing industry, thus generating a 'shift in authority' within the trade unions away from the salaried cadre of full-time professional officials (Royal Commission 1968; Terry 1983). By the end of the 1970s, shop stewards had spread to the public sector, and there may have been as many as 250,000 of them active in Britain (Clegg 1979).

Shop stewards, or workplace, or office, representatives as they are sometimes called, are often the first point of contact for union members. They have responsibility for recruiting union members and sometimes collect their union subscriptions. Shop stewards bargain with management on behalf of their members and represent their interests, supporting, advising, and standing up for them in the workplace (Coates and Topham 1980). Stewards, then, provide workers with protection at work that they are less able to secure for themselves as individuals.

Stewards derive much of their authority and legitimacy from their closeness to the members they represent in the workplace (Hyman 1975). But their role can often be a thankless one. They are frequently at the beck and call of their members, receive little gratitude for their achievements, but are the target of complaints should they make a mistake (Beynon 1973). Stewards can also be the target of criticism that they are only 'in it for themselves' (Nichols and Beynon 1977); that the job is a way of shirking work, or used as a vehicle for self-advancement. In the manufacturing plant studied by Batstone, Frenkel, and Boraston (1977), stewards who had used their position as a stepping-stone to a supervisor's job came in for criticism from their erstwhile colleagues.

Stewards must decide whether or not to take up with managers issues that have been brought to them by their members. They do not just represent the interests of their members, but actively determine what a legitimate interest is, how it will be handled by the union, and whether or not it will be put to managers (Batstone, Frenkel, and Boraston 1977). A further challenge for stewards is to forge a constructive relationship with managers, while at the same time having to oppose them, and thus fulfil the sometimes unrealistic expectations of their members. Steward interventions, in so far as they are designed to help resolve workplace disputes, may even enhance managerial effectiveness (Turner, Clack, and Roberts 1967). Indeed 1970s legislation, which obliges employers to give shop stewards of recognized unions reasonable paid time off work to attend to their union duties, reflected the prevailing pluralist policy assumption that by accepting and integrating workplace unionism, rather than challenging it, managers could effectively contain industrial conflict.

The rise of white-collar unionism and the increasing influence of the Trades Union Congress

During the 1960s and 1970s, the development of trade unionism in Britain was characterized by two notable trends. First, union membership and organization became more common-place among non-manual, so-called 'white-collar' workers in both the private and public sectors (Blackburn and Prandy 1965). Much of the rapid acceleration in union membership during this period – by 1979 over half the British workforce were unionized – reflected the increased unionization of workers in office-based occupations in sectors such as central and local government administration. Much was made of the success of the Association of Supervisory, Technical and Managerial Staff (ASTMS), now part of the Amicus trade union, in recruiting scientific, professional, and quasi-professional workers. By 'the end of the 1970s nearly 40 per cent of all trade unionists were in white-collar jobs' (Price 1983: 155). This indicates, perhaps, that white-collar workers were developing a sense of working-class consciousness, reflected in their greater propensity to organize collectively in trade unions. An alternative explanation for this growth, however, attributes it to employment restructuring and the development of large-scale enterprises employing non-manual labour, the greater propensity of employers to recognize trade unions, and a supportive public policy environment (Bain 1970).

How can the character of these white-collar unions be understood? It seems that unions of white-collar workers were prepared to act militantly, and take industrial action, but in pursuit of their own material interests (Carter 1985), rather than as an expression of collective solidarity. They were particularly concerned with securing pay increases that maintained their standard of living. Thus trade unionism 'is viewed in this light as a means of keeping ahead of manual workers rather than as an expression of unity with them in fighting for a common cause' (Price 1983: 163). Yet we have already seen that a concern with advancing their narrow, sectional interests has long been a major reason why workers in Britain have organized in trade unions (Hyman 2001b).

The second development concerns the increasingly prominent role enjoyed by the Trades Union Congress (TUC) in British employment relations. As a trade union confederation, which represented the interests of its union affiliates, provided them with services, like education and training for example, and also attempted to regulate their behaviour, the TUC originated in the nineteenth century. During the 1960s and 1970s, however, the growth of state intervention in employment relations (see below) enhanced the stature of the TUC as a conduit to government.

By the end of the 1970s, perhaps the most striking feature of employment relations in Britain was the strength of trade unionism. For example, the aggregate level of trade union membership, and membership density, a term that is used to refer to the proportion of the workforce who are union members, peaked in the late 1970s (see Table 1.1). From the 1980s onwards, though, a series of related political, industrial, and economic changes, which we examine in later chapters, significantly eroded the power of the unions in contemporary employment relations. Having sketched the evolution of trade unionism in Britain here, in Chapter 6 we consider the reasons for the decline in union membership during the 1980s and 1990s, and critically assess efforts designed to improve the representation of workers' interests.

Table 1.1 Trade union membership 1892–1979

Year	Union membership	Union density (%)
1892	1,576,000	10.6
1900	2,022,000	12.7
1910	2,565,000	14.6
1917	5,499,000	30.2
1920	8,348,000	45.2
1926	5,219,000	28.3
1933	4,392,000	22.6
1938	6,053,000	30.5
1945	7,875,000	38.6
1950	9,829,000	44.1
1955	9,741,000	44.5
1960	9,835,000	44.2
1965	10,325,000	44.2
1970	11,187,000	48.5
1975	12,026,000	51.0
1979	13,447,000	55.4

Source: Bain and Price (1983)

SECTION SUMMARY AND FURTHER READING

- Trade unions originated in Britain during the nineteenth century as organizations of generally skilled craft-workers who sought to use their collective power to maintain control over pay and labour conditions. During the late nineteenth and early twentieth centuries, trade unionism grew rapidly with the unionization of many semi- and unskilled workers in industries such as transport and coal mining.

- Trade union membership declined markedly throughout most of the 1920s and 1930s. Economic recession, and the mass unemployment that accompanied it, together with the more assertive anti-unionism characteristic of many employers, eroded the power and influence of the unions. In the new industries, such as light engineering and food processing, union organizing efforts were rather lame.

- The Second World War and the post-war decades saw a major revival of trade union membership under conditions of full employment. Three features stand out: first, the increasing importance of workplace trade union structures and the role of shop stewards in industries such as engineering for example; second, during the 1960s and 1970s trade unionism spread significantly beyond its manual worker roots to white-collar employees, including those in the public sector; third, the role of the Trades Union Congress (TUC) in British employment relations became more prominent.

For the history of trade unionism in Britain, see Clegg, Fox, and Thompson (1964), Clegg (1985), and Hyman (2001b) in particular. Glucksmann (1990) provides a superb account of industrial development in the inter-war years and the central role of women workers, including material on trade union organizing efforts. Terry (1983) and Beynon (1973) focus on workplace unionism and the development of shop stewards' structures. For the expansion of trade unionism during the 1960s and 1970s, see Bain and Price (1983).

1.4 The state and employment relations

Although management and unions are the principal parties in employment relations, it is also important to emphasize the strong, or 'pervasive' (Kelly 1998), influence of the state and its bodies. It is conventional to understand the effects of state activity on employment relations in four ways. First, employment in the state, or public, sector is a major element of contemporary employment relations and at various points in this book we consider some of its distinctive features, such as pay determination for example (see Chapter 7). Second, states enact legislation in the area of employment relations, such as that designed to regulate trade union behaviour (see Chapter 3), or establish minimum wages (see Chapter 7). The European Union is also a source of employment legislation (see Chapter 3). Third, states operate arrangements to assist employers and unions to resolve disputes, notably arbitration and conciliation machinery (see Chapter 9). Fourth, the economic and political programmes followed by the governments of national states also have important implications for employment relations (see below and Chapter 3). In order to understand contemporary employment relations properly, then, it is essential to consider the important influence of the state.

1.4.1 Understanding the role of the state

How, though, can the state be defined, since it can be a rather slippery concept (Miliband 1973)? One of the most popular approaches is that of the German sociologist Max Weber, who understood the state in terms of the monopoly it enjoys over the legitimate use of physical force within certain defined territorial limits (see Pierson 1996). According to one prominent contemporary political scientist, the state is 'a system of relationships which defines the territory and membership of a community, regulates its internal affairs, conducts relations with other states (by peaceful and by warlike means) and provides it with identity and cohesion' (Jordan 1985: 1).

Liberal-pluralist approaches have long dominated attempts to understand the way in which groups mobilize and accrue power, and thus come to have their interests represented by the state (Miliband 1973). As a result, 'the making of public policy by governments is the end-product of a process of negotiation and accommodation in which citizens organized in groups to represent their interests exert pressure to realize their ambitions' (Pierson 1996: 72). While the liberal-pluralist perspective encompasses a variety of distinctive strands, in respect of employment relations the state's role is generally seen to involve maintaining a balance between the competing interests of capital and labour, and accommodating the demands of both. Where an imbalance of power arises, particularly in favour of employers, the state acts, by introducing legislation for example, to ameliorate it.

There are two fundamental problems with liberal-pluralist perspectives. First, they fail to account for the marked tendency of state policy to favour the interests of employers. Second, they assume that state intervention produces an equivalence of power between capital and labour when in reality the odds remain stacked against the latter (Miliband 1973).

However, a rather different assumption underpins new right, or neo-liberal, perspectives, as exemplified by the work of writers such as Hayek that became more prominent during the 1970s and 1980s. From this viewpoint, state intervention is treated as a fundamental threat to liberties; it stifles market forces and is liable to undermine the free society. Whereas liberal-pluralist approaches consider state intervention in the area of employment relations as a largely progressive development, helping to ameliorate the imbalance of power between capital and labour, from a neo-liberal perspective, laws that make it easier for unions to operate endanger the liberties of individual workers and their employers to conduct their affairs in a manner of their own choosing. State regulation is desirable only in so far as it helps to protect and support free markets (see Dunleavy and O' Leary 1987). As we show in Chapter 3, state policy in contemporary employment relations is largely informed by such a perspective.

For a critical, and more sophisticated, appreciation of the role of the state in employment relations it is appropriate to draw upon Marxist perspectives. Although Marx himself did not develop an explicit theory of the state under capitalism (Hyman 1975), two distinct approaches to understanding its role can be inferred from his work. In his early writings, the state is treated as an instrument of class rule by the dominant capitalist interest (see Jordan 1985; Pierson 1996). In this approach, the emphasis is on the coercive, repressive role of the state, and the way in which its offices and policies are designed to undermine trade unions and the interests of labour in general in order to further those of capital. Kelly (1998), for example, suggests that the repression of trade unions, in particular the way in which strike activity is restricted and undermined, demonstrates the importance of the coercive role of the state in employment relations (see Box 1.2).

Yet state policy is not just characterized by the repression of the labour interest. Thus the second broad approach to understanding the role of the state under capitalism that can be inferred from Marx's writings, and that is particularly associated with the Italian Marxist theorist Antonio Gramsci, suggests that in order to maintain the long-term viability of capitalism, states need to win the favour, or consent, of those they govern. This provides a stable and ordered environment within which the capitalist order can flourish (Pierson 1996). From this perspective, then, policies and legislation ostensibly designed to favour the labour interest, such as the nineteenth-century laws restricting the working hours of women and children (see Hyman 1975), in fact benefit capital in the long term. By seemingly favouring the interests of labour, they give the capitalist system, and the exploitative nature of the employment relationship that underpins it, added legitimacy. Thus in order to maintain the long-term viability of capitalism, states adopt policies or enact legislation that runs counter to the short-term interests of business (Dunleavy and O'Leary 1987).

Although Marxism offers a rather sophisticated understanding of the influence of the state on employment relations, suggesting that its approach is characterized by a mixture of coercion and consent (Kelly 1998), the extent to which state policies necessarily support

---

BOX 1.2 UNION REPRESSION AROUND THE WORLD

State repression of trade unions and workers' rights is a marked feature of contemporary employment relations in many countries. The International Confederation of Free Trade Unions (ICFTU) publishes an annual survey of violations of trade union rights around the world. Whereas many countries restrict the ability of trade unions to organize workers in some way, or limit opportunities for collective bargaining, the ICFTU's survey of developments in 2002 demonstrates the violence exhibited towards independent trade unionism in some places. In Zimbabwe, for example, the government of Robert Mugabe engaged in the harassment and intimidation of union activists and representatives of the Zimbabwe Congress of Trade Unions (ZCTU). Wellington Chibebe, its general secretary, was arrested and interrogated. In October 2003, further arrests of ZCTU activists occurred as a result of union opposition to Mugabe's authoritarian regime.

The government of China uses repressive measures to challenge any attempt by workers to form independent trade unions in opposition to the state-controlled official union federation. In 2002, union activists, including Yao Fuxin, were arrested by state authorities on the grounds that they were responsible for organizing 'illegal demonstrations'. He was subsequently given a seven-year prison sentence. The American organization Human Rights Watch (**www.hrw.org**) monitors the suppression of independent trade unionism in China, and the violation of basic labour rights that characterizes employment relations there.

By far the most dangerous place to be a trade unionist, however, is Colombia in South America. In 2002, 184 trade unionists either disappeared or were murdered there. The Colombian government claims that the violence is a consequence of years of civil war and the activities of numerous powerful armed groups of guerillas who control much of its territory. But there is evidence that the Colombian state encourages the killings. According to the ICFTU, it 'not only fails to prevent such crimes, but also fails to ensure that the perpetrators are brought to justice'.

Source: ICFTU (2003)

---

the interests of capital has been questioned. Edwards (1986) contends that it is over-simplistic to view the state as the servant of one class and that state managers, policy-makers, and government officials have to accommodate the interests of both capital and labour. The state does not just respond to demands from capital; it must also react to the concerns of labour. Policy reflects an accommodation between the demands of capital and those of labour, and does not simply flow from the interests of the former. Nevertheless, the state must still operate within a capitalist order, something that shapes, but does not determine, the character of its policies. This is even more pronounced given the imperatives of globalization (see Chapter 2).

Having briefly discussed some of the main theoretical approaches to understanding the state, particularly in relation to its role in employment relations, we now describe how state policy evolved in Britain, with a particular emphasis on the importance of voluntarism. More recent developments since the 1980s are considered in Chapter 3.

1.4.2 Voluntarism and employment relations in Britain

An appreciation of the importance of voluntarism is crucial to understanding the nature of employment relations in Britain. What, then, is meant by the term 'voluntarism'?

In essence, it refers to the general absence of direct state intervention in employment relations and a preference for the terms of the employment relationship to be determined voluntarily by employers and trade unions, without state interference. The roots of the voluntaristic tradition can be traced as far back as the seventeenth and eighteenth centuries. During this period, the development of capitalism in Britain was informed by the complementary ideologies of economic *laissez-faire* and market individualism within which the recognition of private property interests predominated (Fox 1985a; Hyman 1975). Nascent capitalist entrepreneurs were resistant to state intervention in their affairs and preferred, wherever possible, to handle their own affairs. Under the common law, with its emphasis on individual rights, the trade unions, as collective organizations of workers, were treated as criminal conspiracies acting in 'restraint of trade' (Clegg, Fox, and Thompson 1964). As well as 'master and servant' legislation that tied individual labourers to their employer, this made it very difficult for unions to operate without committing criminal or civil offences (Price 1986).

The dominance of market individualism and *laissez-faire* ideologies provided the foundation for the development of 'collective *laissez-faire*' as the dominant state approach to employment relations in Britain, a preference that employers should deal with employment relations matters, and with unions, themselves, without direct intervention by the state (Davies and Freedland 1993). The existing legal framework enabled employers to deal with union activities in ways that did not threaten their interests too severely, and thus obviated the need for more explicit measures.

Why, though, did the trade unions come to place so much faith in voluntarism? They were disinclined to look to the state for legislation that would enhance the labour interest and, given their suspicion of state organs, especially the judiciary, were to develop a considerable attachment to the principle of 'free collective bargaining', based on the strength of their collective organization, as the most effective means of regulating the employment relationship (Flanders 1974).

To a large degree, therefore, the development of employment relations in nineteenth-century Britain was characterized by an abstentionist role on the part of the state, something that was to have a pronounced and longstanding influence during the twentieth century (Hyman 2001b; Kahn-Freund 1964). Some legislation was considered desirable, in the area of health and safety for example. Moreover, during the late nineteenth and early twentieth centuries, the British state sought to accommodate trade unionism and encourage the development of moderate trade unions (MacInnes 1987), by enabling them to organize strikes and industrial action without breaching the common law.

Unlike many other countries, then, the regulation of the employment relationship in Britain came to be determined largely by a combination of collective bargaining and managerial prerogative, without the development of a comprehensive system of statutory employment rights (Fox 1985a; Hyman 2001b). While direct state intervention in employment relations may have been marginal, one should not assume that the British state therefore exercised neutrality in employment relations matters. Rather, its abstentionist role benefited the stronger party, the employer (Hyman 1989). Moreover, ongoing judicial hostility to trade unions – laws were interpreted in ways that benefited employers for example (Fox 1985a; Miliband 1973) – frequently undermined unions' legitimacy.

The system of collective *laissez-faire* that developed in Britain did not mean that intervention by the state in employment relations was entirely absent. Rather, the aim was, so far as possible, to reduce the likelihood of judicial interference (Wedderburn 1986). Moreover, during periods of sustained industrial unrest, such as in the years immediately following the conclusion of the 1914–18 war, the state acted promptly in taking measures designed to repress trade unions and their ability to undertake strike action, including the enactment, in 1920, of an Emergency Powers Act which enabled the state to deal more effectively with large-scale industrial disputes, including the provision of troops as strike-breakers (Geary 1985). During the Second World War, strikes were forbidden by the government lest they disrupted the war effort.

These examples serve to illustrate how the state's role in employment relations is far removed from that of a neutral, disinterested observer. Rather, it is largely concerned with providing an environment in which businesses can thrive, something that in Britain has, for the reasons we have outlined above, generally implied limited direct state intervention in employment relations, but does not rule out a more coercive approach should it be dictated by circumstances (Hyman 1975).

1.4.3 State intervention and employment relations

In the post-war period, there was a notable accentuation in the degree of state intervention in employment relations, something that posed a considerable challenge to the established voluntaristic system. For one thing, both Labour and Conservative governments supported full employment as the principal goal of economic policy. As part of the social-democratic post-war 'consensus', active government intervention to achieve this goal was deemed desirable (Crouch 1995). However, full employment caused upward pressure on wages, generated inflationary pressures in the economy, and consequently damaged economic competitiveness. Thus from the late 1940s onwards, governments sought union agreement, largely through the TUC, to restrain their wage-bargaining behaviour (S. Kessler 1994).

By the time of the 1964–70 Labour governments, these voluntary 'incomes policies' had developed from relatively short-term and *ad hoc* interventions designed to overcome short-term economic difficulties, becoming a characteristic feature of attempts to manage the economy (Crouch 1977). Given that they posed a major challenge to the principle of 'free collective bargaining', the development of incomes policies, which for a period of time during the late 1960s even had statutory force, helped to erode the hitherto dominant voluntarist system (Clegg 1979). Nevertheless, prompted by growing membership discontent, during the late 1960s the unions became more hostile to incomes policies, particularly statutory ones, something that impeded the ability of governments to incorporate and integrate the unions in processes of state economic management (Hyman 1975).

Alongside the development of incomes policies, during the 1960s and 1970s the development and evolution of tripartite arrangements for economic and industrial policy formulation was further evidence not only of greater state involvement in economic planning and management, but also of government efforts to incorporate, with business representatives, union leaderships and the TUC into state policy-making processes (Davies and Freedland 1993). Thus 'tripartism' refers to the participation of unions, employers, and government representatives in operating state institutions. In 1962, for example, the National Economic Development Council (NEDC) was established with government, business, and union participation. While it is important not to overstate the level of union influence during this period (Waddington and Whitston 1995), the trade union movement came to be characterized as a 'governing institution' (Middlemas 1979), or as an 'estate of the realm' (Taylor 1993).

Voluntarism was further eroded during the 1960s and 1970s by the growing statutory regulation of the employment relationship in areas such as redundancy payments, the dismissal of employees, equal pay, and sex and race discrimination. Hitherto, the prevailing assumption was that, apart from some exceptions like health and safety at work, individual employment rights were more effectively secured through collective bargaining. For a number of reasons, including economic efficiency, social change, and pressure from workers for improved rights, this period saw a substantial growth, which continues in the present period, in the 'juridification', that is the regulation of social and economic activity by statute, of the employment relationship (Davies and Freedland 1993; Dickens and Hall 1995).

The involvement of union leaderships and the TUC in the formulation of state policy marked a clear attempt to control the behaviour of the trade unions by involving and incorporating them into the machinery of the state. At a time of considerable economic instability, the capacity of workers 'to disrupt government economic policy inspired a strategy of enmeshing unions in its formulation and administration' (Hyman 1989: 189). The success of such a strategy depended, however, upon the willingness of workers to accept it, something that could not be assumed.

In the area of employment relations policy, the 1974–79 Labour government was dominated by the experience of the so-called 'social contract'. In exchange for legislation designed to promote genuine social reforms, the TUC accepted the need for voluntary wage restraint as a means of reducing inflation and securing improvements in economic competitiveness (Davies and Freedland 1993). To what extent did the social contract resemble the corporatist arrangements characteristic of other European countries? By corporatism, or neo-corporatism as it is referred to in some accounts, we are referring to the way in which government intervention to manage the economy is achieved by integrating, or incorporating, employers' associations and trade unions into state policy-making processes (Davies and Freedland 1993). In particular, employers and trade unions agree to restrain their wage bargaining autonomy in the interest of long-term economic stability and consensus in return for influence in state policy formulation and, for the unions, favourable policy goals.

To a crucial extent, though, the British experience fell well short of genuine corporatism, although it is fair to suggest that corporatist 'tendencies' or 'pressures' were present during this period (Crouch 1977; Davies and Freedland 1993; Strinati 1982). The ethos of voluntarism proved to be rather too resilient to enable corporatism to prosper in Britain, not least because of the reluctance of the TUC and employers' groups to commit themselves to change, as well as their inability to control their affiliates and members. The extent of corporatism in Britain, then, was largely restricted to the institution of *ad hoc*, short-term efforts designed to relieve immediate economic crises, or as a means of conflict avoidance, for which the term 'bargained corporatism' has been deemed appropriate (Crouch 1977, 1979).

Despite its ambitious intentions, in practice the social contract ended up as little more than a conventional incomes policy since, after 1976, the government came under increasing pressure, not least from the International Monetary Fund, which made it a loan condition, to scale back its social policies in order to pursue austerity measures (Marsh 1992). Union support for wage restraint fell away, largely because of the discontent voiced by workers, particularly in the public sector, who were unhappy at the relative decline in their standard of living. This was a major aspect of the wave of industrial action that affected Britain in 1978–79, and which was to become popularly known as the 'winter of discontent'.

The development of corporatist 'tendencies' in the 1970s was part of an attempt by the state to accommodate trade union power, to shape and control it, in order to sustain economic growth and the long-term viability of the capitalist market economy. But it is important to acknowledge the repressive basis of this attempt to incorporate the union interest (Hyman 1989). Importantly, though, union leaders were also influenced by pressure from their members, which inevitably limited the extent to which a whole-hearted strategy of incorporation could ever be realized.

SECTION SUMMARY AND FURTHER READING

- The state exercises an important influence over the conduct of employment relations. We have drawn on perspectives influenced by Marxism to demonstrate that the state is largely concerned with providing an environment in which capital can flourish at the expense of the labour interest. It does this not just through direct repression, but also through the development of measures, such as progressive legislation for example, designed to secure workers' consent and help legitimize the exploitative nature of the employment relationship.

- For many years, the principle of voluntarism, or collective *laissez-faire*, in which the state abstained from directly intervening in relations between employers, employees and trade unions, characterized the role of the state in Britain. While it received the support of employers and unions, voluntarism should not be equated with neutrality on the part of the state. Abstentionism favoured the stronger party in the employment relationship, the employer.

- During the 1960s and 1970s, there was a marked increase in the degree of state intervention in employment relations. The imposition of incomes policies, the development of tripartite arrangements, and the growing statutory regulation of the employment relationship all eroded, but did not significantly undermine, the voluntarist ethos. Although the trade unions were given greater influence over state policy-making this period, it fell well short of genuine corporatism and was largely designed to accommodate trade union power as a means of sustaining economic growth and the long-term viability of the capitalist market economy.

For perspectives on the nature and the role of the state, see Pierson (1996) and Dunleavy and O'Leary (1987). Miliband's (1973) Marxist analysis contains much that is of relevance to an understanding of employment relations. Edwards (1986) and Kelly (1998) both consider the relationship between the state and the nature of employment relations. For voluntarism in Britain, see Flanders (1974) and Hyman (2001b). S. Kessler (1994) examines the development of incomes policies. Davies and Freedland (1993) offer the best account of the growth of state intervention in employment relations during the 1960s and 1970s.

1.5 The nature and development of collective bargaining in Britain

1.5.1 The nature of collective bargaining

In the introductory chapter, we indicated that collective bargaining, as a means of enabling workers to determine the terms and conditions of their employment jointly with management, is an important means of regulating the employment relationship. But what is collective bargaining? It can be considered in both narrow and broad terms. In its narrow sense, collective bargaining is simply a means of determining pay and conditions of employment. Beatrice and Sidney Webb, its first serious students, suggested that it is largely an economic process, the collective equivalent of individual bargaining (Webb and Webb 1920a). By acting collectively through trade unions, semi- and unskilled workers could secure more for themselves from the employment relationship than was possible from their individual efforts.

Collective bargaining, however, is more than just a means of determining employment terms. It also fulfils a broader, political function. Flanders (1975) stressed that collective bargaining is a rule-making process. Not only does it set the terms and conditions on which labour is hired, but it also gives workers, through their unions, rights to challenge and influence managerial decisions over such things as the organization of work. Thus collective bargaining, since it is a process of 'job regulation', is an important means of giving workers voice over matters that affect them in their working lives.

The American writers Chamberlain and Kuhn (1965) identified two strands of this political aspect of collective bargaining. It is a rule-making process, allowing workers collectively to influence the terms of their employment, and also a system of industrial governance, in that it establishes a procedure that enables managements to reach decisions jointly with trade unions. It is inappropriate, therefore, to view collective bargaining simply as a device for determining pay and conditions. Rather, it 'is generally more useful to use the term to cover a broader set of joint regulatory behaviour, embracing all activity whereby employers deliberately permit representatives of employee collectivities to be involved in the management of the employment relationship' (Brown 1993: 197).

For pluralist writers, collective bargaining is the most effective means of regulating the employment relationship. For one thing, it enables workers to exercise influence over decisions that affect them at work. This was a particularly strong theme of the 1960s Donovan Royal Commission which, heavily imbued by the dominant pluralist thinking of the time, stated that where it was properly undertaken 'collective bargaining is the most effective means of giving workers the right to representation in decisions affecting their working lives, a right which is or should be the prerogative of every worker in a democratic society' (Royal Commission 1968: 54). For the pluralists, though, collective bargaining not only gives workers a voice over matters that affect them at work, but is also an important means by which the inherent conflict in the employment relationship can be accommodated or, as it is often put, institutionalized. In other words, the presence of collective bargaining enables managers to contain conflict, to keep it within acceptable limits, and is therefore an effective means of managing employment relations and extending managerial control (Flanders 1975).

The principal radical critique of collective bargaining is that it contains workers' militancy within boundaries that are acceptable to employers. By institutionalizing conflict, it runs counter to the real interests of workers. It is suggested, moreover, that by becoming enmeshed in the process of bargaining with management, unions come to adopt a fundamentally conservative ethos, concerned with the procedural details of negotiations and agreements, rather than with advancing the substantive interests of their members. Whereas workers want to improve their terms and conditions of employment, and to secure greater influence over workplace decisions, in the bargaining process union leaders may prefer to focus upon establishing and maintaining stable relationships with employers, thus sustaining the institutional security of the union, rather than challenging them (Hyman 1989).

In practice, however, one cannot readily distinguish between union leaders' concern with stable and secure bargaining relationships and the desire of their members for improved pay and conditions. Workers have a concern with the security and survival of their union because, without it, they have no means of winning better employment terms. Moreover, the position of union leaders becomes problematic if, in the bargaining process, they are not seen to be delivering benefits for their members (Smith 2001).

1.5.2 The evolution and development of collective bargaining in Britain

Collective bargaining in Britain emerged during the nineteenth century as craft societies, the forerunners of the trade unions, in industries such as printing and engineering for example, eschewed their traditional reliance on trying to regulate employment conditions unilaterally in favour of joint regulation with employers. Initially, bargaining took place at a local or district level but, by 1910, following the path-setting 1898 national agreement in engineering, unions in the shipbuilding, printing, building, and footwear industries, among others, secured national recognition agreements (Clegg, Fox, and Thompson 1964), frequently as a result of industrial action.

In general, collective bargaining found favour among employers, as well as among cautious union leaders, in that it enabled industrial conflict to become 'institutionalized', accommodated and contained within the bargaining relationship. The alternative was continuing instability and disorder as unions struggled to secure a presence. Thus the decision to recognize and bargain with unions reflected an acceptance on the part of employers that a union presence was inevitable: the 'lesser of two evils' (Blyton and Turnbull 2004: 228).

The implications of the 1914–18 war, in particular the growth of union bargaining power, compelled the British government to intervene in employment relations and, in 1917, a committee of inquiry was established under the chairmanship of J. H. Whitley. Its remit, part of broader governmental concern with the conditions for post-war reconstruction, was to examine ways in which relationships between managers and workers could be improved. Five reports were published over a period of two years. The most well-known recommendation was that collective bargaining arrangements, in the form of Joint

Industry Councils (JICs), should be established at a national level across all industries, supplemented by joint committees at lower levels.

Even though many of the new JICs soon became moribund, government intervention had nonetheless accentuated the trend towards industry-wide bargaining (Hyman 1975). During the inter-war years, economic depression meant that the development of collective bargaining was gradual, but the 1939–45 war provided a further stimulus. The maintenance of orderly and stable employment relations was considered to be an important contribution to the war effort.

1.5.3 Collective bargaining in the public sector

The development of national-level, multi-employer collective bargaining was a particularly noteworthy feature of employment relations in the public sector. For example, in 1919 the Burnham committee was established. Based on Whitley principles, it provided a forum within which schoolteachers' pay could be negotiated between representatives of the local authority employers and the teaching unions, and conflicts between them resolved, without the need for disruptive strikes and industrial action. Nevertheless, it is important not to underestimate the role played by teachers, through the National Union of Teachers (NUT), in agitating for a national system of pay bargaining (Ironside and Seifert 1995).

There are three further things to bear in mind about the implementation of Whitleyism in the public sector. First, its spread was somewhat piecemeal and haphazard (Bailey 1996). Although in some occupations, such as schoolteaching, Whitley-style arrangements were implemented at a fairly early stage, elsewhere their diffusion was gradual. Whitley arrangements were extended to the health sector following the establishment of the National Health Service (NHS) in 1948 (Bach 1999a), and Whitleyism only really became 'entrenched' in the public sector during the 1950s (Carter and Fairbrother 1999).

Second, national collective bargaining machinery, since it set standardized rates of pay and was thus seen to be fair, can be presented as a central feature of the 'model employer' tradition in public sector employment. However, this concealed significant problems of low pay in some parts of the public sector, particularly among women (Winchester and Bach 1995).

Third, it would be a mistake to see harmonious employment relations as the outcome of the development of Whitleyism in the public sector. A study of employment relations in the Royal Dockyards, for example, demonstrates that the implementation and development of Whitleyism did not greatly threaten the traditional pattern of managerial authority. In practice, managers were reluctant to accept the legitimacy of trade unions and collective bargaining (Lunn and Day 1999).

1.5.4 The rise of workplace bargaining

By the 1950s, multi-employer, industry-wide bargaining arrangements dominated the formal system of employment relations in Britain. Of the estimated 80 per cent of employees whose pay was set by collective bargaining, three-quarters were covered by multi-employer agreements either at national or sometimes regional level (Brown, Marginson, and Walsh 1995). However, the predominance of multi-employer bargaining increasingly obscured workplace developments. It was always improbable that employers could effectively exclude union influence from the workplace, not least because of the inadequacies of industry agreements (Hyman 1975; Royal Commission 1968). During the 1950s and 1960s, in a climate of full employment, shop stewards in the engineering industry were able to negotiate with local managers over bonuses, overtime arrangements and incentive payments, and reach settlements that were outside, and in addition to, the industry agreements. Thus 'many managements tended increasingly to settle matters in their own workplace by negotiating through shop stewards rather than through multi-employer bargaining involving their employers' organisation' (Sisson and Brown 1983: 138).

The influence of multi-employer bargaining was inevitably eroded, and there were concerns about the consequences. The increasing gap between the rates agreed by means of industry-level bargaining and the actual earnings of workers, augmented by locally negotiated supplements, or 'wage drift' as it became known (Brown 1973; Royal Commission 1968), was perceived to have inflationary consequences. Added to this, informal workplace bargaining tended to 'sap management control over work' (Brown, Marginson, and Walsh 2003: 200), and generated a multitude of small-scale, often short industrial disputes which, taken together, were deemed by policy-makers to be detrimental to British economic performance.

Although dominated by the experience of the engineering sector, the Donovan Royal Commission (1965–68) found, as we have already observed, that much of the blame for the problems outlined above could be laid at the door of management who, it was asserted, should take a greater degree of responsibility for shaping their own employment relations arrangements (Royal Commission 1968). While the extent of Donovan's influence is questionable – single-employer bargaining was rising in popularity anyway as employers sought to develop organization-specific arrangements – the 1970s saw a diminution in the incidence of multi-employer bargaining.

A study of manufacturing industry undertaken in the late 1970s revealed that while multi-employer agreements continued to be commonplace, in textile production for example, their effectiveness was much diminished (Brown and Terry 1978). While single-employer bargaining had grown rapidly in significance, it had come about not as a result of the 'deliberate rejection of established multi-employer arrangements' but as a 'largely unplanned consequence of piecemeal reform' (Brown 1981: 24).

By the early 1980s, collective bargaining remained the predominant method of pay determination in Britain, with over 70 per cent of employees covered by collective agreements (Daniel and Millward 1983). Although single-employer bargaining had become more common, particularly in manufacturing industry, in large parts of the economy, including the food retail and banking sectors, multi-employer arrangements prevailed. Moreover, employment relations in the public sector was dominated by national, multi-employer collective bargaining based on Whitley principles. Though some criticism of these latter arrangements had been expressed, no fundamental reforms were advocated (Bailey 1996), and generally single-employer bargaining was restricted to a small number of local authorities (Beaumont 1992). Nevertheless, as we demonstrate in Chapter 7, since the 1980s the coverage of collective bargaining has declined markedly, and, outside the public sector, multi-employer bargaining is virtually extinct.

SECTION SUMMARY AND FURTHER READING

- As we have already established in the introductory chapter, collective bargaining is an important means of determining the terms of the employment relationship since it enables employers and unions to reconcile their different interests. Collective bargaining is an economic and political process. It gives employees, collectively organized in unions, the opportunity to influence decisions that would otherwise have remained within the prerogative of managers.

- The main collective bargaining trends in Britain during the twentieth century were the growth in importance of multi-employer bargaining at industry level, the challenge to this formal system of employment relations posed by the development of workplace bargaining, and a subsequent increase in the extent of bargaining activity at company level as employers attempted to exercise greater control.

- In the public sector, the significance of national-level bargaining grew steadily during the twentieth century, associated with the Whitley model.

For the development of collective bargaining in Britain, see Clegg, Fox, and Thompson (1964). Flanders (1975) offers an important consideration of the political nature of collective bargaining. See Sisson (1987) for a study of the attraction of multi-employer bargaining and the rationale for the formation of employers' associations. Beaumont (1992) covers collective bargaining developments in the public sector.

1.6 Worker participation and involvement in historical context

In so far as it allows workers to influence decisions that affect their employment conditions and working environment, collective bargaining may be viewed as a form of participation and involvement (Clegg 1976, 1979). Generally, though, we use terms such as employee involvement and worker participation to refer to other arrangements that enable workers to exercise influence over organizational or workplace decisions, or that allow managers to communicate with their staff. A major problem, however, concerns the diversity of practices that can be accommodated under these labels. There is little commonality between arrangements that enable worker representatives to serve on company boards, for example, and those that allow managers simply to inform their staff about current organizational developments. Thus, 'participation and involvement are somewhat elastic terms and are amenable to a range of definitions' (Marchington and Wilkinson 2000: 342).

1.6.1 Conceptualizing participation and involvement

There are five areas where the potential for differing interpretations and conceptual misunderstandings exist. First, what is the purpose of participation? Is it driven largely by managers, with the aim of eliciting improved worker commitment and thus more output? Or is participation driven from the bottom up, through the collective organization and mobilization of workers, and designed to restrict the exercise of managerial prerogative?

Thus it is important to recognize that terms like 'participation' and 'involvement' are often used in an imprecise way that invites confusion over their real meaning. In a general sense, moreover, participation is something that can be supported by managements, unions and workers alike (Blyton and Turnbull 2004). Nevertheless, some scope for clarity does exist. The term 'participation', for example, may be used to refer to arrangements that give workers some degree of influence over organizational and workplace decisions. The term 'employee involvement' (EI) is more usefully applied to managerial initiatives that are designed to further the flow of communication at work as a means of enhancing the organizational commitment of employees (Hyman and Mason 1995).

Second, it is important to recognize differences over the subject matter, or scope, covered by participation. Does the content of participation encompass such wide-ranging matters as company decision-making, investment policies, planning and future priorities? Or, as is generally more likely, is it restricted to a narrower, perhaps more trivial, range of issues such as the state of the car park or the staff canteen (Marchington et al. 1992)?

Third, following on from this, it is evident that the level at which participation takes place may vary. It can occur at the level of the organization, the workplace or, particularly in respect of teamworking initiatives, the work group. Fourth, participation may be undertaken directly between management and the workforce, or indirectly, by means of workers' representatives, who may, or may not, be trade unionists. Fifth, perhaps the greatest potential for ambiguity concerns the depth, or degree, of participation and involvement. There is a distinction to be drawn between those arrangements that enable workers, or their representatives, to exercise influence over organizational or workplace decisions, and those that simply allow managers to communicate information with their staff.

The most pronounced form of participation, and by far the rarest, is control over the business by workers themselves. Demands for workers' control and industrial democracy were a prominent feature of employment relations in the late nineteenth and early twentieth centuries. During the 1960s and 1970s, though, there was a revival of interest in such matters (Poole 1986). For example, threatened plant closures and job cuts associated with industrial restructuring stimulated a number of 'work-ins' in which workers and their unions attempted to maintain the operation of plants themselves. The most famous instance occurred following the announcement of the closure of the Upper Clyde Shipbuilders yard near Glasgow. Workers and shop stewards occupied the yard for a period of time in order to prevent its closure (Foster and Woolfson 1986).

There was also much interest evinced in how workers' interests could be represented on company boards of directors (Brannen 1983). A government committee of inquiry recommended that union representatives should have equal parity with shareholders on the boards of large companies, with an 'intermediary' group of ostensibly independent directors appointed by mutual consent maintaining a balance between the two sides. Employer opposition and the hostility of influential union leaders, who were concerned about the threat to the primacy of collective bargaining, ensured that the proposals came to nothing. Nevertheless, in 1978–79 union representation was established on the board of the Post Office. An evaluation of this experiment found that while union officials were able to challenge management proposals and take the initiative in the boardroom, they had little influence on corporate decision-making. Not only did the so-called 'independent' directors tend to side with management, but also the union representatives themselves were weakened by internal differences and by their acceptance of the expertise and authority demonstrated by managers (Batstone, Ferner, and Terry 1983).

1.6.2 The development of joint consultation

Having outlined the meanings of, and conceptual difficulties associated with, participation and involvement at work, we now focus on one important aspect, the development of joint consultation arrangements in Britain. Joint consultation has long been a feature, albeit not always a prominent one, of Britain's employment relations landscape. It is a form of participation that is particularly amenable to managers since it renders their prerogatives relatively untouched in as much as they can secure employees' views without being bound by them. Workers 'influence but in no way determine managerial policy and practice' (Poole 1986: 71). In theory, joint consultation committees (JCCs) are seen to be appropriate forums for matters where there is a supposed greater propensity for cooperation and a commonality of interests between management and workers, such as health, safety, and welfare issues, as opposed to the more explicitly conflictual collective bargaining relationship (Clegg 1979; Marchington 1989). However, it is often difficult to maintain a rigid distinction between consultation and collective bargaining, not least because union representatives will attempt to use consultation machinery as bargaining forums. Moreover, as we will consider shortly, the practice of joint consultation varies considerably (Marchington 1989, 1994), something that renders a simple association between JCCs and the regulation of employment conditions where there is a commonality of interest problematic.

Although instances of consultation arrangements can be traced as far back as the nineteenth century (Marchington 1989), the area 'first became a problem of general importance during the 1914–18 war', given the priority accorded to maintaining wartime production in a context of growing industrial unrest and union militancy (Clegg and Chester 1964: 330). Hence, the Whitley Committee and its reports were concerned to establish formal means by which this conflict could be accommodated and contained. By 1921, some seventy-three Joint Industry Councils, and over 1,000 local committees had become established with the purpose of promoting greater industrial cooperation without ceding too much control to the workers and their unions. 'Whitleyism was the officially sponsored compromise with demands for workers control' (Brannen 1983: 41).

During the 1920s and 1930s, though, with the exception of a few major companies, such as ICI for example, the Whitley-based arrangements for joint consultation fell into disuse, not least because, given the less amenable climate for trade unionism, employers were less interested in securing cooperation (Brannen 1983; Clegg and Chester 1964). Once again, however, wartime circumstances, in this case the Second World War, and official backing from the government, stimulated greater efforts to build cooperative relations between managers and workers in the shape of formal workplace consultation arrangements that came to be known as joint production committees (JPCs). By the mid-1940s, some 4,000 JPCs existed in the engineering industry alone (Marchington et al. 1992): 'their agendas covered items relating to production, efficiency, productivity and the like, but excluded anything to do with negotiable issues such as pay' (Marchington 1989: 380).

Although the industries that were taken into state ownership following the war were obliged to establish joint consultation machinery, the incidence of consultation arrangements appears to have declined fairly substantially during the late 1940s and the 1950s (Brannen 1983; Marchington 1989). According to one influential interpretation, this was an inevitable function of the development of workplace bargaining. This made consultation arrangements increasingly redundant since shop stewards preferred to bargain with managers rather than allow themselves just to be consulted (McCarthy 1966). Although some writers argue that the incidence of joint consultation remained relatively stable between the 1950s and 1980s (MacInnes 1985), a significant revival in joint consultation activity appears to have occurred during the 1970s (Brown 1981; Marchington 1989).

It is important, therefore, to emphasize the diversity of joint consultation arrangements; Marchington (1989, 1994) identifies four ideal types. First, they can be operated as an alternative to collective bargaining machinery, particularly in firms where there is no recognized trade union. Second, joint consultation can operate in such a way that it is marginal to the process of collective bargaining, covering relatively trivial welfare issues such as the state of the car parking and canteen facilities. Third, it can be used as a way of competing with, or undermining, the collective bargaining process. In these cases managers will seek to consult, rather than bargain, with a union over as many issues as they can given that, with consultation, as opposed to bargaining, they reserve the right to make the final decisions. Fourth, joint consultation can be operated in conjunction with, or as an adjunct to, the collective bargaining process, encompassing matters on which common interests appear to be more readily apparent. Thus it is clear that the practice of joint consultation cannot be equated with the cooperative relationships between managers and workers in an overly straightforward manner. Indeed, the 'four ideal types... demonstrate that JCCs can take a variety of forms in different workplaces, and that to conceive of consultation as a unified concept is both misguided and simplistic' (Marchington 1994: 683).

What, though, explains the waxing and waning of employer interest in participation initiatives such as joint consultation? Ramsay (1977) proposes the existence of cycles of participation. At particular times, such as 1918–21, and in the 1960s and 1970s, employers foster participation as a means of containing and moderating worker militancy. Participation is embraced as a means of defusing industrial conflict and accommodating workers' demands as part of a more cooperative ethos to managing the employment relationship. The main problem with this approach, however, is that it assumes that the incidence of worker participation has a single causal factor when, in practice, participation initiatives are more likely the outcome of a number of considerations, of which accommodating worker militancy is just one. Nor does the 'cycles' approach explain the increasing interest of employers in improving how they communicate with their employees since the 1980s, a period of pronounced union weakness (Ackers et al. 1992; Marchington and Wilkinson 2000).

Thus the concept of 'waves of interest' in participation has been developed in order to provide a more nuanced explanation of trends in employee involvement and worker participation (Marchington et al. 1992). According to this approach, participation may take different forms and be driven by a variety of motives. Thus 'rather than viewing EI or participation as either absent or present, as some absolute or unidimensional concept, we can analyse a number of different forms or aspects of participation' (Marchington et al.

1992: 25–6). A further advantage of the 'waves of interest' approach is that it does not assume that historical patterns of participation repeat themselves in an overly mechanical way. Rather, 'waves come in different shapes and sizes, and last for different lengths of time in different organizations' (Marchington et al. 1992: 26). The benefits of this approach to understanding employee participation will become evident in later chapters when we consider the increasing interest of employers in communicating with their staff (Chapter 5), developments in employee information and consultation arrangements (Chapter 6), and the experience of workers themselves (Chapter 8).

SECTION SUMMARY AND FURTHER READING

- Perhaps the major problem in respect of worker participation is the diversity of meanings that can be attached to it, from the simple disclosure of information to the control of enterprises by workers. Thus one must exercise great care in interpreting the extent and significance of developments in this area of employment relations. In order to account for variations in the incidence of participation, the concept of 'waves of interest' has been used to capture trends and patterns.

- From a managerial perspective, joint consultation, in so far as it protects management prerogative, is a more satisfactory form of participation. Joint consultation has a long history in Britain. It is often associated with determining aspects of the employment relationship where there is a supposed greater propensity for cooperation and a commonality of interests between management and workers. In practice, however, there is no one model of joint consultation and its use can vary considerably.

For an overview of debates about worker participation and involvement, see Marchington and Wilkinson (2000). Marchington (1989, 1994) considers the history, practice and meanings of joint consultation. Brannen (1983), and Poole (1986) contain much useful historical and conceptual material.

■ **CONCLUSION**

This chapter has served two purposes. First, it has enabled us to analyse the main actors in, and processes of, employment relations: employers and management; trade unionism; the state; collective bargaining; and employee participation and involvement. Taken together, this and the introductory chapter have assessed the nature and components of employment relations in a way that gives contemporary developments covered later on in this book their appropriate context. Second, we have also sought to offer an historical perspective, something that, in so far as it adds more context, further enables trends and issues in contemporary employment relations to be more easily understood.

Without an understanding of managerial prerogative, and of how employers have sought to preserve it when faced with growing union power, it is difficult to understand the management of employment relations. One of the most important features of employment relations in the twentieth century was the rise to prominence of the trade unions. The state traditionally enjoyed little direct influence in Britain's voluntarist system of employment relations, though this changed from the 1960s onwards. Instead, the emphasis was on 'free' collective bargaining between employers, or employers' associations, and trade unions. Between the 1950s and the 1980s, the system of multi-employer bargaining that once dominated in the private sector declined as increasing numbers of employers looked to exercise control over their own employment relations. Finally, the history of employment relations in Britain is characterized by 'waves of interest' in employee participation (Marchington et al. 1992).

The trends and issues identified here inform the analysis of developments in contemporary employment relations considered in later chapters. In most cases, the historical overview offered in this chapter extends to the late 1970s or early 1980s. In many ways, this period was a turning-point, as related economic, political, and organizational reforms altered the employment relations landscape of Britain to a considerable extent. We deal with these changes in the material that follows, particularly in Chapters 2 and 3. Nevertheless, important areas of continuity persist. The historical perspective offered here means that one is better able to appreciate the background to, and significance of, developments in contemporary employment relations.

■ ASSIGNMENT AND DISCUSSION QUESTIONS

1. Why and how do managers seek to retain their prerogative in employment relations?

2. What were the main trends in the development of trade unionism in Britain before the 1980s?

3. Should the state play an active part in employment relations or are such matters best left to employers, trade unions, and workers?

4. What are the advantages and disadvantages of collective bargaining for employers, the state and workers respectively?

5. What forms of employee involvement or participation have been used in organizations where you have worked? What did they cover, and what were their effects?

■ WEBSITE MATERIALS

Visit the companion web site to this book for interesting and updated material at
www.oup.com/booksites/busecon/business

■ CHAPTER CASE STUDY

Managing with unions in the Royal Mail

The Royal Mail is a highly unionized organization with postal workers, both those working in mail centres where post is sorted, and those delivering letters and parcels, represented by the Communication Workers' Union (CWU). Basic rates of pay are traditionally low, and workers depend upon overtime payments and other allowances to bring their earnings up to a reasonable level. In some areas, employees' need to maximize earning opportunities has led to them and the union controlling working arrangements, with managers unwilling or unable to deploy staff in a way consistent with operational efficiency.

Since the late 1980s, Royal Mail has faced increasing competition for its services. Other forms of communication such as email and fax have not reduced the volume of mail, but have limited its potential increase. Private delivery operators have taken some business from the organization, however, and, as a result of an EU Directive, it is now required to compete on cost and service quality with private providers. In response to this increased competition, Royal Mail has sought to introduce, with union agreement, initiatives that would reduce overtime working, remove inefficient working practices, improve service quality, and implement a shorter working week. Managers and union representatives at each workplace were required to negotiate their own detailed agreements to implement the necessary changes.

Implementation has, however, proved unpopular, even though a small majority of workers voted in favour of the national agreement. In many areas, staff who stood to lose the most voted against the principle of new working arrangements. Even where detailed workplace agreements had been reached by managers and union representatives, workers refused to accept their implementation. Between 1999 and 2001, there were episodes of industrial action by postal workers opposed to the new arrangements. Of the several hundred stoppages of work, the overwhelming majority were unofficial, that is taken without the support of the CWU leadership. These instances of industrial action were typically 'localized', based on just one workplace. However, on some occasions the action has spread, often where staff in one mail centre have been required to sort mail diverted to it from another location where a strike was in progress.

Front-line managers are portrayed as authoritarian, directing employees and closely monitoring their work: 'body watchers' as they often describe themselves. Their permission is needed before an employee can go to the toilet, or get a drink of water. The application of misconduct rules or procedures for dealing with sickness absence were seen by them as measures to punish employees in a mechanistic manner. Union representatives do not accept any commitment to the business objectives of the Royal Mail or the need to change. Any proposals by management for change are typically rejected 'out of hand'. Similarly, they protect their local autonomy from the national union, and often oppose agreements that national officials have negotiated with the company. Thus a culture has emerged where managers intimidate employees, and union representatives antagonize managers who are unable to stand up to them. Meanwhile, there is little evidence of the Royal Mail succeeding in achieving its agenda for change.

Source: Sawyer, Borkett, and Underhill (2001)

Case discussion questions

1. What factors have led to the current state of employment relations in the Royal Mail?

2. What interventions would improve management–union relations in the organization?

PART 2

Contemporary Employment Relations in Context

2 Employment relations in the contemporary economy   51

3 The politics of employment relations   83

4 Social divisions and employment relations   115

CHAPTER 2
Employment relations in the contemporary economy

CHAPTER OBJECTIVES

The main objectives of this chapter are to:

- examine the implications of developments associated with the rise of the so-called 'new' economy for employment relations

- assess the impact of economic globalization and the activities of multinational companies on employment relations

- examine the factors that influence how multinational companies transfer employment relations practices across national borders

- assess the significance and nature of international labour standards, and the implications for workers in developing countries

---

2.1 Introduction

In this chapter, we examine the implications for employment relations of developments in the contemporary economy. In a capitalist market economy, employers buy the capacity of workers to engage in productive effort, or their latent labour power, in the labour market. Having hired someone, moreover, an employer must realize that worker's latent effort, by securing his or her compliance and gaining his or her consent, so that he or she is able to contribute appropriately to the production of goods and services. Changes in the economic context, by altering the power held by the parties, exercise a profound influence on the character and conduct of employment relations, particularly as organizations come under pressure to reduce labour costs, and increase the output of their staff, in order to maintain their competitiveness. To what extent do growing competitive pressures influence contemporary employment relations? We focus on two main developments in contemporary economic life: implications of the so-called 'new' economy, and the effects of economic globalization.

2.2 Employment relations in the 'new' economy

One of the most important influences on contemporary employment relations concerns developments in the British economy, especially the changing composition of employment. During the latter part of the twentieth century Britain underwent a process of de-industrialization, something that saw the decline of staple industries such as coal mining, iron and steel making, and shipbuilding, and also the erosion of the country's manufacturing capacity. While the continuing importance of manufacturing industry as a source of economic dynamism should not be overlooked (Ackroyd and Proctor 1998), there has been a pronounced shift in employment in favour of the service sector – in banking, finance, retailing, leisure and hospitality, for example, and also in the public services (Beynon 1997).

What have been the implications of these developments for employment relations? While it is important to recognize the diversity of its employment arrangements, the 'old industrial economy of Britain' was responsible for employing 'large numbers of highly unionized workers employed on full-time contracts' (Beynon 1997: 37), who were mainly men. The decline of employment levels in primary and manufacturing industries resulted in a large rise in economic inactivity and unemployment, particularly among men, since the increasing number of (frequently part-time) service sector jobs tend to be taken up by women (Bradley 1999). Thus high concentrations of male unemployment arose in the industrial regions of Britain, such as South Wales and North-East England (Nolan and Slater 2003). Moreover, de-industrialization eroded the membership and power of unions since many of the industries in decline were strongholds of trade unionism. Unions generally have a much weaker presence in the increasingly important private service sector.

What are the salient features of the 'new' economy, and what are their implications for employment relations? In the first place, the 'new' economy is supposedly characterized by a diminution in the significance of the employment relationship, given the increasing number of people who apparently work without one, as autonomous and independent self-employed, freelance contractors for example. Second, economic change is held to be transforming the nature of work itself, with the increasing significance of occupations based on the manipulation of knowledge. Third, the growth of flexible employment patterns, such as part-time and temporary work, is presented as advantageous both for employers, since it enables them to manage labour more efficiently, and workers, who are able to exercise more choice over their working arrangements. In the following sections we expose such claims to critical scrutiny, and demonstrate that the most prominent feature of employment relations in the contemporary economy is the growing power of capital relative to labour.

2.2.1 The end of the employment relationship?

One of the most prominent features of debates about the development of the 'new' economy concerns the supposedly greater significance of work undertaken by self-employed, freelance contractors who are not subject to the disciplines of an employment relationship. This is celebrated as a positive development since it signals that people are increasingly escaping the shackles of the employment relationship and looking to secure the independence that comes with working for oneself (Handy 1994; Leadbeater 1999).

The number of people in self-employment grew substantially during the 1980s, from 5 per cent to more than 10 per cent of the workforce, or over 3 million people (Hakim 1988; Nolan and Wood 2003). Self-employment was supported by successive Conservative governments who viewed its growth, and also that of small businesses in general, as the mark of a dynamic and competitive economy in which enterprise thrived (Goss 1991). While there is evidence that for some people, younger entrants to the labour market for example, the decision to become self-employed was a function of the absence of alternative job opportunities in a climate of high unemployment (MacDonald and Coffield 1991), in many cases it was a positive choice (Hakim 1988).

In their study of self-employed translators, Fraser and Gold (2001) found that independence and autonomy were highly prized characteristics of their working arrangements. More than three-quarters of those surveyed expressed no wish to work for a company directly as an employee. However, female translators were much more likely to have become freelance contractors because they had been obliged to do so by a 'change of circumstances', in particular the need to earn a living while raising a family. This demonstrates that the choices enjoyed by people in such situations are, given their domestic circumstances, frequently limited in practice.

Moreover, freelance translators tend to establish a wide client base. Over one-third worked for ten or more clients. Given a growing demand for translation services, such workers enjoyed considerable autonomy since they were not dependent on a small number of companies for work. This is contrasted with a study of freelance editors and proofreaders by Stanworth and Stanworth (1995), who found that these people generally worked for just one or two publishing clients and were reliant, and therefore over-dependent, on them for commissions. Thus the degree of control and autonomy enjoyed by freelance contractors varies according to such factors as their market situation (Fraser and Gold 2001).

One should not exaggerate the extent to which self-employment is stimulated by a desire for independence, autonomy, and control on the part of workers. By far the most significant factor responsible for the growth of self-employment during the 1980s was the changing pattern of labour use by employers, particularly their increased preference for sub-contracting arrangements as a way of reducing employment costs (Cully et al. 1999; Hakim 1988; Rees and Fielder 1992). Even the freelance translators studied by Fraser and Gold (2001) were able to work as self-employed contractors only because many large companies and European organizations had shut down their in-house translating arrangements, preferring to externalize such services.

Sub-contracting arrangements have a long history, especially in the construction industry. Often, sub-contract workers may undertake the same functions as a direct employee. In the construction industry, for example, 'people work as bricklayers or steel erectors or labourers on the large building sites of companies like Costain and Tarmac. They are paid by the company and to all intents and purposes are employees; but the companies do not recognise this relationship' (Beynon 1997: 33). While this is done primarily for cost savings, it leaves the workforce, hired on short-term contacts, manifestly more exposed and vulnerable. Workers are obliged to bear more of the risks and costs of employment, given the unwillingness of companies to enter into a long-term and direct relationship with them.

As contractors, workers do not benefit from the full range of employment rights. Moreover, although workers are often dependent upon client companies for work, these companies have no reciprocal obligations to them beyond the terms of the immediate contract.

One of the most popular forms of self-employment is the franchise arrangement. Under the 'business format' type of franchise, in exchange for a hefty fee, franchisees are provided by the franchiser company with a business format that they then operate as if it were their own business (Felstead 1991). The case study of a milk delivery company undertaken by O'Connell Davison (1994) demonstrates that franchising cannot be equated with genuine self-employment, and that it can be used as a means of extending management control. In order to reduce costs, the company in question did away with direct employment on its milkrounds, obliging the delivery staff to operate as self-employed contractors. While the company made major cost savings, it was no longer required to make National Insurance or pension contributions for example, the 'very one-sided' franchise contract instituted 'some very specific controls over how franchisees must organize their work' (O'Connell Davison 1994: 29, 30), including the wearing of an appropriate uniform. Thus the 'contract is seen as an effective substitute for what would once have been a job description and allows management to closely prescribe the day-to-day activities of the franchisee just as it would have controlled the activities of direct employees' (O'Connell Davison 1994: 32). Unlike Felstead (1991), who uses the term 'controlled self-employment' to describe the work situation of franchisees, based on her study of milk distribution, O'Connell Davison (1994) prefers to conceptualize franchise arrangements as a type of employment relationship, albeit one that leaves workers more exposed and vulnerable.

Despite the claimed benefits of self-employment, and of freelance working arrangements, since the early 1990s the number self-employed has been relatively stable. According to official figures, in 2003 the total number in Britain was under three and a half million, some 12 per cent of the total workforce, hardly a sign of the growth of a 'new' economy (Nolan and Slater 2003). While favourable market conditions may give self-employed workers some degree of control over their work, as in the case of the freelance translators for example, most depend on clients for work and thus enjoy little real autonomy. This is particularly the case for homeworkers (see Box 2.1). Much so-called 'self-employment', moreover, is simply disguised employment, as in the case of the milk delivery company studied by O'Connell Davison (1994). The employment relationship remains by far the most important means of organizing work in the contemporary economy.

2.2.2 Occupational change and the rise of the knowledge worker

A second feature of debates about the changing nature of work in the 'new' economy concerns the extent to which occupational change, the rise in the number of professional and managerial jobs in particular, has rendered conventional understandings of employment relations redundant. It is an area of longstanding interest. During the 1960s, the concept of 'post-industrialism' was developed by the American writer Daniel Bell as a means of analysing how technological change generated an increase in professional, managerial, and technical occupations, within which jobs were more highly skilled and inherently more satisfying for those who undertook them, relative to declining manual labour (Kumar 1986).

BOX 2.1 HOMEWORKING IN BRITAIN

Advocates of the 'new' economy often emphasize that developments in information technology, the use of email and internet facilities in particular, give people more opportunities to work from home, offering them greater autonomy and flexibility over their working lives, and liberating them from the rigid shackles of the traditional workplace (e.g. Leadbeater 1999). Studies of homeworkers suggest, however, that such a 'rosy picture' may be unjustified given that they are a highly differentiated group (Felstead and Jewson 2000). Those who 'sometimes' work from home, often male managers and professional employees for example, people given the opportunity to do so largely as a benefit, should be distinguished from those who 'mainly' work at home, frequently low-paid women workers undertaking routine manual labour with minimal discretion. In 1998, 680,000 people worked 'mainly' at home, some 2.5 per cent of the workforce (Labour Research 2001).

Such work generally attracts low pay, often based on output, or 'piecework', and is characterized by poor and exploitative working conditions. Felstead and Jewson (2000: 91) cite the example of a woman who received £3.50 for every 100 bows she made from material provided by her employer, something that would take her at least six hours. A 2004 study by Oxfam, the Trades Union Congress and the National Group on Homeworking – *Made at Home* – found that workers often receive no maternity pay, sick pay, or paid holidays, and earn as little as 73 pence an hour for making Christmas crackers (Oxfam 2004a).

Since there are problems with its enforcement, many homeworkers have not benefited from the National Minimum Wage. Employers, and other providers of work, have also been able to overestimate the pace at which homeworkers can assemble products, and thus publish theoretical hourly rates of pay that are unattainable in practice. In 2004, the government responded to concerns that many homeworkers were not receiving the minimum wage by tightening up the regulations governing piecework to ensure that 'fair piece rates' operate, based on the hourly minimum wage rate.

While evidence for such a change was decidedly lacking, during the 1980s there was a revival of post-industrial thinking, linked to the related concepts of 'post-Fordism' and 'flexible specialization' (Kumar 1995). At the heart of the former is the notion that the Fordist, mass-production-based economy was in terminal decline as a result of a transformation in the organization of capitalism, most notably technological change and the emergence of less predictable patterns of demand (Castells 1996). For Kumar (1995), flexible specialization is at the 'heart' of post-Fordism. New technology, the use of computer-controlled machinery in manufacturing in particular, enables firms to meet more unpredictable demand in a way that renders jobs more highly skilled, offering greater autonomy and control for those undertaking them (see Piore and Sabel 1984; Wood 1989).

While the flexible specialization thesis suggested that technological and economic change encouraged a new and more harmonious relationship between employers and workers in which conflict was rendered increasingly archaic, there are considerable doubts about its overall value. For one thing, it rests upon an over-simplistic view of the so-called mass-production economy; in many industrial sectors in Britain, such as food production for example, Fordist production techniques were never dominant (Pollert 1988a; Smith 1989). Moreover, there is little evidence for the emergence of a cadre of highly skilled, functionally flexible workers who benefit from good employment conditions. The flexible specialization thesis fails to recognize that for many, including those in the expanding service sector, an area it generally ignores, the introduction of new technology in banks, offices, and supermarkets, for example, often reduces autonomy and intensifies work (Hyman 1991; Poynter 2000).

Since the mid-1990s, there has been a further revival of post-industrial thinking based on the view that technological change and innovation increasingly generates jobs that demand higher levels of knowledge on the part of those who undertake them. The more widespread use of information technology and the rise of the internet as a business tool oblige companies increasingly to rely on workers' knowledge, not their labour, as a means of competitive advantage (Castells 2001).

It is assumed that the rise of the information-based, knowledge economy, in which jobs will increasingly be of a managerial, professional, and technical kind, reduces the need for traditional management approaches, and erodes the potential for conflict in the employment relationship. Not only is extensive management control redundant in the new, knowledge economy, but also greater cooperation between employers and their employees is inevitable given the harmony of interests that arises between them. Thus 'the new economy is identified with a fresh pattern of work relations free from long-standing hierarchical and conflictual employment relations' (Nolan and Slater 2003: 77).

There are two major problems with this approach to assessing the nature of occupational change. First, the 'knowledge work' concept is a very crude and unsatisfactory tool for analysing the nature of contemporary jobs (Thompson and Warhurst 1998). Can it be applied equally to a call-centre operator, who relies upon information technology during the course of her work, and an information systems manager working for the same company? Much so-called 'knowledge work' consists of rather basic, routine, and mundane data-processing activities that are founded on the manual labour of workers rather than what they contain in their heads.

This is evident from Poynter's (2000) study of workplace change in the finance sector. Technological innovation, such as the development of call centres for example, combined with the search for competitive advantage, had prompted a polarization of jobs. A relatively small proportion of workers who were involved with developing information technology capabilities, or employed in the sales and marketing functions, enjoyed greater autonomy in their jobs. The majority of workers, mainly women whose jobs involve routine data processing and handling customer enquiries, experienced a decline in the conditions of their work such that they resembled the assembly-line process characteristic of industrial society.

The second problem concerns the assumption that the labour market in Britain is characterized by a rapidly growing proportion of people in professional, managerial, and technical occupations. While there has been a growth in the number of software engineers and computer programmers, among the fastest-growing occupations during the 1990s were hairdressing, nursery nurses, sales assistants, and data input clerks. Much of the expansion of professional occupations has occurred as a result of restructuring in the public sector, changes to the delivery of education and health services for example (Nolan and Slater 2003).

Assertions about the greater predominance of highly skilled jobs in the economy should be treated with due caution. Currently there are approximately 10.5 million manual workers in Britain, nearly two-fifths of the workforce, a number that has barely altered since the start of the 1990s. 'Add to this figure other long-standing service jobs, for example clerical and secretarial work, and the size of the "traditional" labour force soars to 17 million' (Nolan and Wood 2003: 170), appproaching two-thirds of the total workforce.

The concept of the 'new' economy, characterized by a greater degree of 'knowledge' work, is therefore highly misleading (Nolan and Wood 2003). Moreover, it serves to obscure the realities of wage labour in a capitalist market economy. There is evidence that, as private sector companies experience ever-greater competitive pressures, and public sector organizations are increasingly constrained by budget limitations, employment relations in the contemporary economy is marked by the efforts of employers to secure more work for less reward from their employees. This is amply demonstrated in Beynon et al.'s (2002) assessment of developments in seven public and private sector organizations. The behaviour of managers towards workers was strongly influenced by pressure to comply with exacting short-term financial targets in a way that was inimical to the development of long-term, stable, and secure employment relationships. Workers were increasingly treated as if they were 'commodities', to be used and disposed of as determined by organizational needs. Based on this evidence, the potential for conflict in the employment relationship seems to be growing rather than diminishing.

2.2.3 A flexible labour market?

A third feature of debates about the development of a so-called 'new' economy concerns the more widespread use by companies of 'flexible' or 'non-standard' labour. In particular, the use of part-time and temporary staff is associated with the growing proportion of employment in service sector jobs, such as in retail, banking, and finance (Felstead and Jewson 1999). By using part-time and temporary staff, rather than full-time and permanent employees, employers are able to align production or service delivery with anticipated demand and thus manage labour more efficiently. Since the 1980s, moreover, the greater use of flexible working by employers has attracted strong support from both Conservative and Labour governments. The former viewed it as a key component of its attempt to initiate a more competitive, dynamic, and flexible economy based on a deregulated labour market (Bradley et al. 2000; Brown 1997). Labour broadly shares this perspective although, as we will see in Chapters 3 and 4, it has also made greater efforts to encourage flexible working as a means of stimulating more 'family-friendly' employment arrangements.

We have already used the terms 'flexible' and 'non-standard' to describe those part-time and temporary working arrangements that differ from the perceived full-time, permanent norm. But there are problems with both. The term 'flexible' implies that employers take on, and discard, workers with impunity and use them in a range of ways. Yet survey data reveal that part-time workers not only seem to have greater job security than their full-time equivalents but also are less likely to be used flexibly (Gallie et al. 1998: 172). The term 'non-standard' working assumes an established, 'standard', model of full-time and permanent employment against which we can compare. Not only are such so-called 'standard' employment arrangements a relatively recent phenomenon (Felstead and Jewson 1999), but traditionally they were also more likely to apply to certain, relatively privileged groups of workers, typically white skilled males (Bradley et al. 2000).

Women make up the overwhelming majority of workers holding part-time jobs, though there are some indications that part-time jobs are increasingly held by men (Robinson 1999). One of the most powerful arguments in favour of flexible employment arrangements is that, in addition to being convenient for employers, they allow people to exercise greater choice over their own working hours. Thus part-time working is popular among women because it enables them to combine employment with family commitments (Hewitt 1993). Robinson (1999) suggests that temporary jobs are often taken voluntarily since they are seen as a potential route into full-time employment. In some interpretations, temporary work assignments are viewed in an unambiguously positive manner, as a means by which workers can liberate themselves from the constraints of a full-time, permanent job and, by selling their services to a 'portfolio' of different clients, exercise greater choice over their working lives (Handy 1994; Leadbeater 1999).

The 'flexible firm' model (Atkinson 1984) posits a more strategic approach to labour utilization on the part of organizations, principally through the articulation of 'core' and 'peripheral' groups of workers. It proposes that core employees will benefit from relative job security, receive good pay, conditions, and benefits, and be highly skilled, while being functionally flexible. In other words, flexibility among valued core employees is achieved by enabling them to become multi-skilled, capable of undertaking a range of jobs. Around the core rests a peripheral group of non-standard workers, part-time, and agency workers, people on fixed-term contracts and sub-contractors who are more disposable and whose numbers can be adjusted to meet variations in demand, in a way that insulates the privileged core employees.

It would seem that flexible employment arrangements not only benefit workers, but also enable organizations to manage labour more efficiently, helping them to respond more effectively to fluctuations in demand for their products or services. However, there are a number of problems with the propositions that, first, the contemporary economy is characterized by a recent dramatic rise in the incidence of flexible employment, and, second, that part-time and temporary jobs are unambiguously beneficial for those who undertake them.

For one thing, the growth of flexible employment arrangements has been gradual and halting. The main developments have been: a decline in the proportion of full-time, permanent jobs, part of a long-term trend; an expansion in the number of part-time jobs, though again this began before the 1980s; and a more modest increase in temporary employment that has, however, stabilized since the early 1990s (see Robinson 1999; Nolan and Slater 2003). During the 1980s and 1990s, then, the labour market in Britain did not see 'employment shifts which are dramatically out of line with historical experience' (Robinson 1999: 91).

To what extent do part-time and temporary workers really enjoy choice over their employment arrangements? There is evidence that schoolteachers undertake temporary teaching assignments largely because they have been unable to secure a permanent position (Grimshaw, Earnshaw, and Hebdon 2003). Many women are confined to relatively low-paid, poor quality part-time employment because of an absence of other alternatives. Thus the emphasis on 'choice' pays insufficient heed to constraints such as childcare responsibilities (Beynon 1997; Felstead and Jewson 1999). There is plentiful evidence of people, women workers in particular, being trapped in low-paid, part-time jobs that generally offer few opportunities for advancement compared to full-time ones (Bradley et al. 2000; Nolan and Walsh 1995).

While the use of temporary workers and those on fixed-term contracts is by no means a widespread feature of the labour market in Britain, it is important nonetheless to recognize the diverse nature of temporary work, and that the people who undertake it cannot be treated as a homogeneous group. Gallie et al. (1998) distinguish 'short-term temporary workers', whose jobs are typically under a year in length, from 'fixed-term contract' workers, whose employment generally lasts for between one and three years. Workers in the former category, often people recruited for organizations by employment agencies, have fewer opportunities to develop their careers and suffer from greater job insecurity than those in the latter, for example university researchers, whose pay and employment conditions are similar to their permanent counterparts.

The use of fixed-term contracts is most common in the public services, especially health and education, where funding uncertainties and budgetary constraints often conspire to make it difficult for employers to offer staff a permanent contract (Hunter et al. 1993; Robinson 1999). The case studies of a local authority, 'Councilco', and a health trust, 'Healthco', undertaken by Beynon et al. (2002), show that while managers wanted to offer permanent contracts to new staff, funding difficulties prevented them from doing so.

A notable feature of the labour market in Britain is the operation of private employment agencies that supply organizations with short-term staff. The agency employs the workers, or hires them as ostensibly self-employed contractors, thus sparing the organization from the costs, such as holiday pay, and duties that come with being an employer. In theory, workers can choose whether or not they want to take on an assignment, thus enabling them to work in a flexible manner of their own choice. In reality, however, the mutuality embodied in this vision of the temporary assignment is rarely evident. In his study of temporary agency working in Leeds and Telford, Forde (2001) discovered that agencies reward those people whom they perceived to be good performers with regular assignments. Workers who refused assignments, however, are less likely to be offered future ones.

Using agency-supplied staff transfers more of the costs and risks of employment from the organization to the worker (Forde 2001; Ward et al. 2001), since the former explicitly repudiates any of the obligations and responsibilities that would underpin an employment relationship, rendering the latter very much more vulnerable. Studies of temporary workers highlight the irregularity of their earnings and, for those who are designated as self-employed, the absence of paid holidays and other benefits (Grimshaw, Earnshaw, and Hebdon 2003).

Short-term, financial pressures upon companies to reduce their headcounts, that is the number of staff they directly employ, encourage the use of agency workers, who can thus be conveniently excluded from the official tally (Beynon et al. 2002). Companies also use agencies to 'screen' potential employees (Ward et al. 2001). For example, the pharmaceutical company, 'Pillco', studied by Bradley (1999), did not recruit any production workers itself. Rather, it took them on initially through an agency, and only once they had demonstrated a satisfactory work record did the company employ them directly.

Using agency labour may, however, present its own problems for managers. Beynon et al. (2002) examined the extensive use of agency workers in the Consumer Division of 'Telecomco', a provider of telecommunications services. Within the workplace divisions arose between those workers who were directly employed by the company and those hired as 'temps'. While organizations might aspire to relieve themselves of the responsibility of managing labour through the use of temporary staff, in reality managers are obliged actively to manage all of the workers under their control and differences in pay and conditions between groups of workers doing the same job can be disruptive.

Finally, it is apparent that the flexible firm model is an unsatisfactory means of analysing the way in which employers manage labour. For one thing, it assumes that the 1980s was a decade in which there was a rapid growth in the extent of flexible working when in fact change was more gradual and long-term (Dex and McCulloch 1997; Felstead and Jewson 1999; Pollert 1988b). Nor should one assume that ostensibly core workers are necessarily multi-skilled and functionally flexible in the positive manner implied by Atkinson's model since this appears to be a characteristic of only a minority of workplaces (Ackroyd and Proctor 1998). Moreover, the flexible firm model presents an overly crude distinction between a core and periphery when, in reality, there is a considerable heterogeneity within these categories (Gallie et al. 1998; Ward et al. 2001). For example, we have already highlighted the diversity of temporary work arrangements.

Despite receiving qualified support from some writers (Proctor et al. 1994), the flexible firm model has been criticized for overstating the degree of strategic intent that underpins employers' decisions about labour use. Employers generally hire temporary staff not as part of an explicit strategy but in order to align the size of their workforce to meet changes in the level of demand, to acquire specialist skills, to cover short-term absences or, as in the case of the public sector, because funding constraints mean they cannot increase their permanent headcount (Cully et al. 1999; Hunter et al. 1993). Moreover, it is not clear whether Atkinson's model was advanced as a description of existing organizational practice, as a prediction of how organizations would change their practice, or as a programme for organizations that did wish to change – three conceptually distinct approaches (Pollert 1988a).

The popularity of the flexible firm model during the 1980s and 1990s was a function of the prevailing political and economic climate, one in which trade union power was in decline (Pollert 1988b). It reflects the increased concern with management as the primary actor in employment relations, and of how managers can use their enhanced prerogative to effect change. In doing so, it deflects attention from the most significant aspect of how companies have pursued greater employment flexibility. This is the way in which they have sought to render their workforces more pliable as competitive pressures impel them to manage labour more efficiently. In their analysis of seven organizations from the private and public sectors, Beynon et al. (2002) show how flexibility in practice meant the erosion of established norms and practices as managers responded to market pressure to reduce costs. 'With the vagaries of the market behind them, HR managers have sent a clear signal to workers that they are disposable and that previous employment terms do not count' (Beynon et al. 2002: 248). In a climate where trade unions have been much weakened, the way in which flexibility has been enacted, then, reflects a shift in the balance of power between capital and labour, in favour of the former.

SECTION SUMMARY AND FURTHER READING

- There has been no fundamental transformation of employment relations consistent with the notion of a 'new' economy. The number of people who are self-employed is a rather small proportion of the total workforce. Much self-employment, moreover, is disguised employment. Thus the employment relationship is still of fundamental importance to the functioning of the contemporary economy.

- Wage labour in Britain is dominated by routine manual and non-manual work, with both the growth and the significance of managerial and professional occupations being of rather less importance than is often assumed. Given the way in which workers are increasingly treated by organizations as commodities, and thus inherently disposable, the potential for conflict is an important feature of contemporary employment relations.

- It is important not to exaggerate the extent of the increase in flexible employment arrangements in Britain. Although many workers choose to take part-time or temporary jobs, often their choices are constrained by a lack of appropriate alternatives, especially among women who have childcare responsibilities. The use of temporary labour highlights the way in which employers are impelled, given pressure to reduce costs, to render their workforces more pliable, since competitive pressures impel them to manage labour more efficiently.

See Bradley et al. (2000: Chapter 3) for a critical assessment of debates about 'non-standard' or 'flexible' working. Other useful sources include Dex and McCulloch (1997), Felstead and Jewson (1999), and Robinson (1999). Both Nolan and Slater (2003), and Nolan and Wood (2003) draw on reliable data in respect of labour market developments and occupational change to challenge the notion of a 'new' economy. Beynon et al. (2002: 151–8, 243–8) consider issues pertaining to the management of temporary labour.

2.3 Employment relations in a global economy I: multinationals and the management of employment relations

The growing degree of global economic integration, or economic 'globalization' as it is often called, is one of the most important contemporary influences on employment relations. What, then, do we mean by the increasingly fashionable concept of globalization? Although economic activity has long spread across national borders, it is suggested that since the 1970s, in particular, there has been a major increase in the extent of economic interconnectedness on a worldwide scale, facilitated by innovations in information technology and communications facilities, and the break-up of the Soviet bloc (Castells 1996; Dicken 2003; Held et al. 1999). We start this section by examining the broad implications of globalization for employment relations. This is followed by a discussion of the significant role enjoyed by multinational companies (MNCs) in the globalization process, and an analysis of the influences on employment relations within them.

2.3.1 Globalization and employment relations

The globalization of economic and business activity has four key features: growing levels of international trade in goods and services; the increasing volume of international financial transactions and the transformation of world financial markets; an acceleration in the amount of foreign direct investment (FDI) in the global economy; and the enhanced

---

BOX 2.2 GLOBALIZATION AND MIGRATION

Migration, the movement of people across regions, national borders, or even continents, is a phenomenon of longstanding historical significance. Along with political and cultural changes, economic globalization, though, has facilitated an increase in the extent to which people are willing and able to migrate. The impact of migration on 'receiving' countries is a source of particular political controversy. In Britain, for example, the government has taken ever more severe measures to restrict the entry of unwanted 'economic migrants', people who travel in search of opportunities to improve their lives, without official sanction, as a way of demonstrating its toughness on immigration policy.

Yet without the presence of widespread migrant labour key areas of the British economy would immediately run into trouble since such people frequently fill jobs that indigenous workers are unwilling to take. The presence of migrant workers is extensive in the agriculture and food-processing industries, for example, where they constitute a cheap source of labour for employers, enabling the major supermarket chains to keep prices low while at the same time improving their profitability. A 2003 report by the Trades Union Congress – *Migrant Workers: Overworked, Underpaid and Over Here* – revealed the extensive degree of exploitation experienced by many migrant workers, including extremely low levels of pay. In March 2004, an investigation by *The Guardian* newspaper highlighted the gruelling conditions endured by Chinese workers who, organized by gangmasters, were hired by agencies to work in the food-processing factories of eastern England, and received half the wages of their indigenous counterparts. The existence of such people is rarely acknowledged except when a tragedy occurs, such as the deaths of twenty Chinese cocklepickers at Morecambe Bay in 2004. The Transport and General Workers' Union has campaigned for greater protection for such workers and, despite the lack of government interest in the issue, played a major part in prompting the development of legislation designed to regulate the affairs of unscrupulous gangmasters.

---

importance and power of MNCs, often as sources of FDI themselves (see Bradley et al. 2000: 18–19; Dicken 2003; Held et al. 1999). Moreover, globalization is associated with an increase in the incidence of migration by workers around the world (see Box 2.2).

It is claimed that economic globalization, in so far as it enables the greater mobility of capital, places constraints upon the capacity of individual nation-states to regulate their economies (e.g. Gray 1998; Strange 1996), to support employment levels for example. Yet the extent of economic globalization, and also the way in which it is held to constrain the policy options of national states, have been questioned. According to Hirst and Thompson (1999), the current level of openness in the world economy is not without precedent. Nation-states, moreover, retain considerable powers over economic decision-making (Held et al. 1999; Weiss 1997). The concept of globalization, then, is often used rhetorically by national governments as a means of persuading people that, given the enhanced mobility of capital and the pressures of global competition, deregulated labour markets and weakened trade unions are essential attributes of a competitive economy. Thus globalization may be interpreted as a 'myth', developed in such a way that it 'exaggerates the degree of our helplessness in the face of contemporary economic forces' (Hirst and Thompson 1999: 6).

The process of global economic integration is not a neutral force, but one that is a feature of the development of capitalism (Bradley et al. 2000). Moreover, it has been fostered by influential international agencies like the International Monetary Fund (IMF) as a 'neo-liberal' project, based on what Stiglitz (2002) refers to as the 'Washington Consensus'. Thus governments, particularly those in developing countries, are pressured to liberalize markets, privatize state assets, and reduce taxation as a means of stimulating economic growth and competitiveness.

What are the implications for employment relations? In order to compete more effectively in a more globalized environment, the neo-liberal agenda determines that countries should seek to deregulate their labour markets and promote greater employment flexibility (Debrah and Smith 2002; Leisink 1999), although, as Stiglitz (2002: 84) points out, when the promoters of the 'Washington Consensus' use the term 'labour market flexibility' they generally mean 'lower wages and less job protection'. Thus the process of economic globalization has been underpinned by a neo-liberal reform imperative. It holds that deregulated labour markets, and greater employer flexibility over jobs, wages and working conditions, are essential conditions for enhanced economic competitiveness. This threatens existing national systems of employment relations regulation and the role of trade unions (Eaton 2000).

The continuing erosion of economic barriers, symbolized by the 1995 establishment of the World Trade Organization (WTO), a body set up to promote and manage the liberalization of trade relations between nation-states, poses major challenges to workers and trade unions around the world. According to one interpretation, it 'will increase pressures to cut costs in order for businesses to stay competitive and, therefore, put still more downward pressures on labour costs and working-class incomes in particular' (Moody 1997: 134). Although proponents of free trade claim that economic globalization produces greater prosperity (Wolf 2004), as a process of capitalist restructuring along neo-liberal lines, it has the potential to erode workers' pay, rights, and conditions in a fundamental way.

Globalization may also contribute towards the growing 'convergence' of employment relations systems around the world. The concept of 'convergence' was originally used to refer to the way in which the process of industrialism, with its associated technical and institutional arrangements, such as collective bargaining for example, generated greater uniformity in employment relations systems across nation-states (Kerr et al. 1962). The recent acceleration and intensification of global economic activity may, however, be responsible for accentuating pressures towards convergence around a new employment relations 'paradigm' based upon deregulated labour markets, employment flexibility, weak or decentralized collective bargaining arrangements, and powerless trade unions (Eaton 2000).

In spite of the challenges posed by economic globalization, it is important to acknowledge the resilience of national systems of employment relations, something that is an obstacle to the convergence process and thus a source of divergence between nation-states (Ferner and Hyman 1998; Rubery and Grimshaw 2003). For example, Hall and Soskice (2001) distinguish between 'liberal market economies', such as Britain and the United States, and 'co-ordinated market economies', such as Germany. The former are characterized by the predominance of a neo-liberal policy agenda such that the 'result should be some weakening of organized labour and a substantial amount of deregulation, much as conventional views predict' (Hall and Soskice 2001: 57). However, among the 'co-ordinated market economies', deregulatory pressures are more likely to be constrained, or at least moderated, by the presence of robust national-level employment relations systems. Here trade unions and centralized systems of collective bargaining are less brittle in the face of pressures for enhanced flexibility. Some writers express the need to treat the concepts of 'convergence' and 'divergence' with caution. There are important sectoral differences across countries for example (Katz and Darbishire 2000). Nevertheless, the employment relations effects of economic globalization are felt more acutely in those countries, like Britain and the United States, whose governments are more favourable to neo-liberal policy imperatives.

2.3.2 Globalization and multinational companies

Multinational companies have long been a feature of the international business environment. Since the beginning of the 1990s, though, the scale and scope of their activities have grown markedly and, as a result, they have contributed substantially to the process of economic globalization (Edwards and Ferner 2002; Muller-Camen et al. 2001). Investment flows from multinationals, rather than by patterns of trade between different countries, increasingly dominate international economic activity (Held et al. 1999; Hirst and Thompson 1999). Companies including Coca-Cola, Microsoft, and IBM have been able to develop a massive worldwide presence, not only benefiting from the growing interconnectedness of the global economy, but also, through their activities, helping to stimulate it still further. The fast-food industry, in particular, is dominated by MNCs (Royle and Towers 2002).

While it is easy to cite examples of prominent multinationals, and industries in which they predominate, how can they be conceptualized? We use the term to refer to companies that invest in, and are thus directly responsible for, foreign subsidiaries beyond the boundaries of their national territorial base, although this underplays the increasing importance of cross-border mergers and acquisitions as a source of economic internationalization (Held et al. 1999). According to one authority, by the late 1990s there were some 53,000 MNCs, responsible for at least 448,000 foreign subsidiaries, in existence (UNCTAD 1998). The British economy, in particular, is dominated by the activities of multinationals since it is a notably open, and attractive, venue for investment by overseas companies. By the turn of the last century, 'over 18,000 foreign firms were operating in Britain, more than 5,000 of which had 1,000 or more employees' (Ferner 2003: 85).

One of the most striking features of how multinationals operate is their retention of an important home base. There is little evidence for the emergence of 'transnational' corporations, those that are genuinely global in character and able to organize their activities without regard to the influence of their country of origin (Dicken 2003; Hirst and Thompson 1999). As we will see below, the country-of-origin effect represents an important influence on the way in which employees are managed.

Nevertheless, multinationals can integrate their operations on a worldwide scale, particularly through the use of global production chains (Hyman 1999). Kim Moody observes that the US car company General Motors can make use of improved transport facilities to 'use Mexican-produced parts in cars assembled in Michigan and sold throughout the USA or Canada, or Spanish-made body stampings and/or Czech-made engines in a car produced in eastern Germany and sold in western Europe' (Moody 1997: 69). This example illustrates the cost savings that MNCs can accrue by re-locating their production activities. The erosion of economic barriers, in a neo-liberal, deregulatory context, enhances the capacity of multinationals to mount operations in environments where labour costs are cheaper, employment regulation weaker, and workers more quiescent (Held et al. 1999: 255).

Concerns have arisen, then, about the ability of multinationals to subvert national-level employment regulations that obstruct their interests. In the fast-food industry, for example, companies like McDonalds often enjoy a level of power sufficient to enable them to avoid employment regulations, especially those governing collective bargaining and employee rights to information and consultation, that do not suit them (Royle and Towers 2002). Countries frequently offer MNCs incentives, including the relaxation of employment regulations, as a means of attracting investment (Leisink 1999), or of preventing it from going elsewhere. Multinationals can shrewdly use the threat of withdrawal, of disinvestment, to secure government favour, or to control their employees' behaviour.

Thus writers have discussed the potential for MNCs to engage in 'regime competition' (Streeck 1997). This refers to the way that multinationals base decisions about investment, or disinvestment, on the relative attractiveness of a country's employment 'regime', that is its set of employment laws and regulations. In order to attract investment in an increasingly internationalized economy, then, governments come under pressure to relax the supposed regulatory burden for fear that if they do not do so, MNCs will transfer their activities to countries that will. In Britain, government policy in this area has been dominated by a concern to promote the benefits to companies of its relatively deregulated labour market as a means of trying to attract inward investment by MNCs (Ferner 2003). Ironically, the weakness of its employment protection regime renders Britain more vulnerable to the negative effects of disinvestment than most of its European counterparts since multinationals can cease operations there more easily. Thus MNC investment in Britain has something of an 'easy come, easy go' character to it (Muller-Camen et al. 2001).

For a number of reasons, it is doubtful that 'regime competition' has been responsible for a significant worsening of employment conditions within developed countries (Debrah and Smith 2002). To multinationals, relative labour costs are rarely as important as easy access to consumer markets. Moreover, MNCs will often not only be concerned with how cheaply they can hire workers, but also with matters such as workforce skills and qualifications (Marginson et al. 1995). Nevertheless, competitive pressures, and the need to trim costs, mean that many British companies are increasingly looking abroad for cheaper sources of labour (see Box 2.3 for example). This aspect of the globalization process, then, potentially renders many British workers more insecure, vulnerable, and exposed.

2.3.3 Influences on employment relations in multinational enterprises

What factors influence how employment relations operates within MNCs and, in particular, the extent to which they are able to transfer practices across national borders and, by implication, undermine national-level systems? Multinationals may prefer to develop organization-based approaches to managing employment relations, with the aim of securing a greater level of corporate control. This can undermine systems of multi-employer bargaining, something that appears to have occurred in the Swedish engineering industry for example (Marginson and Sisson 1996).

The extent to which a multinational is capable of transferring employment relations practices from its home base to its foreign subsidiaries, through 'forward diffusion' as it is

> **BOX 2.3** GLOBALIZATION AND THE GROWTH OF THE INDIAN CALL-CENTRE INDUSTRY
>
> One of the most prominent, and controversial, aspects of the way in which economic globalization affects employment is the growth of the call-centre sector in India. Since the early 1990s, the call-centre market in Britain has expanded considerably and, by 2004, employed 435,000 people. Since 2001, however, many major companies, including BT, Norwich Union, Lloyds TSB, Prudential, and Abbey Bank, have re-located some of their call-centre and other customer service operations overseas, principally to India. In October 2003, for example, the HSBC bank announced that 4,000 customer service jobs would be lost in Britain by the end of 2005 as a result of its plans to switch some operations to India, China, and Malaysia. Improvements in communication and information technologies enable companies to move jobs involving things like customer relations, telemarketing, payment processing, insurance claims, and credit card and loan applications to locations where labour is considerably cheaper. In India, wages are between 10 and 15 per cent of those offered in Britain. Moreover, firms can benefit from a highly educated and well-motivated pool of English-speaking labour. In 2004, the Indian call-centre industry employed 180,000 people and was growing at 20 per cent per annum. In 2003, the Communication Workers' Union (CWU) estimated that up to 200,000 jobs in Britain were threatened by the transfer of call-centre operations to India.
>
> Such developments have prompted vigorous trade union campaigns designed to ensure that jobs stay in Britain. The CWU, for example, has organized protests in opposition to BT's plans to transfer operations in India. To the fury of the unions, the British government claims that the extent of the transfer of jobs to India has been exaggerated. Moreover, it expects the call-centre industry to continue expanding in Britain, taking on an additional 200,000 workers between 2004 and 2007. In May 2004, Patricia Hewitt, the secretary of state for trade and industry, saluted the 'vibrant' call-centre industry in Britain. However, the fate of many people's jobs, lost or threatened by corporate relocation decisions, is a stark indication of the implications of economic globalization for employment in the developed world. Opportunities to transfer jobs in areas such as accounting, legal services, and IT support to countries like India are, if not already underway, under active consideration.

called, is a prominent contemporary topic for discussion. How far do national-level systems of employment relations oblige multinationals to adapt their practices to conform to local circumstances? The framework developed by Edwards and Ferner (2002) is helpful in enabling us to examine the extent to which MNCs can diffuse employment relations practices to their foreign subsidiaries (also see Edwards 2004). They identify four influences on the way in which employment relations is managed in multinationals: the effect of their country of origin; the 'economic dominance' effect; the degree to which the MNC is globally integrated; and the characteristics of the host country environment.

A country-of-origin effect

The first key influence to consider when examining the management of labour in any multinational is the effect of its country of origin. In other words, to what extent do the characteristics of the national employment relations system of the MNC's home-country affect practices in its foreign subsidiaries? Where multinationals attempt to export their home-country practices in a direct and explicit manner it is often associated with an 'ethnocentric' management style (Perlmutter 1969). In other words, the MNC attempts to replicate in its foreign subsidiaries the management techniques that prevail at home, making little attempt to adjust them to the nature of the host-country environment.

It is evident that 'the country of origin exerts a distinctive effect on the way labour is managed in MNCs' (Edwards and Ferner 2002: 97). This can be seen clearly in the activities of American multinationals since they tend to embody an ethnocentric approach. Anthony Ferner (2003) traces the twentieth-century history of innovation by American multinationals operating in Britain. He points to the leading role of companies such as Ford in developing standardized mass-production techniques, and the elaboration of distinctive company-based personnel policies. American companies, such as Kodak and Heinz for example, eschewed multi-employer bargaining, preferring to bargain with unions over pay and conditions themselves. There is also a long history of attempts by American multinationals to exclude trade unions from their British subsidiaries (Gennard and Steuer 1971). As we will see in Chapter 5, US companies are particularly resistant to unionization, as demonstrated by the opposition of companies such as Amazon to union recognition.

A global dominance effect

Second, MNCs originating in countries that are relatively dominant in the global economy, particularly the United States at the present time, may find it easier to diffuse employment relations practices to their foreign subsidiaries. Multinationals, as we have already seen, generally retain a home base, something that generates the country-of-origin effect. But this effect is accentuated by the characteristics of the home country's national business system in such a way that it enables, or constrains, the MNC's capacity to diffuse its employment relations practices to foreign subsidiaries (Ferner 1997).

What do we mean by the 'national business system' concept? It refers to differences in the way in which capitalism is organized across countries. We have already contrasted 'liberal' market economies such as the United States and Britain with 'coordinated' market economies, of which Germany is a prime example (Hall and Soskice 2001). In the liberal market approach, often referred to as the 'Anglo-Saxon' model, the national business system tends to be characterized by a more short-termist financial system in which companies are obliged by shareholder pressure to maximize immediate profitability and thus produce quick returns. This emphasis on enhancing short-term shareholder value often renders it difficult for companies to construct long-term, cooperative relations with their employees. Contrast this with the approach characteristic of the coordinated market economies in which companies benefit from more long-term financial arrangements, are less prone to shareholder pressure to maximize short-term profits, and are thus more capable of instituting a more consensual style of managing employment relations (see Albert 1993).

Given the neo-liberal character of the globalization process, it is proposed that MNCs whose home base is in one of the countries where the national business system is more 'Anglo-Saxon', the United States in particular, will be better able to diffuse their practices to foreign subsidiaries. There is some evidence, moreover, that in order to compete more effectively in world markets, MNCs from other countries, France and Germany for example, are taking on some of the characteristics of the liberal model in a process of

'Anglo-Saxonization' (Ferner and Quintanilla 1998; Marginson 2000). This refers to a 'convergence in MNC structure and behaviour around a model of international operation typical of highly internationalized British or US MNCs' (Ferner and Quintanilla 1998: 711).

In a study of German multinationals operating in Britain and Spain, Ferner and Quintanilla (1998) discovered that pressure to enhance shareholder value increasingly dominated management decision-making processes in companies such as Siemens. Nevertheless, they continued to exhibit certain features, such as the aim of managing employees consensually and the desirability of avoiding job losses, that distinguished them from a truly 'Anglo-Saxon' approach. Thus a country-of-origin effect, in this case a German one, moderated the process of 'Anglo-Saxonization'.

A global integration effect

A third influence concerns the degree to which the MNC is integrated on a global basis. In other words, the 'more that firms adopt a truly global perspective, the greater is the possibility that they act as bearers of "best practice" and thereby contribute to the globalization of production' (Edwards et al. 1996: 41). Moreover, the greater the degree of integration, and in particular the standardization of products and services on a global basis, the easier it is for multinationals to undertake detailed scrutiny of, and thus be able to compare, the respective performance of each of their subsidiaries (Marginson and Sisson 1994; Rubery and Grimshaw 2003). MNCs in this position enjoy the scope to make 'coercive comparisons' between plants operating in the same, or different, countries (Mueller and Purcell 1992).

What is meant by the concept of 'coercive comparisons'? Briefly, it is argued that multinationals can use intricate financial, productivity, and output data to make detailed comparisons of the performance of their respective plants. These can then be used to exert pressure on workers and unions in plants that are found to be under-performing to increase their work effort or accept more flexible working arrangements as a means of catching up. Where the MNC is more globally integrated, then, it may be better able to challenge established national-level employment relations arrangements and resist unionization (Edwards et al. 1996).

Yet it is important not to exaggerate the implications of global integration for employment relations. By no means do 'all MNCs aim for, let alone have achieved, a globally-integrated production or operations strategy' (Rubery and Grimshaw 2003: 219). One should not assume that MNCs are supremely rational entities that are always capable of acting in a calculative and predictable manner. Just like any other organization, an MNC is characterized by the presence of power relations, something that may constrain its ability to secure the compliance of its foreign subsidiaries (Edwards, Rees, and Coller 1999; Ferner and Edwards 1995). See, for example, Martin and Beaumont's (1999) study of the Scottish subsidiary of 'Cashco', a US-owned manufacturer of cash registers. While the company philosophy was marked by hostility towards trade unions, since the plant was successful local managers were able to forge a distinctive approach to employment relations, one that included a more consensual relationship with the unions.

A host-country effect and reverse diffusion

The fourth factor that affects a multinational's ability to diffuse employment relations practices to its foreign operations is the influence of the host-country environment, that in which a subsidiary is located. The characteristics of the host country are of paramount importance in understanding the way in which labour is managed in multinational subsidiaries (Muller-Camen et al. 2001). This is apparent from the experience of Japanese companies operating in Britain, such as the car manufacturer Nissan, whose activities are marked, it is suggested, by an innovative approach to managing work and employment relations based on practices commonplace in their home country. This includes ways of managing work and employment relations based on extensive worker participation, forms of management that encourage high commitment and cooperative relationships with trade unions (see Oliver and Wilkinson 1992).

Case studies demonstrate, however, that in Britain the management of employment relations in these firms is often dominated by an absence of high commitment approaches, a concern to exclude or marginalize the influence of the unions, and a reliance on getting workers to comply with managerial commands (Danford 1999; Delbridge 1998; Garrahan and Stewart 1992). There is evidence that British managers are suspicious of policies that encourage greater worker participation, fearing that their own power would be undermined (Broad 1994). Although it seems that Japanese firms are more likely to experiment with novel employment relations approaches than are indigenous British ones, the diversity of practice, and the lack of evidence for the existence of a distinctive Japanese model (Elger and Smith 1994; Ferner 2003), is suggestive of an important host-country influence.

To what extent do multinationals engage in the 'reverse diffusion' of employment relations practices across their operations? Hitherto in this section, our emphasis has been on the 'forward diffusion' of practices by MNCs to their foreign subsidiaries. The concept of reverse diffusion refers to the way in which subsidiaries are used to experiment with innovative employment relations practices, with the aim of transferring them back to the home country or throughout the MNC as a whole (Ferner and Varul 2000).

Studies show that reverse diffusion is somewhat rare. Only two of the ten MNC examined by T. Edwards (2000) practised it, and these were both globally integrated firms. In their study of German subsidiaries operating in the UK, however, Ferner and Varul (2000) identified the presence of reverse diffusion in half of them, especially where the integration of international product lines predominated. It would seem that the range of practices subject to reverse diffusion is somewhat limited, with innovations in work organization, management development techniques, and systems of performance management more likely to be transferred in this way (T. Edwards 1998, 2000; Ferner and Varul 2000). This highlights a more general point concerning the ability of MNCs to transfer employment relations practices either through forward or reverse diffusion. Those practices that are less likely to be subject to national-level regulation, such as employee involvement techniques, work organization arrangements, and methods of management development, are more easily transferred. It is often more difficult for MNCs to diffuse practices in the areas of employee representation and pay determination since these tend to be more tightly regulated by national legislation.

How, then, does reverse diffusion operate? In his study of a Japanese MNC, Edwards (1998) found that it was facilitated by the firm's corporate headquarters, usually by indirect means, through the use of 'unobtrusive controls'. Nevertheless, these were reinforced using 'coercive comparisons' as a means of initiating change. Ferner and Varul (2000: 130) found that reverse diffusion operated 'casually as a result of informal information flows'. However, they do highlight the presence sometimes of more explicit and formal machinery 'which could be used to identify vanguard practices in subsidiaries and to diffuse them to other parts of the corporation'.

To what extent, though, have German MNCs operating in Britain been able to use the advantages of a more deregulated employment relations system to diffuse novel practices throughout the firm and especially to their more regulated home-country environment? Theoretically, German multinationals could use their British plants as 'vanguard' subsidiaries (Ferner and Varul 2000), as 'a focal point for the introduction of [employment relations] innovations, with potential feedback effects' (Tüselmann et al. 2003: 341), helping them to escape from some of the rigidities of their more regulated German home-country environment. There is some evidence that German MNCs operating in Britain tend to adapt to the characteristics of their environment, by not recognizing trade unions for example, something that runs counter to practice in their home-country (Guest and Hoque 1996). The German car manufacturer BMW, for example, did not recognize a union at its Rolls-Royce plant near Chichester in Sussex when it opened in 2003. Yet further research confirms the resilience of a home-country effect. While German MNCs are becoming more internationalized, and are increasingly taking on some of the characteristics of their 'Anglo-Saxon' counterparts, they are doing so in a way that 'remains basically German' (Ferner and Varul 2000: 137). Thus it is important to recognize the continuing importance of national diversity in employment relations systems and the way in which it shapes efforts by MNCs to transfer practices across borders.

SECTION SUMMARY AND FURTHER READING

- Although its extent and novelty has been questioned, the process of economic globalization has important implications for employment relations. In particular, the erosion of economic barriers between countries has been impelled by a neo-liberal ideology which holds that deregulated labour markets, and greater employer flexibility over jobs, wages, and working conditions, are essential conditions for improvements in competitiveness.

- Multinational companies have not only been an important catalyst of economic globalization but they are also among its principal beneficiaries. They may use their economic power to weaken national-level employment regulations as the price of investment. The effect on working conditions is, however, unclear given that multinationals' location decisions are based on a range of relevant matters and not solely labour force costs.

- The transfer, or 'diffusion', of employment relations practices across a multinational company's subsidiaries is moderated by a 'country-of-origin effect', the extent of its home country's dominance in the world economy, the degree to which it operates as a globally integrated entity, and the character of the 'host-country' environment. The influence of a host-country effect suggests that national diversity remains an important feature of contemporary employment relations despite the imperatives of globalization.

The most rigorous and informative books on globalization are Dicken (2003) and Held et al. (1999). For a sceptical perspective on the significance of the globalization phenomenon, see Hirst and Thompson (1999). Bradley et al. (2000: Chapter 1) offer a brief and critical overview of globalization debates. For the employment relations implications of globalization, see Leisink (1999), and Rubery and Grimshaw (2003: Chapter 9). Rubery and Grimshaw (2003: Chapter 8) examine the activities of the multinationals. Ferner (2003) offers an overview of MNC influence on employment relations in Britain. For further information about the diffusion of employment relations practices by multinationals, see Edwards and Ferner (2002), and Edwards (2004).

2.4 Employment relations in a global economy II: multinationals and the debate on international labour standards

What effect does the activity of multinational companies (MNCs) have on jobs and employment relations in developing countries, given the attractiveness of such locations as a source of cheap labour costs? From the 1950s to the 1970s, East Asian countries such as Taiwan and Singapore were particularly popular as production locations. As their wages and living standards rose more recently, however, China, Indonesia and Cambodia, which offer extremely low labour costs, have become more popular investment locations. In this section, we consider whether or not there is a global 'race to the bottom' in respect of labour standards as multinationals, in search of lower production costs, look for cheaper sources of labour. We also consider the increasing interest in, and varieties of, international labour standards and also the extent to which they can help to regulate the employment relationship on a global basis.

2.4.1 A global 'race to the bottom'?

There is a vigorous debate concerning the extent to which the activities of MNCs in poor countries exploit workers there and are thus undesirable. Wages are often very low, the hours long, and working conditions poor. However, by investing in these countries, and creating jobs, MNCs create employment opportunities, generating prosperity, and thus enabling people who might otherwise be destitute to earn a living and improve their economic situation.

One would be mistaken in assuming that interest in the activities of MNCs in developing countries is of relatively recent origin. During the 1960s and 1970s, the 'New International Division of Labour' (NIDL) concept was advanced as a means of understanding the location decisions of multinational companies (Fröbel, Heinrichs, and Kreye 1980). This theory proposed that 'industrial capital from the core was moving to the periphery as "world-market factories" were established producing manufactured goods destined for export' (Cohen 1991: 125). In other words, MNCs from the 'core' industrialized countries of Western Europe and North America actively sought out low-cost manufacturing locations in the 'periphery' – Brazil, Mexico and South Korea in particular – taking advantage of relatively cheap and largely non-unionized unskilled and semi-skilled workforces to produce goods for world markets (Munck 1988). In these countries, production, typically of electric and electronic goods, toys, clothing, and shoes, became concentrated in special areas, sometimes known as 'free production zones' or, more popularly, 'export processing zones' (EPZs).

As a location incentive, manufacturers in these zones are often exempted from aspects of the country in question's employment, environmental, and taxation laws. In her book *No Logo*, Naomi Klein estimates that 124 export processing zones exist worldwide, with some 18 million workers employed within them (Klein 2000). Perhaps the best known is the 'maquiladora' system in Mexico along that country's long border with the United States. Established in the 1960s, it enables foreign companies, particularly those from the United States, to own and operate production facilities in Mexico, where labour costs are much lower, and export the finished goods back to their home country (Munck 1988). By 1997, over 3,500 maquiladora plants existed and some 900,000 workers were employed within them (Klein 2000).

Although the manufacture of textiles and electronics goods by a largely female workforce dominated at first, during the 1980s and 1990s the big US car-makers invested in new production facilities in Mexico, though not always in the maquiladora zone. Moody (1997) focuses on the 1986 establishment of a Ford/Mazda assembly plant. He observes that the 'workforce of 1,600, which proved to be as efficient as any in the US, cost about $2 an hour per worker in wages, benefits, and taxes, or about $7 million a year. A comparable workforce in a US Ford plant would have cost $30 an hour or nearly $100 million a year' (Moody 1997: 129). As Moody (1997) wryly notes, the cars sell for about the same price as if they were made in the United States.

The NIDL theory can be criticized in a number of respects. Investment flows tend to be predominantly between advanced industrialized societies, for example (Marginson and Sisson 1994). Moreover, location decisions may be influenced more by the need to be close to key markets rather than by labour costs (Edwards et al. 1996). Nevertheless, the increasing internationalization of economic activity, facilitated by substantial improvements in information technology, transport links, and communications networks, provides MNCs with more favourable opportunities to relocate production in such a way that labour costs are substantially reduced. In 2003, for example, Proctor and Gamble closed its plant near Portsmouth, England, moving the production of female sanitary products to China. In the United States and Europe, major organizations, like aircraft manufacturer Boeing and the manufacturing conglomerate ABB, have relocated production to foreign locations where labour costs are lower, with the loss of thousands of jobs in their home countries (Held et al. 1999; Moody 1997).

To what extent has this trend affected jobs and employment relations in the advanced industrialized societies of Europe and North America? It is suggested that the resulting decline in demand for labour, particularly unskilled labour, has kept wages in check and generated greater pay inequality (Wood 1994). However, while economic globalization has stimulated a shift in the balance of power between capital and labour in favour of the former (Held et al. 1999), its effects cannot be understood without reference to political factors. The policies that governments in the United States and Britain, in particular, have enacted to undermine trade unionism, and the anti-union ideology of many employers, have done more than globalization to challenge the established systems of employment relations in these countries (Hirst and Thompson 1999).

In respect of rich countries, then, evidence that globalization has induced a 'race to the bottom' in respect of labour standards is somewhat ambiguous. How, though, has it affected jobs in developing countries? On the one hand, globalization enthusiasts contend that workers in poor countries benefit from the prosperity generated by free trade and MNC investment. While the jobs they create are poorly paid by the standards of developed countries, the opportunities globalization gives to people, especially women, who would otherwise be entrenched in poverty, means that it should be welcomed. Moreover, MNCs, and their suppliers, tend to offer higher wages and better working conditions than do indigenous firms. In this interpretation, then, the proposition that globalization results in a 'race to the bottom' in respect of labour standards is nonsensical; rather, the investment it generates creates jobs, economic opportunities, and the potential for prosperity in places where they would otherwise be absent (Bhagwati 2004; Wolf 2004).

On the other hand, it is purported that the global sourcing strategies of many manufacturers have, as part of a 'race to the bottom', eroded labour standards (Tsogas 2001). Thus a considerable amount of controversy has arisen regarding the alleged 'sweatshop' conditions endured by workers in developing countries, particularly those employed by sub-contractors in one of the many EPZs, who make goods for famous global companies.

The giant US retailer Wal-Mart, for example, which owns the supermarket chain Asda in the UK, is well known for the effort it expends to find ever-cheaper goods, something that has led it to source an increasing proportion of its wares from China, where wages are tiny relative to those in North America or Europe. A 2004 Oxfam report shows in some detail how the pressure Wal-Mart puts on its suppliers in developing countries squeezes workers' conditions and undermines their rights. It offers the example of a US-owned factory in Kenya that supplies Wal-Mart with jeans. The retailer 'pushes down the price it pays by getting quotations from several global sourcing agents and challenging the factory to match the lowest price'. Its buyers, moreover, closely monitor the production process, and suggest ways of reducing costs. The result is that the 'workers are left to face the squeeze. Excessive hourly production targets are almost impossible to reach. Few dare complain'. Although in principle the factory respects the workers' right to join a trade union, in April 2003, when there was a strike over pay, most of the union members were sacked (Oxfam 2004b).

Poor working conditions and labour rights abuses are especially prevalent in the increasing number of EPZs around the world. A 1996 report by the International Confederation of Free Trade Unions (ICFTU 1996) highlighted the systematic violation of national labour laws evident within them, including the avoidance of minimum wage legislation, non-compliance with basic health and safety standards, and examples of child labour. The document cites numerous cases of anti-union repression in EPZs in such countries as Honduras and Guatemala in Central America, much of it undertaken with the implicit support of national governments. They accept violations of their own labour laws as part of the price to be paid for attracting foreign investment.

In the late 1990s, the Canadian writer Naomi Klein investigated EPZs in the Phillipines where workers endured low pay and poor working conditions making goods for the export market. She visited the Cavite free-trade zone that covers nearly 700 acres to the south of the capital Manila. Here, Klein discovered over 200 factories employing some 50,000 workers engaged in producing goods for IBM, Nike, and Gap, among others. She found that the 'management is military-style, the supervisors often abusive, the wages below subsistence and the work low-skill and tedious' (Klein 2000: 205). In one case, that of a factory making computer screens for IBM, overtime working was rewarded with a doughnut and a pen. Abuses of labour rights were commonplace. Any 'workers who do attempt to organize unions in their factories are viewed as troublemakers, and often face threats and intimidation' (Klein 2000: 213). Perhaps most telling, however, was the prevailing climate of insecurity that characterized the zone. The government, factory owners, and workers were all aware of the inherently precarious nature of the jobs that multinational investment delivered and realized how easily they could be transferred elsewhere should multinationals find alternative, cheaper sources of production.

There are indications that some MNCs, such as Nike for example, have responded to trade union and consumer campaigns against sweatshop labour by instituting codes of conduct, which establish minimum labour standards that their suppliers are obliged to respect. Some improvements in pay and working conditions have occurred as a result (Connor 2002). However, MNCs are reluctant to submit themselves, and their supply chains, to independent scrutiny (Oxfam 2004b), and there is some scepticism about the genuineness of their commitment to preventing abuses of labour rights. Despite its assertions to the contrary, Nike has been dogged by allegations that in Cambodia many of its products are made using child labour (BBC 2000), and there is also evidence that the production of sportshoes for Nike and Adidas in Indonesia is based on poverty wages and violent anti-unionism (Connor 2002).

In theory, as Stiglitz (2002) observes, economic globalization, by promoting freer trade and greater levels of FDI, has the potential to increase the standard of living of many of the poorest people on the planet. In practice, however, people in developing countries have received relatively little economic benefit from globalization; the countries of the industrialized world, and especially their companies, have profited the most. Multinationals vigorously manage supply chains in order to secure cheaper sources of production, something that results in considerable downward pressure on the pay and conditions of workers, and sustained union repression, among the myriad contractor and sub-contractor factories, often located in EPZs, that make the goods for relatively affluent western consumers. Whether this is leading to a 'race to the bottom' in terms of labour standards, though, is questionable, as we see below.

2.4.2 Regulating international labour standards

Since the late 1980s, three factors have contributed to a marked increase of interest in international labour standards: the growing internationalization of economic activity, and the prominent role played by MNCs; concerns about the implications of a 'race to the bottom', particularly for jobs and working conditions in the developing world; and, related to this, the assertive campaigning by the American trade union movement against the deleterious social and employment implications of global free trade (Compa 2001; Tsogas 2001).

As a tripartite organization, comprising representatives of governments, trade unions and employers' organizations, the International Labour Organization (ILO) has long-established conventions that its member countries are invited to ratify. Among other things they oblige those countries that have ratified them to arrange for the eradication of child labour (Convention 138, 1973), and to respect the right of workers' freedom of association, to organize in trade unions and to bargain collectively (Conventions 87, 1948, and 98, 1949). However, members are not obliged to ratify any of the conventions and many do not do so (Leisink 1999). About one-third have not ratified the convention outlawing child labour, for example. Moreover, the ILO lacks an effective means of ensuring that countries that ratify a convention actually comply with it in practice (Rubery and Grimshaw 2003).

Nevertheless, since the late 1990s the ILO has taken on a more active role in the propagation of international labour standards (Elliott and Freeman 2003). In 1998, it published a Declaration of Fundamental Principles and Rights at Work. This incorporated eight ILO conventions covering freedom of association and the right to collective bargaining, the elimination of forced or compulsory labour, the abolition of child labour, and the elimination of workplace discrimination. All member states are required to comply with these obligations even if they have not ratified the relevant convention. The ILO still lacks any real powers to guarantee compliance (O'Brien 2002). Instead, it aims to 'promote labour standards through technical assistance and development policies, and to work with member states on how to implement the fundamental rights included in the declaration' (Rubery and Grimshaw 2003: 244).

The principal criticism of attempts to regulate labour standards on a global basis is that they are protectionist. Enthusiasts for globalization and free trade contend that setting international labour standards obstructs the efforts of developing countries that wish to use one of their key competitive advantages, low labour costs, to attract investment and pursue economic growth. By setting minimum employment rights, which developing countries are less likely to be able to meet, this hinders free trade and unfairly protects companies and workers in the developed world from the rigours of global competition, leading to fewer job opportunities, and less prosperity in poorer countries. Jobs in EPZs might offer low pay and undesirable working conditions by the standards of rich nations, but the workers who undertake them are generally better off than if they had remained as agricultural or domestic labourers. Thus efforts to determine minimum international employment rights are misplaced and counterproductive (Bhagwati 2004; Wolf 2004).

Nevertheless, the case for international labour standards does not rest on economic grounds alone. Rather, they are often advanced as a means of stimulating social justice, including dignity at work, something that has informed the perspective of the ILO in particular (Leisink 1999). Moreover, the assumption that international labour standards are necessarily prejudicial to economic competitiveness has not gone unchallenged. They can often be made context-specific. Freedom of association – the right of workers to organize and join trade unions – while ostensibly a universal standard, can be tailored to the circumstances and legal system of individual countries (Leisink 1999).

Globalization enthusiasts contend that since the presence of trade unions increases labour costs in developing countries, and thus impedes investment, restrictions on union activity are rational, and indeed desirable, if competitiveness and prosperity are to be advanced (Bhagwati 2004; Wolf 2004). But such an approach fails to appreciate that a union presence could work to the benefit of employers (Elliott and Freeman 2003). Unions may encourage firms to seek other, potentially more advantageous, ways of generating improvements in labour productivity rather than simply by exerting downward pressure on wages and conditions. Countries like South Korea, for example, have experienced tremendous economic growth in recent decades, stimulated largely by capital investment and skills development, rather than by intensive, low-wage production techniques (van Roozendaal 2002).

There are some interventions, such as the abolition of child labour for example, that might be seen as basic, and thus universally applicable, human rights regardless of context. There is an argument that while child labour may be undesirable, it is nonetheless an indispensable feature of economic and social development in some societies because the additional wages are a vital contribution to family income. However, it is doubtful that economic development is contingent upon the practice of widespread child labour. Rather, its existence helps to keep wages low to the advantage of unscrupulous employers (Tsogas 2001).

The assumption that a system of international labour standards is inimical to globalization, free trade, and increased prosperity is far too simplistic. Indeed, in so far as it has the potential to raise living standards in poorer nations, and give the internationalization of economic activity greater support and legitimacy in richer ones, a system of international labour standards can be regarded as an integral feature of the globalization process (Elliott and Freeman 2003).

2.4.3 Approaches to international labour standards

How, then, can we distinguish between different ways of establishing international labour standards? Four main approaches can be identified: unilateral, bilateral, regional, and multilateral methods (Tsogas 1999, 2001). By 'unilateral' labour standards we are referring to the voluntary efforts of MNCs in establishing, and getting their suppliers to abide by, corporate codes of conduct governing employment practices and working conditions. These became increasingly commonplace in the United States during the 1990s, particularly within the sportswear and fashion industries, as companies responded to trade union campaigns and consumer pressures for reform. Nike, for example, claims its code dates back to 1991. In its current form, it obliges contractors not to employ workers aged below 18 in the production of footwear or below 16 in the production of clothing goods, accessories, and equipment. Nike is also a member of the Fair Labor Association (FLA), a body that also includes Puma and Reebok within its membership. The FLA publishes is own code of conduct which, as well as requiring member firms to ensure that their suppliers comply with local labour laws, also mandates them to respect workers' rights to organize in trade unions and bargain collectively.

In Britain, the Ethical Trading Initiative (ETI), which includes Tesco, Marks and Spencer, and W H Smith among its members, as well as the Trades Union Congress (TUC) and leading non-governmental organizations like Oxfam, fulfils a similar function. Its 'base code' requires its member companies to source their products from suppliers who, among other things, respect workers' rights to form trade unions and pay 'living wages', defined as 'enough to meet basic needs and to provide discretionary income'.

However, the extent to which corporate codes of conduct, that of course have no legal force, can generate effective international labour standards is questionable. For example, we have already seen that in 2000, despite Nike's claims to the contrary and the provisions of its code of conduct, some of its suppliers appear to have still been using child labour in Cambodia (BBC 2000). Many US retailers instituted codes of conduct only because of consumer pressure and not from a genuine commitment to improving working conditions in the developing world (Compa 2001); they are sometimes established with the aim of improving a company's public relations image (O'Brien 2002). Nevertheless, in the face of vigorous anti-sweatshop and other activist campaigns, companies have taken steps to strengthen their codes and subject them to a greater degree of independent scrutiny (Elliott and Freeman 2003).

'Bilateral' types of labour standards are those that are incorporated into trade agreements between individual countries or groups of countries. Both the European Union (EU) and the United States, for example, operate Generalized System of Preferences (GSP) regimes whereby developing countries are given favourable trading rights in exchange for agreeing to abide by minimum labour standards. In respect of the US regime, there is some evidence that the GSP process may have had a positive impact on employment conditions. It led to the first union recognition agreement in Guatemala's EPZ factories, for example (Compa 2001). However, the GSP process is extremely susceptible to political interference. According to Tsogas (2001: 109), 'no close ally of the United States has ever been removed from the GSP programme'. Thus it would be unwise to expect that bilateral types of international labour standards will do much to improve employment conditions worldwide.

Essentially, 'regional' types of labour standards are by-products of the development of free-trade agreements between groups of countries, of which the EU's 'social dimension', discussed in Chapter 3, and the North American Free Trade Agreement's (NAFTA) labour side agreement are the most prominent (see Box 2.4).

Finally, the appropriateness of 'multilateral' types of international labour standards, those that are included as part of global trade agreements under which a country can be penalized by means of sanctions if it does not abide by an agreed set of minimum rules, has recently become a source of much controversy. Following years of negotiations, in 1995 the World Trade Organization (WTO) was established with the purpose of determining a global framework within which free trade could flourish. In some quarters, within the US labour movement for example, the formation of the WTO was viewed as an opportunity to enact a multilateral set of labour standards linked to free trade (Tsogas 2000; van Roozendaal 2002). The Clinton administration came under strong pressure from American trade unions to insist upon the inclusion of a 'social clause' within the WTO agreement. Following sustained opposition from many developing countries, who were hostile to what they interpreted as blatant protectionism, the WTO, in its 1996 Singapore Declaration, announced that a social clause would not be forthcoming.

Nevertheless, labour activists, particularly those in the United States, continued to campaign for the inclusion of a social clause. The 1999 WTO meeting in Seattle, which was arranged to accelerate the liberalization of global trade, was the target of massive protests, not just by representatives of worldwide labour, but also from other groups opposed to the neo-liberal thrust of the globalization process. While the Seattle talks resulted in no further progress being made in respect of world trade liberalization, the activities of the protestors nonetheless ensured that debates about international labour standards received greater publicity (Tsogas 2001).

BOX 2.4 THE NORTH AMERICAN FREE TRADE AGREEMENT AND LABOUR STANDARDS

The North American Free Trade Agreement (NAFTA) was instituted in 1994 as a free trade area incorporating the United States, Canada, and Mexico. As a result of pressure generated by American unions, the US government, under the presidency of Bill Clinton, insisted upon, and achieved, a side agreement governing labour conditions – the North American Agreement on Labor Cooperation (NAALC). It obliges the three governments to ensure that certain stated principles, such as the freedom of workers to organize in trade unions, are promoted within their own national-level employment regimes (Teague 2003). National Administrative Offices in each of the three countries deal with complaints that national labour laws have been transgressed in some way in one of the other countries.

There is evidence that the process has encouraged some slight improvements in employment rights in parts of the Mexican *maquiladora* sector. However, NAALC 'does not tie any of the participating countries to international labour standards. Nor does it have the capacity to make extra-national labour market rules' (Teague 2003: 441). In effect, all NAALC does, then, is offer a mechanism to ensure that the three governments comply with their own respective domestic labour legislation. Unlike the European Union's 'social dimension', which, as we see in Chapter 3, involves a degree of supra-national regulation of employment relations, that is above the level of the nation-state, NAALC 'appears to have been deliberately designed to prevent supranational forms of regulatory or policy action on labour matters' (Teague 2003: 448). One should thus not put any faith in the capacity of this agreement to initiate substantial improvements in labour standards. Rather, it was established to overcome opposition to NAFTA, a free trade agreement that enormously benefits American multinationals operating in Mexico.

2.4.4 Globalization and labour internationalism

To a large extent, therefore, the efforts of union activists, workers, and associated campaigning groups are vital to the development of an effective international regime governing labour standards and to withstanding the neo-liberal character of the globalization process. Historically, Cold War divisions impeded efforts to build global labour solidarity (Cohen 1991; Tsogas 2001). Since the early 1990s, and the end of the Cold War, the American trade union movement in particular has been able to pursue a more progressive foreign policy agenda, one that is markedly different from the somewhat crude anti-communism that had characterized it hitherto (Compa 2001).

Perhaps a more enduring obstacle to the articulation of international union solidarity concerns the influence of protectionist attitudes among trade unions in developed countries (Rubery and Grimshaw 2003). Workers' organizations in, and the governments of, developing nations perceive that the hostility towards globalization and free trade evinced by union movements in the rich countries stems from a concern to prevent the export of jobs, and thus protect living standards, at the expense of their workers. However, the run-up to Seattle, and its aftermath, witnessed important links being forged between trade unions and labour activists from developed countries in North America and Europe and their counterparts in the developing world, based on a shared understanding that the global regulation of labour standards was imperative to worldwide improvements in living standards and working conditions (Compa 2001; Waterman 2001).

Globalization, in so far as it represents the development and expansion of a neo-liberal capitalist order on a massive scale, may, given the pressure under which it puts workers, create the conditions for its own demise as they mobilize to challenge and contest it (see Chapter 9). There is already plentiful evidence from countries such as South Korea, Indonesia, and Brazil to suggest that economic development, and entry into the capitalist global system, generates the conditions that make the emergence of vigorous independent trade unionism viable (see Moody 1997). Thus it would be a mistake to assume that globalization will invariably weaken trade unionism around the world. Instead, it may prompt the emergence of a more progressive international union agenda, based on a common need to regulate effectively labour standards around the world. Viewed from this perspective, then, the notion that globalization is generating a 'race to the bottom' in respect of labour standards is seriously misplaced (Silver 2003).

SECTION SUMMARY AND FURTHER READING

- For decades, some multinational companies have shifted production activities to parts of the world where they can benefit from the cost savings generated by cheap labour. However, the increasingly intensive competitive pressures associated with the process of economic globalization have stimulated renewed efforts by companies to source their products from areas of the world with lower labour costs.

- Among developing countries, there is ample evidence that globalization has undermined labour standards. Multinational companies, particularly those responsible for clothing and sportswear brands, use their economic power to squeeze the margins of their suppliers, resulting in the erosion of pay and working conditions, and attacks on independent trade unions.

- This has generated renewed interest in the desirability of regulating labour standards on an international basis. Though open to criticism that they hinder economic growth in a way that unfairly protects jobs in developing countries, international labour standards can stimulate improved social and economic well-being. The voluntary efforts of MNCs themselves, however, are unlikely to be very effective, and much depends upon the extent to which trade unions and workers' groups worldwide are able to campaign and mobilize around the issue of enhanced workers' rights.

Naomi Klein reports on conditions in an EPZ in the Phillipines (Klein 2000: Chapter 9). The International Confederation of Free Trade Unions (ICFTU) publishes reports on labour abuses worldwide and campaigns for better working conditions (**www.icftu.org**), as do non-governmental organizations such as Oxfam (**www.oxfam.org**). The Fair Labor Association (USA) and the Ethical Trading Initiative (UK) both promote good labour standards among their member companies (**www.fairlabor.org** and **www.ethicaltrade.org**). For further material on international labour standards, see the work of George Tsogas (1999, 2000, 2001), and the overview provided by Rubery and Grimshaw (2003: Chapter 10). See the companion website for further information about the labour standards debate and links to other relevant websites.

■ CONCLUSION

Perhaps the most notable theme to have emerged from our assessment of the implications of economic change for contemporary employment relations is the extent to which the competitive pressures associated with a capitalist market economy have impelled employers to find ever more efficient ways of managing labour, resulting in downward pressure on labour conditions. In Britain, this can be seen, for example, in the preference of employers for flexible working arrangements that make workers more 'disposable' (Beynon et al. 2002). For workers, the outcomes of this intensification of market competition are greater job insecurity and higher workloads, matters we consider in Chapter 8, as employers seek to shift the terms of the wage-work bargain in a direction favourable to their own interests. On a global scale, the efforts of powerful multinational companies to undermine national systems of employment relations, and to shift production to locations where it is cheaper to employ staff, are major consequences of the process of economic globalization. Moreover, the erosion of labour standards in the developing world is further evidence of how the neo-liberal process of economic globalization, as an intensification of capitalist relations, often undermines workers' interests.

Economic change, then, far from inducing a more cooperative character to employment relations, has made the potential for conflict in the employment relationship more starkly apparent. For many workers in developing countries, who produce clothes, shoes, and other consumer items for western markets, conditions are often extremely poor, and their jobs precarious. The conflict of interest that lies at the heart of the employment relationship is perhaps most readily apparent in the export processing zones and their like, which are increasingly dotted around the developing world.

Although the relentless process of capitalist restructuring and the associated intensification of competitive pressures described in this chapter would appear to be wholly advantageous to employers, one would be mistaken in assuming that they have made both national systems of employment relations and organized labour impotent. For one thing, we have established that, despite the convergence pressures associated with globalization, national-level diversity remains an important feature of contemporary employment relations. Furthermore, the conditions under which labour operates make the mobilization of workers, and their organization in trade unions, increasingly viable. As long as the exploitative capitalist employment relationship endures, workers will endeavour to combine and look to secure improvements by means of collective action.

■ ASSIGNMENT AND DISCUSSION QUESTIONS

1. To what extent do people working as freelancers or sub-contractors have more control over their labour than would be the case if they were employees?

2. Discuss the proposition that part-time and temporary working arrangements benefit both employers and workers.

3. What are the main factors that influence the ability of multinational companies to transfer employment practices across national borders?

4. 'Investment in developing countries by multinational companies leads to improvements in living standards by providing opportunities for paid employment that would otherwise not be available. Such investment should therefore be encouraged.' Discuss.

5. Should there be minimum labour standards that multinational companies must observe in all countries where they operate? Why?

■ WEBSITE MATERIALS

 Visit the companion web site to this book for interesting and updated material at
www.oup.com/booksites/busecon/business

■ CHAPTER CASE STUDY

Union organization of 'atypical' workers

One characteristic of contemporary employment is the number of workers employed on fixed-term and similar contracts. These include semi- and unskilled casual workers in industries such as hospitality and road haulage, and those with specialist technical skills, for example people working in journalism, and television and film production. The nature of such employment means that they may work for several different employers in the course of a relatively short period of time. This, then, is a very different relationship from that of the majority of employees who have 'open-ended' contracts with one employer. While some may work alongside a substantial number of permanent staff, others, for example in film production, may comprise the majority, or even the whole of the workforce. For trade unions, such types of work pose particular challenges in respect of recruitment and representation and, in some cases, the type of service they provide.

Trade unions normally rely on local representatives, for example shop stewards, or work colleagues, to recruit new workers into membership. Such representatives may not exist where the majority of staff are on fixed-term contracts, or, where they do, they may focus on recruiting and representing permanent staff. Furthermore, workers may consider the costs of union membership not to be worthwhile if their period with any individual organization is relatively short. Even where unions succeed in recruitment, the intermittent nature of working arrangements often means that workers allow their membership to lapse when they stop working for that employer.

As well as finding alternative recruitment methods, unions may need to provide specific services that remain valuable to workers while they are between assignments. This might include a reduced level of subscription for these periods, access to training to maintain skills and knowledge which will continue to make them attractive to employers recruiting both temporary and permanent staff, and specific legal advice relevant to non-standard employment. Heery et al. (2004) point out that such services may provide a substitute to the benefits that would otherwise be available from employers. These include sickness and maternity benefits, health insurance, and pension advice. They also note that some unions provide information on job vacancies.

The possible absence of any existing workplace representatives, as noted above, raises questions about how unions can fulfil their traditional representational role on behalf of these workers, in grievance and disciplinary hearings for example. The appointment or election of a 'temporary representative' is one possibility, or full-time union officers might fulfil such a role. However, the former may not possess the depth of skills and knowledge needed to be fully effective, while full-time officers may have competing demands on their time. Where temporary workers are employed alongside permanent staff, shop stewards may not see the interests of mobile workers as a priority compared to their role in representing employees of the organization.

Sources: Adam-Smith (1997); Heery et al. (2004)

Case discussion questions

1. What are the problems faced by trade unions in representing the interests of atypical workers, and how might these be overcome?

2. Does this group of workers offer unions a means of increasing their membership, and of demonstrating the relevance of unionization to all categories of workers?

CHAPTER 3
The politics of employment relations

CHAPTER OBJECTIVES

The main objectives of this chapter are to:

- understand the implications for employment relations of developments in public policy

- examine how Conservative and Labour governments have influenced the conduct of employment relations since the 1980s

- understand the implications of European Union policy for employment relations, and assess whether its involvement amounts to the emergence of supra-national employment regulation

- examine the relationship between the Labour party and the trade unions

- consider the internal politics of, and democracy within, trade unions

3.1 Introduction

In this chapter, the second of those that seek to contextualize contemporary employment relations developments, our concern is with the political dimension of the subject area. One of the most distinctive features of the subject is that it is highly politicized; in other words, employment relations arrangements, institutions, and processes are infused by, and cannot be understood without reference to, politics. The wage-work bargain itself is a political phenomenon since, as we saw in the introduction to this book, the employment relationship is a power relationship and thus cannot be understood simply as an economic process. Moreover, employment relations exists within a political context, as we saw in Chapter 1. In this chapter, we consider the implications of contemporary public policy developments, and explore the nature and significance of the European Union's influence over employment relations. The very existence of trade unions, as the collective embodiments of workers' pressure to combine and thus challenge employers from a position of enhanced strength, is a sign of political activity. Thus we also need to consider the politics of trade unionism. This chapter, then, aims to help readers more readily appreciate the importance of politics in employment relations.

3.2 State policy and employment relations: a contemporary assessment

In Chapter 1, we examined the role of the state in a capitalist society, focusing on the implications for the conduct of employment relations. Perhaps the most notable trend of the last half of the twentieth century was the growth of state intervention and the concomitant erosion of voluntarism. How, though, did state policy evolve under the Conservative administrations of the 1980s and 1990s, and what impact did Labour make after being returned to government in 1997?

3.2.1 Public policy under the Conservatives: towards neo-liberalism?

On entering office in 1979, the Conservative government's economic policy was dominated by a concern to reduce inflation through tight control of the money supply, and an explicit abandonment of the objective of full employment. It placed a greater emphasis on the free play of market forces as a source of enhanced economic competitiveness, rejecting Keynesian methods of demand management as a tool of economic policy. Moreover, the Conservatives had little regard for tripartite methods of economic policy formulation and, over time, abolished most of the state institutions that exemplified tripartism (Crouch 1995). Thus there was a 'distancing of unions from the corridors of power' (Davies and Freedland 1993: 427).

The trend towards increasing juridification of employment relations did, however, continue under the Conservatives, although with a markedly different emphasis as they oversaw a large-scale programme of employment relations reform, by means of six major Acts of Parliament between 1980 and 1993, largely designed to weaken the trade unions. This constituted 'probably the most single-minded and sustained attack on the position of a major and previously legitimate social force to have been undertaken anywhere under modern democratic conditions' (Crouch 1996: 120). Excessive union power was perceived to be a major constraint on British economic competitiveness; thus the reform of the unions was central to attempts to boost the economy. Among other things, the legislation severely restricted the ability of trade unions to undertake lawful industrial action (see Chapter 9), enabled employers to sue unions for damages in certain circumstances, prohibited the operation of closed shop arrangements (see Chapter 1), regulated the operation of union political funds (see below), and mandated that trade union general secretaries and members of their governing bodies, their executive committees, be elected in secret postal ballots (see below).

Prior to entering office, the Conservatives had given little thought to the reduction of union power, beyond the desirability of doing so (Dunn and Metcalf 1996), though the lessons of the fate of Edward Heath's Conservative administration, which, in the early 1970s, had attempted a wide-ranging transformation of employment relations, and failed, weighed heavily in Conservative thinking (Marsh 1992). What, then, were the Conservatives' principal aims in reforming the legislation governing unions and employment relations in Britain? First, they wished to reduce the power of trade unions in the economy (Davies and Freedland 1993; Martin et al. 1995). Second, Conservative governments were eager to diminish the scope for legitimate political activity by trade unions, something that also involved an attempt to challenge the links between the unions and the Labour party (Davies and Freedland 1993). A third aim of the Conservatives' legislative programme was to promote greater internal democracy within trade unions, to restore membership control of union policies and leaderships, and thus, it was anticipated, instil greater moderation in union behaviour (DE 1983; Martin et al. 1991, 1995). Fourth, there was also a clear desire to challenge the collective power of the unions; legislative measures made it easier for individual members both to dissent from, and challenge, collective decision-making processes (Davies and Freedland 1993; McIlroy 1991; Martin et al. 1991; Metcalf 1994).

The scale of the Conservative governments' legislative reform of employment relations during the 1980s and 1990s is suggestive of a marked shift towards the repression of union activity by the state, something that also extended to the use of its powers to combat industrial disputes (see Box 3.1). It has been suggested that Conservative policy towards the

---

BOX 3.1 THE DEFEAT OF THE 1984–85 MINERS' STRIKE

Conservative governments of the 1980s and 1990s did not rely solely on the reform of employment law to suppress trade unionism, as the experience of the 1984–85 miners' strike demonstrates. In March 1984, the leadership of the National Union of Mineworkers (NUM), under Arthur Scargill, called for a national strike in order to defeat the National Coal Board's (NCB) plan, backed by the government, to close twenty pits with the loss of over 100,000 mining jobs. Miners in Yorkshire walked out and were followed by those in other regions, including Scotland and South Wales. The strike was to last for a year. Controversially, the NUM's leadership did not authorize a ballot, largely on the basis that the strike was underway anyway, and many miners in areas where the pits were not under threat of closure, Nottinghamshire for example, only participated reluctantly.

Throughout the course of the dispute, the extensive powers of the state were deployed to ensure that the miners were defeated. In the years preceding the strike, the government had made arrangements for alternative energy supplies, and had built up coal stocks in preparation for a lengthy struggle. A special cabinet sub-committee was instituted, chaired by the prime minister, Margaret Thatcher, to oversee the state's response once the strike had started. Figures associated with the Conservative party, like businessman David Hart for example, helped to arrange support for miners who wished to return to work, and assisted the formation of a breakaway union, the Union of Democratic Mineworkers (UDM) in Nottinghamshire. They also backed legal actions by NUM members against their union for breaching its own rules by not holding a ballot. Eventually, in October 1984 the union had its assets seized, or 'sequestrated', by the courts.

The resources of the Security Service, MI5, were used to undermine the strike's effectiveness; it had an agent placed within the NUM's leadership. Extensive, military-style policing tactics, including the use of roadblocks on motorways, were deployed to prevent NUM pickets from travelling around the country blocking the supply of coal to electricity-generating plants, and obstructing efforts to return to work. Nearly 9,000 miners were arrested in 1984 as a result. In March 1985, after holding out for a year, the NUM called off the strike and organized a return to work, having failed in its attempt to use industrial action to prevent the pit closure programme.

Sources: Beynon (1985); Milne (2004)

unions was based upon the writings of the right-wing political scientist Friedrich Hayek. He viewed unions as coercive organizations that used their illegitimate collective power to put pressure on employers to concede improvements in pay and conditions that distorted the free operation of market forces, thus generating adverse economic outcomes, including higher inflation and greater unemployment. While the Conservatives' legislation may have been cumulative and incremental, Wedderburn (1989) suggests it was nonetheless informed by a coherent set of neo-liberal values and principles associated with the 'new right'.

In his analysis of the 1980s legislation restricting the ability of unions to undertake strike action, Auerbach (1990) prefers, however, to highlight the pragmatic and opportunistic aspects of Conservative policy-making. Rather than reflecting a purposive neo-liberal ideology, the anti-union laws tended to be passed in response to particular events or were influenced by prevailing circumstances. For example, the measures designed to restrict 'unofficial' industrial action that were included in the 1990 Employment Act resulted from a series of industrial disputes in transport the previous year.

A reasonable conclusion is that the Conservatives' legislative programme was founded upon a combination of ideology and political opportunism (Davies and Freedland 1993; Dickens and Hall 1995). According to one set of observers, the 'Conservatives begun with a coherent "step-by-step" introduction of reforms which degenerated after 1984 into a haphazard insertion of fragments of a neo-Hayekian anti-union ideology in response to various industrial disputes and initiatives from interested parties' (Undy et al. 1996: 75). Some measures, though, such as the undermining of the closed shop for example, do seem to have been driven more by ideology than others (Davies and Freedland 1993). Yet the opportunistic character of much of the Conservatives' later legislative interventions demonstrates that, while the policy regime had become much more repressive, the resilience of the unions compelled the state to respond to particular challenges to its authority as and when they arose (Davies and Freedland 1993).

One of the main assumptions that underpinned the Conservatives' policy agenda during the 1980s and 1990s was that the scale and the scope of trade union activity needed to be heavily restricted in order to secure a more deregulated labour market, something that was considered crucial to British economic competitiveness. It is perhaps ironic, therefore, that such a major degree of state intervention, designed to repress the trade unions, was a necessary precondition for a freer, more liberalized labour market. Indeed, as far as the political scientist Andrew Gamble (1988) is concerned, the use of the state's coercive power to undermine those interests, in particular the trade unions, that would otherwise challenge and obstruct the development of a free market economy is, from a new right perspective, both rational and entirely justified.

To what extent did the Conservatives' reforms weaken union power in Britain? It has been suggested that they were only able to enact such restrictive policies because of the degree to which the unions had been weakened by economic developments, such as job losses in manufacturing and increasing levels of unemployment (Dunn and Metcalf 1996). Nevertheless, the sheer scale of state repression of the unions during this period, of which the legislation was but one part, significantly challenged the legitimacy of trade unionism in Britain. How far, then, did the 1997 and 2001 Labour governments reverse the more explicitly repressive nature of state policy that characterized the Conservatives' approach to employment relations, informed, as it was, to a degree by a neo-liberal ideological perspective that viewed trade unions as obstacles to economic competitiveness?

3.2.2 Labour and employment relations in Britain 1997–2005

The landslide election victory enjoyed by the Labour party in May 1997, and its subsequent re-election in the general election June 2001, raises two related questions about the development of employment relations in Britain: to what extent did the nature of state policy shift away from the anti-union approach of the Conservatives, and, following on from this, how far can 1997 be characterized as a 'turning point' (R. Taylor 1998) in British employment relations?

Having originally opposed the Conservatives' legislative changes, during the early 1990s, the Labour party, following a string of election defeats, revised its employment relations policies, and came to favour retaining most of them. This formed part of a broader shift in Labour party policy towards the endorsement, and indeed the celebration, of a dynamic, free market economy (Coates 2000; Driver and Martell 1998; Hay 1999). In particular, Labour developed a notably enthusiastic acceptance of the desirability of a deregulated labour market as a source of economic competitiveness, a marked convergence with the neo-liberal policies that had been followed by the previous Conservatives governments (McIlroy 2000a).

How, then, did state policy in the area of employment relations develop after 1997? Following the election of the Labour government some immediate and highly symbolic interventions were made that were favourable to the trade unions, including the restoration of union rights at the Government Communications Headquarters (GCHQ) (R. Taylor 1998). While no attempts were made to revive the tripartite arrangements of the 1960s and 1970s (Crouch 2003), it is evident that union leaders and the Trades Union Congress (TUC) secured better access to government ministers than they had enjoyed under the Conservatives, although even as a 'high-profile insider' union success was limited to stopping 'the tide of anti-union legislation' (McIlroy 2000b: 9). Indeed, compared to the lobbying influence of business interests, to which the Labour government appears to have been 'particularly susceptible' (Undy 1999: 322), the results of the TUC's efforts were somewhat modest during Labour's first term (McIlroy 2000a, 2000b). Nevertheless, the TUC maintained its support for the Labour government, for one thing because its reluctance to countenance a broader vision of trade union activities and goals left it with little alternative (McIlroy 2000a), but also because the Labour's legislative programme, by increasing the juridification of employment relations (see Dickens and Hall 2003), held out the promise of a major expansion in the scope of employment rights.

Four imperatives governed Labour's legislative programme in employment relations. First, it was concerned to build greater social partnership between employers and trade unions (Brown 2000), something that informed the development of proposals, incorporated into the 1999 Employment Relations Act and discussed in Chapter 5, obliging employers to recognize a union for collective bargaining where this is wanted by a majority of the workforce (DTI 1998). Labour, however, adopted an explicitly unitary perspective on social partnership, one that envisaged employment relations as being about the development of a 'harmony of interests' (Howell 2004); a union presence is viewed as legitimate only in so far as it helps to enhance business competitiveness (McIlroy 2000a). Thus Labour's vision of social partnership was one in which trade unions exist only as weak and powerless employment relations actors, dependent upon the goodwill of employers (Smith and Morton 2001).

Second, Labour articulated the need for greater 'fairness' in employment relations, particularly through the establishment of minimum employment standards (Heery 1997a), though this theme became a less prominent feature of its policy agenda once it entered government (McIlroy 2000a; Smith and Morton 2001; Waddington 2003a). Nevertheless, one can point to important policy initiatives like the National Minimum Wage (NMW), introduced in 1999, as evidence of Labour's commitment to creating a more extensive system of individual employment rights (see Chapter 7). Yet the Labour government continued to articulate the benefits of Britain's 'flexible' labour market, and the potential threat to economic competitiveness of extending employment protection beyond a minimum floor of rights (Coates 2000).

Third, Labour fashioned a more supportive approach to the regulation of employment relations by the European Union (EU) than was the case with the Conservatives, the most evident feature of which was the government's signing of the 'social chapter' after entering office in 1997 (Dickens and Hall 2003: 129; Undy 1999). As later chapters will show in more detail, the result of this was to increase markedly the scope of juridification in employment relations with EU-derived legislation on such matters as parental leave, information and consultation rights for employees, and new rights for part-time and fixed-term contract workers. Yet Labour often introduced, or 'transposed', EU legislation reluctantly and, where possible, with opt-outs from key provisions, as in the case of the Working Time Directive for example (see Chapter 7). The 'minimalist' approach to transposing EU directives (Howell 2004; McKay 2001) accords with the emphasis Labour placed on the appropriateness of a flexible, deregulated labour market as a means of sustaining economic competitiveness and 'the need to maintain relations with business' (Waddington 2003a: 342).

The fourth feature of Labour's employment relations programme was the increased emphasis accorded to developing 'family-friendly' policies, designed to improve the balance between home and paid work responsibilities (McKay 2001), not least as a means of improving women's labour market prospects. For example, in its 2002 Employment Act Labour enhanced both maternity and paternity leave provisions, introducing paid paternity leave for the first time, and gave workers the right to request flexible working arrangements. While we will critically assess Labour's policy interventions in this area in more detail in Chapter 4, the extent to which Labour was genuinely committed to securing change in this area is, given its reluctance to legislate effectively against excessive working hours (see Chapter 7), perhaps questionable. Dickens and Hall (2003) suggest that Labour may be more at ease promoting 'family-friendly' policies, given the greater scope for consensus that exists, than it is in engaging with collective employment relations matters.

How, then, can the nature of state policy under the 1997 and 2001 Labour administrations be interpreted? Clearly, Labour's legislative programme constituted a marked shift in emphasis from the approach taken by the Conservatives (Dickens and Hall 2003). Nevertheless, Labour retained just about all of the Conservative anti-union legislation, and the scope of the legal regulation of the trade unions remains highly restrictive in a way that contravenes international labour norms (McKay 2001; Smith and Morton 2001).

Thus while important changes undoubtedly occurred, these need to be set against a 'background of underlying continuity' (Hyman 2003: 55). What, then, explains the Labour governments' reluctance to challenge the policy legacy that they inherited from their Conservative predecessors? In order to answer this question it is necessary to examine more deeply the ideological basis of Labour's policy agenda.

Much has been written about the concept of the 'third way' as a policy guidebook for left-of-centre governments, not least by its originator, the sociologist Anthony Giddens (Giddens 1998). Briefly, he distinguishes between the 'old left', or 'classic social democracy', which is characterized by an emphasis on state intervention, collectivism, Keynesian demand management polices, the goal of full employment, and a limited role for markets, and the 'new right', or 'neo-liberalism', in which minimal state regulation and the free play of market forces are the dominant features. It is argued that social and economic transformation, in particular the rise of global interconnectedness, render the policy assumptions of the 'old left' and the 'new right' increasingly redundant. The 'third way', then, is presented as a means of renewing and adapting social democracy to the contemporary world (Favretto 2003; Giddens 1998). A political programme based on 'third way' principles would, for example, eschew state intervention as a means of generating full employment, but rather seek to establish favourable economic conditions within which businesses are better able to create jobs, while also seeking to moderate the social dislocation created by deregulated markets.

In much of Giddens's work, there is very little that is of direct relevance to employment relations beyond a general concern that inequality is best addressed through 'social inclusion' rather than by state intervention in the labour market, and the trade unions barely receive a mention (Giddens 1998; Undy 1999; Waddington 2003a). Crouch (2001) argues that the third way concept is of no relevance to understanding Labour's employment relations policies since these can be relatively easily classified as either 'social democratic', like the minimum wage, 'neo-liberal', such as the emphasis on the deregulated labour market as a source of economic competitiveness, or some mixture of the two.

In Giddens's later writing, however, some of the implications of 'third way' thinking for employment relations become rather clearer. In *Where Now for New Labour?* (Giddens 2002), he expresses support for the Conservatives' labour market reforms, and emphasizes the desirability of competitive market economies in which the presence of low-paid and casualized jobs is acceptable as long as individuals are given opportunities to move out of them. Giddens recommends, moreover, that in order to govern effectively Labour must challenge 'sectional' interests, like trade unions, especially if it is to secure successful reform of the public services (Giddens 2002). Thus it is clear that, in respect of employment relations, the 'third way' approach closely resembles the deregulatory and anti-union imperatives of neo-liberal policy prescriptions.

While its overall coherence should not be overstated (Dickens and Hall 2003), Labour's employment relations policies were based on an unreflective acceptance of the premise that processes of economic globalization tightly constrain the extent to which nation-states can regulate their own economies and labour markets (Driver and Martell 1998; Hay 1999; McIlroy 1998). Labour's employment relations policy programme differs from the approach taken by its Conservative predecessors in some important ways. However, interventions ostensibly designed to improve employment rights and to ease the position

---

BOX 3.2 NEO-LIBERALISM AND EMPLOYMENT RELATIONS IN NEW ZEALAND

By no means was the UK government the most enthusiastic proponent of neo-liberal policies during the 1980s and 1990s. Prior to the 1980s, economic policy in New Zealand was dominated by the pursuit of full employment, and the use of Keynesian techniques of demand management with which to achieve it. The public policy environment was extremely favourable to trade unionism. Unions benefited from a system of 'compulsory unionism', and the existence of very centralized arrangements for collective bargaining. Following its 1984 election victory, the Labor government, in particular the finance minister Roger Douglas, who was supported by a cadre of enthusiastic and dedicated officials, forced through a series of free market reforms, including the dismantling of the welfare state, the privatization of state-owned industries, and labour market deregulation, to an extent unprecedented elsewhere among the advanced industrialized societies.

   The neo-liberal reforms were extended by the right-wing National government, elected in 1990. The 1991 Employment Relations Act did away with the system of national-level collective awards and agreements, which had been the bases of union power, and encouraged employers to establish individual contracts with their staff. The result was a massive fall in the level of trade union membership, and a huge decline in the coverage of collective bargaining. More generally, the neo-liberal programme of reforms generated increases in poverty, inequality, and unemployment. Moreover, it failed to deliver economic prosperity to the people of New Zealand. According to John Kay, 'the country experienced the worst economic performance of any rich state' (Kay 2003: 45). After 1999, a left-of-centre Labor/Alliance government halted, and partially reversed, the neo-liberal reforms, and enacted legislation more supportive of collective bargaining and trade unionism.

Sources: Harbridge, Crawford, and Hince (2002); Kelsey (1995)

---

of trade unions were pursued only in so far as they did not challenge the prevailing neo-liberal assumption that deregulation is the most effective means of generating improvements in economic competitiveness, something that has also influenced policy developments elsewhere (see Box 3.2). After 1997, the explicitly repressive approach to unions that was formulated under the Conservatives was modified, rather than reversed, making it difficult to see that year's election victory by the Labour party as a real turning point in employment relations.

SECTION SUMMARY AND FURTHER READING

• During the 1980s and 1990s, Conservative governments used the machinery of the state, most notably through the enactment of repressive legislation, to undermine the power and legitimacy of the trade unions. Although it was informed by a neo-liberal ideological agenda, the opportunistic basis of the Conservatives' legislative programme is evident.

• The 1997 and 2001 Labour governments instituted some important changes in employment relations policy, notably the development of new statutory protections in the area of individual employment rights. There was no extension of the programme of anti-union legislation that was enacted under the Conservatives.

- Labour did, however, retain the overwhelming bulk of the anti-union legislation it inherited from the Conservatives, and its employment relations policy interventions were designed not to upset employers. This reflects an uncritical acceptance that economic competitiveness is contingent upon deregulated labour markets, making substantial improvements to union and workers' rights undesirable.

For a critical overview of the Conservative's anti-union legislation, see McIlroy (1991). The most accessible and informative account of public policy developments under Labour is offered by Dickens and Hall (2003). The annual review articles in the *British Journal of Industrial Relations* are also very useful; in particular, see Undy (1999), Brown (2000), McKay (2001), and Waddington (2003a). Finally, for insightful understandings of the implications of Labour for employment relations, see McIlroy (2000a), and Howell (2004).

3.3 Employment relations and the politics of European integration

In recent years, the influence of the European Union (EU) on employment relations has grown markedly, especially since 1997 when the newly elected Labour government under Tony Blair brought Britain under the auspices of the 'social chapter'. To what extent, then, has supra-national regulation, that is regulation above the level of the nation-state, become a significant feature of employment relations in Europe? Further, is it possible to identify a process of convergence within European employment relations? In other words, has growing supra-national regulation begun to erode differences between national systems of employment relations in Europe such that a common model can increasingly be identified? We will return to these questions when we assess the impact of the EU on employment relations below. Before that we critically examine the progress of the EU's so-called 'social dimension', the implications of economic and monetary union, and the process of European-level 'social dialogue'. See Box 3.3 for details of relevant EU institutions.

3.3.1 The 'social dimension' to European integration

The EU was instituted as the European Economic Community (EEC), or the 'Common Market' as it became popularly known, in 1957 when France, Italy, West Germany, as it then was, and the Benelux countries acceded to the Treaty of Rome. Britain joined the EEC sixteen years later. As its name suggests, the EEC was designed as a vehicle for greater economic cooperation across Western Europe, as a means of promoting market integration. Apart from provisions designed to improve cross-border labour mobility and pay equality between men and women (Gold 1993; Martin and Ross 1999), the Treaty of Rome covered social and employment matters relatively briefly. It referred to issues like improvements in working conditions, but these were considered relevant only in so far as they enhanced the operation of the common market and supported economic integration (Hall 1994; Teague 1999).

BOX 3.3 THE INSTITUTIONS OF THE EUROPEAN UNION

Employment relations in Britain is increasingly influenced by the policies of the European Union (EU). There are four principal EU institutions. The European Commission, comprising representatives of each of the twenty-five member states, is responsible for promoting and effecting legislation, and monitoring its progress. The European Court of Justice (ECJ) deliberates on matters of EU law, and on issues that are of EU-wide significance. The European Parliament, made up of directly elected members from all twenty-five EU countries, has traditionally lacked much influence though it can now obstruct and amend legislation in some areas. Most power, however, rests with the Council of Ministers. It represents the interests of member state governments, and is the principal decision-making body of the EU.

In respect of employment relations, though, one must also acknowledge the role of the 'social partners', bodies representing the interests of employers and unions at EU level. There are a number of employers' organizations. Founded in 1958, the Union of Industrial and Employers' Confederations of Europe (UNICE) represents the interests of private sector employers; the Confederation of British Industry (CBI) is one of its thirty-seven affiliates. Since 1998, UNICE has worked in cooperation with another employers' organization, the European Association of Craft, Small and Medium-Sized Enterprises (UEAPME), which represents the interests of small and medium-sized employers. The European Centre of Enterprises with Public Participation and of Enterprises of General Economic Interest (CEEP) represents public sector employers in more than twenty countries.

The European Trade Union Confederation (ETUC) is the social partner that represents the interests of the trade unions. Founded in 1973, it encompasses nearly eighty national union confederations, including the British TUC, from thirty-five different countries. The ETUC supports the activities of eleven European Industry Federations (EIFs), bodies that represent the interests of trade unions in specific industrial sectors, such as the European Metalworkers' Federation in engineering for example.

In the early stages of the EEC's development, then, little attention was paid to the 'social dimension' of European integration, embracing employment-related matters, as well as social protection and benefits (Bridgford and Stirling 1994; Leat 1998). Although the EEC was established in part from a desire to eliminate the possibility of armed conflict in Europe, it was advanced largely as a market-building project, designed to stimulate the economic capacities of Western European nation-states and thus help them to compete more effectively with the increasingly dominant United States economy (Hyman 2001a; Martin and Ross 1999).

By the 1970s, there was a greater concern to give the EEC a more active social and employment dimension, something that resulted in the 1974 'Social Action Programme'. Although the process of economic cooperation and market integration appeared to have been relatively successful, influential politicians, such as the West German chancellor Willy Brandt, considered that the EEC was too distant from the concerns of the populace, and action was needed to secure its legitimacy. The development of a social dimension, therefore, 'was seen as a particularly important way to deepen the political and social foundations of the union' (Teague 1999: 140). The Social Action Programme produced legislation, in the form of directives, concerning such matters as the protection of workers in redundancy situations and when their employer was subject to a change of ownership, sex discrimination, and pay equality between men and women. However, this 'burst of activity was shortlived' (Martin and Ross 1999: 317); because of employers' opposition, no agreement was reached on proposals to enhance employee participation in company decision-making for example (Gold 1993). Moreover, the onset of economic recession impeded the development of the Social Action Programme such that by the end of the 1970s it had ceased to have any real significance (Hall 1994; Martin and Ross 1999).

The 1979 election of Margaret Thatcher's Conservative government in Britain also posed an obstacle to the development of social and employment policy by the EEC, since at that time directives required the unanimous support of all the member states. Given its deregulatory policy agenda, the Conservatives were, unsurprisingly, opposed to extending the competence of the EEC in matters relating to employment relations on the basis that such interventions would damage economic competitiveness (Hall 1994; Teague 1989). Nevertheless, during the 1980s and 1990s Conservative governments were often frustrated by the obligation to adjust British law to comply with directives that had been enacted under the Social Action Programme, such as in the area of redundancy consultation for example (Hall and Edwards 1999).

The British government's hostility notwithstanding, from the mid-1980s onwards the social dimension was revived, and indeed accelerated, under the auspices of the then president of the European Commission, the former French finance minister Jacques Delors. The activities of the European Community were increasingly dominated by the prospect of the 1993 completion of the Single European Market. Thus a central motivating force underpinning the increased emphasis given to social and employment policy during this period was the need to secure support for, and the legitimacy of, further economic integration in Europe (Bridgford and Stirling 1994; Hall 1994; Martin and Ross 1999). Moreover, without some movement towards a 'level playing field' in respect of social and employment rights, the ability of multinational corporations to re-direct investment, and therefore jobs, to locations where labour costs were lower, or 'social dumping' as it became known, would otherwise go unchecked (Smith 1999).

The prospect of the single market inspired a major institutional innovation in European Community (EC) decision-making, one which was to have major implications for employment relations policy. The 1987 Single European Act (SEA) enabled the Council of Ministers to determine certain matters by 'qualified majority voting' (QMV). Individual member states were accorded a certain number of votes within the Council of Ministers – Britain now has twenty-nine, for example. Matters that were subject to QMV, those 'which have as their object the establishment and functioning of the internal market' (Bridgford and Stirling 1994: 77), needed to attract a certain number of votes in order to progress. Although most employment matters remained subject to the need for unanimous agreement among the member states if they were to go forward, under the SEA, measures relating to improvements in the working environment, including health and safety at work, were covered by QMV. By the latter half of the 1980s, then, there was a growing acknowledgement that a more robust social and employment policy agenda was beneficial to the development and success of economic integration, and was not something that should be marginalized (Davies and Freedland 1993).

The adoption of the social charter, in 1990, and the enactment of a further programme of social action that accompanied it, demonstrates the extent of this increasing interest in the development of social and employment policy. The social charter, which Britain, alone among EC member states, refused to support was a declaration of intent, a political statement, rather than a concrete set of legislative proposals, and covered such areas as improvements in living and working conditions and information, consultation and participation rights for workers (Martin and Ross 1999; Teague 1999). Moreover, it also provided the basis for a legislative action programme that encompassed seventeen draft directives, mostly in the area of health and safety, including the regulation of working time (Bridgford and Stirling 1994), something to which Britain was deeply opposed (Davies and Freedland 1993; Hall 1992).

It would be a mistake, though, to overstate the significance of this activity in the area of social and employment policy. For one thing, as Mark Hall (1994: 297) contends, the proposed measures did not 'venture very far beyond the [European] Commission's long-standing social policy agenda'. Thus they did not presage a significant extension of EC intervention in the regulation of employment relations (Teague 1999). Moreover, the development of the social dimension remained subordinate to the process of market integration, and was articulated largely as a means of attracting support for it within European labour movements (Martin and Ross 1999).

Nevertheless, the British Conservative government was profoundly opposed to the expansion, however limited, of the European Community's competence in the area of social policy (Davies and Freedland 1993). As a result, the 1993 Treaty of European Union, agreed in 1991 in the Dutch town of Maastricht, in fact comprised two distinct documents. One included a new 'social chapter' that extended QMV to a range of social and employment matters, including information and consultation rights for workers, and was signed by all the member states except Britain. The other, which Britain signed, left it out. The social chapter was adopted by Britain in 1997, following the victory of the Labour party in that year's general election. See Box 3.4 for details of the major EU directives in the area of employment policy that have been enacted since 1993.

Although the implications of particular directives for employment relations in the UK will be considered in later chapters, it is necessary to assess the overall progress of the EU's social dimension. On the one hand, its provisions, those associated with the implementation of the social chapter in particular, have been broadly welcomed by British trade unions, who see them as an important counterweight to the more neo-liberal policy approach favoured by Conservative and Labour governments. On the other hand, the social dimension is not a very effective means of enhancing workers' rights (Wedderburn 1995), and the legislation that it has invoked is often much less rigorous than that which already existed in most member states. Key aspects of employment relations policy, such as collective bargaining and the right of workers to associate in trade unions for example, still come within the prerogative of individual member states.

The limited progress of EU social and employment policy is, however, not particularly surprising given that it has been subordinated to the process of market integration. Indeed, the principal aim of the Maastricht agreement was to lay the ground for economic and monetary union; 'social policy was peripheral' (Martin and Ross 1999: 319). The EU is, then, as it always has been, primarily a vehicle for the promotion of market integration, an institution whose policies are favourable, in the main, to the large multinational corporations that have benefited from the removal of economic and other barriers within Europe

---

BOX 3.4 MAJOR EUROPEAN UNION DIRECTIVES IN THE AREA OF EMPLOYMENT RELATIONS
SINCE 1993

- The Directive on the Adaptation of Working Time (1993): provides for the regulation of working hours, rest breaks, and holiday periods (see Chapter 7).
- The European Works Council Directive (1994): provides for the establishment of transnational information and consultation arrangements in multinational companies operating in Europe (see Chapter 6).
- The Parental Leave Directive (1996): provides for minimum standards of maternity and paternity leave provision within the EU, including the provision of at least two weeks of unpaid paternity leave (see Chapter 4).
- The Directive on Equal Rights and Treatment for Part-Time Workers (1997): prohibits employers from giving part-time workers less favourable pay and conditions than equivalent full-time staff (see Chapter 4).
- The Fixed-Term Contract Workers Directive (1999): prohibits employers from giving workers on fixed-term contracts less favourable pay and conditions than equivalent permanent staff (see Chapter 4).
- The Framework for Equal Treatment in Employment and Occupations Directive (2000): prohibits direct or indirect discrimination on grounds of religion or belief, disability, age, or sexual orientation (see Chapter 4).
- The National Information and Consultation of Employees Directive (2002): provides for information and consultation arrangements among firms employing fifty workers or more (see Chapter 6).

(Hyman 2001a). The principal justification for the development of the social dimension rested upon the extent to which it could support, and add legitimacy, to the process of economic union.

By the late 1990s, the level of EU interest in social and employment policy initiatives seemed to have diminished markedly. According to Paul Teague (1999: 150), the European Commission 'appears to have opted for relatively modest labour law proposals rather than the promotion of genuinely supranational initiatives', and demonstrates a preference for voluntary agreements, through a process of 'social dialogue' between employers and unions (see below) rather than legislative enactment. The publication of the Charter of the Fundamental Rights of the European Union in 2000, one of whose chapters covers rights at work, including the right to fair and just working conditions, collective bargaining, and to take strike action, may be a sign that the social dimension has not entirely stalled (see Weiss 2002). Although the adoption of the EU Constitutional Treaty, agreed by the member states in June 2004, would give it legal force, the Charter is, however, designed not to override national-level legislative arrangements.

3.3.2 Economic and Monetary Union and employment relations

Perhaps the most notable feature of the Maastricht Treaty of European Union was the impetus it provided for the process of market integration, in particular by setting out the convergence criteria for Economic and Monetary Union (EMU). What, then, have been the implications of EMU for employment relations? This is a matter of some relevance given the establishment of the single currency, the Euro, though not yet in the UK. The first aspect of EMU to be addressed concerns its place in the process of European integration; it is important to bear in mind that, whatever its implications for social and employment policy, the main outcome of the agreement forged at Maastricht was to accelerate the EMU process (Martin and Ross 1999).

In order to satisfy the conditions for EMU, member states were required to meet a rigid set of rules, or criteria, to facilitate the convergence of their economies. One of these was an obligation, supported by the 1996 Growth and Stability Pact, to keep budget deficits normally to within 3 per cent or less of Gross Domestic Product (Whyman 2002). Governed by a new European Central Bank (ECB), this policy was designed to impose strict price stability across Europe and thus mitigate inflation (Teague 1998). Its effect was to bind 'Europe to a highly restrictive policy regime to prevent inflation whatever the cost in unemployment' (Martin and Ross 1999: 320; Moss 2001). A further implication of EMU was that national governments lost the capacity to adjust the value of their currency as a means of generating improvements in economic competitiveness. Given the restrictions on budget deficits, which impedes their ability to borrow money as a way of expanding their economies, governments may therefore be obliged to pursue alternative methods of facilitating growth, those that promote austerity, in particular through greater deregulation and flexibility, reductions in public expenditure, and downward pressure on wage costs (Levitt and Lord 2000; Martin and Ross 1999).

There are four main implications of EMU for employment relations in Europe. First, the large extent to which, as a means of facilitating market integration, the EMU process has further marginalized the EU's social dimension has become clear. The priority accorded to EMU has been at the expense of more active social and employment policy interventions and is, then, a major cause of the erosion in significance of the social dimension (Crouch 2000; Martin and Ross 1999; Moss 2001).

Second, austerity measures resulted in major industrial conflict across Europe during the 1990s as governments took the necessary steps to comply with the Maastricht convergence criteria. Unions mobilized to resist such measures, especially proposed reductions in public expenditure, in a number of countries, including Italy, France, and Germany (Ferner and Hyman 1998).

A third implication of EMU for employment relations concerns the extent to which its deflationary emphasis encourages governments to promote wage moderation, especially in the public sector. One result was that during the 1990s many countries saw the establishment of so-called 'social pacts' between government and union movements, in order to facilitate the greater coordination of wage bargaining outcomes, and thus reduce the prospect of disruptive industrial conflict. Thus one result of the movement towards EMU was the apparent revival of corporatist arrangements in countries such as Italy, Belgium, Germany, and the Netherlands (see Crouch 2000; Ferner and Hyman 1998; Regini 2000; Whyman 2002). The main problem with these social pacts, however, was that they offered very little to union movements, and were established largely as a means of muting union resistance to the stringent economic policies that were necessary to facilitate EMU. Thus they did not constitute corporatism as it is commonly understood since the bargain between states and their labour movements was too heavily weighted in favour of the former (Regini 2000; Teague 1998, 2000; Whyman 2002).

The fourth and perhaps the most notable implication of EMU is the extent to which, by deepening the process of economic integration within Europe, and facilitating the greater mobility of capital, it has undermined established employment relations arrangements, particularly centralized bargaining activity. The establishment of a unified economic and monetary area, within which there is a single currency, not only accentuates competitive pressures, but it also enables employers to play countries off against each other more easily in the pursuit of increased competitiveness. As a result, there is pressure on national-level unions to concede greater employment flexibility, in particular the decentralization of bargaining activity to company level. According to Marginson and Sisson (2001: 20), 'the restructuring and rationalization that is accompanying EMU is stimulating processes of internal change as management comes under pressure to make its employment and working arrangements more competitive'. Nevertheless, there are signs that EMU may be a factor influencing national unions to develop cross-border bargaining relationships, thus strengthening their organizational capacities at a European level – in the communications, printing and media industries for example (Gennard and Newsome 2001). In general, though, such progress is somewhat slow, subject to employer opposition, and characterized by considerable diversity of practice (Marginson and Sisson 2004). Therefore it is more accurate to refer to the gradual emergence of a European 'dimension' to, rather than 'level' of, collective bargaining (Marginson and Sisson 2002).

3.3.3 The pursuit of social dialogue

The limited progress of 'social dialogue' (EU-level discussions between the social partners – trade union bodies and employers' organizations – with the aim of reaching agreement on relevant matters of social and employment policy) is a further indication of the weakness of the EU's social dimension, relative to the accelerating pace of market integration. During the 1960s and 1970s, the European Commission supported various initiatives as part of its aim to facilitate 'the participation of supra-national interest groups in [European Community] policy-making' (Hall 1994: 293), including the formation of industry-level joint committees that provided a forum for union bodies and employers' groups to discuss relevant matters of mutual interest even though, as far as the main employers' organization UNICE (Union of Industrial and Employers' Confederations of Europe) was concerned, binding agreements were out of the question (Carley 1993; Gold 1993; Waddington and Hoffman 2003).

During the 1980s, though, the European Commission, under the presidency of Jacques Delors, took action to promote social dialogue as an integral part of the social dimension. This followed the difficulties associated with gaining political support for legislative action, not least as a result of British hostility (Carley 1993; Keller 2003). Following a series of informal tripartite talks conducted during 1985 under the aegis of the European Commission, the 1987 Single European Act obliged the Commission to encourage the development of social dialogue between the social partners at European level (Bridgford and Stirling 1994; Carley 1993). It was anticipated that legislative proposals in the field of social and employment policy would stand more chance of success if they already had the support of the trade unions and employers' organizations (Hall 1994; Teague 1989).

Social dialogue received a further boost from the 1993 Maastricht Treaty of European Union. It provided for the conclusion of 'framework agreements' between the social partners. In areas where directives had been proposed, trade unions and employers' organizations at EU level were given an opportunity to reach an agreement themselves that could then be taken forward and adopted as legislation. The Maastricht Treaty also provided for agreements between the social partners that could be implemented voluntarily across the EU member states without the need for legislative action (Keller and Sörries 1999).

What, then, have been the results of the social dialogue process between the social partners at EU level? On the one hand, it appears to have been rather successful. Although there was a failure to reach an agreement regarding European Works Councils, obliging the European Commission to intervene and take forward the relevant legislative proposals, directives regulating parental leave, and the rights of part-time and fixed-term contract workers were all enacted by QMV following agreement between the social partners (Keller and Sörries 1999; Waddington and Hoffman 2003). On the other hand, however, these were matters that the European Commission was determined to legislate on anyway. The participation of UNICE, which opposed the negotiation of such agreements in principle, was predicated upon a belief that, since such legislation was inevitable, by becoming involved in the process of negotiating an agreement it might at least be able to secure something more favourable to its interests (Keller 2003; Keller and Sörries 1999). The significance of such social dialogue has, then, been somewhat limited.

The conclusion of voluntary agreements through social dialogue at EU level has been characterized by even more difficulty. While the aim of the European Trade Union Confederation (ETUC) has been to use the social dialogue process to facilitate collective bargaining at a European level, UNICE is reluctant to participate in any meaningful dialogue precisely because it is fearful of this developing. By the end of 2003, only one voluntary agreement existed, that which was concluded in 2002 covering teleworking arrangements, and it is unclear how compliance with its provisions can be enforced across the EU (Keller 2003). Nevertheless, the European Commission remains committed to extending and strengthening the social dialogue process (European Commission 2002), seemingly at the expense of legislative action. It is important not to be too critical of the development of social dialogue, since the mere fact that it happens at all is significant. Moreover, 'it has to be acknowledged that the outcome is regarded by trade unions in many EU countries as a considerable improvement on national conditions, given the very diverse levels of social policy regulation in Europe' (Waddington and Hoffman 2003: 53).

As it is currently constituted, however, social dialogue is a less effective means of regulating employment relations at EU level, and of promoting workers' rights, than legislation (Mahnkopf and Altvater 1995). Moves to substitute social dialogue for legal enactment therefore run the risk of eroding the already feeble social dimension of European integration.

What has been the progress of social dialogue between the social partners at industry sector level? From the 1960s onwards, the European Commission fostered the development of 'joint committees' in industries where the establishment of the common market had particular implications, although they were rather ineffectual since the resulting 'joint opinions' tended to be weak statements of intent rather than robust programmes for action. The main outcomes of these committees appear to have been the organization of joint studies and seminars (Carley 1993). Nevertheless, sector-level informal working parties also developed under the aegis of the European Commission; these brought out 'a slowly growing number of voluntary, non-binding declarations and general recommendations' (Keller 2003: 127).

In 1998, the European Commission reformed the industrial-level structure through the establishment of sectoral dialogue committees in those industries where the social partners submitted a joint request. This resulted in the establishment of twenty-five such bodies, including all of the former joint committees and most of the informal working parties (Keller 2003; Keller and Bansbach 2000; Leisink 2002). In general, then, the 'new structure was nothing but a copy of the old one or a linear continuation of former patterns' (Keller 2003: 130). There have been instances of sector-level agreements being struck as a result of social dialogue, for example over the regulation of working time for specific occupations in the transport industry (Keller and Bansbach 2000; Waddington and Hoffman 2003).

Overall, however, the progress of social dialogue at sectoral level has been rather limited. Although the ETUC has taken steps to pursue greater activity in this area, its 1999 decision to facilitate the greater coordination of collective bargaining at industry level by fourteen European Industry Federations in particular (Keller and Bansbach 2000), the effectiveness of such initiatives has been undermined by the absence of an equivalent level of commitment among employers (Waddington and Hoffman 2003). For one thing, employers' organizations have been reluctant to enter into the social dialogue process. Moreover, in some industrial sectors, including construction for instance, employers' representative structures are rather weak, thus inhibiting their capacity to engage in effective dialogue (Keller and Sörries 1998; Leisink 2002).

Therefore the development of social dialogue at sectoral level has been rather tentative, with progress only having been achieved in the transport industry, where agreements regulating working time for specific occupations have been established, or in sectors where the implications of EU policy, such as the opening up of telecommunications markets, have been particularly important (Leisink 2002). Although Teague (2001) acknowledges the weaknesses of the social dialogue process, he argues that it does have some positive effects, in so far as it facilitates greater cross-national understandings within and between the social partners. However, it is evident that the process has produced little by way of substantive outcomes and, according to some observers (e.g. Hyman 2001b; Keller 2003), it is doubtful whether it ever will. The slow pace of progress towards genuine social dialogue is, then, a stark reminder of the subordinate role of social policy within the EU relative to the very much more significant process of market integration (Keller and Bansbach 2000).

3.3.4 Towards the supra-national regulation of employment relations in Europe?

Returning to the questions posed at the start of this section, how far has supra-national regulation become a feature of employment relations in Europe, and to what extent does this signal a diminution in the distinctiveness of national systems and the resultant growth of convergence? Despite much rhetoric about the EU's social dimension, our analysis has demonstrated the large extent to which it has been subordinate to powerful pressures of market integration. From this perspective, the social dimension has been a rather marginal aspect of the process of European integration. EU legislation in the area of social and employment policy and the development of social dialogue have done little to counter the enhanced scope enjoyed by multinational companies to benefit from the removal of economic and political barriers and to organize themselves on a European scale. While European integration has the potential to enable unions to develop effective cross-border bargaining networks, business has been its main beneficiary (Hyman 2001a; Martin and Ross 1999; Moss 2001).

The 2004 enlargement of the EU, with the accession of ten new member states, is likely to marginalize the social dimension of European integration still further. Generally, the governments of the accession states, many of them former components of the Soviet bloc – Poland, Hungary, and the Czech Republic for example – are sympathetic to neo-liberal, deregulatory policy approaches. However, it is too early to draw firm conclusions and the eventual outcome may be somewhat less straightforward (Meardi 2002; Scott and Foster 2003).

A further objection to the notion that the supra-national regulation of employment relations has been a major feature of the process of European integration lies in a recognition that while the EU is most assuredly not a traditional nation-state, it is not really a supra-national one either (Hyman 2001a; Teague 2001). Much of the power over decision-making within the EU remains vested, through the Council of Ministers, in national governments. The social partners, moreover, rely heavily on the European Commission for support and lack legitimacy among those they purport to represent. This is a major obstacle to the development of supra-national regulation at the EU level since, for the most part, employment relations continues to be rooted in the activities and experiences of social actors, workers, trade unions, and employers, who operate within, and are influenced by, arrangements that are confined to particular nation-states (Hyman 2001a).

EU institutions and processes of decision-making tend to be remote from the consciousness of workers and their employers (Hyman 2001a), something that is exacerbated by the 'complexity and elitist bias of decision-making' (Moss 2001: 128), thus reducing their legitimacy. Moreover, the sheer diversity of national systems of employment relations within Europe implies that the emergence of a supra-national dimension is bound to be tentative (Teague 2001), thus rendering the process of convergence sluggish at best. At present, there is little likelihood of any major deviation from this state of affairs; for example, even with the establishment of the single currency and the development of a system of European Works Councils (see Chapter 6), genuine European-level collective bargaining remains a remote prospect (Marginson and Sisson 2001). While the process of European integration has notably influenced employment relations in a number of major respects, it has not resulted in a significant level of supra-national regulation, thus limiting the extent of real convergence.

SECTION SUMMARY AND FURTHER READING

- During the 1980s, the development of the 'social dimension', encompassing legislation in areas such as working time, and information and consultation rights for workers, became an increasingly important aspect of the EU. Nevertheless, it remained subordinate to the process of market integration and was progressed largely in so far as it legitimized economic union.

- Thus the development of the EU has been dominated by the process of market integration, in particular the establishment of Economic and Monetary Union (EMU). Not only does EMU aid the ability of multinational companies to operate at a supra-national level, and thus exert pressure to erode established national systems of centralized bargaining, it also constrains national governments' policy-making options, encouraging them to pursue deregulatory policies and secure wage restraint.

- The outcomes of 'social dialogue' between trade unions and employers at the European level have, until now, been of limited significance relative to the economic advantages enjoyed by multinational companies as a result of European integration.

- While the influence of the EU on employment relations has been considerable, its interventions have not engendered the supra-national regulation of the employment relationship in Europe. In particular, the resilience of national diversity in employment relations precludes any significant move towards convergence along a common model.

For a general overview of the role and influence of the EU on employment relations, see Leat (1998), although be aware that it is slightly dated now. For the history of the 'social dimension', see Hall (1994), and the more critical analysis offered by Martin and Ross (1999). Teague (1999) contains much relevant employment relations material. Foster and Scott (2003a) contains important chapters on social dialogue and the implications of EMU. For further perspectives on EMU and employment relations, see Marginson and Sisson (2001), and Whyman (2002).

3.4 The politics of trade unionism I: trade unions and the Labour party in Britain

At the beginning of the twentieth century, the leading trade unions of the time, along with a group of prominent socialists, played a key role in establishing the Labour party in Britain. In this section, we examine the evolution of the relationship between Labour and the unions. What are its main features and what influence, if any, do the unions have within the Labour party in contemporary Britain?

3.4.1 The politics of labourism

The 1918 Labour party constitution formally entrenched trade union influence within its structure and organization; affiliated unions were given 'effective control over the new party machine' (Flanders 1975: 34). In what came to be known as 'labourism', though, a rigid demarcation was established between the milieu of parliamentary politics, the arena for Labour politicians, and that of industrial affairs, in which the unions had a legitimate interest. Thus 'union leaders have normally been happy to abstain from any initiating role in the formulation of general Party policy' and restricted their influence accordingly (Hyman 1989: 44). A further aspect of labourism is the priority that is given to parliamentary politics and the authority of the party leadership in the House of Commons (Flanders 1975; Hyman 1983). According to Ralph Miliband (1972: 375), union leaders conceived of themselves as 'representatives of organized labour, involved in a bargaining relationship, notably over industrial and economic issues, with their political colleagues in the Labour party, and not in the least as political rivals'. The predominance of Labourism as an ideology, allied to the political conservatism of union leaderships, gave the Labour party's political programme a non-socialistic character in which radical ideas were generally downplayed in favour of incremental, pragmatic reforms, accommodating capitalism rather than seeking to challenge it (Hyman 1975).

For most of the twentieth century, then, the trade unions exerted a powerful, and moderating, influence over the politics of the Labour party. Three features of the way in which the trade unions and the Labour party became 'symbiotically linked' (Thorpe 1999) are particularly worthy of attention. First, the unions, their officials, and their members provided a considerable proportion of the necessary organizational activities essential to the effective functioning of the party. Second, through their affiliation fees, the funding of election campaigning, and the sponsorship of Labour MPs, the unions provided much of the Labour party's funds (Alderman and Carter 1994). Third, the unions provided the Labour party with 'political ballast'; the leadership came to rely upon the support of the trade unions whenever it was necessary to defeat left-wing challenges to its policies (Minkin 1991). Such 'industrial discipline' (Miliband 1972) was regularly displayed at the annual conference when union leaderships were able to use their 'block vote', that is the aggregated votes of their supposed affiliated membership, to support the official position of the party leadership.

Traditionally, then, the unions deferred to the party leadership on most issues. During the 1950s and 1960s, though, union leaders came under increasing pressure from members and activists to pursue more radical policies, and strains began to emerge in the relationship between the party and the trade unions. A generation of more left-wing union leaders, including Jack Jones of the Transport and General Workers' Union (TGWU) were more vocal in their opposition to Labour policies of wage restraint that damaged the interests of workers (Thorpe 1999).

Following Labour's 1970 election defeat, successful efforts were made to rebuild party–union relations. However, the collapse of the social contract upset them again since the Labour government faced increasing opposition to wage restraint from the unions once more (see Chapter 1). The influence of the so-called 'winter of discontent' in 1978–79, a symbolic and highly charged manifestation of the breakdown of the relationship between the Labour party and the trade unions, was to endure for at least the next two decades. The Conservatives used it as a device to challenge the legitimacy of the unions' proximity to the Labour party; for the self-styled Labour party 'modernizers', the winter of discontent signified the unelectability of a political party that was over-dependent on the trade unions.

3.4.2 Challenging the relationship between the Labour party and the trade unions

During the 1980s and 1990s, the relationship between the Labour party and the trade unions became the subject of critical scrutiny in two distinct ways. First, as part of its legislative programme of trade union reform, Conservative governments attempted to depoliticize the trade unions, by challenging the legitimacy of the unions' links with the Labour party and also by seeking to undermine their more general political campaigning activities (McIlroy 1991; Martin et al. 1995). The 1984 Trade Union Act obliged trade unions operating political funds to win the support of their members for such arrangements in a ballot at least once every ten years.

Many unions, even those that were not affiliated to the Labour party, maintained political funds and used them for general campaigning purposes. The 1984 legislation, then, posed a direct threat to the ability of unions to campaign on issues such as privatization and social policy. However, the results from the first round of political fund ballots conducted in the mid-1980s were 'an outstanding success for the trade union movement' (Leopold 1986: 300). Not only did all the unions with political funds vote to keep them, often with very large majorities in support, but seventeen new ones were also established. The Conservatives, who judged that members were opposed to the political activities of their unions and should be given an opportunity to halt them, clearly did not expect such an outcome. Such positive support for political funds appears to have been the result of 'government miscalculation, membership loyalty, understanding of the necessity of union political activities and careful imaginative campaigning by the unions themselves' (McIlroy 1991: 99). In the second round of ballots, undertaken between 1994 and 1996, the retention of political funds once again received the strong support of members who appreciate the ability of their union to undertake campaigning activities (Leopold 1997).

The second source of pressure to reform the relationship between the Labour party and the unions came from within the party itself. During the 1980s, the Labour leadership 'reasserted its political autonomy from the unions', a return to the tradition of labourism being something that received the approval of most union leaders who were content to return to the days when their main role was to help resist the adoption of radical policies (Marsh 1992: 162). Following the disastrous election performances of the 1980s, however, the Labour leadership tentatively began to distance the party from the unions, a process that accelerated after a fourth successive defeat in 1992. The union link was perceived to be unpopular with the electorate since it gave the impression that the Labour party was too beholden to one special interest group (Alderman and Carter 1994). Self-styled Labour 'modernizers', such as Peter Mandelson, criticized what they saw as the failures of Labour governments of the 1960s and 1970s, citing an over-dependence on the unions as a major problem (Mandelson and Liddle 1996).

From 1992 onwards, and particularly after Tony Blair became leader in 1994, the Labour party sought to reduce its dependency on the unions for financial support, and looked instead for donations from business and wealthy individuals (Leopold 1997; Osler 2002). Moreover, the Labour leadership introduced measures designed to reduce the influence of the trade unions within the party's internal structures and decision-making processes, though it remained careful to avoid antagonizing the unions too much since they were still important as a source of funds and organizational support (McIlroy 1998). In 1995, for example, the union share of the vote at the party's annual conference was reduced from 70 per cent to 50 per cent. The conference, moreover, became less important once a new National Policy Forum was established as the principal policy-making body, with union representatives comprising about a sixth of its membership. Union leaders acquiesced in these changes, mostly uncomplainingly. They considered a reduced role and influence within the party to be a price well worth paying if it helped to deliver a Labour election victory, and the promise of a less hostile political environment than had been the case under nearly two decades of Conservative government (McIlroy 1998).

3.4.3 Labour in government: the state of the union–party relationship since 1997

The importance of trade union affiliation to the Labour party was clearly displayed at the 1997 general election when Labour's landslide victory was secured with the help of massive donations of funds for campaigning and organization (McIlroy 1998). Nevertheless, once Labour entered government union influence within the party continued to diminish. In 1998, the trade union presence on the Labour party's ruling thirty-two member National Executive Committee (NEC) was reduced from seventeen (a majority) to just twelve (Ludlum and Taylor 2003). If anything, however, during Labour's first term in office between 1997 and 2001, the party–union relationship became stronger, despite the preference among some left-wing union activists for the policies of the breakaway Scottish Socialist and Socialist Labour parties.

For one thing, as McIlroy (2000a: 26) observes, the unions still control 50 per cent of the vote at Labour's annual conference (although its power has been considerably eroded), retain a significant proportion of the seats on the NEC, and enjoy representation on the National Policy Forum. 'At every level', he contends, 'the unions remain an appreciable if diminished feature of the New Labour landscape'. Labour's attempts to secure funds from corporate donors and wealthy individuals were rather unsuccessful, not least because of the controversy aroused by some of the donations. During its first term in office, then, Labour's dependency on the unions for funds grew, especially once a general election, expected in 2001, loomed. Indeed, the campaigning efforts of the unions were 'central to Labour's retention of almost all its 146 key seats in 2001, and thus to its massive second victory' (Ludlum and Taylor 2003: 734).

Moreover, the 'political ballast' that the unions give to the Labour party, helping to defeat left-wing challenges to the party leadership, continued to be a significant feature of Labour's first term in office. In meetings of the National Policy Forum during 1999 and 2000, for example, the Labour leadership was able to win support for its position on such matters as pension policy and constitutional reform largely because of the support of union representatives (Ludlum and Taylor 2003). Unions continued to exercise their block votes and influence in ways that supported the Labour leadership, often in quite controversial circumstances. One of the best examples of this was the election of Labour's candidate to head the newly established Welsh Assembly. The backing of some unions, including the Amalgamated Engineering and Electrical Union (AEEU – now Amicus), which did not ask its members for their views, was crucial to the victory of Tony Blair's favoured candidate (McIlroy 2000a). Union leaders were also supportive of, and grateful for, some of Labour's policies, such as the enactment of new laws providing for a minimum wage and enabling union recognition. It seems that 'the health of the labour alliance of unions and party had revived by the end of New Labour's first term' (Ludlum and Taylor 2003: 737).

From 2001 onwards, however, the relationship between the trade unions and the Labour party became increasingly strained (Ludlum and Taylor 2003; Waddington 2003a). For one thing, some of the features of the Labour government's policy programme proved rather unpalatable to the unions, in particular its concern with extending the influence of private sector businesses in the delivery of public services, through arrangements such as the Private Finance Initiative (PFI). The unions expressed concern, and increasingly anger, about what they perceive as the potentially detrimental implications for service provision, and the threats to public sector workers' pay and conditions (Waddington 2003a). A second source of strain concerns government policy towards employment relations. The unions were frustrated at the reluctance of the Labour government to strengthen union rights, and by its support for the virtues of a deregulated labour market as a source of economic dynamism (Ludlum and Taylor 2003).

A third source of strain in the relationship between the unions and the Labour party after 2001 concerned changes in the make-up of union leaderships as union members

---

BOX 3.5 THE TRADE UNIONS AND THE LABOUR PARTY 2001–05: A GROWING RIFT?

Since 2001, there have been signs of a growing rift between the Labour party and its affiliated trade unions as the latter became increasingly disenchanted with the Labour government's policy programme. During 2004, two unions disaffiliated from the Labour party. Having already reduced its financial support for the Labour party, in 2003 the Rail Maritime and Transport (RMT) union's annual conference voted to allow its branches to support other political parties, including the Scottish Socialist party (SSP), Plaid Cymru in Wales, and the Green party. Some of its Scottish branches subsequently chose to affiliate to the SSP – a breach of Labour's rules. Consequently, early in 2004, the RMT was expelled from the Labour party.

During 2002 and 2003, activist pressure to disaffiliate from the Labour party was evident within a number of other unions, though it was strongest within the Fire Brigades Union (FBU) – a reflection of membership discontent with the government's handling of their pay dispute (see Chapter 9). At the union's June 2004 annual conference, FBU delegates voted to sever its link with the party. Many of the major union affiliates, including Unison and the GMB general union, have instituted reviews of their links with the Labour party while also reducing the level of their financial support. However, most union leaderships, including that of Unison, which represents workers in the public services, have strenuously resisted efforts to break with the Labour party, fearing that such an outcome would prejudice their political influence, and thus lose the unions a voice within government. In the summer of 2004, the unions and the Labour leadership struck a deal at a policy forum held at the University of Warwick. In exchange for union support at the general election expected in 2005, Labour agreed to enact limited improvements in employment rights, an extension to the statutory minimum annual leave entitlement for example. Whether this was just a temporary accord, something that kept the conflict between Labour and the unions under wraps until after the election, or the start of more long-lasting period of cooperation, remains to be seen (see Kampfner 2004).

increasingly elected leaders willing to be more critical of government policy. One of the most significant examples of this was the 2002 defeat of the incumbent Ken Jackson, one of the Labour leadership's most uncritical supporters within the union movement, by Derek Simpson, in the election to be general secretary of the Amicus–AEEU trade union. The emergence of a new cadre of union leaders, who are willing to be more critical of Labour policy, is partly the result of membership dissatisfaction over the direction of government policy. One of its outcomes is internal pressure within many unions for the amount of money they give to Labour to be reduced, although by the beginning of 2005 only the Rail, Maritime and Transport union (RMT) and the Fire Brigades Union (FBU) had broken with the party entirely (see Box 3.5).

These pressures, combined with the ambivalence about the need for the union link held by influential elements of the Labour leadership, meant that by 2003 the party–union relationship was at a 'low ebb' (Waddington 2003a: 352). Nevertheless, in the absence of other means of financial backing the Labour party remains heavily reliant on the unions for funds, and also for organizational support. In the run-up to the 2005 general election, Labour and the unions sought ways of reconciling their conflicting goals. While they may seek to reduce the level of their contributions, it seems unlikely that most union affiliates will sever their links with the party.

SECTION SUMMARY AND FURTHER READING

- The longstanding, and frequently strained, relationship between the trade unions and the Labour party is one that has been dominated by the politics of labourism. Historically, union leaders ceded influence over party policy for autonomy in industrial affairs. Moreover, their political conservatism was often mobilized to support the Labour leadership and defeat left-wing challenges, thus helping to moderate party policy.

- During the 1980s, Conservative governments enacted legislation that was designed to depoliticize the unions, though this was unsuccessful. Despite efforts by the Labour leadership to reduce the influence of the unions within the party, their financial and campaigning contributions were important factors in Labour's 1997 and 2001 landslide election victories.

- During Labour's first term in office, between 1997 and 2001, the relationship between the Labour party and the unions appears to have been strengthened. After 2001, however, the Labour government's neo-liberal policy agenda, including the extension of private sector involvement in the delivery of public services, and its emphasis on the importance of deregulated labour markets as a source of economic dynamism, caused relations with the trade unions to become increasingly strained.

The classic, and lengthy, account of the relationship between the trade unions and the Labour party is Minkin (1991). For a more concise historical perspective, and one that covers a shorter time period, Thorpe (1999) is recommended. Much of Ralph Miliband's *Parliamentary Socialism* (Miliband 1972), a robust critique of the reformist basis of Labour party policy, is relevant today. There are two good studies of recent developments in the relationship between Labour and the unions available: see Ludlum and Taylor (2003); and McIlroy (1998).

3.5 The politics of trade unionism II: union democracy and the internal politics of the unions

Two related considerations inform this examination of the internal political activities of the trade unions. First, trade unions are characterized by conflict over their goals and the appropriate means of achieving them. Like any organization, then, the process of decision-making in unions invariably has a political dimension (Morgan 1997). Trade unions, though, as vehicles for the mobilization of members' interests, are inherently more highly politicized, since their policies and decisions should reflect the wishes of the membership. This brings us to the second point, which is that trade unions aspire to be democratic bodies. In a strict sense, democracy implies 'rule by the people' (McIlroy 1988). In the case of the trade unions, then, one might conceive of union democracy as 'the extent to which the actions of union leaders are constrained by the needs and wishes of their members' (Heery and Fosh 1990: 15).

But the concept of union democracy is a nebulous one (Morris and Fosh 2000). For one thing, should the emphasis be placed on ensuring membership participation in the process of reaching decisions? A possible weakness of this approach is that it may militate against speedy and efficient outcomes. Or is it sufficient simply that the policies enacted by union leaders reflect the wishes of the broad mass of members, with their active involvement in the development of those policies being relatively marginal? While this approach may be more administratively efficient, without the provision of effective safeguards there is a danger that union members will lose their influence over leadership policies. Following a section in which three perspectives on union democracy are considered, we focus on the implications of attempts by 1980s Conservative governments to reform processes of union decision-making.

3.5.1 Understanding trade union democracy

Drawing on previous studies in this field (Child, Loveridge, and Warner 1973; Undy et al. 1996), we demonstrate that three alternative ways of conceptualizing democracy in trade unions exist. Union democracy can be understood with reference to the degree of membership participation, the level of administrative efficiency, or the extent to which members express their wishes by voting in ballots.

First, union activity is underpinned by a participative rationale, in which democracy can be said to exist in so far as decisions are based on the direct influence of, and contributions from, members. This was a particular feature of the nineteenth-century local trade societies. Given their very small size and exclusive membership, they were characterized by a form of 'primitive democracy' in which the active involvement of members was relatively straightforward (Webb and Webb 1920a). In his study of the Lancashire cotton unions during the nineteenth and twentieth centuries, Turner (1962) distinguished between 'open' and 'closed' unions. Whereas the former increased in size by incorporating a relatively wide range of occupations, the latter remained elite, small-scale, craft-based trade societies, or 'exclusive democracies', in which the homogeneity of members and their interests made widespread membership participation possible and encouraged self-discipline.

As trade unions increased in size, however, 'primitive' or 'exclusive' democracy became more difficult to sustain since a larger and more heterogeneous membership made the development of an administrative apparatus necessary for the purposes of efficient organization, and to mediate between competing demands on union resources. The reluctance of members to participate in the affairs of their union, something that has been a longstanding feature of union history (e.g. Goldstein 1952), may result in an unrepresentative minority of activists dominating decision-making processes. Nevertheless, one cannot understand the mobilization and articulation of interests within trade unions without some reference to the vital role of membership participation. In approaches to trade union democracy that place an emphasis on the importance of members' participation in union affairs, officials and leaders are characterized as delegates, enacting members' wishes as they have been articulated through collective decision-making processes, and subordinate to them (Fairbrother 1984).

Second, given the difficulties of securing membership participation in large unions, the administrative rationale holds that trade union leaders and officials use their knowledge, skills, and expertise to deliver appropriate benefits to their members, thus serving their interests. Trade unionism, then, is not an 'exercise in self government' (Allen 1954: 15). In this perspective, the emphasis is on speed of decision-making, efficiency, and the skills of the professional union official as a means of meeting the needs of members. Thus 'union leaders are democratic in so far as they represent the economic interests of their members *vis-à-vis* the employers', something that does not require membership participation (Martin 1985: 225). In larger and more diverse unions, particularly 'open' ones, the need to restrict the scope for membership activity is more acute given the likelihood of disputes arising between different groups of members with conflicting interests (Hyman 1975).

In the context of declining trade union membership, there was much interest during the 1980s and 1990s in how unions can administer their affairs more efficiently in ways that serve the interests of their members and attract new ones. The development of a more service-oriented, 'managerial unionism', in which union officials enjoy a more forthright role, has been identified. Thus trade unions concentrate on delivering services and benefits to members as individuals, and use consumer-style methods, including market research techniques, to identify membership priorities (Heery 1996; Heery and Kelly 1994).

The main problem with the emphasis on administrative rationality as a means of conceptualizing union democracy is the assumption that the means of decision-making in unions, that is how decisions are effected, are unimportant as long as union policies reflect members' concerns. In the case of trade unions, though, the way in which interests are articulated, the means of decision-making that is, have a major influence upon, and cannot be distinguished from, the outcomes in terms of policies (Hyman 1975). There is, then, a 'false dichotomy between union purposes and union democracy' (McIlroy 1988: 130), since, given the tendencies towards oligarchy that exist within trade unionism (see below), a low level of membership participation tends to beget more conservative policy orientations. In the case of managerial unionism, for example, the emphasis upon the role of expert officials delivering efficient services to individual members implies a narrowing in the scope of legitimate trade union activity. In particular, it de-emphasizes the role of unions as collective bodies of workers that mobilize to challenge employers.

The third perspective that can be applied to understanding democracy in trade unions is that which focuses upon the operation of ballots as a means of ensuring that union policies reflect members' wishes. In this liberal-pluralist approach, resembling the parliamentary model, representative democracy predominates. Members' interests are secured largely by the periodic election and re-election of union leaders, and by ensuring that decisions are decided by ballots. Thus elected union leaders are the representatives of their members, rather than their delegates, and enjoy wider scope to determine union goals based on their expertise and electoral mandate. There have been many studies examining the conditions for robust representative democracy within trade unions, in particular the existence of competition for posts, the scope for the organization of opposition parties or factions, and the characteristics of their electoral arrangements (e.g. Edelstein and Warner 1975; Lipset, Trow, and Coleman 1956; Martin 1985; Undy et al. 1981).

There are two major problems with this liberal-pluralist conception of union democracy. First, the emphasis on ballots militates against active membership participation in union affairs. According to Richard Hyman (1975: 76), it 'involves reducing popular involvement to the periodic participation in elections, in which a choice is possible between rival candidates'. Second, one of the implications of the liberal-pluralist model is that union leaderships are periodically challenged in elections by organized opposition parties that, if successful, constitute the new leadership. Although some unions resembled this model, for example the engineering union in which all official positions were elected and electoral competition between left-wing and right-wing candidates was rife (Hyman 1983; Undy et al. 1981), in general it is an inappropriate one for understanding union democracy (Edelstein and Warner 1975; Seifert 1984). Historically, the operation of organized opposition groups within British trade unions has either been absent, or prohibited by their rules (Hyman 1975).

Whereas it is generally inappropriate to refer to the existence of 'parties' in British trade unions, a degree of factionalism has long been prevalent (Clegg 1979; Hyman 1983; Seifert 1984). In so far as they challenge and constrain union leaderships, the existence of organized factions can be an important component of union democracy (Martin 1985). What, though, is the difference between 'parties' and 'factions'? The latter are more fluid and transient affairs, often consisting of temporary alliances between groups who have joined together to challenge the union leadership on a particular policy issue. See, for example the activity of the 'Not on the Agenda' (NOTA) group within the Communication Workers' Union (CWU) during the 1990s. This was an alliance of activists of differing political persuasions that developed in order to put pressure on the CWU leadership to oppose the introduction of new management techniques, including teamworking, in the Royal Mail (Gall 2001). Thus it is important to recognize that unions are politically charged bodies in which policy goals may be subject to major conflict, often on ideological grounds. In order to understand the internal politics of trade unions, it is necessary to look beyond their electoral machinery, and the other arrangements that constitute their formal systems of government. The large degree to which unions are sites of political and ideological conflict (Darlington 2002; Gall 2001), in which members articulate, and officials and activists influence interests in a complex and often contested way, must also be acknowledged.

Perhaps the most significant problem with the representative democracy concept as it is applied to the trade unions is the risk that union leaders not only use the privileges of their position to resist legitimate challenges to their authority, but also that their interests become divorced from those they are supposed to be representing. Although his main concern was with the internal affairs of political parties, in the early part of the twentieth century the political scientist Robert Michels developed the concept of the 'iron law of oligarchy' as a means of capturing the phenomenon whereby the interests of elected leaders come to diverge from those of their members. Union leaders, by virtue of their position, become conservative in their orientation, looking, in particular, to maintain constructive relationships with employers rather than mobilizing to challenge them (Hyman 1989). It is evident that oligarchic pressures exist within British trade unions – see, for example, the powerful role of general secretaries relative to their elected executives in unions such as the TGWU (McIlroy 1988). A strength of the oligarchy thesis, moreover, is its acknowledgement that unions, and their internal arrangements, are influenced by the characteristics of employment relations under capitalism, something that restricts their leaderships' scope for manoeuvre (Hyman 1983). Thus union leaders encounter powerful constraints on their activities that encourage conservatism.

But it is too crude to portray trade unions as bodies within which a conflict of interest between leaders and ordinary, or 'rank and file', members prevails (Heery and Fosh 1990; Hyman 1975, 1989). While there are powerful external constraints on trade unions that encourage their leaders to develop moderate, conservative policies, they nonetheless need to retain the support, loyalty, and election votes of their members. This may prompt a more radical agenda. Thus unions 'can only grow away from their members to a certain extent' and 'there is a constant struggle in unions between democracy and oligarchy' (McIlroy 1988: 143). A further implication of the presence of both oligarchic and democratic pressures within trade unions is that they are characterized by a 'two-way system of control' (Hyman 1975). While leaders try to use their authority to mobilize support for official union policies, they are nonetheless also obliged to respond to, and are influenced by, the collective wishes of their members.

All unions, then, are to varying degrees influenced by participative, administrative, and representative democratic rationales. None of them, on their own, is a satisfactory model for conceptualizing union democracy. Indeed it is doubtful, given the external pressures unions face, that pure democracy in unions is at all feasible; according to Hyman (1989: 158–9), 'its attainment will always be partial and always against the odds'. During the 1980s, however, Conservative governments enacted legislation designed to enhance the responsiveness of union leaders to their members. What measures did they introduce and what were their effects?

3.5.2 'Giving unions back to their members': the Conservative reform of union government

Before the 1980s, the principal influence on the internal government of trade unions was the content of their own rulebooks (Miller 1986). A major concern of the Conservatives was to reform the internal government of trade unions, to improve democracy by 'giving unions back to their members' (Martin et al. 1995). This policy was based on an assumption that the moderate mass of trade union members was being led astray, or coerced, by militant union leaderships into taking unnecessary industrial action, and thus their voice needed to be heard, principally through a greater role for ballots (McIlroy 1991). As the previous discussion shows, this was a presumption that ran counter to most of the academic work in the field. Indeed, the Conservatives' real aim seems to have been to use the rhetoric of individual member rights as a way of undermining collective union power, thus reducing the effectiveness of trade unionism (Martin et al. 1995; Smith and Morton 1993).

The 1980 Employment Act made funds available to unions on a voluntary basis to facilitate the use of ballots; they were little used though (Undy and Martin 1984), not least because of union opposition to Conservative employment relations policy in general. However, after 'their victory in the June 1983 general election, the Conservative Party placed trade union reform at the centre of its legislative programme for 1983–4' (Undy and Martin 1984: 43). The initial outcome was a 1983 discussion paper, *Democracy in Trade Unions* (DE 1983). It castigated the existing electoral procedures in the trade unions, and criticized their reluctance to reorganize themselves in a more democratic way. As a result, 'all too often it is evident that the policies which are being pursued do not reflect the views and interests of the members' (DE 1983: 1). The ensuing 1984 Trade Union Act mandated that union general secretaries and executive bodies be subject to periodic election in a ballot. It was reinforced by the 1988 Employment Act, which made postal ballots mandatory in union elections, established a special commissioner to assist members with complaints against their union, and gave members the right not to be unjustifiably disciplined by their union, for example suspension for not heeding a strike call.

What, then, were the effects of this legislation concerning the internal government of the trade unions? In general the balloting provisions do not appear to have been too much of a constraint on trade union behaviour, and may have helped to reinforce the authority of union leaderships in so far as they gave decisions added legitimacy (Undy et al. 1996). There is no evidence that they encouraged moderation, in fact rather the opposite. By the mid-1990s, just two unions had seen sitting general secretaries defeated in a ballot, and there were specific issues in both that had been influential (Martin et al. 1995; Undy et al. 1996). Overall, and especially since 2000, the balloting provisions, have, if anything, favoured radical challenges to conservative leaders, the 2002 success of Derek Simpson over Ken Jackson in the contest for the general secretaryship of the Amicus–AEEU engineering union being a prime example. In thinking that more effective balloting arrangements would induce greater union moderation, Conservative politicians were, then, profoundly mistaken. If anything, union leaders tend to exert a moderating influence on a generally more militant membership.

It is also doubtful whether the Conservatives' interventions enhanced democracy within the trade unions. Research studies demonstrate that the legislation, given the complexity of its demands, stimulated greater centralization of authority in the unions, enhancing their administrative rationality in a way that benefited union leaders, but diminished members' participation in union affairs (Martin et al. 1995). The 'result of the change was, therefore, not increased union democracy, but a shift towards popular autocracy' (Undy et al. 1996: 261). The approach of the Conservatives was largely predicated upon a liberal-pluralist assumption that equates democracy with the presence of periodic election ballots. Such an emphasis on representative democracy is, though, an unsatisfactory way of ensuring that democratic pressures in unions are enhanced, given the significance of, as we have seen, the administrative and participative imperatives that underpin union behaviour.

SECTION SUMMARY AND FURTHER READING

- Like all organizations, trade unions are politicized bodies, but as vehicles for mobilizing and channelling the diverse and sometimes contradictory interests of their members, they are distinguished by the large amount of political and ideological conflict that informs their activities and policies.

- The concept of trade union democracy is a complex one, and can be interpreted with reference to the participative, administrative, and representative rationales informing union systems of government. None of these perspectives, by themselves, enables union democracy to be adequately conceptualized. It is better to consider union democracy as an ideal, to be worked towards, rather than something that can ever be attained in practice.

- Despite the presence of oligarchic pressures within trade unions, that is the tendency for their leaders to become overly cautious and conservative, and thus promote interests that may run counter to their more radical members, the Conservatives considered that the reverse was true. Militant union leaders were viewed as coercing their more moderate members into taking disruptive industrial action. However, legislation designed to 'give unions back to their members' appears to have generated greater centralization of much union decision-making.

For a classic analysis of union democracy, one that uses the toleration of factions as its framework, see Martin (1985). Hyman (1975: Chapter 3) offers a most sophisticated analysis of the possibilities of, and constraints upon, union democracy. See Fairbrother (1984) for the case for a participatory approach. For an analysis of the effects and implications of the Conservatives' reform of union government, see Undy et al. (1996: Chapters 5 and 7). See the companion website for a further discussion of factionalism within British trade unions, the influence of left-wing political groups in particular.

■ CONCLUSION

This chapter has examined the highly politicized nature of employment relations. We have considered the influence of state policy, and the implications of greater European integration for employment relations. One thing that will be evident is the large extent to which the British state and the EU have been concerned with developing and enacting policies that provide businesses with a supportive environment in which they can pursue growth more readily. The Conservatives' legislative reforms of the 1980s and 1990s, for example, were impelled by a belief that excessive union power was an obstacle to economic competitiveness, and that greater labour market deregulation was a necessary, and indeed desirable, component of wealth creation. Although Labour has made some notable policy interventions that are ostensibly designed to favour workers and trade unions, in general they have been enacted in such a way that they do not conflict with the assumption that, given greater economic globalization, deregulated labour markets and weak trade unions are necessary components of a competitive economy. At the supra-national level, the impetus of the EU's 'social dimension' has dwindled markedly, a further reflection of its inferior status relative to the process of market integration.

It would be reasonable to suppose, therefore, that the nature of Labour and the EU's respective policy agendas is to maintain and extend the power of capital by accommodating, containing, and incorporating workers' and unions' interests, as opposed to the more obviously repressive approach taken by the Conservatives during the 1980s and 1990s. Yet it is important not to underplay the efforts expended by the trade unions in shaping the public policy agenda. Within the EU, for example, policy-makers are often sensitive to union activities and initiatives. Moreover, Labour's domestic programme of employment relations reform was strongly influenced by the efforts of the union movement to ensure that favourable policies were enacted. Thus it is important to recognize that the decisions made by state policy-makers, and those in supra-national bodies like the EU, are not entirely concerned with supporting the aims of capital, but may also be disposed to the labour interest.

Towards the end of the chapter, we examined the politics of trade unionism in Britain. Unions are politically charged bodies in which policy goals may be subject to major conflict, often on ideological grounds (Darlington 2002; Gall 2001). Indeed, one cannot properly understand trade union behaviour without an appreciation of their political nature, including the close relationship many of them have with the Labour party, and the role of factions. Although trade unions are ostensibly, and aspire to be, democratic bodies, the concept of union democracy is not a straightforward one and can be viewed from a number of different perspectives. One of the most notable contemporary concerns within trade unions is how to enhance the contribution of women, and other groups, within union affairs. This is something we examine in Chapter 4 when we assess the implications of social divisions for employment relations.

■ ASSIGNMENT AND DISCUSSION QUESTIONS

1. Identify the main implications of neo-liberal policies for employment relations.

2. Assess the extent to which the Labour governments of 1997 and 2001 continued the public policy approach begun by preceding Conservative governments.

3. How far is the idea of the 'third way' useful in explaining recent public policy developments in employment relations?

4. Provide arguments either for or against the proposition that 'the EU should concern itself only with trade and related matters and leave employment matters to individual member states'.

5. What is meant by the 'social dimension' of the EU? How successful has the EU been in achieving its social objectives?

6. Discuss the view that trade unions would be more effective in achieving their aims if they were not so closely identified with the Labour party.

7. Do trade unions need to be democratic to serve their members' interests?

■ WEBSITE MATERIALS

Visit the companion web site to this book for interesting and updated material at
www.oup.com/booksites/busecon/business

■ **CHAPTER CASE STUDY**

Trade unions and the Euro

The establishment of Economic and Monetary Union (EMU), with its attendant strict controls to maintain low inflation, has had a significant impact on the daily lives of workers and their families in those countries that have adopted the single currency – the Euro. The potential effect of EMU on their members has prompted trade unions across Europe to consider whether or not they should support entry into the Euro by their respective countries. Their response has been varied: no more so than among public sector unions whose members may bear the brunt of economic policies pursued by governments to maintain compliance with the Stability and Growth Pact's requirements on public sector borrowing.

Foster and Scott (2003b) investigated the views of public sector unions towards EMU both in countries that had joined, and those that, to date, had not. They characterize union approaches under four broad headings. First, there are the 'Enthusiasts'. Public sector unions in Ireland are most typical of those holding this view. The country has received considerable benefits to its economy, and to the standard of living of the population, as a result of membership of the EU. It has developed a strong national-level social partnership in employment relations that has allowed the impact of economic controls to be mediated in terms of their effect on workers.

The second stance is labelled as the 'Altruists'. This tends to be the dominant position of public sector unions within the EU. It accepts that the impact of EMU will have short-term negative implications for the state sector. However, the belief here is that, in the longer term, EMU will deliver an improved economic situation, leading to greater prosperity, eventually benefiting those working in the state sector.

The 'Sceptics', at best, are resigned to the need for EMU, but have significant fears for the level of social provision that countries will be able to afford. Associated with this concern is the fear of job losses within the public sector. French unions are portrayed as most typical of the sceptical view, and the country has witnessed industrial action aimed at halting government proposals that could damage workers' employment terms, over reduced public sector pensions for example.

The final approach identified by the authors is the 'Resisters'. This view can be seen within the UK public sector unions, where entry to EMU is opposed because of the claimed loss of national sovereignty over public spending. Resistance is deemed necessary so that control over welfare spending remains in the hands of national governments. From this perspective, EMU is part of a neo-liberal challenge to labour market regulation and trade unions.

Foster and Scott (2003b) also highlight the large body of resistance to EMU that may exist among populations, including union members, throughout Europe. Even where union leaderships have been broadly supportive of EMU, many unionists have opposed entry. For example, the referendum in Denmark rejected adopting the Euro even though the public sector union supported the proposal. Unions should not assume members will unquestioningly follow their leaders' advice.

Case discussion questions

1. What are the benefits and disadvantages to trade unions and their members of Economic and Monetary Union?

2. What might be the implications for unions that develop policy in this area without taking into account their members' views?

CHAPTER 4

Social divisions and employment relations

CHAPTER OBJECTIVES

The main objectives of this chapter are to:

- explain the nature of workplace inequality, and to consider the implications for employment relations

- consider the extent, nature, and implications of employer-led initiatives designed to reduce disadvantage, including equal opportunity policies, and the diversity management approach

- assess public policy and legislative developments designed to challenge disadvantage in employment

- examine employer efforts to promote work–life balance initiatives

- consider the efforts made by trade unions to represent the interests of workers from disadvantaged social groups

---

4.1 Introduction

Following on from Chapters 2 and 3, in which we examined employment relations in the contemporary economy, and the politics of employment relations respectively, this chapter, the third of those that aim to analyse contemporary employment relations developments in a broader context, focuses on the influence of social divisions. By this we mean aspects of disadvantage and inequality that are socially constituted, that reflect people's shared social characteristics, gender for example. The aim of this chapter is to provide you with a good knowledge of the nature, and principal features, of inequality and disadvantage in employment relations, and to enable you to develop a critical understanding of the main ways in which they have been addressed.

4.2 Workplace inequality and employment relations

For many years, the principal focus of studies of workplace inequality concerned the so-called status divide between manual and non-manual workers. In this section, we consider the extent to which occupational and organizational changes have eradicated such inequality in British workplaces. We also direct our attention to the importance of other manifestations of inequality at work, those based on shared social characteristics such as gender. After reading this section, you will be better placed to appreciate the relevance of social divisions to employment relations in contemporary Britain.

4.2.1 Inequality at work and the status divide

One of the most prominent aspects of inequality in British employment relations is the status divide that has long existed between manual, blue-collar workers and their non-manual, white-collar 'staff' counterparts. In manufacturing industry, for example, manual workers traditionally enjoyed the least favourable terms and conditions of employment, including a longer working week, shorter holidays, and fewer fringe benefits. In the 1960s, many firms had different canteen facilities for their manual and non-manual employees. Ninety per cent of manual workers were fined if they were late for work, whereas only a minority of non-manuals, and few managers, had to endure such a penalty (Wedderburn and Craig 1974). Non-manual work, largely undertaken in an office environment, was associated with higher status, better terms and conditions of employment, and greater job security. White-collar employees were more likely to benefit from sick pay arrangements, and enjoy longer holidays, a shorter working week, greater opportunities for promotion, and more autonomy at work (Price 1989).

What accounts for this higher status accorded to white-collar, non-manual staff? By virtue of the closer relationship they had with their employers, relative to manual workers, non-manual employees were considered to be more committed to the aims of the organization, possessed greater intrinsic motivation, generated by relatively high job security and career development opportunities in particular, and were thought to be more trustworthy as a result (Fox 1974; Lockwood 1958; Price and Price 1994). Detailed control of their work was largely unnecessary. Thus 'greater proximity to the functions of the employer brought with it higher social status and greater privileges in conditions of employment' (Price 1989: 277). Manual workers, however, were subject to a much more regimented employment regime, with strict controls over matters including working time, attendance and discipline, since they were thought to exhibit less organizational commitment (Price 1989).

Since the 1980s, though, there has been an apparent trend towards the 'harmonization' of employment conditions in Britain, something that is supposed to have caused the status divide between manual and non-manual employees to have markedly declined in significance (Russell 1992). Organizational restructuring, in particular the demand for greater workplace flexibility, challenges traditional occupational patterns, and the established distinction between manual and non-manual employees (Bradley et al. 2000). Moreover, much of the impetus for reform is identified with the activities of foreign-owned multinationals in Britain, such as the American company Johnston and Johnston for example. In their concern to enhance flexibility and employee commitment, and to generate a more cooperative employment relations environment, such firms have sought to extend the benefits traditionally enjoyed by non-manual employees to their manual counterparts (Price 1989; Price and Price 1994). In many cases, this has resulted in the conclusion of single-status agreements, where all employees, regardless of their job role, enjoy the same conditions of service and fringe benefits (Bassett 1987). Perhaps the best-known of these single-status agreements is that which was reached in local government in 1997. It established a single pay spine for manual, and administrative, professional, clerical, and technical (APC&T) staff, and it harmonized basic working conditions such as working time and holiday entitlement. The implementation of this agreement across the country, however, has not been smooth, not least because of complaints that it has been insufficiently funded (Bach and Winchester 2003).

It is important to acknowledge the 'patchy and variable' extent of harmonization in Britain, and the durability of the status divide (Price 1989: 274; Price and Price 1994; Bradley et al. 2000). Inequality remains an enduring feature of British workplaces. According to one manual worker: 'They [managers] assume you're stupid because you're a production worker. There's no prospects' (quoted in Bradley et al. 2000: 143). In the authors' own institution, the status divide is a prominent feature of how employment relations is managed. Take holiday entitlement for example. Academic staff enjoy thirty-five days annual leave. For white-collar staff, holiday entitlement is dependent upon their position in the salary scale and their length of service, but the maximum possible is twenty-eight days. Manual workers, though, have a basic allowance of twenty days, rising to twenty-three days after five years service, and twenty-five days after ten years service.

Survey data show that manual workers now benefit from greater task discretion and enjoy more responsibility over how they undertake their tasks. Nevertheless, they have fewer opportunities for training, are more closely monitored and controlled at work, and have less job security than their white-collar counterparts (Gallie et al. 1998). Although occupational change has rendered the distinction between manual and non-manual employees less important than it once was, not least because of the growth of non-manual jobs in the economy, the status divide remains a durable feature of British employment relations. In terms of access to fringe benefits and control over working time, to take two examples, inequalities between white-collar occupations appear to be the most prominent source of division in British workplaces, suggesting a polarization of jobs within growing non-manual employment (McGovern and Hill 2003).

4.2.2 Social disadvantage and workplace inequality: towards a broader agenda

One of the main weaknesses of the traditional, institutional approach to employment relations was its emphasis on arrangements in male-dominated manual work environments that were characterized by the presence of a strong trade union and collective bargaining (Greene 2003). Consequently, the role of women workers, the relationship between men and women at work, and the ways in which these influenced employment relations have often been rather neglected (Wacjman 2000). Instead, 'there is a tendency to treat workers as homogeneous, with this homogeneity based around male experience' (Greene 2003: 308).

But gender, the 'lived relationships between men and women through which sexual differences and ideas about sexual differences are constructed' (Bradley 1996: 82), exercises an important influence on the conduct of employment relations.

Although we focus on gender divisions at work in this section, this should not imply that other social divisions are less important. In spite of changing social attitudes and growing tolerance about people's sexual orientation, reports of discrimination against lesbian and gay workers persist (see Bairstow 2004). Age discrimination at work appears to be rife in Britain, notwithstanding evidence of the advantages of employing older workers (see Box 4.1). There is a long history of discrimination against disabled people in employment, who are especially prone to unemployment or segregation in poorly paid, low-skilled jobs as a result (Barnes 1992). Disadvantage on grounds of 'race' and ethnicity is also a feature of employment in Britain. The unemployment rate for Black Caribbean men, for example, is twice that for white men (Modood et al. 1997).

For reasons of space, however, in this section we concentrate on the pattern of gender inequality and disadvantage at work. Historically, women were generally channelled by employers, often with the support of male-dominated trade unions, into poorly paid, low-skilled jobs that offered few opportunities for promotion (Bradley 1989), or were excluded from the workforce entirely. There is evidence of progress towards gender equality in contemporary Britain. For one thing, greater numbers of women now undertake paid employment; in 2002 women made up 45 per cent of the employed workforce

---

BOX 4.1 AGE DISCRIMINATION AT WORK

Discrimination against workers on the grounds of their age, or 'ageism' as it is popularly called, has attracted an increasing amount of interest in Britain (see Glover and Branine 2001). There are claims that organizations that make effective use of older workers gain business benefits. The retail chain B & Q, for example, asserts that its policy of recruiting staff who are beyond the normal age for retirement has led to reduced absenteeism, improved punctuality, and better customer service. Where workers perceive that they have been discriminated against on the grounds of their age, it can produce negative work attitudes and behaviours (Snape and Redman 2003). Nevertheless, 'discrimination against older workers is deeply embedded in the cultures, policies and practices of many organizations' (Taylor and Walker 1998: 74). In 2003, British Airways cabin crew protested against company rules that forced them into retirement at the age of 55.

Before taking office in 1997, Labour had promised to introduce legislation outlawing age discrimination. Once in government, however, it opted for a voluntary approach, publishing a code of practice, *Age Diversity in Employment*, in 1999. Among other things, the code urged employers not to use age as a criterion when advertising job opportunities. Voluntary methods seem to be rather ineffective as a means of challenging discrimination against older workers (Snape and Redman 2003). The charity Age Concern, for example, suggests that age discrimination may have become more prevalent since the publication of the code of practice. European Union legislation, though, has forced the government to act. The 2000 EU framework directive on equal treatment in employment and occupations obliges the British government to legislate to outlaw discrimination on grounds of age by 2006, making mandatory retirement ages unlawful, for example, unless they have some objective justification.

(Duffield 2002). Moreover, growing numbers of women have secured entry to hitherto male-dominated professional and managerial jobs, in areas such as education (Crompton and Sanderson 1990; Walby 1997). As a result, 'women's over-representation in lower-grade and less well-paid occupations has been reduced, and their representation in professional and managerial occupations has increased' (Crompton 1997: 46).

Yet the progress towards gender equality at work should not be overstated (Bradley et al. 2000). For one thing, although it has been eroded, the segregation of jobs and occupations based on gender remains a marked feature of contemporary employment relations. It is conventional to distinguish between 'vertical' and 'horizontal' gender segregation (Hakim 1979), although in practice the two are related (Bradley 1999). Vertical segregation refers to the over-representation of women in relatively poorly paid and low-skilled jobs at the bottom of organizational hierarchies, and their under-representation in executive and managerial roles. Horizontal segregation applies to the over-representation of women in particular occupations, such as that of supermarket cashier for example, and their under-representation in others.

Contemporary employment relations is characterized by gender segregation in respect of work and occupations (Bradley 1999; Greene 2001; Munro 1999). Relative to males, female managers are under-represented in over two-thirds of workplaces (Cully et al. 1999). In respect of manual jobs, horizontal segregation is pronounced, 'with men dominating, for example, in construction, transport and metalwork while women remain clustered in female specialisms as care assistants, hairdressers and cashiers' (Bradley et al. 2000: 83). Although female participation in the labour force has grown, much women's employment is concentrated in poorly remunerated, part-time jobs in the service sector where opportunities for career progression are very limited (Dickens 2000a; Hakim 1996), and which are often depicted as being less important than full-time ones. In the Post Office, for example, the male-dominated trade union sought to exclude the largely female part-time workforce from access to overtime arrangements, and thus better wages, on the grounds that their earnings were less important than those of full-time employees (Jenkins, Martinez Lucio, and Noon 2002).

The persistence of gender segregation at work is perhaps one of the main reasons why the gender pay gap has proved to be so resilient. This is the difference between the average earnings of men and those of women, and is a major aspect of gender disadvantage. In 2004, for full-time employees this gap was nearly 20 per cent, meaning that average earnings for female employees are little more than 80 per cent of those of men (IDS 2004a). According to Hakim (1996: 150–1), studies of particular occupations 'indicate that vertical job segregation accounts for virtually all the difference'. In other words, women earn less on average than men because they are over-represented among poorly remunerated jobs at the bottom of organizational hierarchies. For Hakim (1996), the concentration of women in low-paid, part-time jobs largely reflects women's own choices; many women choose not to pursue organizational careers to the same degree as men, but focus on their family responsibilities, perhaps combining them with part-time employment.

Yet the existence of vertical segregation does not adequately explain the resilience of the gender pay gap. There is evidence that 'male-dominated jobs tend to be paid at a higher level than female-dominated jobs of an equivalent level of skill and qualification' (IDS 2003: 13). Thus those jobs that are largely undertaken by women are undervalued and not accorded as much importance as those that are primarily filled by men, even when, objectively, they appear to be equally, or perhaps more, demanding. Occupations and jobs that are primarily the preserve of women are treated as less important, not so highly skilled, and thus attract less pay than those that are largely filled by men (Dex, Sutherland, and Joshi 2000). Moreover, pay systems often operate in ways that disadvantage women at work, by linking earnings to length of service for example (McColgan 1997).

A further, more fundamental problem with Hakim's notion that gender segregation at work, and thus the gender pay gap, reflect the choices exercised by many women (Hakim 1996) is that it pays insufficient heed to the structural constraints that inhibit women from advancing in organizations, in particular the ways in which men attempt to exercise power over, and exclude, them (Bradley 1999). Gender disadvantage is still a significant feature of contemporary employment relations in Britain. In the remainder of this chapter, we examine how far organizational equal opportunities initiatives, public policy and legislative interventions, and trade union activities have respectively challenged inequality and disadvantage at work.

SECTION SUMMARY AND FURTHER READING

- Inequality at work has long been manifested in the status divide, something that harmonization initiatives have done little to eradicate. Nevertheless, divisions within non-manual labour now seem more important than those between manual and non-manual positions.

- Nevertheless, a broader conceptualization of social divisions at work is desirable, one that considers the implications for employment relations of disadvantage based on age, sexual orientation, disability, race and ethnicity, and gender. Gender inequality at work is reflected in the persistence of job segregation and the lower earnings of women, relative to those of men.

There are some good studies of developments in female employment; Crompton (1997), Bradley (1999), and Bradley et al. (2000: Chapter 4) are particularly recommended. See the companion website for additional information about the gender pay gap, and contemporary efforts designed to reduce it.

4.3 Managing equality and diversity at work

In this section, we are concerned with organizational initiatives designed to challenge inequality and disadvantage at work. Equal opportunities policies are the main tool used by employers to promote equality in the workplace. How can such interventions be understood and why have they become so commonplace? Given the relative ineffectiveness of equal opportunities in practice, there has been an increasing amount of interest in the concept of managing diversity as a means of challenging disadvantage at work. But how far does this approach differ from conventional equal opportunities policies, and is it more likely to promote equality in the workplace? It will become evident that organizational initiatives on their own are unlikely to erode inequality and disadvantage at work.

4.3.1 Understanding equal opportunities policies

Since the 1970s, employers have increasingly committed themselves to the pursuit of equal opportunities, in particular by styling themselves as 'equal opportunity employers', and enacting formal equal opportunities (EO) policies (Dickens 2000a; Jewson et al. 1995; Liff 2003). According to data from the 1998 Workplace Employment Relations Survey (WERS), 67 per cent of workplaces in Britain with ten or more employees are covered by an equal opportunities policy of some kind (Anderson, Millward, and Forth 2004). Among larger organizations, they appear to be almost universal (IDS 2004b). Whereas in the past, equal opportunities policies were generally restricted to the areas of sex and race, there is evidence that, under the influence of legislation, they are increasingly covering disability, age, and sexual orientation (Liff 2003).

Generally, organizational EO policies are characterized by a 'liberal' approach to tackling inequality at work (Jewson and Mason 1986). This refers to an emphasis on the use of formal procedures, in respect of recruitment, selection, and promotion decisions for example, designed to ensure that people are accorded equal treatment regardless of their social characteristics (Jewson and Mason 1986; Kirton and Greene 2000; Liff 1999). Equality, then, is delivered through the use of bureaucratic methods that encourage managers to treat people as if they are the same, reducing the salience of social differences (Liff 1999; Liff and Wacjman 1996).

There is, therefore, an overwhelming emphasis on the development of a 'level playing field' (Webb 1997), so that workers are treated in the same way. As applied to the recruitment and selection of staff, for instance, 'procedures are set up to attempt to ensure that candidates are chosen on the basis of their suitability for the job on meritocratic grounds' (Kirton and Greene 2000: 106); supposedly the best person is chosen for the job irrespective of their social characteristics. Why, though, have equal opportunities policies become so commonplace among British organizations? Compliance with the law is the most significant influence on organizational practice (IDS 2004b); equal opportunities policies are designed to ensure that the organization is less liable to actions on grounds of sex, race and, more recently, disability, religious belief, and sexual orientation. Moreover, the pursuit of equal opportunities has also been informed by a belief that inequality and unfair discrimination at work are inherently undesirable and, in the interests of social justice, should be eradicated (Davies and Thomas 2000). Since the 1980s, however, the social justice rationale for equality action has been eclipsed by the one that stresses the advantages to businesses of reducing inequality and disadvantage in the employment relationship (Dickens 1994, 1997, 1999, 2000a).

There is no one business 'case' for equality action. Rather, it is proposed that the promotion of equality will, to varying degrees, generate certain business advantages (Dickens 1994; Liff 2003). These include being able to draw on a wider pool of talent when recruiting employees, retain important staff, benefit from the contribution of groups whose skills and potential contribution might otherwise have been neglected, match the characteristics of customers, and sustain a positive corporate reputation (Dickens 2000a; IDS 2004b; Liff 2003). Since the desirability of equality action is bound up with its potential contribution to improving organizational performance, business arguments may be more effective in generating positive reform, in particular by securing the commitment of managers, than the social justice rationale (Dickens 1994; Liff 2003). Employer-led bodies such as Opportunity Now (formerly Opportunity 2000) and Race for Equality are at the forefront of articulating the business benefits of equality action, in the respective areas of sex and race.

The adoption and development of organizational EO policies have made a positive difference to the position of some groups of workers, particularly relatively well-off women who are better able to gain access to managerial and professional jobs (Webb 1997). This is evident in the case of the airline company studied by Rutherford (1999). It was a founder member of Opportunity 2000 and, over a long period of time, had developed a range of sophisticated equal opportunities practices, job-sharing arrangements for example, designed to increase the number of women in management roles. Yet the proportion of women in senior management roles remained stubbornly low, largely, it seems, because of an assumption that such jobs required excessive working hours, something that was difficult to reconcile with women's family responsibilities.

4.3.2 Equal opportunities policies: a critical assessment

There are four main problems with equal opportunities policies as tools for challenging discrimination and disadvantage at work. The first is that they are often merely rhetorical statements of intent that help to conceal the presence of discriminatory workplace practices (Kirton and Greene 2000: 188). In other words, the presence of a formal policy need not have much of an effect at all on employment relations processes and arrangements. Only 'lip service', then, is paid to equality (Dickens 2000a). Just because there is an equal opportunities policy in place should not be taken as a sign that unfair discrimination is absent (Aitkenhead and Liff 1991). The experiences of the black trade union activists studied by Healy, Bradley, and Mukherjee (2004) were marked by incidents of racial discrimination, even in companies that were noted for their positive pursuit of equal opportunities. Moreover, equal opportunities policies are often just 'empty shells'. This means that in many workplaces covered by a formal equal opportunities policy, there are either few practices to support it or, if there are, they are restricted to certain groups of workers, such as the ability to undertake job-sharing for example (Hoque and Noon 2004).

A second problem with organizational equal opportunities policies is that their focus is often rather narrow, concerned with assisting women managers break the 'glass ceiling' and secure more senior positions. This was apparent in the case of the airline discussed above (Rutherford 1999). However, employers are largely uninterested in developing interventions that would benefit the many more female workers who are employed in jobs characterized by low pay and poor working conditions, and whose prospects are obstructed more by the presence of a 'sticky floor' rather than a glass ceiling (Cockburn 1991; Dickens 1997). This is evident within the National Health Service (NHS). A member of Opportunity 2000, the NHS has pursued a gender equality agenda that prioritizes increasing the proportion of women in professional and managerial jobs. Such an approach, however, has 'little relevance to women in clerical and administrative grades, much less ancillary workers such as cleaners, catering staff and health-care assistants' (Richards 2001: 27).

The third obstacle to the progress of employer-led equality initiatives concerns the attitudes and behaviour of, often male, line managers. Equality initiatives are often treated as unimportant, or even resisted, by managers who see them as an infringement upon their prerogative (Kirton and Greene 2000). Collinson, Knights, and Collinson (1990), for example, discovered that when recruiting new employees line managers are reluctant to comply with procedures designed to secure equal treatment. This may be exacerbated during periods of organizational restructuring since equality initiatives can become marginalized. This is apparent from a study of organizational change in a civil service agency that, among other things, gave line managers more discretion over equal opportunities. Although a minority of managers did take the opportunity to progress these issues, most had only a 'hazy perception of the role they were expected to play in maintaining and developing' equal opportunities (Cunningham, Lord, and Delaney 1999: 70), and some expressed downright hostility. According to one female employee, when equality issues are raised: 'The standard sort of reaction [in management meetings] is the raised eyebrows and an "Oh gawd, not this again, what a waste of time, here we go again with something else to complain about", you know' (quoted in Cunningham, Lord, and Delaney 1999: 71).

Linked to this, the fourth weakness of equal opportunities policies as devices designed to reduce unfair discrimination at work is that they generally fail to challenge those features of the cultures and structures of organizations that privilege men. This is evident in the case of a high street bank. The company had a longstanding formal commitment to equal opportunities and was a founder member of Opportunity 2000. In practice, however, major barriers to women's progress existed. Managers were expected to undertake excessive working hours, something of a problem for women with family responsibilities. Moreover, it was assumed that once they had children, women would lack the appropriate level of organizational commitment necessary for promotion. If a woman expressed an interest in flexible working, so as to combine work and family responsibilities more easily, this was taken as a sign that she was not interested in pursuing a career. Thus management in the organization, especially senior roles, was dominated by men. 'Formal equality statements expressed concern about this situation but there were far more powerful informal practices which reinforced it' (Liff and Ward 2001: 30).

It is important not to underplay the significance of equal opportunity initiatives in British workplaces. In some areas they have fostered a 'climate of equality', enabling women to challenge long-established structures of job segregation (Bradley 1999). By itself, though, employer-led equality action is a rather weak means of challenging such discrimination in employment (Dickens 2000a). A major source of this weakness is that it is underpinned by an assumption that equality is best promoted on the basis that it delivers important business benefits.

Yet there are a number of problems with this approach. For one thing, employers may focus their efforts on improvements in areas where it is easier to secure change, or where the business benefits are more easily identifiable (Dickens 1999). This explains the popularity of initiatives designed to erode the glass ceiling and increase the proportion of female managers in senior positions. Challenging long-established patterns of job segregation and low pay, which operate to the disadvantage of women workers in particular, is a much more complicated and difficult area and will not be in the interests of employers who secure important cost advantages by maintaining a pool of cheap, low-paid female labour (Dickens 1994). In such cases 'a business case can be articulated against [equal opportunities] action' (Dickens 1999: 10). A further problem is that the supposed business benefits of equality action may be difficult to identify at an organizational level (Colling and Dickens 1998).

They are also likely to be of a relatively long-term character, something that is problematic given the pressure on organizations to deliver short-term performance gains (Kirton and Greene 2000). Equality initiatives, then, are more likely to be perceived by employers as business costs, rather than as investments that can help to enhance organizational performance, and are liable to be withdrawn if no advantage is apparent (Dickens 2000a). As a result, employer-led efforts to challenge inequality at work are bound to be 'partial' and 'selective' (Dickens 1997), varying between organizations and over time according to managerial preferences, and not those of disadvantaged employees.

4.3.3 Towards managing diversity?

In contrast to the emphasis on equal treatment and fair procedures that characterizes the liberal model of equal opportunities approaches, interventions designed to produce equal outcomes are at the heart of the radical model. 'It seeks to intervene directly in workplace practices in order to achieve a fair distribution of rewards among employees, as measured by some criterion of moral value and worth' (Jewson and Mason 1986: 315). The radical model recognizes that structural factors particular to certain socially disadvantaged groups inhibit their participation in employment, for example women's greater share of domestic responsibilities (Webb and Liff 1988). Thus equality 'of access is an illusion while the white, male, full-time worker with few domestic responsibilities is the norm' (Kirton and Greene 2000: 107). Positive action, then, such as the setting of employment quotas for example, is necessary if equality at work is to be achieved.

The main problem with the radical approach is that it invites the complaint that certain groups of workers are the unworthy beneficiaries of 'special treatment', something that may erode support for equality initiatives. Nor does it 'promise any improvement *in the nature of the organisation itself*' (Cockburn 1989: 217, original italics). Instead, Cockburn (1989) proposes that it is more useful to distinguish between 'short' and 'long' equality agendas. Whereas the short agenda is concerned with rather superficial managerial interventions designed to improve equality of opportunity, at its longest the equal opportunities agenda should be a transformative programme, dedicated to challenging the power of privileged groups of white, male employees. It recognizes that 'disadvantage can be perpetuated through an organization's structure, culture and practices, rather than just through the biased decision-making of managers . . .' (Liff 2003: 440), and that it is these that should be reformed.

One of the claims made for the managing diversity approach is that it holds out the promise of transformative organizational change as a means of eroding disadvantage in employment (Blakemore and Drake 1996). The managing diversity approach has become increasingly influential, particularly in the United States, as a means of challenging discrimination and disadvantage in the employment relationship (Davies and Thomas 2000; Liff 2003; Webb 1997). What, then, are the main assumptions that underpin, and the principal characteristics of, the managing diversity model? Whereas the liberal equal opportunities approach emphasizes the importance of equal treatment and sameness as the best way of reducing disadvantage, the managing diversity model contends that equality is more effectively secured by acknowledging and lauding differences between employees (Kandola and Fullerton 1994). 'In contrast to equal opportunities approaches, which aim for workplaces where an individual's sex and race is of no greater significance than the colour of the eyes in determining the treatment they receive, the core idea behind managing diversity seems to encourage organizations to recognize difference' (Liff 1997: 13). How might a managing diversity approach differ in practice from one based on equal opportunities? Liff (1999: 68) uses the example of employee appraisals. Managers operating within the confines of a liberal equal opportunities approach would seek to ensure that there is no bias in the assessment criteria for measuring employee performance that might disadvantage members of a particular social group. In an organization that focuses on managing diversity, however, managers would reconsider the very nature of the criteria used to establish effective performance.

Within the managing diversity approach, the emphasis on individual differences stands in marked contrast to the primacy of tackling group-based disadvantage that is central to liberal equal opportunities programmes (Liff 1997). Thus there 'is a move away from the idea that different groups should be assimilated to meet an organizational norm' (Kirton and Greene 2000: 109), one which is often, of course, based on the experiences of men (Liff and Wacjman 1996). A further aspect of the managing diversity approach, which distinguishes it from an equal opportunities one, is that it is supposedly more attractive to managers (Liff 1997). The emphasis on managing individual employees, and of realizing their potential in a way that benefits the business, is something that managers, who would otherwise be sceptical of the value of equal opportunity initiatives, are able to appreciate. In contrast to the equal opportunities approach, which is often perceived as an external imposition, managing diversity is more easily aligned with, and supportive of, the needs of the business (Ross and Schneider 1992).

Thus the managing diversity approach would appear to constitute a firmer basis for managerial action on equality than traditional equal opportunities approaches; it may generate business benefits. *The Guardian* newspaper, for example, claims that its own commitment to managing diversity enables it to secure more advertising from like-minded organizations (IDS 2004b). The most profound claim for the approach, though, is that if organizations are to acknowledge and manage individual differences effectively, and thus realize the full potential of their employees, they should review the way they operate. Underpinning the managing diversity approach, therefore, is the assumption that an organization must 'recognize that *it* has to change to adapt to employee differences rather than simply expecting employees to fit in with its pre-existing practices' (Liff 1999: 68).

Managing diversity, then, appears to hold out the potential for a transformation in employer attitudes towards equality, consistent with the 'long' approach discussed above. In reality, however, it promises significantly more than it delivers. There are three major problems with the managing diversity model. First, in practice it is difficult to distinguish between equal opportunities and managing diversity approaches. In her study of BT, for example, Liff (1999) found evidence of managing diversity in action, including efforts to restructure jobs to make them more attractive to female graduates. But these co-existed alongside more conventional equal opportunities initiatives, including job-sharing arrangements. In this case, then, there was no 'radical separation between equal opportunities and managing diversity approaches' (Liff 1999: 72). The latter may involve little more than a simple re-labelling of conventional EO initiatives (Kirton and Greene 2000: 112), perhaps to make them more palatable to managers.

Second, the managing diversity approach has been criticized for offering a 'sanitized' and 'unthreatening' perspective on workplace differences (Webb 1997: 163). It is a model that is designed to be comfortable for managers, not to challenge their assumptions or prejudices. The emphasis on individuals, moreover, means that pressure to change potentially discriminatory organizational practices is often absent, since they do not have the collective power to effect reforms enjoyed by socially disadvantaged groups (Kirton and Greene 2000; Webb 1997). As a result, understandings of 'differences', and of whether and how they should be valued, generally come within the prerogative of managers, who may support diversity only as long as it delivers explicit organizational benefits, or does not cost them anything (Kirton and Greene 2000; Webb 1997).

Third, although in theory the managing diversity approach holds out the promise of transformative organizational change in order to enable individual differences to be recognized and valued, in practice it generally leaves established beliefs and practices unchanged (Dickens 2000a). It is rarely used to challenge those longstanding features of organizations that systematically privilege white men, and thus contribute to employment disadvantage and inequality (Liff 1997). Despite a commitment to managing diversity, the international computer systems manufacturer studied by Webb (1997) continued to function in ways that disproportionately benefited male employees. Vertical job segregation was pronounced. Male managers simply assumed that women were uninterested in promotion; they did not recognize that the absence of facilities such as childcare arrangements, for example, hindered the advancement of women. Diversity, then, 'may have more to do with corporate image-building than with the kind of interventions designed to facilitate more egalitarian work organization and increased inclusion of women' (Webb 1997: 166). Like conventional equal opportunities approaches, to which they often bear a marked resemblance, managing diversity policies, are, given their status as employer-led methods of generating change, somewhat weak interventions for challenging workplace inequality.

SECTION SUMMARY AND FURTHER READING

- There has been an increase in the extent and coverage of equal opportunities policies among organizations in Britain. Such policies are characterized by a liberal approach to challenging disadvantage in employment, in which the importance of using formal procedures to ensure equality of treatment is emphasized, and have contributed to an increase in the number of women in professional and managerial jobs.

- However, since their rationale is largely one of business self-interest, employer-led initiatives are often restricted in their focus, doing little to assist women segregated in low-paid jobs for example. Nor do they challenge male-dominated organizational power structures that operate to disadvantage women.

- The managing diversity approach is concerned with how organizations can manage and take advantage of individual differences. In practice there is often some overlap with traditional equal opportunities approaches. Moreover, the model does not challenge those aspects of organizational structure and culture that continue to privilege white males.

For an overview of the issues pertaining to managing equal opportunities and diversity in organizations, see Kirton and Greene (2000: Chapters 5, 8 and 9). Jewson and Mason (1986) develop the concepts of 'liberal' and 'radical' approaches to understanding equal opportunities. In her critique of their approach, Cynthia Cockburn (1989, 1991) prefers to use the 'short' and 'long' agendas of equal opportunities. Linda Dickens outlines the weaknesses of business self-interest as a rationale for equal opportunities (see Dickens 1994, 1997). For critical insights about the managing diversity phenomenon, Liff (1997), Liff and Wacjman (1996), and Webb (1997) are especially recommended.

4.4 Public policy, equality at work, and the work–life balance

This section is concerned with examining the implications of the principal legislative interventions designed to challenge inequality and disadvantage at work, and the public policy assumptions that characterize them. Following an analysis of the way in which the legislation evolved between the 1970s and the 1990s, we consider the changes enacted by the 1997 and 2001 Labour governments. One of Labour's main themes is the desirability of reconciling work and family life, through the promotion of a better 'work–life balance'. We finish this section by critically assessing organizational policy and practice in this important area of contemporary employment relations.

4.4.1 Public policy and equality legislation in Britain

During the 1970s, legislation designed to promote equality at work helped to erode the voluntarist basis of employment relations in Britain. The 1970 Equal Pay Act, which came into effect fully in 1975, provided for equal pay between men and women when engaged in 'like work'. Also in 1975, the principle that pregnant women be entitled to a period of paid maternity absence was established. The 1975 Sex Discrimination Act made direct and indirect discrimination against women in employment unlawful. Direct discrimination refers to circumstances where a man or woman is not considered for employment, or for promotion, or a pay rise, among other things, purely because of their sex. The concept of indirect discrimination, however, concerns the situation where a condition of employment is applied 'to both sexes of a kind such that the proportion of one sex who can comply with it is considerably smaller. An example might be when a police force specifies that all candidates for the post of police officer must be two metres tall' (Cockburn 1991: 28–9).

Similarly, the 1976 Race Relations Act prohibited direct and indirect discrimination in employment on the grounds of race. Two state bodies, the Equal Opportunities Commission (EOC) and the Commission for Racial Equality (CRE), were established to promote, monitor, and provide guidance on the new anti-discrimination legislation. They emphasized the desirability of equal opportunities in employment, stipulating the importance of a liberal approach based on the need for fair procedures in personnel management, for example in recruitment and selection practices (Dickens 2000a).

Pressure from campaigning groups and trade union activists was an important impetus for the enactment of legislation in this area (Cockburn 1991). It eradicated many of the more blatant discriminatory practices that had existed hitherto (Dickens 2000a). Nevertheless, the union movement's enthusiasm for equal pay was constrained by a desire not to upset existing pay structures, most of which operated largely to the benefit of men (Dickens 1992; O'Donovan and Szyszczack 1988). Yet the equal pay legislation did cause the gender pay gap to close somewhat during the 1970s, an effect that was, however, of a rather short-term nature (Dickens 1992; O'Donovan and Szyszczack 1988).

As we saw in Chapter 3, the Conservative governments of the 1980s and 1990s favoured a deregulationary public policy approach, one based on the desirability of giving employers greater control over their own employment relations arrangements. In the area of equality, the Conservatives largely eschewed legislative interventions as a means of effecting change in favour of voluntary employer- and market-led efforts (Dickens 1997; Webb 1997). Thus they promoted 'a privatized route to equality, with an emphasis on individual organizations deciding what is in their interests' (Dickens 1999: 11). The principal exception was the 1995 Disability Discrimination Act, which obliged large employers to make 'reasonable adjustments' to facilitate the access of people with disabilities, the result of many years of campaigning by pressure groups and disabled activists (Liff 2003).

Yet the Conservative's efforts at avoiding further state intervention in the area of equality at work were stymied by the obligations of Britain's membership of the European Economic Community (EEC) (Davies and Freedland 1993; Dickens and Hall 2003). During the 1980s and 1990s, the 'need for British law to give effect to European equality law and for judges to interpret national legislation in the light of such law protected this area of legislation from the Conservative's deregulationary thrust and led to a strengthening of the national equality legislation in a number of areas' (Dickens 1997: 285). One example in particular stands out. The 1976 Equal Treatment Directive obliged the Conservatives to amend the Equal Pay Act, which they eventually did in 1983, giving women workers the right to equal pay with men where they perform work of 'equal value'. This extended the scope for women workers to make equal pay claims since the basis of comparison was no longer whether or not they could demonstrate that their jobs were the same as those of men who were being paid more, something that could be difficult to establish in the many organizations where job segregation by sex was commonplace, but was based on the comparative value of what could be different jobs. It stimulated successful claims from, for example, female supermarket checkout operators who demanded equal pay with largely male warehouse workers in the same organization, who had hitherto earned more, on the basis that the skills demanded of their respective jobs were of similar worth.

Notwithstanding such European initiatives, even in the 1990s the framework of legislation in Britain comprised a set of rather weak and ineffective instruments for promoting equality at work. Dickens (1992) suggests that there are two main problems with the sex equality legislation. First, the procedures for claiming equality are inadequate. Individual women who experience discrimination or disadvantage are encouraged to submit a complaint to an employment tribunal. Yet even in the minority of cases where a complaint is upheld, the remedy, in the form of monetary compensation is usually less than £10,000 (Willey 2003). The employer, moreover, is under no obligation to eradicate the discriminatory practice that caused the complaint (Dickens 1994, 1997).

Although the EOC and the CRE possess investigatory powers, these are rarely used and there are limitations on their ability to enforce changes (Kirton and Greene 2000). The extent to which the establishment of a Commission for Equality and Human Rights, incorporating the EOC, CRE, and other relevant bodies, will change this situation remains to be seen.

Second, the liberal, equal treatment approach that underpins the legislation leaves the structural causes of inequality and disadvantage at work largely unchallenged. It eschews any kind of positive action designed to promote greater equality. The emphasis on establishing a level playing field, upon which, in theory, men and women can compete on the same terms, fails to appreciate the extent to which the rules of the game conform with the experiences of men (Dickens 1992).

4.4.2 Public policy, equality and the 1997 and 2001 Labour governments

In turning to the public policy framework since 1997, it is important to consider the equality implications of Labour's employment relations policies in general. The introduction of the National Minimum Wage (NMW), for example, advantaged low-paid women workers in particular (see Chapter 7). The predominant theme underpinning Labour's equality policies, though, was the encouragement given to promoting 'family-friendly' employment policies and a better 'work–life balance'; on giving as many people as possible, especially women and lone parents, the opportunity to reconcile their family responsibilities with undertaking paid employment, something that is presented as being advantageous to businesses (McKay 2001). Thus the most significant piece of legislation that Labour enacted in the area of employment relations during its first term, the 1999 Employment Relations Act and its associated regulations, increased maternity leave for women, and provided new entitlements to parental leave, and time off work for family emergencies. The minimum period of maternity leave was raised from fourteen to eighteen weeks; both men and women were given the right to take up to three months' unpaid leave on the birth of a baby or the adoption of a child; and employees also became able to take unpaid time off work in order to manage family crises, such as the sickness of a child.

However, these initiatives were largely driven by the need to comply with European Union legislation, the 1996 Parental Leave Directive in particular (Dickens and Hall 2003; McColgan 2000b). As we saw in Chapter 3, on coming to power in 1997 the Labour government adopted the EU's social chapter. As a result, it was obliged to incorporate the provisions of the directive into British law. A further piece of European equality legislation, the 1997 Part-Time Workers Directive, giving part-time workers, who of course are largely women, an entitlement to terms and conditions of employment that are no less favourable than comparable full-time workers, was introduced in 2000 (McColgan 2000a).

The way in which these directives were introduced into British law was controversial, in large part because of the very narrow, or 'minimalist', approach that the government took when implementing them. Legislation introducing parental leave, for example, did not go beyond the minimum standards provided for by the directive, meaning that it would be limited to three months and, more importantly, be unpaid (McColgan 2000b). The government's approach was heavily influenced by the belief that the legislation should prompt voluntary initiatives by employers who would recognize the business benefits of providing enhanced parental leave opportunities (Hardy and Adnett 2002; Roper, Cunningham, and James 2003). McKay (2001) cites instances of agreements between employers and unions that provide for enhanced parental leave, such as the introduction of paid paternity leave for fathers in the Crown Prosecution Service. Where there is no union presence that can exert pressure on employers to enact improvements, though, the provision of enhanced parental leave and other 'family-friendly' policies may be more difficult to secure (Hyman and Summers 2004).

The main weakness of the 2000 Part-Time Workers (Prevention of Less Favourable Treatment) Regulations, which implemented the Part-Time Workers Directive in Britain, is the requirement that part-time workers who experience disadvantage in employment must identify appropriate full-time workers as comparators. The level of job segregation in Britain, though, which means that part-time workers generally do not undertake the same jobs as full-timers, makes such comparisons problematic (McKay 2001), resulting in few part-time workers being in a position to benefit from this legislation (McColgan 2000a).

Labour's reluctance to implement European legislation in a way that builds upon the minimum provisions contained in the respective directives reflects its unwillingness to antagonize powerful business interests, as articulated by the Confederation of British Industry (CBI) for example, that oppose legislative interventions which increase the level of employment regulation. While the Labour government may have adopted the EU's social chapter, its insistence that European directives are implemented in such a way as render them largely ineffective in practice, and also its refusal to introduce legislation to outlaw age discrimination, despite promising to do so when in opposition, invites comparisons with the approach taken by its Conservative predecessors (McColgan 2000b).

After 2000, though, and especially after it was elected to a second term of office in June 2001, Labour advanced the equality agenda in two important respects. First, there was a notable widening of the scope of the anti-discrimination legislation. Some of these changes resulted from domestic policy developments. For example, one response to the report of the Macpherson inquiry into the murder of the black teenager Stephen Lawrence was a new Race Relations Act, in 2000, that among other things obliges public sector employers to actively promote race equality (Fredman 2001). In 2004, moreover, disability discrimination was extended to cover all employers, following on from the establishment of a Disability Rights Commission (DRC), established along the same lines as the EOC and CRE. Mostly, however, the impetus for reform has again been generated by EU legislation, in particular a 2000 framework equality directive that extends the grounds on which discrimination is prohibited to sexual orientation and religious belief, in 2003 (Vickers 2003), and age, in 2006. See Box 4.2 for EU action concerning the 'mainstreaming' of equality action.

Second, there has been a grudging shift towards improved statutory provision in respect of family-friendly policies. The 2002 Employment Act included a number of relevant provisions that came into effect in April 2003. Among other things, it extended maternity leave provision to a minimum of twenty-six weeks, increased statutory maternity pay by a third, introduced two weeks paid paternity leave, and provided for paid leave on the adoption of a child. It also established the right of parents of young, or disabled, children to have a request for flexible working arrangements, such as moving from full-time to part-time employment, to be taken seriously by their employer.

BOX 4.2 MAINSTREAMING EQUALITY IN THE EUROPEAN UNION

Equality action by the European Union (EU) is not confined just to legislative measures; it has also sought to promote greater equality in employment through 'mainstreaming' initiatives. What does the concept of equality mainstreaming mean? It 'can be summarized as the integration of equality considerations into all aspects of policy formulation, implementation and evaluation' (Bell 2004: 252). Mainstreaming implies the need for positive action to improve the employment position and prospects of people from disadvantaged social groups; that changes to institutions and practices are necessary in order to secure equality, even if this has been difficult to achieve in practice (T. Rees 1998). Since the 1980s, the European Commission has fostered the development of a number of action programmes designed to improve the labour market position of women and, in 1996, it mandated that a gender perspective should inform all EU decision-making. Although initially restricted to addressing gender-based inequality, mainstreaming has now been expanded to cover other forms of employment disadvantage, including race and disability (Bell 2004).

What explains the growing concern on the part of the government with developing a more family-friendly working environment in Britain? In one respect, it can be seen as an outcome of the increasing 'awareness of the difficulties in reconciling paid work and discharging family commitments [that] have helped to lead to a changing policy climate in the UK, where concerns about the effects of long working hours on parental responsibilities and relationships with children are being expressed' (Hyman et al. 2003: 220). But government policy is also driven by another imperative, one that is based on encouraging workers with family responsibilities, especially women and lone parents, to take up paid employment (Taylor no date).

The new right of parents to request flexible working arrangements has attracted a large amount of attention. It was first mentioned in a 2000 government consultation paper, *Work and Parents: Competitiveness and Choice* (DTI 2000), before, in 2001, an employer-led 'Work and Parents Taskforce' was charged with developing an approach that would be acceptable to businesses. The legislation obliges employers to consider an employee's request for flexible working seriously. They are entitled to refuse on business grounds, if it would result in a substantial increase in costs, for example. Reports suggest that the right has been rather effective in provoking positive and constructive responses from employers when requests have been made. Nevertheless, a quarter of workers have their requests refused outright, even when all it involves is minor adjustments to starting and finishing times. Of the two-thirds of workers who do have their request granted, or who reach a compromise with their employer, over a quarter experience a reduction in their salary or job status as a result (Maternity Alliance 2004). One commentator accuses the government of enacting 'sound bite' employment legislation in this area. The introduction of the right to request flexible working arrangements has attracted a lot of favourable comment, but it is unlikely to lead to significant changes in organizational practice (Anderson 2003).

The relevant provisions of the 2002 Employment Act improve on the minimum requirements of the Parental Leave Directive. Moreover, in February 2005, the government proposed increasing the amount of paid maternity leave and extending the right to request flexible work arrangements to adult carers and parents of older children, should Labour be elected to a third term in office. Yet government policy was characterized by a determination not to antagonize employers who, by virtue of vigorous lobbying efforts, have successfully prevented some proposed policy initiatives from becoming legislation. For example, although membership of the EU obliged Britain to implement the 1999 Fixed-Term Work Directive, which, following its introduction in 2002, gives employees working on fixed-term contracts the right to no less favourable employment terms and conditions than comparable, permanent staff, the government has vigorously opposed EU attempts to extend its coverage to staff supplied by agencies.

On the whole, the Labour government favoured employer-led efforts when it comes to promoting equality at work, with legislative action treated as an undesirable last resort when voluntary efforts fail (Roper, Cunningham, and James 2003). Little was done, then, to oblige employers to eradicate discriminatory practices at work. The system remains geared towards the readiness of individual workers who experience disadvantage to submit complaints to employment tribunals, with little hope of adequate redress even if they win their case (Dickens and Hall 2003). The idea is that equality action is best fostered by a relatively light touch legislative regime within which employers are encouraged, because it is in their own interests, to take voluntary initiatives to promote equality. We have already outlined the weaknesses of business arguments for equality at work. To what extent, though, has the government's message that, by instituting family-friendly policies, or by promoting a work–life balance, employers can realize important business benefits informed organizational practice?

4.4.3 Managing the work–life balance: a critical assessment

We have already used the terms 'family-friendly' and 'work–life balance' extensively without adequately assessing what they mean, and how they might differ. The 'family-friendly' label has been used to describe a wide variety of different practices that may assist parents and carers reconcile their work with their domestic responsibilities, including, among other things, maternity and paternity leave, childcare facilities, job-sharing arrangements, and other forms of flexible working. Yet it is an 'elastic' term, something that can be used to refer to 'systems that are supportive of families; policies that actively promote and benefit workers with families; or a package of "perks" which are simply an "add-on" to other employment extras' (McKee, Mauthner, and Maclean 2000: 558).

The term 'work–life balance' has increasingly been favoured over 'family-friendly', including by the British government, not least because it implies a focus on workers in general, not just those with hefty family responsibilities. In so far as it assumes that workers should enjoy greater control over when, where, and how they undertake their jobs (Felstead et al. 2002), the work–life balance approach has some potentially far-reaching implications. The main problem with the concept, though, is the assumption that a distinction can easily be made between people's 'work' and 'lives' (Scholarios and Marks 2004). In reality, of course, they overlap and interact with each other in subtle, complex, and dynamic ways. As we will see below, moreover, it seems that people's duties at work increasingly affect, and constrain, the way in which they undertake the rest of their lives.

The British government has, as we have seen, emphasized the business benefits of family-friendly and work–life balance policies in order to stimulate voluntary initiatives by employers. It is claimed that their presence can raise staff morale, reduce absenteeism, aid the retention of skilled employees, and make recruitment easier (HM Treasury and DTI 2003: 20). The government's own work–life balance website features case studies of organizations that have benefited from introducing change. BT, for example, claims that the introduction of flexible working hours has enabled it to improve staff retention (DTI no date). The Work Foundation runs the Employers for Work–life Balance Forum, which displays details of successful initiatives. At Lloyds TSB, for example, all employees can apply to change their working hours to fit in with their domestic responsibilities (Work Foundation no date).

There is some research evidence that employers accept the business rationale for family-friendly and work–life balance policies. A study of the Scottish oil and gas industry, for example, demonstrates that innovation is particularly evident in large multinational companies. These had developed job-sharing and flexible working arrangements, among other things, which helped them compete for, and retain, skilled staff (McKee, Mauthner, and Maclean 2000). In the hospitality industry, recruitment and retention difficulties encouraged some major employers to invest in flexible working arrangements in order to hold on to women staff with young children (Doherty 2004). Yet most employers remain to be convinced of the business case for family-friendly and work–life balance policies, given the additional business costs that they impose (Roper, Cunningham, and James 2003). Small and medium-sized companies, for example, are particularly circumspect when it comes to developing formal procedures, tend to judge individual cases on their merits, and prefer less formal means of enabling valued staff to benefit from flexible working arrangements (Dex and Scheibl 2001).

For a number of reasons, it is doubtful that voluntary action by employers alone will lead to the widespread adoption of robust family-friendly and work–life balance policies in a way that promotes gender equality at work. For one thing, despite all the rhetoric about supposed business benefits, survey evidence demonstrates that 'whilst demand for better balance by employees has grown, employers have yet to treat work–life balance as a priority' (Hyman and Summers 2004: 421). Those employers that have initiated changes, moreover, tend to restrict them to arrangements that enable workers to vary the times at which they start and finish work (Hyman and Summers 2004; Hyman et al. 2003). Work–life balance policies are often presented by employers, and perceived by employees, as perks, additional benefits that may be, and indeed are, withdrawn, or at least not accorded as much importance, in periods of economic difficulty (Doherty 2004; Hyman and Summers 2004; Lewis 1997). If seen as perks, moreover, policies directed at workers with family responsibilities can be a cause of disaffection among staff who do not enjoy access to them (Nolan 2002).

Even when work–life balance policies exist in an organization, it cannot be assumed that they will promote equality between men and women at work. Indeed, they may reinforce disadvantage. Women who undertake flexible working, especially part-time employment, may be perceived by male managers as lacking the requisite commitment to the job and the organization necessary for promotion. This was particularly evident in the firm of chartered accountants studied by Lewis (1997). She found that organizational commitment was largely equated with time spent at work. Female employees who were unable to match the number of hours at work put in by their male counterparts, or were on reduced hours, were seen as less promotable. Speaking of a female employee, one male senior manager commented that: 'She's a good manager, but she won't be promoted. She doesn't have the commitment . . . doesn't put in the time' (quoted in Lewis 1997: 16).

Unsurprisingly, then, there appears to be a 'take-up gap' in respect of work–life balance practices (Kodz, Harper, and Dench 2002). Even in organizations where they exist, employees, both male and female, sometimes shun them, and are reluctant to damage their careers by appearing less committed. A further obstacle to the take-up of such practices is that they often come under the control of line managers who may be reluctant to allow employees to make use of them (Hyman and Summers 2004), in spite of what the organizational policy might say.

Perhaps the most significant constraint on the effectiveness of work–life balance policies, though, concerns the way in which the increasing demands of work disrupt people's family lives. Excessive working hours (see Chapter 7), and greater work intensity (see Chapter 8), mean that jobs increasingly intrude upon, and upset, family life in what has come to be known as the 'negative spillover' effect (see Hyman and Summers 2004; Hyman et al. 2003; Kodz, Harper, and Dench 2002; Nolan 2002; White et al. 2003). Consequently, the 'gap between enlightened rhetoric about the need for a readjustment in the work–life "balance" and the reality in most workplaces remains disturbingly wide' (Taylor no date: 15).

SECTION SUMMARY AND FURTHER READING

- Legislation governing equality in work and employment developed during the 1970s in particular. Nevertheless, the legislation was a rather ineffective means of promoting equality at work; it rarely obliged employers to effect positive change. During the 1980s and 1990s, the Conservative governments were obliged to enact further measures as a result of the need to implement European directives and to respond to campaigns by activists.

- After being returned to office in 1997, Labour promoted the family-friendly polices and the need for greater work–life balance in employment. It provided for improved maternity rights, introduced the concept of parental leave, implemented paid paternity leave for fathers, and gave working parents the right to request flexible working arrangements. Much of the new legislation was introduced in order to comply with relevant European directives, and was often implemented in a rather narrow, or minimalist, way. While Labour then took steps to improve the statutory provision, it did so in a very tentative manner, with an emphasis on using legislation to goad employers into voluntary action.

- The Labour government emphasized the business benefits to employers of introducing family-friendly polices and working arrangements that help to promote a better work–life balance. Although there is some evidence that business self-interest is an effective source of reform in some cases, overall the take-up of family-friendly and work–life balance practices are low. Studies point to the numerous obstacles that inhibit the provision and use of such arrangements.

For further information about the legislative framework governing equality in Britain, see Kirton and Greene (2000), Dickens (2000a), and Willey (2003: Chapters 4, 5, 6 and 13). The public policy assumptions that inform the legislative framework, and the nature and content of the legislation itself, are critically assessed by Dickens (1992), Dickens and Hall (2003), and McKay (2001). Hyman and Summers (2004) offer the best critical analysis of employers' work–life balance policies; for an insightful case study see Lewis (1997).

4.5 Trade unions, collective bargaining, and the pursuit of workplace equality

As previous sections make clear, both voluntary interventions by employers and legislative measures enacted by governments are of limited effectiveness in challenging discrimination and disadvantage in employment. What difference, then, can trade union representation and collective bargaining make? In this section, we examine the extent to which equality considerations inform the contemporary bargaining agenda, and how far unions have progressed in recognizing and representing the interests of workers from disadvantaged social groups. The emphasis is largely on gender equality, which is where most union activity has been concentrated. Such efforts present major challenges for the unions, which have traditionally been reluctant to accept that 'industries, organizations and occupations are comprised of diverse groups of employees, whose interests may at times converge, but at others diverge' (Kirton and Greene 2000: 160). Should unions focus their efforts on representing their women members as workers, with their gender considered irrelevant, as women workers, who might have particular employment relations interests separate from those of men, or as women, addressing the multitude of concerns that affect their lives? To begin with, though, we consider the regressive role of trade unions in the area of equality and the factors that have compelled them to change.

4.5.1 Trade unions and the equality agenda

There is a long history of women's activity in trade unions. Between 1906 and 1926, for example, the National Federation of Women Workers 'organized more women, fought more strikes and did more to establish women trade unionists than any organization' (Boston 1980: 60). It challenged the low pay and poor working conditions that characterized female employment in parts of the clothing industry for example. In general, though, the activities of the largely male-dominated trade unions supported and reinforced gender inequality and disadvantage at work. For one thing, during the nineteenth and early twentieth centuries unions often colluded with employers to exclude women from skilled, and therefore more highly paid jobs, helping to reinforce patterns of occupational segregation and a sexual division of labour that privileged the work of men over that of women (Bradley 1989). Union collective bargaining priorities, moreover, reflected dominant male assumptions concerning the inferior value of women's labour. Since men were presented as the principal family wage earners, or 'breadwinners', women's earnings were thereby considered less important, and thus only a 'secondary wage' or 'pin money'.

The extent of these assumptions was evident in a series of seven workplace studies undertaken in 1980. Union representatives commonly believed 'that most women who went out to work were earning a secondary wage and that therefore the fact that they were paid less than their male fellow workers was not a problem' (Charles 1986: 164). It is important to recognize, therefore, that historically the trade unions were largely uninterested in promoting gender equality at work. Indeed, their activities may 'prop up those very mechanisms in the organization of work which makes patterns of gender segregation so difficult to break down' (Rees 1992: 85).

One of the main reasons for the traditional conservatism of the unions in this area is that they are organizations whose decision-making structures were, and often still are, dominated by men (Cockburn 1991). What explains the under-representation of women within trade unions? The principal reason is that union organization and activity reflected the traditional dominance of men in paid work, in a way that led to the exclusion of women (Cunnison and Stageman 1993). Thus unions tended to operate in ways that privileged the interests of men, and developed an overly masculine culture within which women, and their interests, were marginalized.

The way in which trade unionism functions makes it difficult for women to pursue union careers or to become active in decision-making structures. The rarity of childcare arrangements, for example, means that women's domestic responsibilities often preclude them from attending union meetings (Ledwith et al. 1990). Moreover, due to members' demands, union officials often have excessive workloads. The ways in which their jobs are structured, though, makes them difficult to combine with family responsibilities (Kirton 1999; Watson 1988). Thus there are a series of obstacles pertaining to the masculine norms and assumptions that govern how unions operate which inhibit the participation and representation of women in trade unions (Cockburn 1987, 1991; Rees 1990). Unsurprisingly, therefore, on the rare occasions when they did make an effort in this area, unions traditionally found it difficult to integrate and represent the interests of their female members effectively (Kirton 1999).

Whatever they might have said in their formal policy statements, until the 1970s the trade unions generally had an abject record on the issue of race. According to one commentator, 'history shows the record of the trade union movement to be characterized at worst by appalling racism and often by an indefensible neglect of the issues of race and equal opportunity' (Wrench 1986: 3). During the 1940s and 1950s, the increasing proportion of black migrant workers in the workforce, originating from places such as the Caribbean for example, met with a hostile reception from many unions who worried that immigrants would be used by employers as a cheap source of labour, and as replacements for striking workers (Wrench 1987). In many workplaces, white trade unionists often supported, or at least did not challenge, practices that excluded and disadvantaged black workers. Despite its formal denunciations of discrimination, until the 1970s the Trades Union Congress (TUC) opposed efforts to combat race-based disadvantage since these would 'discriminate against the white membership' (Wrench and Virdee 1996: 245).

However, trade union attitudes towards, and responses to, race-based disadvantage were rather complex (Lunn 1999). The unions came under increasing pressure from their own activists to improve their policies and practices, though discrimination against black workers was not entirely eradicated from the union movement (Phizacklea and Miles

1980; Wrench 1987). They continued to be under-represented in trade union decision-making structures, despite being more likely than white workers to be union members (Wrench 1987). Moreover, trade unions have experienced problems in trying to recruit and organize ethnic minority workers, largely because of the difficulties they have striking and sustaining relationships with community groups and activists (Wrench and Virdee 1996).

Historically, therefore, trade union practices and collective bargaining activity have often operated to the detriment of women and black workers. Since the 1980s, though, the unions have, albeit rather slowly and unevenly, sought to represent the interests of an increasingly diverse workforce more effectively, those of women in particular. They have done so for three related reasons. First, economic change has eroded the traditional heartlands of trade unionism in male-dominated manufacturing industry. Employment growth has been concentrated largely in the service sector, which is characterized by high levels of female employment. The unions have been compelled, therefore, to respond by re-orienting themselves as more female-friendly organizations (Liff 2003).

Second, with the decline of male-dominated manual industries, trade unionism, then, is increasingly concentrated in areas, such as public sector occupations like schoolteaching, that are disproportionately populated by female employees (Colling and Dickens 2001). Traditionally much lower, the proportion of women workers who are union members is now just about the same as it is for men. Between 1991 and 2001, the proportion of men who are union members fell from 41 to 29 per cent of the workforce; for women the fall was less marked, from 32 per cent to 28 per cent. The figure would be higher for women if they were not over-represented in part-time employment where union membership tends to be lower (Bewley and Fernie 2003).

Third, influenced by feminism, women themselves have challenged the male-dominated structures and decision-making processes of trade unions (Colgan and Ledwith 2002; Cunnison and Stageman 1993). 'If women's interests are better represented by trade unions today it has not been because of any natural trend but because of a concerted struggle by women themselves to defeat male self-interest' (Cockburn 1991: 111). In the sections that follow, then, we examine the effectiveness of union efforts to represent the interests of a diverse membership, beginning with the topic of equality bargaining.

4.5.2 Equality bargaining

Perhaps 'the most important indication of changed union behaviour . . . [is] an increased willingness to incorporate equality demands within collective bargaining' (Colling and Dickens 2001: 142). In a broad sense, we take equality bargaining to refer to initiatives undertaken by trade unions that are designed to reduce the employment disadvantage of particular groups, women workers in particular, by means of interventions directed at employers. An equality 'agenda' can be distinguished from an equality 'dimension'. The former refers to where unions develop a separate set of bargaining demands that are specifically designed to favour women workers, for example improved childcare arrangements. The concept of the equality dimension, however, seeks to ensure that the equality implications of all bargaining topics, including pay for example, are recognized (Dickens 2000b).

We have already seen that in the past union bargaining priorities and activities discriminated against women at work by systematically undervaluing the contribution of their labour. Unions, moreover, often support pay structures, those that accord high value to length of service for example, that disadvantage women. However, while collective bargaining has done much to sustain workplace inequality, it also has the potential to erode it (Cockburn 1991). Women who are in workplaces that are covered by collective agreements enjoy better pay and employment conditions, greater job security, and improved access to family-friendly working arrangements than those who are not (Bewley and Fernie 2003; Colling and Dickens 1998).

In recent years, the concept of equality bargaining has attained greater significance as trade unions have sought to represent the interests of their women members more effectively (Colling and Dickens 1989). Unions may be more capable of securing equality action on the basis of social justice, rather than for narrow, insecure, and partial business reasons (Colling and Dickens 1998). Through trade union action, collective bargaining may give women workers greater influence over their pay and employment conditions. It 'provides a way of giving women a voice; an ability to define their needs and concerns and to set their own priorities for action' (Dickens 2000b: 197). Male and female workers enjoy many shared interests, such as a concern with securing pay rises for example. Women, however, express a particular concern that issues such as job sharing be given greater priority on union bargaining agendas (Bradley 1999; Kirton 1999).

In recent years, many unions have been active in promoting and articulating equality issues as priorities for collective bargaining, including demands for pay equality between men and women, and greater access to family-friendly working arrangements (Bewley and Fernie 2003; Cunnison and Stageman 1993). Perhaps the most effective union action has been in the area of equal pay. Groups of largely female workers, such as speech therapists for example, have benefited from pay rises generated by successful union equal value campaigns (Bradley 1999). Trade unions, then, have sometimes been able to use legislative measures, and the threat of potential discrimination claims on a mass scale, to secure employer action (Colling and Dickens 1998).

Yet unions have emphasized the pursuit of women's equality far more so than that of other groups, such as black workers for example (Kirton and Greene 2000). Moreover, there is evidence that union representatives, particularly at the local level, do not recognize that issues that are of specific concern to women workers, such as childcare arrangements, are appropriate topics for collective bargaining. The bargaining agenda often fails to incorporate an equality dimension. As a result, such a 'restricted agenda serves to promote lack of interest in unions, since they appear irrelevant to the experiences of workers and of the workplace' (Munro 1999: 196).

The presence of female union representatives, though, may ensure that women's issues are incorporated within a union's bargaining agenda. Female officials 'are more likely to make a priority of issues such as equal pay, childcare, maternity leave and sexual harassment in collective bargaining' (Heery and Kelly 1988: 502; see also Dickens 2000b). However, the greater incidence of female representatives in decision-making bodies in the public services union, Unison, does not appear to have markedly increased the extent to which issues relevant to women are promoted. Experienced men continued to dominate meetings, leading to equality issues often being marginalized (McBride 2001). This suggests that we need to assess how far unions have altered their representative structures, and the way in which their decision-making processes operate, to accommodate the interests of a diverse membership.

4.5.3 **Representing diversity in trade unions**

In assessing the extent and nature of changes to the unions' internal representative arrangements and structures, it is useful to employ, in modified form, the distinction between liberal and radical approaches discussed earlier in this chapter. The liberal approach is concerned with reducing the barriers to women's, and members of other disadvantaged group's, participation in trade unions; by removing discriminatory practices it seeks to establish a 'level playing field' (Kirton and Greene 2002). Measures, including the appointment of equality or women's officers and ensuring that union meetings are made more accessible, by offering childcare facilities for example, have been taken in order to help promote equality of access (Colgan and Ledwith 2002). See Box 4.3 for details of how the unions have sought to represent the interests of their lesbian and gay members.

The liberal approach characterizes the approach of most trade unions to the way in which they promote internal equality. Its main weakness, however, is its failure to challenge male-dominated union power structures that often operate in ways that disadvantage women. There are two problems in particular. First, female union representatives can find it difficult to operate effectively in roles that are characterized by norms and assumptions derived from men's experiences. The excessive number of hours required by union work militates against the involvement of women who have childcare responsibilities for example (Kirton 1999).

Second, there is plenty of evidence that the male-dominated nature of trade unionism contributes to an environment in which women often face hostility, and sometimes outright sexism, when attempting to undertake their responsibilities (Cockburn 1991). A study of the experiences of senior female representatives within the Manufacturing

---

BOX 4.3 REPRESENTING THE INTERESTS OF LESBIAN AND GAY MEMBERS IN BRITISH
TRADE UNIONS

Samantha Bairstow studied the way in which trade unions in Britain represent the interests of their lesbian and gay members (Bairstow 2004). She found evidence of the existence of a dual approach in union practice. Some unions were characterized by bottom-up, activist-led efforts to secure change. This made for a more participatory, informal, and inclusive approach to the advancement of lesbian and gay interests. In others, though, the development of internal structures for lesbian and gay representation was a more top-down, leadership-driven affair. In these cases, links between lesbian and gay representative structures and mainstream union decision-making bodies seem to be more effectively realized. The problem here, however, lies in ensuring that centralized and bureaucratic union initiatives are sensitive to the particular needs of gay and lesbian members. Unions are also using their educational facilities and programmes to build awareness of the issues facing lesbian and gay members, and to secure effective representation of their interests. There is little evidence of concerted resistance to these developments on the part of more conservative union members and officials. Most members, for instance, do not appear to be interested. Nevertheless, Bairstow (2004) does suggest that unions are sometimes uncomfortable with, or uncertain about, dealing with issues relating to sexual orientation.

Science and Finance Union, now part of Amicus, revealed that sexist attitudes and behaviour were commonplace. One female representative claimed that:

It's still a male culture, right from the top. There are too few women in positions of real power in unions. I think that most trade union meetings, if a new woman went along to one, she'd turn round and walk straight back out again – it's like a boys' club. (quoted in Kirton 1999: 216)

Given the persistence of male-dominated decision-making processes and cultures, in recent years there has been a growing recognition that liberal measures are an ineffective means of securing the effective participation of under-represented groups, such as black and women members, in trade unions, and that more radical interventions may be necessary (Healy and Kirton 2000). The radical approach implies that positive action is required in order to enable union members from disadvantaged social groups to participate in trade unions and thus have their interests represented more effectively (Kirton and Greene 2002). It encourages the need for direct intervention 'in organizational practices to achieve fair representation and a fair distribution of rewards' across disadvantaged groups (Colgan and Ledwith 2002: 171).

The most significant measures that come under the 'radical' label are, first, the provision of special seats, or 'reserved seats', for representatives from particular social groups, mainly women workers, on union decision-making bodies and, second, the establishment of internal structures that enable members from disadvantaged groups to organize and represent themselves through what is known as 'self-organization' (Virdee and Grint 1994). Both of these interventions challenge established assumptions about the nature of union democracy (see Chapter 3). Reserving seats for, say, women members goes against the tradition, central to the notion of representative democracy, that union representatives should be elected on behalf of the membership as a whole, and not owe their places to the electoral support of particular groups. Allowing some groups of workers to self-organize, on the basis of their social characteristics rather than their collective identity as workers, runs counter to traditions of participatory democracy in unions (McBride 2000; Terry 1996).

The presence of reserved seats on union decision-making bodies has become more common in trade unions, though they are still limited to a minority (Kirton and Greene 2000). The public services union, Unison, which has a very high female membership, is the most prominent example. Its emphasis on 'proportionality' in decision-making structures is designed to ensure that women are elected to representative positions in proportion to the number of female members. The principle of 'fair representation' in Unison takes proportionality a stage further, with the aim being to secure an appropriate number of elected representatives who are employed in low-paid jobs. One assessment indicates that proportionality 'has enabled women's systematic inclusion within' Unison and led to 'dramatic increases in women's access to the decision-making area' (McBride 2001: 69).

Nevertheless, the provision of reserved places in union policy-making bodies is not without its problems. Trade unionists, including some women, dislike its potential divisiveness (Bradley 1999: 186). This raises the question of how far women, and other socially disadvantaged groups, have specific interests that can only be articulated by representatives of their own kind. A further problem with reserved places is that those women who take them up are often made to feel inferior; they can be treated as second-class union representatives whose contributions should be limited to issues that specifically concern women members and thus can be easily marginalized (Colgan and

Ledwith 2002; Kirton and Healy 1999). Conversely, women who have been elected to general, non-reserved seats often feel an obligation to speak on behalf of their entire constituency, male and female, leading them to play down the significance of issues that are specific to women (Healy and Kirton 2000; McBride 2000). Perhaps the most fundamental criticism of reserved seats, though, is that although their presence advances the representation of individual women within trade unions, they are less effective in promoting the interests of women as a disadvantaged social group. In other words, tinkering with policy-making structures in a way that enables more women to participate as individuals does little to challenge the embedded, and collectively generated, male-dominated norms and assumptions that determine union action (McBride 2000, 2001).

Few unions have innovated with self-organization as a means of enabling disadvantaged social groups to participate and thus secure effective representation of their interests. Unison has the most sophisticated set of practices in respect of self-organization. Black, disabled, lesbian and gay, and women members all have the opportunity to self-organize (McBride 2000; Terry 1996). What, then, is meant by 'self-organization' in trade unions? It refers to arrangements that provide a separate space for collective organization and action by union members and activists, on the basis of their shared social characteristics. In order to secure more effective representation, it offers a means by which members from disadvantaged social groups can work together, separate from established union decision-making structures, to pursue their collective interests. Whereas reserved seats focus on improving representative democracy in unions, self-organization is designed to enhance the participation of members from disadvantaged groups. It enables them to work together, constructing 'a sense of identity, political consciousness, confidence and solidarity and to develop and practice activist skills' (Colgan and Ledwith 2002: 178). Self-organization, therefore, explicitly challenges the notion that workers are a homogeneous group with a single set of common interests that can be articulated and represented by a trade union unproblematically. It recognizes that workers, by virtue of belonging to particular social groups, may have diverse interests, and that traditional approaches to participatory democracy in trade unions, which assumed a commonality of interest, are therefore inappropriate.

Studies of self-organization in practice show that, while it is still rare in British trade unions, it nonetheless gives members and activists a forum that they can use to develop participation, and to bring issues that specifically concern them on to the union agenda (Colgan and Ledwith 2000; Parker 2002). Black members' networks, for example, are not only an effective way of stimulating involvement and participation, but also serve to encourage greater discussion of race equality issues within a trade union context (Bradley, Healy, and Mukherjee 2002). Self-organization arrangements may also serve to generate union activism, giving members a sense that they are able to effect changes that benefit their working lives. In her study of gay and lesbian self-organization in Unison, Colgan (1999) demonstrates how self-organization challenges discriminatory attitudes and practices within trade unions, producing a more inclusive union agenda.

The positive effects of self-organization may, however, be limited in practice. For one thing, it relies upon the willingness of members to participate in union affairs, something that cannot be assumed. Moreover, apart from in Unison, separate organizing is generally limited to women (Kirton and Greene 2002). Where the links with established policy-making bodies are tenuous, self-organization can lead to the interests of disadvantaged social groups being marginalized. Autonomy, then, may foster exclusion (Colgan and Ledwith 2002), particularly if powerful union interests feel challenged. In Unison, for example, those policy issues discussed in the women's self-organized groups rarely made it on to the agenda of the powerful mainstream decision-making bodies (McBride 2000, 2001). Thus 'the predominant model of self-organization within Unison is of a pressure group whose comments are welcome but not necessarily taken into consideration' (McBride 2001: 172). While there is some evidence that the relationship between the self-organized groups and established decision-making may improve over time (Colgan 1999), self-organization may reinforce, rather than ameliorate, the under-representation of disadvantaged groups within trade unions.

SECTION SUMMARY AND FURTHER READING

- Historically, trade unions have often supported employment arrangements and bargaining priorities that sustain and reinforce discriminatory employment practices to the disadvantage of women and black workers. Although the decline of the trade unions, their white, male-dominated heartlands in particular, has prompted a change of attitudes since the 1970s, much of the pressure for reform has come from union members and activists themselves.

- Collective bargaining has increasingly been used by the trade unions as a vehicle for advancing equality at work. How far the rise of equality bargaining has transformed union approaches is, however, questionable, since there is evidence of a more restricted trade union agenda sometimes existing in practice.

- Trade unions have undertaken efforts to improve the representation of members from disadvantaged social groups within their internal structures. Their initiatives have, however, been of a largely liberal kind, concerned with establishing equal treatment. More radical approaches, such as the provision of reserved seats and, more rarely, arrangements for self-organization, may be more successful in advancing equality within trade unions, though there are obstacles to their likely effectiveness.

For an overview of trade unions and equality at work, see Kirton and Greene (2000: Chapter 7). Cunnison and Stageman (1993) use a series of case studies to examine how unions have changed their policies and practices in order to respond to the demands of women members and activists. The most recent study of equality bargaining issues is Colling and Dickens (2001). For details of practices in Unison, see Terry (1996), and McBride (2000). See Colgan and Ledwith (2002) for debates on reserved seats and self-organization in general.

■ **CONCLUSION**

In this chapter, we have demonstrated that inequality and disadvantage, based on social divisions, are important features of contemporary employment relations. Like Chapters 2 and 3, the material discussed in this chapter shows the influence of environmental factors on employment relations. Thus relationships between employers and employees at work cannot simply be understood in the context of the workplace, but are informed by wider economic, political, and social influences that transcend particular employment situations. For example, although the practice of trade unionism is clearly founded upon collective values and the need for unity to combat hostile employers, it has also often been concerned with excluding groups of workers, such as women for example, in order to advantage a privileged male minority. Nevertheless, unions have come under pressure to operate more inclusively, not least because their traditional constituencies, male-dominated industries based on manual labour, have dwindled in significance. Thus unions have taken up the interests of women workers and other socially disadvantaged groups more readily, and have altered their structures to enable them to be more effectively represented.

Union activity in these areas, while not without its difficulties, is an important catalyst for greater equality in contemporary employment relations. Employer-led efforts, based on a rather narrow and insecure conception of the business advantages of equality action, can be of limited effectiveness. Equal opportunities policies, which emphasize the need to treat everybody the same regardless of their social characteristics, are strong on rhetoric, but often short on action. The managing diversity model, despite its ostensibly more transformative approach, does little to challenge socially generated disadvantage and inequality at work, and is often, in practice, little different from the more conventional equal opportunities agenda. A trade union presence, though, can exert pressure on employers to deliver a more effective set of equality policies, such as better family-friendly policies for example.

Equality action at organizational level occurs within, and is informed by, a legislative framework. While Britain has had anti-discrimination and equality laws since the 1970s, in general they lack effectiveness; the liberal, equal treatment values that underpin the legislation preclude positive action, and employers are rarely obliged to undertake initiatives that promote equality, even if they are found to be operating discriminatory practices. After 1997, Labour governments encouraged organizations to adopt family-friendly policies and work–life balance arrangements for their staff, although they were extremely reluctant to compel businesses to improve their practices. Robust equality action by employers is therefore dependent upon both a stronger legislative framework and the presence of a trade union that has made a commitment to effecting positive change in this area.

■ ASSIGNMENT AND DISCUSSION QUESTIONS

1. What is meant by the concept of the 'status divide' at work?

2. Prepare arguments in support of, or in opposition to, the view that 'women are paid less than men because their domestic and family responsibilities mean that employers receive a lower level of organizational commitment from them relative to men'.

3. Should employers have any concern with equal opportunities at work? Why?

4. Why might employers be more sympathetic to 'diversity management' than to the liberal equal opportunities approach?

5. Discuss the view that public policy in the area of equal opportunities is more concerned with governments 'being seen to be doing something' than with tackling fundamental inequality at work.

6. Why have trade unions been slow to respond to the particular problems of disadvantaged groups at work?

■ WEBSITE MATERIALS

Visit the companion web site to this book for interesting and updated material at
www.oup.com/booksites/busecon/business

■ **CHAPTER CASE STUDY**

Employer attitudes to employees' work–life balance

A growing body of legislation aims to allow employees to balance the demands of their paid work with that of their home and family responsibilities. However, the extent to which any additional provisions are available to workers depends upon the views that employers hold on the issue: are they seen as a burden, or things that can provide specific benefits to business through employees having greater job satisfaction?

One survey sought to identify how UK employers viewed this matter. The authors identified three phases in the approach taken by employers. Phase one is where organizations have given little or no thought to the matter, beyond normally adhering to legal requirements. In phase two, employers develop formal policies and practices to ensure that workers are more able to balance work–life demands. Organizations may obtain some business benefits as a result. Firms that have reached phase three strategically undertake a major change in their culture and employment arrangements. In such organizations, an employee's 'work' and 'life' are not seen as matters to be 'traded' against each other. Rather, full organizational and management support for a genuine work–life balance for employees is seen to add value to the business through the identification of work inefficiencies, and new and better forms of work organization.

The survey reported findings from 138 organizations, and the researchers estimate that the results covered over 650,000 workers. The findings suggest that there is little evidence of organizations moving towards a phase three approach. Over one-third of respondents were located in phase one: limited attention had been given to the issue beyond meeting provisions of the legislation. Almost half of the organizations saw work–life balance as a social issue and that any business benefits were a 'bonus'. Only around one-fifth of, typically large, employers saw the matter as a genuine business issue and could be classed as phase three organizations. Even among these, though, there was evidence that while employers believed benefits flowed to the firm, they were not able to identify any specific advantages.

In terms of the policies and practices that organizations had developed in this area, the majority focused on 'family-friendly' matters such as maternity leave and pay. The companies that had provisions beyond those required by law typically provided additional pay rather than longer leave, which would be important in balancing parental and work responsibilities. Only around 10 per cent of firms provided workplace nurseries or similar assistance with childcare. Beyond family-related practices, over half offered an employee assistance programme or similar service concerned with confidential counselling for employees.

In many cases, these benefits were not a right for workers but subject to a manager's discretion, and there is evidence that managers were not readily willing to use such discretion in favour of the employee. In reviewing their evidence, the researchers conclude that 'achieving a work–life balance for the majority of employees in the UK is only likely if more comprehensive legislation is introduced' and that 'advocates of the business case (for work–life balance) have some way to go in convincing managers of the merits of their argument' (Adam-Smith and Copestake 2001: 8).

Source: Adam-Smith and Copestake (2001)

Case discussion questions

1. Why do managers appear reluctant to introduce comprehensive policies and practices to support the work–life balance of their employees?

2. What are the possible consequences for workers who are unable to effectively balance the demands of their work and non-work responsibilities and interests?

PART 3

Key Issues in Contemporary Employment Relations

5 Managing employment relations   147

6 Representation at work   177

7 Contemporary developments in pay and working time   207

8 Experiencing employment relations   237

9 Conflict and employment relations   267

CHAPTER 5

Managing employment relations

CHAPTER OBJECTIVES

The main objectives of this chapter are to:

- examine how management has utilized the more favourable economic and social climate to challenge the role and influence of trade unions

- consider the implications for employment relations of the statutory procedure for union recognition

- explore the extent to which the rise of human resource management has transformed the management of employment relations

- analyse how employment relations is managed in firms that do not recognize trade unions

- consider the tensions inherent in management's need both to control employees' behaviour and performance, and to elicit their commitment and cooperation

---

5.1 Introduction

In this chapter, we consider contemporary developments in the management of employment relations. Surprisingly, until recently the management of employment relations in Britain received little attention from researchers and writers in the area. Although the employment relationship must, by definition, comprise two parties – employer and employee – our understanding of how the former managed it was rather undeveloped (Clegg 1979). The principal areas of interest were the collective organization of employees in trade unions, and the features of the bargaining relationship that existed between employers' associations and trade unions. Since the 1980s, though, with changes in the economic and political climate having prompted union decline, there has been a much more sustained 'focus on management as the prime mover in industrial relations, both in terms of organizational practice and in the amount of academic research' (Marchington and Harrison 1991: 286). Rather than having to react to, and accommodate, trade unionism, managers would appear to enjoy an environment in which they are much better able to innovate in respect of employment relations.

5.2 **Challenging unions**

Since the 1980s, the changes in the economic and political environment discussed in Chapters 2 and 3 have made it easier for employers to challenge the influence of trade unions, compounding the fundamentally unitary preferences of managers (Poole and Mansfield 1993). Managers no longer found it essential to reach pragmatic accommodations with the unions in order to contain their power. Given its well-known anti-union philosophy, the fast-food chain McDonalds is by no means representative of employers in Britain in general; however, the comment of one of its senior managers symbolizes the trend of increased 'employer militancy' (Kelly 1998).

Unionization has risen its ugly head over the years, but you know, we feel that we don't need unions. I think we've seen that the unions' power within business has been eroded quite considerably over the last 15 years, we've managed to get rid of them. (quoted in Royle 2000: 110)

Even where they had hitherto encouraged a union presence, such as in the Cadbury's Bourneville plant for example, during the 1980s, managers attempted to undermine, and even extinguish, a formal union presence (Smith, Child, and Rowlinson 1990). In this part of the chapter, we examine the ways in which employers in Britain have sought to challenge trade unionism, and consider the implications of the statutory union recognition procedure introduced in 2000.

5.2.1 **Union exclusion in Britain**

Perhaps the most obvious measure of union exclusion in Britain is the substantial fall in the incidence of union recognition that occurred during the 1980s and 1990s, particularly in the private sector. As can be seen from Table 5.1, union recognition in the public sector generally held up rather well; the most significant falls occurred in the private sector, where, by the end of the 1990s, unions were recognized for collective bargaining purposes in just a quarter of workplaces. Interestingly, Table 5.1 also shows that the decline in the incidence of union recognition in the private sector seems to have taken off not in the early 1980s, but in the latter half of that decade. This suggests that employers did not

Table 5.1 Percentage of workplaces with a recognized union 1980–98

	All workplaces	Private manufacturing	Private services	Public services
1980	64	65	41	94
1984	66	56	44	99
1990	53	44	36	87
1998	42	30	23	87

Workplaces with twenty-five or more employees.

Sources: Cully et al. (1999); Machin (2000); Millward et al. (1992).

take immediate advantage of the more favourable political and economic climate to launch an assault on union power, but were rather more tentative in their approach, perhaps under the influence of the Conservative anti-union legislation.

For most of the twentieth century, an employer's decision to recognize a union, or not to recognize one, was a voluntary matter, influenced, of course, by the organizing efforts of workers and unions. In general, employers were never legally obliged to deal with a union. In theory, employers could withdraw recognition from, or 'derecognize', trade unions as they saw fit. Perhaps the most striking feature of the 1980s, then, was the somewhat limited extent of union derecognition (Claydon 1989, 1996; Gall and McKay 1994).

While outright union derecognition was rare, it was not unimportant, with incidents concentrated in certain sectors such as magazine and newspaper publishing and the maritime industry. One of the best-known examples in the newspaper industry was the withdrawal of union recognition by Rupert Murdoch's News International, owner of *The Times, The Sunday Times, The Sun*, and the *News of the World* titles, prompting a bitter industrial dispute in 1986–87 (Littleton 1992). In magazine publishing, the removal of union recognition rights was seen by managers as crucial since it gave them greater flexibility to cope with more competitive market conditions (Gall 1998). Although complete derecognition was rare, and where it did occur it was largely an opportunistic response by managers to declining union membership and organization, 'partial' derecognition, the withdrawal of collective bargaining rights from particular groups of workers, such as managers in the financial services industry for example, was perhaps more common (Claydon 1996; Gall and McKay 1994).

By the early to mid-1990s, though, it seemed that a 'cumulative trend towards derecognition might be emerging' (Claydon 1996: 163). It became increasingly common in the oil and chemicals industries in particular, and even extended to the Fawley oil refinery (Smith and Morton 1994), which, thirty years previously, had been celebrated as the epitome of pluralist employment relations (Flanders 1964). Nevertheless, by the mid-1990s the derecognition trend appears to have been reversed; fewer instances of it arose and these were offset by an increasing number of new recognition agreements (Gall and McKay 1999).

By itself, the extent of union derecognition insufficiently accounts for the overall decline in union recognition in Britain during the 1980s and 1990s. A more significant factor was the increasing incidence of non-recognition by employers in new workplaces (Cully et al. 1999; Machin 2000; Millward 1994; Millward, Bryson, and Forth 2000). In 1998, 32 per cent of workplaces that had been in existence for twenty-five years or more recognized a trade union. Just 18 per cent of new workplaces, those that were under 10 years old, did so (Cully et al. 1999). Newly established workplaces operating in growing sectors of the economy, such as high-tech industries, are unlikely to recognize unions in the first place (Findlay 1993; McLoughlin and Gourlay 1992). Thus the decline in union recognition can be ascribed to the policies of more assertive employers, who, aided by a supportive economic and political environment, were increasingly unwilling to countenance a union presence within their operations (Kelly 1998).

While not as prominent as the headline fall in union recognition, even where unions retained a formal workplace presence managers became keener to challenge their role. This was not in general by means of an outright, aggressive anti-union policy, or what could be referred to as a 'macho management' approach (Edwards 1987). Rather, managers, tentatively at first, increasingly sought to erode the influence of unions in situations where, because of the size of union membership for example, outright derecognition was not feasible. New methods of direct communications techniques, between management and employees, such as team briefings for example, were designed to encourage greater organizational loyalty and commitment, and to foster among the workforce a sense of identification with the company (Edwards 1987; Storey 1992). Such innovations were a key feature of the shift towards greater employee involvement within the workplace, which, while perhaps not designed explicitly to undermine trade unionism, nonetheless contributed to its declining influence (Marchington and Parker 1990). However, it is doubtful whether management-controlled communications initiatives can offset the diminution of collective voice provided by robust trade unionism, and there is frequently a gap between formal policy and the reality of involvement, or rather the lack of it, on the ground (Marginson et al. 1988; Millward 1994).

Where union membership levels are high, it is likely to be more trouble than it is worth, in terms of potential disruption, to try to exclude unions entirely (Storey 1992). Added to which, many employers 'do not have an alternative set of employment relations policies that they can realistically hope to put in place of those agreed with trade unions' (Sisson and Storey 2000: 193). Case study evidence from the food industry shows, moreover, that managers may not have the wherewithal to develop sophisticated new techniques of employment relations management in established workplaces, and are constrained by traditional arrangements (Scott 1994). In situations where unions retain a formal presence, or where it is not practical to exclude them entirely, managers have sought to challenge their influence and marginalize their role (Marchington and Parker 1990), 'reducing the disadvantages' of a union presence in order to enhance managerial prerogative (Purcell 1991: 37). During the 1980s and 1990s, some employers looked to mitigate the perceived problems of multi-unionism, recognition of more than one union, by signing 'single union agreements', or 'sweetheart' deals, with unions that made a virtue of their cooperative approach. In 1985, for example, the Nissan car manufacturer chose, following a union 'beauty contest', to recognize the potentially more amenable engineering union, rather than a potentially more militant competitor (Garrahan and Stewart 1992). In Chapter 6, we examine the trend towards 'partnership agreements' between employers and unions, a further example, perhaps, of the way in which employers may, for pragmatic reasons, uphold union recognition, but seek to shape the relationship in a manner that better suits their interests.

5.2.2 Statutory union recognition in Britain

Except for the 1970s, when statutory procedures existed for a time (see Beaumont 1981), before 2000, employers were never under a legal obligation to recognize a union. The third statutory recognition procedure to be introduced in Britain was enacted by the 1999 Employment Relations Act (ERA 1999), and came into effect in June 2000. It is important to appreciate the different context into which it was introduced, compared with its 1970s predecessors. These were established at a time of growing union membership and power, and were in part the outcome of a concern to avoid disruptive industrial action as unions used strikes, for example, to pressurize employers into conceding recognition. The employment relations landscape of the late 1990s, however, was quite different; barely a third of the workforce, for example, were union members. The 1997 Labour government's commitment to introduce a measure that would oblige employers to recognize a union where the majority of the workforce wanted it (DTI 1998) was the outcome of trade union pressure within the Labour party itself to secure favourable legislation that might help them to regain some of their lost ground. The Trades Union Congress (TUC) anticipated that the new statutory recognition procedure could produce as many as a million new trade union members.

The introduction of the new statutory recognition procedure would, at first glance, appear to be a distinctly union-friendly act (see Box 5.1). It was enacted, however, in a way that was largely favourable to employers (Smith and Morton 2001; Wood and Godard 1999). For example, the procedure does not apply where there are fewer than twenty-one employees. Even if an employer is obliged to recognize a union by means of the statutory route, the scope of bargaining is limited to pay, hours, and holidays. There are also no guaranteed outcomes since the right to recognition is limited to the 'right to invoke a procedure' (Brown et al. 2001: 183).

The government's preference for voluntary agreements underpinned the legislation (Brown et al. 2001; Oxenbridge et al. 2003). The statutory procedure was to prevail only if an employer and union were unable to reach a deal themselves. Indeed, its main effect seems to have been to stimulate voluntary union recognition by employers (TUC 2003b; Wood, Moore, and Ewing 2003; Wood, Moore, and Willman 2002). According to one estimate, between October 2000 and October 2002 over 730 new recognition deals were signed, most of them voluntary ones, a marked increase on the preceding period (TUC 2003b). More recently, though, there has been a diminution in the pace of recognition agreements, a result of there being fewer easy union targets, and growing employer resistance (IRS 2004; TUC 2004).

By April 2004, the statutory recognition procedure had generated just eighty-nine new agreements (Central Arbitration Committee 2004). Among the companies that have

---

BOX 5.1 THE STATUTORY RECOGNITION PROCEDURE IN BRITAIN

Under the procedure, if a union has a recognition claim for a particular group of workers dismissed by the employer it can make an application to a state body, the Central Arbitration Committee (CAC), which decides if the claim is a valid one for the purposes of the statutory procedure. It does not apply where fewer than twenty-one workers are employed. CAC must also determine whether there is sufficient support for unionization among the workforce; at least 10 per cent must be union members with the likelihood that a majority of the workforce would vote in favour of union recognition in a ballot. If these tests are met, and no other union is recognized for the group of workers in question, then CAC can mandate union recognition if 50 per cent or more of the relevant workers are in union membership, or it can order a ballot of the workforce. To secure recognition, a union must win approval from a simple majority of those voting, as long as this constitutes a threshold of 40 per cent of the relevant workforce.

signed recognition deals with trade unions as a result are: Kwik Fit, the car repairer; Virgin Atlantic, the airline; and Alldays convenience stores; with the agreement between the car manufacturer Honda and the AEEU–Amicus engineering and electrical union, covering some 4,000 workers at its Swindon plant, perhaps being the most notable of those reached through the statutory procedure in the first four years of its existence. The preference for voluntary agreements demonstrates that in some cases unions have been successful in putting pressure on employers to concede recognition without needing to invoke the statutory procedure, though its existence is clearly an influence. While there have been cases of employers having initiated recognition themselves, in order to benefit from a 'sweetheart deal' with a moderate trade union (Gall 2003a), this has not been a major trend (Wood, Moore, and Ewing 2003).

The extent to which some employers will go to resist unionization should not be under-estimated though. Extensive opposition to union recognition persists, but aggressive anti-union behaviour akin to the 'union-busting' approaches favoured in the United States (see Box 5.2) does not appear to be all that common, though it may be growing (Gall 2003a, 2004). In one study, the researchers reported that half of the companies they visited had tried to prevent a formal union presence from becoming established, often because of the antagonism exhibited by senior managers towards unions (Oxenbridge et al. 2003). Some companies have adopted a hard-nosed, aggressive strategy of 'union suppression', whereas others have developed a more 'substitutionist' approach (Gall and McKay 2001). In the case of the former, managers may use intimidation to curtail unionism, claiming, for example, that union recognition could threaten the viability of the workplace and thus cost jobs, and also by dismissing union activists (Gall 2003a). The substitutionist approach, however, is designed to hinder unionization by providing employees with alternative, in-house methods of representation such as a company council.

Well-known companies like BSkyB, the satellite television programmer, Borders, the US-owned retail book chain, Ryanair, the self-styled 'low cost' airline, and Bodyshop, the 'ethical' manufacturer and retailer of cosmetics, have been at the forefront of resistance to union recognition in recent years using either 'suppressionist' or 'substitutionist' approaches, or sometimes a mixture of both. (Gall 2003a; Gall and McKay 2001). In 2000 and 2001, Amazon, the online bookseller, conducted a vigorous campaign against union-ization at its distribution centre near Milton Keynes. During 2001, negotiations with the Graphical Paper and Media Union (GPMU) broke down amid complaints of anti-union activity by the company, before a rather controversial in-house ballot showed the majority of the workforce to be opposed to unionization. Given such opposition to trade unionism, and the way in which the relevant legislation was designed not to antagonize employers, it seems unlikely that the statutory union recognition procedure will generate a revival of trade unionism on its own. Although it may have a small symbolic impact (Oxenbridge et al. 2003), given that it signals a shift away from the more overt anti-unionism of the Conservative's legislative programme, the statutory recognition procedure is, like the rest of Labour's public policy agenda, imbued by a belief that robust, independent trade unionism is inimical to labour market flexibility.

BOX 5.2 ANTI-UNIONISM IN THE UNITED STATES

Visceral hostility towards trade unionism and collective bargaining has been a longstanding feature of employment relations in the United States, despite the existence of a statutory recognition procedure, offering an instructive comparison with the British experience. Attempts by trade unions to gain recognition for collective bargaining purposes have generally been met by robust employer opposition, something that seems to have increased since the 1970s (see Adams 1995; Logan 2001).

Some insight into the kinds of problems encountered by workers when attempting to exercise their right to organize in trade unions can be gained from an examination of the fast-food industry where 'union-busting techniques' are commonplace. In his book on the fast-food industry, *Fast Food Nation* (2002), Eric Schlosser details some of the methods used by McDonalds to remain free of the unions. It uses, for example, managerial 'flying squads', comprising experienced senior managers, who descend upon a restaurant to encourage the workforce to desist from unionization, by means of threats if other approaches fail to do the trick, as soon as a hint of union activity emerges (Schlosser 2002).

But perhaps the most infamous anti-union firm in the US is the giant retailer Wal-Mart, now the owner of Asda in Britain. In the early days of the company, Wal-Mart's founder, Sam Walton, engaged a 'professional union-buster' in an effort to prevent unionization (Ortega 1999: 87). According to one worker, when the Teamsters union tried to organize a distribution centre Walton told the staff 'that if the union got in, the warehouse would be closed . . . people could vote any way they wanted, but he'd close her right up' (Ortega 1999: 107). Unsurprisingly, the union failed to get enough support to win recognition. Wal-Mart has fine-tuned its anti-union approach over the years, vigorously resisting any attempts by unions to organize its stores, often by means of heavy-handed tactics. When Ann Bertelli, a photo-processing clerk, tried to form a union at her store in Massachusetts she was dismissed (Ortega 1999: 354–5). Departmental manager Kathleen Baker and her fellow workers were upset when Wal-Mart raised the wages in all of its stores in the Minneapolis area, except for theirs. In her own time, Baker drafted a petition that requested an equivalent rise, and had it signed by eighty workers. When it came to the attention of the store manager, Baker was summarily dismissed for: 'negatively affecting team concept and store performance . . . misuse of company payroll [gathering signatures while at work] . . . and use of Company Assets (typewriter) for personal use' (quoted in Ortega 1999: 358). In November 2002, union activists staged anti-Wal-Mart rallies in a number of US cities in order to protest against the company's employment relations record, and to bring the campaign for better pay and working conditions, and the right to union representation, to wider public attention.

SECTION SUMMARY AND FURTHER READING

- Although some employers derecognized trade unions during the 1980s and 1990s, this form of union exclusion was rare. Newly established workplaces operating in growing sectors of the economy, such as high-tech industries, were unlikely to recognize unions in the first place.

- In organizations where unions retained a formal presence, managers tried to diminish their role and influence through the propagation of new direct communications techniques.

• In September 2000, a statutory union recognition procedure was introduced in Britain. It obliges an employer to recognize a union for collective bargaining purposes where a majority of the workforce want it. The procedure, however, was implemented so as not to antagonize employers. Despite the more favourable climate for the trade unions, employer anti-unionism remains a feature of British employment relations.

For data on union recognition levels in Britain, see Cully et al. (1999), and Machin (2000). The best overview of union derecognition in the 1980s and early 1990s is Claydon (1996). See Royle (2000) for insights concerning the anti-union tactics adopted by one well-known American multinational. For the impact of the statutory union recognition procedure in Britain, see Wood, Moore, and Willman (2002), and Oxenbridge et al. (2003).

5.3 Human resource management and employment relations

The extent to which, given the diminution of union power during the 1980s and 1990s, managements have been able to develop new, innovative techniques for managing employees is an important question. The terms 'personnel management' and 'personnel manager' have increasingly been replaced by 'human resource management' (HRM) and 'human resource manager' in organizational vocabularies. While there is evidence that organizations have been taking the way in which their employees are managed more seriously (Sisson 1993), how far does this represent a transformation in the management of employment relations in Britain? Three related questions underpin our assessment of HRM and employment relations. First, is HRM simply a re-ordering, or a re-packaging of traditional personnel management activities under a new title, one that is more attractive to senior managers? Second, alternatively, has the arrival of HRM brought about a transformation in how employees are managed in British firms, constituting a novel and more innovative approach to the management of employment relations? Third, following on from this, if new techniques of managing employees can be identified, to what extent are they consistent with the longstanding concern of managers to assert their prerogatives, though under a perhaps more benign guise? We begin our assessment of the implications of HRM for employment relations by examining its nature and the factors that influenced its development.

5.3.1 The rise of human resource management

In order to comprehend the purported distinctiveness of the HRM, it is necessary to consider the underpinning policies that drive an HRM approach, and the practices that constitute it. In the first major study to consider its implications for employment relations, Guest (1987) identified four HRM policy goals: integration; commitment; flexibility; and quality.

First, HRM is held to be distinctive from personnel management in so far as it puts a greater emphasis on the fit between employment policies and the overall business objectives of the organization. Such an approach recognizes the important role played by line managers in supporting and implementing appropriate HRM practices (Wood 1995). Strategic integration, moreover, also refers to 'the extent to which the various personnel policies cohere and provide a consistent and comprehensive focus' (Guest 1996: 9). Thus HRM is seen to consist of a mutually supportive and interlocking set of employment practices that, taken together, make an important contribution to business goals. Second, the enhancement of individual employees' commitment to the organization is central to the HRM approach. This is based on the 'assumption that committed employees will be more satisfied, more productive and more adaptable' (Guest 1987: 513). Third, HRM enables organizations to become more adaptable, principally by encouraging and reinforcing employment flexibility, and thus the more effective utilization of labour. Fourth, it is assumed that the more elaborate approach to managing employees embodied by an HRM approach is more capable of delivering enhanced business performance since, given the imperative to build commitment and flexibility, the use of high-quality employment polices is rendered essential (Guest 1987).

Commitment is perhaps the only one of the four policy goals that poses a direct threat to the role of the unions, in so far as it seeks to bind individual employees to the firm, and thus facilitate a more unitary ethos (Guest 1987, 1989, 1995). The 'increasing adoption of HRM-type practices and, in particular, the targeting of the individual, have two objectives: to win "hearts and minds", and to demonstrate the relative ineffectiveness of trade unions' (Sisson 1993: 208). In contrast to the traditional personnel management approach, which tended to rely upon bureaucratic methods, such as the provision of regular pay increments for example, to enforce control in the workplace, under an HRM regime the emphasis is placed more on techniques for managing organizational culture (Bach and Sisson 2000; Legge 2005; Storey 1992). While the concept of 'organizational commitment' is not without its problems (Guest 1987), it should be evident that the rise of HRM, especially its unitary ethos, and the emphasis it places on managing individual employment relationships, may be linked to the weakening of trade unionism discussed in the last section.

Based on these policy goals, then, one can make an attempt to distinguish those features associated with HRM, thus making it distinctive from a personnel management approach. These include: the preference for individual contracts instead of collective bargaining; the reduced emphasis placed on conflict, and consequently less of a need to accommodate it; pay systems linked to performance rather than fixed grades; the marginalization of workplace unionism; a more sustained attempt to involve employees, through the greater incidence of direct communications techniques; and the increased use of teamworking (Storey 1992).

There is, then, a sharp contrast between the unitary ethos of HRM, where the role of unions is very much played down, and the purportedly more pluralist character of traditional personnel management in which the emphasis is on managing with, and accommodating, trade unions. Under HRM, it would appear that managing employment relations is not so much about containing trade unionism, but rather is more concerned with how the way in which employees are managed can contribute to business performance.

A considerable amount of ambiguity surrounds the meaning of HRM (Blyton and Turnbull 1992; Sisson 1993). In some interpretations, it is presented as a metaphor, with the messages it carries being more important than the actual practices used (Keenoy and Anthony 1992). Perhaps the most significant ambiguity concerns whether one should conceptualize HRM in 'soft' or 'hard' terms (Storey 1992). In 'hard' HRM, the emphasis is placed on managing employees as a resource, a factor of production, to be used, and discarded, in a way that supports organizational objectives. In contrast, the 'soft' approach to HRM, 'while still emphasizing the importance of integrating HR policies with business objectives, sees this as a way of treating employees as valued assets, a source of competitive advantage through their commitment, adaptability and quality . . .' (Legge 2005: 105). Thus the emphasis is on building business performance through the involvement and development of employees. However, these contrasting approaches are not necessarily mutually exclusive (Legge 2005), and we examine the rather limited evidence for the existence of 'soft' HRM below.

But what, though, accounts for the emergence of HRM? Conceptually, it would appear to be based on two distinctive intellectual approaches (Storey 1992). One is the growth of interest in the nature and dynamics of corporate strategy, and of the way in which an organization's resources can contribute to its objectives. HRM is also based on the revival of a human relations approach to understanding organizational behaviour, one which emphasizes how sophisticated managerial techniques can enhance the motivation, commitment, and job satisfaction of workers to the benefit of the organization (Walton 1985).

In 1980s Britain, certain economic trends provided fertile soil for the emergence of HRM, in particular growing international competition, the importation of novel employment relations arrangements by foreign companies, particularly those from the Far East, and the increasing emphasis on flexibility and quality as sources of competitive advantage (Blyton and Turnbull 1992). More importantly, perhaps, the unitary and individualistic ethos of HRM accorded with the political climate of the time, one in which the trade unions, given the decline in their power, and the hostility exhibited towards them by the Conservatives, were on the retreat (Bach and Sisson 2000; Blyton and Turnbull 1992; Keenoy and Anthony 1992; Legge 2005). Interestingly, there is evidence that the impetus for the development of HRM techniques came not from personnel managers, who were largely content with operating within the parameters of established pluralist approaches, but as important by-products of organizational restructuring and changes in production methods driven by line and general managers (Storey 1992). The vocabulary of HRM, and its strategic and unitary assumptions, would appear to be more attractive to senior managers than personnel management (Sisson and Storey 2000).

5.3.2 **HRM in practice**

Although there is evidence that, from the late 1980s onwards, managements were taking a more sophisticated approach to the way in which their human resources are managed (Sisson 1993), including in the public sector (see Box 5.3), the extent to which this represented a transformation is questionable. Organizations appear to have adopted particular elements of the HRM approach, those that were most appropriate to their immediate needs, especially direct communications methods, in an *ad hoc* and opportunistic way (Legge 2005). Overall, the shift towards an HRM approach in Britain has been

---

BOX 5.3 TOWARDS A NEW PUBLIC MANAGEMENT?

For many years, the management of employment relations in public sector organizations was characterized by the dominance of centralized, highly bureaucratic procedures, which were determined from above, and national collective bargaining machinery. Consequently, the role of the personnel management function was largely restricted to the implementation of standardized procedures and national agreements, with very little scope for discretion (Bach 1999b; Beaumont 1992; Farnham and Giles 1996). During the 1980s, however, Conservative governments enacted policies that stimulated the role and authority of managers in the public sector: the emphasis on better value for money and customer service; the devolution of decision-making to smaller business units; and the encouragement of a greater strategic awareness in a context of rigorous financial targets (Winchester and Bach 1999). Such was the degree of apparent change in the way in which public sector organizations were run, that a new term, the 'new public management' (NPM), came to be used to refer to it (Hood 1991).

NPM comprises three key dimensions. First, it refers to the growth of a stronger, more robust managerial function within public sector enterprises. Second, NPM is closely associated with the devolution of managerial responsibility for decision-making to business units. Third, it is characterized by the development of a more market-oriented approach to the delivery of public services, based on an assumption that competitive pressures can improve their quality (Bach and Della Rocca 2000). Thus the rise of NPM is associated with an increase in managerial authority in the public sector, the elaboration of more sophisticated managerial approaches, and the greater use of management techniques imported from the private sector (Winchester and Bach 1999).

Evidently, NPM shares many of the characteristics of an HRM approach to managing employment relations in so far as the emphasis is placed upon managing people in a more purposive way, with the aim of generating flexibility, and enhancing commitment, in order to raise business performance (Bach 1999b). Like HRM in general, though, NPM, is beset by an important contradiction. The market-based reforms to public services which it has accompanied have created greater insecurity among employees, and lowered their morale to such an extent that commitment and flexibility are rendered increasingly difficult to secure (Bach 1999b).

---

gradual and tentative, with few organizations wholeheartedly adopting a commitment-based 'soft' HRM strategy (Bach and Sisson 2000).

The one area where employers have made considerable progress in altering their employment relations arrangements is in the growing incidence of direct communications techniques, part of an approach which, ostensibly, is designed to promote employee involvement at work, and thus generate greater individual commitment (Marchington et al. 1992; Sisson and Storey 2000). However, as we will see in Chapter 8, managers generally exhibit a marked reluctance to act upon employees' suggestions.

Although there is some evidence that where the practices associated with HRM exist they have a positive influence on job satisfaction (Guest 1999), the limited scope of employee involvement, and the way it is used to limit rather than enhance employees' influence at work, suggests that the existence of 'soft' HRM is somewhat rare in Britain (Bach and Sisson 2000; Legge 2005). Case study research demonstrates, moreover, that the distinction between 'soft' and 'hard' HRM may be meaningless anyway.

Most of the 'Leading Edge' organizations studied by Gratton et al. (1999) claim to have adopted the 'soft' HRM approach. For example, they stressed the importance of developing employees as individuals, and of providing them with training opportunities. But the training was often related to the narrow, immediate requirements of the job, and not of much benefit to employees in the long term. Moreover, where the importance of individual development was attested, it was done in such way that it helped to legitimize increasingly limited employment and promotion opportunities. Thus the emphasis was placed on giving employees the necessary skills to self-manage their own careers in situations where the organization was, for financial reasons, less able to offer security of employment.

There may have been a lot of 'soft' rhetoric exhibited by the Leading Edge organizations, 'but the underlying principle was invariably restricted to the improvement of bottom-line performance' (Gratton et al. 1999: 56–7). While the 'soft' HRM model implies that business objectives can be more effectively realized if an emphasis is placed upon developing employees, and fostering their commitment, in practice the organizations predominantly viewed their employees as costs, and thus to be minimized. The language of 'soft' HRM was important since it helped to obscure the commodity status of employees. Thus 'even if the rhetoric of HRM is "soft", the reality is almost always "hard", with the interests of the organization prevailing over those of the individual' (Gratton et al. 1999: 57).

Based on such evidence, then, it would be unwise to claim that HRM has transformed employment relations in Britain. Competitive pressures, and the need to enhance short-term financial performance, preclude many organizations from investing in the kind of sophisticated, progressive management techniques necessary to foster greater organizational involvement and commitment. More fundamentally, perhaps, it is unclear how far managers are able to eschew a traditional concern with upholding their prerogatives in such a way that it enables a significant level of genuine employee involvement to become established (Scott 1994).

In the United States, HRM emerged as an approach to managing the employment relationship in firms without a union presence (Kochan, Katz, and McKersie (1986). A feature of the development of HRM in Britain is that the practices most associated with it are more commonly found in unionized organizations rather than non-union ones. If one sees the use of HRM practices as part of the broader efforts of employers to marginalize union influence in British organizations, though, then this should not come as a great surprise; where unions are absent they are simply not seen as necessary (Kelly 1998). In respect of firms that do not recognize a trade union, the absence of both union voice arrangements and, outside a small number of large companies, HRM-style employee involvement mechanisms suggests the existence of a harsh, or 'bleak house' environment with workers treated as 'factors of production' (Millward 1994; Sisson 1995).

5.3.3 **HRM and performance**

One of the most distinctive aspects of an HRM approach to managing employment relations is held to be the emphasis on managing human resources in a way that produces enhanced business performance. This contrasts with the traditional approach in which the priority was to manage with, and accommodate the effects of, trade unionism and collective bargaining. Since the mid-1990s, a lot of the academic work in the area of HRM has examined the extent to which the presence of so-called 'high commitment', or 'high involvement', practices produce a positive impact on organizational performance, largely influenced by studies undertaken in the United States where such an approach to the subject has become commonplace (Godard and Delaney 2000; Guest 1997).

Why has there been such a growth of interest in the relationship between HRM and organizational performance in Britain? The quest for business credibility on the part of practitioners engaged in personnel activities is an important influence since, historically, this function was largely seen as a cost and not a source of added business value. If the presence of sophisticated HRM practices can be demonstrated to have a positive impact on the financial bottom-line of organizations, then this not only helps to justify the existence of a specialist personnel or human resource function, but also enhances its status (Millward, Bryson, and Forth 2000). This, then, has encouraged interest in 'the search for a Holy Grail of establishing a causal link between HRM and performance' (Legge 2001: 23).

What, though, are the 'high commitment' or 'high performance' management practices and how, according to those who have studied them, does their presence boost business performance? At a general level, the high-commitment approach embodies 'recruitment practices which aim to attract and select highly committed and flexible people; internal labour markets which reward commitment and training with promotion and job security; [and] methods of direct communication and involvement such as team briefing, team working and quality circles' (Wood and Albanese 1995: 222).

In respect of specific practices, the 1998 Workplace Employee Relations Survey examined the incidence of fifteen, including the presence of: guaranteed job security; regular appraisals; teamworking; personality tests in recruitment and selection; formal off-the-job training; formal grievance and disciplinary procedures; and group-based team briefings with feedback (Cully et al. 1999: 81). While different studies rarely refer to the same set of specific practices when assessing the impact of the high-commitment management approach, a problem to which we return below, in general they encompass an emphasis on employment security, training, sophisticated recruitment and selection techniques, flexible job design and teamworking, and robust arrangements for employee involvement (Sisson and Marginson 2003).

How, though, is it suggested that such practices impact positively on the organizational bottom-line? First, the elaboration of sophisticated recruitment, selection, and training and development techniques produces better quality employees who are thus more productive (Truss 2001). Second, the high-commitment management approach helps to generate an increase in employees' 'discretionary work effort', with positive implications for performance (Huselid 1995). To the extent that they develop a greater sense of identification with the organization, and are more involved in decisions that affect them in the workplace, employees will, it is assumed, perform better and be more productive (Wood and de Menezes 1998).

The positive impact of the so-called high-commitment or high-performance management practices is, it is argued, more pronounced when they are used not in an idiosyncratic, *ad hoc* way, but in a mutually supportive fashion, or in 'bundles' (MacDuffie 1995). Teamworking arrangements, for example, should produce better results where they are operated in combination with appropriate recruitment and selection and reward practices. Research studies in the United States demonstrate that high-commitment management practices, particularly where they are used in bundles, and in combination with a flexible system of work design, do have a positive impact on business performance (Huselid 1995).

According to some survey data, during the 1990s the presence of high-commitment practices appeared to become more commonplace among British organizations, since managers began to take their human resources more seriously (Cully et al. 1999; Wood and de Menezes 1998). Such studies demonstrate that HRM, contrary to the scepticism about its prevalence expressed above, may be more common than had otherwise been appreciated. Data from the 1998 Workplace Employment Relations Survey, moreover, reveal an association between the use of high-commitment practices and workplace financial performance in private sector companies, though there are few signs of the existence of coherent bundles (Guest et al. 2000; Ramsay, Scholarios, and Harley 2000).

Unsurprisingly, personnel practitioners welcome evidence that the presence of certain HR practices is associated with better workplace financial performance, since it would appear to give them a more integral role within organizations. But how valid are the suppositions that, first, the use of high-commitment management practices has become more commonplace and, second, that their presence generates improved business performance? There are five major problems with such propositions.

First, the extent of high-commitment management in Britain has been questioned. Just two per cent of workplaces operate more than two-thirds of the fifteen practices identified by the 1998 Workplace Employment Relations Survey (Bach and Sisson 2000).

Second, how distinctive are the practices associated with the high-commitment approach anyway? Can the presence of formal grievance and disciplinary procedures, for example, really be seen as evidence of the high-commitment model, or are they simply characteristic features of contemporary good practice in personnel (Bach and Sisson 2000; Godard and Delaney 2000)?

Third, the assumption underpinning the high-commitment approach, that improvements in business performance result from better quality of working life for employees, because it raises their productivity, is questionable. There is some evidence, Danford et al.'s (2004) case study of an aircraft manufacturer for example, that improvements in performance result from heavier workloads, without any of the benefits that are supposed to accrue to employees from new ways of working. Although survey evidence demonstrates that high performance under HRM regimes is not simply a function of a coercive managerial approach (Ramsay, Scholarios, and Harley 2000), since the management of the employment relationship is characterized both by the need to exercise control over employees and to secure their consent, something we return to later on in this chapter, efforts to demonstrate a direct relationship between managerial practices, employees' experiences and business perform-ance are likely to be in vain.

Fourth, much of the research which links high-commitment management with business performance treats human resource practices as formal managerial interventions, readily identifiable and thus, when presented as variables, making the effects of their presence supposedly easy to measure. But the management of the employment relationship is a process; it possesses a dynamic, and should not be reduced to a set of formal practices. How these function in workplaces, where, for example, managers and workers contest their operation, or interpret them in different ways from those intended, is a much more complex and less easily measurable matter. A case study of Hewlett-Packard, a firm characterized by an ostensibly sophisticated HRM approach, found that despite the presence of a formal system of measuring employees' performance against company set targets, informal methods, such as ensuring they got noticed, were more effective in pursuing career advancement (Truss 2001).

Fifth, the conceptual assumptions and research methodology that underpin studies of the relationship between HRM and performance raise doubts about the high-commitment paradigm. There is no consensus on what practices constitute a high-commitment approach, the specification and measurement of business performance are often somewhat rudimentary, and they rely upon responses from managers who, unsurprisingly, offer a biased and partial perspective, and may know little of how the practices they identify are interpreted in the workplace (Godard and Delaney 2000; Legge 2001). While there may be an association between HRM and business performance, it is not necessarily a causal one. What about the likelihood that firms that are financially successful are better placed to deploy more sophisticated, and costly, management techniques? Thus 'much of the research on HR "high commitment/performance" practices and organizational performance is at best confused and, at worst, conceptually and methodologically deeply flawed' (Legge 2001: 31).

How, then, should HRM, and its impact on employment relations be understood? While it is clear that some changes have occurred, the growth of direct communications arrangements for example, these hardly amount to a transformation of the way in which employment relations is managed in Britain. They occurred in part because the decline of trade unionism opened up opportunities for innovation, but, more commonly, have been elaborated because of a desire to challenge union influence. While the increasing interest in the relationship between HRM and business performance stems, as we have suggested, from personnel practitioners eager to justify their role, it is also a function of change within the academic world, since researchers have been encouraged to eschew studies of the relationship between management and labour, and to focus more on how employment relations can influence economic competitiveness (Legge 2001).

SECTION SUMMARY AND FURTHER READING

- In so far as its emphasis is on how organizations can develop more sophisticated management techniques to raise employees' commitment, and thus improve business performance, the emergence of HRM in the 1980s appeared to challenge the traditional way in which employment relations was managed in Britain.

- The extent of any transformation has, however, been somewhat limited. In general, significant innovation has been restricted to the growth of direct communications arrangements, and even these are generally very circumscribed in their scope. The distinction between 'soft' and 'hard' HRM is of limited use given the way in which practices associated with the former are often used to mask a less benign reality. It is perhaps better to consider the rise of HRM, given the unitary assumptions that underpin it, as part of a general trend towards challenging the influence of the trade unions.

- Although there has been much recent interest in how HRM, and so-called high-commitment or high-performance practices in particular, can enhance business performance, the research on which it is based is riddled with conceptual and methodological problems.

Legge (2005) is the best critical assessment of the HRM phenomenon. Storey (1992) sensitively considers the emergence, characteristics, and implications of HRM based on case study research. For a more recent general overview of developments, see Bach and Sisson (2000). Gratton et al. (1999) use case study research to provide a splendid analysis of the limits and contradictions inherent within a commitment-based HRM approach. Finally, see Sisson and Marginson (2003) for an overview of the debates about HRM and performance, and Legge (2001) for a vigorous critical assessment.

5.4 Managing employment relations in non-union environments

For many years, the employment relations characteristics of firms without a formal union presence barely featured in studies of employment relations. There were some exceptions, such as the analysis of foreign-owned companies operating in Britain for example (e.g. Gennard and Steuer 1971). Until the 1980s, though, studies of employment relations were overwhelmingly dominated by analyses of the roles of trade unions, employers, and employers' associations, and the relationships between them. Companies without union recognition were, if they were large ones, treated as idiosyncratic and given some brief consideration (e.g. Clegg 1979), or, in the case of the many small firms where no formal union presence existed, largely ignored. Since the mid-1980s, however, there has been something of a change in emphasis, not least because of the sharp decline in union recognition in Britain. Nevertheless, studies of employment relations in non-union environments, particularly in private services, remain far from commonplace. This reflects difficulties researchers have in gaining access to firms, especially smaller ones, in order to collect data, and the continuing emphasis in employment relations on developments in the unionized part of the economy. Nevertheless, the growing proportion of new workplaces without a formal union presence has provided the catalyst for a more considered appreciation of how employment relations is managed in non-union firms.

5.4.1 Sophisticated HRM and non-union firms

Perhaps the most important question about the employment relations arrangements of non-union firms, especially large ones, is the extent to which they exemplify a sophisticated HRM approach to managing employees. Given the absence of a formal union presence, how far, then, have managers been able to reshape the relationship with employees in such a way that commitment and cooperation have come to transcend conflict in the employment relationship? Notwithstanding the evidence that HRM practices are more commonly found in unionized, rather than non-unionized, workplaces, in some interpretations the rise of non-unionism in Britain 'has been closely linked with the emergence of new techniques of human resource management' (McLoughlin and Gourlay 1994: 23).

The association between HRM practices and non-unionism stems largely from the experience of companies like IBM in Britain, and its 'open' management style, single status policy, robust communications, and emphasis on managing employees as individuals, and providing them with superior benefits (Bassett 1987), and developments in the United States. A study of an IBM plant in Greenock, Scotland, found that the company had 'erected a sophisticated system of industrial relations to enable it to function without the necessity of recognizing trade unions . . .' (Dickson et al. 1988: 510). During the 1970s and 1980s, the growing non-union sector in the United States became the focus of increasing attention not least because it was thought that such companies embodied a superior, more enlightened way of managing their human resources (Foulkes 1980).

Two key features of employment relations in large non-union firms can therefore be identified. First, in so far as employees' pay, conditions, and benefits exceed those that could be won by union activity, the sophisticated HRM approach may be considered as a 'substitute' for trade union organization. Unions are therefore simply unnecessary, and indeed their presence would disrupt the cooperative and harmonious relationship between managers and workers that has been so carefully fostered. See the three case studies of non-unionism in the high-tech sector in Britain undertaken by McLoughlin and Gourlay (1994), for example. Although there were significant variations in the companies' approaches to managing employment relations, an overarching theme was the perceived irrelevance of trade unions. With the exception of manual staff in one of the firms, there was little evidence that workers were dissatisfied with their employment arrangements to the extent that a union presence would be considered desirable. According to one of the computer staff in one of the firms: 'The company has always challenged me and is a fun company with a very open management style. I have never considered the need for a trades union' (quoted in McLoughlin and Gourlay 1994: 115). What, then, would be the purpose of a trade union in such an environment? Thus firms that operate sophisticated HRM policies in the absence of a formal union presence, often style themselves as 'non-union', rather than 'anti-union'. Managers claim not to oppose trade unions in principle, but simply cannot see any need for them given the favourable pay, conditions, and benefits enjoyed by employees.

The second key feature of employment relations in large non-union firms is held to be the emphasis on individualism; that members of staff are treated by managers as individuals, contrasting with the collective representation of employees in unionized environments, something which is thus rendered unnecessary. The computer firm IBM is often presented as the archetypal non-union firm in this respect. It 'refuses to recognize unions, not because of their potential nuisance value, but because their collectivism runs wholly counter to the company's fundamental individualist philosophy' (Bassett 1987: 164). According to a manager in another high-tech firm, 'the staff see it to their advantage to be treated as individuals . . . the type of work they do is such that it calls for an individual approach' (McLoughlin and Gourlay 1992: 680).

It would seem, then, that a combination of sophisticated HRM with an individualistic management style may not only provide workers with superior quality of employment, but is also an effective way of preventing trade unions from gaining a foothold. The extent to which such an approach exists, beyond a small number of high-profile companies in high-tech industries is, however, questionable. It is striking how often the experience of

IBM is cited by writers keen to demonstrate the advantages of the benefits of a non-union, sophisticated HRM approach. The reluctance of employees to embrace trade unionism is often not a reflection of progressive management policies, but more the result of an inability to see what value union membership could offer them or, in some cases, an aversion to trade unions (Dundon and Rollinson 2004; McLoughlin and Gourlay 1994).

It is also evident that an individualistic approach to managing employees is difficult to uphold in practice, not least because it is extremely costly to maintain. Much of the available evidence would suggest that while 'procedural individualization' is an important trend in British workplaces, 'substantive individualization' is much rarer (Brown et al. 2000). What, then, is the difference between 'procedural' and 'substantive' individualization? The former refers to the absence of collective procedures, generally involving trade unions, as a means of determining employment contracts, an increasing trend since the early 1980s. 'Substantive' individualization, however, 'the differentiation of contractual terms within the organization' (Brown et al. 2000: 627), is far from commonplace. Indeed, there appears to be a 'high degree of standardization of employment contracts within British workplaces, so far as both pay and non-pay entitlements are concerned' (Brown et al. 2000: 620). This was evident in 'Knowco', a company specializing in the provision of IT skills training and consultancy that, while supposedly following a sophisticated HRM approach, nonetheless relied upon standardized contracts for employees. Substantive individualization, then, is 'potentially extremely expensive to pursue since, for it to be meaningful, it requires the management capacity to negotiate, monitor and review a portfolio of individual contracts' (Colling 2003: 387).

Employers' claims to be 'non-union', rather than 'anti-union', should be treated with caution given that 'professions of neutrality' towards unions may often mask a more oppositional and antagonistic approach (Clegg 1979: 102; Dundon and Rollinson 2004; Knox and McKinlay 2003). Marks and Spencer, for example, claims that it does not oppose unions, but that its staff do not need one. However, in the UK the company does its utmost to undermine any union organizing efforts (Blyton and Turnbull 2004).

From our discussion of the implications of human resource management for employment relations, it should also be clear that 'sophisticated HRM' is often a benign façade obscuring the more authoritarian reality. In the steel company 'Ministeel', for example, the elaboration of HRM techniques was part of a policy designed to exclude the union from the workplace, and there were complaints from trade unionists of intimidation (Bacon 1999). In a study of a large retail store, the researchers discovered that the espoused sophisticated human relations policy obscured a more complex, and less benign, reality. They found evidence of, among other things, poor communications, low job satisfaction, and gender discrimination in respect of pay and promotion opportunities (Turnbull and Wass 1998: 108).

The difficulties inherent in sustaining a sophisticated approach to the management of employees are also evident from a case study of a non-union chocolate works. In the early 1980s, senior managers attempted to initiate a transformation in the way in which employees were managed, eschewing the traditional autocratic style in favour of a more sophisticated approach which, among other things, sought to give employees more responsibility over their work and to 'build a culture in which individuals felt responsible for contributing to the success of the wider organization' (Scott 1994: 122). This was not enough, though, to overcome the traditional character of employment relations, in particular the reluctance of managers to disavow authoritarianism, something that limited the propensity of workers to engage with the new approach. Even in situations where there is no union presence, important barriers exist which hinder attempts by managers to engender a sophisticated HRM approach, not least the reluctance of managers themselves to embrace the implications of change.

5.4.2 Employment relations in small firms

It is rare to find a formal union presence within small firms. According to the 1998 Workplace Employee Relations Survey, just 12 per cent of workplaces with between ten and twenty-four employees have a recognized union present. Where the owner works full-time on the premises, it is just 7 per cent (Cully et al. 1999).

Two problems affect any assessment of employment relations in small firms. First, difficulties of access make it hard to obtain adequate data regarding employment practices and employees' attitudes. Nevertheless, we are now able to draw upon a range of high-quality research studies that illuminate our understanding of employment relations in small firms (e.g. Goss 1991; Holliday 1995; Marlow 2002; Moule 1998; Rainnie 1989; Ram 1994). Second, the diverse nature of the small business sector must be respected, even to the extent of questioning whether it is a discrete 'sector' in its own right at all (Scase 1995). We can, however, draw out some common themes.

Perhaps the most notable feature of the work undertaken on small firms has been to expose the myth that employment relations is inherently harmonious since, based on data used by the Bolton Committee of Enquiry on Small Firms in the early 1970s, for many years this was the accepted wisdom (Bolton 1971). The committee's report equated the low level of union activity within small firms with an absence of conflict. It also claimed that the low pay and inferior physical working conditions characteristic of small firms were more than made up for by the benefits that accrue to employees from being in close proximity to their employer (Bolton 1971). Thus arose the 'myth' that when it comes to employment relations small is beautiful, something that 'sunk deep into the consciousness of academics, government and media' (Rainnie 1989: 25).

While it became influential among policy-makers, the 'industrial harmony' thesis has now been subjected to a considerable amount of criticism by academic researchers (e.g. Goss 1991; Rainnie 1989; Ram 1994). Rather than seeing small as 'beautiful', given the relatively high level of worker dismissals and workplace accidents occurring in small firms, it is perhaps more appropriate to see it as 'brutal' (Rainnie 1989). Importantly, though, studies that question, and in effect demolish, the 'industrial harmony' thesis do not simply replace one over-simplistic view, that employment relations in small firms are inherently harmonious, with another, that management autocracy is unconstrained and that pay and conditions are poor (Goss 1991; Rainnie 1989).

Such investigations move away from a simple association between size of firm and employment relations characteristics, and incorporate other factors such as the influence of product and labour market factors. For example, Goss (1991: 73) suggests that the nature of employment relations in small firms can be understood with regard to two related dimensions: first, the extent to which the employer is dependent on his or her employees, and vice versa; and, second, the degree to which employees have the capacity, individually or collectively, to challenge the power of their employer. Using these two dimensions, it is possible to produce four distinct categories that 'reveal the complexity and diversity of employment relations in small businesses' (Goss 1991: 86).

First, the term 'fraternalism' can be applied to situations where employers work with their employees and, principally because of tight labour market conditions, are highly dependent upon them. Such a situation 'gives all the appearance not only of industrial harmony but also of egalitarianism' (Goss 1991: 74), and is likely to be found in professional services where key employees enjoy generally favourable terms and conditions of employment.

Second, where 'paternalism' prevails there is a greater degree of difference between the employer and his or her employees than under fraternal arrangements, given the lower dependency of the former on the latter. Such 'differentiation of employer and employed is at the heart of paternalism' (Goss 1991: 76). At the same time, the employer attempts to generate among the workforce a sense of identification with the firm. The unequal nature of the employment relationship is legitimized by reference to the 'bonds of mutual duty and obligation' (Goss 1991: 77) held to exist between the employer and the workforce, and which frequently extend into the wider community.

Third, in situations where employers are relatively little dependent on their employees and where, partly as a consequence, the power of employees is somewhat constrained, 'benevolent autocracy' is the likely result, as in printing firms for example. Without scarce skills, workers are more vulnerable to the actions of their employer, though this is unlikely to take the form of crude coercion since characteristics of the paternalistic approach can be an effective means of securing managerial legitimacy.

Fourth, where the emphasis is on workers as a cost, to be hired and fired according to the vagaries of the market, with no preference on the part of employers for stability, and with vulnerable, often female workers from ethnic minorities, who are highly dependent upon the employer for paid work, then 'sweating' is commonplace. In such environments, clothing manufacturing for example, 'passive acquiescence' is often the only tactic workers can pursue (Goss 1991: 84).

There can be little doubt that the work of Rainnie (1989) and Goss (1991) has greatly improved our understanding of employment relations in small firms, though by their nature typologies do not capture the dynamism of employment relations. An important study of employment relations in small Asian-owned firms in the West Midlands clothing industry, Monder Ram's (1994) *Managing to Survive*, focuses on the dynamic nature of the employment relationship, conceptualizing it as a 'negotiated order'. Ram (1994) discovered that to portray employment relations in these firms as autocratic was far too simplistic an approach. Rather, even in an environment where one might expect sweating to prevail, managerial authority was bounded by the need to construct and reconstruct bargains with workers over the pace of work tasks, and the wages payable for undertaking them. Space for 'informal accommodations' was created by the workers' intricate knowledge of the production process, given the imperative for a steady flow of output. Thus 'workers were not passive in the face of authoritarian managements; they would endeavour to alter the terms of the effort bargain if they felt that they were not "fairly" rewarded' (Ram 1994: 122).

Further studies demonstrate the broader relevance of the finding that the employment relationship in small firms is 'socially negotiated', though 'bound by market constraints' (Marlow 2002: 39). In their examination of 'WaterCo', a company that supplies water facilities to offices and other locations, Dundon and Rollinson (2004: 91) found that even in the absence of a trade union, 'workers were not passive recipients of the conditions they experienced. Rather, they exerted influence in return and, in so doing, partially shaped how management regulated the employment relationship'. Nevertheless, while it is important to highlight the limits of managerial control, bounded as it is by product and labour market factors and also by the accommodations that are required to elicit workers' cooperation within the workplace, one should not overlook the superior power of the employer in the employment relationship (Marlow 2002), something that is more obvious in the absence of a trade union.

Studies show that small firm employers have a pronounced hostility towards trade unions, seeing them as a potential obstacle to their ability to run the business as they like (Rainnie 1989). One of the owner-managers interviewed in a study of manufacturing businesses in the East Midlands told the researcher: 'I'll never be told what to do by a bloody trade unionist; this is my business . . .' (Marlow 2002: 33). Owner-managers often prefer to keep their employment relations informal. Thus employment arrangements within the firm come to be based 'mainly on unwritten customs and the tacit understandings that arise out of the interactions of the parties at work' (Ram et al. 2001: 846). Informality does not just refer to the unconstrained use of prerogative by the employer in the absence of joint regulation or statutory provisions. Instead, it is a process, one that is influenced by the ongoing mutual accommodations reached by employers and employed, and the characteristics of the product and labour market environments (Ram et al. 2001).

There is some evidence of a growing degree of formality in small firm employment relations. The 1998 Workplace Employment Relations Survey revealed, for example, that 68 per cent of workplaces with between ten and ninety-nine employees reported the presence of an individual grievance procedure and 70 per cent reported the existence of a disciplinary procedure (Cully et al. 1999: 263). The existence of such procedures is one thing, how they are used is quite another. A study of small manufacturing firms revealed a pronounced reluctance on the part of owner-managers to use formal procedures since 'they would disrupt the informal negotiated nature of the employment relationship' (Marlow 2002: 34). There is also some evidence that ostensibly 'formal' procedures, such as in the area of discipline for example, can be used in a somewhat 'informal' way, since managers use them simply as a way of 'going through the motions', having already decided the outcome in advance (Earnshaw, Marchington, and Goodman 2000). This demonstrates that while managerial prerogative in small firms is restricted by the need to reach accommodations with employees, and by product and labour market factors, it nonetheless exists, and is pronounced. While employment relations in small firms may not be wholly autocratic, by no means can it be said to be harmonious.

SECTION SUMMARY AND FURTHER READING

- Employment relations in large non-union firms would appear to be characterized by the presence of sophisticated HRM policies that focus on the effective management of individual employment relationships. In practice, though, there are limits to the individualization of employment relations, and such an approach may mask an anti-union philosophy.

- The widely held view that employment relations in small firms is inherently harmonious has been challenged by a number of authoritative studies. These have revealed the diversity of employment relations, and the factors, such as product and labour markets, that contribute to it.

- While a trade union presence is rare within small firms, and owner-employers often display a marked antipathy to unions, even here there are limits to managerial prerogative. Many employment relations arrangements are the outcome of an ongoing process of bargaining between managers and workers, though this should not lead one to disregard the superior power of the employer in the employment relationship.

There is still a limited amount of work available on non-unionism. The assessment by Blyton and Turnbull (2004) is highly recommended. Dundon and Rollinson (2004) provide four case studies of non-union employment relations in practice. For small firms, the overview provided by Scase (1995, 2003) is a good starting point. Beyond this, the work of Al Rainnie (1989), David Goss (1991), and Monder Ram (1994) respectively has done much to improve our understanding of small-firm employment relations. For two good, shorter studies, see Moule (1998), and Marlow (2002).

5.5 Conceptualizing the management of employment relations

Historically, a defining feature of the management of the employment relationship was its pragmatic or opportunistic character, typified by a preference for relatively unsophisticated personnel practices (Gospel 1992). The growing influence of management as an employment relations actor, however, has generated an increasing amount of interest in how its role should be understood, mainly through a consideration of management 'style'. This 'implies the existence of a distinctive set of guiding principles, written or otherwise, which set parameters to and signposts for management action regarding the way employees are treated and how particular events are handled' (Purcell and Ahlstrand 1994: 177).

The starting point for most analyses of management style in employment relations is the distinction between 'unitary' and 'pluralist' approaches made in the 1960s by Alan Fox (Fox 1966). The unitary style is characterized by an assumption that the employer and employees share common goals, and that the presence of unions would bring conflict and disorder to an otherwise harmonious workplace environment. The pluralist approach accepts that employers and employees may have different interests in the employment relationship, and that unions have a legitimate role in articulating them. As we have already established, though, employers often recognize trade unions for pragmatic reasons, in response to particular circumstances, notably union power, rather than from a genuine belief in the virtues of a pluralist approach.

In the period since Alan Fox articulated the distinction between unitary and pluralist approaches, a number of writers have refined the concept of managerial style. It is evident that the nature of the relationship between management and unions in unionized organizations may vary. In some organizations, the retail giant Tesco for example, which has forged a 'partnership' agreement with the union (see Chapter 6), an explicitly cooperative relationship has been forged whereas in others, and here the Royal Mail comes to mind (Gall 2003c), relations are more adversarial.

5.5.1 Management style in non-union firms

Much of the recent interest in the concept of management style has centred on attempts to understand the diversity of employment relations approaches in non-union firms. By examining the extent to which employees are treated as individuals, and managed in a sophisticated way aimed at releasing their potential, Purcell and Ahlstrand (1994) were able to distinguish between three styles of management in non-union environments. Companies like IBM, which appear to use a range of personnel practices designed to promote the development of their employees as individuals, are typified by a 'sophisticated human relations' style. In 'paternalist' firms, however, of which Marks and Spencer was traditionally held up as a leading example, there tends to be a history 'of welfare-based personnel policies which seek to emphasize loyalty on the part of employees, often by means of reasonably generous fringe benefits and pay levels' (Purcell and Ahlstrand 1994: 180). 'Traditional' firms follow a 'cost minimization' approach in which employees are essentially treated as commodities to be hired, and then discarded, according to the dictates of the market.

How appropriate is it to classify the management style in non-union firms in this way given the gap that exists, for example, between the espoused rhetoric of sophisticated HRM and the often less benign reality? In 'Ministeel', elements of a sophisticated human relations approach co-existed with more traditional coercive methods of managing the employment relationship (Bacon 1999). Styles of management should perhaps be seen, then, as characteristic tendencies, rather than as mutually exclusive approaches (Edwards 1987).

An alternative way of classifying non-union firms has been used in a study of new workplaces. The researchers examined whether or not firms had a clear HRM strategy, and also the take up of HRM practices. From this, they were able to identify four management approaches: 'good' firms, those which espoused a clear HRM strategy and made extensive use of a range of HRM practices; firms with no HRM strategy and a low uptake of HRM practices were the 'bad face of non-unionism'; the 'lucky' firms were those that had no HRM strategy but, by chance, operated a large number of HRM practices; 'ugly' firms had a clear strategy but made little use of HRM practices and, being 'efficiency driven', must be 'bleak environments in which to work' (Guest and Hoque 1994).

Although it is claimed that the 'good' firms, those that have a clear HRM strategy and make use of a wide range of supporting practices, and which were found to be the most common type, have better performance outcomes (Guest and Hoque 1994), there are a number of problems with this method of classifying non-union firms. For one thing, it comes from a very limited sample of firms in the manufacturing sector. Moreover, it is entirely based on the responses of managers (Kelly 1998), informants who are often unreliable when it comes to reporting workplace developments. It is unwise to assume that the reality of employment relations matches up with managerial rhetoric (Turnbull and Wass 1998).

5.5.2 Typologies of management style: a critique

Typologies have their uses in employment relations, to capture the diversity of small firms for example (Goss 1991), but they tend to present a rather static picture of employment relations and, in respect of the management of the employment relationship, over-emphasize the degree of consistency evident in managerial approaches. Two features of the employment relationship constrain the capacity of managers to develop consistent approaches in respect of the management of labour.

First, managers need to exercise control over employees while at the same time gaining their cooperation. Understandably, the ways in which managements exert control over their employees have been a longstanding feature of workplace studies. For example, a distinction has been made between two types of managerial control strategy: 'direct control', in which managers closely regulate and supervise the activities of workers; and 'responsible autonomy', where control is exercised by deliberately ceding to workers some degree of discretion over how they carry out their work tasks (Friedman 1977). In order to sustain management prerogative, organizations have been compelled to design ever more sophisticated techniques; the growth of formal personnel policies and procedures can be seen as an attempt to secure 'bureaucratic control' (Edwards 1979). The rise of HRM, given the extent to which it is concerned with securing organizational culture change, is, in some interpretations, a more robust and, in so far as it is concerned with manipulating the meaning employees attach to their work, a more insidious way of securing managerial control (Willmott 1993).

In service industries, where the relationship between the employee and the customer is a key source of competitive advantage, managers have been obliged to develop novel techniques in an attempt to exercise control (see Box 5.4). This may, for example, involve using customers themselves (Korczynski 2002). Some companies use fake, or 'mock', customers. Their job is to establish that employees are fulfilling their role in the prescribed manner while pretending to be consumers (Fuller and Smith 1991). In some sectors, most famously the airline industry, but also in call centres, companies have attempted to control the operation of the service encounter through the manipulation of workers' feelings or emotions (Hochschild 1983; S. Taylor 1998). Delta Airlines, for example, used wide-ranging and sophisticated training methods to ensure that its cabin crew acted appropriately, in particular by smiling, in all of their interactions with customers. Thus 'the emotional style of offering the service is part of the service itself' (Hochschild 1983: 5).

Managerial efforts to secure employee compliance in these ways are, however, always going to be frustrated and thus incomplete. The nature of the employment relationship as a wage-work bargain invariably limits the scope of managerial prerogative, and also provides workers with opportunities to challenge managerial control. Even in service industries, where workers' conduct is often highly prescribed, there is generally sufficient space for workers to behave in ways that do not accord with management expectations (Korczynski 2002). Therefore in understanding how the employment relationship is managed, it is important not to over-simplify by concentrating solely on managerial attempts to secure control (Hyman 1987; Storey 1985).

BOX 5.4 TIPPING AS A SOURCE OF MANAGEMENT CONTROL?

In some parts of the economy, restaurants for example, customer tips, as part of the 'total reward system' for front-line customer service staff, are viewed as an important component of workers' remuneration since they offset low rates of basic pay (Mars and Mitchell 1976). The practice of tipping, moreover, particularly where it has been 'institutionalized', that is become a standard and accepted feature of workplace life, can serve to enhance managerial control of customer service workers, such as waiting staff for example. In a study of the 'Central Restaurant Group', Ogbonna and Harris (2002: 730–1) noted that the use of tipping was an 'integral part of reward', and had 'a long history in the organization', a reflection of its founder's belief that 'the best way to generate enthusiasm, loyalty and the required customer service behaviour from front-line staff was in encouraging them to keep their own tips'. Three main reasons underpinned the institutionalization of tipping in Central Restaurant Group. First, as a motivational tool it helped to improve employees' performance. Second, it allowed the company to pay a low basic wage, helping to keep labour costs down. Third, it enabled management to maintain control, albeit indirectly, over employee behaviour during the customer service encounter.

The institutionalization of tipping in Central Restaurant Group served to reinforce managerial control over employee behaviour in three ways. First, competition for tips encouraged an ethos of self-interest among the workforce, and thus impeded the development a collective consciousness. Second, by keeping basic pay low managers fostered among the waiting staff a sense of dependency on the tips. Third, the company used a number of means, including communications processes, to promote its approach to tipping. Since tips comprised a substantial proportion of their earnings, workers were, understandably, supportive of the Central Restaurant Group's approach. Many gave it as the main reason for working there. Moreover, union attempts to represent them came to nothing after senior management threatened to do away with tipped income if workers agreed to be unionized. Nevertheless, there was some dissatisfaction among workers over the behaviours it was felt necessary to produce in order to receive tips. Managers sometimes encouraged flirting, a form of potentially exploitative sexual labour, as a means of keeping customers happy. Ogbonna and Harris (2002: 742) suggest that such activity is a 'degrading and debasing' feature of front-line customer service work, and that workers feel obliged to 'prostitute' themselves in exchange for the possibility of additional tipped income. They conclude, however, that despite the high level of management manipulation inherent in the institutionalization of tipping, and its potentially exploitative implications, workers nonetheless used the system for their own ends. They were not the passive dupes of managers, but rational and calculative actors aware of what they needed to do to maximize their earnings.

In order to realize the efficient production or delivery of goods and services, managers must secure a degree of legitimacy, or consent, among those they manage (Legge 2005), something that, according to some interpretations, may also be viewed as means of control (Burawoy 1979). Nevertheless, 'management strategy is always a blend of consent and coercion, though the nature of that blend varies between companies and between the various levels within each company hierarchy' (Fox 1985b: 66). In Britain, consent was traditionally secured by means *of ad hoc* accommodations with trade unions (Hyman 2003). Yet even in non-union environments, managers must operate in such a way as to gain the cooperation of, and thus secure legitimacy among, those they manage, as was evident in the firms studied by Ram (1994). Other studies demonstrate how workers, collectively, exert an influence over the way in which employment relations is managed even in the absence of a trade union (Dundon and Rollinson 2004; McLoughlin and Gourlay 1994). Typologies of management style, therefore, cannot adequately capture the complexity of how employment relations is managed in practice (Dundon and Rollinson 2004).

A second factor that hinders managerial consistency concerns the tension that is created by the dual function of labour in a capitalist market economy. On the one hand, employees, as the firm's human resources, are central to the realization of corporate objectives, and thus improvements in their loyalty, motivation, and commitment are essential if the organization is to be financially successful. Managers, then, are obliged to design and implement sophisticated and potentially costly personnel techniques in order to secure the dedication of their employees; in other words to foster a sense of dependency. On the other hand, however, since labour costs often comprise a large proportion of an organization's budget, the workforce often bears the brunt of efforts to reduce expenditure. Moreover, the nature of the capitalist market economy means that firms constantly search out cheaper ways of producing goods and delivering services (Hyman 1975), something that makes employees inherently disposable. A study of employment relations in Esso's oil refinery at Fawley, for example, highlighted the tension that existed between the imperative to cut labour costs as a means of enhancing productivity, something that involved workforce reductions, and the need to secure greater employee commitment as a means of generating flexibility (Ahlstrand 1990). Thus the management of labour in a capitalist economy is beset by contradiction (Legge 2005). Managements have to reconcile two seemingly conflicting interests, 'to cut costs to the bone and yet at the same time promote the security, autonomy and teamwork, which are the conditions for innovation into new markets, products and services' (Sisson and Storey 2000: 29).

5.5.3 Managing employment relations in a market economy

Financial imperatives, and the need constantly to keep labour costs under control, are a major obstacle to the development of a sophisticated HRM approach within firms operating in Britain. The case of Hewlett-Packard, a firm with an espoused sophisticated HRM approach, is instructive. Intense competitive pressures compelled the firm to reduce its workforce, resulting in increased pressure and lower morale among those who remained. Inevitably, such feelings influenced the perceptions and behaviour of employees, thus ensuring that HRM techniques were rendered less effective (Truss 2001).

The dominance of short-term pressures on companies to improve their financial performance is particularly acute in Anglo-Saxon economies such as Britain (see Chapter 2) and, given that it is associated with new forms of accounting and techniques of financial control, has been exacerbated by the widespread popularity of the multi-divisional organizational structure (Batstone 1988; Marginson et al. 1988). A study of British manufacturing firms revealed the importance of finance-based forms of control and how this encouraged a particular form of labour flexibility, one founded upon the intensive use of relatively unskilled workers, rather than one which is contingent upon use of a better developed, more committed workforce (Ackroyd and Proctor 1998). Thus the nature of the capitalist market economy, reinforced by the widespread adoption of tight financial and accounting controls in British companies, is a key obstacle to the development of a high-commitment management approach.

Two contradictions, then, the need to exercise control over employees as well as to secure their consent and cooperation, and the desirability of treating employees as resources to be developed and the obligation to consider them as commodities to be discarded should it be necessary, are inherent features of the way in which employment relations is managed in capitalist market economies. They pose immense challenges to organizations which are keen to manage employment relations in a long-term, purposive, or 'strategic' way (Hyman 1987). In Chapter 1, we discussed the unsophisticated way in which employment relations was traditionally managed in Britain, influenced, as it was, by certain characteristics of the product and labour market environment (Gospel 1992). The contradictions in the management of the employment relationship we have highlighted here, though, point to the inevitability of opportunism. For Hyman (1987: 30), 'there is no "one best way" of managing these contradictions, only different routes to partial failure'. In other words, management can never enjoy complete control over employment relations, and the results of their interventions may differ substantially from the intended outcomes.

■ CONCLUSION

What, then, are the salient aspects of the way in which contemporary employment relations is managed? Clearly, pressures to sustain and expand the scope of managerial prerogative, and thus diminish the influence of trade unions, are prevalent features. Although instances of outright union derecognition were relatively uncommon, employers nonetheless took advantage of the more favourable economic and political climate of the 1980s and 1990s to challenge the influence of trade unions. Among newly established workplaces, union recognition was rare; whereas in organizations where unions did retain a formal presence, managers attempted to erode their influence, through the development of direct communications techniques for example. The responses of some employers to the introduction of the statutory recognition procedure demonstrates the persistence of anti-union values.

In so far as they represent a reinforcement of managerial authority, albeit within a benign rhetoric in which commitment and flexibility are proclaimed, the managerial techniques associated with the rise of HRM have further challenged the influence of the trade unions. The activities of those non-union firms that espouse a sophisticated HRM approach, moreover, reveal them to be often concerned with preventing a union presence from becoming established, something that makes the distinction between 'non-unionism' and 'anti-unionism' approaches difficult to uphold in practice (Blyton and Turnbull 2004).

Although attempts to expand the scope of managerial prerogative is a defining feature of the way in which employment relations is managed, the very nature of the employment relationship, as a 'negotiated order', means that it is inevitably limited in practice. In order to realize the efficient production of goods and services, managers must only seek to exercise control over their employees, but are also compelled to win their consent and cooperation. Even within small, non-union work-places, where 'passive acquiescence' is all that might be expected from employees (Goss 1991), employers are obliged to secure a degree of legitimacy from them in order to operate efficiently. Thus the scope of managerial prerogative is inherently limited by the nature of the employment relationship as a wage-work bargain.

The need to exercise control over employees, as well as gain their cooperation, is an important contradictory feature of the management of employment relations. As such, it militates against consistency in managerial interventions, making the elaboration of a purposive, or strategic, approach difficult to pursue in practice. This is reinforced by a further contradictory feature of the way in which the employment relationship is managed in capitalist market economies, that which exists between the desirability of treating employees as resources, whose skill, commitment and dedication contribute to raising organizational performance, and the need to consider them as commodities, to be discarded should competitive pressures dictate it.

These contradictions render consistency in managerial approaches, such as the pursuit of HRM, difficult to achieve in practice. An espoused policy goal of high commitment may be undermined by the effects of more intense competitive pressures, leading to job cuts, insecurity, and a lowering of employee morale. Despite a more favourable climate, then, and the dramatic decline of trade unionism, it is clear that there has been no real transformation in the way in which employment relations is managed in contemporary Britain.

■ ASSIGNMENT AND DISCUSSION QUESTIONS

1. Why and how have employers been able to weaken the influence of trade unions?

2. Discuss the view that employers should not be obliged to recognize a trade union under any circumstances.

3. In theory, why might 'high-commitment practices' lead to improved business performance? What are the practical obstacles?

4. Do you agree with the view that in non-union firms management practices are aimed at preventing unions from gaining a foothold by providing a substitute for the role of a trade union? Why?

5. Why is it a mistake to argue that employment relations in small firms is either inherently harmonious, or characterized by autocracy, and poor pay and conditions?

6. What arguments have been put forward to support the view that employers cannot take a longer-term, strategic approach to the management of employment relations? Explain whether you agree or disagree with these arguments.

■ WEBSITE MATERIALS

Visit the companion web site to this book for interesting and updated material at
www.oup.com/booksites/busecon/business

■ **CHAPTER CASE STUDY**

Human resource management and the hotel industry

Human Resource Management (HRM) is claimed to offer organizations a new and improved approach to the management of the employment relationship. Through its 'key levers' of sophisticated recruitment and selection techniques, the appraisal of employees' performance linked to individualized payment strategies, and communication with workers, it offers a route to enhanced employee commitment to the organization's business objectives. The focus of HRM on delivering improved quality would seem to be particularly relevant to sectors such as the hotel industry that claim to rely on good customer service by employees as a means of securing competitive advantage.

Studies undertaken in the hotel sector paint very different pictures of the extent to which HRM, and its associated focus on techniques that enhance employee commitment, has replaced the traditional emphasis on managerial and cost control in the industry. Hoque (1999) compared large hotel companies with similar sized manufacturing firms, where most research on the use of HRM has been undertaken, to identify whether any differences existed between them on the use of HRM. Based upon managers' replies to questionnaires, he notes a significant adoption by hotel companies of the principles of HRM. More of them, compared to manufacturing businesses, had developed a formal HR strategy that was integrated with their business strategy. Moreover, the key levers of HRM themselves were integrated with each other such that there was a clear link between, for example, performance appraisal and reward systems. Furthermore, the use of HR practices to support the strategy, such as selection criteria, terms and conditions, training, consultation, and communication, were as likely, and, in some cases, more likely to be found among hotel companies than in manufacturing firms.

Other studies, however, suggest a different reality. That by Adam-Smith, Norris, and Williams (2003) covered both large hotels, often part of a group, and smaller businesses, and examined the views not only of managers, but also the experience of workers in the industry. The researchers identified a largely reactive approach to the management of labour, aimed at meeting customer demands while also minimizing costs. Workers suffered from work intensification through the need to cover staff shortages, and through having to switch to other duties as required by managers. There was little evidence of flexibility derived from investment in training to multi-skill workers. Few organizations had introduced merit pay based upon employee performance: rather, most payment systems were unsophisticated. Pay enhancements, for example, to train new employees or to undertake some minor supervisory responsibilities, were often introduced in an *ad hoc* manner, rather than as the result of a planned employment strategy. The management of employment relations in many hotels is characterized by a considerable degree of informality rather than by strategic intent.

Case discussion questions

1. Why might the HRM approach to managing the employment relationship be attractive to hotel companies?

2. What factors might inhibit its take-up in such firms?

CHAPTER 6

Representation at work

CHAPTER OBJECTIVES

The main objectives of this chapter are to:

- examine the ways in which trade unions represent the interests of workers
- consider the effectiveness of non-union arrangements for the representation of workers' interests
- assess the implications for employers and trade unions of 'partnership agreements'
- evaluate the extent to which adoption of the organizing unionism model could enhance workers' interests

---

6.1 Introduction

In this chapter, we examine how the interests of workers are represented. In Britain, workers have traditionally had their interests represented by means of the 'single channel' of trade unionism. However, declining unionization levels have reduced the extent to which workers enjoy effective representation of their interests independent from their employer. In order to understand developments in the representation of workers, we need to consider both how unions have sought to respond to the decline in membership, and alternative forms of worker representation.

What, though, are workers' interests? How can they be defined? In order for a union, or indeed any body, to represent the concerns of workers it helps to know what they are. This may seem obvious; surely workers want higher pay? But non-economic issues, such as job security for example, may sometimes be an equally, if not more important, demand. The concept of workers' 'interests' is extremely ambiguous, incorporating a potentially diverse and complex set of issues. Moreover, is it in the interest of workers to challenge, or to cooperate with, their employers? While there is always the potential for conflicting interests in the employment relationship, workers also have a concern with ensuring that their employer is successful, since their job and wages depend on it (Kelly 1998). When reading this chapter, then, it is important to recognize that workers' interests are rarely unambiguous.

6.2 Trade unions, worker representation, and the rise of a 'representation gap'

In Chapter 1, we provided an overview of the development of trade unions in Britain and an outline of their principal functions. In Chapter 3, we considered the nature of union government, and assessed the various ways in which the concept of union democracy can be understood. Here, we examine how trade unions represent the interests of workers, demonstrate the extent of union decline in Britain, and assess the factors that contributed to it.

6.2.1 Trade unions and the representation of workers' interests

There are four main ways in which trade unions represent the interests of workers. First, unions insure workers against difficulties and problems that arise during the course of their working lives. In Chapter 1, we observed that the provision of friendly benefits was a major function of the early unions of skilled workers (Webb and Webb 1920a). During the twentieth century, the importance of friendly benefits as a union function declined markedly, not just because collective bargaining became the principal way in which unions sought to regulate the employment relationship, but also because the state's role in providing welfare benefits, like unemployment assistance for example, expanded considerably.

Nevertheless, one of the defining features of union organization is that it reflects the wishes of workers collectively to insure, or protect, themselves against problems at work. This was evident from a 1990s study of public sector trade unionism in the north-east of England undertaken by one of this book's authors. Organizational restructuring in the health service and local government generated a more assertive style of management, increased pressure on employees, and produced a climate of job insecurity. Unsurprisingly, then, the need for protection at work was an important determinant of union membership. According to one member: 'It is a necessity to be a union member in today's economic climate as a safeguard against employers attempting hardline proposals which may be unreasonable – a safeguard against hardline tactics'. While union membership may be predicated on workers' demands for insurance against individual problems at work, it is something that is achievable only through robust collective organization (Williams 1997).

The second way in which unions represent the interests of workers is by bargaining on their behalf with managers over pay and other terms and conditions of employment. We considered the nature and development of collective bargaining in Chapter 1. Importantly, collective bargaining is not just an economic process, concerned with setting the terms on which workers are hired, but it is also a political activity since it enables workers, through their union representatives, to influence, and thus regulate jointly with managers, workplace decision-making (Flanders 1975). Contemporary trends in collective bargaining activity are discussed in Chapter 7.

In our introduction to the role of the unions in Chapter 1, we traced the evolution of the shop steward role in British employment relations. The third way in which unions represent the interests of workers concerns the activities of stewards and workplace union representatives. They are generally the first point of contact for union members, and act to advocate their interests to managers, supporting and standing up for them in the work-place (Coates and Topham 1980). One problem is that stewards are essentially concerned with representing the (sometimes narrow and sectional) interests of their own members, hindering union efforts to expand their membership base. Moreover, the way in which stewards represent their members' interests is often shaped by their assumptions about the kinds of issue that are legitimate for union action. Munro's (1999) study of shop steward organization among ancillary staff in the health service demonstrates the influence of a relatively narrow 'trade union agenda' dominated by the concerns of male workers. This affects stewards' behaviour in that they ignore issues of particular importance to women workers, such as childcare provision for example.

Fourth, unions do not just represent the interests of their members in the workplace, but also in the broader political arena. Indeed, by seeking to advance the interests of workers in general, and not just those of their members, unions act as a 'sword of justice' (Flanders 1975), by campaigning for effective laws governing employment rights for example. In Chapter 3, we considered the influence of unions in the Labour party. The enactment of the National Minimum Wage in 1999 (see Chapter 7), the culmination of a successful campaign run within the party by some trade unions to secure a manifesto commitment to introduce it, demonstrates how unions can use political channels to advance workers' interests. Unions have increasingly looked to alternative, broader ways of representing workers' interests politically, other than through the Labour party. For example, in the 1990s the union movement campaigned to improve the rights and employment conditions of mostly non-unionized, part-time workers (Heery 1998b).

6.2.2 Declining unionization in Britain and the 'representation gap'

While trade unionism has traditionally constituted the 'single channel' by which workers have had their interests represented in Britain, declining levels of unionization have stimulated discussion about the extent to which people enjoy effective representation at work. During the 1980s and 1990s, trade union membership fell by more than 5 million; by 2000, fewer than 30 per cent of British workers were union members. While the presence of a trade union does not guarantee that workers will have effective representation, the absence of the protection that a union can provide has diminished the extent of their 'representation security' (Burchell, Ladipo, and Wilkinson 2002). While there are signs that the decline in union membership may have bottomed out, some two-thirds of workers in Britain have no access to independent means of interest representation.

Although the decline in the level of union membership has attracted much attention, it has to be seen in the context of the broader diminution of joint regulation as a means of regulating the workplace. In Chapter 5, for example, we considered the falling incidence of union recognition during the 1980s and 1990s. The decline in the level of collective bargaining coverage is discussed in Chapter 7. Union workplace organization has also been rendered less effective by the increased preference of managers to by-pass shop stewards, and to communicate with workers directly (Marchington and Parker 1990; Storey 1992). In 1980, union representatives were present in 53 per cent of workplaces. By 1998, it was only a third (Millward, Bryson, and Forth 2000). Successive Conservative governments reduced the influence of the unions over the formulation of public policy (Heery 1998c).

Table 6.1 Trade union membership and density in Great Britain 1980–2003

	Union membership	Density (%)
1980	12,239,000	54.5
1985	10,282,000	49.0
1990	8,835,000	38.1
1995	7,193,000	28.9
2000	7,153,000	27.1
2003	7,136,000	26.4

Employees in employment.

Sources: Palmer, Grainger, and Fitzner (2004); Waddington (2003b)

Although the 1997 Labour government partly restored the trade unionism's 'insider' status, the unions were kept at a distance, treated as simply another pressure group among many rather than as a partner in the labour movement (McIlroy 2000a).

Nevertheless, membership decline is perhaps the starkest indication of the collapse of the union movement's fortunes (see Table 6.1). In 1979, there were over 12.5 million union members in Britain, some 53 per cent of the workforce. By the late 1990s, membership had fallen to just 7 million, meaning that fewer than 30 per cent of employees were union members (Waddington 2003b). What caused this decline? Six factors are considered here.

First, it is sometimes suggested that social change, in particular the diminution of class as a source of social identity, and the rise of an ethos of individualism, has eroded the collectivism that traditionally underpinned people's motivation to unionize (Bassett and Cave 1993). Yet such a view is based on a profound misunderstanding of the basis of trade unionism. In particular, it ignores the large extent to which union practice has always been informed by a complex mix of individualistic and collective orientations. Moreover, survey data suggest that collective reasons are important in influencing workers' decisions to join unions (Waddington and Whitston 1997).

A second, more persuasive explanation for union membership decline is that it has been caused by the changing composition of employment in Britain. The compositional approach asserts that, since the 1980s, employment has been contracting in areas where unions are strong and increasing in areas where unions are weak. Thus the number of full-time, male-dominated jobs in large manufacturing enterprises, where unionization tends to be commonplace, has dwindled considerably. Most employment growth has been in the private services sector, where jobs are often held by women on a part-time basis, and where unions are relatively weak. The main problem with the compositional approach, though, is that many of the trends that supposedly weaken trade unionism, such as increasing levels of employment in the service sector for example, or the rise in the number of part-time jobs, existed in the 1970s when union membership grew (Metcalf 1991). Moreover, the trend towards so-called flexible employment is much exaggerated, as we saw in Chapter 2, and workers in part-time jobs are by no means inimical to unionization (Walters 2002).

Third, to what extent have economic factors, in particular the incidence of unemployment, affected the level of union membership in Britain? During the early 1980s, the sharp fall in unionization coincided with a dramatic increase in unemployment. Not only are unemployed workers unlikely to uphold their union membership, but those still in employment may be wary of unionization if it is perceived as jeopardizing their jobs. The problem with this explanation for union membership decline, however, is that it continued, albeit at a slower rate, during the late 1980s, when employment levels were rising (Metcalf 1991). This suggests that there is no straightforward relationship between the incidence of unemployment and the overall level of union membership (Waddington 2003b).

Fourth, while the changing composition of employment has clearly contributed to union membership decline (note the sharp fall in the level of unionization in the early 1980s when millions of jobs were lost in manufacturing industry for example (see Table 6.1)), other factors were also influential, not least increased employer hostility. In Chapter 5, we considered the efforts managers made to avoid unions entirely, particularly in new workplaces, or, where this was not feasible, to weaken their influence by using techniques associated with human resource management, for example.

The capacity of managers to undermine union power, though, was underpinned by a fifth factor, the hostility directed by successive Conservative governments towards the trade unions – what Waddington (2003b) calls a 'neo-liberal assault' on trade unionism. We considered the nature of Conservative policy on employment relations in Chapter 3. Although some writers argue that the anti-union legislation enacted by the Conservatives was largely responsible for union membership decline during the 1980s (Freeman and Pelletier 1990), much of it occurred before the changes in the law could take effect. The anti-union laws were introduced more easily because the unions had already been weakened by other factors (Waddington 1992, 2003b). Nevertheless, the Conservatives established a political climate that helped to undermine the legitimacy of the unions, giving managers more confidence to exclude them from workplaces. Trade unionism was rendered less effective, making union membership less attractive to workers. Thus 'the impact, either directly or indirectly, of the Conservative political project had a wide-ranging influence on the decline in unionization' (Waddington 2003b: 219).

The sixth and final factor we need to consider concerns the activities of the unions themselves. Much of the decline in the level of unionization can be attributed to the failure of unions to organize in new workplaces, and thus gain recognition from employers in expanding areas of the economy (Machin 2000). Clearly, the hostile industrial and political climate impeded the ability of the unions to expand their constituencies. But the unions themselves were reluctant to embark on vigorous recruitment and organizing drives, for reasons we will discuss later on in this chapter. Between the mid-1980s and mid-1990s, union efforts at dealing with the membership crisis were largely focused on improving individual membership benefits, or creating economies of scales through mergers (Heery 1996; Willman 1989), not with organizing new recruits.

In summary, then, the overall fall in the level of union membership during the 1980s and 1990s was the result of a complex combination of factors (Waddington 2003b). Although compositional changes and increasing unemployment levels caused a dramatic fall in union membership during the early 1980s, by the latter part of that decade the effects of the Conservative's legislative changes were beginning to take effect, fostering a climate within which the exercise of managerial prerogative was strengthened, and union confidence undermined.

Since the late 1990s, the decline in the overall level of trade union membership has stabilized, although the proportion of employees who are union members has still fallen slightly; growth in the numbers in employment has outstripped the minor increase in union membership (see Palmer, Grainger, and Fitzner 2004). What has caused the fall in trade union membership to level off? Clearly, the Labour governments offered a less hostile public policy climate than their Conservative predecessors, even if, as we saw in Chapter 3, it was far from being pro-union. Employment growth is an additional factor. In particular, there has been a marked increase in the number of new jobs in the public services, a sector where the level of unionization is robust. Moreover, as we see later on in this chapter, some unions are devoting more resources to organizing workers.

Nevertheless, the overall level of union membership is at its lowest level since the late 1930s (Waddington 2003b). This has prompted a considerable amount of interest in the implications for workers' interests and how they are represented. The diminution of trade unionism has, in some interpretations, generated a 'representation gap' (Towers 1997). Although the statutory union recognition procedure has generated an increase in the number of recognition agreements (see Chapter 5), its overall importance should not be overstated. In the rest of this chapter, we consider the implications for worker representation of three developments in contemporary employment relations, and whether or not they are likely to close the representation gap: the evolution of non-union systems of employee representation, including works councils; the increasing number of partnership agreements between employers and unions; and the articulation of an organizing model of trade unionism.

SECTION SUMMARY AND FURTHER READING

- Trade unions represent the interests of workers by providing them with protection, or insurance, against problems that affect them at work, bargaining collectively with employers on their behalf, acting as a workplace advocate, and in the broader, political arena.

- Since the 1970s, there has been a marked fall in the overall level of trade union membership in Britain. While the outcome of a combination of factors, including the changing composition of employment and employer policies of union exclusion, the hostile anti-union policy climate propagated by Conservative governments was a prominent cause of union decline.

- While the fall in overall union membership is perhaps the starkest dimension of union decline, it is just one aspect of the broader diminution of union power, something that also includes the contraction of collective bargaining coverage and dwindling numbers of workplace union representatives. The result has been a growing 'representation gap' across British workplaces.

For an overview of union membership trends and the factors that influence them, see Waddington (2003b). The Department of Trade and Industry produces an annual study of trade union membership data (see Palmer, Grainger, and Fitzner 2004). For a study of the rise of the representation gap in Britain and the United States, see Towers (1997).

6.3 Non-union forms of employee representation

The scale of the crisis of employee representation in Britain has raised questions about whether the 'single channel' of trade unionism and collective bargaining necessarily guarantees workers influence over their working lives (Frege 2002; Rogers and Streeck 1995). Would a system of works councils, as is found in many European countries, be an effective alternative? The German 'dual system' of employee representation (see Box 6.1), based on the formal separation of collective bargaining from participation rights, has received a considerable amount of attention as a result (Beaumont 1995; Towers 1997). While not going so far as to advocate the introduction of works councils, by exploring various ways in which employee representation could be improved in non-union companies, during the 1990s the Trades Union Congress (TUC) began to acknowledge, in the face some internal opposition, that the British union movement's previous commitment to the 'single channel' of trade union representation was no longer viable (Gospel and Willman 2003; Hyman 1996; TUC 1995).

Since then, the hitherto dominant 'single channel' model has increasingly come to be eroded in Britain largely because of the need to comply with European Union (EU) directives in the area of information and consultation rights for workers. In this section,

---

BOX 6.1 THE SYSTEM OF WORKS COUNCILS IN GERMANY

Collective bargaining in Germany is largely conducted at multi-employer level between trade unions and employers' associations. Works councils, however, which can be established in all private sector companies with five or more employees and which enjoy specific rights to information, consultation, and codetermination, are technically independent from the unions. Codetermination, which in effect allows the works council the right to reject management proposals, applies to 'social' issues, including payment methods, overtime arrangements, and the allocation of working hours. Works councils have information and consultation rights over matters pertaining to, among other things, the working environment, job design, and new technology; and information rights on financial issues (Jacobi, Keller, and Müller-Jentsch 1998: 210; Müller-Jentsch 1995: 58–9). Works councillors are elected by the entire workforce, have a term of office of four years, and are obliged by law to cooperate with management 'in a spirit of mutual trust' for the benefit of employees and the establishment. While the powers of works councils should not be overstated, their existence places considerable limits on the ability of managers unilaterally to reform working conditions (Hyman 1996: 71). Nevertheless, their formal separation notwithstanding, there is a strong 'mutual dependence' between the unions and the works councils (Jacobi, Keller, and Müller-Jentsch 1998: 212; Müller-Jentsch 1995). Moreover, despite being prohibited from being involved in collective bargaining, in some instances works councils negotiate improvements to industry-level collective agreements (Tüselmann and Heise 2000).

then, we assess the phenomenon of non-union of employee representation in Britain, explain why it is such a relevant contemporary topic, and consider the nature and significance of European Works Councils (EWCs), cross-border arrangements for employee information and consultation in multinational companies operating in Europe.

6.3.1 Factors influencing the development of non-union forms of employee representation in Britain

There is nothing new about non-union systems of employee representation. In Chapter 1 we examined the nature and history of joint consultation arrangements in Britain and acknowledged that they can exist in unionized and non-unionized firms alike. Nevertheless, it appears that many employers are increasingly looking to establish some kind of 'company council' machinery through which they can inform and consult with employee representatives. Much of this new interest appears to have been generated among firms without union recognition, despite evidence that only about one-fifth of private sector non-union workplaces have some kind of joint consultation system in place (Cully et al. 1999: 224).

What is driving this concern? There is some evidence that information and consultation arrangements have been developed as a means of realizing managerial objectives. It is thought that where employees have some influence, or 'voice', over decisions that affect them at work, then this can generate positive business benefits. For example, the Pizza Express chain of restaurants established an employee forum in the aftermath of a damaging dispute concerning its failure to comply with the National Minimum Wage regulations governing tips. Management considered that a more open, transparent, and rigorous system of communications could be used to demonstrate to staff that Pizza Express was in fact a decent employer and enhance business performance (Cooper 2001; IDS 2002).

The extent to which such a 'business case' enables employees to have their interests adequately represented at work is questionable, however. It runs counter to the long-established assumption that 'the basis for employee participation lies in employee rights to have their views and interests taken into account in managerial decision-making; that is, the fundamental point of employee participation is to shape employer rather than employee attitudes and behaviours' (Hall and Terry 2004: 216). The outcome of employee representation arrangements that are driven primarily by a desire to improve organizational performance is a highly restricted form of employee voice, over which management enjoy significant control (Hall and Terry 2004).

Moreover, union avoidance is generally a more important motivation to develop a system of non-union employee representation. In Britain, the enthusiasm of non-union companies for systems of collective employee representation is partly linked to the introduction of the statutory union recognition procedure discussed in Chapter 5, and is best understood as an attempt to avoid unionization. Gall and McKay (2001: 103) note that 'consultative' or 'representative' forums are more commonplace in situations where the employer is keen to resist a union presence. The system of employee 'advocates' at the Body Shop, for example, was established in the context of a recognition campaign by the Transport and General Workers' Union (TGWU). At 'Aeroparts', the aerospace company studied by Lloyd (2001: 323), an Employee Council was established 'explicitly as a mechanism for union substitution', after the trade unions there were derecognized following a change in company ownership. Although the principal stated objective of the 'employee forum' at Pizza Express was to improve internal communications, and thus increase employee commitment, it is evident that managers were also concerned that allowing employee grievances to go unvoiced might have provided a union with an opportunity to establish a presence.

However, EU legislation is perhaps the most important factor that has influenced the growth of non-union forms of employee representation. In 1994, the European Court of Justice ruled that legislation obliging employers to inform and consult with employee representatives on certain specific issues, when proposing to undertake a major redundancy exercise for example, applied not just to firms that recognized trade unions, as the then Conservative government had tried to insist, but also to those that did not (Hall and Terry 2004). Thus non-union firms that plan to make twenty or more redundancies over a three-month period are obliged to inform and consult with elected representatives of the workforce (see Hall and Edwards 1999). Further EU-derived legislation provides non-union employers with an incentive to establish arrangements that enable them to inform and consult with elected employee representatives.

Regulations introduced in 1996 oblige employers to inform and consult with their staff in the area of health and safety. Although in this case, the legislation permits them to consult with employees directly, and not necessarily indirectly through a system of elected representatives, it nonetheless appears to have generated an increase in formal consultation arrangements for health and safety in small, non-union workplaces (Millward, Bryson, and Forth 2000: 117). The 1998 Working Time Regulations (see Chapter 7) established the 'workforce agreement' concept, something that was also a feature of later legislation on parental leave (see Chapter 4). Workforce agreements 'are intended to offer employers without union recognition agreements the same flexibility in the application of the Regulations as that available through collective agreements with trade unions' (Hall and Terry 2004: 209).

In public policy terms these developments are rather significant (Dickens and Hall 2003; Hall and Edwards 1999). For one thing, under certain circumstances employers are now obliged to establish formal information and consultation arrangements, involving elected employee representatives, a marked shift in emphasis away from the previously voluntarist approach. Second, although 'piecemeal' and 'issue-specific' (Dickens and Hall 2003), the legislation nonetheless starts to erode the hitherto dominant single-channel system of employee representation in Britain. In summary, then, 'in terms of the law and practice Britain has moved decisively down a multi-channel road, but has been left with a fragmented system of information, consultation and representation' (Gospel and Willman 2003: 148).

6.3.2 Non-union systems of employee representation: a lack of an effective voice?

Research studies demonstrate that non-union systems of employee representation, such as company councils, are generally ineffective at representing employees' interests. For one thing, they lack legitimacy among the workforce, being seen as too closely controlled by managers. Thus employees do not enjoy an independent 'voice'. Lloyd's (2001) case study of 'Aeroparts' amply demonstrates the lack of independent power that characterizes non-union systems of employee representation. Office workers were cautiously favourable about the Employee Council, perceiving it to increase communications, and improve relations with management. This was largely due to the inactivity of their union when it had been recognized, or because workers had not been union members anyway. Any initiative, however modest, was considered to be an improvement.

Shopfloor workers, however, overwhelmingly wanted to see a return to union representation. The Employee Council did not have the power, the independent power free from managerial control, that the trade union had enjoyed. Thus it was not an effective constraint on managerial prerogative. As one front-line manager admitted, 'since the introduction of the EC [Employee Council] the company have managed to bulldoze through any policy they feel fit, with hardly any kickback from employees', and that the 'things I do now, I wouldn't have dreamt of doing in a trade union environment because I know I can get away with it' (quoted in Lloyd 2001: 322).

Company councils, precisely because they are management tools, rarely have the power to influence managerial decision-making, and are thus viewed by employees as ineffective arrangements for expressing their voice at work. In his study of non-union employee representation at the Eurotunnel call centre, Gollan (2003) discovered that managers largely saw the company council as a vehicle for communicating information to staff rather than giving them voice. Most employees surveyed 'stated that the company council was not effective in representing general employee interests' (Gollan 2003: 537).

In another case, that of 'Liftco', the non-union consultative committee was held up by the company as evidence of its participatory style of management. A large majority of employees voted against unionization in a recognition ballot. However, the economic recession of the early 1980s meant that 'Liftco' needed to cut costs. It proposed reductions in working time, redundancies, and a pay freeze, and sought employees' views on the latter directly, by-passing the consultative committee. The committee's employee representatives all resigned, claiming that it had been ignored. Systems of non-union representation may be feasible when business conditions are favourable, but lack the independent power to challenge the employer when jobs, pay and conditions are threatened (Terry 1999).

Overall, then, it is evident that non-union company councils do not give employees effective representation at work. These forums are generally management devices to improve internal communications, rather than arrangements for giving employees genuine influence, thus enhancing, rather than restricting, managerial prerogatives. Nevertheless, we should not assume that dissatisfaction with non-union forms of employee representation necessarily equates to a demand for unionization. In the case of Eurotunnel, for example, some employees would have preferred a company council that had teeth to union representation (Gollan 2003).

6.3.3 The implementation of the Information and Consultation Directive

To what extent will the implementation of a further piece of EU legislation, the Information and Consultation Directive, from April 2005, strengthen the way in which employees' interests are represented in British workplaces? At the present time, all we can do is set out the background to the legislation, consider its main details, and discuss any potential implications. For some years, the Labour government opposed the progress of a proposed directive that would oblige employers to establish permanent arrangements for informing and consulting with their workforces on such matters as the firm's business prospects, changes in employment levels and structures, and the organization of work, threats to job security, and the like. By 2002, however, it found itself unable to block the measure since, under the system of qualified majority voting, there was insufficient opposition on the EU's Council of Ministers to prevent it from being enacted.

Nevertheless, the government came under a lot of pressure to ensure that the directive was implemented in a way that was favourable to business. 'The major employers' organizations lobbied for and supported the UK government's opposition to the Directive, and once it became clear that opposition was no longer tenable argued, successfully, for a flexible, minimalist approach to its implementation' (Hall and Terry 2004: 221). Accordingly, the government's consultation paper argued strongly against a 'single, static model for information and consultation' and the inappropriateness of a 'one size fits all' approach in the British context. Instead, the legislation should enable organizations 'to develop their own arrangements tailored to their particular circumstances, through voluntary agreements' (DTI 2003a: 5). The legislation specifies that employers must negotiate with employee representatives over the establishment of information and consultation arrangements where 10 per cent of the workforce request it, but may be able to rely on existing arrangements, which can include direct forms of involvement, if they go unchallenged by staff. The government won agreement that the directive could be implemented in stages. It will apply to firms with 150 or more employees in 2005; full coverage, for all firms with fifty or more employees, will not come until 2008.

Although the government has tried to implement the legislation in a way that minimizes its impact, the potential implications are far-reaching (Hall and Terry 2004). For one thing, employee representation is increasingly influenced by legislative measures (Terry 2003). Research evidence demonstrates that a large proportion of non-union firms do not operate standing arrangements for informing and consulting with employees (Welch and Williams 2004). Although trade unions do not so far seem to have enjoyed much success in capturing company councils, exposing their ineffectiveness, and using them as a springboard for the extension of unionization in non-union firms (Hall and Edwards 1999), any expansion in the incidence of information and consultation arrangements might enable them to secure a presence in companies from which they would otherwise be excluded (Hyman 1996). Given the minimalist way in which it has been implemented, though, the legislation is unlikely to close the representation gap in the immediate future. Hall and Terry (2004) suggest that the 10 per cent threshold to trigger a request may be a major obstacle. They also point out that employers may be able to rely on getting employees to agree to 'direct forms of information and consultation', rather than by means of elected representatives (Hall and Terry 2004: 220), something that could strengthen management prerogative rather than enhance the employee voice. Whatever the outcome, though, the significance of the Information and Consultation Directive should not be underestimated.

6.3.4 European Works Councils

Have European Works Councils (EWCs), transnational forums for information provision and consultation, generated enhanced employee representation? While a few bodies existed beforehand, mainly in French companies, a 1994 European Union directive mandated that 'community-scale' undertakings, defined as those with at least 1,000 employees in the countries covered by the directive, including at least 150 in each of two or more countries, establish a mechanism for informing and consulting employee representatives about transnational issues. Under Article 13 of the directive, multinational companies were given two years to establish voluntary mechanisms, which could be 'tailored to the circumstances of the enterprise' (Carley and Hall 2000: 105). As the 1996 deadline approached, there was 'frantic activity' as companies looked to put appropriate arrangements in place and thus avoid the possibility of having a more rigid model imposed upon them under Article 6 of the directive (Cressey 1998).

Some 400 'Article 13' agreements were eventually concluded and, overall, by 2000 nearly 600 EWCs had been established (Carley and Hall 2000; Marginson et al. 1998). The Conservative government's 'opt-out' from the European Union's 'social chapter', reversed by Labour in 1997, formally meant that initially British workers were excluded from the scope of the directive. In practice, however, many British companies, including Sainsbury's, Stagecoach, United Biscuits, and NatWest, which had a substantial presence in other European countries and were thus obliged to set up EWCs for staff there, extended their coverage voluntarily.

The bus and rail company Stagecoach anticipated that the EWC directive would apply in Britain. In 1997, it invited trade unions in Britain and Sweden, where it also had a major presence, to participate in the process that would establish an EWC. A draft agreement was signed in the spring of 1998, and the first meeting of the EWC took place in October the same year. Elected employee representatives from Stagecoach's bus and train operations in Britain, and from its businesses in Sweden, Finland and Portugal, met with managers under the chairmanship of the group chief executive (IRS 1998a).

The EWC directive was eventually transposed into British law in January 2000. Managements are required by the directive to hold annual meetings with elected employee representatives. They must provide information on, among other things, the performance of, and prospects for, the business, the financial situation, and investment plans. Consultation is limited by the directive to 'the exchange of views and establishment of dialogue' (Carley and Hall 2000: 105), and few companies have gone further than this (Marginson et al. 1998: 25). Panasonic, for example, emphasized that the scope of its EWC is strictly limited to 'consultation' as it is defined in the directive (Kalman 1999).

Thus it is difficult to see how EWCs, as they are currently constituted, can be much of a restraint on managerial decision-making (Ramsay 1997). Indeed, during its development the scope of the directive was diluted by employer opposition, something that had proved inimical to previous attempts to initiate employee participation at European level (Ramsay 1997), its final provisions thus being a 'judiciously crafted political compromise' (Hyman 1996: 75).

But what has been the impact of the EWC directive? While robust trade union representation on many EWCs, something not specified by the directive, has given most of these bodies a degree of independence (Marginson et al. 1998), overall they act to reinforce managerial power rather than to widen the scope of employee influence over company decision-making. Generally, Article 13 agreements are managerially led devices to stimulate improved business performance and, in Britain, may be used as a way of advancing and legitimizing non-union systems of employee representation (Cressey 1998; Wills 1999). Panasonic, for example, needed to put in place arrangements for the selection of employee representatives from its non-unionized sales company. Instead of extending union recognition, it chose to establish a new non-union consultative committee from which the EWC delegates could be nominated (Kalman 1999). The limited nature of consultation in EWCs has already been highlighted; thus there is a tendency for them to become just another vehicle for communicating with employees. At McDonald's, for example, the EWC 'is just another institution to be captured for management; another method of "getting the message across" ' (Royle 2000: 193).

There are further factors, moreover, that limit the representational capacity of EWCs. Language barriers and national differences of interest have inhibited collaboration between representatives from different countries (Wills 2000), and many EWC agreements initially did not make any provision for representatives' training, something that may, however, have improved (Gilman and Marginson 2002; Miller and Stirling 1998). Multinational companies have many opportunities to dilute the scope of EWCs. The majority of 'employee' representatives on the McDonald's EWC are, in fact, salaried managers. Among other things, the fast-food chain has exerted strict control over the structure and organization of EWC meetings, has limited, through the use of 'dubious' election methods, the presence of trade union members among its EWC representatives, and has prevented the holding of 'pre-meetings' which representatives can use to discuss tactics before the EWC event itself (Royle 2000).

All this suggests, then, that EWCs are unlikely to transform the prospects for employee representation in Britain. This is clear from Wills's (2000) case study of the operation of the EWC in an un-named multinational manufacturing and merchanting company. Genuine consultation was rare; managers came to EWC meetings to report on decisions that had already been made. Delegates had no opportunity to challenge managerial decision-making or to influence decisions. According to a frustrated British representative: 'We should be able to challenge things. What happens now is we are just told things. The unions put forward an alternative plan and the company ignores it. That surely isn't right?' (quoted in Wills 2000: 94).

Thus, an 'EWC does not give employees the power to alter decision-making, nor does it provide the means to intervene in corporate life', rather it offers 'a new forum for managers to inform their staff' (Wills 2000: 102). While in some cases the development of an EWC may allow for the interests of employees to be significantly advanced at European level, this is something which is strongly influenced by the characteristics of the company's 'home' country. The scope and powers of EWCs based in British companies tend to be more limited than others (Gilman and Marginson 2002; Lecher and Rüb 1999). While British unions may increasingly be able to use EWCs to build networks of international cooperation and information-sharing, in the final analysis there should not be too much faith in the capacity of these bodies to secure effective pan-European employee representation.

SECTION SUMMARY AND FURTHER READING

- The growth of the representation gap in Britain has generated an increasing amount of attention concerning the extent to which the 'single channel' of union representation remains an effective means of enabling workers to exercise voice at work.

- Although there is a business case for systems of non-union employee representation, a desire to avoid unions and compliance with the law appear to be more pronounced reasons for the development of 'company council' arrangements in Britain. They are typically established in order to enhance managerial prerogatives and undermine trade unionism, not to give employees adequate independent representation of their interests.

- The Information and Consultation Directive is the latest, and potentially most far-reaching, piece of legislation, derived from the European Union, concerned with enhancing the rights of employees to be informed and consulted about matters that affect them at work.

- EWCs have the potential to enhance employee influence over company decision-making. However, they tend to be used narrowly as an extra channel that managements can use to communicate with staff.

For a general overview of debates pertaining to works councils, see Rogers and Streeck (1995). Hall and Terry (2004) offer the best guide to the evolving statutory framework of information and consultation rights in Britain. Terry (1999), Lloyd (2001), and Gollan (2003) provide critically informed case studies of non-union company councils in practice. Wills (2000) provides an excellent in-depth case study of an EWC. Royle's (2000) critical analysis of the McDonalds EWC is also well worth reading.

6.4 Partnership agreements

While there is nothing new about cooperative industrial relations (Kelly 1998; Towers 1997), one of the most striking trends since the early 1990s in Britain has been the growth in significance of more explicit partnership agreements reached between employers and trade unions. One of the main reasons why the partnership approach has generated so much interest in Britain is the novelty of the concept. Elsewhere in Europe the term 'social partnership', while it is employed with some flexibility, is commonly used to refer to the relationship between employers and unions (Ferner and Hyman 1998). Why has the concept of 'partnership' become so popular? What are the characteristics of the partnership agreements?

6.4.1 Partnership agreements in Britain

Although the explicit concept of 'partnership' between employers and unions has traditionally been somewhat alien to Britain, there are signs of a surge of interest as greater numbers of partnership agreements are signed, involving such well-known companies as Barclays Bank and Legal and General. Perhaps the most prominent agreement was that signed in March 1998 by the leading supermarket chain Tesco, Britain's largest private sector employer, and the Union of Shop, Distributive and Allied Trades (USDAW). Tesco managers contended that employee representation methods in the company were no longer appropriate for the more competitive and dynamic environment in which the retailer operated, and which demanded greater employee flexibility and commitment. They were also concerned that the ritualized process by which the annual pay rise was agreed – it involved a ballot of union members – generated adversarialism, and that non-union members lacked an adequate voice. The company considered a range of options, one of which was to derecognize USDAW, even though more than a half of store staff are union members (IRS 1999).

The partnership agreement was developed over several months with the help of academics at Cranfield School of Management, and received the support of USDAW members in a ballot. The agreement comprises nine 'pillars of partnership', including 'effective representation', 'genuine consultation', 'reliable communication', 'sharing values and culture', and a 'sharp business focus' (IRS 1999). As part of the desire to allow all employees a voice, consultative staff forums were established in all Tesco stores, to which non-union employees could be elected, although each must include a union representative. These workplace forums send representatives to three regional forums, and these elect the national forum that is responsible for discussing the annual pay review, and other major business issues (Tailby and Winchester 2000). Following the conclusion of the partnership agreement, USDAW benefited from an increase of nearly 20,000 in its Tesco membership, and a 20 per cent rise in the number of its workplace representatives (Haynes and Allen 2001).

This case study of a well-known partnership agreement is a useful starting point for an assessment of the components of partnership, a consideration of why such an approach has become so popular, and an analysis of its outcomes. The Tesco experience suggests that partnership encompasses both broad principles and concrete practices (Guest and Peccei 2001). USDAW has maintained its presence in the company, but has lost its monopoly of employee representation, and has given management greater scope to secure employment flexibility. Critics inside the union have accused USDAW of being too cooperative with Tesco, and have complained about the overly collaborative nature of the partnership agreement (IRS 1999).

Studies of partnership deals indicate that they generally include: a shared commitment on the part of the unions and management to business success; employer guarantees about job or employment security; union agreement to more flexible working practices; and new forms of information and consultation arrangements, perhaps to the extent that unions are involved in strategic business decision-making (Kelly 2004; Terry 2004). For example, trade union agreement to new forms of employee involvement and representation, including the abandonment of the commitment to the 'single channel' of union representation, and an acceptance of greater job flexibility, are staple elements of the partnership proposals promoted by the British Involvement and Participation Association (IPA 1992; Coupar and Stevens 1998). In exchange, managements are encouraged to offer employees enhanced security of employment, though not necessarily job security, a greater stake in the financial success of the company, and broader information provision and consultation rights.

6.4.2 Why partnership?

Employers have largely generated pressure for partnership (Oxenbridge and Brown 2002), as the case study of Tesco demonstrates. What do they gain from such an approach? Two related factors have encouraged employers' interest in partnership, though in Britain the effect of the changed political climate should not be discounted, as will be discussed below. First, research in the United States appears to demonstrate that cooperative management–union relationships can ease the introduction of new working practices and boost business performance in the 'mutual gains enterprise' (Kochan and Osterman 1994; Towers 1997). The adoption of a partnership approach can assist managerial efforts to secure, and gain support for, organizational change (Martinez Lucio and Stuart 2002; Oxenbridge and Brown 2002). For example, United Distillers initiated a partnership approach with the trade unions following a decision to transform production techniques, under the banner of its 'Towards World Class' change programme. In the case of Barclays Bank, senior managers viewed a partnership agreement as essential in order to retain the cooperation of the union, Unifi, and thus avoid potentially highly damaging industrial action during a period of intense restructuring (Wills 2004b).

Second, there is a presumption that if organizations want greater effort and commitment from their staff, then, in the interests of 'mutuality', they should give them opportunities to express their views (Guest and Peccei 2001). But it is not only companies that have tried to engender partnership. The British Labour government has been a strong advocate of such an approach (DTI 1998), as was discussed in Chapter 3, something that may have contributed to the interest of employers (Ackers and Payne 1998). In 1999, it made over 2 million pounds available from a 'partnership fund' to support joint workplace projects (Terry 2004). According to prime minister Tony Blair, speaking in 2000 at the TUC's Partners for Progress conference, partnership is 'about modernisation and getting rid of old class legacies, it's about trust and co-operation and it's about bringing employee relations into line with a company's business position' (Danford, Richardson, and Upchurch 2002: 1–2). For the British government, then, partnership is conceptualized in an explicitly unitary fashion (Ackers and Payne 1998). If there is a role for the unions, it is a very restricted one, limited to working with businesses in a cooperative way in order to improve competitiveness.

Why, then, have the unions embraced the partnership approach so readily, since, at first glance, it does not appear to be a very attractive proposition for them? In the case of Tesco, the union was concerned to maintain a presence in a company that employed a large proportion of its members. The possibility of derecognition would have weighed heavily in influencing the union's policy. In an otherwise hostile environment, partnership appears to guarantee the unions a presence, a degree of institutional security, and some, however limited, influence in organizational decision-making (Tailby and Winchester 2000). According to a leading representative of the Manufacturing Science and Finance Union (now Amicus) in a National Health Service hospital, partnership enhances union input to the benefit of employees:

We've got an opportunity to go in and comment on and respond to policies even before they have been offered as a formal paper. We can contribute to drafting them and I think that's what partnership means. It means taking full account and giving full weight to the staff side and their views. (quoted in Danford, Richardson, and Upchurch 2002: 20)

BOX 6.2 PARTNERSHIP AT BORG WARNER

Studies of partnership agreements that consider how far they benefit employees are rare. Suff and Williams (2004), though, asked employees at Borg Warner in South Wales, a manufacturer of specialist components and systems for vehicles that has developed a celebrated partnership approach with the Amicus trade union, about whether or not they had benefited from it. The 1997 agreement, known as the 'Margam Way', after the location of the plant, comprises a ten-point plan that, among other things, emphasizes the importance of transparency and good communications. Managers and union representatives cited the positive impact of partnership, in particular the way in which the development of cooperative relations enabled the business to grow.

What were employees' views, though? How did they experience partnership in practice? Most of those surveyed (57 per cent) thought it had improved their working lives, and had enabled the union to participate more effectively in organizational decision-making. Thus there was general backing for the partnership approach. Nevertheless, despite the emphasis on communications many staff felt that they had limited influence over decisions that affected them at work. While partnership had increased their job security, in general people considered themselves to be insecure, a reflection of the competitive market environment and the history of job losses in the plant. Job satisfaction was high; generally employees did not see this as a product of the partnership agreement. Although partnership had clearly cemented the reputation of Borg Warner as a 'good' employer, employees nevertheless exhibited a low level of trust in management.

In this case, a partnership agreement had secured important benefits for employees, and the plant had remained open, ensuring that jobs were saved. However, the level of cooperation between management and employees was strictly bounded, and fell well short of that proposed by the 'mutual gains' model. In the context of a market economy, in which workers have to be treated as disposable, as well as dependable, it is doubtful whether genuine partnership can ever be realized in practice.

The benefits of partnership appear to make it a very enticing prospect for all the parties to the employment relationship, though studies of the outcomes for employees are quite rare (see Box 6.2 for an exception). For employers, it has a positive impact on business performance (Knell 1999; Marks et al. 1998). The unions maintain a presence and have enhanced opportunity to influence organizational decision-making, and employees gain 'a better psychological contract and greater voice' (Guest and Peccei 2001: 332). In the case of Barclays, for example, the company is better able to 'implement change through consultation with the union, so making better decisions and minimizing obstruction to change', while Unifi secures 'employer support for its role and activities in the bank' (Wills 2004b: 335). Who, then, could possibly be opposed to partnership?

6.4.3 **Partnership: a critique**

Proponents of partnership agreements claim that they do not threaten trade unionism (Knell 1999). A closer examination of the evidence indicates that this is far from the case. For one thing, the representational capacity of the unions is often weakened by partnership. The role of the unions under partnership regimes may be restricted to an entitlement to be consulted about developments, rather than a right to bargain over them (Terry 2004).

Moreover, as has already been noted, management almost always drives partnership, often with the threat of union derecognition, or major workforce reductions, hanging in the background if the unions do not concur. This was the case at both United Distillers and Allied Domecq, where partnership was initiated by the respective companies 'as part of a restructuring and closure package' (Marks et al. 1998: 217). As noted above, Tesco considered union derecognition as one of the alternatives to the partnership agreement (IRS 1999).

Within the labour movement, support for partnership is strongest among union leaderships and full-time officers, who may sign agreements over and above the heads of shop stewards. At Allied Domecq, for example, the company deliberately by-passed shop stewards and reached agreement with union full-time officers and convenors (Marks et al. 1998). While these deals give unions 'institutional security', that is they help to secure a formal presence for the union at an organizational level, they nonetheless shift the balance of power firmly in favour of management.

In the case of Barclays, for example, although Unifi secured greater access to, and influence over, organizational decision-making, this generated its own tensions. From the point of view of its members and activists, senior union representatives were too closely identified with managerial decisions. Therefore the union did not seem to be fighting on behalf of its members' interests as strongly as it ought to have done; it appeared to have developed a relationship with the bank that was too cosy and cooperative. According to one union member:

How it seems to be working is that the union hierarchy go and have their meeting and discussions with the bank, negotiate whatever and they come back to me as a union member and say, 'this is what's been offered to you, this is the option, how do you feel about it?' I don't think we're actually consulted when it comes down to making any sort of hard-and-fast decisions as to what our contracts are going to look like. (quoted in Wills 2004b: 340)

Thus, one of the main dangers of partnership for the trade unions concerns the distance that is potentially opened up between those union representatives who are party to managerial decision-making, and use their position to influence it, and the members, who may become disillusioned about the extent to which, as they view it, the union is really representing their interests in opposition to management (see Oxenbridge and Brown 2004).

A further problem with partnership agreements is evident in Taylor and Ramsay's (1998) case study of the 'Megashop' supermarket chain. They demonstrate that by giving managers greater scope to restructure working practices, partnership deals may act as enabling agreements, allowing managers to intensify work without effective restraint. Partnership agreements, because they have been jointly concluded, even if it is by senior officials on the union side, have a level of legitimacy that makes them difficult to counter, even when they have detrimental results for the employees and undermine workplace unionism. According to one worker at Megashop: 'They [managers] are in a people-oriented business but they do not treat all the people they deal with equally. They bend over backwards for the customers but they treat us like shit!' (quoted in Taylor and Ramsay 1998: 131). When shop stewards tried to represent workers' grievances, they were rebuffed, told by managers that their actions ran counter to the provisions of the partnership agreement. Trade unionism, 'in the short term, is acceptable as long as it does not interfere with managerial prerogatives on the shop floor' (Taylor and Ramsay 1998: 137). At United Distillers, a shop steward explained how partnership had strengthened management power:

The people who work with us day in day out in the office or on the lines haven't changed, and these people are still going to manage us in the way that they always have, except now they have got an agreement which the union signed up to and they will beat us with it. (quoted in Marks et al. 1998: 221)

Not only do partnership agreements enhance management prerogative, but they may also weaken union organization in the workplace. At the NHS hospital referred to above, the distance between senior union representatives, who were involved in high-level policy formulation and committee work, and their members increased. This had a detrimental effect on the ability of the union to represent and mobilize workers in opposition to management (Danford, Richardson, and Upchurch 2002). In their case study investigation of partnership in the Scottish spirits industry, Marks et al. (1998) also demonstrate how partnership agreements weaken shop-floor union organization.

How committed are managers to genuine partnership with the trade unions anyway? Agreements are generally concluded on the terms of the employer who would, ideally, prefer to manage in a non-union environment, but is willing to make a pragmatic compromise (Bacon and Storey 2000; Kelly 1998). Indeed, it should not be assumed that 'partnership' entitles the union to a presence at all. The British Labour government emphasized the desirability of building partnerships between employers and employees, not trade unions (Hyman 2001b); and a survey of managers' attitudes to partnership revealed that they did not envisage much of a role for the unions (Guest and Peccei 1998).

6.4.4 Partnership: an assessment

These critical points notwithstanding, there are some signs that partnership agreements may, in a very limited way, enhance the scope of employee representation. Not only do they offer the unions some security and help to stimulate membership growth, as at Tesco, but they may also encourage a broadening of the bargaining agenda, to include quality of working life issues such as 'family-friendly' working practices, for example (Heery 2002; Terry 2004).

Moreover, the inherent ambiguity of the partnership concept may provide the unions with an opportunity to extend their organizational capacity. In Barclays, for example, the union benefited from a greatly enhanced system of workplace representation that extended union organization to parts of the company from which it had hitherto been absent (Wills 2004b). There is no accepted definition of the 'partnership' term, and it can be used both in a pluralist sense, as the trade unions do, and a unitary one, as do the government and employers (Guest and Peccei 2001). For Ackers and Payne (1998: 546), such vagueness may be an asset for the unions. They may even be able to use the notion of 'partnership' rhetorically, as a way of extending their organizations in circumstances where it would otherwise be difficult.

There is some evidence that this is may be occurring. The public services union Unison has extended learning opportunities for its members as a result of 'partnership' with some employers, who contribute towards the costs. But this is explicitly not a form of cooperative unionism. The provision of learning opportunities has enhanced the attractiveness of the union to potential members, increased existing members' identification with the union, and strengthened collective organization (Munro and Rainbird 2000). In some circumstances, then, a partnership approach need not be inimical to effective trade unionism and the representation of workers' interests.

Nevertheless, the overall assessment must be a negative one. Since they are arrangements that are designed to buttress existing, formal management–union relations, partnership agreements do little for the millions of workers without access to union representation. Kelly (2004) observes that union organizing campaigns resulting in new recognition agreements have been more effective than partnership in extending unionization, and thus eroding the representation gap. It is widely acknowledged, moreover, that partnership delivers little real employment security (Oxenbridge and Brown 2002). Generally, the partnership agenda is firmly under the control of managements. Even though agreements may state that legitimate differences of interest exist, 'that is about all they do say, and the language is otherwise overwhelmingly unitarist in flavour' (Terry 2004: 212). While it is important to recognize that it may at least help to secure a trade union presence, partnership is a largely managerial initiative, one that reflects the general weakness of the union movement (Terry 2004), and does little to close the representation gap in British workplaces.

SECTION SUMMARY AND FURTHER READING

- Since the early 1990s, there has been a marked trend towards the conclusion of 'partnership agreements' in British companies. In general, workers are promised security of employment, though this is almost always qualified, and new forms of employee involvement and representation, in exchange for greater job flexibility.

- While partnership agreements can enhance the unions' 'institutional security', that is they may be allowed some limited influence over organizational decision-making, this comes at the expense of workplace trade unionism, which is weakened by the shift in the balance of power in favour of management. Nevertheless, the inherent ambiguity of the partnership concept can in certain circumstances be used by unions to secure greater influence.

For a discussion of the characteristics and benefits of partnership agreements, see Coupar and Stevens (1998). Towers (1997) puts the concept of partnership in an international context, linking it to the emergence of more explicitly cooperative management – labour relations in the United States. Tailby and Winchester (2000) provide an overview of developments in Britain. There are good, detailed case studies of partnership available, for example at United Distillers and Allied Domecq (Marks et al. 1998), and Barclays Bank (Wills 2004b) respectively.

6.5 Organizing unionism

In 1899, the Workers' Union's first full-time district organizer, Will Buchan, initiated a recruitment drive at Sir Thomas Lipton's City Road warehouses in London. The 1,300 workers were badly paid, and experienced poor working conditions. As Hyman (1971: 19) reports: 'Girls worked a 10-hour day with only one half-hour break, carrying heavy loads in unhealthy conditions; often they fainted, and the time lost was deducted from their wages'. Perhaps unsurprisingly, Buchan's attempts to organize these workers met with considerable success at first, and a new branch of the Workers' Union was established. As the union become more powerful, however, Lipton took measures to undermine its position, and dismissed many of the leading union activists among the workforce. By early 1900, union organization in the warehouses had collapsed (Hyman 1971).

6.5.1 Trade unions and recruitment

The Workers' Union was to go on to become one of the most important general unions in Britain during the first two decades of the twentieth century, eventually to become a part of the Transport and General Workers' Union (TGWU). Nevertheless, its failure to secure a presence, because of intense employer hostility, at Lipton's warehouses in 1899, demonstrates that the process of organizing workers into unions can be a daunting task. By the second half of the twentieth century, union organizing activity had dwindled markedly in Britain (Beaumont and Harris 1990). Since the overall level of union membership, which was rising in most years, appeared to be determined principally by extraneous factors such as the business cycle and the public policy climate, and not by trade union activities themselves (Bain and Price 1983), it is scarcely surprising in retrospect that unions marginalized recruitment activity, even though such a reactive approach may have encouraged membership passivity (Hyman 1989). Understandably, unions tended to focus on providing representational services to existing members, a 'servicing' approach, rather than organizing in new areas.

Given that there was some evidence to suggest that a union's policies could positively influence its membership levels (Undy et al. 1981), the precipitous decline in union membership of the 1980s impelled some unions to pursue explicit growth strategies. While this mainly took the form of 'market-share' unionism, whereby unions sought to gain members through mergers and amalgamations, thus increasing their share of the existing 'market' for trade union members without actually extending it (Willman 1989), by the early 1990s recruitment activity was gaining a higher priority.

One of the few unions to experience membership growth during the 1980s was the shop-workers' union, USDAW. While this was partly a reflection of increasing retail employment, the union's own recruitment efforts were the principal cause of its positive performance. From 1986 onwards, for example, USDAW officers were mandated to spend a certain proportion of their time on recruitment activity (Upchurch and Donnelly 1992). While the TUC's recruitment drives in Trafford Park, Manchester, and London's Docklands were conspicuous failures, the TGWU's 'Link Up' strategy deserves a more considered assessment. Launched in 1987, its main objectives were to increase membership in workplaces where the union already had recognition; to prioritize the recruitment of categories of workers who had previously been neglected by unions, such as part-time and temporary workers; and to build stronger links with the wider community. While the TGWU made some important recruitment gains, the success of the 'Link Up' strategy was limited. The union found recruiting workers to be relatively straightforward, but keeping them as members was more difficult. There was also internal opposition to the increased emphasis on recruitment from officials who were resistant to change (Snape 1994). Most union officials' expertise lies in supporting and providing services to existing members, not in going out and finding new ones. This is something that has long inhibited recruitment activity in both Britain and the United States (Bensinger 1998; Kelly and Heery 1994).

Since the mid-1990s, however, in Britain and elsewhere, there has been an increased emphasis on how unions themselves can rebuild their strength through intensive and focused recruitment activity. Why has 'organizing unionism' become so pronounced? What are its characteristics? And what are the implications for the representation of workers' interests?

6.5.2 Why organizing unionism?

In Britain, the development of organizing unionism has been impelled by three factors. First, policy has been influenced by developments in Australia and, more importantly, the United States (New Unionism Project 1998). Second, a greater emphasis on organizing workers into trade unions formed part of the 'relaunch' of the TUC during the 1990s (Heery 1998c). Third, it has now been firmly accepted by most unions that people join them for collective reasons (Waddington and Whitston 1997). Given the multitude of problems that workers experience in the workplace (see Chapter 8), there would appear to be considerable scope for collective mobilization, and the revival of union representation in the workplace.

The origins of organizing unionism in Britain can be traced to the 1996 launch of the TUC's 'New Unionism' project, one of the objectives of which was to 'promote organizing as the top priority and build an organizing culture' (TUC 1997: 39). While it was considered important to build union membership among the 4 million workers in Britain based in unionized workplaces but who were not members themselves, particularly in the short term, the TUC considered that this would not be enough to revive trade unionism on its own. Rather, the unions needed to 'break into new jobs and industries' and 'sharpen unions' appeal to "new" workers, including women, youth and those at the rough end of the labour market' (TUC 1997: 39). Thus the adoption of the organizing approach marked a recognition of the limitations of servicing unionism as a source of union resilience. The TUC acknowledged that some unions had enhanced their recruitment activities. However, influenced by the development of organizing unionism in the United States and Australia (Bensinger 1998; TUC 1997), it argued that a more strategic, encompassing approach was needed if unions were to recapture their vitality. What, then, are the principal characteristics of organizing unionism?

First, it is necessary to distinguish 'organizing' from 'recruitment'. With the latter the recruiter simply enrols the worker into the union and leaves it at that; 'organizing', however, goes further and, recognizing that retaining existing members can often be more difficult for unions than recruiting new ones, involves an ongoing process of developing and strengthening workplace organization (Heery et al. 2000c). In the United States, the 'union building' approach, in which existing members play an active part in organizing initiatives, has been shown to be more effective in expanding trade unionism (Bronfenbrenner and Juravich 1998).

Organizing unionism has also spread to New Zealand, where it has enjoyed some initial success. Following the introduction of a new law that heavily circumscribed union activity, in 1994 the Service Workers' Union (SWU), which mainly represented workers in low-paying jobs in the healthcare, cleaning, and hospitality sectors, initiated an organizing approach. The adoption of this new strategy was not determined by the union's leadership in isolation, but in the context of a commitment to, and a history of, building unionism from the bottom-up and of actively involving members and union activists themselves in the process of organizing. As Oxenbridge (1997: 21) explains, 'SWU leaders' values centred around the political education of members and a belief in the power of grassroots organizing methods which translated into a commitment to resourcing organizing reform initiatives'.

Second, organizing unionism is characterized by an emphasis on the unionization of groups of workers that the unions have largely neglected in the past, and who frequently suffer from labour market disadvantage. In Britain, the TUC has emphasized improvements

---

BOX 6.3 'JUSTICE FOR JANITORS' IN SOUTHERN CALIFORNIA

Perhaps the most notable example of the efforts of American unions to expand their memberships through 'organizing' has been the campaign to build trade union strength among office cleaning workers, or 'janitors', in Los Angeles, popularized by Ken Loach in his film *Bread and Roses* (2000). In the 1980s, competitive pressures encouraged building owners to contract out their cleaning activities, increasingly to non-unionized operators who were able cut costs by undercutting union pay rates and worsening conditions. Even though the office cleaning industry boomed in this period, union membership declined. Contractors preferred hiring 'cheap' and ostensibly 'controllable' immigrant workers from Mexico and Central America.

The Service Employees International Union (SEIU) launched the 'Justice for Janitors' campaign in Southern California in 1988. After two years, it had enjoyed considerable success, including a recognition agreement at the Century City office complex in west Los Angeles. How was this achieved? First, many of the largely immigrant workers themselves were favourable to trade unionism. Not only were they becoming acutely conscious of their disadvantaged labour market position, and wanted to do something about it, but many also had activist backgrounds in their home countries. Moreover, the presence of dense community networks allowed trade unionism, once introduced, to flourish. Second, the SEIU itself played a crucial 'top-down' role in strategically planning the organizing campaign. The union devotes a major proportion of its budget – up to 25 per cent – to recruitment activity, in effect using resources gained from its existing members to find new ones. Third, Justice for Janitors used innovative organizing techniques to forge unionization. Significantly, union organizers eschewed the traditional route to gaining union recognition in the United States – building up membership before workers are balloted, in a 'representation election', to determine whether or not they want a union to bargain on their behalf. Instead, they used public demonstrations and 'in-your-face' campaigns to call for 'justice' and 'dignity' for janitorial workers, causing embarrassment for the companies using the offices. Thus pressure was put on the contractors, and also the building operators, to recognize and bargain with the union.

Following its initial success, during the 1990s the Justice for Janitors campaign stalled somewhat. The principal challenge that faced the union was whether to focus on consolidating its membership base or to concentrate on organizing new workers. Nevertheless, in 2000 the Justice for Janitors campaign secured another notable victory after mobilizing public opinion in support of a successful campaign for a pay rise.

Sources: Erickson et al. (2002); Fisk, Mitchell, and Erickson (2000); Waldinger et al. (1998)

to the representation of part-time and young workers (Heery 1998b; TUC 1997). In the United States, though, the organization of immigrant workers, particularly those from Latin America, is seen as crucial to the revival of the trade unions (see Box 6.3), notwith-standing the poor record of American unions in this area (Figueroa 1998; Milkman 2000; Moody 1997).

Third, perhaps the most distinctive feature of organizing unionism is the use of a special-ized cadre of officials, whose task is to build union organization. After investigating the operation of the Organizing Institute in the United States and the Australian Congress of Trade Unions' 'Organizing Works' programme, in 1998 the TUC established an 'Organizing Academy', the purpose of which is to give union-sponsored trainees a year-long training programme combining classroom-based learning and real-life organizing activity with their union sponsors. 'The intended result is to produce a cadre of "lead organizers" who can plan and manage organizing campaigns and promote the cause of organizing across the British trade union movement' (Heery et al. 2000b: 400). The characteristics of the trainees differed somewhat from those of traditional union officers. Most trainees were women under 30 years of age, who had a broad range of campaigning experience outside the union movement, though the majority had been union members (Heery et al. 2000b: 404). Thus it was anticipated that these individuals would, on completing their training, become dedicated union organizers who would be able to use their skills to expand union organization in Britain.

Fourth, following on from this, the use of trainees has been associated with innovative organizing tactics (Heery et al. 2000b). One of the most distinctive features of organizing unionism is the use of novel techniques to encourage unionization. These include 'mapping' the workforce in particular establishments, identifying those workers who are more sus-ceptible to trade unionism, and the choice of particular 'levers' or grievances that 'lead' union organizers can use to build support (Heery et al. 2000a: 40). In the United States, there has sometimes been a moral dimension to organizing initiatives as unions campaign on the basis of giving workers 'justice' or 'dignity', as in the case of the Justice for Janitors example (see Box 6.3).

6.5.3 Organizing unionism: an assessment

Since it was only launched in 1996, perhaps it is too soon to deliver a verdict on the impact of organizing unionism in Britain. Nevertheless, it already appears to have had a positive impact in some workplaces. At 'TypeCo', a call centre run by a voluntary organization which provides services for the deaf, the Communication Workers' Union built up a considerable membership base following the 1997 launch of an organizing drive, though without gaining recognition from the employer. Supported by a 'lead organizer' from the Academy, a member-led 'organizing committee' has generated union support by campaigning on 'winnable' issues which were causing discontent among staff, such as the abuse of telephone operators by callers (Heery et al. 2000a: 45–6).

There are, however, signs that the development of organizing unionism may prove to be somewhat limited. Case study research demonstrates that while progress is possible, it requires a considerable amount of investment on the part of the unions involved (e.g. Simms 2003). The take-up of the model in Britain has been restricted to a small number of 'vanguard' unions and therefore remains a 'minority trend' (Heery et al. 2000a; Heery 2002). The Iron and Steel Trades Confederation (ISTC), originally an iron and steel industry union, and the Graphical Paper and Media Union (GPMU), in the printing and publishing industries and now part of Amicus, were the most prominent advocates of organizing unionism. The former, for example, increasingly presented itself as a 'community' union, and indeed is now part of the Community trade union, and has actively recruited new members in a variety of different industries, including food manufacturing and electronics assembly, in those parts of the country where iron and steel making was previously dominant (Heery et al. 2000c).

While unions are taking recruitment more seriously, by employing more specialized officials for example (Heery et al. 2000c), the extent to which organizing unionism has been adopted remains questionable. Most unions have tried to consolidate their existing membership bases rather than attempt to take the resource-intensive step of seeking to organize workers in 'new jobs and industries', as the TUC had anticipated, and as the ISTC has attempted (Heery et al. 2000c; TUC 1997). Rather than taking up the organizing model wholesale, interested unions appear to have used selected elements of it in their recruitment campaigns, those that are most appropriate to their particular circumstances. Person-to-person recruitment has been the most popular approach, while workforce mapping appears to be relatively rare. Some use of the moral discourse of 'dignity' and 'justice' has been reported. The TGWU's recruitment drive among restaurants in London's Covent Garden district was accompanied by pressure to establish a 'Respect at Work Zone'. Nevertheless, British unions have blanched at the overly evangelistic tone of some American organizing campaigns (Heery et al. 2000b; Heery et al. 2000c).

Nor should it be assumed that organizing unionism commands universal support within the British trade union movement. Those union officials whose expertise is based on servicing existing members have understandably felt threatened by the increased emphasis on organizing, perceiving it as an added burden on top of their already heavy workloads, and thus a form of work intensification. This was the case in the MSF union, now a part of Amicus, where the adoption of the Organizing Works initiative, and the emphasis on recruitment, resulted in other aspects of union activity, which might also have contributed to the development of union organization, being sidelined (Carter 2000).

Leading British trade unions, including the TGWU and the GMB general union, have not been involved in the Organizing Academy. They have been wary of the enhanced role being carved out by the TUC in this area, seeing it is a potential threat to their autonomy (Heery et al. 2000b). This highlights one of the central tensions in the organizing unionism approach; as a form of 'managed activism' (Heery et al. 2000c) it is a top-down approach to stimulate collective mobilization in the workplace. Although without some degree of coordination from above it is difficult to see how unions can mobilize effectively to improve people's working lives, initiatives designed by union leaderships to boost work-place unionism may be of limited effectiveness since they are perceived to be bureaucratic interventions and thus lack support on the ground (Carter 2000). There is evidence, more-over, that union leaderships may be wary of committing themselves to a full-blown organizing approach, viewing it as an obstacle to the development of a cooperative relationship with employers (Taylor and Bain 2003).

What, then, are the implications of organizing unionism for the representation of workers' interests? The approach has an ostensibly inclusive character, given that a leading objective is to expand union organization into areas where it has hitherto been weak and thus offer representation to workers who would previously have lacked it. However, most British unions have been reluctant to adopt organizing unionism wholeheartedly and have preferred to concentrate on building membership in areas of existing strength (Heery et al. 2003: 61). Perhaps the most notable effect of the unions' dalliance with organizing, then, has been to reinforce their 'institutional security', in much the same way as the partnership approach has. This is not, of course, something that should be derided. Robust trade unionism is vital to the effective representation of workers' interests, and those who accept that there is an inherent imbalance of power in the employment relationship should welcome anything that secures a union presence. The challenge for the unions is how they can expand their representative capacity to cover the millions of British workers without the means of independent and effective representation at work.

SECTION SUMMARY AND FURTHER READING

- Influenced by developments in the United States, since the mid-1990s in Britain there has been a renewed emphasis placed upon organizing workers by trade unions as a way of expanding their influence.

- The 'organizing unionism' model, however, is held to differ from traditional union recruitment effort in a number of key respects. First, it is concerned with 'union building', that is the ongoing development of workplace organization, and not just recruitment on its own. Second, it is designed to attract into union activity workers who have previously been marginalized by the union movement. Third, it involves specially trained union organizers. Fourth, it uses novel organizing techniques such as 'workplace mapping'.

- The diffusion of organizing unionism in Britain has so far been somewhat limited. Most unions remain conservative in their recruitment priorities. Moreover, attempts to initiate novel organizing campaigns have come up against internal obstacles, since many within the unions see them as top-down devices to curtail their autonomy.

The dynamics of organizing unionism in the United States are discussed in two edited collections, Bronfenbrenner et al. (1998), and Milkman (2000). See Gall (2003d) for some useful British case studies. The series of articles written by Heery and his colleagues (Heery et al. 2000a, 2000b, 2000c) is also very useful for details of unions' organizing efforts.

■ CONCLUSION

In this chapter, we have focused upon how workers' interests are represented. For many years in Britain, the trade unions have been responsible for representing workers' interests. By virtue of their collective organization, unions can provide individuals with protection, or insurance, against problems at work. They also bargain with management on behalf of their members, seeking to alter the terms of the wage-work bargain in favour of their members. Unions operate in the workplace itself, where the union representative, or shop steward, not only negotiates with management, but also advises, supports, and represents his or her members. Finally, unions represent the interests of workers in the wider political arena, by influencing the legislative process for example.

Nevertheless, the complex nature of workers' interests poses considerable challenges for unions as they attempt to carry out their representative functions. Workers generally want protection for themselves as individuals, but this requires collective action to be effective. Unions must therefore demonstrate their relevance to individuals, while at the same time operating as a collective agency on behalf of what may be a considerably diverse membership. Thus effective trade unionism depends upon the extent to which the unions are able to translate diverse, individual interests into collective action (Hyman 1994b).

Moreover, unions frequently face difficulties when seeking to construct a broader representative agenda. Campaigning on political and social issues can lead to discontent among members who, understandably, would prefer their union to concentrate its resources on representing their 'sectional' interests in the workplace rather than waste money, as they see it, on irrelevant causes. Thus unions are caught between narrow and broad understandings of interest representation (Hyman 1994b).

Perhaps the most important implication of this overview of employee representation in the workplace is that it is not representation mechanisms, by themselves, that give workers influence over the decisions which affect their working lives, but those that are effective (Kelly 1998). Works council arrangements, at least in Britain, are generally used as management tools to improve communications, or to avoid a union presence. They lack the power and legitimacy of agencies that are independent of the employer, like trade unions, and thus do not help to offer workers adequate representation of their interests.

Although a trade union presence is a necessary condition of effective representation, it is not a guarantee. Invariably unions must strike a cooperative relationship with employers, if only to secure a presence, while at the same time acting to challenge their interests. The concept of 'partnership' has become popular among union leaderships specifically because, in a hostile environment, cooperation with employers is seen as the only way of guaranteeing 'institutional security'. But is this in the interests of their members? Clearly a union presence, however constrained, is important. Without it, workers would have limited defences against threats to their pay and employment conditions. Partnership agreements may, though, not only damage workplace union organization, but may also allow managers greater scope to intensify work, without providing any real job security.

Finally, workers' interests are not constant, but are fluid, and subject to ongoing adjustments as the characteristics of their environments change. The process of interest representation does not simply mean that trade unions act on behalf of, or 'for', their members. Unions themselves play an active part themselves in shaping, influencing, and controlling the interests of workers and thus exercising power 'over' them (Hyman 1975). In one sense, organizing unionism may be viewed as a kind of 'managed activism' (Heery et al. 2000c), something that enhances the power of union leaderships. Unions are to a large extent, however, agencies that embody the collective power of their members. Not only does this limit the authority of union leaderships, since policies depend for their effectiveness on mobilization from below, but it also highlights, once again, the tension between the presence of oligarchic tendencies and the pressure for democratic participation that characterizes all trade union activity.

■ ASSIGNMENT AND DISCUSSION QUESTIONS

1. Prepare arguments either in support of, or opposition to, the following proposition: 'workers no longer need to be represented at work by a trade union or other body since, in the twenty-first century, management fully take account of the needs and views of workers when making decisions that affect them'.

2. What factors accounted for the decline in union membership in the UK during the 1980s and 1990s?

3. How might company or employee councils meet the representational needs of workers? What are the limitations of such bodies?

4. Why do some employers that recognize trade unions appear to be in favour of partnership agreements with them? What do workers and unions gain from such arrangements?

5. You have been asked to advise a trade union on how it might go about recruiting younger workers into membership. In small groups, or by talking to friends, identify what younger people want from work and explain what unions could do to meet these needs.

■ WEBSITE MATERIALS

Visit the companion web site to this book for interesting and updated material at **www.oup.com/booksites/busecon/business**

■ CHAPTER CASE STUDY

e-unions

In common with many commercial and other voluntary organizations, trade unions at both national and local levels have developed websites to publicize their activities to members, non-members, and the wider public. The relative cheapness of communication offered by the web provides unions with an additional means of attracting members to complement existing recruitment methods. However, the web may offer unions the opportunity to improve and increase services, and indeed some have suggested that it could herald the advent of 'virtual unions'.

   Two immediate advantages of the web to unions concern recruitment, and organizing in small and/or non-union workplaces. The average age of union members continues to increase, and they find it difficult to reach out to younger workers. However, these workers are more likely than their older colleagues to use the internet and be more comfortable with using it. To attract such workers, unions will need to identify issues that are relevant to them to encourage access of union sites. For existing union members, the web offers them a route to discover information about both union activities, and those of their employer. In those firms where membership is insufficient to achieve employer recognition, the web provides a means of establishing a permanent presence for workers that would otherwise be difficult and expensive for unions to maintain. Bulletin boards, chatrooms, and online question-and-answer pages, free of any possible victimization from management, may offer an effective, low-cost alternative to direct personal contact in these companies. Only a small number of committed activists is needed to set up and maintain these pages.

The provision of these services can be developed by trade unions at the national level. Email offers members a convenient way of requesting expert advice unconstrained by 'office hours'. Specific information can be made available to local workplace representatives rapidly. For example, the TUC and the union for building workers have weekly e-bulletins and forums for health and safety representatives on risks to workers. Services can be differentiated to appeal to non-members with further 'password-protected' information available only to existing members.

Two further organizational benefits are claimed for unions using the web. First, it can enhance internal democracy by disseminating information and improving communication between the union's leadership and members. Following the tentative steps being taken in the UK for national and local government elections, the web could also be used for union ballots on industrial action and leadership elections. Second, in industrial disputes, unions could use their website to present their case to members, the media, and the public, and to engender support from other unions, both nationally and internationally. More tantalizingly, the web can be used as a weapon in disputes, for example by flooding an employer's website with messages in support of the union's case: so-called 'cyber-disruption'.

Sources: Diamond and Freeman (2002); Greene, Hogan, and Grieco (2003)

Case discussion questions

1. Can the virtual union become a reality?

2. What are the possible limitations and disadvantages to unions that become increasingly reliant on the internet to extend their organizing capacity?

CHAPTER 7

Contemporary developments in pay and working time

CHAPTER OBJECTIVES

The main objectives of this chapter are to:

- provide an overview of the contraction of collective bargaining in Britain, and to assess the extent of managerial freedom to determine pay and conditions of employment, and develop innovative wage payment techniques

- explore the reasons for the resilience of collective bargaining as an influence on the terms of the wage-work bargain in the British public sector

- assess the extent to which greater managerial control has contributed to widening pay inequality in Britain

- consider the extent to which statutory regulation, in particular the National Minimum Wage and the Working Time Regulations, protects workers, and acts to constrain managerial prerogative

---

7.1 Introduction

The concept of the wage-work bargain, as we demonstrated in the Introduction of this book, is central to understanding the nature of the employment relationship. In exchange for the promise of wages, workers agree to engage in productive labour. This is not a one-off transaction, though. The terms of this open-ended bargain are subject to an ongoing process of adjustment and contestation. Since an employer does not pay for a worker's labour, but rather his or her capacity to labour, or potential labour power, the job of managing employment relations is invariably characterized by contradictory tendencies. Managers, as we saw in Chapter 5, must not only secure employees' compliance, but also elicit their cooperation, in order to realize the production of goods and services. Moreover, the wage-work bargain is as much a struggle over working time, and how it is used by employers to secure productive effort from workers, as it is over pay.

The imbalance of power in the employment relationship makes the effective representation of employees' interests at work something best achieved collectively by means of independent trade unions, as we demonstrated in Chapter 6. However, with the diminution of union power in Britain we would expect managers to enjoy greater discretion over the employment relationship, subject of course to the inherent limits to managerial control we highlighted in Chapter 5. This chapter explores how far, and the ways in which, such contemporary developments in employment relations have influenced the terms of the wage-work bargain, with regard to pay and working time in particular.

7.2 The changing pattern of pay determination in Britain

In this section, we examine contemporary trends in pay determination in Britain. One of the most notable recent developments in employment relations has been the diminished importance of collective bargaining as a pay-setting tool, and the resulting increase in the level of managerial discretion over pay. To what extent have managers been able to innovate in methods of pay determination? Performance-based approaches have become increasingly popular. Nevertheless, there is little evidence to suggest that managers have used the greater latitude they enjoy over pay determination very effectively. We finish the section by examining the resilience of collective bargaining, including multi-employer arrangements, in the British public sector. While the importance of collective bargaining as a means of determining pay has declined, it continues to influence earnings for millions of workers in many organizations.

7.2.1 The contraction of collective bargaining in Britain and the rise of managerial discretion over pay

Two major trends have characterized the development of collective bargaining in Britain since the beginning of the 1980s: a substantial decline in the coverage of collective bargaining, and the almost complete disappearance of multi-employer bargaining from the private sector. By the end of the 1990s, just two-fifths of all employees were covered by collective bargaining, compared to over two-thirds in the early 1980s, and barely a fifth of those employed in private services (Cully et al. 1999). Not only did the coverage of collective bargaining decline in the 1980s and 1990s, but, where it remained, its scope was often eroded. What this means is that in situations where unions continued to negotiate with employers over pay and conditions, the range of issues subject to joint regulation has narrowed (Brown et al. 2000). There is some evidence, though, that where they have a presence, unions can exert an important influence over the ability of managers to organize work (Millward, Bryson, and Forth 2000).

Why, then, did the extent and coverage of collective bargaining decline so precipitously during the 1980s and 1990s? A number of factors were at work. Conservative governments discouraged collective bargaining, a reflection of their espoused belief in individualism. Collective bargaining was portrayed as an archaic process that, in so far as it restricted managerial flexibility, undermined business performance. There was also a compositional effect. The changing composition of the workforce, in particular the increasing proportion of employees working in the private services sector, where collective bargaining had never been widespread anyway outside a few sectors such as food retailing, contributed to the diminution of collective bargaining. Moreover, collective bargaining is rare in new work-places, those established since the early 1980s.

The most important cause of the overall fall in collective bargaining coverage, though, was the diminution of union power. Not only were unions increasingly unable to secure bargaining arrangements in new workplaces, but employers also attempted, often success-fully, to exclude them from existing ones, in an effort to forge more individualistic relations with their staff. It should not be forgotten that collective bargaining had always been something that managers were willing to accept, often reluctantly, as a way of avoiding disruption. Thus the decline in collective bargaining coverage was a reflection of the deter-mination of management to extend its prerogative to the area of pay determination, some-thing that was enabled by, and further contributed to, the frailty of the union movement.

The second major collective bargaining trend in Britain during the 1980s and 1990s was the almost complete disappearance of multi-employer bargaining in the private sector, with the exception of a few industries such as electrical contracting (see Box 7.1). In 1998, just

---

BOX 7.1 THE SURVIVAL OF NATIONAL BARGAINING IN THE ELECTRICAL CONTRACTING INDUSTRY

Although increasingly rare, national, multi-employer bargaining survived in some parts of the private sector in the 1990s, including the electrical contracting industry. The sector encompasses firms and self-employed contractors that install and wire electrical systems in homes and businesses. During the 1960s, the Electrical Contractors' Association (ECA), the employers' association for the industry, and the leadership of the electricians' union, now a part of the Amicus trade union, established a close working relationship borne out of a mutual concern to purge workplace union militancy. Set up in 1966, the Joint Industry Board (JIB), made up of an equal number of employers' and union representatives, not only regulated pay, hours, and holidays, but also certified training and provided insurance cover and other benefits.

During the 1980s and 1990s, increasing competitive pressures, and the growth in the numbers of self-employed, challenged the 'viability of national regulation' (Gospel and Druker 1998: 257). Never-theless, the JIB system survived into the 1990s. Why was this? The nature of the industry, comprising a large number of small firms, was one factor. Multi-employer bargaining, as we saw in Chapter 1, ostensibly allows employers to save on the much of the cost of dealing with unions. It can also help to take wages out of competition, an important consideration given that the skills profile of the workforce could result in pay leapfrogging as firms compete with each other for qualified staff. The leaders of the electricians' union, too, favoured national bargaining since it facilitated widespread recognition from employers and 'further reinforced their central control', thus helping to 'contain political challenges mounted by disaffected members' (Gospel and Druker 1998: 262).

These reasons were not enough on their own, however, to sustain national bargaining. The most important factor was that many employers continued to welcome the stability and predictability in employment relations engendered by the JIB system. Moreover, the presence of the JIB itself, given that it developed an increasingly important role in the electrical contracting industry, particularly over matters relating to training, further helped to maintain joint regulation. Thus for relatively small firms in competitive product markets, who rely on a skilled workforce, multi-employer bargaining, in so far as it engenders stability in employment relations, may continue to be attractive in some sectors.

5 per cent of non-managerial employees had their pay set in this way (Cully et al. 1999). Where collective bargaining prevails in the private sector, it is now much more likely to be undertaken at single-employer level. Although the importance of multi-employer bargaining had been dwindling well before the 1980s, that decade saw the termination of national agreements across a range of sectors, including retail banking, engineering, and food retailing (Brown and Walsh 1991; Brown, Marginson, and Walsh 1995). This trend continued into the next decade in such a way that multi-employer bargaining 'which had greatly diminished in importance in the 1980s, became even more of a rarity in the 1990s' (Cully et al. 1999: 228).

Although the Conservatives disliked the perceived rigidity and inflexibility of multi-employer bargaining, the principal cause of its decline was the ambition of firms to align pay more closely with business performance, and to exert greater control over pay outcomes in a more competitive environment. Without control over their own bargaining arrangements, firms found it difficult to secure increasingly necessary flexibility over pay (Brown and Walsh 1991; Brown, Marginson, and Walsh 2003). In the publicly owned water industry, for example, until the late 1980s multi-employer bargaining was preferred since it helped to counterbalance union power, preventing 'leapfrogging' in pay settlements. In other words, the unions were unable to move from organization to organization bidding up pay rates. However, in the period leading up to privatization of the water industry in 1989, national bargaining arrangements were terminated. The ostensible cause was the withdrawal of Thames Water from the industry agreement. Across the sector, however, there was a growing realization that as private sector organizations, operating in a more commercial environment, and governed by the imperative for profitability, the new water companies would need to secure greater control over their own employment relations and, in particular, arrangements for managing pay and performance (Ogden 1993).

What, then, are the implications of the contraction of collective bargaining in Britain? How do employees have their pay determined, if not through the process of collective bargaining? In the private sector the most notable trend has the growing extent to which pay is subject to unilateral regulation by management (Brown, Marginson, and Walsh 2003; Millward, Bryson, and Forth 2000). The findings of the 1998 Workplace Employment Relations Survey (WERS 98), presented in Table 7.1, show the proportion of employees covered by particular pay-setting arrangements. As can be seen from Table 7.1, multi-employer bargaining in the private sector is rare, with just 5 per cent of employees having their pay determined by this method. It remains common, however, in the public sector, covering over a third (35 per cent) of employees. Moreover, the WERS findings considerably undervalue the significance of collective bargaining in the public sector. Table 7.1 shows that over a third (35 per cent) of public sector employees have their pay determined by 'some other method', for example by pay review bodies. As we see below, the pay review body system should perhaps be seen as part of the bargaining process, rather than a substitute for it (Burchill 2000).

Perhaps the most telling feature the data presented in Table 7.1, then, is the degree to which pay-setting decisions rest with management, either in the workplace, or at a higher level. Almost a half (48 per cent) of employees in all workplaces, and nearly two-thirds (65 per cent) of those in the private sector, have their pay determined unilaterally by management. Indeed, pay is set by collective bargaining in only a fifth of private sector workplaces

Table 7.1 Percentage of non-managerial employees covered by particular pay-setting arrangements, by workplace sector 1998

	All workplaces	Private sector	Public sector
Multi-employer bargaining	14	5	35
Single employer bargaining	15	14	16
Workplace bargaining	7	9	3
Set by management at the workplace	26	37	3
Set by management at a higher level	22	28	8
Individual negotiation	2	2	0
Set by some other method	14	4	35

Workplaces with twenty-five or more employees.
Source: Cully et al. (1999: 108)

(Cully et al. 1999: 109). The large extent to which managers now appear to enjoy latitude over pay-setting arrangements raises some important questions. How have managers used this greater freedom? And how far have they been able to eschew the apparent rigidities of collective bargaining, and thus design innovative pay systems that enhance flexibility, commitment, and performance? One of the most well-known developments concerns the increasing use of payment systems that relate an element of an employee's pay to a measure of their performance.

7.2.2 The implications of performance-related pay

Incentive-based payment systems, that link an element of workers' pay to a measure of their output, have a long history in employment relations. Managers are often attracted to them since they seem to be a relatively straightforward way of securing more effort from workers without the need for close supervision (Brown and Walsh 1994). In practice, though, such arrangements rarely operate as effectively as managers anticipate. Workers, for example, may restrict their output, in order to maximize the earnings of them all as a group, and not go flat out in pursuit of a higher individual wage. Moreover, the effect of incentive payments on motivation is rarely unambiguous (Brown, Marginson, and Walsh 2003); the demotivation resulting from a failure to be awarded an expected wage bonus, for example, may outweigh any motivational advantages.

Nevertheless, there has recently been an increasing amount of interest among employers in how pay can be made contingent upon performance, even though, if anything, as we shall see, the use of performance-related pay (PRP) may have a demotivating effect (Brown, Marginson, and Walsh 1995). What, then, is PRP? The term refers to payment systems in which an element of an employee's remuneration is based, over a given period of time, upon an often subjective assessment of the quantity and quality of his or her work, normally by an immediate manager, set against a series of targets. Its use in white-collar jobs in particular represents a shift away from pay based on job grade or length of service 'towards relating pay more directly to individual characteristics' (Kessler and Purcell 1995: 350), particularly in the public sector where PRP schemes have become somewhat popular (Bach 2002; White 1999). While some PRP schemes fell into disrepute during the 1990s, largely because of operational problems, the enthusiasm of many managers does not appear to have diminished; the 'onward march' of PRP continues, with reports of its demise apparently having been 'greatly exaggerated' (Kessler 2000: 280). Employees, too, generally support the principle of PRP (Marsden and French 1998), though, as we shall see, they are often highly disparaging about how it is implemented.

What is the purpose of PRP? Why have managers been so concerned to relate pay more directly to employees' performance? Kessler and Purcell (1995) suggest that three sets of managerial goals provide the rationale for PRP. First, managers use it as a way of stimulating pay flexibility. PRP ostensibly gives them greater latitude to restructure pay systems so that they support organizational objectives, though this is rarely done in a strategic way. The second set of goals relates to the desirability of enhancing employee motivation, commitment, and loyalty. If pay is made more contingent upon their performance, then it is presumed that employees will identify with, and become more attached to, managerially determined organizational goals.

In his study of PRP in four local authorities, Heery (1998a) identified a contradictory rationale underpinning the decision to adopt PRP. On the one hand, managers sought to use it to gain greater employee compliance; PRP could help to reduce shirking and augment management control. On the other hand, the implementation of PRP was also seen as a way of generating culture change, towards a climate in which an ethos of flexibility and commitment predominated. Perhaps this should not be surprising given that the management of the employment relationship is driven by the need to secure employee compliance, as well as elicit their commitment, as we saw in Chapter 5.

In addition, managers use PRP as a way of challenging collective bargaining arrangements and marginalizing the influence of trade unions. In some cases, such as with the derecognition of unions for managerial grades at British Telecom, there is 'an unambiguous attempt by management to use performance pay to undermine the collective dimension of industrial relations' (Kessler and Purcell 1995: 358–9). In the case of one national newspaper company, 'NewsCo', the implementation of a PRP scheme was explicitly designed to undermine union power, eliminate collective bargaining, and thus enhance managerial prerogative (I. Kessler 1994). Evidence from a study of greenfield sites in Ireland demonstrates that PRP schemes, in so far as they marginalize collective bargaining and individualize pay-setting arrangements, undermine joint regulation, thus 'posing an explicit challenge to collectivism in employment relations' (Gunnigle, Turner, and D'Art 1998: 574).

Yet the existence of PRP is not incompatible with a trade union presence. While a desire to reduce the influence of trade unions and collective bargaining is a major rationale for the adoption of PRP schemes, there is evidence that a union presence can help to regulate how they are implemented, and shape the details (Heery 1997b). In the case of 'PharmCo', a pharmaceutical company that until privatization in the 1980s had been in the public sector, the unions jointly regulated the implementation of PRP with management. The effect was to dilute the initial aim of management for a scheme in which pay progression was determined solely by performance, and most staff continued to receive annual increments (I. Kessler 1994).

When implementing PRP, managers must take into account the reactions of employees. Heery (1998a: 85), in his study of local government, considers that 'PRP has been the subject of a tacit exchange between managers and employees, in which managers have refrained from an exacting application of formal procedures for fear of alienating employees'. This helps to explain, for example, the reluctance of managers to give employees low perform-ance ratings. Like any management initiative in employment relations, then, the imple-mentation of PRP is conditioned by the need to elicit employees' cooperation as well as their compliance.

To what extent, though, is PRP effective, in managerial terms, as a way of increasing employees' motivation, and thus their levels of performance? Key features of PRP schemes, such as the manipulation of performance targets, the subjective evaluation of performance by managers, and the fact that the performance element to pay is generally a very small pro-portion of overall earnings, conspire to reduce their effectiveness (Kessler 2000). Added to which, PRP, given that it generates variations in earnings between employees, has the potential to create jealousies and erode staff morale. If anything, then, in practice PRP schemes may have a greater demotivating effect than a motivating one, as can be seen from the experiences of two government agencies, the Inland Revenue and the Employment Service (Marsden and French 1998). Although most employees supported the principle of PRP, in general they were highly critical of the way in which the respective schemes operated in practice. In the Employment Service, for example, the individual performance targets were a source of discontent since it was difficult for employees, given that they had insufficient control over their workloads, to attain them. It was widely felt, moreover, that managers manipulated the performance review process to give higher ratings to favoured employees. In both organizations, PRP appears to have led to a significant decline in morale, caused jealousies, and reduced the level of cooperation between managers and employees.

There are two further aspects of how PRP schemes operate. First, in the public sector it would seem that the introduction of performance pay has been driven not so much by a concern with improving employees' motivation, commitment, and loyalty, but by a need to cut wage bill costs. PRP is associated with a significant increase in workloads as fewer staff are required to take on more tasks and work harder (Foster and Hoggett 1999; Marsden and French 1998). Thus it can be seen as a way of attempting to secure greater work effort in a context of staff reductions. Second, as the cases of the Inland Revenue and the Employ-ment Service show, PRP is often implemented in such a way that it is perceived by employ-ees to be unfair. The principle of PRP is widely understood to be fair; in practice, however, it is bound to disrupt established pay arrangements and, in doing so, upset existing norms of fairness and the sense of legitimacy that they create, something which forms the basis of workplace order. Thus any alterations to pay-setting arrangements, particularly those that link an element of pay to performance in some way, unless handled very carefully and with due sensitivity, seem likely to have a demotivating effect (Brown and Nolan 1988; Brown and Walsh 1994; Brown, Marginson, and Walsh 2003).

7.2.3 The resilience of established pay-setting arrangements?

The experience of PRP schemes suggests that the need to win the consent of employees places important constraints upon managerial discretion over how pay is determined.

Nevertheless, there has been some discussion about the extent to which payment schemes have become more sophisticated, and thus conform with a human resource management (HRM) approach to managing employees. The use of the term 'reward', rather than pay, refers to innovative methods of remunerating employees that assist the achievement of organizational goals. Rather than basing pay on relatively unsophisticated criteria, such as the number of hours employees spend at work each week, for example, or their length of service, reward schemes may offer employees greater flexibility over their methods of remuneration, or align wages with their performance at work, individually, or sometimes as members of a team. For Druker and White (1999: 13), the management of reward 'is one of the key levers to be deployed in the pursuit of effective HRM. If pay is to "deliver the goods" in terms of HR strategy, then it must be structured . . . in order to meet HR objectives'. Thus the way in which pay is managed must not only be aligned with, and supportive of, broader HRM objectives, but also be integrated with the overall strategic goals of the organization. Should this be the case, then, one would expect pay to be more closely aligned with the characteristics of individual employees, or contingent on business performance.

Following our assessment of the nature of HRM in Chapter 5, it should come as no surprise that management-inspired innovations in respect of pay arrangements have been somewhat limited. Even PRP, despite its attractiveness to managers, not least as a way of undermining collectivism, is far from common, as is the individualization of pay more generally (Arrowsmith and Sisson 1999). An overview of developments in the management of pay highlights the 'relatively durable' character of established practices, 'and certainly the absence of any daring new departures' (Kessler 2000: 283). While high-profile instances of innovations such as competency or team-based pay have been reported, their overall significance appears to be limited. Thus the strategic reform of pay systems is something that managers have been reluctant to attempt. They prefer to tread carefully, and restrict their efforts to incremental, minor adjustments (Kessler 2000).

What, then, explains the absence of significant innovation in the way in which pay is managed, despite the apparently increased freedom of managers to effect change? Three factors would appear to be important. First, managers are reluctant to bear the risks of innovation. We have already seen how the introduction of PRP can disrupt employment relations, by undermining established norms of fairness and the legitimacy they offer. Managers are wary about making changes to existing payment systems. The 'tried and tested nature of arrangements, it seems, invests them with a high degree of legitimacy in the eyes of managers and employees' (Arrowsmith and Sisson 1999: 66). Second, external pressures limit the capacity of managers to innovate in respect of pay arrangements. Although profitability is an important determinant of pay settlements, the significance of two longstanding influences – cost of living and comparability – continued well into the 1990s, despite the diminution of collective bargaining (Ingram, Wadsworth, and Brown 1999). In other words, firms' decisions over pay settlements are constrained by the need to offer rises that are in line both with inflation, and with what other, comparable, groups of workers have been awarded. Third, following on from this, there is evidence of a sector effect in respect of pay. What this means is that similarities between firms operating in the same industry sector can be identified. Arrowsmith and Sisson (1999) found this to be the case after examining arrangements and trends in two sectors – printing and the NHS – where multi-employer bargaining prevailed, and two others – engineering and retailing – where it did not. Although pay was determined within the firm in the latter two sectors, this did not seem to have resulted in organizational outcomes that were noticeably different. Employers 'in each of the four sectors, it seems, continue to move like ships in a convoy' (Arrowsmith and Sisson 1999: 63). Managers may aspire to freedom in determining pay, but they do not appear to have made much use of it (Arrowsmith and Sisson 1999: 70).

7.2.4 The resilience of multi-employer bargaining in the public sector?

While the extent of unilateral regulation of pay by managements has undoubtedly risen, by no means does this imply that collective bargaining in Britain has become extinct. Some two-fifths of employees have their pay determined largely by collective bargaining. While employers may have challenged the influence of the trade unions, union recognition for collective bargaining purposes remains commonplace among large private sector companies. The giant retailer Tesco, for example, has a formal bargaining relationship with a trade union, one that, as we saw in Chapter 6 has been reconstructed as a 'partnership agreement'. In the public sector, collective bargaining, generally by means of multi-employer arrangements, continues to exert a powerful influence over the determination of pay.

Multi-employer bargaining is a significant feature of employment relations in the British public sector. The resilience of national bargaining in the public sector (Corby 2000), despite Conservative attempts to undermine it, is striking. Conservative policy was founded upon the belief that the devolution of operational decision-making to local managers would make employment relations more 'responsive to the needs of managerial efficiency and labour market conditions, and more sensitive to employee performance' (Winchester and Bach 1999: 45). The restructuring of many public services, such as the 1991 creation of NHS trust hospitals, was designed in large part to stimulate local bargaining, and also to undermine the national power bases of the major public sector trade unions.

However, with the exceptions of the Civil Service, where responsibility for pay determination has been devolved to individual executive agencies, such as the Benefits Agency for example, and further education colleges, where national bargaining has been eroded (see Box 7.2), significant decentralization has been limited. 'Across the public services, more decentralized and flexible arrangements for pay determination . . . have developed but in a piecemeal, uneven and often inconsistent way' (Bach and Winchester 2003: 299). Why, then, were attempts to decentralize bargaining in the public sector largely unsuccessful, and why have national bargaining arrangements proved to be so resilient? In some areas, structural factors have impeded decentralization. Schools, for example, are generally too small to be able to handle their own employment relations effectively (Ironside, Seifert, and Sinclair 1997). Despite attempts in the 1990s to stimulate local bargaining in the NHS, it was challenged by a combination of management ambivalence and union opposition (Carr 1999; Thornley 1998). The Treasury, moreover, was reluctant to cede control over pay outcomes. Thus a tension exists between the objective of devolving decision-making and the necessity of maintaining central control over the public sector paybill (Carter and Fairbrother 1999; White 1996; Winchester and Bach 1999).

Furthermore, the operation of pay review bodies has 'contributed to the resilience of national systems of pay determination' (Bach and Winchester 1994: 273). What, though, are pay review bodies? Briefly, they are ostensibly independent institutions, whose

---

BOX 7.2 THE EROSION OF NATIONAL BARGAINING IN THE FURTHER EDUCATION SECTOR

Apart from the civil service, where the more direct role of government as employer appears to have been critical, the only other part of the public sector in Britain where national bargaining has been significantly eroded is the further education sector in England and Wales. Until 1993, further education colleges came under the control of their respective local authorities, which were the employers of college staff. Pay rates were negotiated nationally between representatives of the local authorities and the appropriate trade unions. Conditions of service were also determined by multi-employer bargaining at national level. The national 'Silver Book' agreement – as it was called because of the colour of its cover – among other things set upper limits on the number of teaching hours that lecturers could work on a weekly and annual basis.

In 1993, the colleges were taken out of local authority control and, in a process called 'incorporation', became employers of college staff in their own right. Although the arrangements would change, there was no expectation that national bargaining would cease. It was anticipated that the newly established College Employers' Forum (CEF), an employers' association which took on the job of representing the colleges' employment relations interests, would continue to negotiate agreements with the unions which would then apply throughout the sector. The CEF's leadership, however, developed an ambitious reform agenda. Since college budgets were to be squeezed, it proposed replacing the Silver Book with a 'flexible' contract that placed no specific limitations upon college lecturers' workload. This provoked a lengthy and bitter industrial dispute as the main lecturers' union tried to resist the imposition of new contracts. While some colleges were able to impose the CEF's contract, many introduced, either unilaterally or after negotiations with local union representatives, a version of their own which included some workload limits. By the end of the 1990s, then, a large variety of different contractual arrangements existed in the sector.

Pay remained formally subject to national bargaining, although the inability, or reluctance, of many colleges to implement annual recommended awards in full, or at all in some cases, because of purported financial difficulties, led to an increasingly disparate set of pay rates across the sector as well as a number of industrial disputes. Since 2000, attempts have been made by the employers and the unions to reinforce the authority of national agreements linked to the availability of more funds for the sector. It has proved difficult, though, to reinstate their influence given the diversity of employment arrangements present in the college sector.

Source: Williams (2004)

---

members are appointed by the government, which, after evaluating appropriate data and submissions from interested parties such as trade unions, make non-binding recommendations to the government on pay increases, and any other relevant matters within their remit. Since the 1960s, pay review bodies have covered some groups of public sector employees, such as doctors and dentists. However, since nurses, along with 'professions allied to medicine', including midwives and health visitors, and schoolteachers' pay became subject to review body recommendations, in 1983 and 1991 respectively, their role has understandably attracted greater prominence. In 2002, prison officers were also given a pay review body.

Pay review bodies were established for nurses and schoolteachers following key industrial disputes in the health service and in education. In respect of nurses, the then Conservative government was shaken by industrial action in the NHS during 1982. By establishing a pay review body for nurses and professionals allied to medicine, it anticipated 'that these groups would never again join other health-service workers in a sector-wide pay campaign' (Bach 1999a: 107–8). The Burnham bargaining machinery, which had hitherto regulated bargaining over schoolteachers' pay, was abolished by the government in 1987 as a 'punishment for extensive industrial action in the mid-1980s' (Bailey 1996: 137). Given that the government had promised to restore bargaining arrangements, the announcement that from 1991 onwards schoolteachers' pay would be subject to a pay review body process appears to have been somewhat unexpected (Ironside and Seifert 1995; White 2000).

While not perhaps an ideal option, for the government the two main attractions of pay review bodies are, first, that they offer a 'more stable and less conflictual system of pay determination than existed previously' (White 2000: 94), and second, that they give the impression that the government is an indifferent bystander, allowing it to avoid being drawn into potentially messy employment relations issues. Thus the pay review body system may be viewed as a more than adequate substitute for traditional collective bargaining arrangements in so far as it mitigates industrial conflict in key public sector occupations.

How, then, is one to interpret the implications of the pay review bodies? Their presence has undoubtedly hindered the development of local bargaining arrangements since pay recommendations generally apply across the board. In respect of pay outcomes, it would seem that public sector occupations whose pay awards are the outcome of pay review board recommendations do better than those who are covered by traditional bargaining arrangements. Moreover, the review body process can boost the legitimacy of trade union arguments. Perhaps the biggest losers are public sector employers who have to bear the cost of implementing pay awards but have little influence over the process by which they are enacted (Bach and Winchester 2003).

But how should the pay review body process itself be understood? In some interpretations, it is treated as a form of pay determination that is distinct from collective bargaining. Analyses of the WERS data omit workers covered by pay review body machinery when calculating collective bargaining coverage in the public sector. Thus nurses and schoolteachers are treated as if they are excluded from bargaining coverage, which, unsurprisingly, according to this measure, has dwindled considerably since the early 1980s, from 95 per cent of employees in 1984 to 64 per cent in 1998 (Cully et al. 1999; Millward, Bryson, and Forth 2000). Such an interpretation has been challenged, however, by the argument that, rather than acting as a 'substitute' for the collective bargaining process, pay review bodies, as a kind of third-party intervention, are in fact 'part of it' (Burchill 2000: 155). In other words, the review bodies mediate between the claims of the unions, representing the collective interests of their members, and the counter-claims of the employer representatives; recommendations 'may be more or less favourable to one or other of the two main groups but are generally not too distant from either', and are implemented by the government with due regard to the unions' bargaining power, with the possibility of industrial action should the unions be dissatisfied with the outcome (Burchill, 2000: 152). Just because the parties do not meet with each other directly over a single negotiating table does not invalidate its status as bargaining. The concept of 'arms' length bargaining' would therefore appear to be the most appropriate way of classifying the review body process (Winchester and Bach 1995).

Finally, it is important to be aware that the resilience of formal national bargaining arrangements across most of the public sector has disguised significant changes within many workplaces. Faced with pressures to improve service delivery, make cost savings, and improve efficiency, public sector managers have made some headway in re-shaping the wage-work bargain for some groups of workers. They have 'concentrated on altering the utilization and composition of the staff employed, increasing work intensity and "re-profiling" the work-force to meet short-term budgetary constraints' (Bach and Winchester 1994: 276). This has been particularly evident within the NHS where the creation of the post of healthcare assistant (HCA) has enabled managers to gain much sought after flexibility. Unlike qualified nursing staff, the pay and conditions of HCAs are determined locally, often unilaterally by management, though sometimes with union involvement (Grimshaw 1999: 302).

The increased use of HCAs, whose pay and conditions are not subject to nationally agreed awards, has often been part of initiatives to 're-profile' the workforce, or to change its 'skill-mix' – in effect a device to increase the proportion of lesser-paid, and thus cheaper, HCAs at the expense of qualified, and more expensive, nursing staff. Thus 'the resilience of national pay determination has disguised significant changes in employment practices at workplace level' (Bach 1999a: 112). Moreover, the opening up of public services to private sector providers increasingly undermines national pay and conditions of service agreements. In education, for example, the operators of city academies, new types of school that are partially funded and run by private companies, are, in principle, able to set their own terms and conditions of employment for schoolteachers. While national, multi-employer bargaining in the public sector has proved to be remarkably resilient, increasing private sector involvement in the delivery of public services may erode it in future.

SECTION SUMMARY AND FURTHER READING

- Since the 1980s, multi-employer bargaining in the private sector has become a rarity. In order to secure greater flexibility over their own employment relations, employers increasingly prefer to bargain with trade unions themselves. Moreover, the contraction of collective bargaining coverage in the private sector means that the majority of employees in Britain have their pay determined unilaterally by management.

- Though it may not be all that common, a large amount of attention has been devoted to PRP and its implications. Managers find arrangements that associate pay with performance attractive; they help to secure the commitment of employees to business goals. While sometimes designed to undermine collectivism, PRP is not inimical to joint regulation and trade unionism. Nevertheless, despite the apparently greater freedom they enjoy to reform pay systems and influence pay settlements, managers have been reluctant to upset existing, 'tried-and-tested' arrangements.

- In the public sector, formal multi-employer bargaining arrangements have been somewhat resilient, despite attempts to challenge them. The operation of pay review bodies for key groups of workers, a form of 'arms' length bargaining', is an important contributory factor. The apparent resilience of formal machinery at national level may, however, disguise important changes in the workplace, such as 're-profiling' and 'skill-mix' initiatives, designed to alter the wage-work bargain in favour of the employer.

Collective bargaining trends in Britain since the 1980s are amply covered by Brown and Walsh (1991), and Brown, Marginson, and Walsh (1995, 2003). For overviews of developments in pay determination, see Brown and Walsh (1994), Brown, Marginson, and Walsh (2003), and Kessler (2000). Marsden and French (1998) report on the findings of a study of PRP in the public services, and Heery's (1998a) careful and sophisticated analysis of PRP in local government is also recommended. Arrowsmith and Sisson (1999) consider the durability of established pay-setting processes. There are now several good overviews of employment relations developments in the public sector: Bach and Winchester (2003), White (1999), and Winchester and Bach (1999) are particularly recommended.

7.3 Pay inequality, low pay, and the National Minimum Wage

One of the main implications of the diminution of collective bargaining as a pay-setting mechanism in Britain, and the consequent increase in managerial discretion, has been the growth of pay inequality. There is a strong relationship between low pay and gender, with women concentrated in low-paying occupations. In this respect, the 1999 introduction of the National Minimum Wage (NMW) was a significant legislative development. For Simpson (1999: 1), it was the Labour government's 'most radical and far-reaching reform of employment rights'. Following an opening section in which we consider the growth of wage inequality and the problem of low pay, we assess the means by which low pay has been regulated, and the impact of the NMW in the period since its inception.

7.3.1 Pay inequality in Britain

A significant trend in Britain since the early 1980s has been the growth of pay inequality. By this we mean that the gap between high earners and low earners has widened considerably. Between 1979 and 1996, the earnings of the bottom 25 per cent of male wage earners fell from 80 per cent to 73 per cent of median average earnings, while for the top 25 per cent they rose from 125 per cent to 138 per cent (Kessler and Bayliss 1998: 227). According to Machin (1999: 185), pay gaps 'between the rich and poor have widened since the late 1970s, with wage inequality reaching the highest levels experienced in the twentieth century'. The growth of inequality, then, has largely been fuelled by the way in which pay rises for high and relatively high earners have far outstripped the increases for people on more modest earnings. With the exception of Ireland, where wage inequality also rose, in the rest of the European Union it largely remained stable or even diminished (Machin 1999).

Although the growth of pay inequality may have slowed in the 1990s (Machin 2003), why has it been so pronounced in Britain? For one thing, it is clear that high earners, in particular senior executives, have been able to attract ever-higher levels of remuneration relative to others (see Box 7.3). But this is only part of the story. Changes in the economy and the labour market, in particular new technology and increased wage premiums that

---

BOX 7.3 DIRECTORS' PAY AND THE GROWTH OF PAY INEQUALITY

One of the contributory factors to the growth of pay inequality in Britain has been the ever-increasing level of remuneration enjoyed by executives of public limited companies. According to a survey by *The Guardian* newspaper, in 2001 boardroom pay rose by 17 per cent; in the following year, it increased by 23 per cent, some seven times greater than the growth in average earnings for all employees. Instances of what some trade union leaders have referred to as 'fat-cat' pay arrangements abound. In 2003, for example, a director of the HSBC bank was appointed on a deal that would give him £37 million over the three years of his contract. Business groups, such as the Institute of Directors, claim that companies are operating in a global market for talent, and thus need to offer high basic salaries, and also the prospect of share options and generous bonuses, in order to attract key executives. Nevertheless, since the size of a director's remuneration package signals their importance relative to others, status would appear to be a major influence on boardroom pay. One feature of executive pay that has caused widespread concern, moreover, is that directors frequently receive large pay-offs on leaving their companies, regardless of their performance. A former chief executive of the insurers Royal & Sun Alliance, for example, was given a pay-off of over £2 million despite a fall of 90 per cent in the company's share price, and the loss of some 12,000 jobs.

The British government has been reluctant to legislate and restrict fat-cat pay. During the 1990s, both Conservative and Labour administrations encouraged self-regulation, in particular the adoption of the Cadbury, Greenbury, and Hampel codes of practice which, among other things, recommended the establishment of dedicated remuneration committees made up of non-executive directors, and greater transparency and disclosure of directors' pay arrangements. The presumption was that it was for the shareholders of companies to challenge excessive and unjustified pay awards. Further controversial fat-cat pay deals have, however, prompted the Labour government to introduce legislation. Shareholders have been given the opportunity to vote on directors' remuneration arrangements at company annual general meetings. In 2003, shareholders of the pharmaceutical firm Glaxo-SmithKline voted down the £22 million pay-off due to chief executive Jean-Pierre Garnier should his contract be terminated. Such votes, though, are merely voluntary, and companies can ignore them if they wish. The government, in its 2003 discussion paper *Rewards for Failure*, suggests that further legislation may be necessary to ensure that directors' pay-offs are in some way based on company performance, for example.

---

can be attracted by more highly qualified workers, are also important factors. However, 'when we take an international perspective the countries which have seen the largest rises in inequality are those where the importance of labour-market institutions in wage setting has declined most' (Machin 1996: 63). In other words, the diminution of trade union power and collective bargaining have been important influences on the growth of earnings inequality (Brown, Marginson, and Walsh 2003). Where collective pay-setting institutions are robust, and particularly where they are centralized, they can act to compress pay differentials, especially if the unions are strongly committed to the pursuit of equality, as in Scandinavia for example (Robson et al. 1999; Rubery and Edwards 2003).

Thus the presence of powerful trade unions, and strong, centralized collective bargaining arrangements, can act to lessen the problem of low pay, though not so much for women (Dex, Robson, and Wilkinson 1999). How, though, is low pay defined? Is there a particular level below which we can say pay is low? Or is low pay a relative concept, something that can only be measured in relation to the general level of earnings characteristic of a particular society? For example, a British worker earning £2.00 per hour would consider herself to be low-paid; an Indonesian worker on the same rate might think herself somewhat well off. Studies of low pay prefer to treat it as a relative concept (e.g. Rubery and Edwards 2003). What measure, then, should be used? The Organization for Economic Cooperation and Development (OECD) defines low pay as a level of earnings that falls below two-thirds of median average full-time earnings. The profusion of different measures can sometimes make international comparisons difficult, especially if they restrict the analysis to full-time earnings, since low pay is often a feature of part-time jobs (Rubery and Edwards 2003) which are largely populated by women. Low pay is also more common in small businesses than in larger ones, and also in certain occupations, such as hospitality, private social care, retail, clothing and textile manufacturing, and hairdressing.

7.3.2 The regulation of low pay

Broadly speaking, there are two main ways in which low pay is regulated in modern economies, by collective agreements, or by means of a statutory minimum wage (Rubery and Grimshaw 2003). In the case of the first of these arrangements, a floor of wages is generally set by collective bargaining on an industry-by-industry basis, such as in Germany for example, with governments sometimes having the power to extend the settlement to all employers in the sector, even those that are not directly party to the agreement. Centralized systems of bargaining can often be quite effective ways of regulating low pay, and of impeding the growth of wage inequality, especially for men (Bazen and Benhayoun 1992; Robson et al. 1999). The second type of arrangement, a statutory minimum wage, exists in countries such as France, Spain, Portugal, and, since the late 1990s, in Ireland and Britain too.

But the NMW, which took effect in Britain from April 1999, is by no means the first way in which the British state has acted to regulate low pay. Fair Wages Resolutions, for example, which originated in 1891, obliged employers to respect minimum standards when working on public sector contracts, largely to prevent unfair competition arising from the undercutting of wages (Bercusson 1978; Metcalf 1999b). In the early 1980s, the Conservative government repealed them. In 1993, the Conservatives also abolished the remaining wages councils, which, for a large part of the twentieth century, had fixed wage rates, and sometimes employment conditions, in a range of low-paying sectors. They were seen as outdated and anachronistic institutions which inhibited labour market flexibility, were ineffective at tackling poverty and, given that they priced workers out of jobs, hindered employment growth (Dickens et al. 1993; Rubery and Edwards 2003).

Research into the impact of the abolition of the wages councils found evidence of widening pay distribution, and an absence of any positive impact on employment (Lucas and Radiven 1998). According to a study of the hospitality industry, pay subsequently fell in a third of establishments; one employer welcomed the greater 'flexibility' that the removal of the wages councils had brought, meaning that he could 'get away with paying lower wages' (Lucas and Radiven 1998: 11). Thus we are presented with a stark indication of how the weakening of the institutions of labour market regulation, driven by Conservative governments of the 1980s and 1990s, contributed to increasing wage inequality. The Labour government elected in 1997, however, initiated an important change of direction by establishing, for the first time ever, a National Minimum Wage, 'belatedly bringing Britain in to line with the rest of the industrialized world' (Brown 2000: 309).

7.3.3 The National Minimum Wage in Britain

Labour's commitment to an NMW was the outcome of protracted debates and struggle within the party as supporters of the policy, particularly within some trade unions, tried to overcome the traditional ambivalence towards statutory wage-fixing that had characterized attitudes within much of the labour movement. Labour's 1992 general election manifesto included a promise to implement a minimum wage to be set at a half of male average median weekly earnings, excluding overtime. Despite losing the 1992 election, Labour retained its commitment to introduce a minimum wage. However, following the 1994 election of Tony Blair as Labour party leader, there was a subtle, but significant, shift in policy. Instead of promising to establish a minimum wage at a specific rate, Labour now advocated giving the job of recommending a level to a dedicated body to be put in place for the task. Following its 1997 election victory, the Labour government set up a Low Pay Commission (LPC), comprising employers' and union representatives, as well as academic experts.

Once it had determined what aspects of pay could be counted towards the NMW, tips left on the table by customers are excluded for example, perhaps the most significant tasks which faced the LPC were to recommend a minimum rate, and to determine which workers would be entitled to receive it. The LPC proposed that all workers aged 21 and over should be covered by the full NMW rate, at a 'deliberately prudent' (Metcalf 1999a) £3.60 per hour. It also recommended a lower 'development' NMW rate of £3.20 per hour which should be paid to workers aged between 18 and 20, and also to any worker in the first six months of a job on condition that their employer provides them with formal training based upon externally accredited qualifications. The government accepted these recommendations, but made two adjustments. First, the lower NMW rate was introduced at £3.00 per hour for young workers. Second, it was extended to cover 21 year olds. Since their introduction in 1999, the NMW rates have been changed, or 'uprated', several times, as can be seen from Table 7.2. In October 2004, the government introduced a new, lower rate of £3.00 per hour that applies to 16 and 17 year olds. Trade unions and the LPC (LPC 2004) had expressed concern about the very low pay levels earned by some workers in this age group.

The method of uprating the NMW has proved controversial. Formally, the LPC, drawing on research and evaluation studies, recommends a new rate to the government, which, if it agrees, then implements the rise. The absence of an annual uprating mechanism, however, leaves the NMW rates open to political interference. A second area of criticism concerns the lower, or 'subminimum', NMW rates for younger workers, a topic that appears to have caused a considerable amount of discussion within the LPC itself (Metcalf 1999a). What was the rationale for these differential rates? Although it was expected that in the longer term the youth development rate should be linked to a programme of relevant skills training (LPC 1998, 2000, 2001b), it was introduced largely because of a concern that if young workers were to be covered by the main NMW rate it would make them too expensive for employers to hire, thus significantly damaging their labour market prospects (Metcalf 1999a). Research on the effects of minimum wages in the United States demonstrates, however, that subminimum rates of pay for young workers are not only unpopular among

Table 7.2 National Minimum Wage rates 1999–2005

	Workers aged 22 and over	Workers aged between 18 and 21
April 1999	£3.60	£3.00
June 2000	No uprating	£3.20
October 2000	£3.70	No uprating
October 2001	£4.10	£3.50
October 2002	£4.20	£3.60
October 2003	£4.50	£3.80
October 2004	£4.85	£4.10
October 2005	£5.05	£4.25

employers, largely based on the belief that they would not be able to attract workers at such low wages, but that they also appear to have no discernible positive impact on employment (Card and Krueger 1995; Katz and Krueger 1992).

Use of the subminimum rates in Britain is far from extensive. In a study of the textiles industry, Heyes and Gray (2001) found that forty-eight out of the fifty-three workplaces they studied paid 18–21 year olds an hourly rate that was greater than the development rate. The reluctance of employers to use the lower rate for young workers is something that has been identified elsewhere (e.g. LPC 2003). There are difficulties recruiting, motivating, and retaining younger workers at rates of pay that are below the main 'adult' NMW level; many managers view it as unfair to discriminate against them on the grounds of age (Williams, Adam-Smith, and Norris 2004).

A further area of criticism, one that came from many trade unions and campaigning organizations for the low paid, was that the main rate of £3.60 per hour was set at far too low a level. It 'was roughly equivalent to half of male median earnings, in contrast to the level of two-thirds of the median which is the widely accepted measure of low pay' (Rubery and Edwards 2003: 461). The LPC appears to have taken a deliberately cautious stance in its recommendations, favouring the introduction of an NMW at a relatively low level, just in case there were any adverse effects on the economy, and, through regular upratings, building from there. But how far has such an approach benefited the low paid? Although some 1.3 million workers appear to have been immediate beneficiaries of pay rises brought about by the NMW, the policy itself was not designed to eliminate low pay but, as a statutory floor of wages, only to 'reduce its extent and intensity' (Rubery and Edwards 2003: 466).

The NMW, then, was implemented in such a way that it would not be overly disruptive for employers. It is entirely consistent, therefore, with the business-friendly ideology that shaped Labour's employment relations policies. While its interventions were not insignificant, as we saw in Chapter 3 they were too often implemented in a 'minimalist' way, designed not to inconvenience employers too greatly. Based upon her experiences of a series of low-paying jobs, including cleaning hotels and working in a care home, the journalist Fran Abrams challenged the assumptions upon which the introduction of the minimum wage was based. She referred to the NMW as 'an old-fashioned political stitch-up, set at a level which would ensure the lowest possible level of protest from employers without enraging the unions sufficiently for them to cause real trouble' (Abrams 2002: 170). The NMW policy is clearly a marked contrast with the deregulatory labour market policies enacted by the Conservatives during the 1980s and 1990s (Adam-Smith, Norris, and Williams 2003). Its impact, however, is likely to have been somewhat constrained by the characteristics of its implementation. What remains to be considered now, therefore, are the effects of the NMW since it was introduced in April 1999.

7.3.4 **The impact of the National Minimum Wage**

Prior to the implementation of the NMW, there were some well-informed, and many not so well-informed predictions of its likely effects both on employment in low-paying sectors of the economy and also on the economy in general. Before, during, and after the 1997 general election, both the Conservative party and many business organizations opposed the minimum wage policy claiming that it would push up inflation, and would have such an adverse impact on employment that hundreds of thousands of jobs were at risk. The simple economic reasoning behind these claims is that any rise in the price of labour, wages that is, will, without a corresponding increase in productivity, reduce employers' demand for it. Alternatively, firms will pass on the higher costs of adapting to the NMW to customers in the form of higher prices. Such problems would be exacerbated if, as critics of the minimum wage expected, other groups of workers were to secure corresponding increases in their wages in order to preserve their relative position in the pay hierarchy or, in other words, restore their existing pay 'differentials'.

Yet contrary to these expectations, the introduction of the NMW appears to have had little adverse effect on the British economy; it arrived with a 'whimper rather than a bang' (Dickens and Manning 2003: 202). The impact on inflation was negligible, and employment levels in many low-paying sectors of the economy, such as hospitality and retail for example, rose, rather than fell, once the minimum wage took effect (LPC 2001a). Three factors appear to have eased the introduction of the NMW. First, the low level at which the NMW was set meant that most firms, even in low-paying sectors of the economy, were unaffected directly by its introduction and many of those that were found the necessary increases in wage rates easily affordable. Second, the NMW was introduced in a period of robust economic growth. Increasing demand for hospitality services, for example, led to a tightening of the labour market, often pushing up wages to well above the NMW rate (Adam-Smith, Norris, and Williams 2003).

Third, was it ever likely that a wholesale process of upholding differentials would occur? The unions have a weak presence in low-paying sectors of the economy, so there would be little pressure to restore differentials from that quarter. It also seems unlikely that wage rises in one sector will necessarily fuel demands for equivalent treatment in others (Rubery and Edwards 2003). Furthermore, since it is their position within the pay hierarchy that generally matters to workers, rather than the scale of the gap between them and others, then firms have the ability to narrow, or 'squeeze', differentials when responding to the NMW. The authors came across an example of this in a holiday resort where the introduction of the NMW compelled the company to raise the pay of chalet attendants and their lower-paid assistants in order to comply with the statutory minimum wage. However, once the new rates came into effect the gap between the attendants and their assistants was no longer as great as it had been prior to the change.

While these factors have clearly limited the impact of the NMW, a further explanation of why it has not created a 'labour market shock', in the manner expected by some (Brown and Crossman 2000), concerns the nature of employment relations in low-paying firms. Studies of the impact of the NMW in low-paying sectors of the economy generally show most firms to have been unaffected directly by the introduction of the statutory floor of wages (Adam-Smith, Norris, and Williams 2003; Heyes and Grey 2001; Undy, Kessler, and Thompson 2002). They also reveal that even where firms were required to raise wages in response to the NMW, there was generally little impact on employment levels. For many firms, frequently small businesses operating on tight margins, there is no further scope to reduce their workforce since they already operate with the minimum number of staff necessary to function. In the clothing and knitwear industries employment was falling, but this was largely a consequence of greater foreign competition (Undy, Kessler, and Thompson 2002).

Among firms that have been directly affected by the minimum wage, perhaps the most noticeable way in which they have attempted to recoup the costs of higher wages, particularly in clothing manufacturing where piecework incentives have been eroded, has been through increased workloads and greater supervision (Heyes and Grey 2001; Undy, Kessler, and Thompson 2002). The minimum wage also appears to have caused some firms to invest in new technology as a way of boosting productivity and thus recouping costs. But this has been rare. Indeed, the most striking feature of firms' responses to the NMW has been the absence of any pattern other than that its introduction does not appear to have been overly traumatic. How, then, did the minimum wage come to be accommodated so relatively easily?

The key to understanding the relatively muted impact of the NMW rests upon an appreciation that firms in low-paying sectors of the economy, where formal arrangements for determining pay are uncommon, have the ability to respond to changes in their environment, such as the introduction of a minimum wage, in a dynamic way (Edwards and Gilman 1999). In other words, the high level of informality that characterizes the management of employment relations in small firms means that employers enjoy considerable freedom to juggle the terms of the wage-work bargain in order to respond to external challenges. In the hospitality industry, for example, employers are well used to operating with less than a full complement of staff, not least because of high turnover levels and the need to keep costs under control. The introduction of the NMW, in so far as it raises costs, has not transformed this situation, but merely encouraged employers to tinker with it (Adam-Smith, Norris, and Williams 2003).

Thus, far from being a shock to firms in low-paying sectors of the economy, the minimum wage is simply a further influence among the many that shape the employment relationship. It is unlikely that a consistent pattern of responses to the NMW will be identified, particularly with it being set at such a low level. Rather, affected firms will react in idiosyncratic and diverse ways, influenced by the characteristics of their product and labour market environments (Gilman et al. 2002; Ram et al. 2001). A study of the impact of the NMW in small firms demonstrated that, while the establishment of a statutory floor of wages often raised their costs, its arrival 'did not provide a shock sufficient to jolt employers or workers out of their customary practices and habits' (Arrowsmith et al. 2003: 451–2).

Finally, what has the NMW done to stem the growth of wage inequality in Britain? As was indicated above, some 1.3 million workers, over two-thirds of them women, seem to have benefited from the introduction of the NMW in that before 1999 they were paid below what would become the statutory minimum rates. Not only did the NMW close the divide between higher male and lower female average earnings – the 'gender pay gap' – by a whole percentage point in the year after it took effect, the biggest movement for ten years, but it also appeared to have caused a slight reduction in overall pay inequality (Rubery and Edwards 2003: 464). This effect may, however, only have been a temporary one. The excessive growth in pay levels of largely male executives at the top of the pay hierarchy, caused the gender pay gap to increase again in 2002 and has thus helped to render the NMW ineffective as a way of combating inequality (IDS 2003). In summary, then, the minimum wage has undoubtedly been of great benefit to many low-paid, generally female workers who have seen a rise in their pay. It has done little, however, to offset pay inequality in Britain, which, in the early 2000s, continued to grow.

SECTION SUMMARY AND FURTHER READING

- Since the 1980s, wage inequality in Britain has grown markedly, in contrast to most other EU countries. It has been caused in part by the erosion of collective bargaining coverage, though excessive pay rises for high earners and economic and technical changes were also contributory factors.

- There are two broad ways in which low pay can be regulated, either by some form of statutory minimum wage, or by means of comprehensive collective agreements which provide a floor of wages on an industry basis. The latter appears to be a more effective way of tacking wage inequality, especially among men.

- The first National Minimum Wage (NMW) was introduced in Britain in April 1999, although until the 1990s the system of wages councils had hitherto provided protection in some low-paying industries. The main NMW rate was initially set at a rather low level, £3.60 per hour, something which made it more acceptable to business leaders.

- The NMW has not had any adverse economic consequences, and has been accommodated by firms in low-paying sectors of the economy with relative ease. Its contribution to reducing wage inequality appears to have been slight.

Machin (2003) provides a good overview of trends in wage inequality in Britain. The best analysis of low pay, attempts to regulate it, and the implications of the NMW is offered by Rubery and Edwards (2003). For an account of the way in which the Low Pay Commission handled its task from a notable advocate of a cautious and prudent approach to the NMW, see Metcalf (1999a). The Low Pay Commission has produced five reports, one of which, in 2001, was in two parts. These should be available in all good libraries, with the more recent also accessible online at: **www.lowpay.gov.uk.** Fran Abrams (2002) has written a book that details what it is like to work in low-paid jobs. Finally, for studies of the impact of the NMW in particular sectors, see Arrowsmith et al. (2003), and Adam-Smith, Norris, and Williams (2003).

7.4 Developments in working time

Working time – its length, its pattern, and its use – is a central concern of employment relations, although it is often overlooked in textbooks (Sisson and Storey 2000). This is somewhat odd since, as was discussed in the introductory chapter of this book, the principal feature of the employment relationship is the exchange of wages for latent labour power – an employee's capacity to work. When a job is started it is not the employee's labour that an employer is buying, but, in effect, his or her time. It is then the task of the employer to ensure that this time is used productively (Arrowsmith and Sisson 2000: 303). Moreover, working time has long been an issue on which trade unions have campaigned, for a shorter working week in particular. In order to understand contemporary employment relations properly, then, it is essential to consider trends in working time, and also how it is regulated.

The issue of working time has recently attracted an increasing amount of interest, to such an extent that it may even exceed pay in its importance as an employment relations topic. There are three reasons for this. First, it is suggested that employers are seeking innovations in how working time is organized as a way of generating efficiencies. Second, concerns have been expressed about the harmful effects of excessive working time in Britain, or what has popularly become known as the 'long hours culture'. Third, in 1998 the British government introduced the Working Time Regulations (WTR), as a result of a European Union (EU) directive, which ostensibly places legal limits upon the number of hours that can be worked. Before we consider these developments, it is necessary to consider working time and employment relations in general.

7.4.1 Working time and employment relations

The organization of working time by employers was critical to the development of capitalist industrialization during the late eighteenth and nineteenth centuries. Since it helped employers to develop a new ethos of factory discipline, the clock was a crucial component of the rise of the factory system (Noon and Blyton 2002; Pollard 1968; Thompson 1967). Although workers did not submit meekly to the new industrial capitalist order, attendance at work, for a specified period of time governed by the clock, became the norm.

Like any other aspect of the employment relationship, attempts by employers to control working time have always been challenged. Absenteeism is the most prominent way in which employees can appropriate working time (Ackroyd and Thompson 1999). It will be examined in more detail, as a potential manifestation of conflict in the employment relationship, in Chapter 9. But there are other ways in which workers have manipulated working time to suit their interests.

In particular, in workplaces based around production lines workers have an opportunity to exert control over their working time, by working 'back up the line' for example. This refers to the process, commonplace in vehicle manufacturing at one time (e.g. Turner, Clack, and Roberts 1967), by which an increase in the pace of work enables workers to generate short, informal rest breaks as the production line catches up. This is particularly effective in situations where workers are able to manipulate job timings set through work study techniques. If workers can slow a job down and make it look difficult when it is being measured, this is likely to result in a 'loose' rate, making it easier to accumulate informal rest periods if they revert to their normal, faster pace or, alternatively, allowing them to work more leisurely, at the pace set for the work study engineers, without any loss of pay (Roy 1952). While it may have become harder for workers to manipulate working time to their advantage, attempts to do so remain an important feature of the employment relationship.

Thus not only is working time is an important feature of the employment relationship, but it is also one that is contested between the employer and employee. This can be seen in the long-running attempts by workers, collectively through trade unions, to shorten the length of both the working day and the working week. Although nineteenth-century campaigns by prominent liberal philanthropists helped to secure reduced working hours for women and child workers, it is important to recognize that legislation was largely the outcome of working-class pressure for reform (Arrowsmith 2002). The reduction of working time has been an aim of organized labour ever since, if not always a central one. Working time has been a key source of contestation between unions and employers, and campaigns to reduce its length were 'fundamental to the organization of the working class and the development of labour solidarity' (Arrowsmith 2002: 114). During the 1980s and 1990s, for example, engineering unions in Germany and Britain successfully used industrial action to reduce the length of the working week, to thirty-five hours in the case of the former. However, this often came at a price as employers conceded lower hours in return for greater flexibility over the utilization of working time (Hyman 2001b; McKinlay and McNulty 1992). Nevertheless, trade unions have an important role in successfully campaigning for, and wresting from employers, reductions in working time, and also paid holiday entitlement (Green 1997).

7.4.2 Trends in working time

Having considered the importance of working time in employment relations, and the way in which trade union efforts have been directed at reducing it, what, then, have been the main trends? Historically, the overall trend in Britain, at least until the 1990s, was towards the reduction in the average number of weekly working hours for full-time employees. Nevertheless, reflecting the large extent to which working time reductions were the outcome of struggles and campaigns by organized labour, it was 'manifested in sporadic discrete jumps punctuated by long periods of stability' (Green 2001: 58). However, in the early 1990s this trend came to an end, and may even have been reversed, resulting in British full-time employees having the longest average working week in the EU (see Table 7.3), and creating significant concerns about the rise of a so-called 'long-hours culture' (Arrowsmith 2002).

Taken as a whole, though, the average length of the working week in Britain is unremarkable relative to other EU countries. While the working week of full-time employees is particularly lengthy, the high number of part-time jobs in Britain means that there is a notable 'dispersion' of working hours (Green 2001): some work many hours in an average

Table 7.3 Number of hours usually worked each week by full-time employees in selected EU countries 2002

United Kingdom	43.3
Greece	41.0
Spain	40.4
Sweden	39.9
Belgium	39.3
The Netherlands	38.9
Italy	38.5
France	37.7

Source: EIRO (2004a)

week, whereas others may only work for a few. Women in Britain, who dominate part-time jobs, work the fewest hours of any EU country, with the exception of the Netherlands; male workers, however, 'top the European league' (Green 2001: 59). Data from the 1998 Workplace Employment Relations Survey highlight some interesting characteristics of the lengthy working week in Britain (see Cully et al. 1999: 154–8):

- 13 per cent of employees reported usually working more than forty-eight hours a week;
- one-third of employees reported usually working more than forty hours a week;
- 22 per cent of male employees work more than forty-eight hours per week;
- 5 per cent of female employees reported usually working more than forty-eight hours a week, though they are still more likely to undertake more of the household chores than their male partners;
- the long working week is particularly commonplace among managers, professionals, and operative and assembly workers;
- 37 per cent of male managers and 21 per cent of female managers reported usually working more than forty-eight hours per week.

What, then, has caused the lengthening of the average working week? Three factors seem to be significant. First, competitive pressures, which have impelled many businesses to find ways of increasing output while freezing, or even reducing, staff numbers, have had an effect. Thus employees, particularly those in white-collar jobs, especially professionals and managers, are obliged to work more hours, usually unpaid, to make up the slack. Second, unlike other EU countries where statutory limits on working time are commonplace (see Box 7.4 on France), legal regulation has traditionally been 'minimal' in the UK (Arrowsmith and Sisson 2000: 304). Moreover, the trade unions which, through collective bargaining, had been a major influence on the shortening of the working week, suffered a significant reduction in their power during the 1980s and 1990s. Third, employment relations in Britain is characterized by a remarkably high incidence of overtime working, paid, usually at a higher, premium rate, or unpaid work undertaken in excess of the 'normal' working day or week.

BOX 7.4 THE 35-HOUR WORKING WEEK IN FRANCE

The regulation and control of working time has long been a central concern of trade unions in France, and a prime source of contestation in employment relations. For much of the twentieth century, reductions in working hours, either through legislation or employer concessions, were the outcome of intense periods of mobilization and struggle by organized labour (Jefferys 2000). Following the 1981 election of François Mitterrand as president of France, and the establishment of a coalition government of socialists and communists, a 1982 law fixed the maximum working week, before overtime payments apply, at thirty-nine hours, with the progressive reduction to thirty-five hours as a longer-term aim, and increased the minimum period of paid annual leave to five weeks.

Although a 1996 law provided employers with incentives to shorten the working week voluntarily, realization of the 35-hour limit had to await the 1997 election of a Socialist government under the premiership of Lionel Jospin. While it had never really disappeared from the political agenda, working time 'was now back with a vengeance' (Jefferys 2003: 141–2). The first 'Aubry' law of 1998, named after its ministerial sponsor, offered incentives for employers who negotiated 35-hour agreements that created jobs. The second 'Aubry' law of 2000 made the maximum 35-hour week mandatory for all those working in firms with more than twenty employees.

The ostensible aim of the legislation was to create job opportunities, and thus reduce the level of four million unemployed. Perhaps some half a million new jobs were generated between 1997 and 2001. By 2001, full-time employees in France worked an average of 38.3 hours per week including overtime, the lowest of any EU country. But the legislation was also driven by another imperative, 'that of a continuing process of state modernization of industrial relations in which working time was held out as bait' (Jefferys 2003: 142). The aim, then, was to encourage firms to negotiate workplace agreements with local union representatives over the more flexible use of working time. This would, it was hoped, not only stimulate workplace bargaining, and thus challenge the authority of the unions and their national power bases, but also enhance productivity through the more intensive use of working time. Understandably, therefore, many manual workers, who bore the brunt of such flexibility initiatives, were rather restrained in their support of the 35-hour week. In February 2005, the by now right-wing government proposed that the 35-hour limit should be relaxed.

Sources: Jefferys (2000, 2003)

This highlights something very important about the pattern of working time in Britain: the length of the 'normal' or 'basic' working week has continued to decline. The main reason why full-time employees in Britain work more hours than their counterparts elsewhere in the EU is because of the high level of overtime that is worked (Harkness 1999). The preponderance of overtime has long attracted a degree of criticism. Flanders (1975) viewed the existence of 'systematic overtime' as a sign of managerial irresponsibility; it was a particularly inefficient, albeit easy, way of securing increases in output without hiring new staff or, more importantly, investing in capital machinery, and thus stifled innovation. Workers welcomed the opportunity to undertake overtime since it enabled them to supplement their low basic wages. In the 1950s and 1960s, then, overtime working became 'institutionalized', particularly among male manual workers (Arrowsmith 2002). This refers to the way in which overtime came 'to be accepted as a habit – as a way of life in industry – for which all kinds of justifications are then invented'. It gained 'a self-perpetuating character' (Flanders 1975: 56).

Overtime working remains commonplace in Britain (Arrowsmith and Sisson 1999), and has had a significant effect upon the lengthening of the working week. According to data from WERS 98, 53 per cent of employees usually do overtime each week. One of the most interesting trends concerns the rising incidence of unpaid overtime – some two-thirds of managers and professionals who undertake overtime receive no reimbursement for the additional hours worked (Kodz et al. 2003).

It would appear that an ongoing reliance on overtime, and a marked absence of innovation, have characterized the attempts by employers to re-arrange working time in such a way that it generates greater flexibility. Certainly, there has been a trend towards greater diversity in working time arrangements as hitherto 'standard' nine to five, Monday to Friday working becomes less commonplace (Noon and Blyton 2002; Rubery and Grimshaw 2003). For example, increasing numbers of people work what used to be called 'unsocial hours', in the evening or on weekends, since competitive pressures oblige businesses, particularly in the expanding service sector, to open for longer periods.

One of the most prominent innovations concerns 'annualized hours' arrangements. While they vary in their detail, the main feature of such schemes is the specification of a certain number of hours to be worked by an employee in any given year, in exchange for a guaranteed wage. The main benefit of annualized hours for employers is that it enables them to manage peaks and slumps in demand for a product over a year without having to resort to the use of expensive overtime when it is high, or having workers sitting around idle when it is low. Given that, for the employer, the aims of introducing annualized hours are to secure flexibility and eliminate overtime, employees are, understandably, often wary, even though overall working time may fall. Managers may pledge that the average guaranteed wage will leave most employees better off, but the loss of overtime may have a significant negative impact on the income of some (see Heyes 1997), and a greater likelihood of 'unsocial hours' working may prove problematic for people, usually women, who have childcare responsibilities (Rubery and Grimshaw 2003).

These developments notwithstanding, in general British employers have been reluctant to innovate in respect of working time arrangements. Annualized hours schemes are not widespread, overtime working continues to be commonplace, and 'employers on the whole remain slow to adopt a comprehensive approach to working time as a tool for competitive advantage' (Arrowsmith and Sisson 2000: 309; see also Arrowsmith and Sisson 1999).

7.4.3 The legal regulation of working time

As was mentioned above, in Britain, unlike elsewhere in the EU, except for legislation restricting the hours of women and children, the legal regulation of working time was traditionally very limited. By the end of the 1980s, though, there was increasing concern within the European Commission that working time needed to be addressed across the EU as a health and safety measure (Bridgford and Stirling 1994). Membership of the EU, then, obliged the British government to implement the 1993 Working Time Directive, something that was done by means of the 1998 Working Time Regulations. John Major's Conservative government tried to obstruct its implementation, arguing that, as a 'social' measure, it could only be enacted through the so-called 'social chapter', from which Britain, because of its Maastricht 'opt-out', was exempt. In 1996, the European Court of Justice (ECJ) ruled that the directive was, as the European Commission maintained, a 'health and safety' measure and thus fell outside the 'social chapter', was subject to Qualified Majority Voting and, having thus been enacted, had to be extended to Britain. Nevertheless, Tony Blair's Labour government, which took office in 1997, was able to win some significant concessions when the WTR were implemented in 1998.

The main features of the WTR are featured below, as they apply to adult workers:

- they provide for a maximum 48-hour average working week, inclusive of overtime, normally calculated over a 17-week reference period;
- they provide for workers to have at least 11 consecutive hours of rest in any 24-hour period;
- they allow workers a minimum rest period of at least 24 consecutive hours in any 7-day period;
- they allow workers at least a 20-minute unpaid break from work in any 6-hour period;
- they place restrictions on nightworking;
- and they provide for a minimum of 4 weeks' paid annual leave.

Although employers raised concerns about the requirement to keep records of time worked by employees, the three most notable features of the way in which the WTR were implemented were the exclusion of certain groups of workers, the potential for individual derogations or 'opt-outs' from their coverage, and the provision of a qualifying period for annual leave entitlement. Workers in the transport industry, for example, were excluded from the scope of the directive, though this is something that has subsequently been partly rectified by a further EU directive that the British government enacted in 2003. More controversial was the provision that employees, by means of an 'individual agreement' with their employer, can exempt themselves from the 48-hour weekly limit. While trade unions, by means of collective agreements, and elected company or works councils, by means of 'workforce agreements', can negotiate flexibilities in certain other aspects of the WTR, only in Britain were individual opt-outs established. In respect of paid annual leave, in 2001 the ECJ ruled that the 13-week qualifying period before being entitled to it was unlawful, thus allowing workers the opportunity to accrue leave entitlement from the day they start a job.

What has been the impact of the WTR? To what extent has the legislation countered the trend towards increased working hours? In respect of rest periods, research shows that most employers comply with their legal obligations, and that some organizations have made minor adjustments to nightwork arrangements. Most importantly, though, the use of 'individual agreements', to opt out of the 48-hour maximum working week, appears to be widespread (Goss and Adam-Smith 2001). Research studies demonstrate that some employers use them automatically, obliging employees to sign opt-out clauses during their induction (Barnard, Deakin, and Hobbs 2003; Neathy and Arrowsmith 2001). The Trades Union Congress (TUC) claims that employers put pressure on employees to 'agree' to opt out (EIRO 2003).

As a result 'it seems unlikely that . . . the WTR will initiate a radical break with the UK's established practice of working time' (Goss and Adam-Smith 2001: 207). The widespread use of individual, collective, and workforce agreements suggests the presence of 'pragmatic collusion'. Both workers and their employers have a vested interest in ensuring that the WTR are kept weak, and that excessive working hours continue (Barnard, Deakin, and Hobbs 2003). Workers either need the additional income provided by paid overtime or, where it is unpaid, do the extra work in order to ensure that they keep their jobs, or are well regarded for promotion purposes. Employers, as we have seen, are reliant on overtime working as a key means of securing workplace flexibility.

The fall since the 1990s in the proportion of people working an excessive number of hours, particularly male full-time employees, does not seem to have been caused by the introduction of the WTR (Green 2003). Moreover, many workers in Britain continue to endure a long working week. The TUC claims that 4 million workers usually work more than 48 hours per week (EIRO 2003). In 2003, the European Commission launched a review of the provision for individual agreements. The British government and business groups such as the Confederation of British Industry (CBI) lobbied vociferously for its retention on the grounds that, without it, employers would enjoy less flexibility over working time arrangements, and thus be rendered less competitive. In September 2004, the Commission proposed that individual opt-outs could be retained subject to certain conditions, most notably by agreement with a union. While the TUC wants to see the opt-out provision ended altogether, the CBI complained that the Commission's proposals would, if enacted, allow unions too much influence over whether or not workers can work for more than 48 hours in an average week (EIRO 2004b). In May 2005, the European Parliament voted to scrap the opt-out entirely. The British government responded by vowing to ensure that it stays in place. Whatever the future for the individual opt-out, without more comprehensive change in the organization of work and the system of employment relations it is unlikely that the WTR, however well intentioned, will counteract the widespread practice of overtime working in Britain.

SECTION SUMMARY AND FURTHER READING

- Working time, and its regulation, is a key issue in employment relations, being a central feature of the employment relationship. It has long been a prime source of contestation between employers and unions.

- The historical trend towards the reduction in the length of the working week, in large part the result of union struggle, appeared to be reversed for full-time employees in 1990s Britain as the average number of working hours worked each week began to rise.

- Overtime working is the principal reason why people work excessive hours in Britain. Perhaps as a result, employers have been somewhat reluctant to innovate in the area of working time arrangements.

- In contrast to the minimal way in which working time has traditionally been regulated by the law in Britain, the implementation of the 1998 Working Time Regulations represent a marked departure. However, the impact of the 48-hour week provision has been limited because of the ease with which employers can secure opt-outs.

Two good overviews of working time as an employment relations issue are Arrowsmith (2002), and Arrowsmith and Sisson (2000). The former concentrates on the historical evolution of working time as a source of contestation between employers and unions; the latter focuses on the how working time is managed in modern organizations and, in particular, suggests a lack of innovation. Harkness (1999), and Green (2003) present data on trends in working time. Goss and Adam-Smith (2001) consider the limited impact of the Working Time Regulations.

■ CONCLUSION

One of the most important aspects of contemporary employment relations in Britain is the diminished significance of collective bargaining in the private sector. Nevertheless, collective bargaining, at multi-employer level, remains commonplace in the public sector, especially if the pay review body system is considered as a form of 'arms' length bargaining' (Winchester and Bach 1995). What have been the main implications of the contraction of collective bargaining coverage in Britain? This chapter considered three particularly noteworthy developments. First, the increased extent of unilateral regulation of the terms of the wage-work bargain by management was identified. However, managers do not appear to have used their apparent new-found freedom to innovate very much in pay and working time arrangements. Rather, they prefer to rely on established, tried-and-tested approaches, such as the reliance on overtime for example. In attempting to pursue changes in employment relations, managers are constrained by the need to secure their legitimacy among the workforce. This is very important since it demonstrates that, even though the power of the trade unions has declined substantially, the wage-work bargain remains relevant as a way of conceptualizing the employment relationship, and that limits to the exercise of managerial prerogative exist.

Second, although other factors have played a part, the decline of collective bargaining as a means of determining pay in Britain has contributed to the growth of pay inequality since the 1980s. Moreover, as we established in Chapter 1, collective bargaining is not just a pay-setting mechanism; its presence also allows workers a say, or voice, over decisions that affect them at work. The diminution of trade union power has enabled managers to secure changes to the wage-work bargain in ways that are to the advantage of the employer. In particular, the lengthening of the working week for full-time workers has been caused in part by the erosion of joint regulation in the workplace. In Chapter 8, we will examine the implications for work effort and intensity.

Third, the implementation of the Working Time Regulations and the National Minimum Wage in Britain are significant developments as statutory interventions designed to regulate low pay and working time. Such regulation of the employment relationship by statute is a weak substitute for collective bargaining. The minimum wage was set at a deliberately low, or cautious, level that was designed to alleviate the most extreme cases of low pay in a way that would not be disruptive to employers. Given the scope for opt-outs enjoyed by employers, it seems unlikely that the Working Time Regulations have, until now, done much to challenge excessive working hours in Britain. Thus statutory regulation of the employment relationship is, by itself, not an adequate replacement for joint regulation as a means of securing improved pay and conditions for workers.

■ ASSIGNMENT AND DISCUSSION QUESTIONS

1. Identify the reasons for the decline in collective bargaining coverage in Britain since the 1980s.

2. Why did British private sector firms withdraw from multi-employer bargaining? Why has it remained significant in the public sector?

3. What are the advantages and disadvantages of performance-related pay for employers?

4. Why have employers not been more innovative in devising new pay and working time arrangements?

5. Does pay inequality between the highest and lowest paid reflect an abuse of power by those at the top of organizations, or simply the market rate for different jobs?

6. Prepare a case either in support of, or against, the existence of the National Minimum Wage.

7. Why have the Working Time Regulations not had a major impact on the typical working hours of British workers?

■ WEBSITE MATERIALS

Visit the companion web site to this book for interesting and updated material at
www.oup.com/booksites/busecon/business

■ CHAPTER CASE STUDY

The National Minimum Wage and the hairdressing industry

The British hairdressing industry employs over 100,000 staff, of whom two-thirds are female. It is comprised of many small firms, has a high proportion of young workers, and makes significant use of part-time employment. These characteristics are typical of low-paying industries and means that the introduction of the National Minimum Wage (NMW) in 1999 was likely to have a major effect on the hairdressing sector. The image of hairdressing is one of a low-paying industry. Consequently, many employers report difficulties in filling vacancies from suitably qualified applicants, particularly for junior positions. However, once staff qualify as stylists earnings can be relatively high. Moreover, the fairly lengthy entry period on low pay does not seem to deter those who have firmly decided on a career in the sector. Nonetheless, younger workers do feel that their pay should be higher, particularly in relation to what their friends earn in other occupations.

Between 1998 and 1999, when the NMW was established, it is estimated that average hourly rates of pay for all employees in hairdressing rose from £3.56 to £4.17, a rise of over 17 per cent. For those at the lower end of the earnings hierarchy, predominantly younger workers, hourly rates increased by almost 50 per cent from the 1998 rate of £2.11 per hour. Further significant increases in hourly rates were reported over the following two years. The group of workers most dramatically affected by the introduction of the NMW were, thus, younger workers who are typically employed as shampooists, trainee stylists, and receptionists. While they received a significant increase in pay, redundancies were reported among 18–21 year-old workers in larger hairdressing salons. Employers claimed that they needed to earn revenue at three times the cost of wages to make continued employment viable, and that the work of these younger staff was not economically viable. Job losses among younger workers in smaller salons was not as commonplace, probably because there was less flexibility in staffing levels. There has subsequently been a rise in the number of younger workers in the industry, perhaps indicating that the earlier response of larger employers was something of an over-reaction. It will be interesting to see if the NMW rate for 16 and 17 year olds, introduced in 2004, has a similar effect on employment in the industry.

The NMW was introduced at a time when the hairdressing industry was buoyant, and little has changed since 1999 in this respect. Thus, the most common response was to increase prices to customers. Little evidence emerges that employers undertook any strategic review of their businesses or people management practices as a result of the NMW. Those salons that had achieved Investor in People (IIP) status appeared to more easily absorb the requirements of the NMW. With its emphasis on training, staff communication, and customer care, IIP status is most likely to be found in firms with a proactive management style.

Source: Druker, Stanworth, and White (2002)

Case discussion questions

1. What does this case study show us about the impact of the NMW on both employers and workers?

2. In what other ways might employers have responded to the introduction of the NMW?

CHAPTER 8
Experiencing employment relations

CHAPTER OBJECTIVES

The main objectives of this chapter are to:

- assess the extent to which management policies of employee participation and involvement allow workers to influence workplace decisions

- appreciate how management imperatives for discipline are experienced by workers

- develop an understanding of the nature of the redundancy process and its implications for workers' feelings of job insecurity

- examine the reasons why workers in Britain are working harder, and to consider the implications of this process of work intensification

---

8.1 Introduction

Managerial accounts of workplace life change increasingly dominate the contemporary employment relations agenda, linked to the emergence of human resource management (HRM) as an area of study. Accounts of HRM that consider the implications of managerial interventions for workers are somewhat rare; exceptions include Gratton et al. (1999), and Guest (1999). Yet the employment relationship is not only something that is regulated by employers, it is also experienced by workers. A proper assessment of developments in contemporary employment relations must acknowledge that the employment relationship *is* a relationship and that it is characterized by the potential for conflicting interests as well as by cooperation. In this chapter, then, we draw upon a range of up-to-date quantitative and qualitative research findings to demonstrate both the extent to which an understanding of workers' experiences of the employment relationship are a relevant matter for investigation, and also how they can differ markedly from those of their employers.

8.2 Developments in employee involvement and participation

We have already examined the nature of employee involvement and participation (in Chapter 1), indicated that the use of direct communication techniques is held to be integral to the sophisticated HRM approach (in Chapter 5), and considered the way in which trade union representation enables workers to exercise voice over workplace decisions (in Chapter 6). Here, though, we investigate workers' experiences of involvement and participation in contemporary employment relations. Our starting point, however, is the increasingly espoused managerial concern to communicate directly with their employees, and to involve them more in workplace decision-making, enhancing their levels of motivation and commitment, and thus realizing improvements in business performance (see Marchington 2001; Marchington and Wilkinson 2000). Together with the diminution of union voice arrangements (Millward, Bryson, and Forth 2000), it means that employee involvement 'and participation are increasingly characterized by being management rather than union driven and by the underlying aim of increasing commitment and seeking competitive advantage' (Sisson and Storey 2000: 93).

8.2.1 Communicating with employees

During the late 1980s and early 1990s, both case study and survey evidence pointed to the rising use of direct communications techniques such as team briefings and briefing groups for example (Millward 1994; Storey 1992), a trend that appeared to persist through to the end of the 1990s (Cully et al. 1999).

In Table 8.1, we present data from the 1998 Workplace Employee Relations Survey (WERS 98) showing the increasing incidence of arrangements that enable managers to communicate directly with employees. While the 'cascading' of information downwards via the management chain was present in three-fifths of workplaces during the 1980s and 1990s, over the same period there was a distinct increase in the use by organizations of regular meetings and newsletters as devices for communicating with their employees.

Table 8.1 Percentage of workplaces where particular methods to communicate with employees are used

	1984	1990	1998
Management chain	62	60	60
Regular newsletters	34	41	50
Regular meetings	34	41	48
Team briefings	36	48	61

Workplaces with twenty-five or more employees.

Sources: Cully et al. (1999); Millward et al. (1992)

By 1998, moreover, team briefings, involving the verbal communication of information between a line manager or supervisor and his or her work group, occurred in over 60 per cent of workplaces.

There also appears to have been an increase in the incidence of arrangements that allow employees to communicate their views 'upwards' to managers. In 1998, a third of workplaces operated suggestion schemes, representing a small increase since the 1980s, but in nearly two-fifths of workplaces the existence of 'problem-solving groups', sometimes known as quality circles, where employees came together to 'solve specific problems or discuss aspects of performance or quality', was reported (Cully et al. 1999: 66). Given the initial failure of quality circles to take root in the 1980s, largely due to managerial indifference (Hill 1991b), this is a potentially significant development. According to Gallie et al. (1998), for example, quality circles are a particularly effective means of stimulating employee involvement.

The increasing incidence of downwards and upwards communications arrangements in British workplaces would, then, appear to signal a significant change in employment relations, given that before the 1980s communication channels, largely in the form of consultation machinery, were, in many organizations, dominated by the unions. But the evidence on direct communications and employee involvement must be handled with some care. For one thing, there is evidence that communications techniques can be used to enhance managerial control rather than involve employees. In a Japanese-owned plant manufacturing televisions, for example, Delbridge (1998) notes the large extent to which the company used its extensive communications arrangements to influence workers' behaviour so that it conformed to managerial expectations, particularly in matters pertaining to quality. Moreover, while there has been an increase in the extent of such arrangements, there is plenty of evidence to suggest that the largely top-down character of communication limits the degree to which employees are able to influence decisions that affect them at work (Cully et al. 1999; Millward 1994).

'Downward' communications arrangements, those that refer to the flow of information from managers to employees, dominate. A study of a group of 'Leading Edge' companies, including Citibank, Hewlett-Packard, and W H Smith, found that while many employees felt well informed about their company's objectives, and the ways in which it was attempting to achieve them, few considered they had any influence themselves. Opportunities for employees to communicate their ideas, concerns, and suggestions upwards were scarce (Gratton et al. 1999). There is plenty of case study evidence that the flow of information is generally one-way, from managers to workers, with the latter afforded few opportunities to express their voice.

In the non-union chocolate works studied by Scott (1994), for example, managers considered that the regular bi-monthly 'job involvement meetings' (JIs) not only gave them the opportunity to keep the workforce informed about the company's performance, changes in company practice, and other relevant matters, but also enabled the workers to communicate their feelings and views. In reality, however, most workers did not believe that the JIs served this dual purpose, and saw them as a one-way, top-down method of delivering messages. Some workers, moreover, were worried about the consequences of communicating their views. One of them, for example, emphasized that he worked for a 'good company', but

. . . I haven't got long to go and I don't want any trouble. Once at a JI I spoke my mind to the manager. Two weeks later I found myself being transferred to another job and I reckon that speaking out cost me £50 a week in wages that I could have earned. Some managers are alright [*sic*], but others you've got to watch. (quoted in Scott 1994: 116)

Unsurprisingly, there is little evidence that, as a form of employee involvement, direct communications initiatives, despite their prevalence, impact much on employees' organizational commitment, or their performance at work (Marchington 2001), though there is a suggestion that they may be effective as a means of influencing management behaviour (Bryson 2004). Managers prefer to restrict communication to sharing information with employees, and are reluctant to respond positively to their suggestions (Cully et al. 1999; Gallie et al. 1998). In so far as managers use communication techniques to influence workplace behaviour in ways that they deem desirable, such as the need to prioritize quality for example, it is inappropriate to characterize such employee involvement initiatives as interventions that widen the scope of workers' influence over decision-making. Rather, they are better envisaged as a means of enabling managers to uphold their prerogatives, and to restrict the influence of employees, especially where they are organized in trade unions.

8.2.2 Employee participation and the reorganization of work

Having considered the incidence and implications of downward and upward forms of direct communications, we now assess the extent to which the experience of workers in contemporary employment relations has been influenced by new forms of task-based participation. In this section, therefore, we examine relevant innovations in the organization of work – in particular quality management, teamworking, and empowerment initiatives – and judge how far their presence provides workers with greater autonomy and discretion over the way in which their work is undertaken, thus resulting in genuine participation. It is suggested that giving employees greater influence and voice over the organization of work, and changes in work processes, are essential if companies are to secure the levels of commitment necessary for the production of high-quality goods and services, and thus thrive in increasingly competitive global markets (see Boxall and Purcell 2003). As discussed in Chapter 5, forms of task-based participation, teamworking arrangements in particular, are among the major best practice HRM interventions that are thought to deliver improvements in business performance (Marchington and Wilkinson 2000).

In the previous section, we noted the development of quality circles as a kind of problem-solving group, and thus a form of upward communication, and their potential effect on employee involvement. During the 1990s, however, many organizations came to acknowledge the importance of quality as a source of competitive advantage, and instituted more rigorous systems of quality management, often associated with the concept of Total Quality Management (TQM) (Hill 1991a; Wilkinson et al. 1997). The characteristic feature of a TQM approach is that quality is something that is built into all aspects of the process of production or service delivery. Consequently, all workers should take responsibility for the quality of their own contribution, and constantly seek ways of improving it. Although its managerialist emphasis may be an obstacle, effective TQM, then, is arguably contingent upon greater employee participation and involvement. It is 'supposed to place a greater emphasis on self-control, autonomy and creativity, expecting active cooperation from employees rather than mere compliance' (Wilkinson et al. 1992: 5). In a study of four organizations that were 'pioneers' of TQM, for example, Hill (1995) observed that workers enjoyed greater influence over their work tasks as a result.

One of the main ways in which organizations have sought to enhance the quality of their employees' contributions is through some form of teamworking arrangement. Teamworking potentially enables workers collectively to organize and manage part of the process of production or service delivery without the need for direct supervision by management. In so far as it holds out the promise of a significant increase in the degree to which workers are able to exercise an influence over the organization of their work, the presence of self-managed teams is perhaps the 'ultimate in direct participation' (Marchington and Wilkinson 2000: 349). In his study of organizational change in one of Pirelli's plants, for example, Clark (1995) found that the overwhelming majority of employees enjoyed greater job satisfaction and more autonomy at work as a consequence of the establishment of self-supervised teams. The benefits of teamworking were also evident to one white-collar worker in a utilities company: 'Business improvement teams/working groups...have expanded my awareness of other business unit issues. I've gained problem-solving experience, and also job satisfaction, that you are achieving something in the short term, fixing it in the short term' (quoted in Hudson 2002: 54).

Thus TQM and teamworking complement one another in so far as improvements in the quality of production, or the delivery of services, may be associated with innovative work practices that enhance employee involvement and participation. This has prompted consideration of whether or not such developments have enabled employees to become 'empowered'. What, then, is meant by the concept of 'empowerment' in the workplace? It comprises two related aspects. First, empowerment is held to involve the devolution to workers of some supervisory responsibilities that hitherto would have come under the auspices of managers. Second, following on from this, the presumption is that workers will enjoy greater autonomy at work and, in particular, more discretion over the way in which their jobs are performed (Cunningham and Hyman 1999).

To what extent, then, have workers experienced greater involvement and participation as a result of innovations in the organization of work? If we look at the implications of TQM, for example, there is evidence that organizations use quality management systems to secure the subordination of workers, and thus extend managerial control (Delbridge 1998; McArdle et al. 1995). In these critical perspectives, TQM, as an explicitly management tool, is portrayed as a means of enforcing employee compliance with corporate policies and of stifling their independent collective organization, rather than as a means of enhancing involvement and participation.

Other studies demonstrate, however, that TQM initiatives can increase workers' involvement. As part of its efforts to establish a greater customer orientation, the supermarket chain 'Shopco', for example, used its 'Service Excellence' programme to extend the discretion of its front-line employees. Although staff welcomed the changes, the extent of their autonomy was nonetheless rather limited, to decisions on customer refunds for example (Rosenthal, Hill, and Peccei 1997). More generally, it is apparent that TQM initiatives, while they may slightly increase employee involvement and participation over the performance of job tasks, do so within boundaries set firmly by management and are associated with the stricter imposition of managerial control, in particular over discipline and standards of performance (Edwards, Collinson, and Rees 1998; C. Rees 1998; Wilkinson, Godfrey, and Marchington 1997).

Critical interpretations of teamworking arrangements suggest that they are interventions designed to serve the interests of management, rather than increase employee involvement and participation. In their study of work organization and employment relations in the Nissan car plant near Sunderland in north-east England, Garrahan and Stewart (1992) observed that the peer pressure to fulfil production quotas evident among the factory's teams could be interpreted as 'management by stress'.

But what do we mean by 'teams' anyway? The WERS 98 researchers discovered that some kind of teamworking arrangement was present among the largest occupational group in nearly two-thirds of British workplaces. Genuine participation, however, is predicated upon the existence of semi-autonomous, self-managing work teams, where workers elect their own supervisors or team leaders, and collectively decide how to organize their work. These are present in only a tiny minority (3 per cent) of workplaces (Cully et al. 1999). Thus one cannot equate teamworking with worker participation in an overly straightforward manner. In the service sector, for example, teams are generally no more than 'administrative work groups of individual workers under the jurisdiction of one supervisor' (Korczynski 2002: 134).

There is also evidence that managers use teamworking initiatives as a means of extending their control over labour. In his study of a plant manufacturing car components, Danford (1998) shows that the company introduced teamworking in order to undermine workers' influence over the production process. The new arrangements enabled management to institute flexibility on its terms, rather than those of the workers, exercise greater control over the way in which work tasks were undertaken, and raise effort levels. According to one of the workers:

As I see it, the management have bought in all these fancy new ideas but they're all the same really. Every one is about squeezing more work out of less men. You can forget all the pretty words, they're about making you work harder it's as simple as that. (quoted in Danford 1998: 421)

In respect of empowerment, there is now a widespread body of research evidence suggesting that real power is seldom transferred from management to workers. Rather, workers are generally given a relatively small amount of additional discretion, such as in the case of 'Shopco' for example (Rosenthal, Hill, and Peccei 1997), within boundaries that are tightly regulated by managers (Beynon et al. 2002). In a study of the restaurant chain TGI Fridays, for example, Lashley (2000) discovered that waiting staff were encouraged to accept customer requests for variations to standard menu products, deal with, and rectify, customer complaints themselves, and to customize their uniforms. Nevertheless, such discretion was constrained by the existence of tightly prescribed rules governing service delivery, such as maximum waiting times between courses for example.

Workers, then, are often sceptical about the prospects for empowerment. According to an office worker in a utilities company:

Empowerment . . . it empowers you to do what you think you should do after you've been asked to do it. . . . It's a load of rubbish. It's OK when you're there [at the training centre], but as soon as you get back you realize that you are not empowered at all. It's different for the top bosses. (quoted in Hudson 2002: 55)

The concept of empowerment is rather misleading in that it suggests that workers enjoy greater power over workplace decision-making when often all it involves is a relatively minor expansion in people's job tasks. (Marchington and Wilkinson 2000).

Despite the evidence that it generates greater job satisfaction, improved levels of commitment, and better business performance, the principal obstacle to worker participation, and the transfer of real power from managers to workers, is the concern of the former with upholding their prerogatives, and their unwillingness to cede control to the latter (Broad 1994; Geary 2003; Marchington and Wilkinson 2000). In his study of a frozen food factory that had hitherto been characterized by a rather authoritarian style of management, Scott (1994) accounts for the failure of an initiative designed to give part of its workforce more autonomy. When the workers failed to behave in ways that entirely accorded with management's expectations, the latter quickly reverted to a less participatory approach.

Work reorganization initiatives of the kind we have discussed here have, then, largely failed to transform employment relations in Britain, not only because of an ongoing managerial concern with the control of labour, but also due to a failure on the part of management to ensure that reforms are pursued in a consistent and coherent manner (Edwards, Geary, and Sisson 2002; Marchington and Wilkinson 2000). Where significant change has occurred, such as in the case of an aluminium plant operated by Alcan for example, it is as a result of certain conditions being present, such as a consensual employment relations climate, a genuine management commitment to reform, and the process-based nature of the industry which, since it gave workers space and time to collaborate, made teamworking arrangements viable (Edwards and Wright 1998; Geary 2003). Not even in this case, though, were managers able to secure high organizational commitment.

Overall, then, while new methods of work organization do seem to have stimulated some degree of greater employee involvement in most cases, it is often accompanied by tighter managerial control of performance and discipline, and greater pressure on workers to work harder (Edwards, Collinson, and Rees 1998; C. Rees 1998; Wilkinson, Godfrey, and Marchington 1997). Thus the employment relationship, and the balance of control and consent that characterizes it, has been not been transformed by new working practices.

SECTION SUMMARY AND FURTHER READING

- The extent to which employers communicate with their workers has risen markedly in recent years, though it tends to be limited to keeping them informed of developments. Not only do workers appear to have few opportunities to influence organizational and workplace decisions, but communication techniques, as explicitly managerial interventions, are also used to uphold managerial prerogative.

- Innovations in work organization, such as quality management techniques and teamworking arrangements for example, seem to result in relatively minor increases in the discretion which workers exercise in their jobs.

- It would be a mistake, however, to assume that they have brought about a genuine shift in power, away from managers and towards workers, since the extent of the latter's discretion is generally quite narrow, and exists within a framework of more intensive forms of managerial control over performance.

For an overview of developments in employee participation and involvement, see Marchington (2001), and Marchington and Wilkinson (2000). Geary (2003), and Edwards, Geary, and Sisson (2002) are particularly good on task-based participation. See Gratton et al. (1999) for case study evidence of the preference of managers for downward communications. Cunningham and Hyman (1999) offer a sound analysis of the concept of empowerment; Lashley's (2000) case study of empowerment at TGI Friday's is also recommended.

8.3 Discipline at work

Workplace discipline has always been a somewhat neglected area in studies of employment relations (Fenley 1986). Yet an appreciation of the dynamics of workplace discipline is crucial to developing an understanding of contemporary employment relations. For one thing, the ability of managers to discipline workers for breaches of workplace rules, and impose sanctions upon them where appropriate, is an integral feature of the exercise of managerial prerogative. In one interpretation, then, the operation of workplace discipline is characterized as 'the most vivid and crude expression of managerial power over employees' (Fenley 1986: 16). Moreover, as we will consider below, the exercise of managerial discipline is a defining feature of many employees' lives in so far as it influences their activities and behaviour at work.

The approach adopted here, then, differs from the managerialist perspective that is generally offered by those HRM texts that cover workplace discipline. These tend to treat discipline as a technical activity, in as much as they give advice on how to establish appropriate disciplinary procedures within the confines of the relevant legislation, and, in particular, on how to avoid successful claims for unfair dismissal. Our aim, however, is to offer a more critical appreciation of workplace discipline, emphasizing its salience to the experience of workers in contemporary employment relations, and the way in which it signals the inherent potential for conflict in the employment relationship.

8.3.1 Workplace discipline and employment relations

Based on the work of P. Edwards (1989, 1994, 2000), we can identify three 'faces' of, or ways of understanding, discipline in the workplace. Taken together, the first, those actions undertaken by management when breaches of workplace rules occur, such as the application of sanctions for example, and the second, the elaboration of formal procedures within organizations for dealing with disciplinary matters, are central to conventional approaches to understanding discipline at work. In general, formal disciplinary procedures, which now exist in all bar the smallest of organizations, set the appropriate standards of conduct expected from employees and delineate areas of unsatisfactory activity, provide a process that managers should use to investigate allegations of offending behaviour, outline the constitution of the disciplinary hearing, including the right of employees to voice their response to any allegations made against them, and indicate the relevant sanctions to be used in the event of a confirmed breach of discipline. For minor offences, such as a small number of illegitimate absences, the penalty might be a verbal warning by an employee's immediate supervisor. Where the offence is repeated, or in instances of gross misconduct, which can include matters such as sexual harassment for example, the disciplinary procedure might provide for summary dismissal.

Although the 2002 Employment Act provides for a mandatory 'minimum' disciplinary procedure where one does not exist, in general organizations are at liberty to design a system that suit their needs. The only significant constraint is the guidance on appropriate procedures published in the Advisory, Conciliation and Arbitration Service's code of practice (ACAS 2003b), which can be used for comparative purposes in employment tribunal hearings. The emphasis that is often accorded to disciplinary procedures, when discussing discipline at work, should not divert attention from the fact that these are explicitly managerial tools designed to serve managers' interests (Fenley 1986). Disciplinary procedures, then, largely reflect managerial aspirations and, moreover, by formalizing the application of workplace discipline, help persuade employees to accept the rules elaborated within them. Far from eroding managerial prerogative, then, in so far as they give managerial rules added legitimacy, disciplinary procedures can extend it.

What, then, is meant by the third 'face' of discipline? In his various contributions, P. Edwards (1989, 1994, 2000) emphasizes that workplace discipline is about more than the existence of formal disciplinary procedures. Rather, the rules that govern workplace behaviour are, he contends, constituted and reconstituted as part of an everyday process of negotiation within the office or the factory. Thus what 'the rule is cannot be discovered from the rule-book. Day-to-day experience will create standards which may differ sharply from official rules' (P. Edwards 2000: 318). Drawing on the seminal work of American sociologist Alvin Gouldner, who distinguished between different types of workplace rules which, depending on their nature, were either ignored, supported, or obeyed (Gouldner 1954), Edwards argues that the 'day-to-day understandings' between managers and workers have as much of an influence on the experience of employment relations as the formal rule-book, if not more so. Thus discipline is 'part of a continual negotiation of order, not just a technical activity' (Edwards 1994: 564).

Long-established workplace norms, then, can exert an important influence on the rules that govern behaviour. In the docks, for example, workers used to be able to deploy their collective power to regulate employment relations in ways that suited their interests (Mellish and Collis-Squires 1976). More recently, however, attention has shifted to the way in which managers are able to bend the rules in the interests of workplace efficiency and their own prerogative.

Andrew Scott (1994) offers a good example of this in his account of employment relations in a non-union chocolate factory. On coming across evidence that workers were leaving to go home before the end of a shift, and without tidying the changing room, managers instituted a 'first and last hour' rule. Anyone leaving the production line during the first and last hours of their shift without their manager's approval would receive a written warning. During the first few weeks of the new rule's existence, a number of workers received warnings as a result of breaching it. Having to ask permission to go to the toilet, for example, was, for the workers, a distasteful experience, and most considered the rule to be 'silly' and 'unfair' (Scott 1994: 113). Nor did the rule find favour among all the managers. They 'found it inconvenient and tiresome to spend two hours of each day making sure their staff did not slip away without permission and, moreover, they sensed that shop floor relations were not as friendly as they had been before the rule was introduced' (Scott 1994: 113). Not all managers, then, enforced the rule, though its continued existence in the rule-book meant that it could always be re-imposed should they wish to enforce their authority more rigorously at any time.

This example demonstrates that workplace rules are contingent upon the relationship between managers and workers. Discipline, then, 'means more than the application of sanctions by management. It also refers to the ways in which day-to-day understandings are negotiated between workers and managers: some rules are treated more seriously than others, and there is a process of shopfloor negotiation which defines which rules are respected and which are not' (Edwards and Whitston 1994: 320). Workplace rules are not laid down by managers, and then obeyed by workers, in an overly clear-cut manner. Rather, they are interpreted, and then adjusted, by managers and workers as part of the continuing process of negotiation and re-negotiation that characterizes the employment relationship.

8.3.2 Disciplinary procedures

Although discipline at work should not be equated simply with the existence of formal disciplinary policies and procedures, in order to understand how workers experience workplace discipline it is important to consider, and, moreover, critically evaluate, their operation. The growth of formal disciplinary procedures between the late 1960s and late 1970s was a particularly striking phenomenon (P. Edwards 1994, 2000). Before this period, only a relatively small proportion of firms possessed their own disciplinary procedures (Anderman 1972; Fenley 1986; Henry 1982), though some used those operated by their employers' association. By 1984, however, formal disciplinary procedures were evident in over 90 per cent of establishments (Edwards 1989).

What, then, explains this rapid process of formalization? The growth in the statutory regulation of the employment relationship was a crucial factor, in particular 1970s legislation giving employees protection from unfair dismissal. Firms that use appropriate procedures for investigating an alleged breach of discipline that results in an employee being given the sack are less likely to lose an unfair dismissal hearing. More recent legislation – the 2002 Employment Act – obliges all firms to notify employees of their procedures or, where they do not exist, the new minimum disciplinary procedures provided for in the legislation. When a dispute arises in a firm without its own procedure, an employment tribunal will presuppose the existence of the 'mandatory' statutory model when adjudicating whether or not a decision to dismiss is fair or unfair.

There is evidence that the unfair dismissal provisions prompted a formalization of disciplinary procedures in many organizations, including, more recently, small firms (Evans, Goodman, and Hargreaves 1985; Goodman et al. 1998). It would be a mistake, however, to exaggerate the influence of legislation as a catalyst for the growth of formal disciplinary procedures (Edwards 1994). During the 1970s, many firms, as we saw in Chapter 1, formalized their arrangements for managing employment relations in general as a means of accommodating workplace militancy and of taking control over their own employment relations. In the case of discipline, though, the trend towards formalization helped to bolster managerial authority, not least because by following formal procedures managers found that workers accepted their decisions more readily, since they were accorded added legitimacy.

As we have already observed, disciplinary procedures are to all intents and purposes management procedures (Clegg 1979; Dickens et al. 1985; Earnshaw et al. 1998; Evans, Goodman, and Hargreaves 1985). A recognized trade union might be consulted about the constitution and contents of a procedure, but it is rarely given the opportunity to negotiate (P. Edwards 2000). In non-union firms, it would appear that employees are given few opportunities to contribute. Goodman et al. (1998: 543) found that with the exception of a small number of unionized organizations, in the companies they studied there was a 'virtual absence of employee or employee representative consultation or involvement in the design and introduction (or revision) of the written disciplinary procedures'.

Disciplinary procedures, therefore, are explicitly managerial tools. Moreover, by giving legitimacy to disciplinary and dismissal decisions, their existence buttresses managerial authority rather than erodes it. They help to define managerial authority in the area of discipline, and enable workers to understand more clearly the boundary between appropriate and inappropriate standards of behaviour (Goodman et al. 1998). In his study of a British-based Japanese television plant, 'Nippon CTV', Delbridge (1998) demonstrates the effectiveness of disciplinary rules in regulating workplace order. During induction, new recruits are instilled with the need to comply with the firm's rules, particularly those concerning absenteeism and punctuality.

It is wrong to assume, however, that the formalization of disciplinary practice in Britain has provided workers with added protection against arbitrary discipline. Managers frequently fail to follow their own procedures. In their survey of tribunal decisions, Earnshaw et al. (1998) found evidence of numerous procedural irregularities in the way in which firms had dismissed employees, not least a reluctance to give them a chance to voice their side of the story in advance of the decision to dismiss. In their study of workers' experiences of the disciplinary process, Rollinson et al. (1997) encountered among their respondents a strong sense that managers had assumed their guilt even before the hearing had commenced, and paid little attention to anything they said in mitigation. There is also case study evidence from small firms which suggests that managers make up their minds to dismiss an employee before the disciplinary hearing gets underway (Earnshaw, Marchington, and Goodman 2000). Although 'formalism and due process have spread widely, when it comes to the actual practice of disciplinary action many employers, it seems, do not use their procedures' (P. Edwards 2000: 322).

Research studies demonstrate, moreover, that managers often interpret disciplinary procedures in a 'flexible' manner (Earnshaw, Marchington, and Goodman 2000; Goodman et al. 1998). Where they have some sympathy with the worker concerned, or knowledge of an individual's personal affairs, managers may choose to have a private, informal conversation, and thus resolve the issue without instituting formal proceedings. But this can give rise to inconsistencies should someone else charged with a similar offence be treated less leniently. The existence of formal procedures in respect of discipline, then, 'still leaves a great deal of discretion to management in deciding what is acceptable conduct and how it is to be enforced' (Edwards 1994: 572).

8.3.3 **The resilience of discipline**

To what extent has the nature of discipline changed over time? We might expect the use of disciplinary sanctions to have declined, as managements prefer more progressive means (such as motivating staff and gaining their commitment) of regulating the workplace. Perhaps, moreover, the use of discipline has also become less punitive in nature, based on punishing employees for breaches of workplace rules, and more corrective, aimed at helping employees to identify any failings, thus improving their behaviour. The principal components of the punitive approach to workplace discipline are an emphasis on getting workers to obey management's rules for fear of the punishment, such as dismissal, that would result from any failure to comply (Fenley 1998). This can be contrasted with a 'corrective' approach. This is founded upon the assumption that the purpose of disciplinary action against workers is to improve, or correct, their behaviour, and is associated with the proper use of appropriate procedures as a means of delivering 'natural justice' (Fenley 1998). One influential body of work, which has been termed the 'consensus' approach (Henry 1982), contends that, over time, management's use of discipline has evolved from a punitive to a corrective style (Anderman 1972).

This is, however, a somewhat crude argument. While discipline was often maintained by dismissal, or the threat of dismissal, in the early factories (Pollard 1968), there is also evidence which suggests that management style in early industrial organizations was more eclectic than the 'consensus' theory purports. Some relied heavily on paternalist approaches to the management of labour, for example (P. Edwards 2000; Edwards and Whitston 1989). Moreover, based on their case study of disciplinary practice on the railways, Edwards and Whitston (1994) demonstrate that it is wrong to assume that a punitive approach to discipline has been superseded by a corrective one. Instead, they highlight the important influence of financial pressures on the use of discipline. In periods when finances are tight, managers tend to adopt a tighter approach to discipline, and are more likely to impose disciplinary sanctions. In the 1980s, managers attempted to assert their authority, by taking a harder line on absenteeism for example. Thus the use of discipline ebbs and flows according to financial pressures. As a result, 'disciplinary systems have not evolved towards a more corrective style and . . . punitive strands remain a significant component of current practice' (Edwards and Whitston 1994: 335). In practice, it is difficult to make too hard and fast a distinction between the punitive and the corrective approach within organizational practice (P. Edwards 2000).

What, though, has been the impact of human resource management on the practice of discipline in British firms? It might be assumed that the elaboration of new management techniques, aimed at generating increases in workers' effort by involving them, motivating them and eliciting their commitment, makes conventional modes of discipline increasingly redundant. Since they identify more readily with managerial aims, workers do not need to be threatened with punishment or encouraged to correct their behaviour; rather, they are inherently less likely to act in ways that conflict with their managers, thus maintaining self-discipline. Given the doubts expressed in Chapter 5 about the significance of HRM as a new employment relations paradigm, perhaps we should treat claims that conventional approaches to discipline are no longer appropriate with scepticism. But what does the evidence tell us?

One of the most significant aspects of the use of disciplinary sanctions is the variation that exists between sectors. According to WERS 98, across all industries there was an average of 2.9 disciplinary sanctions per 100 employees in the previous year (Cully et al. 1999: 128). In some sectors, such as manufacturing, and transport and communications for example, the figure was much higher. The use of disciplinary sanctions is lower in organizations where there is a greater union presence. Not only does the presence of a trade union help to resolve disputes informally, before the formal disciplinary procedure is initiated, but it also offers workers protection from arbitrary and unwarranted management allegations (Edwards 1995a; Knight and Latreille 2000).

Although a trade union presence has a marked impact on the use of disciplinary sanctions, the same cannot be said for HRM. Analyses of WERS 98 and its 1990 predecessor show that there is little evidence of a link between the use of those practices associated with HRM and the incidence of disciplinary sanctions (Edwards 1995a; Knight and Latreille 2000). Thus there are no grounds for asserting that self-discipline has transcended more traditional approaches. In general, studies demonstrate that the punitive approach to handling discipline remains a common feature of contemporary employment relations (Edwards 1995a). This is evident from a study of workers who had experienced being disciplined. 'For a large proportion of those formally disciplined, the process was not seen as a persuasive one designed to get them to observe rules, but as an event which gave the manager an opportunity to take retribution, or administer a deterrent to limit future transgressions' (Rollinson et al. 1997: 298). There is evidence, moreover, that managers are taking a harder approach to discipline in some areas, particularly over absenteeism (Edwards 1994; Edwards and Whitston 1993). Some employers use discipline as a means of challenging the effectiveness of union organization (see Box 8.1). Thus it would appear that any 'idea of a progressive trend from punishment through correction to self-discipline is thus far too simple' (P. Edwards 2000: 336).

BOX 8.1 DISCIPLINE AND THE VICTIMIZATION OF TRADE UNIONISTS

The case of Greg Tucker, a union representative for the Rail Maritime and Transport (RMT) union, not only demonstrates that discipline is used as a means of attempting to enforce managerial control, but also indicates that formal rules can be interpreted flexibly, to suit the interests of management, where necessary. In this instance, however, management's efforts largely backfired. South West Trains (SWT) employed Tucker as a train driver. In June 2001, he returned to work from a period of unpaid leave of absence after standing as a Socialist Alliance candidate in that month's general election. On his first day back in the driving seat, Tucker was recorded breaking the line speed limit by a relatively small amount on two occasions, and was disciplined. In spite of evidence that other drivers breached speed limits by far greater amounts without suffering such a serious penalty, SWT dismissed Tucker from his driving job, and demoted him to ticket inspector on less than half the salary. An employment tribunal overwhelmingly found in favour of Tucker, and lambasted SWT management. The 'exceptional penalty' of demotion, it noted, was 'entirely disproportionate' for such 'minor' and inadvertent errors. The real reason for SWT management's hostile treatment of Tucker was opposition to his union activities. Indeed, SWT has something of a reputation for victimizing trade union representatives and activists.

SECTION SUMMARY AND FURTHER READING

- Discipline at work is about more than just the contents of formal disciplinary procedures and the sanctions that apply to breaches of organizational rules. It also refers to the way in which workplace behaviour is governed by the informal rules that are generated by the day-to-day understandings arising from the relationship between managers and workers.

- Since they are explicitly management tools, the operation of formal disciplinary procedures, which are now widespread, generally reinforces, rather than erodes, managerial prerogative in the workplace. Furthermore, managers often enjoy considerable discretion in the application of formal discipline.

- There is little evidence for a trend away from punitive towards corrective approaches to discipline at work. Nor does there seem to have been much of a move towards self-discipline which one would associate with the development of HRM. Instead, a punitive approach to the way in which discipline is handled remains a commonplace feature of contemporary employment relations.

P. Edwards (2000) offers the most extensive and thorough analysis of discipline at work. Rollinson et al. (1997) provide a rare study of workers' experience of being disciplined, and Earnshaw, Marchington, and Goodman (2000) examine the operation of disciplinary procedures. The ACAS Code of Practice on Disciplinary and Grievance Hearings is available at: www.acas.org/publication/pdf/CP01.pdf.

8.4 Redundancy and insecurity

Losing one's job, or the threat of losing one's job, is perhaps the most unsettling of experiences for workers in contemporary employment relations. In this section, we consider the functions and process of redundancy, and its implications for workers, before assessing the dynamics of workplace insecurity.

8.4.1 Redundancy, public policy, and employment relations

Prior to the 1960s, the term 'redundancy', which normally means the collective dismissal of employees, scarcely registered in British employment relations. Nevertheless, the term started to become more widely used as some employers, who wanted to reduce employment levels, used financial payments to compensate workers for the loss of their jobs (Fryer 1981; Mukherjee 1973). Unions often strongly opposed management proposals to discharge employees and, in situations where dismissals appeared to be unavoidable, insisted on 'last-in, first-out', or 'LIFO', as the principal selection criterion. In other words, those who had the least length of service with the firm would be chosen to go first.

Policy-makers, however, increasingly viewed the strength of union opposition to such dismissals as an obstacle to the efficient functioning of the economy since something needed to be done to encourage workers in declining industrial sectors to move to parts of the economy that were experiencing growth. Thus the stated aim of the 1965 Redundancy Payments Act (RPA) was to promote economic efficiency by enabling the more rational use of labour in a climate of full employment (Mukherjee 1973). It defined the concept of redundancy as a dismissal resulting from the employer ceasing to carry out its business 'or because a cessation or diminution of work of a particular kind had occurred' (Fryer 1981: 152). The legislation also acknowledged that workers held property rights in their jobs, stipulating that cash compensation, in the form of severance payments based on age and length of service, be awarded to those made redundant by their employer (Anderman 1986). Although the 1965 Act appeared to satisfy the twin rationales of stimulating greater economic efficiency, while at the same time providing displaced workers with cash compensation for the loss of their jobs, it was nonetheless infused by 'a clear managerial agenda' (Turnbull and Wass 1997: 30). The legislation was underpinned by a desire to make it easier for employers to dismiss employees, in that it was designed to reduce both union opposition to dismissals and the workplace disputes that they often provoked (Fryer 1981). Thus the RPA was dominated by a 'predominantly management frame of reference' in as much as it strengthened managerial prerogative in the area of dismissals, and thus helped to legitimize them (Fryer 1973: 11).

The evolution of policy and practice since the 1960s clearly demonstrates the large extent to which the redundancy provisions strengthen the hand of managers when instituting dismissals. Judicial interpretations of the relevant legislation have largely supported the supremacy of managerial prerogative over redundancy decisions (Turnbull 1988; Turnbull and Wass 1997). The concept of redundancy, moreover, has been treated increasingly loosely, to such an extent that it is taken to apply to an employer's decision that fewer employees are required to undertake particular work, without any obligation to demonstrate that the amount of work has in fact diminished (Lewis 1993: 72). The up-front financial costs of making severance payments are rarely onerous for employers (Turnbull 1988); in 2004, the maximum statutory payout that an individual could receive was just over £8,000. Redundancy has therefore become a popular means of instituting efficiency savings, through cuts in labour costs, and has become far removed from its original stated purpose of improving the economy-wide supply of labour.

The process of redundancy also enables managers to restructure their workforces in ways that benefit the employer's interest. It 'is a time when new standards can be laid down as the organization gears up to operating in a changed environment' (Lewis 1993: 39). In particular, management exercises control over the redundancy selection criteria and can use them to streamline their workforces in a desirable manner through the use, for example, of supposedly more objective factors, such as performance, ability, skills, and disciplinary and attendance records, rather than LIFO. The redundancy provisions, then, are used in ways that enhance organizational flexibility and competitiveness, and do little to provide workers with job security. Indeed, they may actively erode it (Turnbull 1988; Turnbull and Wass 1997), as we shall now go on to see.

8.4.2 The process and experience of redundancy

Having discussed the public policy background, in this section we consider the contemporary salience of redundancy in employment relations, since it 'is probably the most evocative and fear-inducing form of organizational change for many workers' (Worrall, Cooper, and Campbell 2000: 648). In particular, we examine the implications for workers of the substantial discretion enjoyed by managers over the decision to shed labour, who should be dismissed, and how and when they should go.

Redundancies have become an established part of the employment relations landscape, linked in particular to the economic recessions of the early 1980s and early 1990s when millions of workers lost their jobs as a result of business closures and rationalization programmes (Gallie et al. 1998). Although the incidence of redundancy in Britain appears to have diminished since the early 1990s, official data do not include other measures used to reduce staff numbers, such as so-called early retirement for example, which may be a form of disguised redundancy (Worrall, Cooper, and Campbell 2000). There is plenty of evidence, moreover, which suggests that redundancy, and the threat of being made redundant, is salient to the experience of workers.

Seventeen of the twenty organizations studied by Burchell et al. (1999) had instituted redundancy programmes in the preceding five-year period, with several having done so more than once. In their study of the aerospace industry in south-west England, Danford, Richardson, and Stewart (2003) demonstrate the extent to which large-scale redundancies, linked to rationalization initiatives following changes of ownership, decimated employment levels in many workplaces across the region. During the 1990s, the number of skilled manual workers employed by BAE Systems, for example, was more than halved. Major reductions in employment are not confined just to the manufacturing sector. Rationalization initiatives in financial services, for example, including the slimming down of branch networks, appears to have also generated significant numbers of job losses (Hudson 2002). Even in a relatively buoyant overall economic climate, then, fears of redundancy are seemingly 'well founded' (Turnbull and Wass 2000).

Perhaps the most striking aspect of redundancies is the way in which they are now used by organizations to shed labour even when they are performing relatively successfully (Blyton and Turnbull 2004). You will recall that in public policy terms the ostensible aim of redundancy was to encourage the movement of workers from declining industrial sectors of the economy to new, expanding ones. Increasingly, however, redundancy programmes seem to be initiated not because there has been a diminution in what workers are expected to do, but as a means of generating cost savings, or of instituting greater workplace flexibility (Hudson 2002; Worrall, Cooper, and Campbell 2000). In so far as they enable firms to 'downsize', redundancies, then, are often viewed as central to realizing organizational efficiencies, even when the workload remains constant. Hudson (2002: 47) offers the example of a further education college in which 'downsizing had been achieved by making permanent teaching staff redundant and re-employing them as part-time agency workers and also by contracting out the catering and security functions'.

We have already observed that the decision to make redundancies is generally one that is in the prerogative of managers. Key features of the redundancy process, moreover, are also subject to managerial control, often to the detriment of certain groups of workers. In the case of the docks, for example, Turnbull and Wass (1994) observed that older workers, those who were medically restricted in some way, and thus unable to undertake a full range of tasks, and union activists were over-represented among those selected for redundancy.

In respect of the redundancy selection criteria, there is evidence that managers may override supposedly objective scoring systems in order to exercise discretion over who stays and who goes. In their study of redundancies among defence-related firms in Scotland, Donnelly and Scholarios (1998) found that in one case, workers were awarded points based on their performance. Other criteria, however, appeared to influence the selection process in a way that was perceived as unfair. According to one former employee: 'The selection method was sick to say the least. I was picked out for one and a half days ill in seven years with the company, the same week I got my assessment sheet and my total points were 28 out of 30' (quoted in Donnelly and Scholarios 1998: 332).

One of the ways in which management can intensify their control over redundancy exercises is to encourage workers to depart voluntarily with the promise of an enhanced cash payment if they agree to go of their own volition. This must seem odd. One would assume that voluntary redundancy, as opposed to being made compulsorily redundant, at least gives workers some discretion. In reality, however, it is not as simple as that. There is evidence, from the coal-mining industry for example, that ostensibly voluntary redundancy programmes are subject to managerial influence over selection (Wass 1996). Furthermore, managers enjoy the right to refuse applications for voluntary redundancy from people whom they would prefer to stay on, particularly if they have 'certain skills, knowledge or capabilities deemed essential to the firm' (Turnbull and Wass 1997: 33).

As opposed to this, they may actively encourage, and indeed impose, voluntary redundancy on people they do want to be rid of. Thus it is not inappropriate to refer to the concept of 'forced' voluntary redundancy in many cases (Turnbull 1988). Donnelly and Scholarios (1998) encountered a number of instances where simply enquiring about the possibility of voluntary arrangements resulted in the workers concerned being targeted for compulsory redundancy. In some cases, the alternative to voluntary redundancy is the acceptance of new terms and conditions of employment that provide for more flexible working and limit pay increases (Hudson 2002). In the docks, for example, in the aftermath of a major strike called against the government and employers' decision to terminate a national agreement covering conditions of service, many workers felt that the onerous terms of their new contracts made it impossible for them to remain. According to one worker: 'The amount of money was irrelevant really. For me it didn't matter if it was £10,000, £20,000 or £30,000. The choice was something or nothing, because there was nothing for me in the docks after the strike' (quoted in Turnbull and Wass 1994: 497). In practice, then, there is often little to distinguish voluntary from compulsory redundancy (Burchell et al. 1999). Indeed, the term 'voluntary redundancy' may be 'something of a misnomer' (Turnbull 1988; Turnbull and Wass 1997), in so far as it communicates the misleading impression that workers can exercise much choice over whether they go or not.

Evidently, redundancy exercises offer managers an opportunity to strengthen their prerogative and, moreover, institute efficiency gains at the expense of workers' jobs. This is largely unaffected by the obligation to consult with representatives of the workforce (see Box 8.2). In a review of practice in three sectors, the docks, steel industry, and coal mining, Turnbull and Wass (1997) demonstrate that redundancy exercises enabled managers to secure work effort at less cost to the employer. In particular, workers who had been made redundant were then re-hired, on a self-employed, contract, or casual basis on drastically

---

BOX 8.2 REDUNDANCY CONSULTATION IN PRACTICE

Where employers propose to dismiss twenty or more employees they are obliged to consult with union representatives if the organization recognizes a trade union, or, if it does not, with elected employee representatives. The consultation should, according to government advice, 'be in good faith with a view to reaching an agreement, ought to encompass ways of avoiding dismissals, any means of reducing the number of people due to be dismissed and alleviating the consequences of the redundancies (see Hall and Edwards 1999: 312–13). Although in theory organizations are liable to financial penalties if they do not engage in adequate consultation, in practice the obligation to consult is rarely an obstacle to the management of redundancy (White 1983).

There is some evidence that appropriate consultation, especially where union representatives are involved, encourages managers to reform their proposals. In one case, for example, following a consultation exercise, the company made voluntary arrangements available having initially decided upon a compulsory redundancy programme (Hall and Edwards 1999). Nevertheless, the decision to make redundancies is generally taken before any consultation commences (Turnbull and Wass 2000). Moreover, firms often avoid their obligation to consult and 'operate outside the law by using voluntary severance arrangements and offering enhanced severance payments' (Turnbull and Wass 1997: 32).

---

inferior conditions of service. In these cases, then, redundancy exercises were used to alter the terms of the wage-work bargain in a way that was advantageous to employers.

Those who have been made redundant often face a period of unemployment or are forced to accept jobs that offer worse pay and conditions than those to which they are accustomed (Donnelly and Scholarios 1998; Harris 1987; Turnbull and Wass 1997, 2000). Generally, the people who are most likely to be made redundant, older workers for example, or those with health problems, are those who have relatively greater difficulty in finding new ones (Turnbull 1988; Turnbull and Wass 1997). Understandably, then, the ease with which employers can make people redundant in Britain, relative to other European countries, and the large extent to which managers enjoy prerogative over the redundancy process, shapes the experience of workers in important ways and is, it would seem, a major source of job insecurity.

8.4.3 Job insecurity

A high level of job security is often cited as one of the most important features of jobs in so far as it enables people to carry on with their working lives without the fear of redundancy and its adverse consequences. Historically, though, the jobs of manual workers were often far from secure. Employers frequently used fluctuations in the level of demand for their products as a reason for suspending production and sending staff home – laying them off – without pay. This worker at Ford's Halewood plant on Merseyside in the late 1960s protested about the uncertainty that this generated: 'Look, we've been laid off this afternoon and we haven't even been told that officially. They tell you nothing. All your pay can be stopped and they tell you nothing. That's typical of this firm' (quoted in Beynon 1973: 156).

Since the mid-1990s, however, there has been a marked increase of interest in the extent to which employment in Britain has become more insecure (Burchell et al. 1999). This is linked to two developments in particular. First, the pressures generated by the neo-liberal economic restructuring associated with the globalization process (see Chapter 2) appear to have contributed to a stronger climate of insecurity (Elliot and Atkinson 1998). Richard Sennett, for example, proposes that the ascendancy of a system of flexible capitalism, in which companies are exposed to more sustained competitive pressures, and are expected to produce ever-faster returns for their shareholders, means that they are increasingly unable to offer long-term security to their employees, eroding trust, loyalty, and commitment. Given its short-term nature, then, neo-liberal capitalism creates vulnerability and undermines the features of working life that once enabled people to fashion careers and structure their lives (Sennett 1998).

Second, the rise in perceptions of job insecurity is also associated with the growth of non-standard, or flexible, employment patterns (see Chapter 2). Since these arrangements are intended to make the workforce more disposable, it is unsurprising that workers are rendered more vulnerable and insecure. Conley (2002) examined the job insecurity experienced by care workers and newly qualified teachers who were employed by local authorities on temporary contracts. According to Max, a temporary local authority care worker: 'If you have a family you can't plan long term. You can't plan a holiday, you can't plan what is going to happen six months down the road. You can't plan whether you are going to have a job tomorrow. It is just a nightmare' (quoted in Conley 2002: 730).

While the attention accorded to job insecurity ensures that the experience of workers receives due emphasis (Heery and Salmon 2000b), there is considerable scepticism about its significance in contemporary employment relations. We have already seen, in Chapter 2, that the growth of temporary employment has been somewhat limited. According to the WERS 98 data, moreover, most employees, 60 per cent in fact, considered their jobs to be secure, whereas only one-fifth did not (Cully et al. 1999: 167). The assumption that non-standard employment relations arrangements are an inherent source of insecurity has also been questioned (Charles and James 2003).

Moreover, studies of job tenure, that is the length of time people stay in their jobs, reveal that generally it is rather stable. Although men did experience a slight fall in the average length of time they spent in their jobs between the 1980s and 1990s, women's job tenure, perhaps because they were more likely to return to work after taking maternity leave, increased markedly (Gregg and Wadsworth 1995; Gregg, Knight, and Wadsworth 2000). The number of workers in long-term employment, people who have been in their present jobs for at least ten years, has also grown (Doogan 2001). A study of workers' perceptions of insecurity found that at the aggregate level little change could be detected between 1986 and 1997. However, certain groups of workers, such as managers and professionals, did report a marked increase in insecurity (Felstead, Burchell, and Green 1998). Thus one commentator challenges assumptions that job insecurity in Britain has increased significantly; rather, it 'seems to be confined to certain articulate groups such as well-qualified professionals' (Robinson 2000: 37).

Yet tenure is not a very good measure of job security. In a more uncertain and insecure environment workers may prefer to hang on to their current job, rather than look to change it and thus expose themselves to greater risk (Burchell 2002). A more refined approach to understanding job insecurity would adopt a broader measure than simply job tenure, and incorporate the subjective feelings of employees themselves, in particular the prospect of losing their jobs, and the consequences of job loss for their livelihoods (Burchell 2002; Burchell et al. 1999). The perceived cost of losing one's job is a major source of insecurity, given the resulting likelihood of worse employment conditions in a new one, or even unemployment (Turnbull and Wass 2000).

Thus insecurity can be understood as a 'property of jobs', linked to matters such as job tenure and the risk of losing one's job, and as a 'property of the subjective experience of employees'. In order to appreciate the insecurity phenomenon properly, however, it is also necessary to consider it as a 'property of the environment' (Heery and Salmon 2000b: 12–13). In other words, we need to examine the way in which changes in the broader economic, political, and institutional contexts have contributed to greater job insecurity. In particular, higher levels of job insecurity can be explained by the greater exposure of organizations and their employees to market forces, which is a consequence of the rise of a neo-liberal capitalist order, with its preference for deregulated labour markets as a means of delivering improvements in economic performance. Rising insecurity, then, is not a function of jobs, or even of labour market restructuring. It 'is the outcome of a conscious strategy of government that arises from attempts to increase the productivity and competitiveness of the economy' (Doogan 2001: 439).

The extent to which exposure to market forces has contributed to greater job insecurity is particularly evident within the British public services. Since the 1980s, in many areas, especially in local government and the health service, the delivery of public services has been subject to the processes of competitive tendering and market testing, often resulting in them being operated by private sector contractors. While not all workers have been disadvantaged by a change in their employer (Foster and Scott 1998), there is plenty of evidence to suggest that, given the need to secure efficiency gains, contracting out and market testing lead to reductions in employment levels, and erode people's terms and conditions of employment (Allen and Henry 1996; Colling 1999; Morgan, Allinton, and Heery 2000). More generally, restructuring initiatives in the public sector have contributed to workers' insecurity, as one civil servant observed: 'Like everybody else, in the back of your mind, worries about the future, redundancies. At one time the Civil Service was considered the most secure job, once you were in you were in for life, but like everything else that's changing' (quoted in Bradley 1999: 123).

Relative to the private sector, the level of job insecurity in the public sector is still rather low. Nevertheless, restructuring initiatives, and the growth of private sector involvement in service delivery in particular, given its potential to erode pay and employment conditions, have generated greater insecurity for public sector workers (Morgan, Allinton, and Heery 2000).

By adopting a broader perspective on job insecurity, one that both examines workers' subjective experiences and stresses the important influence of changes in the wider environment, we have seen that it has become an increasingly pertinent feature of contemporary employment relations (Burchell et al. 1999; Heery and Salmon 2000b). Not only does insecurity damage the psychological health and well-being of workers, but there is evidence that, in so far as morale suffers, it may also undermine organizational effectiveness (Mankelow 2002; Wichert 2002).

SECTION SUMMARY AND FURTHER READING

- Redundancy is a salient feature of contemporary employment relations given the extent to which organizations use it as a means of shedding jobs and thus delivering efficiency gains. For those workers who have been made redundant, the aftermath is often characterized by periods of unemployment, or employment in jobs that offer worse pay and conditions than they had hitherto been accustomed to.

- Managers have considerable scope to exercise their prerogative during redundancy programmes. Not only do they enjoy discretion over the decision to shed labour, who should be dismissed, and how and when they should go, but they also are rarely hindered by the obligation to consult with trade union or employee representatives.

- Job insecurity has become an increasingly salient part of day-to-day experience of workers in contemporary employment relations. It is not associated with changes in job tenure or labour market restructuring so much as the development of a more neo-liberal, market-based economic climate that renders workers more disposable.

For a managerial perspective on redundancy, see Lewis (1993). Based on industry studies, Turnbull and Wass (1997) provide a more critical interpretation of management's control of the redundancy process, situating it within an assessment of the public policy framework. Donnelly and Scholarios (1998) offer a rare study of workers' experiences of redundancy. For job insecurity, see the collection of essays in Heery and Salmon (2000a), and also the findings of the Joseph Rowntree-funded research study of twenty case study organizations (Burchell 2002; Burchell et al. 1999).

8.5 The intensification of work

Having discussed trends in pay and working time in Chapter 7, developments in one further feature of the wage-work bargain remain to be assessed – how is working time utilized by employers? What do workers do when they are at work, and how intensively, or with how much effort, do they perform their jobs? This is an important area of analysis since the concept of 'effort' is critical to employment relations. Employers, when they hire workers, as we now know, buy their potential labour power, or their capacity to engage in productive effort. How this latent effort is then used is subject to an ongoing process of negotiation and re-negotiation between managers and workers.

8.5.1 Work intensification in Britain

Problems of measurement render judgements of work effort difficult to calculate with any degree of certainty (Green 2001; Nichols 1986). While one can attempt to measure the speed at which a job is undertaken, its physical and mental intensity is personal to the individual performing it, and is thus an inherently subjective phenomenon. Nevertheless, 'the strength and consistency of worker opinions on questions of effort support the argument that effort levels have indeed risen' (Noon and Blyton 2002: 111). Studies of work effort indicate that work became more intensive in the 1980s. Even though a European-wide phenomenon, the trend in the UK has been particularly notable, and appears to have contributed to an increased amount of physical and psychological stress among workers (Burchell et al. 1999). Both survey and case study evidence highlighted the growth in work intensification during the 1980s as employers sought improved flexibility in the utilization of labour (Elger 1990). Based on interviews with workers in four case study companies, Edwards and Whitston (1991) detected evidence of some work intensification – the jobs of railway platform staff, for example, demanded greater effort.

The trend towards greater work intensification appears to have continued throughout the 1990s (Green 2001: 63), as is clear from a number of relevant research studies. Gallie et al. (1998: 223) discovered a 'marked increase in the intensity of work effort over the last decade'. While this was most likely due to a rise in the level of skill required in carrying out certain jobs, the resulting work intensification was nonetheless a source of work strain. Three-quarters of employees responding to WERS 98 agreed that their job requires them to work very hard, while two-fifths claimed never to have sufficient time to complete their work. A quarter of the sample worried about their work outside working hours (Cully et al. 1999: 171). The WERS researchers also found that women were more likely to claim they worked harder than men, perhaps because they are more likely to undertake the majority of household chores and have to balance this with paid employment, and that work intensity was a notable feature of public sector employment, particularly for workers in education (Cully et al. 1999: 172–3).

Perhaps the most substantial evidence we have about the growth of work intensification in 1990s Britain comes from research undertaken in twenty workplaces from both the private and public sectors funded by the Joseph Rowntree Foundation (Burchell 2002; Burchell et al. 1999). The researchers asked employees whether the speed of their work, and the effort they expended in undertaking it, had increased or decreased. Sixty-four per cent of employees reported an increase in the speed of their work; 61 per cent claimed an increase in effort. Only 5 per cent of employees thought the speed of their work had decreased; and just 4 per cent reported a reduction in the effort required by their jobs. Even though it seems not to have increased any further since the late 1990s (Green 2003), work intensification remains an integral feature of employment relations in contemporary Britain. See Box 8.3 for evidence from the airline industry.

8.5.2 The causes and effects of work intensification

But what has caused greater work intensification? Perhaps jobs have become more intrinsically satisfying, with workers more willing to exert additional effort as a result? Gallie et al. (1998), for example, contend that work intensification is linked to increasing skill levels. There is also case study evidence that some employees now enjoy greater responsibility and discretion in their jobs, making them harder, yes, but also more challenging (see Beynon et al. 2002: 280–1). While the importance of such 'supply-side' factors should not be entirely discounted, the bulk of the research evidence suggests that the demand from employers for greater work effort is the major cause of increases in the intensity of work. In sum, greater competitive pressures impel employers to pursue

---

BOX 8.3 HRM AND WORK INTENSIFICATION IN THE AIRLINE INDUSTRY

The airline industry is intensely competitive, and prone to major fluctuations in demand that can lead to problems of over-capacity. Moreover, so-called 'low-cost' providers such as EasyJet and Ryanair increasingly threaten established operators like British Airways. Boyd (2001) surveyed over 900 cabin crew from scheduled and charter airlines based in the UK. She discovered that intense competitive pressures encouraged operators to adopt an approach to managing staff that was so dominated by the imperative to reduce costs that it intensified workers' labour, damaged their health, and potentially undermined safety standards. Boyd's respondents reported that the pursuit of efficiency savings dominated the way in which companies managed cabin crew numbers and their shift patterns. Airlines may choose to operate services with fewer cabin crew, for example, and sometimes just with the minimum legal requirement. The work of cabin crew is very intensive, and contributes to numerous health problems, including fatigue, backache, and stress. According to one worker: 'Every year we are expected to carry out more services, more flights with less crew, minimum hours off in between – how long do management expect us to continue working to a high standard of service without cracking up?' (quoted in Boyd 2001: 448).

On short-haul routes in particular, brief turnaround times between incoming and outgoing flights, often less than thirty minutes, create added strains for cabin crew. Pressure to sell products to passengers also contributes to their workload: '. . . we spend eight out of ten services running around like headless chickens. During turnaround we are treading on cleaners and caterers while getting the aircraft ready for the next sector. Our endeavour to satisfy the passengers means that we compromise safety' (quoted in Boyd 2001: 447).

---

greater flexibility and ruthlessly manage costs in such a way that the same number of employees, or fewer, are obliged to produce ever greater quantities of work (Burchell 2002; Green 2001).

In their analysis of seven private and public sector case study organizations, Beynon et al. (2002) emphasize the large extent to which demands for enhanced organizational competitiveness and efficiency savings drove managers to intensify the labour of their staff. For the private sector companies, the obligation to satisfy the expectations of financial institutions, and thus enhance shareholder value, resulted in pressure to prune staff numbers as a means of taking out costs. Although the public sector organizations were not subject to the disciplines of the stock market, budget cuts compelled them to manage their employment relations in an overly commercial manner. Indeed, the researchers 'were struck by the way managers at the two public sector organizations were often more concerned about performance pressures than were their private sector counterparts' (Beynon et al. 2002: 266).

Thus managers come under increasing pressure to increase the work effort of their staff as a means of realizing improvements in competitiveness. Job cuts often result in the workload having to be shared out between the remaining employees. When, for example, managers in a further education college were made redundant, lecturers were obliged to take on their public relations and marketing duties (Hudson 2002). Notwithstanding some evidence of an increase in job discretion and responsibilities (Beynon et al. 2002;

Gallie et al. 1998), Hudson (2002) discovered that in most cases when workers' jobs are expanded, they are expanded in a 'horizontal' rather than a 'vertical' direction. In other words, workers are expected to take on more tasks at a similar level of skill rather than benefit from an enhancement of their skills base. According to a customer assistant in a supermarket: 'My job title changed from cashier to customer assistant ... it just means that we can do the packing role as well if we see the red light go; cashiers and packers all have the same name now' (quoted in Hudson 2002: 45).

In front-line service work, moreover, where people have responsibility for dealing with customers, managers may use this relationship as a means of extracting greater work effort from staff. The telecommunications company studied by Beynon et al. (2002), for example, had given greater priority to service quality considerations, and expected its workers to be more sensitive to customer needs – an added source of pressure.

As well as the work intensification created by financial considerations, compelling organizations to operate with fewer staff who are given added duties and responsibilities, performance management systems and targets are an added source of workload pressure. In his study of employment relations in two financial services companies and two public sector organizations, Poynter (2000: 216) notes the extent to which managers now use sophisticated performance management techniques to increase the work effort of their staff, and to enhance their own control. Within financial services, for example, the use of performance targets is an effective means of generating faster work rates, not least because in some areas employees faced the threat of disciplinary action should their output be deemed unacceptable. According to Shona, a mortgage processor working for a financial services company in Glasgow: 'There is so much pressure with the phone calls from the branches. ... In a way the real pressure comes from the daily statistics sheet. They can not measure how much we work from the screens but they can from the daily statistics sheets' (quoted in Baldry, Bain, and Taylor 1998: 173).

Developments in information technology enable managers to monitor the performance of their employees, and thus control their work rate more easily (Baldry, Bain, and Taylor 1998). In office-based environments, for example, computerization allows managers greater freedom to organize the flow of work in a way that reduces the ability of workers to manipulate their effort. According to a union representative in a financial services company:

Instead of you picking and choosing which bit of work you want to do, when you finish the piece of work and you press a button to say I have finished this piece of work, it just brings up the next bit. There's no question of you having a break. ... (quoted in Danford, Richardson, and Stewart 2003: 107)

Call centres are environments where the use of information technology enables managers to control the pace of work and monitor staff with particular ease, a source of work intensification. According to one worker:

The major pressure is ... the calls ... and that is understandable because we work in a call-centre environment, and you also get the pressure ... because you haven't got time to literally stand up and do what you need to do or take two minutes. You feel as though you're under pressure by taking the calls because it [the indicator] could be flashing 'there's eight minutes of calls waiting' which is quite regular in the evening. (quoted in Beynon et al. 2002: 289)

As we have already noted, the level of work intensification in the public sector has been particularly acute, a function of the restructuring of the public services, enhanced performance pressures, and the development of new management techniques. It is clear that changes in the public sector, most notably a more market-based approach to the delivery of services, has, in a context of tight budgetary constraints imposed by the Treasury, been a major source of increased work intensity. Harriet Bradley interviewed workers in a hospital for her book *Gender and Power in the Workplace* (1999). At the time of the research the hospital was preparing a bid to become a Self-Governing Trust. The process appears to have increased concern to reduce costs in a way that generated work intensification. According to a male charge nurse:

The workload's too much, staffing loads are deplorable. I personally feel as though that money is the name of the game . . . being just out to cut costs at all costs. I know I could be doing a better job if I had the resources. . . . It's beyond a joke, you're just pushed and pushed and pushed. (quoted in Bradley 1999: 118)

A further aspect of the restructuring of the public sector in Britain, the contracting out of some services, such as schools meals provision and refuse collection, to the private sector has also intensified the effort of many of the workers involved in delivering them. In order to increase productivity, and thus generate profitability in what are labour-intensive activities, private sector providers may reduce the numbers of staff employed, and raise the work pace and the number of job tasks of those who remain (Colling 1999).

The reform of management in the public sector, and the introduction of techniques associated with the 'new public management', which were discussed in Chapter 5, also appears to have been a cause of work intensification. Research studies demonstrate that performance targets are used intensively in the public sector, perhaps more so than in private companies, constituting a significant source of pressure on staff (Beynon et al. 2002; Poynter 2000). In the Benefits Agency, a civil service executive agency in the UK responsible for welfare payments, researchers discovered that the implementation of teamworking and performance-related pay, based on the subjective appraisal of staff by managers, had caused profound changes in two of the three offices they studied: 'It is difficult to convey fully the atmosphere of intense stress and low morale caused by an acute intensification of workloads and individual appraisal uncovered by our interviews within the [Benefits Agency] . . . [the] overriding impression was of an organization at breaking point' (Foster and Hoggett 1999: 30–31, 31).

Research studies consistently point to a process of work intensification in Britain since the 1980s both in the private and public sectors. For employees, the principal causes are 'increased competition and shareholder influence in the private sector, and reduced Treasury funding in the public sector, leading to downsizing, but with an expectation that the reduced number of employees would still achieve the same quantity of work' (Burchell 2002: 76). Coupled with technological innovations that allow managers enhanced control over the pace and flow of work, and the reduction in the influence of the trade unions, which might otherwise act as a countervailing force, the result is a pronounced intensification of work for many people in Britain.

What, though, are the effects of work intensification? For organizations, it seems that the conditions for increases in the levels of trust and cooperation necessary to stimulate long-term, real improvements in economic performance are unlikely to exist. The evidence, on both working time, which we considered in Chapter 7, and work effort, examined here, indicates that many employers prefer to 'sweat' their staff, generating short-term improvements in output by intensifying workloads or using overtime. For workers, increasing workload pressures are a potential source of distress, and may result in both physical and psychological damage (Burchell et al. 1999; Wichert 2002). To have situations where, as observed by some researchers, workers are unable to leave their desks to take refreshments, is unlikely to be healthy (Baldry, Bain, and Taylor 1998). The following quotations, the first from a call-centre operator, and the second from a further education lecturer, encapsulate the psychological and physical damage of excessive work pressures on individuals.

I know a lot of people are off with stress. Because you get customers on the telephone and I have seen women sit there and cry because of the calls they are getting. . . . In this job women get sworn at and cry. (quoted in Beynon et al. 2002: 281)

So many people are going home with work to do that they haven't really got time to do. I find myself going home feeling physically exhausted, although I've hardly done anything physical. (quoted in Nolan 2002: 122)

It is rare for textbooks on employment relations and human resource management to consider the issue of work intensification, its causes, and its effects. The evidence reviewed here, however, demonstrates that it is an integral feature of contemporary employment relations and is central to the day-to-day experience of many workers.

SECTION SUMMARY AND FURTHER READING

- Although there are difficulties associated with measuring how much effort people expend in their jobs, there is nonetheless overwhelming evidence that since the 1980s there has been a general process of work intensification in Britain.

- While an increase in their job responsibilities may in part have led some people to work harder, the principal causes of work intensification are the growing competitive pressures upon organizations that have compelled them to increase staff workloads, the extensive use of new systems for managing performance, linked to developments in information technology, and, in the public services, myriad major restructuring initiatives.

- It is unlikely that work intensification of the kind seen in Britain since the 1980s will generate long-term improvements in economic performance. Moreover, there is increasing evidence of its detrimental consequences for workers' morale, health, and well-being at work.

For an overview of trends in work intensification, see Green (2001). There are two main sources of case study evidence with regard to work intensification. Beynon et al. (2002) examine six private and public sector organizations, while the findings of the Joseph Rowntree-funded research study of twenty organizations are reported in Burchell et al. (1999), Burchell (2002), and Hudson (2002).

■ CONCLUSION

In this chapter, we have examined four important aspects of contemporary employment relations – employee involvement and participation, discipline at work, redundancy and job insecurity, and work intensification – in order to consider the experiences of employees. In general, they are better informed about organizational and workplace decisions, and sometimes enjoy a limited degree of increased discretion over how they undertake their jobs, albeit within strict boundaries. They have, however, little genuine influence over decisions that affect them at work, and there is evidence that managerial control over the wage-work bargain has intensified. Following on from this, the use of workplace discipline is an integral means of sustaining managerial control in the workplace. Formal procedures give employees little protection from the arbitrary exercise of managerial discipline. Moreover, a punitive approach to workplace discipline continues to mark this aspect of contemporary employment relations.

Management control over the decision to make redundancies, and the means by which they are undertaken, is also a prominent feature of contemporary employment relations. In a context of greater competitive pressures, which oblige organizations to search continually for efficiency savings, redundancy exercises are used largely as a means of cutting costs through the shedding of labour. One of the main consequences is a marked increase in the level of job insecurity in Britain. This is amplified by the neo-liberal character of contemporary capitalism, and its preference for deregulated labour markets, something that enhances the disposability of the workforce. Redundancies, and job losses in general, are a function of the pressure on organizations to operate in a leaner, more efficient manner with an emphasis on the need to make cost savings on an ongoing basis. For many workers the result is that they are expected to work harder. Work intensification is one of the most salient features of contemporary employment relations in Britain, given growing competitive pressures on organizations that cause them to increase staff workloads, the extensive use of new systems for managing performance, linked to developments in information technology, and, in the public services, major restructuring processes.

In general, then, the experience of employees in contemporary Britain is marked by an increased exposure to work intensification, insecurity, and a tightening of managerial control over their behaviour, with limited opportunities to influence decisions that affect them at work. The economic and political circumstances outlined in Chapters 2 and 3 of this book give employers greater opportunity to shift the terms of the wage-work bargain in their favour, to the detriment of employees' interests. The latter are not passive actors, though, as the discussion of union organizing efforts in Chapter 6 demonstrates. Nevertheless, the material presented in this chapter demonstrates the basic antagonism that marks the relationship between an employer and employee. How the potential conflict this generates manifests itself in practice is the subject of the next chapter.

■ ASSIGNMENT AND DISCUSSION QUESTIONS

1. Why do managers prefer downward forms of communication to other forms of employee involvement?

2. How do workers experience teamworking and empowerment initiatives? What can managers do to make such processes more effective?

3. What factors influence whether or not a 'disciplinary rule' at work will be enforced by managers?

4. Discuss the proposition that: 'discipline should be about correcting an employee's behaviour to the standards expected by management rather than be a means to impose punishments'.

5. In what ways do redundancy exercises potentially strengthen managerial control of the workplace?

6. What is meant by 'work intensification'? What factors contribute to workers feeling they have to work harder? Have you experienced any of these factors?

■ **WEBSITE MATERIALS**

 Visit the companion web site to this book for interesting and updated material at
www.oup.com/booksites/busecon/business

■ **CHAPTER CASE STUDY**

One service, two types of worker?

After being elected to government in 1997, Labour avoided re-nationalizing those industries, such as coal, telecommunications, gas, electricity, and water supply that had been privatized by its Conservative predecessors. Rather, its belief has been that regulation of public sector services is more important than ownership. In terms of policy on those areas such as health, education, and local government that remain in the public sector, Labour has endorsed private sector involvement, seeing such 'partnerships' as a means of delivering better services without requiring the investment of significant public funding.

One mechanism to achieve this policy has been the Private Finance Initiative (PFI). Here, a private sector firm agrees to provide public services in return for a fee. To date, PFIs cover prisons, roads, and hospitals. Another measure promoted by the government is the outsourcing of contracts where private sector firms employ staff and provide a specific service, for example, cleaning, to the public sector organizations. Staff working in such companies come from two sources: those transferring from public sector employment which had previously provided the service, and newly recruited workers. The pay and other employment conditions of the former are protected by the Transfer of Undertakings (Protection of Employment) Regulations (TUPE) which requires the private sector employer to employ them those on terms that are no worse then those they received in their public sector employment. New recruits are given no such protection, and employers are free to offer different terms and conditions. Since employment accounts for the majority of costs in these businesses, perhaps up to 75 per cent, firms looking for savings have an incentive to cut staffing levels and provide worse employment conditions for new staff in order to win and retain contracts.

This had led to the emergence of a two-tier workforce. Staff working alongside each other and doing the same tasks may be paid differently simply because of the date on which they started work. While evidence about the extent of the two-tier workforce is limited, unions representing staff have claimed that it is a significant problem, and there have been incidents of industrial action in

PFI businesses over the issue. It appears that those most likely to be employed on worse terms and conditions are low-paid, semi- and unskilled staff, and that women workers are more adversely affected than men.

In response to union demands that this issue be tackled, the government introduced a code of practice that would govern the terms and conditions of workers employed by firms providing services to local government. This specified that new recruits working alongside employees transferred from local authorities should receive an 'employment package' which was no less favourable in overall terms to those ex-public sector workers. In addition, recognized unions, or elected workforce representatives if no union is recognized, must be consulted on the employment terms offered to new recruits. Since the code's introduction, there have been no reported disputes. However, controversy in the health service over the two-tier workforce led, in 2004, to the government applying similar principles to other areas, such as defence and health. While accepting the need for broad comparability, employers maintain that they need some degree of flexibility over pay and conditions since they have to organize their work differently. Without this, they argue, they will be unable to deliver the level of service demanded by the government.

Sources: BBC News, October 2001, September 2002; *The Guardian*, March 2002, February 2003, February 2004 (various dates)

Case discussion question

1. Should employers be forced to provide terms and conditions to new recruits at an artificially high level simply because other employees' terms are protected?

the popularity of the term 'wildcat strike' to describe such activity (Gouldner 1955). However, unofficial strikes cannot be treated as if they are spontaneous; their occurrence reflects the ongoing efforts of employees to resist potentially damaging changes to their working conditions, or to improve their position and power, in the context of the wage-work bargain (Cronin 1979). Such activity demands organization, and hence calculation. The preponderance of unofficial strikes in the Royal Mail, for example, reflects managerial attempts to realize efficiency gains, through the implementation of new working methods among other things, and the efforts of employees to resist them. Such activity is generally organized by local union representatives, with or without the knowledge of the formal union hierarchy, who use it to challenge management initiatives. Thus 'unofficial strikes in [Royal Mail] are predominantly organized, premeditated and not spontaneous' (Gall 2003c: 168).

Two implications arise from the purposeful and organized nature of strike activity. First, the notion sometimes advanced by governments and employers that strikes are abnormal, a deviation from the normal character of stable, ordered, and peaceful employment relations, cannot be upheld. In the context of an exploitative employment relationship, the withdrawal of their labour by employees is a rational form of behaviour designed to achieve a particular purpose, to alter the terms of the wage-work bargain in a way, or ways, favourable to them (Hyman 1977). Nevertheless, it is important not to present strikes as examples of rational, purposive activity simply in the context of collective bargaining; they also reflect the capacity of workers to act collectively, to mobilize in pursuit of their interests through the vehicle of a trade union (Cronin 1979; Hyman 1989).

This highlights the second main implication of the strike being an activity that is both purposeful and organized, that is the importance of the collective organization of workers in trade unions. Without the presence of a strong union that is able to mobilize workers, organize the action and coordinate resistance to employer efforts to defeat it, effective strike activity is hard to uphold (Edwards 1983, 1995b; Hyman 1989).

Strikes are often taken as a measure of the level of industrial conflict because they are apparently easy to quantify. There are three main ways of ascertaining the level of strike activity in any given period, usually over the course of a year. The duration of strike activity is measured by calculating the numbers of working days not worked due to strike activity. The breadth of strike activity is calculated by measuring the number of workers involved, and its frequency is determined by totalling up the number of strikes, or stoppages, in any given year. In Britain, unless the total number of days not worked amounts to 100 or more, stoppages involving fewer than ten workers, or lasting less than one day, are excluded from official data (Monger 2004).

The measure of strike activity used can influence one's perception of trends in strike levels. In 1996, for example, a national dispute in the Royal Mail contributed to a threefold increase in the number of working days lost due to strike activity over 1995. The number of recorded stoppages, however, barely rose. Thus, measured by frequency, the level of strike activity in 1996 was similar to that of the previous year. However, the duration, and also the breadth, of strike activity was very different. While official strike data can be used constructively to map trends in strike activity over time (Edwards 1995b), they should nonetheless be treated with caution (Hyman 1977). Managers sometimes do not record strikes, for example (Batstone, Boraston, and Frenkel 1978).

9.2.2 The declining level of strike activity in Britain

A prominent feature of recent employment relations in Britain has been the diminution in the level of strike activity since the 1970s. While the 1980s were characterized by occasional large-scale strikes, in industries such as steel making and coal mining, as workers and their unions fought rationalization initiatives that threatened their jobs, livelihoods, and communities (Gilbert 1996), by the 1990s the amount of strike activity had fallen to very low levels indeed (Edwards 1995b). This decline continued into the latter part of that decade, and the early years of the twenty-first century. For example, 1997 saw the lowest number of working days lost due to strike activity, 235,000, while the smallest number of strikes, just 133, was recorded in 2003. The average figures reported in Table 9.1, though, conceal notable annual fluctuations in strike activity. In 2002, for example, over 1.3 million working days were lost largely as a result of two major public sector strikes involving local government workers and firefighters. The decline in the level of strike activity is an international phenomenon. Nevertheless, it has been more pronounced in Britain than elsewhere (Waddington 2003b).

What factors have caused the incidence of strike activity to fall to such low levels in contemporary Britain? Clearly, the changing composition of employment has been influential. Levels of employment in traditionally strike-prone industries, such as coal mining and the docks for example, have fallen considerably. Job growth has been concentrated in private sector service industries where trade unionism is weaker and strike action less commonplace. There is also some evidence that economic factors have contributed to the declining level of strike activity. During the 1980s, for example, a combination of relatively low inflation and high unemployment appears to have reduced the number of strikes (Edwards 1995b). The former reduces the incentive for strike action, since employees do not feel that their standard of living is threatened by rising prices, whereas the latter invokes a greater fear of the consequences of losing one's job as a result of going on strike.

Table 9.1. The level of strike activity in Britain 1946–2003

	Strikes	Workers involved (000s)	Days not worked (000s)
1946–52	1,698	444	1,888
1953–59	2,340	790	3,950
1960–68	2,372	1,323	3,189
1969–73	2,974	1,581	12,497
1974–79	2,412	1,653	12,178
1980–85	1,276	1,213	9,806
1986–89	893	781	3,324
1990–96	325	275	973
1997–2003	182	260	515

Annual averages.

Sources: Edwards (1995b); Monger (2004)

What, though, has been the effect, if any, of the way in which employment relations is managed? Given the limited impact of human resource management techniques (see Chapter 5), and also considering the nature of people's experiences of contemporary employment relations (see Chapter 8), it seems doubtful that the level of strike activity has diminished because workers are more contented. The potential for conflict in contemporary employment relations is as pronounced as it ever has been, if not more so. What does seem to have changed, though, is that many employers are managing employment relations more assertively. They are fostering a workplace climate in which it is made apparent to employees that, given greater competitive pressures, their cooperation is essential in order to prevent job losses, and the erosion of pay and working conditions (Edwards 1992).

The level of strike activity has fallen as a consequence of the changing balance of power between organized labour and capital. The decline in their membership and organizational capacities has rendered the union movement less capable of undertaking effective industrial action. Many union leaders have placed their faith in partnership and cooperative employment relations as the route to greater influence largely, as we saw in Chapter 6, because they are operating from a position of weakness. Perhaps the most important constraint on the power of unions to organize effective strike action is the highly restrictive legal framework, something we consider below. Much strike action now occurs in the public sector where union organization continues to be somewhat robust (Mathieson and Corby 1999). By the late 1990s and early 2000s, public sector disputes, among post office workers, college lecturers, local government workers, and firefighters in particular, increasingly dominated the strike statistics. Much of their action, moreover, was often relatively short, or discontinuous, in nature, such as a series of one- or two-day strikes for example, something which increases the pressure on the employer while reducing the costs to the employee of striking, in particular loss of wages.

While the amount of recorded strike activity is at historically low levels in Britain, from a global perspective we can see that strikes continue to be an important feature of contemporary employment relations. In a review of strike levels in Western Europe, Gall (1999) suggests that although during the 1980s and 1990s overall strike activity was, relative to the previous two decades, somewhat low, cross-national differences in the way in which data are collected mean that official statistics under-represent the real level of conflict. Moreover, his careful analysis of strike data demonstrates that the level of strike activity is prone to fluctuations and that strikes are therefore not going to vanish (see Box 9.1 on Italy for example).

In so far as it challenges people's working conditions, the process of economic globalization discussed in Chapter 2 both stimulates the extent, and extends the dimensions, of industrial conflict. In countries that have been subject to 'structural adjustment' programmes imposed by global financial institutions, such as Argentina for example, the implementation of neo-liberal policies has generated considerable labour unrest (Silver 2003). Since the 1980s, strikes and protests have occurred in response to the enactment of neo-liberal economic policies, including wage restraint and privatization, in countries such as South Korea, France, and Bolivia, some of which have informed, and developed connections with, the growing worldwide anti-globalization movement, exemplified by the demonstrations at the 1999 World Trade Organization meeting in Seattle (Kingsnorth 2003; Moody 1997; Silver 2003).

BOX 9.1 GENERAL STRIKES IN ITALY

Employment relations in Italy has long been marked by a high incidence of strike activity relative to other countries. Yet the recent history of Italy shows that workers are still capable of mobilizing in large numbers to undertake strike action in order to try to defeat policies that challenge their standard of living. In the three years after it took office in 2001, the policies of Silvio Berlusconi's right-wing government prompted four general strikes. In April 2002, for example, the main trade union confederations organized a one-day strike to campaign against proposed labour market reforms which they claimed would erode workers' rights and damage job security, and have since been enacted. The one-day national strike of November 2004 was called in protest at the Italian government's broader economic policies, in particular its proposal to reduce public spending by massive amounts in order to finance tax cuts and comply with European Union pressure to reduce Italy's budget deficit. Huge demonstrations took place in most of Italy's main cities, with protesters shouting anti-Berlusconi slogans. The strike stopped production at major companies like Fiat, closed many public services, and disrupted public transport. According to Alfonso Pecorao Scanio, of Italy's Green Party, the 'general strike is the best response to the social massacre of this well-to-do government which gives to the rich while heavily cutting services to citizens'. For Romano Prodi, the Italian politician and former president of the European Commission, the 'demonstration is the start of a unified action to get this country back on its feet'.

From a global perspective, it is apparent that strike activity and other forms of labour unrest have not disappeared, but rather are increasingly evident in those countries that have become the principal locations for the production of manufactured goods for western markets. The development of export-oriented manufacturing industries in countries such as China for example, and the concomitant need for cheap labour on a massive scale, generates an environment in which the growth of industrial conflict is a likely development (Silver 2003). There are strong indications that the economic reforms, which are designed to create a capitalist market economy in China, are stimulating widespread labour unrest in many parts of the country, over matters such as unpaid wages for example. Conflict encompasses everything 'from everyday worker resistance, petitions, work stoppages and strikes to public protests, violence, independent unionism and political movements' (Taylor, Chang, and Li 2003: 158). This suggests that in the twenty-first century, labour unrest, including strikes, will in all likelihood remain an important feature of employment relations around the world.

9.2.3 The legal regulation of industrial action in Britain

Unlike many other European countries, in Britain workers have never enjoyed a 'right' to go on strike. Under the common law, based on the notions of freedom of contract and the importance of property rights, workers who strike, or undertake any form of industrial action, generally act in breach of their employment contracts. Trade unions that organize industrial action potentially transgress the common law in a range of areas; most notably they commit the offence of inducing workers to breach their contracts. During the late nineteenth and early twentieth centuries, legislation was enacted that gave unions and their officials immunities from criminal prosecution for organizing industrial action, and from civil proceedings for damages by employers, as long as the action was 'in contemplation or furtherance of a trade dispute' (Wedderburn 1986). The concept of 'immunities' gave the misleading impression that trade unions were above the law, and attracted much judicial hostility (Wedderburn 1991). In practice all they did was ensure that the common law of contract and property rights did not make the conduct of employment relations impossible to uphold in practice (Davies and Freedland 1993). Without these immunities, trade unions would have been in no position to bargain effectively on behalf of their members. The only alternative was a system of positive rights for workers and their unions, something that was contrary to the preference for voluntarism and autonomous self-regulation that characterized employment relations in Britain.

However, during the 1980s and 1990s, the Conservative governments enacted six major pieces of legislation restricting the capacity of trade unions to undertake lawful industrial action. The main focus of their interventions was to reduce the scope of the immunities that enabled unions to organize industrial action within the boundaries of the law (Dickens and Hall 2003; Dunn and Metcalf 1996). Among other things, legislation was enacted that: obliged unions to win majority support for industrial action from the workers concerned in a properly constituted secret postal ballot; prohibited any form of 'secondary' industrial action, meaning that it is only lawful when it involves a 'primary' dispute between workers and their own employer; enabled employers, and other aggrieved parties, to sue a union for damages arising out of unlawful industrial action; and gave employers greater scope to dismiss workers taking industrial action (see Auerbach 1990; McIlroy 1991). The legislation was a major element of the Conservatives' efforts to eradicate the power of the unions in Britain. Although it enacted legislation making it unlawful for employers to dismiss employees undertaking lawful industrial action, and made some of the balloting requirements less onerous for the unions, Labour retained the bulk of the anti-strike legislation it inherited from its Conservative predecessors in government. Given their efforts to promote partnership in employment relations, and not to antagonize the government or employers, trade union leaders appeared reluctant to campaign for greater freedom to organize strikes (McIlroy 1999).

The extent to which the restrictive legal framework weakened the capacity of trade unions to mount effective strikes was evident in a number of high-profile disputes, particularly in the newspaper publishing and transport sectors, during the 1980s and 1990s (Gennard 1984; McIlroy 1991). For the most part, though, employers have been reluctant to invoke the law when facing industrial action by trade unions (Dickens and Hall 2003; Undy et al. 1996: 226). In the Royal Mail, for example, managers generally prefer to avoid the courts when faced with unlawful unofficial industrial action on the basis that legal action would only inflame disputes, making them harder to resolve (Gall 2003c).

Nevertheless, some employers are prepared to request interim labour injunctions, judicial orders temporarily preventing trade unions from undertaking industrial action. Most applications from employers for an injunction are successful, often on very thin, or sometimes no, legal grounds, and few are ever pursued to a full court hearing (Gall and McKay 1996; Wedderburn 2001). Generally, employers apply, or threaten to apply, for injunctions in order to put pressure on unions to settle disputes, or to delay impending industrial action in the hope that the workforce's support for it will dwindle because of the wait (Elgar and Simpson 1993; Evans 1987). The complex legislation governing industrial action ballots gives employers plenty of scope to challenge, and thus delay, any planned action, even if their substantive case turns out to be weak. Such legal cases cost unions a great deal of money. Moreover, 'they reiterate the limits of permissible industrial action; keep unions under pressure; engage the energies of officers and officials; divert attention from organizing effective action; and, where injunctions are granted, dislocate it' (McIlroy 1999: 528–9).

The impact of the legal restrictions on union behaviour is by no means straightforward though. Where workplace union organization is relatively strong, the obligation to hold a ballot before taking industrial action can work to a union's advantage. A large vote in favour, for example, can be used to exert pressure on employers to grant concessions. In situations where they are confident that they have the support of the workforce, canny union officials sometimes use ballots to strengthen their bargaining power in negotiations with employers (Undy et al. 1996). Nevertheless, the constraints the law imposes on industrial action have contributed to a general strengthening of managerial prerogative. In his study of employment relations in an autocomponents factory in South Wales, Danford (1999) demonstrates the large extent to which the legal restrictions on industrial action eroded union resistance to managerial initiatives, and enhanced the capacity of management to secure workplace changes unfavourable to the interests of employees.

It is difficult to quantify the contribution of the restrictive legislative framework to the declining level of strike activity in Britain. Many other European countries have also seen falling strike levels, suggesting that broader economic and industrial trends, the changing composition of the workforce, and the reduction of the number of people employed in 'strike-prone' industries in particular, have exercised more influence (Dunn and Metcalf 1996). Yet the indirect effects of the law, in particular the large degree to which it restricts the capacity of the unions to challenge employers' actions, have certainly contributed to the decline in the incidence of industrial action in Britain over recent decades. Unions are much more hesitant about calling industrial action now than would have been the case before the 1980s.

By retaining the majority of the Conservatives' anti-strike legislation, Labour has ensured that Britain remains in contravention of international conventions that deal with rights at work. In recent years, for example, various International Labour Organization (ILO) committees, as well other international bodies, have expressed concern that Britain's extreme anti-strike legislation negates workers' freedom of association, and undermines the ability of unions to organize workers and bargain effectively (see Ewing and Hendy 2004). British law fails to comply with international obligations in a number of potential respects. For example, the capacity of employers to impose sanctions upon employees undertaking industrial action, up to and including dismissal, is one notable failing. Any employee engaged in unofficial action is not covered by unfair dismissal legislation, and employers also enjoy considerable freedom to dismiss strikers once a twelve-week protected period expires (see Box 9.2). Moreover, the prohibition on all forms of secondary action 'is contrary to international law which stipulates that industrial action is not to be confined to disputes with employers and is, in particular, to be permitted on matters of economic and social policy' (Ewing and Hendy 2002: 91). Although the British government is under no obligation to amend legislation to comply with the ILO's recommendations, interventions

---

BOX 9.2 SACKING EMPLOYEES WHO ARE TAKING LAWFUL STRIKE ACTION

In 1999, Labour made it unlawful for an employer to dismiss employees undertaking lawful industrial action during the first eight weeks of a dispute. Once the eight-week 'protected period' was over, dismissals are lawful only if an employer has made an effort to resolve the dispute. This 'protected period' has since been extended to twelve weeks. The experience of Friction Dynamics, an American-owned car parts plant based in North Wales, demonstrates how the odds are stacked against workers taking strike action, even when it has been lawfully organized by a trade union. In 2001, members of the Transport and General Workers Union (TGWU) employed at the plant went on strike over the employer's proposals to change shift patterns and institute a temporary pay cut. After exactly eight weeks, the employer dismissed the eighty-six strikers. They mounted a picket outside the firm's premises that was to last for two and a half years.

   In 2002, the strikers won their employment tribunal claim for unfair dismissal, and waited for the company to pay the compensation they were due. In August 2003, though, the American owner put the company into liquidation, claiming that the size of its recent losses meant that it could not continue in business. The remaining workers were dismissed. Two weeks later, a new company, called Dynamex Friction, and under the same ownership, took over the business and re-engaged forty workers. Since the company that had been found to have unfairly dismissed the eighty-six workers technically no longer existed, their compensation would have to be provided by the government. Speaking in August 2003, the TGWU's former general secretary, Bill Morris, claimed that the company's closure, and its reappearance under a new name, was 'a tactical manoeuvre designed to avoid making the compensation payments to the eighty-six unfairly dismissed workers and to put the financial burden on to the taxpayers of this country'. In April 2004, the workers finally gained £750,000 compensation, to be shared between them.

---

by international bodies are likely to stimulate further debates about the appropriateness of the current legal framework governing industrial action in Britain.

9.2.4 Conflict at work in contemporary employment relations: insights from mobilization theory

While broader industrial, economic and political factors clearly affect the level of strike activity, it is important to recognize that the causes of strikes are rooted in the dynamics of the relationship between managers and workers in particular workplace environments. Strikes, then, are both social and political phenomena (Batstone, Boraston, and Frenkel, 1978; Hyman 1989). They occur primarily because workers mobilize collectively, in order to resist or influence decisions made by their employers. Thus, their existence constitutes a political challenge to the established order of the organization.

   In order to understand why strikes occur, then, attention must be directed at the way in which workers, organized in trade unions, perceive the need to undertake industrial action, and the effectiveness with which they are able to do so (Shorter and Tilly 1974). Broader structural factors clearly exercise an influence on strike levels in as much as they generate grievances or a more general sense of disaffection, but whether or not such discontent produces a strike in a particular organization or workplace depends upon the mobilizing capacity of the workers involved, as well as their willingness and opportunity to take action (Batstone, Boraston, and Frenkel 1978; Edwards 1995b; Waddington 2003b).

Three implications follow from this understanding that strikes are social and political phenomena, whose manifestation is contingent upon the capacity of workers, organized in trade unions, to mobilize and defend their conditions or challenge their employer, albeit within particular contexts. First, it helps to explain variations in strike activity between different organizations and workplaces. For example, between 1993 and 2002 the further education sector in England and Wales was greatly disrupted by industrial action, but the level of strike activity varied considerably between colleges, reflecting the different mobilizing capacities of the union at different sites (Williams 2003).

Second, since strikes reflect the mobilizing capacity of the workers involved, in the context of antagonistic relations that always have the potential to generate conflict, it can be difficult to identify the causes of a particular dispute (Hyman 1989). In Royal Mail, although strikes are generally called in response to particular incidents, such as the suspension of union representatives for example, their provenance tends to reflect the 'underlying discontent' caused by commercialization pressures and workplace restructuring (Gall 2003c).

Third, the rationale for, and the meaning of, strike action sometimes changes during the course of a dispute. One of the best examples of this was the firefighters' dispute in 2002–03. Although the strikes ostensibly concerned the Fire Brigades Union's (FBU) demand for a full-time annual salary of £30,000, the Labour government, which undermined early efforts to reach a settlement, increasingly saw the dispute as a means of securing far-reaching changes to the organization of the fire service and the nature of its operations. Thus over a period of some months, the basis of the FBU's action changed from a principal concern initially with attaining a hefty pay rise, to a determination to resist major encroachments on firefighters' working conditions and changes to their duties (Burchill 2004).

A focus on the capacity of workers to organize themselves collectively in response to problems at work, and engage in some form of industrial action to redress them, is central to the contribution that mobilization theory makes to an understanding of changes in the level of strike activity in Britain. The fall in the level of strike activity does not reflect greater contentment at work, and thus a diminution of industrial conflict; rather, in the absence of trade unions, discontent is expressed in different forms, as exemplified by the sharp rise during the 1990s in the number of complaints made by aggrieved employees to employment tribunals, concerning matters such as unfair dismissal and discrimination for example (see below). In the largely non-union hotel industry, the unilateral exercise of managerial authority is the source of numerous grievances among employees concerning their perceived unfair treatment, many of which are submitted to tribunals (Head and Lucas 2004). Far from declining, the potential for conflict in employment relations has been increasing. Given evidence that people are willing to act collectively to pursue their interests in society (Kelly 1998), how, then, can the decline in the level of strike activity be explained?

Mobilization theory helps us to understand the social processes that enable, and constrain, the development of collective industrial action. It 'directs our attention to the social relations of the workplace and the processes by which employees perceive and respond to injustice and assert their rights' (Kelly 1998: 51). Thus mobilization theory seeks to explain the circumstances under which individual grievances take on a collective dimension, inform the collective organization of workers, and result in collective industrial action (Kelly 1998: 24).

What, then, is the relevance of mobilization theory to understanding the levels of industrial conflict and strike activity in contemporary employment relations? First, it suggests that the absence of strikes does not imply that industrial harmony prevails in British workplaces. Mobilization theory shows that effective collective action by workers is a highly contingent process, something that takes root in particular circumstances, and often in the face of determined employer opposition, even where a demonstrable conflict of interest exists. Given a supportive political context and legislative framework, employers enjoy plenty of scope to counter-mobilize, and thus impede the capacity of workers to engage in collective action. In the case of Japanese manufacturer 'Nippon CTV' for example, this was done by developing a cooperative relationship with a moderate trade union. Despite the manifest discontent experienced by workers, the company's approach effectively stifled the emergence of any collective action to improve working conditions. Although workers engaged in individual acts of resistance, some refused to wear the company's blue jackets for example, they rarely took on a collective dimension (Delbridge 1998).

The second contribution of mobilization theory is its emphasis that collective action by workers can take a variety of forms and is thus not just restricted to strikes. In non-union environments, for example, where the organization of strikes faces insuperable difficulties, there is evidence that collective action by workers, such as protests over changes to people's jobs for example, may impel managers to re-think their proposals, or even back down entirely (see Dundon and Rollinson 2004; Kelly 1998; Scott 1994). One of the most striking examples of the use by workers of alternative forms of collective industrial action as a means of winning improvements in pay and conditions concerns the Justice for Janitors campaign in the United States (see Chapter 6). Erickson et al. (2002) demonstrate the respective contributions made by street protests, petitions, and the mass picketing of company premises to raising public awareness, and the eventual success of the largely immigrant cleaning workers.

In Britain, innovative forms of collective action have been pioneered by The East London Communities' Organization (TELCO) in partnership with the Unison trade union. As part of its 'living wage' initiative, TELCO campaigns on behalf of low-paid cleaning and catering staff who are employed by contractors on the premises of major organizations like banks and hospital trusts. Its activity, which has involved demonstrations, picketing, and the mass occupation of a branch of the HSBC bank in one instance, is designed to embarrass organizations since public attention is drawn to the low pay and poor conditions endured by many of the people who, indirectly, work for them. While such tactics are as yet rare in Britain, the experience of TELCO highlights the potential way in which community-based initiatives can mobilize around employment issues, and inspire collective action among groups of workers whom trade unions find difficult to organize (Wills 2004a).

The third way in which mobilization theory enhances our understanding of industrial conflict is the importance it attaches to leadership: the role activists play in using the existence of grievances to mobilize workers, and to encourage them into taking collective action in opposition to their employer. This is evident from studies of the call-centre sector that highlight the vast range of grievances and simmering discontent characterizing much of its employment relations. In 'Telecorp', for example, some key activists built on workers' concerns over a number of issues, in particular the poor quality of customer service (the centre dealt with calls to the emergency services), to develop union organization (Bain and Taylor 2000). In the face of management opposition, though, activists often find it difficult to sustain the level of mobilization in a way that enables workers to feel confident that unionization is effective (Bain et al. 2004).

By highlighting the potential constraints on collective action in workplaces, as well as pointing to the features that make it possible, mobilization theory makes an important contribution to our understanding of contemporary employment relations and the nature of industrial conflict. It recognizes that the potential for conflict exists in all employment relationships. Yet the extent to which this latent conflict is expressed, and also the means of its expression, is contingent upon the pattern of relationships between workers and their managers in particular workplace settings, albeit within particular contexts. This is a theme that informs our discussion of non-strike manifestations of industrial conflict in the next section.

SECTION SUMMARY AND FURTHER READING

- Given the inherent potential for conflict that characterizes the employment relationship, it is understandable that strikes, the collective withdrawal by workers of their labour, are a feature of employment relations. They are the most obvious and visible manifestation of industrial conflict. Strikes, whose occurrence generally depends on the existence of union organization, are types of purposive, calculative behaviour in employment relations, designed to pursue a demand, or express a grievance.

- There are a number of ways in which the level of strike activity can be measured, though the accuracy of the data should be treated with caution. Nevertheless, the amount of strike activity in Britain has fallen to very low levels. A number of factors appear to be responsible, including the decline in union bargaining power associated with a more restrictive legal framework. However, the process of economic globalization appears to be intensifying labour unrest in many parts of the world.

- It is important to understand the causes of strikes with reference to the mobilizing capacity of workers and their unions. Mobilization theory can be used to understand the circumstances which generate strikes. Moreover, it also demonstrates that collective action by workers is not just confined to strike action.

The classic introduction to the topic is Hyman's book on *Strikes* (Hyman 1977 and other editions). For strike trends in Britain, see Edwards (1995b), Gilbert (1996), and Waddington (2003b). The government publishes an annual survey of the level of strike activity in *Labour Market Trends* (e.g. Monger 2004). See Silver (2003) for the implications of globalization for labour unrest. Kelly (1998) considers the relevance of mobilization theory. For further information about changes in the legal framework see McIlroy (1991, 1999), and Dickens and Hall (2003).

9.3 Other forms of industrial conflict

While strikes are the most conspicuous form of conflict in employment relations, by no means are they the only one. In this section, then, we broaden our examination of industrial conflict to examine other manifestations of conflict. Following Scott et al.'s (1963) study of the coal mining industry, it is conventional to distinguish between 'organized' and 'unorganized' forms of conflict in the workplace. The latter is distinguished by its spontaneous, individualistic character. Workers respond to the demands of the work environment by undertaking actions that allow them to express their frustration, through committing sabotage for example, or by distancing themselves from the causes of their problems, like going absent, or by quitting their jobs. Organized forms of conflict, though, are imbued with a more formal, collective and purposeful character, undertaken in order to challenge and change managerial decisions, not merely to enable workers to cope with them. Such conflict is 'far more likely to form part of a conscious strategy to change the situation which is identified as the source of discontent' (Hyman 1977: 53). Although a strike is the most obvious manifestation of organized conflict, other forms of collective industrial action short of a strike, including overtime bans and work-to-rules for example, are used by workers collectively, usually in trade unions, to influence organizational decision-making.

We begin this section by examining forms of organized industrial conflict other than strikes, before moving on to explore the various manifestations, and significance, of unorganized conflict. Our discussion will demonstrate that not only is the conventional distinction between organized and unorganized conflict often rather difficult to make in practice, but also that the term industrial conflict itself needs to be used with a considerable degree of caution.

9.3.1 Forms of organized industrial conflict

Forms of organized industrial conflict other than strikes are often referred to as 'action short of a strike', or as 'cut-price' (Flanders 1975) methods of industrial action. While they are types of behaviour designed to disrupt an employer's ability to produce goods and services, as a strike does, they do not involve a complete withdrawal of labour. These are forms of action in which workers mostly continue to undertake their duties. There are three main types of cut-price industrial action. The 'go-slow' occurs in situations where workers carry on performing their jobs, but do so at a much slower pace than normal. The 'work-to-rule' generally involves a refusal by workers to undertake some aspect or aspects of their job that are essential to the normal production of goods, or delivery of a service. In Chapter 7, we noted the high incidence of overtime arrangements in Britain. Since many organizations rely on their workers undertaking overtime in order to maintain production levels, or to ensure that services are maintained, overtime bans, where workers collectively refuse to take on overtime, can be extremely disruptive to the organization.

Like strikes, these forms of industrial action are designed and undertaken with a purpose, to challenge managerial decisions, for example, or to put pressure on the employer to adjust the terms of the wage-work bargain in a way that benefits the workforce. They can be popular. With the possible exception of a refusal to undertake voluntary overtime, and like strike action, these types of behaviour almost certainly constitute a breach of workers' employment contracts (Wedderburn 1992). Nevertheless, they are seen as less risky forms of action than strikes. Moreover, workers do not lose as much as they would if they were to go on strike, and thus not get paid. Like strikes, though, go-slows, working-to rule, and overtime bans require organization and coordination, generally through the activities of a trade union (Edwards 1995b).

While there is some evidence from manufacturing industry of the popularity of overtime bans relative to strike action (Milner 1993b), data from successive Workplace Employment Relations Surveys demonstrate that the incidence of organized forms of industrial actions short of a strike has substantially declined. For example, in 1980 some 10 per cent of workplaces reported the occurrence of at least one overtime ban in the year preceding the survey. By 1990, this had fallen to 7 per cent of workplaces. Only 2 per cent of workplaces reported the occurrence of a work-to-rule (Millward et al. 1992). By the end of the 1990s, non-strike forms of industrial action were, like strikes, rare indeed, and were reported in only about 1 per cent of workplaces. 'Collective action of any kind has . . . virtually disappeared from British workplaces' (Cully et al. 1999: 245).

While its incidence may be rare, cut-price industrial action is nonetheless an effective means by which organized groups of workers can challenge managerial decision-making, express a grievance, or enforce a demand in contemporary employment relations. In 2003, for example, lecturers at London Metropolitan University refused to divulge exam marks to students, or to participate in exam boards, as part of a campaign to improve London weighting allowances. During the late 1990s and early 2000s, schoolteachers enforced effective work-to-rules by refusing to provide cover for absent colleagues, or by refusing to help undertake tests, among other things. While they may be uncommon, examples like these demonstrate that organized industrial conflict should not be equated simply with strike activity.

9.3.2 Forms of unorganized industrial conflict

Clearly, levels of strike activity and also other forms of organized industrial action are, compared to the past, relatively uncommon in contemporary employment relations. Yet the concept of industrial conflict needs to be broadened, to encompass forms of unorganized conflict which, given the diminution of trade union power in Britain since the 1970s, and the concomitant reduction in significance of organized types of action, may be of more relevance. We consider fiddling, sabotage, absenteeism, and quitting, four types of employee behaviour that are often held to exemplify unorganized conflict in employment relations in as much as they are spontaneous or unconsidered acts undertaken by individual workers in order to enable them to cope with the frustrations and pressures of the working environment. Before we do this, however, some initial questions arise that will help to inform the reader's understanding of the nature and dimensions of unorganized industrial conflict.

First, to what extent do the types of worker behaviour considered here conflict with managerial objectives? Can they really be interpreted as industrial conflict, along with more purposeful and organized activities such as strikes and overtime bans for example?

Second, how far are the behaviours associated with so-called unorganized forms of conflict spontaneous, lacking in purpose, and thus distinct from organized activity? Is it wise, therefore, to make a rigid distinction between organized and unorganized forms of conflict? Third, unorganized types of industrial conflict are often portrayed as alternatives to strikes or other manifestations of organized action (Knowles 1952), the implication being that if conflict in the employment relationship is not expressed by means of, say, a strike, it will simply take another form. Are different manifestations of conflict to be regarded as alternatives? Or do they act in concert, complementing one another?

Fiddles

Fiddling can encompass a wide range of illicit activities ranging from employee theft to actions that alter the terms of the wage-work bargain to the benefit of the workers. Much of the early interest in fiddles focused on the latter. Roy (1952) and Lupton (1963) examined the way in which workers, through the process of 'making-out', collectively manipulated piece-rates, that is the amount they were paid per item of production, by regulating their effort. In as much as it influences the wage-work bargain, in a way that runs counter to the interests of the employer, such activities are unambiguously an expression of conflict at work (Edwards 1992).

The term 'fiddling' is also used to describe more illicit behaviours at work. McIntosh and Broderick (1996) examine the practice of 'totting' among refuse collectors, something that was commonplace before the increased work pressures created by the contracting out of the collection service rendered it more difficult to operate. It involved 'sifting through bags and bins in search of "valuables" or "sellables" which were then either kept or sold – many refuse collectors regularly took part in car boot sales' (cited in Noon and Blyton 2002: 238). The most well-known account of employee fiddles is contained in Mars's book *Cheats at Work* (Mars 1982). He examines the way in which the characteristics of particular jobs encourage certain types of employee fiddle to emerge. Supermarket workers, for example, being closely supervised and monitored, tend to be opportunistic in their fiddling behaviour, making the most of opportunities, such as the chance to secure a free bar of chocolate, as and when they arise. Other groups of workers, sales staff for instance, tend to have developed well-articulated and sophisticated fiddling techniques, often collectively, such as the manipulation of expenses claims for example.

Many fiddles, then, are underpinned by a collective ethos and cannot be seen simply as a spontaneous reaction on the part of an individual worker; they are often informed by collectively generated norms and assumptions that govern the limits of what is acceptable, and what is not. Hence there is a difficulty with seeing fiddles as an unambiguously unorganized form of conflict; many of the most effective workplace fiddles are the product of the collective effort by workers to secure for themselves a more favourable working environment, or to increase the rewards from employment. To what extent, moreover, can fiddling be conceptualized as a form of industrial conflict? Workers who participate in fiddles are engaged in activities that would appear to run counter to the interests of their employer, but 'making-out' sometimes operates in ways that support managerial objectives (Edwards 1986). Moreover, one of the most prominent features of studies of workplace fiddling is the often high level of managerial toleration of, or indulgence towards, such behaviour. Why should managers tolerate such activities? For one thing, fiddles help to sustain employee morale in an otherwise mundane working environment, and thus help make the task of supervision less burdensome. In some industries, like hospitality for example, toleration of fiddles enables managers keep wages low. They can also be extremely difficult to eradicate. As long as fiddling is kept within what managers consider to be appropriate limits, and does not overly damage the interests of the business, it is often tolerated on the basis that if challenged it would only reappear in another, perhaps more damaging, guise elsewhere (Edwards 1988; Noon and Blyton 2002; R. Wood 1992).

Sabotage

One of the main difficulties presented by employee sabotage is defining what it is. Sabotage at work, which has been the subject of a number of academic studies (e.g. Brown 1977; Taylor and Walton 1971), is often portrayed rather narrowly as involving the deliberate vandalism or breaking of machinery. The term 'often conjures up the image of people engaged in wilful acts of destruction' (Noon and Blyton 2002: 252). Some writers, however, prefer a broader, more inclusive definition, such that the term sabotage can be used to refer to any type of employee behaviour that does not comply with managerial objectives, such as the fiddles discussed above for example. By this reckoning, incidents of sabotage cannot just be seen as the product of individual frustration with the pressures of work, but may also, in some circumstances, have a collective dimension, being used by organized groups of workers to alter the terms of the wage-work bargain in their favour (Dubois 1979). Rather than acting as an alternative to more conventional forms of industrial action, sabotage may complement them. During 1999, for example, incidents of sabotage were a feature of industrial disputes in Spain. They included 'the cutting of electric cables during a rail dispute, engine drivers destroying the safety mechanism in their cabs, and striking ship-yard workers immobilizing the bridge giving access to the Bay of Cadiz' (Rigby and Marco Aledo 2001: 291).

Given its association with the breaking and destruction of machinery, sabotage is sometimes thought to be something that is specific to manufacturing industry and thus, given the diminution of manufacturing employment in countries like Britain and the United States, of little importance now. Nevertheless, reports of alleged sabotage still occur. In 2001, for example, the US Federal Bureau of Investigation (FBI) was called in to investigate a suspected incident of sabotage involving damaged wiring at Boeing's Renton plant in Washington state, which manufactures the 737 series aircraft. Workers at the plant faced an uncertain future since the company had announced its intention to relocate some production and other activities away from the state.

Incidents of sabotage, broadly-defined, can be found in many parts of the service sector and, in so far as they cause the quality of service offered to customers to deteriorate, potentially damage to the interests of the business (see Box 9.3). In his study of employment relations in McDonalds, Royle (2000) discovered employees engaged in competitions to see which of them could perspire the most over the company's food products. Even the reluctance of customer-facing staff to relate to customers in the approved manner, for example by not smiling when they are supposed to do so (see Fuller and Smith 1991), can be interpreted as a form of sabotage.

BOX 9.3 EMPLOYEE SABOTAGE IN THE CONTEMPORARY SERVICE SECTOR

The most extensive analysis of sabotage in the contemporary service sector is Harris and Ogbonna's (2002) study of four firms in the hospitality industry. They use the term 'service sabotage' to refer to behaviours by workers and managers 'that are intentionally designed negatively to affect service', and report that over 85 per cent of the customer service employees they interviewed admitted to having committed 'some form of service sabotage behaviour' in the preceding week (Harris and Ogbonna 2002: 166, 168). One waiter explained how he might deal with a rude customer: 'There are lots of things that you do that no one but you will ever know – smaller portions, dodgy wine, a bad beer – all that and you serve it with a smile! Sweet revenge!' (quoted in Harris and Ogbonna 2002: 169).

The researchers encountered examples of service sabotage behaviour involving hygiene issues: 'ranging from spitting in consumables to adding dirt to food to spoiling guest rooms in a discreet fashion (an unpleasant example including the wiping of a used tissue around the rim of a drinking glass)' (Harris and Ogbonna 2002: 171). While some of these activities were the product of an attempt on the part of the individual worker concerned to deal with the pressures of the working environment, such as the demands of rude customers for example, others were far from spontaneous affairs, with employees collectively complicit in such behaviours, sometimes with the tacit approval of their managers.

Absenteeism

Dealing with absenteeism appears to be a much greater challenge for managers in contemporary employment relations than confronting strikes. In 2003, some 40 million working days were lost to sickness absence. According to a 2000 study for the Chartered Institute of Personnel and Development (CIPD), over one-third of days not worked because of sickness absence is not due to ill-health at all, amounting to an average of three days off each year for every worker in the country (*The Guardian*, 15 May 2000). Its survey of nearly 1,700 organizations found that the main reasons given by employers for increases in absenteeism were 'changes in workforce morale' and 'workloads'. The annual cost of sickness absence to businesses in Britain is estimated to be at least £13 billion. Absenteeism is more prevalent in the public than the private sector (Cully et al. 1999). Annual sickness absence among employees working for Birmingham City Council, for example, amounts to more than ten days for each worker on average. Some departments are particularly susceptible to absenteeism; in social services the annual rate is in excess of sixteen days on average for each worker (*The Guardian*, 18 February 2004).

These data highlight some important features concerning the role of absenteeism in employment relations. It often reflects workers' dissatisfaction with the conditions of their labour, and can thus constitute a form of withdrawal from work (Hill and Trist 1953, cited in Nichols 1997). The frustrations, pressures, and tensions that confront individuals in the working environment are relieved through the taking of an occasional spontaneous 'sickie'. In this way, absenteeism may be viewed as the archetypal form of unorganized industrial conflict. Yet the observation that absence rates vary, according to sector, organization, and department, suggests that, as a form of industrial conflict, absenteeism cannot be understood purely in individualistic terms. For one thing, studies of absenteeism indicate the presence of absence 'norms', tacitly accepted, perhaps even institutionalized, and collectively held assumptions concerning acceptable levels of attendance. This was traditionally the case in the docks, for example (Turnbull and Sapsford 1992). Moreover, perspectives that treat absenteeism as a means by which individuals withdraw themselves from work generally ignore the powerful influence of structural factors, such as the nature of the work environment, or the incidence of injuries and ill-health at work (Nichols 1997). Where the work process is organized in such a way that workers enjoy little autonomy or control over their labour, or where the pace of work is intense and relentless, such as in some call centres for example, it can damage people's physical and mental well-being (Taylor et al. 2003).

Absenteeism may be used as a tactic by organized groups of workers to alter the terms of the wage-work bargain or to resist managerial challenges to jobs and working conditions. For example, in his study of a plant manufacturing agro-chemicals and dyestuffs, Heyes (1997) demonstrates how the introduction of an annualized hours system undermined the practice of 'knocking'. In one of its manifestations, a worker would report sick in order to generate lucrative overtime opportunities for a colleague. At a later date, the roles would be reversed and the joint proceeds shared. The end-of-chapter case study demonstrates the significance of mass absenteeism as an effective form of industrial action in British Airways.

There are, however, problems with viewing absenteeism as a manifestation of industrial conflict. For one thing, in the majority of cases, absenteeism is the product of ill-health, and not a reaction to unpleasant working conditions, or part of a protest against management decisions. Moreover, the extent to which absenteeism can be conceptualized as a form of industrial conflict often depends upon the context in which it occurs. For the poorly organized women workers in the clothing factories studied by Edwards and Scullion (1982), for example, absenteeism was an 'escape valve', giving them the opportunity to relieve the tensions associated with an authoritarian working environment and the tedium of their jobs, while posing little challenge to managerial control. Within the engineering factories in the study, though, the well-organized male workforce enjoyed an important degree of collective control over the pace of their work, and thus had less of a need to use absenteeism as a means of escaping their jobs.

Quitting

Perhaps the most unambiguously unorganized and individualistic expression of industrial conflict, and the most explicit manifestation of withdrawal from work, is the practice of leaving, or quitting, one's job as a result of unpleasant working conditions. Thus high levels of labour turnover are often interpreted as evidence of a conflict-ridden working environment. In one of the call centres studied by Beynon et al. (2002), managers reported that in the preceding three months 300 staff had resigned, suggesting an annual turnover rate of some 130 per cent. The causes were obvious. For one thing, working conditions were exceptionally onerous. 'Managers talked of "burn-out" and frequently expressed scepticism over whether anyone could effectively perform the job for an extended period' (Beynon et al. 2002: 152). Workers also found the unsocial working hours distinctly unappealing. A further factor was the organization's reliance on large numbers of agency-supplied temporary workers, many of whom left because it was unlikely that they would be offered a permanent contract.

For many workers, particularly those based in industries where unions are weak, and thus more organized forms of conflict inappropriate, resigning from one's job is one of the few ways of expressing one's grievances. In the US fast-food industry, for example, young 'workers generally do not see fast-food work as a long-term career, so quitting is a more common response to dissatisfaction with wages, working conditions, or management than is a collective effort to improve the work' (Leidner 2002: 18).

But there are problems in equating quitting with conflict in an over-deterministic way. For one thing, many workers voluntarily resign their jobs not out of dissatisfaction with the conditions of their labour, but because of superior employment opportunities elsewhere (Edwards 1995b; Edwards and Scullion 1982). A high turnover rate may operate to the benefit of management since it gives them greater flexibility to adjust staff numbers to meet fluctuations in demand, and thus secure control over costs, particularly in labour-intensive customer service industries, like hospitality for example (Adam-Smith, Norris, and Williams 2003). A study of the hospitality industry demonstrates that turnover levels are contingent upon the characteristics of the workforce. Whereas turnover among the bar workers was very high, as businesses competed to recruit a mainly young, student labour force, it was much lower among hotel housekeeping staff. Workers in these positions were mostly mature women whose employment was structured around childcare responsibilities. They enjoyed fewer opportunities to find alternative jobs, had established relatively stable working arrangements, and were thus less likely to consider quitting, even though the conditions of their jobs were no better, and often somewhat worse, than those of the bar workers (Adam-Smith, Norris, and Williams 2003).

9.3.3 'Unorganized' industrial conflict: an assessment

Having considered the main types of so-called unorganized industrial conflict, what conclusions can we draw about the nature of conflict at work? Five points are particularly worthy of note. First, in order to understand the significance of conflict in contemporary employment relations we need to look beyond the level of strike activity, and other cut-price forms of industrial action, and consider the implications of fiddles, sabotage, absenteeism, and quitting. The fall in the number of strikes in Britain cannot therefore be equated with a decline in industrial conflict.

Second, the analytical distinction between so-called organized and unorganized forms of industrial conflict is rarely so clear-cut in practice (Blyton and Turnbull 2004). Seemingly spontaneous and individualistic behaviour, such as absenteeism for example, is often underpinned by collectively established norms governing appropriate levels of absence.

Third, the types of behaviour we have considered as examples of unorganized conflict often appear to operate in ways that benefit managers. They may tolerate a certain amount of fiddling, for example, or some relatively minor sabotage, if it helps them to secure control over the workplace. That such activities occur cannot be taken as evidence of conflict since the way in which they function may not hinder, and can even act to support, management objectives. Moreover, in so far as they enable people to cope more easily with the pressures, demands, and frustrations of their jobs, these activities help to reconcile workers with the exploitative nature of the system of wage labour. Thus a 'given form of behaviour can, then, involve aspects of accommodation and adaptation to a system of work relations as well as being in conflict with or a form of resistance against it' (Edwards 1986: 76). Whether or not a particular type of behaviour can be labelled as conflict depends upon the particular context in which it exists, and the meanings which workers and managers attach to it (Edwards and Scullion 1982).

Fourth, what is meant by the concept of industrial conflict? Quitting one's job because the working environment is particularly unpleasant, for example, or behaving towards customers in a way that does not comply with managerial wishes because one is dissatisfied with one's working conditions, both reflect the antagonism that characterizes the employment relationship. But in general these are expressions of frustration; they are not intended to challenge managerial decisions or to influence the terms of the wage-work bargain in the purposeful manner of a strike or an overtime ban. Thus when referring to the term 'industrial conflict' one needs to be careful to ensure that its meaning is clear.

Fifth, it is clear that rather than acting as alternatives, different manifestations of industrial conflict often complement one another (Turnbull and Sapsford 1992). This can be seen in the case of sabotage incidents, for example, which are sometimes used by groups of workers to supplement other forms of industrial action during the course of a dispute.

SECTION SUMMARY AND FURTHER READING

- Strikes are not the only manifestation of collective industrial action by workers. Industrial conflict can take the form of so-called 'cut-price' forms of industrial action, such as overtime bans for example, or the range of different behaviours that come under the label of 'unorganized' conflict, including fiddling and sabotage among other things.

- The conventional distinction made between 'organized' and 'unorganized' forms of industrial conflict is hard to uphold in practice. Seemingly spontaneous and individual behaviour, such as sabotage for example, is often underpinned by collective norms and expectations. Moreover, it frequently exists in conjunction with, rather than as a substitute for, more ostensibly collective and organized activities.

- One must be cautious about ascribing the label of 'conflict' to behaviours such as fiddling, sabotage, absenteeism, and quitting. They may operate to the advantage of managers. Whether or not such types of behaviour can be classified as conflict depends upon the context in which they occur, and the meanings which the participants attach to them.

For discussions of industrial conflict, how it can be understood, and the various examples of behaviour that constitute it, see Edwards (1988, 1992). Mars's Cheats at Work (Mars 1982) is an engaging analysis of various types of fiddling behaviour. Good overviews of industrial conflict can also be found in Noon and Blyton (2002), and Blyton and Turnbull (2004).

9.4 Resolving disputes in employment relations

It would be inappropriate to discuss industrial conflict without considering the means by which disputes are resolved in employment relations. It can be helpful to distinguish between individual and collective disputes. The former involves the grievances of individual employees, whereas the latter concerns conflict between trade unions and an employer. However, ostensibly individual disputes often have a collective dimension (Dickens 2000c), since the grievances that cause them may be widely expressed in the workforce as a whole. In this section, following a discussion of the characteristics and process of negotiating agreements, we consider the intervention of third parties in resolving conflict, focusing on the activities of the Advisory, Conciliation and Arbitration Service (ACAS) in particular, and examine the role of employment tribunals in settling ostensibly individual disputes.

9.4.1 Negotiating agreements in employment relations

Attempts to resolve disputes in employment relations generally involve some form of negotiated settlement. Negotiations, then, are an important feature of the collective bargaining process; by enabling disputes to be resolved, they help to ensure that industrial conflict is contained, institutionalized, and thus prevented from causing too much disruption. One should not assume that negotiation is appropriate only in situations where there is a collective dispute, that is between an employer and a trade union. The resolution of individual grievances at work is often achieved by means of a negotiated compromise. This demonstrates the relevance of power to the bargaining process. In a non-union environment, without union representation the aggrieved employee enjoys little power to influence the terms of the eventual settlement; where an effective union is present it is more likely that management will be obliged to make concessions.

For present purposes, our analysis of the process of negotiation will focus on its role in resolving collective disputes. Walton and McKersie (1965) distinguish between two broad types of negotiation. Employers and unions sometimes use negotiations in order to address and deal with problems, improvements to the workplace environment for example. This is known as 'integrative bargaining', akin to a joint problem-solving exercise. 'Distributive bargaining', though, is designed to resolve an outstanding issue, such as a union pay claim for example, where there is an explicit dispute.

Staying with distributive forms of bargaining, then, what does negotiation actually involve? In essence, it is a means of resolving disputes by concluding a mutually acceptable agreement. It is a social process in which the parties argue with one another, try to convince each other of the merits of their respective cases, come to appreciate the virtues of their opponent's position, and thus draw closer together so that a settlement is made possible (Martin 1992; Torrington 1991). Without compromises, or 'trade-offs', in which a party will offer to back down in one area in return for a perhaps more important concession from their opponent, negotiation will not resolve a dispute. But each side will attempt to wrest more concessions from its opponents than that which it is obliged to concede in return. As well as being a social process, then, the practice of negotiation exemplifies the struggle for power that characterizes relations between employers and unions.

What determines the extent to which an employer or trade union emerges victorious from a negotiation event? Clearly, the expertise and skills of the participants exercise an influence on the outcome of negotiations, particularly their knowledge of relevant issues, how effectively they can process and handle information, and their ability to persuade their opponent of the strengths of their case. Preparation is also important. Not only do effective negotiators rigorously plan the issues on which they are prepared to trade, in exchange for something more worthwhile, and those they are not, but they also consider the likely arguments and negotiating position of their opponents. The negotiating event itself is characterized by the efforts of each party to influence the attitudes of the opposing sides; adjournments are often useful in helping a party to discuss and, if necessary, adjust its position, and can also help to maintain unity among the negotiating team (Walton and McKersie 1965).

Yet the main factor that influences the outcome of negotiation is the prevailing balance of power between the parties. The concept of bargaining power refers to the ability of a party to induce its opponent to make concessions it would otherwise not entertain. Clearly, the skills and expertise of a negotiating team, and the extent to which they are able to control a negotiation event, are important sources of power (Martin 1992). But the nature of the environment also influences negotiation outcomes. For example, if an employer is struggling to increase capacity to meet a rapid influx of orders, other things being equal, it will be less capable of resisting a union pay demand, given the importance of avoiding potentially disruptive industrial action. Thus environmental variables provide employers and unions with latent bargaining power, the potential to exercise influence over negotiation outcomes. But the extent to which this latent bargaining power is translated into the ability of a party to wrest concessions from their opponents depends upon how effectively they can use it, in other words their mobilizing capacity (Martin 1992).

In a study of a dispute over contracts of employment in the further education sector, Williams (2004) demonstrates the way in which environmental change, the removal of colleges from local authority control in particular, weakened the bargaining power of the main trade union relative to that enjoyed by the college employers. But the main cause of the union's difficulties, and a factor prolonging the dispute, was the superior mobilizing capacity of the employers' leaders, the way that they used the characteristics of the more commercial environment in which the colleges operated, to resist union demands. In this case, initial efforts to achieve a negotiated settlement proved fruitless; the parties were too far apart. But what happens when negotiations fail? How do third parties attempt to resolve disputes?

9.4.2 Disputes procedures and methods of third-party dispute resolution

Procedures for resolving disputes exist in most workplaces; over 90 per cent (Cully et al. 1999) operate grievance procedures which ostensibly enable individual employees to raise problems at work and, in conjunction with managers, to find ways of dealing with them.

Often, though, it is difficult to distinguish between a 'collective' and 'individual' dispute (Dickens 2000c: 71). For example, in Chapter 4 we observed that trade unions have collectivized the ostensibly individual grievances held by female employees concerning pay inequality relative to men.

Procedures for resolving collective disputes, between unions and employers, are a longstanding feature of employment relations in Britain (see Hyman 1972). The 1970s saw a rise in the incidence of disputes procedures (Kessler 1993), a reflection of the pluralist character of reform in employment relations during that period. There is evidence that formal disputes procedures remain an important feature of employment relations in Britain. In 1998, four-fifth of workplaces with a recognized union operated a procedure for dealing with disputes over pay and conditions, the vast majority of which are agreed with the union (Millward, Bryson, and Forth 2000).

What, then, is the purpose of disputes procedures? Generally, they are formal arrangements that set out the method for resolving disputes and, as such, 'provide a framework within which workplace industrial relations are conducted' (Brown 1981: 42). Many procedures make reference to third-party intervention in circumstances where a dispute cannot be settled internally. A 2001 study of sixty-two organizations found that nearly half of them operated procedures that provided for the intervention of conciliation, mediation, or arbitration by an independent third party (IRS 2001). In the prison service, for example, the collective agreement between the employer and the Prison Officers' Association (POA) stipulates that where a dispute cannot be resolved at a local level, it is referred to ACAS for conciliation (see below). If conciliation fails to produce a settlement, then either the national union or the prison service may unilaterally invoke arbitration, which is arranged by ACAS (Corby 2003: 41).

What, then, is meant by the terms 'conciliation', 'mediation', and 'arbitration' as forms of third-party dispute resolution? In the conciliation process, the 'aim is to bring the parties to agreement' (J. Wood 1992: 250). The conciliator works to bring the sides closer together, enabling them to bargain more productively, and thus reach their own agreement. According to a union representative, conciliation is helpful:

… when there is a lack of trust or breakdown of relations. There is an intent or desire to settle on both sides but there is a problem over who backs down or who is seen to move. More often than not it is a way out for both sides without losing face. They can go off and signal that they are prepared to do a deal, but not have to do it face to face. (quoted in Corby 2003: 18)

Mediation is a relatively rare form of dispute resolution in Britain. It is similar to conciliation, but differs in that the third-party has a more active role, with the scope to make recommendations in particular (J. Wood 1992). With the arbitration method the dispute is submitted to a third party, an individual arbitrator, or sometimes an arbitration board, who, after weighing up the arguments of the two sides, and taking into account any other relevant information, decides the issue. It is often used where negotiation and conciliation have both failed to resolve a dispute, particularly in the area of pay.

In general, arbitration awards are not legally binding; like collective agreements in Britain, they are binding in honour only. Disputes procedures that make reference to arbitration will specify whether it can be invoked unilaterally, that is by just of one of the parties, or jointly, that is with the necessary agreement of both. During the 1980s and

1990s, there was increasing interest in the concept of 'pendulum', or 'final-offer', arbitration, in the context of 'new-style' employment relations agreements struck between foreign companies, especially Japanese multinationals, and moderate unions, which were designed to eradicate the need for industrial action (Bassett 1987). Pendulum arbitration 'requires the arbitrator to choose between the employer's final offer and the union's final claim. It does not allow for a compromise' (Lewis 1990: 44). The aim is to moderate both sides' bargaining behaviour since the further they are apart on entering the arbitration stage, the more an individual party has to lose should the arbitrator's decision go against them. Compare this with conventional arbitration where the perception that arbitrators 'split the difference' encourages the parties to make extreme claims (Milner 1993a).

Yet pendulum arbitration remains somewhat rare in Britain, and there are few indications that it is a more effective means of resolving disputes than the conventional approach, or that there is much difference in how they operate (Lewis 1990; Milner 1993a). There is little evidence that conventional arbitration 'splits the difference' in practice (Lewis 1990; Mumford 1996). Moreover, the pendulum approach limits the arbitrators' creativity and room for manoeuvre, precluding their ability to produce compromise deals (J. Wood 1992).

Governments have long recognized the advantages to be gained by facilitating machinery for resolving disputes. State intervention in this area, which dates from the late nineteenth century, was predicated on the need to ensure that potentially harmful industrial action could be resolved without it causing the country too much economic disruption (J. Wood 1992). The use of state-supported conciliation and arbitration facilities for resolving disputes was envisaged as a last resort, to be initiated only with the agreement of both parties once all other methods had been exhausted. The 'emphasis was placed on providing a non-legalistic, flexible system based on voluntarism' (Mumford 1996: 292; Wedderburn 1986). In other countries, the state has often had a more interventionist role (see Box 9.4)

9.4.3 The work of ACAS

The establishment of ACAS in 1975 signalled the rise of a more interventionist approach to dispute resolution by the state. ACAS is a tripartite body, independent of government, and is overseen by a council comprising employers, trade unionists, and academic experts. On its formation, ACAS 'was given the general duty of promoting the improvement of industrial relations, and in particular of encouraging the extension of collective bargaining and the development and, where necessary, the reform of collective bargaining machinery' (Kessler 1993: 220). In particular, it was empowered to provide conciliation facilities, to make any necessary arrangements for mediation and arbitration, and to provide advice on effective personnel and employment relations practice.

Perhaps the most impressive achievement of ACAS is the way in which, as a tripartite body, it managed to endure the period of Conservative rule between 1979 and 1997. As we saw in Chapter 3, not only were Conservative governments hostile to tripartism, but they were also keen to encourage the exercise of greater managerial prerogative, to undermine the power of trade unions, and to challenge the significance of collective bargaining. Thus the pluralist ethos, which during the 1960s and 1970s had encouraged greater state

---

BOX 9.4 THE SYSTEM OF COMPULSORY ARBITRATION IN AUSTRALIA

One of the most distinctive features of employment relations in Australia is the system of compulsory arbitration that operates at both federal and state levels. Arbitration tribunals make legally enforceable pay awards; by the 1980s, federal awards covered one-third of the workforce, and strongly influenced the awards made by state-level tribunals, and the conduct of negotiations between employers and trade unions, resulting in a rather centralized system of industry-level bargaining. For the government, the system of compulsory arbitration was attractive because, as a means of resolving disputes, it helped to stifle industrial conflict.

Since the 1980s, though, the importance of industry awards has declined as successive Australian governments have, as part of their efforts to deregulate the economy and promote greater employment flexibility, encouraged the decentralization of bargaining activity. In particular, since 1996 the right-wing administrations led by John Howard have 'sought to move the system away from a collectivist approach, in which there was a strong role for unions and tribunals, to a more fragmented system of individual bargaining between employers and employees' (Davis and Lansbury 1998: 138). Legislation weakened the role and importance of federal awards, and provided for the development of company-level workforce agreements that could be concluded without the participation of unions. Nevertheless, while the proportion of the workforce whose pay is determined by awards or collective agreements has fallen, the take-up of workforce agreements has been slow, and well over half of employees still have their pay set by awards, or a combination of collective bargaining and awards (Davis and Lansbury 1998; Lansbury and Wailes 2004).

---

involvement in resolving disputes through procedures (Kessler 1993), was supplanted by a unitary emphasis on the primacy of employer action.

Three factors contributed to the resilience of ACAS, its tripartite character notwithstanding. First, it has effectively demonstrated its independence, from government, employers, and the unions alike (J. Wood 1992). Second, ACAS attracts the continued support of many employers. Third, and more significantly, the principal function of ACAS has changed in an important way, from an early focus on the improvement of collective employment relations, and a duty to promote collective bargaining, to a greater concern with resolving individual disputes, and with providing advice about workplace problems (Hawes 2000).

The organization's duty to promote collective bargaining was revoked in 1992. The extent of its collective conciliation activity, helping to resolve collective disputes between an employer and trade union, has declined markedly (Goodman 2000). Nevertheless, in 2002–03 ACAS provided conciliation in over 1,300 disputes (ACAS 2003a). It is closely involved in attempts to resolve high-profile national industrial disputes, such as the one involving the firefighters, their employers, and the government in 2002–03 (Burchill 2004).

How, though, does collective conciliation work? It is, above all, a voluntary process; ACAS cannot compel the parties to cooperate (Goodman 2000). Once underway, the integrity, and therefore the effectiveness, of conciliation work is predicated upon the impartiality of the conciliator, and the need to secure the trust and confidence of both parties (IRS 2001). ACAS conciliators often become involved in a dispute before the formal reference to conciliation is made. By 'running alongside' the dispute, they are able to understand its dimensions, and thus consider potential aspects of a settlement, more quickly (Dix and Oxenbridge 2004). Most conciliation work progresses in a series of so-called 'side meetings', during which the respective parties discuss, hone, and adjust their positions separately in response to the contributions of the conciliator, before they are subject to further bargaining at the negotiating table (IRS 2001).

Conciliators work with each of the parties in order to help them to strike their own agreement. They do this

by acting as an intermediary in the exchange of information and ideas, by keeping the parties communicating, clarifying issues, establishing common ground, identifying barriers to progress, eroding unrealistic expectations, pointing to the costs and disadvantages if the dispute is not settled, developing possible solutions and creating confidence that an acceptable solution will be found. The conciliator has no powers other than those of reason and persuasion. (Goodman 2000: 38)

Employers and unions welcome the way in which ACAS conciliators are able to explain, challenge, and test their negotiating positions and thus open up potential areas of agreement (Dix and Oxenbridge 2004). It should not be assumed, however, that the conciliator makes no contribution to the terms of a deal. In the 2002 local government pay dispute, for example, the principal conciliator produced a number of proposals that ended up forming a major part of the eventual settlement (ACAS 2003a).

ACAS does not mediate or arbitrate in disputes; rather, it refers disputes for mediation or arbitration where appropriate. In 2002–03 it dealt with eighty such requests (ACAS 2003a). ACAS also oversees certain standing arbitration bodies in the public sector, such as in the police service for example (Corby 2003).

As noted above, much of the work of ACAS now concerns disputes between an individual employee and his or her employer. In particular, it is under a statutory duty to offer conciliation when an employee makes a complaint against his or her employer to an employment tribunal. ACAS intervention operates as an 'effective filter', reducing the number of cases dealt with by tribunals (Dickens et al. 1985). About three-quarters of tribunal applications do not reach a hearing. ACAS may resolve a dispute at the conciliation stage by passing on to the complainant an employer's offer of a financial settlement, for example, or by highlighting the potential weaknesses of a case (IRS 2001). Among other things, ACAS conciliators discuss the features of the case with the parties, point out how tribunals have dealt with similar cases in the past, and act as an intermediary between the sides in the production of a settlement. Moreover, they 'often try to get the parties to critically examine their own cases; to consider weaknesses as well as strengths' (Dickens 2000c: 76).

As we see below, the growth in the number of tribunal applications has been a source of increasing concern for employers and the government. Since it makes a major contribution to reducing their workload, individual conciliation activity helps to keep the costs of running the system of employment tribunals under control (Hawes 2000). The main criticism of individual conciliation is that, by encouraging the parties to reach their own settlement before a dispute gets as far as a tribunal, or by encouraging people to withdraw their complaint, it militates against effective justice. In other words, there is 'a conflict between the search for compromise, which is at the centre of conciliation, and the pursuit of rights' (Dickens 2000c: 80). The government's enthusiasm to reduce the number of tribunal cases caused it to put in place a process for individual arbitration in cases of unfair dismissal, although it has been little used so far.

In recent years, the work of ACAS has increasingly been focused not on resolving disputes, but on preventing them. ACAS is frequently used as a source of employment relations advice. In 2002–03, for example, its national telephone helpline dealt with nearly three-quarters of a million enquiries (ACAS 2003a). It also works in an advisory capacity with employers and trade unions on projects designed to improve the quality of employment relations, such as the operation of a joint working party on developing effective bullying and harassment procedures in a health service trust for example (Dix and Oxenbridge 2004; Purcell 2000). When called upon to effect collective conciliation, moreover, ACAS officials sometimes use the resolution of the dispute as a lever to encourage ways of building better long-term relations between employers and unions. While much of its work remains concerned with resolving disputes, ACAS is increasingly focusing on ways of preventing them from occurring in the first place (Dix and Oxenbridge 2004). Despite the decline in the incidence of industrial action in Britain, the inherent potential for conflict in the employment relationship means that the process of dispute resolution, and hence the work of ACAS, remains an important feature of contemporary employment relations.

9.4.4 Resolving individual disputes: the system of employment tribunals

Since the 1960s, employment tribunals, which were called industrial tribunals until 1998, have dealt with individual disputes between an employee and his or her employer, with the number of their jurisdictions having increased markedly over time. Tribunals were originally established to adjudicate disputes over the payment by employers of training levies. In 1965, their scope was extended to cover disputes over redundancy payments. The 1971 introduction of an employee's right not to be unfairly dismissed, though, ensured that the tribunals would secure a long-lasting place in Britain's system of employment relations. The 1968 report of the Donovan Commission had envisaged that a system of labour tribunals, which would adjudicate individual disputes between employees and employers, could provide an 'easily accessible, informal, speedy and inexpensive' means of settling them (Hepple 1992: 92; see also Dickens et al. 1985).

Tribunals, which comprise a legally qualified chair and two lay members, were designed to be free of the perceived encumbrances of conventional legal environments. Applicants are not entitled to legal aid. The 'emphasis on informality and official encouragement to tribunals to eschew legalism is part of the distinguishing of tribunals from the ordinary courts and of promoting simple informal justice' (Dickens et al. 1985: 83).

Reflecting the growth in the scope of employment legislation, over the years tribunals have accumulated an increasing number of jurisdictions: claims relating to sex, race, and disability discrimination; the non-payment of wages; and complaints about the failure of employers to pay the National Minimum Wage. Most claims, though, still concern unfair dismissal. Where such cases are upheld, tribunals can insist upon re-employment. However, financial awards are more commonplace. By the late 1990s, there was growing concern on the part of employers and also the government that tribunals were attracting an excessive number of complaints. In 1980, there were 41,000 applications to tribunals; by 2000–01 the number had reached over 105,000, though it has slightly declined since (ACAS 2003a; Hawes 2000).

Employers, in particular, claim that excessive and unwarranted complaints to tribunals impose a heavy burden since, in contesting them, they incur significant costs in terms of the amount of management time needed to prepare a case, and also legal representation (Emmott 2001). There is some evidence that tribunals may not sufficiently take into account the circumstances of small firms in particular when adjudicating cases, that judgements do not reflect their preference for managing staff in flexible and informal ways (Earnshaw, Marchington, and Goodman 2000). There is also concern that disgruntled employees use the tribunal system to claim unwarranted monetary compensation. Business representatives, Digby Jones, the Director-General of the Confederation of British Industry (CBI) in particular, claim that the rise in the number of tribunal applications reflects a growing 'compensation culture' in Britain in which people are increasingly prone to 'have a punt', and thus secure financial awards to which they are not entitled (EIRO 2001; Shackleton 2002). Right-wing critics of tribunals, and especially the growth in the number of jurisdictions, contend that the regulatory burden they impose on businesses damages economic competitiveness. It is claimed that the 'tribunal system has grown piecemeal to a size where it now imposes significant costs on the economy as a whole – in terms of uncertainty, tension and stress at work, erosion of trust, addition to business costs and, most importantly, discouragement of job creation' (Shackleton 2002: 113).

Governments have tried to reduce the number of complaints to employment tribunals by giving ACAS greater scope to resolve disputes before they reach tribunal, for example. The Conservatives introduced a system of pre-hearing reviews in the 1980s, arrangements designed to filter out weak cases before they reach the tribunal proper. Labour has tightened the pre-hearing review process in a number of ways, with the intention of reducing the supposed burden on the tribunal system (Dickens 2000c). Its most controversial move, however, was the enactment, by the Employment Act (2002), of a policy which obliges discontented employees to use their employer's internal grievance machinery before a tribunal can consider their complaint. There has been some concern that this provision could restrict employees' access to justice.

One of the most prominent charges levelled at the tribunal system is that it is characterized by an excessive amount of legalism, that the tribunals have departed from their original purpose of resolving disputes in a speedy, relatively informal, and non-expensive manner without the formalism of courts of law, the legal arguments that dominate them, and the participation of lawyers. Yet legalism can be interpreted in a positive way in as much as it captures the importance tribunals attach to legal standards, rules, and consistency in their decisions (Macmillan 1999). Perhaps, then, some degree of legalism is inevitable (Dickens et al. 1985), and even desirable. It is somewhat ironic that complaints about excessive legalism in tribunals come from employers since they are more likely to have legal representation than complainants (Dickens et al. 1985; Hayward et al. 2004).

The notion that the rise in the number of tribunal cases reflects the emergence of a 'compensation culture' in which large numbers of employees are willing to 'take a punt' in pursuit of financial gain at the expense of virtuous and over-burdened employers is superficially attractive, but far from the truth, and conceals a more complex set of contributory factors. One, no doubt, is the increasing number of jurisdictions for which tribunals enjoy responsibility. But the growth in the number of complaints to tribunals also reflects rising levels of discontent at work, and that employees have more grievances (Kelly 1998). Only a small fraction of the grievances that could potentially result in a claim to a tribunal actually do so; of those that do, less than a quarter get to a hearing – most are settled or withdrawn beforehand. According to the TUC's Brendan Barber:

I am fed up listening to employers griping about a so-called compensation culture. Tribunal claims do not arise because sacked workers are 'having a punt'. Only around 30,000 claims a year go to a full tribunal hearing. Meanwhile, as many as three-quarters of a million times a year employers get away with actions that could land them in a tribunal. That is the real scandal. (quoted in EIRO 2001)

Linked to this, the rise in the number of applications to tribunals also reflects the growth in the number of people employed in those parts of the private services sector, such as the hospitality industry for example (Head and Lucas 2004), where the management of employment relations is often conducted in a harsh and arbitrary manner by small employers, and unions are weak, which thus tends to generate more claims (Dickens 2000c). The presence of trade unions is associated with lower rates of complaints to tribunals; unions are often able to resolve grievances collectively within the workplace, rendering applications to tribunals unnecessary (Knight and Latreille 2000). The decline in the level of unionization, then, and the increasing proportion of employment in sectors of the economy where unions are weak have been partly responsible for the upsurge in the number of tribunal claims (Hawes 2000). Even right-wing critics of the tribunal system concede that the rise in the number of applications to tribunals partly reflects the decline in unionization (Shackleton 2002: 45).

Generally, tribunal decisions do not inconvenience employers greatly. In fact, they win most cases. Even when complainants win their case for unfair dismissal, the tribunals' power to order their re-employment is rarely used; financial compensation is the most common form of restitution. Contrary to the impression one might have gained from accounts of isolated, but high-profile, sex discrimination cases, which have resulted in professional women receiving large financial settlements, most awards are relatively modest. In 2003, the average financial award across all tribunal jurisdictions was just £4,502 (Hayward et al. 2004), and the average unfair dismissal award is somewhat less. The major weakness of tribunals, then, is not that they place a costly burden on hard-pressed and blameless employers, but rather that it is the failure of the tribunal system to deliver effective industrial justice to the thousands of employees who have legitimate grievances each year, but who rarely gain adequate redress.

SECTION SUMMARY AND FURTHER READING

- Attempts to resolve disputes in employment relations generally involve some kind of negotiated settlement. The nature of any settlement is strongly influenced by the extent of the respective parties' bargaining power. The characteristics of the environment give the parties a degree of latent power, but the outcome of negotiations is largely determined by how effectively they mobilize to make use of it.

- There is a long history of state support for third-party dispute resolution machinery in Britain, in order to ensure that potentially damaging disputes can be settled without causing too much disruption. ACAS provides collective conciliation, and arranges access to mediation and arbitration arrangements in disputes between employers and trade unions. It also offers individual conciliation before complaints by individual employees progress to an employment tribunal hearing. The work of ACAS is increasingly concerned with preventing disputes from arising, in addition to helping to resolve them when they do occur.

• Employment tribunals were conceived as relatively quick, informal, inexpensive, and accessible forums for delivering industrial justice in respect of disputes between an individual employee and his or her employer. The number of jurisdictions has expanded markedly. The government is concerned with reducing the number of complaints that reach tribunals. Business complaints that the tribunal system imposes an excessive burden on employers are misplaced. Rather, the main weakness is its failure to provide justly aggrieved employees with adequate redress.

For perspectives on negotiations and the skills needed for effective negotiation, see Torrington (1991). The historical evolution of third-party arrangements for dispute resolution is covered by Hawes (2000), and J. Wood (1992). ACAS annual reports (e.g. ACAS 2003a) describe its activities in detail. See Towers and Brown (2000) for perspectives on the work of ACAS. The best study of the employment tribunal system is Dickens et al. (1985). See Dickens (2000c) for a more recent perspective.

■ CONCLUSION

Industrial conflict is a major feature of contemporary employment relations. Since the employment relationship is characterized by a 'basic antagonism' between the employer and the employee there is always the potential for conflict to arise (Edwards 1986). The fall in the level of strike activity cannot be equated with a decline in the level of industrial conflict. The low amount of strikes in contemporary employment relations is the product of a number of factors: restrictive government legislation; industrial change, and the reduced significance of 'strike-prone' industries; a more assertive and interventionist managerialism; and the declining level of unionization. Some of these developments, industrial change for example, are an international phenomenon; others, like the restrictive legislative framework, are peculiar to Britain. Thus the declining level of strike activity has not come about because conflict has diminished in importance, but rather it is the expression of a number of political, economic, and industrial developments.

From a global perspective, strikes remain a central feature of contemporary employment relations. Strike activity has not vanished. Instead, it has been subject to a process of relocation so that it is increasingly evident in emerging economies, such as China for example. Moreover, there is evidence that economic globalization is a major source of labour unrest around the world. Therefore the need to understand strikes, how they occur, and how they are resolved, remains of pressing importance in contemporary employment relations. Mobilization theory is an important tool for identifying the factors that contribute to, and also those that constrain, strikes. It also contends that industrial conflict should not be equated with strikes. Other forms of collective labour protest, such as petitions and demonstrations for example, are perhaps more effective ways of redressing grievances for workers in sectors where there is little tradition of robust trade unionism. Moreover, industrial conflict expresses itself in a range of different forms, including so-called 'unorganized' behaviours, such as sabotage and quitting for example.

The significance of conflict in employment relations can be gauged from the large number of employee grievances, very few of which ever become the subject of a formal complaint to an employment tribunal. Given the potential for the employment relationship to generate disputes, knowledge of how arrangements to resolve them operate is of central importance to understanding contemporary employment relations. Although employers complain about the supposed burden of the employment tribunal system, by keeping the potentially damaging consequences of industrial conflict in check, tribunals, and other methods for resolving disputes, contribute to the maintenance of order and stability in employment relations. While the potential for conflict is an inherent feature of the employment relationship, the process of negotiation, and the interventions of third parties, limits its capacity for disruption (Hyman 1975).

■ ASSIGNMENT AND DISCUSSION QUESTIONS

1. Discuss the view that: 'the decline in strike activity means that conflict between employers and workers is not an important feature of contemporary employment relations'.

2. Why has the incidence of strike activity in Britain fallen since the 1970s?

3. How does mobilization theory explain why strikes occur?

4. Thinking about any jobs you have had, were there any occasions when you or a colleague took a day off work without really being ill? What caused you to do this, and what would have persuaded you to go to work instead?

5. Is it sensible to distinguish between 'organized' and 'unorganized' forms of industrial conflict? Why?

6. Should it be compulsory for all disputes to be referred to arbitration, thus making strikes unnecessary? Give reasons for your view.

WEBSITE MATERIALS

Visit the companion web site to this book for interesting and updated material at **www.oup.com/booksites/busecon/business**

■ CHAPTER CASE STUDY

A British Airways case

Faced with increasing competition on both its long-haul flights, by companies such as Virgin Atlantic, and on its domestic and European routes, by EasyJet and Ryanair, over the last decade British Airways (BA) has sought ways of reducing its costs. With employment accounting for about 30 per cent of operating costs, reductions here offered the company a means to increase its profitability. Proposed changes to workers' terms and conditions of employment led to a number of disputes over this period. One famous case in 1997 involved cabin crew staff. The company planned to make changes that would substantially reduce their earnings, and, in response, one of the unions representing employees called them out on strike. On the first day, only 330 workers went on strike. However, over 1,000 telephoned in sick, with a further 1,000 reporting sick during the next two days. The dispute was settled several weeks later, and it was estimated that it had cost the company £124 million in lost revenue.

Following the 11 September attacks in 2001, and with the downturn in the global economy leading to a reduced demand for flights, the company instigated a programme of change that would eventually lead to the loss of 13,000 jobs. In order to meet its need to improve the deployment of staff as a consequence of reduced staffing levels, in 2003 the company linked its annual 3 per cent pay offer to its 2,500 check-in staff to new 'signing-in' procedures, a system used by some 20,000 other BA workers.

Check-in staff are the first contact passengers have with the airline, and are often the ones who bear the brunt of any customer dissatisfaction, for example over flight delays. Their basic rate of pay was £14,000 per annum, and the company estimated that average earnings, including shift payments, were around £19,000. Staff record their shift arrival and departure by signing a paper attendance sheet. A majority of the staff are women, and a substantial number work part-time, most with families. In order to meet domestic commitments, by custom and practice, there is some degree of 'self-rostering', whereby staff swap shift times with colleagues and thus are able to balance home and work commitments. The company claims that the system is abused, with staff leaving early, and colleagues forging their signatures. However, BA was unable to confirm that any staff had been disciplined for the offence.

The company proposed to replace the paper-based system with an electronic swipe card. Negotiations with the unions over the proposal and pay offer broke down and the company unilaterally imposed the new system. On 18 July 2003, around 250 check-in staff spontaneously, and to the surprise of the union, and without its backing, stopped work. Further walk-outs occurred the following day, stranding 80,000 passengers, and requiring the cancellation of over 400 flights in total.

British Airways stated that the new system, common throughout industry, was an attempt to simplify the procedure, and would help in the deployment of staff. However, employees claimed that it was being introduced as a precursor to annualized hours, and pointed out that if no changes to staffing arrangements are planned, then they could see no reason for implementing the system in the first place. An annualized hours system would allow the company to send staff home at quieter times, and require longer working when the airline is busier. Rather than allow staff to balance work and home, the new system would place total discretion over working hours with management, and possibly lead to further redundancies. Unions representing the workers believed the company should have clarified what it intended to use the new system for, should not have imposed it, and should have consulted more with staff and unions. They also point to the reduction in staffing levels through the redundancy programme, which they believed had left BA without sufficient staff to run the airline, and had lowered morale. Employees' fears may be well-founded since the company supplying the system claims that it can increase workforce flexibility, individualize rosters to suit operational requirements, and reduce overtime payments.

Source: The Guardian, July 2003 (various dates)

Case discussion questions

1. Was the 'swipe card' issue the cause of the dispute or the trigger for underlying conflict to become overt?

2. Would you have advised BA to do anything differently?

PART 4

Conclusion

Employment relations: regulating, experiencing, and contesting the employment relationship

The principal aim of this book has been to demonstrate the significance of employment relations in contemporary societies, particularly Britain. In the introductory chapter, we examined the nature of employment relations as a field of study, with specific reference to understanding the characteristics of the employment relationship, in particular the way in which it should be conceptualized as a wage-work, or effort, bargain. This captures the struggle over the terms and conditions of employment that characterizes relations between employers and workers. Consequently, employment relations cannot simply be understood as the study of how jobs are regulated, since such an approach does not adequately capture the dynamic nature of the employment relationship. This book is informed by a view that the subject matter of employment relations must comprise not only how workers experience their employment relationship, but also how they contest and challenge its terms. The purpose of this short, concluding chapter is to draw together some of the main themes of the book to establish the contemporary relevance of employment relations based on the premise that, as a field of study, it is concerned with ways in which the employment relationship is regulated, experienced, and contested.

Regulating the employment relationship

In an important sense, employment relations concerns the means by which the employment relationship is regulated. It is about understanding how the rules that govern employment relationships originate. To some extent, then, employment relations is the study of job regulation (Flanders 1975). In the past, this approach was characterized by an understandable emphasis on the institutions of job regulation (Clegg 1979): the activities of employers, employers' associations, and trade unions; the structure and operation of collective bargaining machinery and consultation arrangements; all within a largely voluntarist public policy framework. In Chapter 1, we offered an historical overview of the development of employment relations in Britain up to the 1980s that focused on these matters. To a very large extent, the study of employment relations used to be devoted to the joint regulation of the employment relationship, by collective bargaining between employers and employers' associations, and trade unions. One of the most prominent trends since the 1980s has been the diminution of joint regulation in Britain as union membership and collective bargaining coverage have both declined. But employment relationships still have to be regulated somehow. Here, drawing on the material presented in earlier chapters, we consider three main developments.

First, as already noted, the decline of joint regulation has been an important feature of employment relations in Britain. In Chapter 7, we considered the contraction of collective bargaining coverage as a means of determining pay, especially in the private sector. This is associated with declining levels of unionization (see Chapter 6), the falling incidence of union recognition during the 1980s and early 1990s (see Chapter 5), the changing composition of industry, such that employment growth has been concentrated in sectors where joint regulation is relatively scarce, and a hostile public policy climate. Nevertheless, one should not underplay the contemporary significance of collective bargaining as a means of regulating the employment relationship. The introduction of a statutory procedure (see Chapter 5) has stimulated a modest increase in union recognition, notwithstanding the opposition of many employers. In Chapter 7, we observed that a number of major private sector employers, such as Tesco and Barclays Bank for example, have revised their relations with trade unions as partnership agreements, although generally these weaken union organization in practice. Collective bargaining is an important means of determining pay and conditions in the public sector, even more so if the operation of pay review bodies is considered as a form of 'arms' length' bargaining (Burchill 2000; Winchester and Bach 1995).

Second, there has been a pronounced increase in the extent to which managements attempt to regulate employment relationships unilaterally. This is evident in the area of pay determination, for example. In Chapter 7, we noted that greater managerial attempts to exercise control over pay is a prominent feature of contemporary employment relations. Managers have taken advantage of a public policy climate that is at best ambivalent about the desirability of strong trade unionism and collective bargaining (see Chapter 3) to challenge the influence of the unions, and sometimes exclude them from their workplaces entirely (see Chapter 5).

We have been careful to assert that managements have *attempted* to regulate the employment relationship unilaterally. Yet the nature of the employment relationship as a wage-work bargain implies that their efforts are invariably influenced by the need to respond to their employees' interests, or to secure their consent and cooperation. Custom and practice expectations remain an important feature of employment relations. In Chapter 9, for example, we observed that managers may be willing to tolerate a certain amount of fiddling activity, or even sabotage, as long as it does not exceed tacitly understood boundaries. The exercise of managerial prerogative, then, is always an aspiration and, given that the employment relationship *is* a relationship in which managers must, to some degree, gain workers' cooperation, can never be fully realized in practice. Nevertheless, there is some evidence, in the area of workplace discipline for example, that managers are more able to manipulate custom and practice understandings to suit their interests better (P. Edwards 2000).

The third main development concerns the increasing degree of statutory regulation of the employment relationship in contemporary employment relations. This is not just the product of national-level legislation, the National Minimum Wage (see Chapter 7) and the statutory union recognition procedure (see Chapter 5) for example. European Union (EU) legislation increasingly affects employment relations in Britain, especially since the Labour government acceded to the EU's 'social chapter' in 1997 (see Chapter 3). The EU's 'social dimension' has, among other things, generated legislation regulating equality at work (see Chapter 4), information and consultation arrangements for employees (see Chapter 6), and working time (see Chapter 7). As we saw in Chapter 2, there are even calls for more rigorous regulation of labour standards on an international basis in order to ameliorate some of the exploitative effects of economic globalization on workers in developing countries.

While the growth in the level of state intervention has been a long-term trend (see Chapter 1), the increase since the 1980s in the quantity of legal regulation has had a marked effect on employment relations in contemporary Britain. The work of the trade unions is increasingly concerned with campaigning for better legal rights for workers, with ensuring that existing statutory protections are upheld, and with using them as a base from which to bargain improvements. In Chapter 4, for example, we examined the way in which some unions have used equal pay legislation to bargain for increases in women's pay (Colling and Dickens 1998).

There are two important features of this growth in the quantity of legal regulation that need to be drawn out. First, in some respects, legislation that ostensibly favours the interests of workers and trade unions is enacted to benefit capital in the long term. In Chapter 3, we saw that the EU's 'social dimension' has been progressed largely as a means of giving the process of market integration, and thus enhanced economic competitiveness, greater legitimacy. Nevertheless, it is important to recognize that pressure for legal enactment also comes from workers, trade unions, and other campaigning groups to which policy-makers are obliged to respond. This was the case with the establishment of the National Minimum Wage in Britain, for example (see Chapter 7). It is therefore unwarranted to treat interventions by the state, and by supra-national bodies like the EU, as automatically benefiting the business interest since policy-makers must accommodate the interests of labour as well as secure the conditions under which capitalism can thrive (Edwards 1986).

The second point concerns complaints from employers that greater legal regulation in employment relations is inimical to business competitiveness, but these do not have much credibility. For one thing, greater regulation can enhance competitiveness by encouraging innovation. Robust regulation of working time, for example, by reducing employers' reliance on overtime, could encourage them to make more effective use of people's normal working hours. Moreover, a significant part of the legal regulation of employment relations in Britain is concerned with undermining the power of the trade unions. In Chapter 9, for example, we highlighted the restrictive legislation governing strikes and industrial action. While there has been a considerable increase in the quantity of legal regulation, its overall significance for employment relations should not be overstated. Labour governments have implemented EU directives in a 'minimalist' way, so that they impose as few constraints on business as possible. This is consistent with the neo-liberal assumptions that characterize Labour's policy framework, in particular the importance of deregulated labour markets as a source of economic competitiveness in a more integrated global environment (Favretto 2003).

It is important not to exaggerate the significance of the increasing amount of legislation on employment relations. Nevertheless, as we have already observed, unions can use the legislation as the basis for more robust joint regulation of the employment relationship. The effectiveness of the statutory union recognition procedure, for example (see Chapter 5), depends more on the extent to which unions can use it as a basis for expanding their organizational capacities than its own intrinsic merits. As we saw in Chapter 4, a union presence tends to enhance the scope and effectiveness of so-called family-friendly policies (Hyman and Summers 2004). Thus the outcomes of greater legal regulation in employment relations are contingent, varying according to the organizational context.

Experiencing the employment relationship

One of the main features of this book has been a concern with examining workers' experiences in contemporary employment relations. The employment relationship is not just something that is regulated, but is also experienced by workers. Moreover, their experiences influence regulation. For example, increasing pay inequality during the 1980s and 1990s, and growing concerns about the effects of low pay on workers in Britain, stimulated campaigning for the National Minimum Wage. In Chapter 4, we demonstrated that the government has tentatively improved the statutory provisions relating to family-friendly working arrangements partly because of increasing concern that workers were experiencing difficulties combining paid employment with family responsibilities.

We have examined the experience of workers in contemporary employment relations in a number of chapters. In Chapter 2, for example, we considered the working arrangements of self-employed, freelance workers. Claims that such groups of workers benefit from greater freedom, autonomy, and control over their work, relative to employees, are rather exaggerated. We also demonstrated the poor working conditions that are often experienced by homeworkers and migrant labourers in Britain. In Chapter 4, we drew on the experiences of workers to show the limited effectiveness of equal opportunities and work–life balance policies in practice. The section on ostensibly 'unorganized' forms of industrial conflict in Chapter 9 was also informed by accounts of workers' experiences.

But our principal assessment of workers' experiences in contemporary employment relations came in Chapter 8. We demonstrated that their interests often differ markedly from those of their employers. Genuine employee involvement and participation tends to be rather limited in practice; workers have few opportunities to influence workplace or organizational decision-making. Our discussion of discipline at work demonstrates that the employment relationship is marked by the exercise of managerial control, that punitive approaches to discipline remain a commonplace feature of employment relations, and also that workplace rules are often the product of custom and practice expectations that derive from the experiences of workers and managers. Job insecurity is an outcome of the way in which the neo-liberal character of contemporary capitalism, and ever-increasing competitive pressures, render workers more disposable. A further outcome is a growing degree of work intensification, something that has also been accentuated by technological developments.

One of the main contributions of this book, then, has been to offer a perspective on contemporary employment relations that differs from conventional human resource management (HRM) texts. These rarely, if at all, consider the experiences of workers and, as a result, often present a rather anodyne and insufficiently sophisticated understanding of what happens in the workplace. But it is important to recognize that employers are not driven solely by a concern with intensifying labour, upholding control, and making workers more easily disposable. The employment relationship is, as we observed in the introductory chapter, inherently exploitative, but it is also characterized by a degree of cooperation. In Chapter 5, we noted that the management of employment relations in market economies is marked by contradiction (Hyman 1987). On the one hand, managers seek to control workers, ensure they comply with instructions, and, should competitive pressures harden, dispose of them if necessary. On the other hand, managers must acquire the consent of the workforce, and accommodate pressures from workers, individually and collectively, if goods are to be produced, or services delivered, efficiently.

Contesting the employment relationship

It is impossible to consider employment relations properly without an adequate assessment of how workers contest the employment relationship. As we have seen, the employment relationship, as a wage-work bargain, is imbued by a struggle over its terms and conditions. Our focus on the experiences of workers demonstrates that, whatever its other character-istics, the employment relationship is marked by a basic antagonism between a relatively powerful employer and a largely powerless employee. Moreover, both individually and, more importantly, collectively, workers have the capacity to challenge and contest the terms of their employment. Thus there is always the potential for conflict in employment relations (Edwards 1986).

This is evident at a number of points in this book. In Chapter 2, for example, we point to a major flaw in the argument that economic globalization, and the activities of multinational companies and their suppliers, invariably give rise to a 'race to the bottom' in terms of labour standards, as workers in developing countries see the conditions of their labour eroded. This is not because multinational investment generates greater prosperity, and thus improves living standards, though this is a popular proposition, especially among advocates of free markets (Bhagwati 2004; Wolf 2004). Rather, globalization, and its implications for poorer countries, may stimulate demand among workers for effective union representation and lay the foundation for a more vigorous labour internationalism (Silver 2003). Our discussion of organizing unionism in Chapter 6 demonstrates the potential for unionization among groups of workers, who often have considerable and well-justified grievances about the way in which they are treated at work, but yet have traditionally not been attracted to trade unions. As we saw in Chapter 5, even in small, non-union firms, where one might expect managerial authority to be absolute, managers must accommodate the demands of workers. They are obliged to negotiate informally with workers over such matters as the organization and pace of work (Dundon and Rollinson 2004; Ram 1994). Workers, then, are never entirely passive actors; they always enjoy some, however limited, capacity to challenge and contest the terms of their employment relationships.

We dealt with the nature of industrial conflict in contemporary employment relations more substantially in Chapter 9. Clearly, the strike is the most visible manifestation of industrial conflict (Hyman 1975). Among the reasons for the decline of strike activity in Britain since the 1970s are: the diminishing proportion of employment in 'strike-prone' industries; the contraction of trade union organization; the articulation of a more assertive management style that aims to make strikes superfluous; and, in particular, the enactment of a whole raft of restrictive legislation. The legal framework places numerous obstacles in the way of trade unions hoping to undertake industrial action, including opportunities for employers to apply to the courts for injunctions that prevent it (Ewing and Hendy 2002).

In Chapter 9, we argued that just because there has been decline in the level of strike activity it does not follow that conflict is no longer an important feature of employment relations. For one thing, there are a variety of behaviours at work that can be encompassed under the umbrella of industrial conflict, including sabotage and absenteeism for example. Whether or not a type of behaviour is classified as evidence of conflict or not, though, depends upon the context in which it arises and the meanings attached to it by participants (Edwards and Scullion 1982). The extent of workplace discontent and the numbers of complaints to employment tribunals substantiate the existence of conflictual relations at work. Mobilization theory, by focusing on how employees acquire a sense of grievance, and the way in which grievances are translated into collective action, suggests that the capacity of unions to organize workers, and mobilize around their discontents, is a crucial determinant of whether or not industrial action occurs (Kelly 1998). Finally, in an international context, strikes and other manifestations of labour unrest remain an important feature of contemporary employment relations.

Since it is an exploitative relationship, which is marked by a basic antagonism between employer and employee, the potential for conflict is an inherent feature of the employment relationship. Nevertheless, this conflict can be contained, by managerial action, jointly agreed procedures, such as negotiations for example, and state policies, in particular legislation governing industrial action. For strikes, or some other form of collective industrial action, to occur depends upon the capacity of unions to respond to grievances and discontent at work by effectively mobilizing workers to challenge their employer.

We have presented the contemporary employment relationship as a complex one. It is a relationship in which the parties cooperate, but also one where they contest its terms. We have considered a range of issues that are relevant to the world of work in the twenty-first century. In doing this, we have sought to avoid providing simple and simplistic answers to the many questions this examination has raised. Rather, we have sought to offer a diagnosis of contemporary employment relations. We hope that this may assist readers in forming their own prognosis.

■ BIBLIOGRAPHY

Abrams, F. (2002). *Below the Breadline: Living on the Minimum Wage*. London: Profile Books.

Ackers, P. (2002). 'Reframing employment relations: the case for neo-pluralism'. *Industrial Relations Journal*, 33/1: 2–19.

Ackers, P. and Payne, J. (1998). 'British trade unions and social partnership: rhetoric, reality and strategy'. *International Journal of Human Resource Management*, 9/3: 529–50.

Ackers, P. and Wilkinson, A. (2003). 'Introduction: the British industrial relations tradition – formation, breakdown and salvage', in P. Ackers and A. Wilkinson (eds), *Understanding Work and Employment: Industrial Relations in Transition*. Oxford: Oxford University Press, 1–27.

Ackers, P., Marchington, M., Wilkinson, A., and Goodman, J. (1992). 'The use of cycles? Explaining employee involvement in the 1990s'. *Industrial Relations Journal*, 23/4: 268–83.

Ackroyd, S. and Proctor, S. (1998). 'British manufacturing organization and workplace industrial relations: some attributes of the new flexible firm'. *British Journal of Industrial Relations*, 36/2: 163–83.

Ackroyd, S. and Thompson, P. (1999). *Organizational Misbehaviour*. London: Sage.

Adams, R. (1995). *Industrial Relations under Liberal Democracy*. Colombia, SC: University of South Carolina Press.

Adam-Smith, D. (1997). 'Atypical workers – typical expectations: on temporary work, temporary workers and trade unions'. *Employee Relations Review*, 3: 3–9.

Adam-Smith, D. and Copestake, Y. (2001). 'Tipping the scales? The business case for work–life balance'. *Employee Relations Review*, 7: 3–9.

Adam-Smith, D., Norris, G., and Williams, S. (2003). 'Continuity or change? The implications of the National Minimum Wage for work and employment in the hospitality industry'. *Work, Employment and Society*, 17/1: 29–45.

Advisory, Conciliation and Arbitration Service (ACAS) (2003a). *Annual Report 2002/03*. London: ACAS.

Advisory, Conciliation and Arbitration Service (ACAS) (2003b). *Disciplinary and Grievance Procedures*. Code of Practice No. 1. Norwich: HMSO.

Ahlstrand, B. (1990). *The Quest for Productivity: A Case Study of Fawley after Flanders*. Cambridge: Cambridge University Press.

Aitkenhead, M. and Liff, S. (1991). 'The effectiveness of equal opportunities policies', in J. Firth-Cozens and M. West (eds), *Women at Work*. Buckingham: Open University Press, 26–41.

Albert, M. (1993). *Capitalism against Capitalism*. London: Whurr.

Alderman, K. and Carter, N. (1994). 'The Labour party and the trade unions: loosening the ties'. *Parliamentary Affairs*, 47/3: 321–37.

Allen, J. and Henry, N. (1996). 'Fragments of industry and employment: contract service work and the shift towards precarious employment', in R. Crompton, D. Gallie, and K. Purcell (eds), *Changing Forms of Employment: Organisations, Skills and Gender*. London: Routledge, 65–82.

Allen, V. (1954). *Power in Trade Unions*. London: Longmans.

Anderman, S. (1972). *Voluntary Dismissals Procedure and the Industrial Relations Act*. London: Political and Economic Planning.

Anderman, S. (1986). 'Unfair dismissals and redundancy', in R. Lewis (ed.), *Labour Law in Britain*. Oxford: Basil Blackwell, 415–47.

Anderson, L. (2003). 'Sound bite legislation: the Employment Act 2002 and the new flexible working "rights" for parents'. *Industrial Law Journal*, 32/1: 37–42.

Anderson, T., Millward, N., and Forth, J. (2004). *Equal Opportunities Policies and Practices at the Workplace: A Secondary Analysis of WERS98*. Employment Relations Research Series No. 30. London: Department of Trade and Industry.

Arrowsmith, J. (2002). 'The struggle over working time in nineteenth- and twentieth-century Britain'. *Historical Studies in Industrial Relations*, 13: 83–117.

Arrowsmith, J. and Sisson, K. (1999). 'Pay and working time: towards organization-based systems?' *British Journal of Industrial Relations*, 37/1: 57–75.

Arrowsmith, J. and Sisson, K. (2000). 'Managing working time', in S. Bach and K. Sisson (eds), *Personnel Management* (3rd edn). Oxford: Blackwell, 287–313.

Arrowsmith, J., Gilman, M., Edwards, P., and Ram, M. (2003). 'The impact of the National Minimum Wage in small firms'. *British Journal of Industrial Relations*, 41/3: 435–56.

Atkinson, J. (1984). 'Manpower strategies for flexible organisations'. *Personnel Management*, August: 28–31.

Auerbach, S. (1990). *Legislating for Conflict*. Oxford: Clarendon.

Bach, S. (1999a). 'From national pay determination to qualified market relations: NHS pay bargaining reform'. *Historical Studies in Industrial Relations*, 8: 99–115.

Bach, S. (1999b). 'Personnel managers: managing to change?', in S. Corby and G. White (eds), *Employee Relations in the Public Services*. London: Routledge, 177–98.

Bach, S. (2002). 'Annual review article 2001: public-sector employment relations reform under Labour: muddling through on modernization?' *British Journal of Industrial Relations*, 40/2: 319–39.

Bach, S. and Della Rocca, G. (2000). 'The management strategies of public service employers in Europe'. *Industrial Relations Journal*, 31/2: 82–96.

Bach, S. and Sisson, K. (2000). 'Personnel management in perspective', in S. Bach and K. Sisson (eds), *Personnel Management* (3rd edn). Oxford: Blackwell, 3–42.

Bach, S. and Winchester, D. (1994). 'Opting out of pay devolution? The prospects for local pay bargaining in UK public services'. *British Journal of Industrial Relations*, 32/2: 263–82.

Bach, S. and Winchester, D. (2003). 'Industrial Relations in the public sector', in P. Edwards (ed.), *Industrial Relations: Theory and Practice* (2nd edn). Oxford: Blackwell, 285–312.

Bacon, N. (1999). 'Union derecognition and the new human relations: a steel industry case study'. *Work, Employment and Society*, 13/1: 1–17.

Bacon, N. and Storey, J. (2000). 'New employee relations strategies in Britain: towards individualism or partnership?' *British Journal of Industrial Relations*, 38/3: 407–27.

Bailey, R. (1996). 'Public sector industrial relations', in I. Beardwell (ed.), *Contemporary Industrial Relations: A Critical Analysis*. Oxford: Oxford University Press, 121–50.

Bain, G. (1970). *The Growth of White-Collar Unionism*. Oxford: Clarendon.

Bain, G. and Price, R. (1983). 'Union growth: dimensions, determinants and destiny', in G. Bain (ed.), *Industrial Relations in Britain*. Oxford: Basil Blackwell, 3–33.

Bain, P. and Taylor, P. (2000). 'Entrapped by the "electronic panopticon"? Worker resistance in the call centre'. *New Technology, Work and Employment*, 15/1: 2–18.

Bain, P., Taylor, P., Gilbert, K., and Gall, G. (2004). 'Failing to organise – or organising to fail? Challenge, opportunity and the limitations of union policy in four call centres', in G. Healy, E. Heery, P. Taylor, and W. Brown (eds), *The Future of Worker Representation*. Basingstoke: Palgrave Macmillan, 62–81.

Bairstow, S. (2004). ' "Outing the unions": sexual identity, membership diversity and the British trade union movement'. Unpublished PhD thesis, University of Portsmouth.

Baldamus, W. (1961). *Efficiency and Effort*. London: Tavistock.

Baldry, C., Bain, P., and Taylor, P. (1998). ' "Bright satanic offices": intensification, control and team Taylorism', in P. Thompson and C. Warhurst (eds), *Workplaces of the Future*. Basingstoke: Macmillan, 163–83.

Barnard, C., Deakin, S., and Hobbs, R. (2003). 'Opting out of the 48-hour week: employer necessity or individual choice? An empirical study of the operation of article 18(1)(b) of the Working Time Directive in the UK'. *Industrial Law Journal*, 32/4: 223–52.

Barnes, C. (1992). 'Disability and employment'. *Personnel Review*, 21/6: 55–73.

Bassett, P. (1987). *Strike Free*. London: Papermac.

Bassett, P. and Cave, A. (1993). *All For One: The Future of the Unions*. London: Fabian Society.

Batstone, E. (1988). *The Reform of Workplace Industrial Relations: Theory, Myth and Evidence*. Oxford: Clarendon.

Batstone, E., Boraston, I., and Frenkel, S. (1978). *The Social Organization of Strikes*. Oxford: Basil Blackwell.

Batstone, E., Ferner, A., and Terry, M. (1983). *Unions on the Board*. Oxford: Basil Blackwell.

Batstone, E., Frenkel, S., and Boraston, I. (1977). *Shop Stewards in Action*. Oxford: Basil Blackwell.

Bazen, S. and Benhayoun, G. (1992). 'Low pay and wage regulation in the European Community'. *British Journal of Industrial Relations*, 30/4: 623–38.

BBC (2000). 'Gap and Nike: No Sweat?' *Panorama*, 15 October.

Bean, R. (1985). *Comparative Industrial Relations*. London: Croom Helm.

Beaumont, P. (1981). 'Trade union recognition: the British experience 1976–1980'. *Employee Relations*, 3/6: 2–39.

Beaumont, P. (1992). *Public Sector Industrial Relations*. London: Routledge.

Beaumont, P. (1995). *The Future of Employment Relations*. London: Sage.

Beaumont, P. and Harris, R. (1990). 'Union recruitment and organising attempts in Britain in the 1980s'. *Industrial Relations Journal*, 21/4: 274–86.

Behrend, H. (1957). 'The effort bargain'. *Industrial and Labor Relations Review*, 10/4: 503–15.

Bell, M. (2004). 'Equality and the European Union constitution'. *Industrial Law Journal*, 33/3: 242–60.

Bensinger, R. (1998). 'When we try more, we win more: organizing the new workforce', in J. Mort (ed.), *Not Your Father's Union Movement*. London: Verso, 27–41.

Bercusson, B. (1978). *Fair Wages Resolutions*. London: Mansell.

Bewley, H. and Fernie, S. (2003). 'What do unions do for women?', in H. Gospel and S. Wood (eds), *Representing Workers*. London: Routledge, 92–118.

Beynon, H. (1973). *Working for Ford*. Harmondsworth: Penguin.

Beynon, H. (ed.) (1985). *Digging Deeper: Issues in the Miners' Strike*. London: Verso.

Beynon, H. (1997). 'The changing practices of work', in R. Brown (ed.), *The Changing Shape of Work*. Basingstoke: Macmillan, 20–54.

Beynon, H., Grimshaw, D., Rubery, J., and Ward, K. (2002). *Managing Employment Change*. Oxford: Oxford University Press.

Bhagwati, J. (2004). *In Defense of Globalization*. Oxford: Oxford University Press.

Blackburn, R. and Prandy, K. (1965). 'White-collar unionisation: a conceptual framework'. *British Journal of Sociology*, 16/2: 111–22.

Blakemore, K. and Drake, R. (1996). *Understanding Equal Opportunity Policies*. Hemel Hempstead: Harvester Wheatsheaf.

Blyton, P. and Turnbull, P. (1992). 'HRM: debates, dilemmas and contradictions', in P. Blyton and P. Turnbull (eds), *Reassessing Human Resource Management*. London: Sage, 1–15.

Blyton, P. and Turnbull, P. (2004). *The Dynamics of Employee Relations* (3rd edn). Basingstoke: Palgrave Macmillan.

Bolton, J. (1971). *Report of the Committee of Enquiry on Small Firms*. London: HMSO.

Boston, S. (1980). *Women Workers and the Trade Union Movement*. London: Davis-Poynter.

Boxall, P. and Purcell, J. (2003). *Strategy and Human Resource Management*. Basingstoke: Palgrave Macmillan.

Boyd, C. (2001). 'HRM in the airline industry: strategies and outcomes'. *Personnel Review*, 30/4: 438–53.

Bradley, H. (1989). *Men's Work, Women's Work*. Cambridge: Polity.

Bradley, H. (1996). *Fractured Identities*. Cambridge: Polity.

Bradley, H. (1999). *Gender and Power in the Workplace*. Basingstoke: Macmillan.

Bradley, H., Erickson, M., Stephenson, C., and Williams, S. (2000). *Myths at Work*. Cambridge: Polity.

Bradley, H., Healy, G., and Mukherjee, N. (2002). *Inclusion, Exclusion and Separate Organisation: Black Women Activists in Trade Unions*, ESRC Future of Work Programme, Working Paper No. 25. Swindon: Economic and Social Research Council.

Brannen, P. (1983). *Authority and Participation in Industry*. London: Batsford.

Bridgford, J. and Stirling, J. (1994). *Employee Relations in Europe*. Oxford: Blackwell.

Broad, G. (1994). 'The managerial limits to Japanisation: a case study'. *Human Resource Management Journal*, 4/3: 52–69.

Bronfenbrenner, K. and Juravich, T. (1998). 'It takes more than house calls: organizing to win with a comprehensive union-building strategy', in K. Bronfenbrenner, S. Friedman, R. Hurd, R. Oswald, and R. Seeber (eds), *Organizing to*

Win: New Research on Union Strategies. Ithaca, NY: ILR Press, 19–36.

Bronfenbrenner, K., Friedman, S., Hurd, R., Oswald, R., and Seeber, R. (eds) (1998). *Organizing to Win: New Research on Union Strategies*. Ithaca, NY: ILR Press.

Brown, D. and Crossman, A. (2000). 'Employer strategies in the face of a national minimum wage: an analysis of the hotel sector'. *Industrial Relations Journal*, 31/3: 206–19.

Brown, G. (1977). *Sabotage*. Nottingham: Spokesman.

Brown, R. (1997). 'Flexibility and security: contradictions in the contemporary labour market', in R. Brown (ed.), *The Changing Shape of Work*. Basingstoke: Macmillan, 69–86.

Brown, W. (1973). *Piecework Bargaining*. London: Heinemann.

Brown, W. (ed.) (1981). *The Changing Contours of British Industrial Relations*. Oxford: Basil Blackwell.

Brown, W. (1993). 'The contraction of collective bargaining in Britain'. *British Journal of Industrial Relations*, 31/2: 189–200.

Brown, W. (2000). 'Putting partnership into practice in Britain'. *British Journal of Industrial Relations*, 38/2: 299–316.

Brown, W. and Nolan, P. (1988). 'Wages and labour productivity: the contribution of industrial relations research to the understanding of pay determination'. *British Journal of Industrial Relations*, 26/3: 339–61.

Brown, W. and Terry, M. (1978). 'The changing nature of national wage agreements'. *Scottish Journal of Political Economy*, 25/2: 119–33.

Brown, W. and Walsh, J. (1991). 'Pay determination in Britain in the 1980s: the anatomy of decentralization'. *Oxford Review of Economic Policy*, 7/1: 44–59.

Brown, W. and Walsh, J. (1994). 'Managing pay in Britain', in K. Sisson (ed.), *Personnel Management* (2nd edn). Oxford: Blackwell, 437–64.

Brown, W., Marginson, P., and Walsh, J. (1995). 'Management: pay determination and collective bargaining', in P. Edwards (ed.), *Industrial Relations: Theory and Practice in Britain*. Oxford: Blackwell, 123–50.

Brown, W., Marginson, P., and Walsh, J. (2003). 'The management of pay as the influence of collective bargaining declines', in P. Edwards (ed.), *Industrial Relations: Theory and Practice* (2nd edn). Oxford: Blackwell, 189–213.

Brown, W., Deakin, S., Hudson, M., and Pratten, C. (2001). 'The limits of statutory union recognition'. *Industrial Relations Journal*, 32/3: 180–94.

Brown, W., Deakin, S., Nash, D., and Oxenbridge, S. (2000). 'The employment contract: from collective procedures to individual rights'. *British Journal of Industrial Relations*, 38/4: 611–29.

Bryson, A. (2004). 'Managerial responsiveness to union and nonunion worker voice in Britain'. *Industrial Relations*, 43/1: 213–41.

Burawoy, M. (1979). *Manufacturing Consent*. Chicago: University of Chicago Press.

Burchell, B. (2002). 'The prevalence and redistribution of job insecurity and work intensification', in B. Burchell, D. Ladipo, and F. Wilkinson (eds), *Job Insecurity and Work Intensification*. London: Routledge, 61–76.

Burchell, B., Lapido, D., and Wilkinson, F. (eds) (2002). *Job Insecurity and Work Intensification*. London: Routledge.

Burchell, B., Day, D., Hudson, M., Ladipo, D., Mankelow, R., Nolan, J., Reed, H., Wichert, I., and Wilkinson, F. (1999). *Job Insecurity and Work Intensification*. York: Joseph Rowntree Foundation.

Burchill, F. (2000). 'The pay review body system: a comment and a consequence'. *Historical Studies in Industrial Relations*, 10: 141–57.

Burchill, F. (2004). 'The UK fire services dispute 2002–2003'. *Employee Relations*, 26/4: 404–21.

Burgess, K. (1980). *The Challenge of Labour*. London: Croom Helm.

Card, D. and Krueger, A. (1995). *Myth and Measurement: The New Economics of the Minimum Wage*. Princeton, NJ: Princeton University Press.

Carley, M. (1993). 'Social dialogue', in M. Gold (ed.), *The Social Dimension: Employment Policy in the European Community*. Basingstoke: Macmillan, 105–34.

Carley, M. and Hall, M. (2000). 'The implementation of the European Works Councils Directive'. *Industrial Law Journal*, 29/2: 103–24.

Carr, F. (1999). 'Local bargaining in the National Health Service: new approaches to employee relations'. *Industrial Relations Journal*, 30/3: 197–211.

Carter, B. (1985). *Capitalism, Class Conflict and the New Middle Class*. London: Routledge and Kegan Paul.

Carter, B. (2000). 'Adoption of the organising model in British trade unions: some evidence from Manufacturing, Science and Finance (MSF)'. *Work, Employment and Society*, 14/1: 117–36.

Carter, B. and Fairbrother, P. (1999). 'The transformation of British public-sector industrial relations: from "model employer" to marketised relations'. *Historical Studies in Industrial Relations*, 7: 119–46.

Castells, M. (1996). *The Rise of the Network Society*. London: Routledge.

Castells, M. (2001). *The Internet Galaxy*. Oxford: Oxford University Press.

Central Arbitration Committee (CAC) (2004). *Annual Report 2003–04*. London: Central Arbitration Committee.

Chamberlain, N. and Kuhn, J. (1965). *Collective Bargaining*. New York: McGraw-Hill.

Charles, N. (1986). 'Women and trade unions', in Feminist Review (ed.), *Waged Work: A Reader*. London: Virago, 160–85.

Charles, N. and James, E. (2003). 'The gender dimensions of job insecurity in a local labour market'. *Work, Employment and Society*, 17/3: 531–52.

Child, J., Loveridge, R., and Warner, M. (1973). 'Towards an organizational study of trade unions'. *Sociology*, 7/1: 71–91.

Clark, J. (1995). *Managing Innovation and Change*. London: Sage.

Claydon, T. (1989). 'Union derecognition in Britain during the 1980s'. *British Journal of Industrial Relations*, 27/2: 214–23.

Claydon, T. (1996). 'Union de-recognition: a re-examination', in I. Beardwell (ed.), *Contemporary Industrial Relations: A Critical Analysis*. Oxford: Oxford University Press, 151–74.

Clegg, H. (1975). 'Pluralism in industrial relations'. *British Journal of Industrial Relations*, 13/3: 309–16.

Clegg, H. (1976). *Trade Unionism under Collective Bargaining*. Oxford: Basil Blackwell.

Clegg, H. (1979). *The Changing System of Industrial Relations in Great Britain*. Oxford: Basil Blackwell.

Clegg, H. (1985). *A History of British Trade Unions since 1889. Volume II: 1911–1933*. Oxford: Oxford University Press.

Clegg, H. and Chester, T. (1964). 'Joint consultation', in A. Flanders and H. Clegg (eds), *The System of Industrial Relations in Great Britain*. Oxford: Basil Blackwell, 323–64.

Clegg, H., Fox, A., and Thompson, A. (1964). *A History of British Trade Unions since 1889. Volume I: 1889–1910*. Oxford: Clarendon.

Coates, D. (2000). 'New Labour's industrial and employment policy', in D. Coates and P. Lawler (eds), *New Labour in Power*. Manchester: Manchester University Press, 122–35.

Coates, K. and Topham, T. (1980). *Trade Unions in Britain*. Nottingham: Spokesman.

Cockburn, C. (1987). *Women, Trade Unions and Political Parties*. London: Fabian Society.

Cockburn, C. (1989). 'Equal opportunities: the short and long agenda'. *Industrial Relations Journal*, 20/3: 213–25.

Cockburn, C. (1991). *In the Way of Women*. Basingstoke: Macmillan.

Cohen, R. (1991). *Contested Domains*. London: Zed Books.

Colgan, F. (1999). 'Recognising the lesbian and gay constituency in UK trade unions: moving forward in UNISON'. *Industrial Relations Journal*, 30/5: 444–63.

Colgan, F. and Ledwith, S. (2000). 'Diversity, identities and strategies of women trade union activists'. *Gender, Work and Organization*, 7/4: 242–57.

Colgan, F. and Ledwith, S. (2002). 'Gender and diversity: reshaping union democracy'. *Employee Relations*, 24/2: 167–89.

Colling, T. (1999). 'Tendering and outsourcing: working in the contract state?', in S. Corby and G. White (eds), *Employee Relations in the Public Services: Themes and Issues*. London: Routledge, 136–55.

Colling, T. (2003). 'Managing without unions: the sources and limitations of individualism', in P. Edwards (ed.), *Industrial Relations: Theory and Practice* (2nd edn). Oxford: Blackwell, 368–91.

Colling, T. and Dickens, L. (1989). *Equality Bargaining – Why Not?* London: HMSO.

Colling, T. and Dickens, L. (1998). 'Selling the case for gender equality: deregulation and equality bargaining'. *British Journal of Industrial Relations*, 36/3: 389–411.

Colling, T. and Dickens, L. (2001). 'Gender equality and trade unions: a new basis for mobilisation?', in M. Noon and E. Ogbonna (eds), *Equality, Diversity and Disadvantage in Employment*. Basingstoke: Palgrave Macmillan, 136–55.

Collinson, D., Knights, D., and Collinson, M. (1990). *Managing to Discriminate*. London: Routledge.

Commons, J. (1924). *Legal Foundations of Capitalism*. New York: Macmillan.

Compa, L. (2001). 'Free trade, fair trade and the battle for labor rights', in L. Turner, H. Katz, and R. Hurd (eds), *Rekindling the Movement: Labor's Quest for Relevance in the Twenty-First Century*. Ithaca, NY: Cornell University Press, 314–38.

Conley, H. (2002). 'A state of insecurity: temporary work in the public services'. *Work, Employment and Society*, 16/4: 725–37.

Connor, T. (2002). *We Are Not Machines: Indonesian Nike and Adidas Workers*. Oxford: Oxfam.

Cooper, C. (2001). 'Talking Italian'. *People Management*, 14 June: 38–41.

Corby, S. (2000). 'Employee relations in the public services: a paradigm shift?'. *Public Policy and Administration*, 15/3: 60–74.

Corby, S. (2003). *Public Sector Disputes and Third Party Intervention*. ACAS research paper 02/03. London: ACAS.

Coupar, W. and Stevens, B. (1998). 'Towards a new model of industrial partnership', in P. Sparrow and M. Marchington (eds), *Human Resource Management: The New Agenda*. London: Financial Times Pitman Publishing, 145–59.

Cressey, P. (1998). 'European Works Councils in practice'. *Human Resource Management Journal*, 8/1: 67–79.

Crompton, R. (1997). *Women and Work in Modern Britain*. Oxford: Oxford University Press.

Crompton, R. and Sanderson, K. (1990). *Gendered Jobs and Social Change*. London: Unwin Hyman.

Cronin, J. (1979). *Industrial Conflict in Modern Britain*. London: Croom Helm.

Crouch, C. (1977). *Class Conflict and the Industrial Relations Crisis*. London: Heinemann.

Crouch, C. (1979). *The Politics of Industrial Relations*. London: Fontana.

Crouch, C. (1995). 'The state: economic management and incomes policy', in P. Edwards (ed.), *Industrial Relations: Theory and Practice in Britain*. Oxford: Blackwell, 229–54.

Crouch, C. (1996). 'Review essay. Atavism and innovation: labour legislation and public policy since 1979 in historical perspective'. *Historical Studies in Industrial Relations*, 2: 111–24.

Crouch, C. (2000). 'National wage determination and European Monetary Union', in C. Crouch (ed.), *After the Euro*. Oxford: Oxford University Press, 203–26.

Crouch, C. (2001). 'A third way in industrial relations?', in S. White (ed.), *New Labour: The Progressive Future*? Basingstoke: Palgrave Macmillan, 93–109.

Crouch, C. (2003). 'The state: economic management and incomes policy', in P. Edwards (ed.), *Industrial Relations: Theory and Practice* (2nd edn). Oxford: Blackwell, 105–23.

Cully, M., Woodland, S., O'Reilly, A., and Dix, G. (1999). *Britain at Work*. London: Routledge.

Cunningham, I. and Hyman, J. (1999). 'The poverty of empowerment? A critical case study'. *Personnel Review*, 28/3: 192–207.

Cunningham, R., Lord, A., and Delaney, L. (1999). ' "Next Steps" for equality? The impact of organizational change on opportunities for women in the civil service'. *Gender, Work and Organization*, 6/2: 67–78.

Cunnison, S. and Stageman, J. (1993). *Feminizing the Unions*. Aldershot: Avebury.

Danford, A. (1998). 'Teamworking and labour regulation in the autocomponents industry'. *Work, Employment and Society*, 12/3: 409–31.

Danford, A. (1999). *Japanese Management Techniques and British Workers*. London: Mansell.

Danford, A., Richardson, M., and Stewart, P. (2003). *New Unions, New Workplaces*. London: Routledge.

Danford, A., Richardson, M., and Upchurch, M. (2002). ' "New unionism", organising and partnership: a comparative analysis of union renewal strategies in the public sector'. *Capital and Class*, 76: 1–27.

Danford, A., Richardson, M., Stewart, P., Tailby, S., and Upchurch, M. (2004). 'Partnership, mutuality and the high-performance workplace: a case study of union strategy and worker experience in the aircraft industry', in G. Healy, E. Heery, P. Taylor, and W. Brown (eds), *The Future of Worker Representation*. Basingstoke: Palgrave Macmillan, 167–86.

Daniel, W. and Millward, N. (1983). *Workplace Industrial Relations in Britain*. London: Heinemann.

Darlington, R. (2002). 'Shop stewards' leadership, left-wing activism and collective workplace union organisation'. *Capital and Class*, 76: 95–126.

Davies, A. and Thomas, R. (2000). 'Gender and human resource management: a critical review'. *International Journal of Human Resource Management*, 11/6: 1125–36.

Davies, P. and Freedland, M. (1993). *Labour Legislation and Public Policy*. Oxford: Clarendon.

Davis, E. and Lansbury, R. (1998). 'Employment relations in Australia', in G. Bamber and R. Lansbury (eds), *International and Comparative Employment Relations* (3rd edn). London: Sage, 110–48.

Debrah, Y. and Smith, I. (2002). 'Globalization, employment and the workplace: diverse impacts?', in Y. Debrah and I. Smith (eds), *Globalization, Employment and the Workplace: Diverse Impacts*. London: Routledge, 1–23.

Delbridge, R. (1998). *Life on the Line in Contemporary Manufacturing*. Oxford: Oxford University Press.

Department of Employment (DE) (1983). *Democracy in Trade Unions*. London: HMSO.

Department of Trade and Industry (DTI) (1998). *Fairness at Work*. London: HMSO.

Department of Trade and Industry (DTI) (2000). *Work and Parents: Competitiveness and Choice*. London: DTI.

Department of Trade and Industry (DTI) (2003a). *High Performance Workplaces: Informing and Consulting Employees*. London: DTI.

Department of Trade and Industry (DTI) (2003b). *'Rewards for failure': Director's Remuneration 1-1 Contracts, Performance and Severance*. London: DTI.

Department of Trade and Industry (DTI) (no date). *Flexible Working*, http://www.dti.gov.uk/bestpractice/assets/flexible.pdf.

Dex, S. and McCulloch, A. (1997). *Flexible Employment*. Basingstoke: Macmillan.

Dex, S. and Schiebl, F. (2001). 'Flexible and family-friendly working arrangements in UK-based SMEs: business cases'. *British Journal of Industrial Relations*, 39/3: 411–31.

Dex, S., Robson, P., and Wilkinson, F. (1999). 'The characteristics of the low paid: a cross-national comparison'. *Work, Employment and Society*, 13/3: 503–24.

Dex, S., Sutherland, H., and Joshi, H. (2000). 'Effects of minimum wages on the gender pay gap'. *National Institute Economic Review*, 173: 80–8.

Diamond, W. and Freeman, R. (2002). 'Will unionism prosper in cyberspace? The promise of the internet for employee organization'. *British Journal of Industrial Relations*, 40/3: 569–96.

Dicken, P. (2003). *Global Shift* (4th edn). London: Sage.

Dickens, L. (1992). 'Anti-discrimination legislation: exploring and explaining the impact on women's employment', in W. McCarthy (ed.), *Legal Intervention in Industrial Relations: Gains and Losses*. Oxford: Basil Blackwell, 103–46.

Dickens, L. (1994). 'The business case for women's equality: is the carrot better than the stick?' *Employee Relations*, 16/8: 5–18.

Dickens, L. (1997). 'Gender, race and employment equality in Britain: inadequate strategies and the role of industrial relations actors'. *Industrial Relations Journal*, 28/4: 282–91.

Dickens, L. (1999). 'Beyond the business case: a three-pronged approach to equality action'. *Human Resource Management Journal*, 9/1: 9–19.

Dickens, L. (2000a). 'Still wasting resources? Equality in employment', in S. Bach and K. Sisson (eds), *Personnel Management* (3rd edn). Oxford: Blackwell, 137–69.

Dickens, L. (2000b). 'Collective bargaining and the promotion of gender equality at work: opportunities and challenges for trade unions'. *Transfer*, 6/2: 193–208.

Dickens, L. (2000c). 'Doing more with less: ACAS and individual conciliation', in B. Towers and W. Brown (eds), *Employment Relations in Britain: 25 Years of the Advisory, Conciliation and Arbitration Service*. Oxford: Blackwell, 67–91.

Dickens, L. and Hall, M. (1995). 'The state, labour law and industrial relations', in P. Edwards (ed.), *Industrial Relations: Theory and Practice in Britain*. Oxford: Blackwell, 255–303.

Dickens, L. and Hall, M. (2003). 'Labour law and industrial relations: a new settlement?', in P. Edwards (ed.), *Industrial Relations: Theory and Practice* (2nd edn). Oxford: Blackwell, 124–56.

Dickens, L., Jones, M., Weekes, B., and Hunt, M. (1985). *Dismissed: A Study of Unfair Dismissal and the Industrial Tribunal System*. Oxford: Basil Blackwell.

Dickens, R. and Manning, A. (2003). 'Minimum wage, minimum impact', in R. Dickens, P. Gregg, and J. Wadsworth (eds), *The Labour Market under New Labour*. Basingstoke: Palgrave Macmillan, 201–13.

Dickens, R., Gregg, P., Machin, S., Manning, A., and Wadsworth, J. (1993). 'Wages councils: was there a case for abolition?' *British Journal of Industrial Relations*, 31/4: 515–29.

Dickson, T., McLachlan, H., Prior, P., and Swales, K. (1988). 'Big Blue and the unions: IBM, individualism and trade union strategy'. *Work, Employment and Society*, 2/4: 506–21.

Dix, G. and Oxenbridge, S. (2004). 'Coming to the table with ACAS: from conflict to co-operation'. *Employee Relations*, 26/5: 510–30.

Doherty, L. (2004). 'Work–life balance initiatives: implications for women'. *Employee Relations*, 26/4: 433–52.

Donnelly, M. and Scholarios, D. (1998). 'Workers' experiences of redundancy: evidence from Scottish defence-dependent companies'. *Personnel Review*, 27/4: 325–42.

Doogan, K. (2001). 'Insecurity and long-term employment'. *Work, Employment and Society*, 15/3: 419–41.

Driver, S. and Martell, L. (1998). *New Labour: Politics after Thatcherism*. Cambridge: Polity.

Druker, J. and White, G. (1999). 'Introduction: the context of reward management', in G. White and J. Druker (eds), *Reward Management: A Critical Text*. London: Routledge, 1–24.

Druker, J., Stanworth, C., and White, G. (2002). *Report to the Low Pay Commission on the Impact of the National Minimum Wage on the Hairdressing Sector*. London: University of Greenwich.

Dubois, P. (1979). *Sabotage in Industry*. Harmondsworth: Penguin.

Duffield, M. (2002). 'Trends in female employment'. *Labour Market Trends*, 110: 605–16.

Dundon, T. and Rollinson, D. (2004). *Employment Relations in Non-Union Firms*. London: Routledge.

Dunleavy, P. and O'Leary, B. (1987). *Theories of the State: The Politics of Liberal Democracy*. Basingstoke: Macmillan.

Dunlop, J. (1958). *Industrial Relations Systems*. New York: Holt.

Dunn, S. and Gennard, J. (1984). *The Closed Shop in British Industry*. London: Macmillan.

Dunn, S. and Metcalf, D. (1996). 'Trade union law since 1979', in I. Beardwell (ed.), *Contemporary Industrial Relations: A Critical Analysis*. Oxford: Oxford University Press, 66–98.

Earnshaw, J., Marchington, M., and Goodman, J. (2000). 'Unfair to whom? Discipline and dismissal in small establishments'. *Industrial Relations Journal*, 31/1: 62–73.

Earnshaw, J., Goodman, J., Harrison, R., and Marchington, M. (1998). *Industrial Tribunals, Workplace Disciplinary Procedures and Employment Practice*. Employment Relations Research Series No. 2. London: Department of Trade and Industry.

Eaton, J. (2000). *Comparative Employment Relations*. Cambridge: Polity.

Edelstein, J. and Warner, M. (1975). *Comparative Union Democracy*. London: George Allen and Unwin.

Edwards, P. (1983). 'The pattern of collective industrial action', in G. Bain (ed.), *Industrial Relations in Britain*. Oxford: Basil Blackwell, 209–34.

Edwards, P. (1986). *Conflict at Work*. Oxford: Basil Blackwell.

Edwards, P. (1987). *Managing the Factory*. Oxford: Basil Blackwell.

Edwards, P. (1988). 'Patterns of conflict and accommodation', in D. Gallie (ed.), *Employment in Britain*. Oxford: Basil Blackwell, 187–217.

Edwards, P. (1989). 'The three faces of discipline', in K. Sisson (ed.), *Personnel Management in Britain*. Oxford: Basil Blackwell, 296–325.

Edwards, P. (1992). 'Industrial conflict'. *British Journal of Industrial Relations*, 30/3: 361–404.

Edwards, P. (1994). 'Discipline and the creation of order', in K. Sisson (ed.), *Personnel Management* (2nd edn). Oxford: Blackwell, 562–92.

Edwards, P. (1995a). 'Human resource management, union voice and the use of discipline: an analysis of WIRS3'. *Industrial Relations Journal*, 26/3: 204–20.

Edwards, P. (1995b). 'Strikes and industrial conflict', in P. Edwards (ed.), *Industrial Relations: Theory and Practice in Britain*. Oxford: Blackwell, 434–60.

Edwards, P. (2000). 'Discipline: towards trust and self-discipline?', in S. Bach and K. Sisson (eds), *Personnel Management* (3rd edn). Oxford: Blackwell, 317–39.

Edwards, P. (2003). 'The employment relationship and the field of industrial relations', in P. Edwards (ed.), *Industrial Relations: Theory and Practice* (2nd edn). Oxford: Blackwell, 1–36.

Edwards, P. and Gilman, M. (1999). 'Pay equity and the national minimum wage: what can theories tell us?' *Human Resource Management Journal*, 9/1: 20–38.

Edwards, P. and Scullion, H. (1982). *The Social Organisation of Industrial Conflict*. Oxford: Basil Blackwell.

Edwards, P. and Whitston, C. (1989). 'Industrial discipline, the control of attendance, and the subordination of labour: towards an integrated analysis'. *Work, Employment and Society*, 3/1: 1–28.

Edwards, P. and Whitston, C. (1991). 'Workers are working harder: effort and shop-floor relations in the 1980s'. *British Journal of Industrial Relations*, 29/4: 592–601.

Edwards, P. and Whitston, C. (1993). *Attending to Work*. Oxford: Blackwell.

Edwards, P. and Whitston, C. (1994). 'Disciplinary practice: a study of railways in Britain, 1860–1988'. *Work, Employment and Society*, 8/3: 317–37.

Edwards, P. and Wright, M. (1998). 'HRM and commitment: a case study of teamworking', in P. Sparrow and M. Marchington (eds), *Human Resource Management: The New Agenda*. Harlow: Pearson Education, 272–85.

Edwards, P., Collinson, M., and Rees, C. (1998). 'The determinants of employee responses to Total Quality Management: six case studies'. *Organization Studies*, 19/3: 449–75.

Edwards, P., Geary, J., and Sisson, K. (2002). 'New forms of work organization in the workplace: transformative, exploitative, or limited and controlled?', in G. Murray, J. Bélanger, A. Giles, and P.-A. Lapointe (eds), *Work and Employment Relations in the High-Performance Workplace*. London: Continuum, 72–119.

Edwards, P., Armstrong, P., Marginson, P., and Purcell, J. (1996). 'Towards the transnational company? The global organisation and structure of multinational firms', in R. Crompton, D. Gallie, and K. Purcell (eds), *Changing Forms of Employment: Organisations, Skills and Gender*. London: Routledge, 40–65.

Edwards, R. (1979). *Contested Terrain: The Transformation of the Workplace in the Twentieth Century*. London: Heinemann.

Edwards, T. (1998). 'Multinationals, labour management and the process of diffusion: a case study'. *International Journal of Human Resource Management*, 9/4: 696–709.

Edwards, T. (2000). 'Multinationals, international integration and employment practice in domestic plants'. *Industrial Relations Journal*, 31/2: 115–29.

Edwards, T. (2004). 'The transfer of employment practices across borders in multinational companies', in A.-W. Harzing and J. Van Ruysseveldt (eds), *International Human Resource Management* (2nd edn). London: Sage, 389–410.

Edwards, T. and Ferner, A. (2002). 'The renewed "American challenge": a review of employment practice in US multinationals'. *Industrial Relations Journal*, 33/2: 94–111.

Edwards, T., Rees, C., and Coller, X. (1999). 'Structure, politics and the diffusion of employment practices in multinationals'. *European Journal of Industrial Relations*, 5/3: 286–306.

Elgar, J. and Simpson, B. (1993). 'The impact of the law on industrial disputes in the 1980s', in D. Metcalf and S. Milner (eds), *New Perspectives on Industrial Disputes*. London: Routledge, 70–114.

Elger, T. (1990). 'Technical innovation and work reorganisation in British manufacturing in the 1980s: continuity, intensification or transformation?' *Work, Employment and Society*, special issue: 67–101.

Elger, T. and Smith, C. (eds) (1994). *Global Japanization?* London: Routledge.

Elliot, L. and Atkinson, D. (1998). *The Age of Insecurity*. London: Verso.

Elliott, K. and Freeman, R. (2003). *Can Labor Standards Improve under Globalization?* Washington, DC: Institute for International Economics.

Emmott, M. (2001). 'Tribunals are judged wanting'. *The Guardian*, 12 March.

Erickson, C., Fisk, C., Milkman, R., Mitchell, D., and Wong, K. (2002). 'Justice for Janitors in Los Angeles: lessons from three rounds of negotiation'. *British Journal of Industrial Relations*, 40/3: 543–67.

European Commission (2002). *The European Social Dialogue: A Force for Innovation and Change*. Brussels: EC.

European Industrial Relations Observatory (EIRO) (2001). 'Employers and unions argue over "compensation culture"', *European Industrial Relations Observatory*, http://www.eiro. eurofound.eu.int/2001/10/inbrief/uk0110106n. html.

European Industrial Relations Observatory (EIRO) (2003). 'Unions back new campaign against long working hours', *European Industrial Relations Observatory*, http://www.eurofound.eu. int/ 2003/10/feature/uk0310104f.html.

European Industrial Relations Observatory (EIRO) (2004a). 'Working time developments – 2003', *European Industrial Relations Observatory*, http://www.eurofound.eu.int/2004/03/update/ tn0403104u.html.

European Industrial Relations Observatory (EIRO) (2004b). 'UK reaction to European Commission working time proposals', *European Industrial Relations Observatory*, http://www.eurofound. eu.int/2004/10/inbrief/uk0410103n.html.

Evans, S. (1987). 'The use of injunctions in industrial disputes May 1984–April 1987'. *British Journal of Industrial Relations*, 25/4: 419–35.

Evans, S., Goodman, J., and Hargreaves, L. (1985). *Unfair Dismissal Law and Employment Practice in the 1980s*. Research Paper No. 53. London: Department of Employment.

Ewing, K. and Hendy, J. (eds) (2002). *A Charter of Workers' Rights*. London: Institute of Employment Rights.

Ewing, K. and Hendy, J. (2004). *Submission by the Institute of Employment Rights to the Joint Committee on Human Rights Inquiry into the Concluding Observations of the UN Committee on Economic, Social and Cultural Rights*. London: Institute of Employment Rights.

Fairbrother, P. (1984). *All Those in Favour: The Politics of Union Democracy*. London: Pluto.

Farnham, D. and Giles, L. (1996). 'People management and employment relations', in D. Farnham and S. Horton (eds), *Managing the New Public Services* (2nd edn). Basingstoke: Macmillan, 112–36.

Farnham, D. and Pimlott, J. (1995). *Understanding Industrial Relations* (4th edn). London: Cassell.

Favretto, I. (2003). *The Long Search for a Third Way: The British Labour Party and Italian Left since 1945*. Basingstoke: Palgrave Macmillan.

Felstead, A. (1991). 'The social organization of the franchise: a case of controlled self-employment'. *Work, Employment and Society*, 5/1: 37–57.

Felstead, A. and Jewson, N. (1999). 'Flexible labour and non-standard employment: an agenda of issues', in A. Felstead and N. Jewson (eds), *Global Trends in Flexible Labour*. Basingstoke: Macmillan, 1–20.

Felstead, A. and Jewson, N. (2000). *In Work, at Home*. London: Routledge.

Felstead, A., Burchell, B., and Green, F. (1998). 'Insecurity at work'. *New Economy*, 5/3: 180–4.

Felstead, A., Jewson, N., Phizacklea, A., and Walters, S. (2002). 'Opportunities to work at home in the context of work–life balance'. *Human Resource Management Journal*, 12/1: 54–76.

Fenley, A. (1986). 'Industrial discipline: a suitable case for treatment'. *Employee Relations*, 8/3: 1–30.

Fenley, A. (1998). 'Models, styles and metaphors: understanding the management of discipline'. *Employee Relations*, 20/4: 349–64.

Ferner, A. (1997). 'Country of origin effects and HRM in multinational companies'. *Human Resource Management Journal*, 7/1: 19–37.

Ferner, A. (2003). 'Foreign multinationals and industrial relations innovation in Britain', in P. Edwards (ed.), *Industrial Relations: Theory and Practice* (2nd edn). Oxford: Blackwell, 81–104.

Ferner, A. and Edwards, P. (1995). 'Power and the diffusion of organizational change within multinational corporations'. *European Journal of Industrial Relations*, 1/2: 229–57.

Ferner, A. and Hyman, R. (1998). 'Introduction: towards European industrial relations?', in A. Ferner and R. Hyman (eds), *Changing Industrial Relations in Europe* (2nd edn). Oxford: Blackwell, xi–xxvi.

Ferner, A. and Quintanilla, J. (1998). 'Multinationals, national business systems and HRM: the enduring influence of national identity or a process of "Anglo-Saxonization"?' *International Journal of Human Resource Management*, 9/4: 710–31.

Ferner, A. and Varul, M. (2000). ' "Vanguard" subsidiaries and the diffusion of new practices: a case study of German multinationals'. *British Journal of Industrial Relations*, 38/1: 115–40.

Figueroa, H. (1998). 'Back to the forefront: union organizing of immigrant workers in the nineties', in J. Mort (ed.), *Not Your Father's Union Movement*. London: Verso, 87–98.

Findlay, P. (1993). 'Union recognition and non-unionism: shifting patterns in the electronics industry in Scotland'. *Industrial Relations Journal*, 24/1: 28–43.

Fisk, C., Mitchell, D., and Erickson, C. (2000). 'Union representation of immigrant janitors in Southern California: economic and legal challenges', in R. Milkman (ed.), *Organizing Immigrants: The Challenge for Unions in Contemporary California*. Ithaca, NY: Cornell University Press, 199–224.

Flanders, A. (1964). *The Fawley Productivity Agreements*. London: Faber & Faber.

Flanders, A. (1974). 'The tradition of voluntarism'. *British Journal of Industrial Relations*, 12/3: 352–70.

Flanders, A. (1975). *Management and Unions*. London: Faber & Faber.

Flanders, A. and Clegg, H. (eds) (1964). *The System of Industrial Relations in Great Britain*. Oxford: Basil Blackwell.

Forde, C. (2001). 'Temporary arrangements: the activities of employment agencies in the UK'. *Work, Employment and Society*, 15/3: 631–44.

Foster, D. and Hoggett, P. (1999). 'Change in the Benefits Agency: empowering the exhausted worker?' *Work, Employment and Society*, 13/1: 19–39.

Foster, D. and Scott, P. (1998). 'Competitive tendering of public services and industrial relations policy: the Conservative agenda under Thatcher and Major, 1979–97'. *Historical Studies in Industrial Relations*, 6: 101–32.

Foster, D. and Scott, P. (eds) (2003a). *Trade Unions in Europe: Meeting the Challenge*. Brussels: Peter Lang.

Foster, D. and Scott, P. (2003b). 'EMU and public service trade unionism: between states and markets'. *Transfer*, 9/4: 702–21.

Foster, J. and Woolfson, C. (1986). *The Politics of the UCS Work-in*. London: Lawrence and Wishart.

Foulkes, F. (1980). *Personnel Policies in Large Nonunion Companies*. Englewood Cliffs, NJ: Prentice-Hall.

Fox, A. (1966). *Industrial Sociology and Industrial Relations*. Research Paper No. 3, Royal Commission on Trade Unions and Employers' Associations. London: HMSO.

Fox, A. (1974). *Beyond Contract: Work, Power and Trust Relations*. London: Faber & Faber.

Fox, A. (1985a). *History and Heritage: The Social Origins of the British Industrial Relations System*. London: Allen and Unwin.

Fox, A. (1985b). *Man Mismanagement* (2nd edn). London: Hutchinson.

Fraser, J. and Gold, M. (2001). ' "Portfolio workers": autonomy and control among freelance translators'. *Work, Employment and Society*, 15/4: 679–97.

Fredman, S. (2001). 'Equality: a new generation?' *Industrial Law Journal*, 30/2: 145–68.

Freeman, R. and Pelletier, J. (1990). 'The impact of industrial relations legislation on British union density'. *British Journal of Industrial Relations*, 28/2: 141–64.

Frege, C. (2002). 'A critical assessment of the theoretical and empirical research on German works councils'. *British Journal of Industrial Relations*, 40/2: 221–48.

Friedman, A. (1977). *Industry and Labour: Class Struggle at Work and Monopoly Capitalism*. London: Macmillan.

Fröbel, F., Heinrichs, J., and Kreye, O. (1980). *The New International Division of Labour*. Cambridge: Cambridge University Press.

Fryer, R. (1973). 'Redundancy, values and public policy'. *Industrial Relations Journal*, 4/2: 2–19.

Fryer, R. (1981). 'State, redundancy and the law', in R. Fryer, A. Hunt, D. McBarnet, and B. Moorhouse (eds), *Law, State and Society*. London: Croom Helm, 136–59.

Fuller, L. and Smith, V. (1991). 'Consumers' reports: management by customers in a changing economy'. *Work, Employment and Society*, 5/1: 1–16.

Gall, G. (1998). 'The changing relations of production: union derecognition in the UK magazine industry'. *Industrial Relations Journal*, 29/2: 151–61.

Gall, G. (1999). 'A review of strike activity in Western Europe at the end of the second millennium'. *Employee Relations*, 21/4: 357–77.

Gall, G. (2001). 'The organization of organized discontent: the case of the postal workers in Britain'. *British Journal of Industrial Relations*, 39/3: 393–409.

Gall, G. (2003a). 'Employer opposition to union recognition', in G. Gall (ed.), *Union Organizing*. London: Routledge, 79–96.

Gall, G. (2003b). 'Marxism and industrial relations', in P. Ackers and A. Wilkinson (eds), *Understanding Work and Employment: Industrial Relations in Transition*. Oxford: Oxford University Press, 316–24.

Gall, G. (2003c). *The Meaning of Militancy: Postal Workers and Industrial Relations*. Aldershot: Ashgate.

Gall, G. (ed.) (2003d). *Union Organizing: Campaigning for Union Recognition*. London: Routledge.

Gall, G. (2004). 'British employer resistance to trade union recognition'. *Human Resource Management Journal*, 14/2: 36–53.

Gall, G. and McKay, S. (1994). 'Trade union derecognition in Britain 1988–1994'. *British Journal of Industrial Relations*, 32/3: 433–48.

Gall, G. and McKay, S. (1996). 'Research note: injunctions as a legal weapon in industrial disputes'. *British Journal of Industrial Relations*, 34/4: 567–82.

Gall, G. and McKay, S. (1999). 'Developments in union recognition and derecognition in Britain, 1994–1998'. *British Journal of Industrial Relations*, 37/4: 601–14.

Gall, G. and McKay, S. (2001). 'Facing "fairness at work": union perception of employer opposition and response to union recognition'. *Industrial Relations Journal*, 32/2: 94–113.

Gallie, D., White, M., Cheng, Y., and Tomlinson, M. (1998). *Restructuring the Employment Relationship*. Oxford: Clarendon.

Gamble, A. (1988). *The Free Economy and the Strong State: The Politics of Thatcherism*. Basingstoke: Macmillan.

Garrahan, P. and Stewart, P. (1992). *The Nissan Enigma*. London: Mansell.

Geary, D. (1985). *Policing Industrial Disputes, 1893 to 1985*. Cambridge: Cambridge University Press.

Geary, J. (2003). 'New forms of work organization: still limited, still controlled, but still welcome?', in P. Edwards (ed.), *Industrial Relations: Theory and Practice* (2nd edn). Oxford: Blackwell, 338–67.

Gennard, J. (1984). 'The implications of the Messenger Newspaper Group dispute'. *Industrial Relations Journal*, 15/3: 7–20.

Gennard, J. and Newsome, K. (2001). 'European co-ordination of collective bargaining: the case of the UNI-Europa graphical sector'. *Employee Relations*, 23/6: 599–613.

Gennard, J. and Steuer, M. (1971). 'The industrial relations of foreign-owned subsidiaries in the United Kingdom'. *British Journal of Industrial Relations*, 9/2: 143–59.

Giddens, A. (1998). *The Third Way*. Cambridge: Polity.

Giddens, A. (2002). *Where Now for New Labour?* Cambridge: Polity.

Gilbert, D. (1996). 'Strikes in postwar Britain', in C. Wrigley (ed.), *A History of British Industrial Relations 1939–1979*. Cheltenham: Edward Elgar, 128–61. .

Gilman, M. and Marginson, P. (2002). 'Negotiating European Works Councils: contours of constrained choice'. *Industrial Relations Journal*, 33/1: 36–51.

Gilman, M., Edwards, P.K., Ram, M., and Arrowsmith, J. (2002). 'Pay determination in small firms in the UK: the case of the response to the National Minimum Wage'. *Industrial Relations Journal*, 33/1: 52–67.

Glover, I. and Branine, M. (eds) (2001). *Ageism in Work and Employment*. Aldershot: Ashgate.

Glucksmann, M. (1990). *Women Assemble*. London: Routledge.

Godard, J. and Delaney, J. (2000). 'Reflections on the "high performance" paradigm's implications for industrial relations as a field'. *Industrial and Labor Relations Review*, 53/3: 482–502.

Gold, M. (1993). 'Overview of the social dimension', in M. Gold (ed.), *The Social Dimension: Employment Policy in the European Community*. Basingstoke: Macmillan, 10–40.

Goldstein, J. (1952). *The Government of British Trade Unions*. London: George Allen and Unwin.

Goldthorpe, J. (1977). 'Industrial relations in Great Britain: a critique of reformism', in T. Clarke and L. Clements (eds), *Trade Unions under Capitalism*. Glasgow: Fontana, 184–224.

Gollan, P. (2003). 'All talk but no voice: employee voice at the Eurotunnel call centre'. *Economic and Industrial Democracy*, 24/4: 509–41.

Goodman, J. (2000). 'Building bridges and settling differences: collective conciliation and arbitration under ACAS', in B. Towers and W. Brown (eds), *Employment Relations in Britain: 25 Years of the Advisory, Conciliation and Arbitration Service*. Oxford: Blackwell, 31–65.

Goodman, J., Earnshaw, J., Marchington, M., and Harrison, R. (1998). 'Unfair dismissal cases, disciplinary procedures, recruitment methods and management style: case study evidence from three industrial sectors'. *Employee Relations*, 20/6: 536–50.

Gospel, H. (1992). *Markets, Firms and the Management of Labour in Modern Britain*. Cambridge: Cambridge University Press.

Gospel, H. and Druker, J. (1998). 'The survival of national bargaining in the electrical contracting industry: a deviant case?' *British Journal of Industrial Relations*, 36/2: 249–67.

Gospel, H. and Willman, P. (2003). 'Dilemmas in worker representation: information, consultation and negotiation', in H. Gospel and S. Wood (eds), *Representing Workers*. London: Routledge, 144–63.

Goss, D. (1991). *Small Business and Society*. London: Routledge.

Goss, D. and Adam-Smith, D. (2001). 'Pragmatism and compliance: employer responses to the Working Time Regulations'. *Industrial Relations Journal*, 32/3: 195–208.

Gouldner, A. (1954). *Patterns of Industrial Bureaucracy*. New York: Free Press.

Gouldner, A. (1955). *Wildcat Strike*. London: Routledge and Kegan Paul.

Gratton, L., Hope-Hailey, V., Stiles, P., and Truss, C. (1999). *Strategic Human Resource Management: Corporate Rhetoric and Employee Reality*. Oxford: Oxford University Press.

Gray, J. (1998). *False Dawn: The Delusions of Global Capitalism*. London: Granta Books.

Green, F. (1997). 'Union recognition and paid holiday entitlement'. *British Journal of Industrial Relations*, 35/2: 243–55.

Green, F. (2001). 'It's been a hard day's night: the concentration and intensification of work in late twentieth-century Britain'. *British Journal of Industrial Relations*, 39/1: 53–80.

Green, F. (2003). 'The demands of work', in R. Dickens, P. Gregg, and J. Wadsworth (eds), *The Labour Market under New Labour*. Basingstoke: Palgrave Macmillan, 137–49.

Greene, A.-M. (2001). *Voices from the Shopfloor: Dramas of the Employment Relationship*. Aldershot: Ashgate.

Greene, A.-M. (2003). 'Women and industrial relations', in P. Ackers and A. Wilkinson (eds), *Understanding Work and Employment*. Oxford: Oxford University Press, 305–15.

Greene, A.-M., Hogan, J., and Grieco, M. (2003). 'Commentary: e-collectivism and distributed discourse: new opportunities for trade union democracy'. *Industrial Relations Journal*, 34/4: 282–9.

Gregg, P. and Wadsworth, J. (1995). 'A short history of labour turnover, job tenure and job security, 1975–93'. *Oxford Review of Economic Policy*, 11/1: 73–90.

Gregg, P., Knight, G., and Wadsworth, J. (2000). 'Heaven knows I'm miserable now: job insecurity in the British labour market', in E. Heery and J. Salmon (eds), *The Insecure Workforce*. London: Routledge, 39–56.

Griffin, J. (1939). *Strikes: A Study in Quantitative Economics*. New York: Colombia University Press.

Grimshaw, D. (1999). 'Changes in skill mix and pay determination among the nursing workforce in the UK'. *Work, Employment and Society*, 13/2: 295–328.

Grimshaw, D., Earnshaw, J., and Hebson, G. (2003). 'Private sector provision of supply teachers: a case of legal swings and professional roundabouts'. *Journal of Education Policy*, 18/3: 267–88.

Guest, D. (1987). 'Human resource management and industrial relations'. *Journal of Management Studies*, 24/5: 503–21.

Guest, D. (1989). 'Human resource management: its implications for industrial relations and trade unions', in J. Storey (ed.), *New Perspectives on Human Resource Management*. London: Routledge, 41–55.

Guest, D. (1995). 'Human resource management, trade unions and industrial relations', in J. Storey (ed.), *Human Resource Management: A Critical Text*. London: Routledge, 110–41.

Guest, D. (1996). 'Human resource management in the United Kingdom', in B. Towers (ed.), *The Handbook of Human Resource Management* (2nd edn). Oxford: Blackwell, 7–25.

Guest, D. (1997). 'Human resource management and performance: a review and research agenda'. *International Journal of Human Resource Management*, 8/3: 263–76.

Guest, D. (1999). 'Human resource management – the workers' verdict'. *Human Resource Management Journal*, 9/3: 5–25.

Guest, D. and Hoque, K. (1994). 'The good, the bad and the ugly: employment relations in new non-union workplaces'. *Human Resource Management Journal*, 5/1: 1–14.

Guest, D. and Hoque, K. (1996). 'National ownership and HR practices in UK greenfield sites'. *Human Resource Management Journal*, 6/4: 50–74.

Guest, D. and Peccei, R. (1998). *The Partnership Company*. London: Involvement and Participation Association.

Guest, D. and Peccei, R. (2001). 'Partnership at work: mutuality and the balance of advantage'. *British Journal of Industrial Relations*, 39/2: 207–36.

Guest, D., Michie, J., Sheehan, M., and Conway, N. (2000). *Employment Relations, HRM and Business Performance*. London: Chartered Institute of Personnel and Development.

Gunnigle, P., Turner, T., and D'Art, D. (1998). 'Counterpoising collectivism: performance-related pay and industrial relations in greenfield sites'. *British Journal of Industrial Relations*, 36/4: 565–79.

Hakim, C. (1979). *Occupational Segregation by Sex*. Department of Employment Research Paper No. 9. London: HMSO.

Hakim, C. (1988). 'Self-employment in Britain: recent trends and current issues'. *Work, Employment and Society*, 2/4: 421–50.

Hakim, C. (1996). *Key Issues in Women's Work*. London: The Athlone Press.

Hall, M. (1992). 'Behind the European Works Councils Directive: the European Commission's legislative strategy'. *British Journal of Industrial Relations*, 30/4: 547–66.

Hall, M. (1994). 'Industrial relations and the social dimension of European integration: before and after Maastricht', in R. Hyman and A. Ferner (eds), *New Frontiers in European Industrial Relations*. Oxford: Blackwell, 281–311.

Hall, M. and Edwards, P. (1999). 'Reforming the statutory redundancy consultation procedure'. *Industrial Law Journal*, 28/4: 299–318.

Hall, M. and Terry, M. (2004). 'The emerging system of statutory worker representation', in G. Healy, E. Heery, P. Taylor, and W. Brown (eds), *The Future of Worker Representation*. Basingstoke: Palgrave Macmillan, 207–28.

Hall, P. and Soskice, D. (2001). 'An introduction to varieties of capitalism', in P. Hall and D. Soskice (eds), *Varieties of Capitalism: The Institutional Foundations of Comparative Advantage*. Oxford: Oxford University Press, 1–68.

Handy, C. (1994). *The Empty Raincoat*. London: Hutchinson.

Harbridge, R., Crawford, A., and Hince, K. (2002). 'Unions in New Zealand: what the law giveth . . .', in P. Fairbrother and G. Griffin (eds), *Changing Prospects for Trade Unionism*. London: Continuum, 177–99.

Hardy, S. and Adnett, N. (2002). 'The Parental Leave Directive: towards a "family-friendly" social Europe?' *European Journal of Industrial Relations*, 8/2: 157–72.

Harkness, S. (1999). 'Working 9 to 5?', in P. Gregg and J. Wadsworth (eds), *The State of Working Britain*. Manchester: Manchester University Press, 90–108.

Harris, C. (1987). *Redundancy and Recession*. Oxford: Basil Blackwell.

Harris, L. and Ogbonna, E. (2002). 'Exploring service sabotage: the antecedents, types and consequences of frontline, deviant, antiservice behaviors'. *Journal of Service Research*, 4/3: 163–83.

Hatton, T. (2004). 'Unemployment and the labour market', in R. Floud and P. Johnson (eds), *The Cambridge Economic History of Modern Britain. Volume II: Economic Maturity 1860–1939*. Cambridge: Cambridge University Press, 344–73.

Hawes, W. (2000). 'Setting the pace or running alongside? ACAS and the changing employment relationship', in B. Towers and W. Brown (eds), *Employment Relations in Britain: 25 Years of the Advisory, Conciliation and Arbitration Service*. Oxford: Blackwell, 1–30.

Hay, C. (1999). *The Political Economy of New Labour: Labouring under False Pretences?* Manchester: Manchester University Press.

Haynes, P. and Allen, M. (2001). 'Partnership as union strategy: a preliminary evaluation'. *Employee Relations*, 23/2: 164–93.

Hayward, B., Peters, M., Rousseau, N., and Seeds, K. (2004). *Findings from the Survey of Employment Tribunal Applications 2003*. Employment Relations Research Series No. 33. London: Department of Trade and Industry.

Head, J. and Lucas, R. (2004). 'Employee relations in the non-union hotel industry: a case of "determined opportunism"?' *Personnel Review*, 33/6: 693–710.

Healy, G. and Kirton, G. (2000). 'Women, power and trade union government in the UK'. *British Journal of Industrial Relations*, 38/3: 343–60.

Healy, G., Bradley, H., and Mukherjee, N. (2004). 'Individualism and collectivism revisited: a study of black and minority ethnic women'. *Industrial Relations Journal*, 35/5: 451–66.

Heery, E. (1996). 'The new new unionism', in I. Beardwell (ed.), *Contemporary Industrial Relations: A Critical Analysis*. Oxford: Oxford University Press, 175–202.

Heery, E. (1997a). 'Annual review article 1996'. *British Journal of Industrial Relations*, 35/1: 87–109.

Heery, E. (1997b). 'Performance-related pay and trade union de-recognition'. *Employee Relations*, 19/3: 208–21.

Heery, E. (1998a). 'A return to contract? Performance-related pay in a public service'. *Work, Employment and Society*, 12/1: 73–95.

Heery, E. (1998b). 'Campaigning for part-time workers'. *Work, Employment and Society*, 12/2: 351–66.

Heery, E. (1998c). 'The relaunch of the Trades Union Congress'. *British Journal of Industrial Relations*, 36/3: 339–60.

Heery, E. (2002). 'Partnership versus organising: alternative futures for British trade unionism'. *Industrial Relations Journal*, 33/1: 20–35.

Heery, E. and Fosh, P. (1990). 'Introduction: whose union? Union power and bureaucracy in the labour movement', in P. Fosh and E. Heery (eds), *Trade Unions and their Members*. Basingstoke: Macmillan, 1–28.

Heery, E. and Kelly, J. (1988). 'Do female representatives make a difference? Women full-time officials and trade union work'. *Work, Employment and Society*, 2/4: 487–505.

Heery, E. and Kelly, J. (1994). 'Professional, participative and managerial unionism: an interpretation of change in trade unions'. *Work, Employment and Society*, 8/1: 1–22.

Heery, E. and Salmon, J. (eds) (2000a). *The Insecure Workforce*. London: Routledge.

Heery, E. and Salmon, J. (2000b). 'The insecurity thesis', in E. Heery and J. Salmon (eds), *The Insecure Workforce*. London: Routledge, 1–24.

Heery, E., Conley, H., Delbridge, R., and Stewart, P. (2004). 'Beyond the enterprise: trade union representation of freelances in the UK'. *Human Resource Management Journal*, 14/2: 20–35.

Heery, E., Simms, M., Simpson, D., Delbridge, R., and Salmon, J. (2000a). 'Organizing unionism comes to the UK'. *Employee Relations*, 22/1: 38–57.

Heery, E., Simms, M., Delbridge, R., Salmon, J., and Simpson, D. (2000b). 'The TUC's Organising Academy: an assessment'. *Industrial Relations Journal*, 31/5: 400–15.

Heery, E., Simms, M., Delbridge, R., Salmon, J., and Simpson, D. (2000c). 'Union organizing in Britain: a survey of policy and practice'. *International Journal of Human Resource Management*, 11/5: 986–1007.

Heery, E., Simms, M., Delbridge, R., Salmon, J., and Simpson, D. (2003). 'Trade union recruitment policy in Britain: form and effects', in G. Gall (ed.), *Union Organizing: Campaigning for Union Recognition*. London: Routledge, 56–78.

Held, D., McGrew, A., Goldblatt, D., and Perraton, J. (1999). *Global Transformations*. Cambridge: Polity.

Henry, S. (1982). 'Factory law: the changing disciplinary technology of industrial social control'. *International Journal of the Sociology of Law*, 10: 365–83.

Hepple, B. (1992). 'The fall and rise of unfair dismissal', in W. McCarthy (ed.), *Legal Intervention in Industrial Relations: Gains and Losses*. Oxford: Blackwell, 79–102.

Herod, A., Peck, J., and Wills, J. (2003). 'Geography and industrial relations', in P. Ackers and A. Wilkinson (eds), *Understanding Work and Employment: Industrial Relations in Transition*. Oxford: Oxford University Press, 176–92.

Hewitt, P. (1993). *About Time*. London: Rivers Oram Press.

Heyes, J. (1997). 'Annualised hours and the "knock": the organisation of working time in a chemicals plant'. *Work, Employment and Society*, 11/1: 65–81.

Heyes, J. and Gray, A. (2001). 'The impact of the National Minimum Wage on the textiles and clothing industry'. *Policy Studies*, 22: 83–98.

Hill, J. and Trist, E. (1953). 'A consideration of industrial accidents as a means of withdrawal from the work situation'. *Human Relations*, 6/4: 357–80.

Hill, S. (1991a). 'How do you manage a flexible firm? The total quality model'. *Work, Employment and Society*, 5/3: 397–415.

Hill, S. (1991b). 'Why quality circles failed but total quality might succeed'. *British Journal of Industrial Relations*, 29/3: 541–68.

Hill, S. (1995). 'From quality circles to Total Quality Management', in A. Wilkinson and H. Willmott (eds), *Making Quality Critical*. London: Routledge, 33–53.

Hinton, J. (1973). *The First Shop Stewards' Movement*. London: Allen and Unwin.

Hirst, P. and Thompson, G. (1999). *Globalization in Question* (2nd edn). Cambridge: Polity.

HM Treasury and Department of Trade and Industry (DTI) (2003). *Balancing Work and Family Life: Enhancing Choice and Support for Parents*. London: HM Treasury/DTI.

Hobsbawm, E. (1968). *Industry and Empire*. London: Weidenfeld and Nicolson.

Hochschild, A. (1983). *The Managed Heart*. London: University of California Press.

Holliday, R. (1995). *Investigating Small Firms. Nice Work?* London: Routledge.

Hood, C. (1991). 'A public management for all seasons?' *Public Administration*, 69/1: 3–19.

Hoque, K. (1999). 'New approaches to HRM in the UK hotel industry'. *Human Resource Management Journal*, 9/2: 64–76.

Hoque, K. and Noon, M. (2004). 'Equal opportunities policy and practice in Britain: evaluating the "empty shell" hypothesis'. *Work, Employment and Society*, 18/3: 481–506.

House of Commons Employment Committee (1994). *The Future of the Unions*. Third Report, Volume II, Minutes of Evidence. London: HMSO.

Howell, C. (2004). 'Is there a third way for industrial relations?' *British Journal of Industrial Relations*, 42/1: 1–22.

Hudson, M. (2002). 'Flexibility and the reorganisation of work', in B. Burchell, D. Ladipo, and F. Wilkinson (eds), *Job Insecurity and Work Intensification*. London: Routledge, 39–60.

Hudson, R. (1989). 'Breaking the mould: the policies of capital, labour and the state in producing social change in North-East England', in R. Hudson (ed.), *Wrecking a Region*. London: Pion, 355–79.

Hunter, L., McGregor, A., MacInnes, J., and Sproull, A. (1993). 'The "flexible firm": strategy and segmentation'. *British Journal of Industrial Relations*, 31/3: 383–407.

Huselid, M. (1995). 'The impact of human resource management practices on turnover, productivity, and corporate financial performance'. *Academy of Management Journal*, 38/3: 635–72.

Hyman, J. and Mason, B. (1995). *Managing Employee Involvement and Participation*. London: Sage.

Hyman, J. and Summers, J. (2004). 'Lacking balance? Work–life employment practices in the modern economy'. *Personnel Review*, 33/4: 418–29.

Hyman, J., Baldry, C., Scholarios, D., and Bunzel, D. (2003). 'Work–life imbalance in call centres and software development'. *British Journal of Industrial Relations*, 41/2: 215–39.

Hyman, R. (1971). *The Workers' Union*. Oxford: Clarendon.

Hyman, R. (1972). *Disputes Procedure in Action*. London: Heinemann.

Hyman, R. (1975). *Industrial Relations: A Marxist Introduction*. London: Macmillan.

Hyman, R. (1977). *Strikes* (2nd edn). Glasgow: Fontana/Collins.

Hyman, R. (1983). 'Trade unions: structure, policies and politics', in G. Bain (ed.), *Industrial Relations in Britain*. Oxford: Basil Blackwell, 35–65.

Hyman, R. (1987). 'Strategy or structure? Capital, labour and control'. *Work, Employment and Society*, 1/1: 25–55.

Hyman, R. (1989). *The Political Economy of Industrial Relations*. Basingstoke: Macmillan.

Hyman, R. (1991). '*Plus ça change?* The theory of production and the production of theory', in A. Pollert (ed.), *Farewell to Flexibility?* Oxford: Blackwell, 259–83.

Hyman, R. (1994a). 'Introduction: economic restructuring, market liberalism and the future of national industrial relations systems', in R. Hyman and A. Ferner (eds), *New Frontiers in European Industrial Relations*. Oxford: Blackwell, 1–14.

Hyman, R. (1994b). 'Changing trade union identities and strategies', in R. Hyman and A. Ferner (eds), *New Frontiers in European Industrial Relations*. Oxford: Blackwell, 108–39.

Hyman, R. (1996). 'Is there a case for statutory works councils in Britain?', in A. McColgan (ed.), *The Future of Labour Law*. London: Cassell, 64–84.

Hyman, R. (1999). 'Imagined solidarities: can trade unions resist globalization?', in P. Leisink (ed.), *Globalization and Labour Relations*. Cheltenham: Edward Elgar, 94–115.

Hyman, R. (2001a). 'The Europeanisation – or the erosion – of industrial relations?' *Industrial Relations Journal*, 32/4: 280–94.

Hyman, R. (2001b). *Understanding European Trade Unionism: Between Market, Class and Society*. London: Sage.

Hyman, R. (2003). 'The historical evolution of British industrial relations', in P. Edwards (ed.), *Industrial Relations: Theory and Practice* (2nd edn). Oxford: Blackwell, 37–57.

Incomes Data Services (IDS) (2002). 'Company Councils'. *IDS Study*, 730.

Incomes Data Services (IDS) (2003). 'The gender pay gap'. *IDS Report*, 873: 11–16.

Incomes Data Services (IDS) (2004a). *IDS Pay Report*, 917: 3.

Incomes Data Services (IDS) (2004b). 'Diversity at work 2004'. *Diversity at Work*, 1: 6–13.

Industrial Relations Services (IRS) (1998a). 'Introducing European Works Councils: travelling along the Stagecoach route'. *Employment Trends*, 667: 11–16.

Industrial Relations Services (IRS) (1998b). 'What do employers' associations offer to members?' *Employment Trends*, 653: 11–16.

Industrial Relations Services (IRS) (1999). 'Partnership delivers the goods at Tesco'. *Employment Trends*, 686: 4–9.

Industrial Relations Services (IRS) (2001). 'We don't need no litigation'. *Employment Trends*, 719: 4–16.

Industrial Relations Services (IRS) (2004). 'A little less union recognition'. *Employment Trends*, 798: 9–16.

Ingram, P., Wadsworth, J., and Brown, D. (1999). 'Free to choose? Dimensions of private-sector wage determination, 1979–1994'. *British Journal of Industrial Relations*, 37/1: 33–49.

International Confederation of Free Trade Unions (ICFTU) (1996). *Behind the Wire: Anti-Union Repression in the Export Processing Zones*. Brussels: ICFTU.

International Confederation of Free Trade Unions (ICFTU) (2003). *Annual Survey of Violations of Trade Union Rights*. Brussels: ICFTU.

Involvement and Participation Association (IPA) (1992). *Towards Industrial Partnership*. London: IPA.

Ironside, M. and Seifert, R. (1995). *Industrial Relations in Schools*. London: Routledge.

Ironside, M., Seifert, R., and Sinclair, J. (1997). 'Teacher union responses to education reforms: job regulation and the enforced growth of informality'. *Industrial Relations Journal*, 28/2: 120–35.

Jacobi, O., Keller, B., and Müller-Jentsch, W. (1998). 'Germany: facing new challenges', in A. Ferner and R. Hyman (eds), *Changing Industrial Relations in Europe*. Oxford: Blackwell, 190–238.

Jefferys, S. (2000). 'A "Copernican Revolution" in French industrial relations: are the times a' changing?' *British Journal of Industrial Relations*, 38/2: 241–60.

Jefferys, S. (2003). *Liberté, Egalité and Fraternité at Work: Changing French Employment Relations*. Basingstoke: Palgrave Macmillan.

Jenkins, S., Martinez Lucio, M., and Noon, M. (2002). 'Return to gender: an analysis of women's disadvantage in postal work'. *Gender, Work and Organization*, 9/1: 81–104.

Jewson, N. and Mason, D. (1986). 'The theory and practice of equal opportunities policies: liberal and radical approaches'. *Sociological Review*, 34/2: 307–34.

Jewson, N., Mason, D., Drewett, A., and Rossiter, W. (1995). *Formal Equal Opportunities Policies and Employment Best Practice*. Research Series No. 69. London: Department for Education and Employment.

Jordan, B. (1985). *The State: Authority and Autonomy*. Oxford: Blackwell.

Kahn-Freund, O. (1964). 'Legal framework', in A. Flanders and H. Clegg (eds), *The System of Industrial Relations in Great Britain*. Oxford: Basil Blackwell, 42–127.

Kahn-Freund, O. (1977). *Labour and the Law* (2nd edn). London: Stevens.

Kalman, D. (1999). 'Collective wisdom'. *People Management*, 25 February: 37–43.

Kampfner, J. (2004). 'The Warwick watershed', *The Guardian*, 2 September.

Kandola, B. and Fullerton, J. (1994). *Managing the Mosaic: Diversity in Action*. London: Institute of Personnel and Development.

Katz, H. and Darbishire, O. (2000). *Converging Divergences: Worldwide Changes in Employment Systems*. Ithaca, NY: Industrial and Labour Relations/Cornell University Press.

Katz, L. and Krueger, A. (1992). 'The effects of the minimum wage on the fast food industry'. *Industrial and Labor Relations Review*, 46/1: 6–21.

Kay, J. (2003). *The Truth about Markets: Their Genius, their Limits, their Follies*. London: Allen Lane.

Keenoy, T. and Anthony, P. (1992). 'HRM: metaphor, meaning and morality', in P. Blyton and P. Turnbull (eds), *Reassessing Human Resource Management*. London: Sage, 233–55.

Keller, B. (2003). 'The European social partners: projects and future perspectives', in D. Foster and P. Scott (eds), *Trade Unions in Europe: Meeting the Challenge*. Brussels: Peter Lang, 115–43.

Keller, B. and Bansbach, M. (2000). 'Social dialogues: an interim report on recent results and prospects'. *Industrial Relations Journal*, 31/4: 291–307.

Keller, B. and Sörries, B. (1998). 'The sectoral social dialogue and European social policy – more fantasy, fewer facts'. *European Journal of Industrial Relations*, 4/3: 331–48.

Keller, B. and Sörries, B. (1999). 'The new European social dialogue: old wine in new bottles?' *Journal of European Social Policy*, 9/2: 111–25.

Kelly, J. (1998). *Rethinking Industrial Relations*. London: Routledge.

Kelly, J. (2004). 'Social partnership agreements in Britain: labor cooperation and compliance'. *Industrial Relations*, 43/1: 267–92.

Kelly, J. and Heery, E. (1994). *Working for the Union: British Trade Union Officers*. Cambridge: Cambridge University Press.

Kelsey, J. (1995). *Economic Fundamentalism*. London: Pluto.

Kerr, C., Dunlop, J., Harbison, F., and Myers, C. (1962). *Industrialism and Industrial Man*. London: Heinemann.

Kessler, I. (1994). 'Performance-related pay: contrasting approaches'. *Industrial Relations Journal*, 25/2: 122–35.

Kessler, I. (2000). 'Remuneration systems', in S. Bach and K. Sisson (eds), *Personnel Management* (3rd edn). Oxford: Blackwell, 264–86.

Kessler, I. and Purcell, J. (1995). 'Individualism and collectivism in theory and practice: management style and the design of pay systems', in P. Edwards (ed.), *Industrial Relations: Theory and Practice in Britain*. Oxford: Blackwell, 337–67.

Kessler, S. (1993). 'Procedures and third parties'. *British Journal of Industrial Relations*, 31/2: 211–25.

Kessler, S. (1994). 'Incomes policy'. *British Journal of Industrial Relations*, 32/2: 181–99.

Kessler, S. and Bayliss, F. (1998). *Contemporary British Industrial Relations* (3rd edn). Basingstoke: Macmillan.

Kingsnorth, P. (2003). *One No, Many Yeses*. London: Free Press.

Kirton, G. (1999). 'Sustaining and developing women's trade union activism: a gendered project?' *Gender, Work and Organization*, 6/4: 213–23.

Kirton, G. and Greene, A.-M. (2000). *The Dynamics of Managing Diversity*. London: Butterworth-Heinemann.

Kirton, G. and Greene, A.-M. (2002). 'The dynamics of positive action in UK trade unions: the case of women and black members'. *Industrial Relations Journal*, 33/2: 157–72.

Kirton, G. and Healy, G. (1999). 'Transforming union women: the role of women trade union officials in union renewal'. *Industrial Relations Journal*, 30/1: 31–45.

Klein, N. (2000). *No Logo*. London: Flamingo.

Knell, J. (1999). *Partnership at Work*. London: Department of Trade and Industry.

Knight, K. and Latreille, P. (2000). 'Discipline, dismissals and complaints to employment tribunals'. *British Journal of Industrial Relations*, 38/4: 533–55.

Knowles, K. (1952). *Strikes – A Study in Industrial Conflict*. Oxford: Basil Blackwell.

Knox, B. and McKinlay, A. (2003). ' "Organizing the unorganized": union recruitment strategies in American transnationals, *c*. 1945–1977', in G. Gall (ed.), *Union Organizing*. London: Routledge, 19–38.

Kochan, T., Katz, H., and McKersie, R. (1986). *The Transformation of American Industrial Relations*. New York: Basic Books.

Kochan, T.A. and Osterman, P. (1994). *The Mutual Gains Enterprise*. Cambridge, MA: Harvard University Press.

Kodz, J., Harper, H., and Dench, S. (2002). *Work–Life Balance: Beyond the Rhetoric*. Institute of Employment Studies Report No. 384. Brighton: IES.

Kodz, J. et al. (2003). *Working Long Hours: A Review of the Evidence (Volume 1: Main Report)*. Employment Relations Research Series No. 16. London: Department of Trade and Industry.

Korczynski, M. (2002). *Human Resource Management in Service Work*. Basingstoke: Palgrave.

Kumar, K. (1986). *Prophecy and Progress: The Sociology of Industrial and Post-Industrial Society*. Harmondsworth: Penguin.

Kumar, K. (1995). *From Post-Industrial to Post-Modern Society: New Theories of the Contemporary World*. Oxford: Blackwell.

Labour Research (2001). 'Study uncovers wide range of homeworkers'. *Labour Research*, February: 25.

Lansbury, R. and Wailes, N. (2004). 'Employment relations in Australia', in G. Bamber, R. Lansbury, and N. Wailes (eds), *International and Comparative Employment Relations* (4th edn). London: Sage, 119–45.

Lashley, C. (2000). 'Empowerment through involvement: a case study of TGI Fridays restaurants'. *Personnel Review*, 29/6: 799–815.

Lazonick, W. (1994). 'Employment relations in manufacturing and international competition', in R. Floud and D. McCloskey (eds), *The Economic History of Britain since 1700* (2nd edn). Cambridge: Cambridge University Press, 90–116.

Leadbeater, C. (1999). *Living on Thin Air*. London: Viking.

Leat, M. (1998). *Human Resource Issues of the European Union*. London: FT Management.

Lecher, W. and Rüb, S. (1999). 'The constitution of European Works Councils: from information forum to social actor?' *European Journal of Industrial Relations*, 5/1: 7–25.

Ledwith, S., Colgan, F., Joyce, P., and Hayes, M. (1990). 'The making of women trade union leaders'. *Industrial Relations Journal*, 21/2: 112–25.

Legge, K. (2001). 'Silver bullet or spent round? Assessing the meaning of the "high commitment management"/performance relationship', in J. Storey (ed.), *Human Resource Management: A Critical Text* (2nd edn). London: Thomson Learning, 21–36.

Legge, K. (2005). *Human Resource Management: Rhetoric and Realities* (2nd edn). Basingstoke: Palgrave Macmillan.

Leidner, R. (2002). 'Fast-food work in the United States', in T. Royle and B. Towers (eds), *Labour Relations in the Global Fast-Food Industry*. London: Routledge, 8–29.

Leisink, P. (1999). 'Introduction', in P. Leisink (ed.), *Globalization and Labour Relations*. Cheltenham: Edward Elgar, 1–24.

Leisink, P. (2002). 'The European sectoral social dialogue and the graphical industry'. *European Journal of Industrial Relations*, 8/1: 101–17.

Leopold, J. (1986). 'Trade union political funds: a retrospective analysis'. *Industrial Relations Journal*, 17/4: 287–303.

Leopold, J. (1997). 'Trade unions, political fund ballots and the Labour party'. *British Journal of Industrial Relations*, 35/1: 23–38.

Levitt, M. and Lord, C. (2000). *The Political Economy of Monetary Union*. Basingstoke: Macmillan.

Lewis, P. (1993). *The Successful Management of Redundancy*. Oxford: Blackwell.

Lewis, R. (1990). 'Strike-free deals and pendulum arbitration'. *British Journal of Industrial Relations*, 28/1: 32–56.

Lewis, S. (1997). ' "Family friendly" employment policies: a route to changing organizational culture or playing about at the margins?' *Gender, Work and Organization*, 4/1: 13–23.

Liff, S. (1997). 'Two routes to managing diversity: individual differences or social group characteristics?' *Employee Relations*, 19/1: 11–26.

Liff, S. (1999). 'Diversity and equal opportunities: room for a constructive compromise?' *Human Resource Management Journal*, 9/1: 65–75.

Liff, S. (2003). 'The industrial relations of a diverse workforce', in P. Edwards (ed.), *Industrial Relations: Theory and Practice* (2nd edn). Oxford: Blackwell, 420–46.

Liff, S. and Wacjman, J. (1996). ' "Sameness" and "difference" revisited: which way forward for equal opportunity initiatives?' *Journal of Management Studies*, 33/1: 79–94.

Liff, S. and Ward, K. (2001). 'Distorted views through the glass ceiling: the construction of women's understandings of promotion and senior management positions'. *Gender, Work and Organization*, 8/1: 19–36.

Lipset, S., Trow, M., and Coleman, J. (1956). *Union Democracy*. New York: Free Press.

Littler, C. (1982). *The Development of the Labour Process in Capitalist Societies*. London: Heinemann.

Littleton, S. (1992). *The Wapping Dispute*. Aldershot: Avebury.

Lloyd, C. (2001). 'What do employee councils do? The impact of non-union forms of representation on trade union organisation'. *Industrial Relations Journal*, 32/4: 313–27.

Lockwood, D. (1958). *The Black-Coated Worker*. London: Allen and Unwin.

Logan, J. (2001). 'Is statutory recognition bad news for UK unions? Evidence from the history of North American industrial relations'. *Historical Studies in Industrial Relations*, 11: 63–107.

Low Pay Commission (LPC) (1998). *The National Minimum Wage: First Report of the Low Pay Commission*. London: HMSO.

Low Pay Commission (LPC) (2000). *The National Minimum Wage: The Story So Far*. Second Report of the Low Pay Commission. London: HMSO.

Low Pay Commission (LPC) (2001a). *The National Minimum Wage: Making a Difference*. Third Report (Volume 1) of the Low Pay Commission. London: HMSO.

Low Pay Commission (LPC) (2001b). *The National Minimum Wage: Making a Difference, the Next Steps*. Third Report (Volume 2) of the Low Pay Commission. London: HMSO.

Low Pay Commission (LPC) (2003). *The National Minimum Wage: Building on Success*. Fourth Report of the Low Pay Commission. London: HMSO.

Low Pay Commission (LPC) (2004). *The National Minimum Wage: Protecting Young Workers*. Fifth Report of the Low Pay Commission. London: HMSO.

Lucas, R. and Radiven, N. (1998). 'After wages councils: minimum pay and practice'. *Human Resource Management Journal*, 8/4: 5–19.

Ludlum, S. and Taylor, A. (2003). 'The political representation of the labour interest'. *British Journal of Industrial Relations*, 41/4: 727–49.

Lunn, K. (1999). 'Complex encounters: trade unions, immigration and racism', in J. McIlroy, N. Fishman, and A. Campbell (eds), *British Trade Unions and Industrial Politics. Volume 2: The High Tide of Trade Unionism, 1964–79*. Aldershot: Ashgate, 70–90.

Lunn, K. and Day, A. (1999). 'Continuity and change: labour relations in the Royal Dockyards, 1914–50', in K. Lunn and A. Day (eds), *History of Work and Labour Relations in the Royal Dockyards*. London: Mansell, 127–50.

Lupton, T. (1963). *On the Shop Floor*. Oxford: Pergamon.

MacDonald, R. and Coffield, F. (1991). *Risky Business? Youth and the Enterprise Culture*. Basingstoke: Falmer Press.

MacDuffie, J.-P. (1995). 'Human resource bundles and manufacturing performance: organizational logic and flexible production systems in the world auto industry'. *Industrial and Labor Relations Review*, 48/2: 195–221.

MacInnes, J. (1985). 'Conjuring up consultation: the role and extent of joint consultation in post-war private manufacturing industry'. *British Journal of Industrial Relations*, 23/1: 93–113.

MacInnes, J. (1987). *Thatcherism at Work*. Milton Keynes: Open University Press.

McArdle, L., Rowlinson, M., Proctor, S., Hammond, J., and Forrester, P. (1995). 'Total Quality Management and participation: employee empowerment, or the enhancement of exploitation?', in A. Wilkinson and H. Willmott (eds), *Making Quality Critical*. London: Routledge, 156–72.

McBride, A. (2000). 'Promoting representation of women within UNISON', in M. Terry (ed.), *Redefining Public Sector Unionism: UNISON and the Future of Trade Unions*. London: Routledge, 100–18.

McBride, A. (2001). *Gender Democracy in Trade Unions*. Aldershot: Ashgate.

McCarthy, W. (1964). *The Closed Shop in Britain*. Oxford: Basil Blackwell.

McCarthy, W. (1966). *The Role of Shop Stewards in British Industrial Relations*. Research Paper No. 1, Royal Commission on Trade Unions and Employers' Associations. London: HMSO.

McColgan, A. (1997). *Just Wages for Women*. Oxford: Clarendon.

McColgan, A. (2000a). 'Missing the point? The Part-time Workers (Prevention of Less Favourable Treatment) Regulations 2000 (SI 2000, No. 1551)'. *Industrial Law Journal*, 29/3: 260–7.

McColgan, A. (2000b). 'Family friendly frolics? The Maternity and Parental Leave etc. Regulations 1999'. *Industrial Law Journal*, 29/2: 125–43.

McGovern, P. and Hill, S. (2003). 'The end of the status divide? Employment conditions in Britain 1992–2000'. Paper presented to the British Universities Industrial Relations Association annual conference, University of Leeds, July.

McIlroy, J. (1988). *Trade Unions in Britain Today*. Manchester: Manchester University Press.

McIlroy, J. (1991). *The Permanent Revolution? Conservative Law and the Trade Unions*. Nottingham: Spokesman.

McIlroy, J. (1998). 'The enduring alliance? Trade unions and the making of New Labour'. *British Journal of Industrial Relations*, 36/4: 537–64.

McIlroy, J. (1999). 'Unfinished business – the reform of strike legislation in Britain'. *Employee Relations*, 21/6: 521–39.

McIlroy, J. (2000a). 'New Labour, new unions, new left'. *Capital and Class*, 71: 11–45.

McIlroy, J. (2000b). 'The new politics of pressure – the Trades Union Congress and New Labour in government'. *Industrial Relations Journal*, 31/1: 2–16.

McIntosh, I. and Broderick, J. (1996). 'Neither one thing nor the other: compulsory competitive tendering and Southburg Cleansing services'. *Work, Employment and Society*, 10/3: 413–30.

McIvor, A. (1996). *Organised Capital*. Cambridge: Cambridge University Press.

McKay, S. (2001). 'Annual review article 2000. Between flexibility and regulation: rights, equality and protection at work'. *British Journal of Industrial Relations*, 39/2: 285–303.

McKee, L., Mauthner, N., and Maclean, C. (2000). ' "Family friendly" policies and practices in the oil and gas industry: employers' perspectives'. *Work, Employment and Society*, 14/3: 557–71.

McKinlay, A. and McNulty, D. (1992). 'At the cutting edge of new realism: the engineers' 35 hour week campaign'. *Industrial Relations Journal*, 23/3: 205–13.

McLoughlin, I. and Gourlay, S. (1992). 'Enterprises without unions: the management of employment relations in non-union firms'. *Journal of Management Studies*, 29/5: 669–91.

McLoughlin, I. and Gourlay, S. (1994). *Enterprise without Unions*. Buckingham: Open University Press.

Machin, S. (1996). 'Wage inequality in the UK'. *Oxford Review of Economic Policy*, 12/1: 47–64.

Machin, S. (1999). 'Wage inequality in the 1970s, 1980s and 1990s', in P. Gregg and J. Wadsworth (eds), *The State of Working Britain*. Manchester: Manchester University Press, 185–205.

Machin, S. (2000). 'Union decline in Britain'. *British Journal of Industrial Relations*, 38/4: 631–45.

Machin, S. (2003). 'Wage inequality since 1975', in R. Dickens, P. Gregg, and J. Wadsworth (eds), *The Labour Market under New Labour*. Basingstoke: Palgrave Macmillan, 191–200.

Macmillan, J. (1999). 'Employment tribunals: philosophies and practicalities'. *Industrial Law Journal*, 28/1: 33–56.

Mahnkopf, B. and Altvater, E. (1995). 'Transmission belts of transnational competition? Trade unions and collective bargaining in the context of European integration'. *European Journal of Industrial Relations*, 1/1: 101–17.

Mandelson, P. and Liddle, R. (1996). *The Blair Revolution: Can New Labour Deliver?* London: Faber & Faber.

Mankelow, R. (2002). 'The organisational costs of job insecurity and work intensification', in B. Burchell, D. Ladipo, and F. Wilkinson (eds), *Job Insecurity and Work Intensification*. London: Routledge, 137–53.

Marchington, M. (1989). 'Joint consultation in practice', in K. Sisson (ed.), *Personnel Management*. Oxford: Basil Blackwell, 378–402.

Marchington, M. (1994). 'The dynamics of joint consultation', in K. Sisson (ed.), *Personnel Management* (2nd edn). Oxford: Blackwell, 662–93.

Marchington, M. (2001). 'Employee involvement at work', in J. Storey (ed.), *Human Resource Management: A Critical Text* (2nd edn). London: Thomson Learning, 232–52.

Marchington, M. and Harrison, E. (1991). 'Customers, competitors and choice: employee relations in food retailing'. *Industrial Relations Journal*, 22/4: 286–99.

Marchington, M. and Parker, P. (1990). *Changing Patterns of Employee Relations*. Hemel Hempstead: Harvester Wheatsheaf.

Marchington, M. and Wilkinson, A. (2000). 'Direct participation', in S. Bach and K. Sisson (eds), *Personnel Management* (3rd edn). Oxford: Blackwell, 340–64.

Marchington, M., Goodman, J., Wilkinson, A., and Ackers, P. (1992). *New Developments in Employee Involvement*. Research Series No. 2. Sheffield: Employment Department.

Marginson, P. (2000). 'The Eurocompany and Euro industrial relations'. *European Journal of Industrial Relations*, 6/1: 9–34.

Marginson, P. and Sisson, K. (1994). 'The structure of transnational capital in Europe: the emerging Euro-company and its implications for industrial relations', in R. Hyman and A. Ferner (eds), *New Frontiers in European Industrial Relations*. Oxford: Blackwell, 15–51.

Marginson, P. and Sisson, K. (1996). 'Multinational companies and the future of collective bargaining: a review of the research issues'. *European Journal of Industrial Relations*, 2/2: 173–97.

Marginson, P. and Sisson, K. (2001). *The Impact of Economic and Monetary Union on Industrial Relations: A Comparative Sector and Company Perspective*. Warwick Papers in Industrial Relations No. 66, University of Warwick.

Marginson, P. and Sisson, K. (2002). 'European dimensions to collective bargaining: new symmetries within an asymmetric process?' *Industrial Relations Journal*, 33/4: 332–50.

Marginson, P. and Sisson, K. (2004). *European Integration and Industrial Relations: Multi-Level Governance in the Making*. Basingstoke: Palgrave Macmillan.

Marginson, P., Armstrong, P., Edwards, P., and Purcell, J. (1995). 'Managing labour in the global corporation: a survey-based analysis of multinationals operating in the UK'. *International Journal of Human Resource Management*, 6/3: 702–19.

Marginson, P., Gilman, M., Jacobi, O., and Krieger, H. (1998). *Negotiating European Works Councils: an Analysis of Agreements under Article 13*. Luxembourg: Office of Official Publications of the European Community.

Marginson, P., Edwards, P., Martin, R., Purcell, J., and Sisson, K. (1988). *Beyond the Workplace: Managing Industrial Relations in the Multi-establishment Enterprise*. Oxford: Basil Blackwell.

Marks, A., Findlay, P., Hine, J., McKinlay, A., and Thompson, P. (1998). 'The politics of partnership? Innovation in employment relations in the Scottish spirits industry'. *British Journal of Industrial Relations*, 36/2: 209–26.

Marlow, S. (2002). 'Regulating labour management in small firms'. *Human Resource Management Journal*, 12/3: 25–43.

Mars, G. (1982). *Cheats at Work*. London: Allen and Unwin.

Mars, G. and Mitchell, P. (1976). *Room for Reform? A Case Study of Industrial Relations in the Hotel Industry*. Milton Keynes: Open University Press.

Marsden, D. (1999). *A Theory of Employment Systems*. Oxford: Oxford University Press.

Marsden, D. and French, S. (1998). *What a Performance: Performance Related Pay in the Public Services*. London School of Economics: Centre for Economic Performance.

Marsh, D. (1992). *The New Politics of British Trade Unionism*. Basingstoke: Macmillan.

Martin, A. and Ross, G. (1999). 'In the line of fire: the Europeanization of Labor representation', in A. Martin and G. Ross (eds), *The Brave New World of European Labor*. Oxford: Berghahn, 312–67.

Martin, G. and Beaumont, P. (1999). 'Co-ordination and control of human resource management in multinational firms: the case of Cashco'. *International Journal of Human Resource Management*, 10/1: 21–42.

Martin, R. (1985). 'Union democracy: an exploratory framework', in W. McCarthy (ed.), *Trade Unions* (2nd edn). Harmondsworth: Penguin, 222–42.

Martin, R. (1992). *Bargaining Power*. Oxford: Clarendon.

Martin, R., Fosh, P., Morris, H., Smith, P., and Undy, R. (1991). 'The decollectivisation of trade unions? Ballots and collective bargaining in the 1980s'. *Industrial Relations Journal*, 22/3: 197–208.

Martin, R., Smith, P., Fosh, P., Morris, H., and Undy, R. (1995). 'The legislative reform of union government 1979–94'. *Industrial Relations Journal*, 26/2: 146–55.

Martinez Lucio, M. and Stuart, M. (2002). 'Assessing the principles of partnership: workplace trade union representatives' attitudes and experiences'. *Employee Relations*, 24/3: 305–20.

Marx, K. (1996). *Capital. Volume I: The Collected Works of Karl Marx and Frederick Engels, Volume XXXV*. London: Lawrence and Wishart.

Maternity Alliance (2004). *Happy Anniversary? The Right to Request Flexible Work One Year On*. London: Maternity Alliance.

Mathieson, H. and Corby, S. (1999). 'Trade unions: the challenge of individualism', in S. Corby and G. White (eds), *Employee Relations in the Public Services: Themes and Issues*. London: Routledge, 199–223.

Meardi, G. (2002). 'The Trojan horse for the Americanization of Europe? Polish industrial relations towards the EU'. *European Journal of Industrial Relations*, 8/1: 77–99.

Mellish, M. and Collis-Squires, N. (1976). 'Legal and social norms in discipline and dismissal', *Industrial Law Journal*, 5/3: 164–77.

Metcalf, D. (1991). 'British unions: dissolution or resurgence?' *Oxford Review of Economic Policy*, 7/1: 18–32.

Metcalf, D. (1994). 'Transformation of British industrial relations? Institutions, conduct and outcomes 1980–1990', in R. Burell (ed.), *The UK Labour Market*. Cambridge: Cambridge University Press, 126–57.

Metcalf, D. (1999a). 'The British National Minimum Wage'. *British Journal of Industrial Relations*, 37/2: 171–201

Metcalf, D. (1999b). 'The Low Pay Commission and the National Minimum Wage'. *The Economic Journal*, 109/February: 46–66.

Middlemas, K. (1979). *Politics in Industrial Society*. London: Andre Deutsch.

Miliband, R. (1972). *Parliamentary Socialism*. London: Merlin.

Miliband, R. (1973). *The State in Capitalist Society*. London: Quartet.

Milkman, R. (ed.) (2000). *Organizing Immigrants: the Challenge for Unions in Contemporary California*. Ithaca, NY: Cornell University Press.

Miller, D. and Stirling, J. (1998). 'European Works Council training: an opportunity missed?' *European Journal of Industrial Relations*, 4/1: 35–56.

Miller, K. (1986). 'Trade union government and democracy', in P. Lewis (ed.), *Labour Law in Britain*. Oxford: Basil Blackwell, 275–303.

Milne, S. (2004). *The Enemy Within: Thatcher's Secret War against the Miners* (2nd edn). London: Verso.

Milner, S. (1993a). 'Dispute deterrence: evidence on final-offer arbitration', in D. Metcalf and S. Milner (eds), *New Perspectives on Industrial Disputes*. London: Routledge, 133–59.

Milner, S. (1993b). 'Overtime bans and strikes'. *Industrial Relations Journal*, 24/3: 201–10.

Millward, N. (1994). *The New Industrial Relations?* Poole: Policy Studies Institute.

Millward, N., Bryson, A., and Forth, J. (2000). *All Change at Work*. London: Routledge.

Millward, N. Stevens, D., Smart, N., and Hawes, W. (1992). *Workplace Industrial Relations in Transition*. Aldershot: Dartmouth.

Minkin, L. (1991). *The Contentious Alliance: Trade Unions and the Labour Party*. Edinburgh: Edinburgh University Press.

Modood, T., Berthoud, R., Lakey, J., Nazroo, J., Smith, P., Virdee, S., and Beishon, S. (1997). *Ethnic Minorities in Britain*. London: Policy Studies Institute.

Monger, J. (2004). 'Labour disputes in 2003'. *Labour Market Trends*, June: 235–47.

Moody, K. (1997). *Workers in a Lean World*. London: Verso.

Morgan, G. (1997). *Images of Organization* (2nd edn). London: Sage.

Morgan, P., Allinton, N., and Heery, E. (2000). 'Employment insecurity in the public services', in E. Heery and J. Salmon (eds), *The Insecure Workforce*. London: Routledge, 78–111.

Morris, H. and Fosh, P. (2000). 'Measuring trade union democracy: the case of the UK Civil and Public Services Association'. *British Journal of Industrial Relations*, 38/1: 95–114.

Morris, M. (1976). *The General Strike*. Penguin: Harmondsworth.

Moss, B. (2001). 'The EC's free market agenda and the myth of social Europe', in W. Bonefeld (ed.), *The Politics of Europe: Monetary Union and Class*. Basingstoke: Palgrave Macmillan, 107–35.

Moule, C. (1998). 'Regulation of work in small firms: a view from the inside'. *Work, Employment and Society*, 12/4: 635–53.

Mueller, F. and Purcell, J. (1992). 'The Europeanization of manufacturing and the decentralization of bargaining: multinational management strategies in the European automobile industry'. *International Journal of Human Resource Management*, 3/1: 15–24.

Mukherjee, S. (1973). *Through No Fault of their Own: Systems for Handling Redundancies in Britain, France and Germany*. London: Political and Economic Planning.

Muller-Camen, M., Almond, P., Gunnigle, P., Quintanilla, J., and Tempel, A. (2001). 'Between home and host country: multinationals and employment relations in Europe'. *Industrial Relations Journal*, 32/5: 435–48.

Müller-Jentsch, W. (1995). 'Germany: from collective voice to co-management', in J. Rogers and W. Streeck (eds), *Works Councils: Consultation, Representation and Cooperation in Industrial Relations*. Chicago: University of Chicago Press, 53–78.

Mumford, K. (1996). 'Arbitration and ACAS in Britain: a historical perspective'. *British Journal of Industrial Relations*, 34/2: 287–305.

Munck, R. (1988). *The New International Labour Studies: an Introduction*. London: Zed Books.

Munro, A. (1999). *Women, Work and Trade Unions*. London: Mansell.

Munro, A. and Rainbird, H. (2000). 'The new unionism and the new bargaining agenda: UNISON–employer partnerships on workplace learning in Britain'. *British Journal of Industrial Relations*, 38/2: 223–40.

Neathy, F. and Arrowsmith, J. (2001). *The Implementation of the Working Time Regulations*. Employment Relations Research Series No. 11. London: Department of Trade and Industry.

New Unionism Project (1998). *Research Bulletin*. No. 2, April. Cardiff: Cardiff Business School.

Nichols, T. (1986). *The British Worker Question*. London: Routledge and Kegan Paul.

Nichols, T. (1997). *The Sociology of Industrial Injury*. London: Mansell.

Nichols, T. and Beynon, H. (1977). *Living with Capitalism*. London: Routledge and Kegan Paul.

Nolan, J. (2002). 'The intensification of everyday life', in B. Burchell, D. Ladipo and F. Wilkinson (eds), *Job Insecurity and Work Intensification*. London: Routledge, 112–36.

Nolan, P. and Slater, G. (2003). 'The labour market: history, structure and prospects', in P. Edwards (ed.), *Industrial Relations: Theory and Practice* (2nd edn). Oxford: Blackwell, 58–80.

Nolan, P. and Walsh, J. (1995). 'The structure of the economy and labour market', in P. Edwards (ed.), *Industrial Relations: Theory and Practice in Britain*. Oxford: Blackwell, 50–86.

Nolan, P. and Wood, S. (2003). 'Mapping the future of work'. *British Journal of Industrial Relations*, 41/2: 165–74.

Noon, M. and Blyton, P. (2002). *The Realities of Work* (2nd edn). Basingstoke: Palgrave Macmillan.

O'Brien, R. (2002). 'The varied paths to minimum global labour standards', in J. Harrod and R. O'Brien (eds), *Global Unions? Theory and Strategies of Organized Labour in a Global Political Economy*. London: Routledge, 221–34.

O'Connell Davidson, J. (1994). 'What do franchisors do? Control and Commercialisation in milk distribution'. *Work, Employment and Society*, 8/1: 23–44.

O'Donovan, K. and Szyszczak, E. (1988). *Equality and Sex Discrimination Law*. Oxford: Basil Blackwell.

Ogbonna, E. and Harris, L. (2002). 'Institutionalization of tipping as a source of managerial control'. *British Journal of Industrial Relations*, 40/4: 725–52.

Ogden, S. (1993). 'Decline and fall: national bargaining in British water'. *Industrial Relations Journal*, 24/1: 44–58.

Oliver, N. and Wilkinson, B. (1992). *The Japanization of British Industry* (2nd edn). Oxford: Blackwell.

Ortega, B. (1999). *In Sam We Trust*. London: Kogan Page.

Osler, D. (2002). *Labour Party PLC*. London: Mainstream Publishing.

Oxenbridge, S. (1997). 'Organizing strategies and organizing reform in New Zealand service sector unions'. *Labor Studies Journal*, 22/3: 3–27.

Oxenbridge, S. and Brown, W. (2002). 'The two faces of partnership? An assessment of partnership and co-operative employer/trade union relationships'. *Employee Relations*, 24/3: 262–7.

Oxenbridge, S. and Brown, W. (2004). 'A poisoned chalice? Trade union representatives in partnership and co-operative employer–union relationships', in G. Healy, E. Heery, P. Taylor and W. Brown (eds), *The Future of Worker Representation*. Basingstoke: Palgrave Macmillan, 187–206.

Oxenbridge, S., Brown, W., Deakin, S., and Pratten, C. (2003). 'Initial responses to the Employment Relations Act 1999'. *British Journal of Industrial Relations*, 41/2: 315–34.

Oxfam (2004a). *Made at Home*. Oxfam Briefing Paper 63. Oxford: Oxfam International.

Oxfam (2004b). *Trading Away Our Rights: Women Working in Global Supply Chains*. Oxford: Oxfam International.

Palmer, T., Grainger, H., and Fitzner, G. (2004). *Trade Union Membership 2003*. London: Department of Trade and Industry.

Parker, J. (2002). 'Women's groups in British unions'. *British Journal of Industrial Relations*, 40/1: 23–48.

Perlmutter, H. (1969). 'The tortuous evolution of the multinational corporation'. *Colombia Journal of World Business*, January–February: 9–18.

Phizacklea, A. and Miles, R. (1980). *Labour and Racism*. London: Routledge and Kegan Paul.

Pierson, C. (1996). *The Modern State*. London: Routledge.

Piore, M. and Sabel, C. (1984). *The Second Industrial Divide*. New York: Basic Books.

Polanyi, K. (1957). *The Great Transformation*. Boston: Beacon Press.

Pollard, S. (1968). *The Genesis of Modern Management*. Harmondsworth: Penguin.

Pollard, S. (1992). *The Development of the British Economy 1914–1990* (4th edn). London: Edward Arnold.

Pollert, A. (1988a). 'The flexible firm: fixation or fact?' *Work, Employment and Society*, 2/3: 281–316.

Pollert, A. (1988b). 'Dismantling flexibility'. *Capital and Class*, 34: 42–75.

Poole, M. (1986). *Towards a New Industrial Democracy: Workers' Participation in Industry*. London: Routledge and Kegan Paul.

Poole, M. and Mansfield, R. (1993). 'Patterns of continuity and change in managerial attitudes and behaviour in industrial relations, 1980–1990'. *British Journal of Industrial Relations*, 31/1: 11–35.

Poynter, G. (2000). *Restructuring in the Service Industries: Management Reform and Workplace Relations in the UK Service Sector*. London: Mansell.

Price, L. and Price, R. (1994). 'Change and continuity in the status divide', in K. Sisson (ed.), *Personnel Management* (2nd edn). Oxford: Blackwell, 527–61.

Price, R. (1983). 'White-collar unions: growth, character and attitudes in the 1970s', in R. Hyman and R. Price (eds), *The New Working Class? White-Collar Workers and their Unions*. London: Macmillan, 147–83.

Price, R. (1986). *Labour in British Society*. London: Routledge.

Price, R. (1989). 'The decline and fall of the status divide?', in K. Sisson (ed.), *Personnel Management in Britain*. Oxford: Blackwell, 271–95.

Proctor, S., Rowlinson, M., McArdle, L., Hassard, J., and Forrester, P. (1994). 'Flexibility, politics and strategy: in defence of the model of the flexible firm'. *Work, Employment and Society*, 8/2: 221–42.

Purcell, J. (1991). 'The rediscovery of the management prerogative: the management of labour relations in the 1980s'. *Oxford Review of Economic Policy*, 7/1: 33–43.

Purcell, J. (2000). 'After collective bargaining? ACAS in the age of human resource management', in B. Towers and W. Brown (eds), *Employment Relations in Britain: 25 Years of the Advisory, Conciliation and Arbitration Service*. Oxford: Blackwell, 163–80.

Purcell, J. and Ahlstrand, B. (1994). *Human Resource Management in the Multi-Divisional Company*. Oxford: Oxford University Press.

Rainnie, A. (1989). *Industrial Relations in Small Firms*. London: Routledge.

Ram, M. (1994). *Managing to Survive*. Oxford: Blackwell.

Ram, M., Edwards, P., Gilman, M., and Arrowsmith, J. (2001). 'The dynamics of informality: employment relations in small firms and the effects of regulatory change'. *Work, Employment and Society*, 15/4: 845–61.

Ramsay, H. (1977). 'Cycles of control: worker participation in sociological and historical perspectives'. *Sociology*, 11/3: 481–506.

Ramsay, H. (1997). 'Fool's gold? European Works Councils and workplace democracy'. *Industrial Relations Journal*, 28/4: 314–22.

Ramsay, H., Scholarios, D., and Harley, B. (2000). 'Employees and high-performance work systems: testing inside the black box'. *British Journal of Industrial Relations*, 38/4: 501–31.

Rees, C. (1998). 'Empowerment through quality management: employee accounts from inside a bank, a hotel and two factories', in C. Mabey, D. Skinner and T. Clark (eds), *Experiencing HRM*. London: Sage, 33–53.

Rees, G. and Fielder, S. (1992). 'The services economy, subcontracting and the new employment relations: contract catering and cleaning'. *Work, Employment and Society*, 6/3: 347–68.

Rees, T. (1990). 'Gender, power and trade union democracy', in P. Fosh and E. Heery (eds), *Trade Unions and their Members*. Basingstoke: Macmillan, 177–205.

Rees, T. (1992). *Women and the Labour Market*. London: Routledge.

Rees, T. (1998). *Mainstreaming Equality in the European Union*. London: Routledge.

Regini, M. (2000). 'Between deregulation and social pacts: the responses of European economies to globalization'. *Politics and Society*, 28/1: 5–33.

Richards, W. (2001). 'Evaluating equal opportunities initiatives: the case for a "transformative" agenda', in M. Noon and E. Ogbonna (eds), *Equality, Diversity and*

Disadvantage in Employment. Basingstoke: Palgrave Macmillan, 15–31.

Rigby, M. and Marco Aledo, M. (2001). 'The worst record in Europe? A comparative analysis of industrial conflict in Spain'. *European Journal of Industrial Relations*, 7/3: 287–305.

Robinson, P. (1999). 'Exploring the relationship between flexible employment and labour market regulation', in A. Felstead and N. Jewson (eds), *Global Trends in Flexible Labour*. Basingstoke: Macmillan, 84–99.

Robinson, P. (2000). 'Insecurity and the flexible workforce: measuring the illdefined', in E. Heery and J. Salmon (eds), *The Insecure Workforce*. London: Routledge, 25–38.

Robson, P., Dex, S., Wilkinson, F., and Salido Cortes, O. (1999). 'Low pay, labour market institutions, gender and part-time work: cross-national comparisons'. *European Journal of Industrial Relations*, 5/2: 187–207.

Rogers, J. and Streeck, W. (eds) (1995). *Works Councils: Consultation, Representation and Cooperation in Industrial Relations*. Chicago: University of Chicago Press.

Rollinson, D., Handley, J., Hook, C., and Foot, M. (1997). 'The disciplinary experience and its effects on behaviour'. *Work, Employment and Society*, 11/2: 281–311.

Roper, I., Cunningham, I., and James, P. (2003). 'Promoting family-friendly policies: is the basis of the government's ethical standpoint viable?' *Personnel Review*, 32/2: 211–30.

Rosenthal, P., Hill, S., and Peccei, R. (1997). 'Checking out service: evaluating excellence, HRM and TQM in retailing'. *Work, Employment and Society*, 11/3: 481–503.

Ross, R. and Schneider, R. (1992). *From Equality to Diversity*. London: Pitman.

Roy, D. (1952). 'Quota restriction and goldbricking in a machine shop'. *American Journal of Sociology*, 5/5: 427–42.

Royal Commission (1968). *Report of the Royal Commission on Trade Unions and Employers' Associations*. London: HMSO.

Royle, T. (2000). *Working for McDonalds in Europe: the Unequal Struggle?* London: Routledge.

Royle, T. and Towers, B. (eds) (2002). *Labour Relations in the Global Fast-Food Industry*. London: Routledge.

Rubery, J. and Edwards, P. (2003). 'Low pay and the National Minimum Wage', in P. Edwards (ed.), *Industrial Relations: Theory and Practice* (2nd edn). Oxford: Blackwell, 447–69.

Rubery, J. and Grimshaw, D. (2003). *The Organization of Employment: an International Perspective*. Basingstoke: Palgrave Macmillan.

Russell, A. (1992). *Harmonisation of Employment Conditions in Britain: Some Causes and Consequences*. Aberystwyth Economics Research Papers, 92–08, Aberystwyth, University College of Wales: Department of Economics and Agricultural Economics.

Rutherford, S. (1999). 'Equal opportunities policies – making a difference'. *Women in Management Review*, 14/6: 212–19.

Samuel, R. (1977). 'The workshop of the world'. *History Workshop Journal*, 3: 6–72.

Sawyer, T., Borkett, I., and Underhill, N. (2001). *Independent Review of Industrial Relations within Royal Mail*, http://www.postcomm.gov.uk/documents/back ground/sawyer.pdf.

Scase, R. (1995). 'Employment relations in small firms', in P. Edwards (ed.), *Industrial Relations: Theory and Practice in Britain*. Oxford: Blackwell, 569–95.

Scase, R. (2003). 'Employment relations in small firms', in P. Edwards (ed.), *Industrial Relations: Theory and Practice* (2nd edn). Oxford: Blackwell, 489–512.

Schlosser, E. (2002). *Fast Food Nation*. London: Penguin.

Scholarios, D. and Marks, A. (2004). 'Work–life balance and the software worker', *Human Resource Management Journal*, 14/2: 54–74.

Scott, A. (1994). *Willing Slaves? British Workers under Human Resource Management*. Cambridge: Cambridge University Press.

Scott, P. and Foster, D. (2003). 'Meeting the challenge?', in D. Foster and P. Scott (eds), *Trade Unions in Europe: Meeting the Challenge*. Brussels: Peter Lang, 11–31.

Scott, W., Mumford, E., McGivering, I. and Kirkby, J. (1963). *Coal and Conflict*. Liverpool: Liverpool University Press.

Seifert, R. (1984). 'Some aspects of factional opposition: rank and file and the National Union of Teachers 1967–1982'. *British Journal of Industrial Relations*, 22/4: 372–90.

Sennett, R. (1998). *The Corrosion of Character*. London: W.W. Norton.

Shackleton, J. (2002). *Employment Tribunals: their Growth and the Case for Radical Reform*. Hobart Paper No. 145. London: Institute of Economic Affairs.

Shorter, E. and Tilly, C. (1974). *Strikes in France*. Cambridge: Cambridge University Press.

Silver, B. (2003). *Forces of Labor: Workers' Movements and Globalization since 1870*. Cambridge: Cambridge University Press.

Simms, M. (2003). 'Union organizing in a not-for-profit organization', in G. Gall (ed.), *Union Organizing: Campaigning for Union Recognition*. London: Routledge, 97–113.

Simpson, B. (1999). 'A milestone in the legal regulation of pay: the National Minimum Wage Act 1998'. *Industrial Law Journal*, 28/1: 1–32.

Sisson, K. (1983). 'Employers' organisations', in G. Bain (ed.), *Industrial Relations in Britain*. Oxford: Basil Blackwell, 121–34.

Sisson, K. (1987). *The Management of Collective Bargaining*. Oxford: Basil Blackwell.

Sisson, K. (1993). 'In search of HRM'. *British Journal of Industrial Relations*, 31/2: 201–10.

Sisson, K. (1995). 'Human resource management and the personnel function', in J. Storey (ed.), *Human Resource Management: a Critical Text*. London: Routledge, 87–109.

Sisson, K. and Brown, W. (1983). 'Industrial relations in the private sector: Donovan re-visited', in G. Bain (ed.), *Industrial Relations in Britain*. Oxford: Basil Blackwell, 137–54.

Sisson, K. and Marginson, P. (2003). 'Management: systems, structures and strategy', in P. Edwards (ed.), *Industrial Relations: Theory and Practice* (2nd edn). Oxford: Blackwell, 157–88.

Sisson, K. and Storey, J. (2000). *The Realities of Human Resource Management*. Buckingham: Open University Press.

Smith, C. (1989). 'Flexible specialisation, automation and mass production'. *Work, Employment and Society*, 3/2: 203–20.

Smith, C., Child, J., and Rowlinson, M. (1990). *Reshaping Work: the Cadbury Experience*. Cambridge: Cambridge University Press.

Smith, P. (2001). *Unionization and Union Leadership: the Road Haulage Industry*. London: Continuum.

Smith, P. and Morton, G. (1993). 'Union exclusion and the decollectivisation of industrial relations in contemporary Britain'. *British Journal of Industrial Relations*, 31/1: 97–114.

Smith, P. and Morton, G. (1994). 'Union exclusion – next steps'. *Industrial Relations Journal*, 25/1: 3–14.

Smith, P. and Morton, G. (2001). 'New Labour's reform of Britain's employment law: the devil is not only in the detail but in the values and policy too'. *British Journal of Industrial Relations*, 39/1: 119–38.

Smith, R. (1999). 'The convergence/divergence debate in comparative industrial relations', in M. Rigby, R. Smith and T. Lawlor (eds), *European Trade Unions: Change and Response*. London: Routledge, 1–17.

Snape, E. (1994). 'Reversing the decline? The TGWU's Link Up campaign'. *Industrial Relations Journal*, 25/3: 222–33.

Snape, E. and Redman, T. (2003). 'Too old or too young? The impact of perceived age discrimination'. *Human Resource Management Journal*, 13/1: 78–89.

Stanworth, C. and Stanworth, J. (1995). 'The self-employed without employees – autonomous or atypical?' *Industrial Relations Journal*, 26/3: 221–9.

Stiglitz, J. (2002). *Globalization and its Discontents*. London: Allen Lane.

Storey, J. (1983). *Managerial Prerogative and the Question of Control*. London: Routledge and Kegan Paul.

Storey, J. (1985). 'The means of management control'. *Sociology*, 19/2: 193–211.

Storey, J. (1992). *Developments in the Management of Human Resources*. Oxford: Blackwell.

Strange, S. (1996). *The Retreat of the State: the Diffusion of Power in the World Economy*. Cambridge: Cambridge University Press.

Streeck, W. (1997). 'Industrial citizenship under regime competition: the case of the European Works Councils'. *Journal of European Public Policy*, 4/4: 643–64.

Strinati, D. (1982). *Capitalism, the State and Industrial Relations*. London: Croom Helm.

Suff, R. and Williams, S. (2004). 'The myth of mutuality? Employee perceptions of partnership at Borg Warner'. *Employee Relations*, 26/1: 30–43.

Tailby, S. and Winchester, D. (2000). 'Management and trade unions: towards social partnership?', in S. Bach and K. Sisson (eds), *Personnel Management* (3rd edn). Oxford: Blackwell, 365–88.

Taylor, B., Chang Kai, and Li Qi (2003). *Industrial Relations in China*. Cheltenham: Edward Elgar.

Taylor, L. and Walton, P. (1971). 'Industrial sabotage: motives and meanings', in S. Cohen (ed.), *Images of Deviance*. Harmondsworth: Penguin, 219–45.

Taylor, P. and Bain, P. (2003). 'Call center organizing in adversity: from Excell to Vertex', in G. Gall (ed.), *Union Organizing: Campaigning for Union Recognition*. London: Routledge, 153–72.

Taylor, P. and Ramsay, H. (1998). 'Unions, partnership and HRM: sleeping with the enemy?' *International Journal of Employment Studies*, 6/1: 115–43.

Taylor, P. and Walker, A. (1998). 'Policies and practices towards older workers: a framework for comparative research'. *Human Resource Management Journal*, 8/3: 61–76.

Taylor, P., Baldry, C., Bain, P., and Ellis, V. (2003). ' "A unique working environment": health, sickness and absence in UK call centres'. *Work, Employment and Society*, 17/3: 435–58.

Taylor, R. (1993). *The Trade Union Question in British Politics*. Oxford: Blackwell.

Taylor, R. (1998). 'Annual review article 1997'. *British Journal of Industrial Relations*, 36/2: 293–311.

Taylor, R. (no date). *The Future of Work–Life Balance*. Swindon: Economic and Social Research Council.

Taylor, S. (1998). 'Emotional labour and the new workplace', in P. Thompson and C. Warhurst (eds), *Workplaces of the Future*. Basingstoke: Macmillan, 84–103.

Teague, P. (1989). *The European Community: the Social Dimension*. London: Kogan Page.

Teague, P. (1998). 'Monetary union and social Europe'. *Journal of European Social Policy*, 8/2: 117–37.

Teague, P. (1999). *Economic Citizenship in the European Union*. London: Routledge.

Teague, P. (2000). 'Macroeconomic constraints, social learning and pay bargaining in Europe'. *British Journal of Industrial Relations*, 38/3: 429–52.

Teague, P. (2001). 'Deliberative governance and EU social policy'. *European Journal of Industrial Relations*, 7/1: 7–26.

Teague, P. (2003). 'Labour-standard setting and regional trading blocs: lesson drawing from the NAFTA experience'. *Employee Relations*, 25/5: 428–52.

Terry, M. (1983). 'Shop steward development and managerial strategies', in G. Bain, (ed.), *Industrial Relations in Britain*. Oxford: Basil Blackwell, 67–91.

Terry, M. (1996). 'Negotiating the government of UNISON: union democracy in theory and practice'. *British Journal of Industrial Relations*, 34/1: 87–110.

Terry, M. (1999). 'Systems of collective representation in non-union firms in the UK'. *Industrial Relations Journal*, 30/1: 16–30.

Terry, M. (2003). 'Employee representation: shop stewards and the new legal framework', in P. Edwards (ed.), *Industrial Relations: Theory and Practice* (2nd edn). Oxford: Blackwell, 257–84.

Terry, M. (2004). ' "Partnership": a serious strategy for the UK trade unions?', in A. Verma and T. Kochan (eds), *Unions in the 21st Century: an International Perspective*. Basingstoke: Palgrave Macmillan, 205–19.

Thompson, E. (1967). 'Time, work-discipline and industrial capitalism'. *Past and Present*, 38: 56–97.

Thompson, P. and Warhurst, C. (1998). 'Hands, hearts and minds: changing work and workers at the end of the century', in P. Thompson and C. Warhurst (eds), *Workplaces of the Future*. Basingstoke: Macmillan, 1–24.

Thornley, C. (1998). 'Contesting local pay: the decentralisation of collective bargaining in the NHS'. *British Journal of Industrial Relations*, 36/3: 413–34.

Thorpe, A. (1999). 'The Labour party and the trade unions', in J. McIlroy, N. Fishman and A. Campbell (eds), *British Trade Unionism and Industrial Politics. Volume 2: The High Tide of Trade Unionism, 1964–79*. Aldershot: Ashgate, 133–50.

Tolliday, S. and Zeitlin, J. (eds) (1991). *The Power to Manage? Employers and Industrial Relations in Comparative-Historical Perspective*. London: Routledge.

Torrington, D. (1991). *Management Face to Face*. Hemel Hempstead: Prentice Hall.

Towers, B. (1997). *The Representation Gap: Change and Reform in the British and American Workplace*. Oxford: Oxford University Press.

Towers, B. and Brown, W. (eds) (2000). *Employment Relations in Britain: 25 Years of the Advisory, Conciliation and Arbitration Service*, Oxford: Blackwell.

Trades Union Congress (TUC) (1995). *Your Voice at Work*. London: TUC.

Trades Union Congress (TUC) (1997). *General Council Report*. London: TUC.

Trades Union Congress (TUC) (2003a). *Migrant Workers: Overworked, Underpaid and Over Here*. London: TUC.

Trades Union Congress (TUC) (2003b). *Trade Union Trends: Recognition Survey*. London: TUC.

Trades Union Congress (TUC) (2004). *Trade Union Trends: Recognition Survey*. London: TUC.

Truss, C. (2001). 'Complexities and controversies in linking HRM with organizational outcomes'. *Journal of Management Studies*, 38/8: 1121–49.

Tsogas, G. (1999). 'Labour standards in international trade agreements: a critical assessment of the arguments'. *International Journal of Human Resource Management*, 10/2: 351–75.

Tsogas, G. (2000). 'Labour standards and the generalized system of preferences of the European Union and the United States'. *European Journal of Industrial Relations*, 6/3: 349–70.

Tsogas, G. (2001). *Labor Regulation in a Global Economy*. New York: M.E. Sharpe.

Turnbull, P. (1988). 'Leaner and possibly fitter: the management of redundancy in Britain'. *Industrial Relations Journal*, 19/3: 201–13.

Turnbull, P. and Sapsford, D. (1992). 'A sea of discontent: the tides of organised and "unorganised" conflict on the docks'. *Sociology*, 26/2: 291–309.

Turnbull, P. and Wass, V. (1994). 'The greatest game no more – redundant dockers and the demise of "dock work" '. *Work, Employment and Society*, 8/4: 487–506.

Turnbull, P. and Wass, V. (1997). 'Job insecurity and labour market lemons: the (mis)management of redundancy in steel making, coal mining and port transport'. *Journal of Management Studies*, 34/1: 27–51.

Turnbull, P. and Wass, V. (1998). ' "Marksist" management: sophisticated human relations in a high street retail store'. *Industrial Relations Journal*, 29/2: 98–111.

Turnbull, P. and Wass, V. (2000). 'Redundancy and the paradox of job insecurity', in E. Heery and J. Salmon (eds), *The Insecure Workforce*. London: Routledge, 57–77.

Turner, H. (1962). *Trade Union Growth, Structure and Policy: a Comparative Study of the Cotton Unions*. London: George Allen and Unwin.

Turner, H., Clack, G., and Roberts, G. (1967). *Labour Relations in the Motor Industry*. London: George Allen and Unwin.

Tüselmann, H.-J. and Heise, A. (2000). 'The German model of industrial relations at the crossroads: past, present and future'. *Industrial Relations Journal*, 31/3: 162–76.

Tüselmann, H.-J., McDonald, F., and Heise, A. (2003). 'Employee relations in German multinationals in an Anglo-Saxon setting: toward a Germanic version of the Anglo-Saxon approach?' *European Journal of Industrial Relations*, 9/3: 327–49.

Undy, R. (1999). 'Annual review article: New Labour's industrial relations settlement: the third way?' *British Journal of Industrial Relations*, 37/2: 315–36.

Undy, R. and Martin, R. (1984). *Ballots and Trade Union Democracy*. Oxford: Basil Blackwell.

Undy, R., Kessler, I., and Thompson, M. (2002). 'The impact of the National Minimum Wage on the apparel industry'. *Industrial Relations Journal*, 33/4: 351–64.

Undy, R., Ellis, V., McCarthy, W., and Halmos, A. (1981). *Change in Trade Unions*. London: Hutchinson.

Undy, R., Fosh, P., Morris, H., Smith, P., and Martin, R. (1996). *Managing the Unions*. Oxford: Clarendon.

United Nations Conference on Trade and Development (UNCTAD) (1998). *World Investment Report*. Geneva: UNCTAD.

Upchurch, M. and Donnelly, E. (1992). 'Membership patterns in USDAW 1980–1990: survival as success?' *Industrial Relations Journal*, 23/1: 60–8.

van Roozendaal, G. (2002). *Trade Unions and Global Governance: the Debate on a Social Clause*. London: Continuum.

Vickers, L. (2003). 'The Employment Equality (Religion or Belief) Regulations 2003'. *Industrial Law Journal*, 32/3: 188–93.

Virdee, S. and Grint, K. (1994). 'Black self-organization in trade unions'. *Sociological Review*, 42/2: 202–26.

Wacjman, J. (2000). 'Feminism facing industrial relations in Britain', *British Journal of Industrial Relations*, 38/2: 183–201.

Waddington, J. (1992). 'Trade union membership in Britain 1980–1987: unemployment and restructuring'. *British Journal of Industrial Relations*, 30/2: 287–324.

Waddington, J. (2003a). 'Annual review article 2002: heightening tension in relations between trade unions and the Labour government in 2002'. *British Journal of Industrial Relations*, 41/2: 335–58.

Waddington, J. (2003b). 'Trade union organization', in P. Edwards (ed.), *Industrial Relations: Theory and Practice* (2nd edn). Oxford: Blackwell, 214–56.

Waddington, J. and Hoffman, R. (2003). 'Trade unions in Europe: reform, organisation and restructuring', in D. Foster and P. Scott (eds), *Trade Unions in Europe: Meeting the Challenge*. Brussels: Peter Lang, 33–63.

Waddington, J. and Whitston, C. (1995). 'Trade unions: growth, structure and policy', in P. Edwards (ed) *Industrial Relations: Theory and Practice in Britain*. Oxford: Blackwell, 151–202.

Waddington, J. and Whitston, C. (1997). 'Why do people join unions in a period of membership decline?' *British Journal of Industrial Relations*, 35/4: 515–46.

Walby, S. (1997). *Gender Transformations*. London: Routledge.

Waldinger, R., Erickson, C., Milkman, R., Mitchell, D., Valenzuela, A., Wong, K., and Zeitlin, M. (1998). 'Helots no more: a case study of the Justice for Janitors campaign in Los Angeles', in K. Bronfenbrenner, S. Friedman, R. Hurd, R. Oswald, and R. Seeber (eds), *Organizing to Win: New Research on Union Strategies*. Ithaca, NY: ILR Press, 102–19.

Walters, S. (2002). 'Female part-time workers' attitudes to trade unions in Britain'. *British Journal of Industrial Relations*, 40/1: 49–68.

Walton, R. (1985). 'From control to commitment in the workplace'. *Harvard Business Review*, 63/2: 77–84.

Walton, R. and McKersie, R. (1965). *A Behavioral Theory of Labor Negotiations*. New York: McGraw-Hill.

Ward, K., Grimshaw, D., Rubery, J., and Beynon, H. (2001). 'Dilemmas in the management of temporary work agency staff'. *Human Resource Management Journal*, 11/4: 3–21.

Wass, V. (1996). 'Who controls selection under "voluntary" redundancy? The case of the Redundant Mineworkers' Payments Scheme'. *British Journal of Industrial Relations*, 34/2: 249–65.

Waterman, P. (2001). *Globalization, Social Movements and the New Internationalisms*. London: Continuum.

Watson, D. (1988). *Managers of Discontent*. London: Routledge.

Webb, J. (1997). 'The politics of equal opportunity'. *Gender, Work and Organization*, 4/3: 159–69.

Webb, J. and Liff, S. (1988). 'Play the white man: the social construction of fairness and competition in equal opportunity policies'. *Sociological Review*, 36/3: 532–51.

Webb, S. and Webb, B. (1920a). *Industrial Democracy*. London: Longmans, Green and Co.

Webb, S. and Webb, B. (1920b). *The History of Trade Unionism* (revised edn). London: Longmans, Green and Co.

Wedderburn, D. and Craig, C. (1974). 'Relative deprivation in work', in D. Wedderburn (ed.), *Poverty, Inequality and Class Structure*. Cambridge: Cambridge University Press, 141–64.

Wedderburn, Lord (1986). *The Worker and the Law* (3rd edn). Penguin: Harmondsworth.

Wedderburn, Lord (1989). 'Freedom of association and philosophies of labour law'. *Industrial Law Journal*, 18: 1–38.

Wedderburn, Lord (1991). *Employment Rights in Britain and Europe*. London: Lawrence and Wishart.

Wedderburn, Lord (1992). 'Laws about strikes', in W. McCarthy (ed.), *Legal Intervention in Industrial Relations: Gains and Losses*. Oxford: Blackwell, 147–208.

Wedderburn, Lord (1995). *Labour Law and Freedom*. London: Lawrence and Wishart.

Wedderburn, Lord (2001). 'Underground labour injunctions'. *Industrial Law Journal*, 30/2: 206–14.

Weiss, L. (1997). 'Globalization and the myth of the powerless state'. *New Left Review*, 225: 3–27.

Weiss, M. (2002). 'The politics of the EU Charter of Fundamental Rights', in B. Hepple (ed.), *Social and Labour Rights in a Global Context: International and Comparative Perspectives*. Cambridge: Cambridge University Press, 73–94.

Welch, R. and Williams, S. (2004). 'Complying with the new employment relations laws? A survey of employers'. *Human Resources and Employment Review*, 2/2: 91–7.

White, G. (1996). 'Public sector pay bargaining: comparability, decentralisation and control'. *Public Administration*, 74/1: 89–111.

White, G. (1999). 'The remuneration of public servants: fair pay or New Pay?', in S. Corby and G. White (eds), *Employee Relations in the Public Services*. London: Routledge, 73–94.

White, G. (2000). 'The pay review body system: its development and impact'. *Historical Studies in Industrial Relations*, 9: 71–100.

White, M., Hill, S., McGovern, P., Mills, C., and Smeaton, D. (2003). ' "High-performance" management practices, working hours and work–life balance'. *British Journal of Industrial Relations*, 41/2: 175–95.

White, P. (1983). 'The management of redundancy'. *Industrial Relations Journal*, 14/1: 32–40.

Whyman, P. (2002). 'British trade unions and Economic and Monetary Union'. *Industrial Relations*, 41/3: 467–76.

Wichert, I. (2002). 'Job insecurity and work intensification: the effects on health and well-being', in B. Burchell, D. Ladipo, and F. Wilkinson (eds), *Job Insecurity and Work Intensification*. London: Routledge, 92–111.

Wigham, E. (1973). *The Power to Manage*. London: Macmillan.

Wilkinson, A., Godfrey, G., and Marchington, M. (1997). 'Bouquets, brickbats and blinkers: Total Quality Management and employee involvement in practice'. *Organization Studies*, 18/5: 799–819.

Wilkinson, A., Marchington, M., Goodman, J., and Ackers, P. (1992). 'Total Quality Management and employee involvement'. *Human Resource Management Journal*, 2/4: 1–20.

Wilkinson, A., Redman, T., Snap, E., and Marchington, M. (1997). *Managing with Total Quality Management*. Basingstoke: Macmillan.

Willey, B. (2003). *Employment Law in Context*. Harlow: Financial Times Prentice Hall.

Williams, S. (1997). 'The nature of some recent trade union modernization policies'. *British Journal of Industrial Relations*, 35/4: 495–514.

Williams, S. (2003). 'Conflict in the colleges: industrial relations in further education since incorporation'. *Journal of Further and Higher Education*, 27/3: 307–16.

Williams, S. (2004). 'Accounting for change in public sector industrial relations: the erosion of national bargaining in further education in England and Wales'. *Industrial Relations Journal*, 35/3: 233–48.

Williams, S., Adam-Smith, D., and Norris, G. (2004). 'Remuneration practices in the UK hospitality industry in the age of the National Minimum Wage'. *Service Industries Journal*, 24/1: 171–86.

Willman, P. (1989). 'The logic of "market share" trade unionism: is membership decline inevitable?' *Industrial Relations Journal*, 20/4: 260–70.

Willmott, H. (1993). 'Strength is ignorance; slavery is freedom: managing culture in modern organizations'. *Journal of Management Studies*, 30/4: 515–52.

Wills, J. (1999). 'European Works Councils in British firms'. *Human Resource Management Journal*, 9/1: 19–38.

Wills, J. (2000). 'Great Expectations: three years in the life of a European Works Council'. *European Journal of Industrial Relations*, 6/1: 85–107.

Wills, J. (2004a). 'Organising the low paid: East London's Living Wage Campaign as a vehicle for change', in G. Healy, E. Heery, P. Taylor, and W. Brown (eds), *The Future of Worker Representation*. Basingstoke: Palgrave Macmillan, 264–82.

Wills, J. (2004b). 'Trade unionism and partnership in practice: evidence from the Barclays–Unifi agreement'. *Industrial Relations Journal*, 35/4: 329–43.

Winchester, D. and Bach, S. (1995). 'The state: the public sector', in P. Edwards (ed.), *Industrial Relations: Theory and Practice in Britain*. Oxford: Blackwell, 304–34.

Winchester, D. and Bach, S. (1999). 'Britain: the transformation of public service employment relations', in S. Bach, L. Bordogna, G. Della Rocca, and D. Winchester (eds), *Public Service Employment Relations in Europe: Transformation, Modernisation or Inertia?* London: Routledge, 22–55.

Wolf, M. (2004). *Why Globalization Works*. New Haven, CT: Yale University Press.

Wood, A. (1994). *North–South Trade, Employment and Inequality: Changing Fortunes in a Skill-Driven World*. Oxford: Clarendon.

Wood, J. (1992). 'Dispute resolution – conciliation, mediation and arbitration', in W. McCarthy (ed.), *Legal Intervention in Industrial Relations: Gains and Losses*. Oxford: Blackwell, 241–73.

Wood, R. (1992). *Working in Hotels and Catering*. London: Routledge.

Wood, S. (1989). 'The transformation of work?', in S. Wood (ed.), *The Transformation of Work*. London: Unwin Hyman, 1–43.

Wood, S. (1995). 'The four pillars of HRM: are they connected?' *Human Resource Management Journal*, 5/5: 49–59.

Wood, S. and Albanese, M. (1995). 'Can we speak of a high commitment management on the shop floor?' *Journal of Management Studies*, 32/2: 215–47.

Wood, S. and de Menezes, L. (1998). 'High commitment management in the UK: evidence from the Workplace Industrial Relations Survey, and Employers' Manpower and Skills Practices Survey'. *Human Relations*, 51/4: 485–515.

Wood, S. and Goddard, J. (1999). 'The statutory union recognition procedure in the Employment Relations Bill: a comparative analysis'. *British Journal of Industrial Relations*, 37/2: 203–45.

Wood, S., Moore, S., and Ewing, K. (2003). 'The impact of the trade union recognition procedure under the Employment Relations Act 2000–02', in H. Gospel and S. Wood (eds), *Representing Workers*. London: Routledge, 119–43.

Wood, S., Moore, S., and Willman, P. (2002). 'Third time lucky for statutory union recognition in the UK?' *Industrial Relations Journal*, 33/3: 215–33.

Work Foundation (no date). *Lloyds TSB: Improving Work–Life Balance for Everyone*, http://www.employersforwork-lifebalance.org.uk/case_studies/lloyds.htm.

Worrall, L., Cooper, C., and Campbell, F. (2000). 'The new reality for UK managers: perpetual change and employment instability'. *Work, Employment and Society*, 14/4: 647–68.

Wray, D. (1996). 'Paternalism and its discontents'. *Work, Employment and Society*, 10/4: 701–15.

Wrench, J. (1986). *Unequal Comrades: Trade Unions, Equal Opportunity and Racism*. Policy Papers in Ethnic Relations No. 5. Centre for Research in Ethnic Relations, University of Warwick.

Wrench, J. (1987). 'Unequal comrades: trade unions, equal opportunity and racism', in R. Jenkins and J. Solomos (eds), *Racism and Equal Opportunities Policies in the 1980s*. Cambridge: Cambridge University Press, 160–86.

Wrench, J. and Virdee, S. (1996). 'Organising the unorganised: "race", poor work and trade unions', in P. Ackers, C. Smith, and P. Smith (eds), *The New Workplace and Trade Unionism*. London: Routledge, 240–78.

■ INDEX

ABB 72
Abbey Bank 66
Abrams, F. 224
absenteeism 227, 283–4
    rules concerning 247
    taking a harder line on 248, 249
abuses 73, 74, 79, 200
ACAS (Advisory, Conciliation and
    Arbitration Service) 245, 289,
    290–3, 294
accession states 100
accommodations 167
    ad hoc 171
    informal 166
    pragmatic 148
Ackers, P. 10, 11, 195
Adam-Smith, D. 224, 232
Adams, R. 153
Adidas 74
adoption 130
adversarialism 169, 191
AEEU (Amalgamated
    Engineering and Electrical
    Union) 104, 106, 111, 152
Aeroparts 184, 186
aerospace industry 252
Age Concern 118
ageism 118
agro-chemicals 284
Ahlstrand, B. 21, 23, 168, 169
aircraft manufacturers 72, 160, 282
airline industry 122, 152, 170, 258
    HRM and work intensification
    in 259
Albanese, M. 159
Albert, M. 67
Alcan 243
Alldays convenience stores 152
Allen, V. 108
Allied Domecq 194
Amazon 67, 152
Amicus 28, 104, 106, 111, 140, 152,
    192, 201
    see also MSFU
Anglo-Saxonization process 67–8
antagonism 9, 10, 286
anti-communism 78
anti-discrimination legislation
    127, 130

anti-globalization movement 271
anti-strike legislation 273, 274
anti-unionism 73, 87, 152, 154, 181
    infamous 153
    violent 74
APC&T (administrative,
    professional, clerical, and
    technical) staff 117
appraisals 125
    regular 159
    subjective 261
apprenticeships 25
arbitration 289, 292
    compulsory 291
    pendulum 290
Argentina 271
arrests 32, 85
Arrowsmith, J. 214, 215, 225, 227,
    229, 231
Asda 73, 153
Asian-owned firms 166
assembly-line work 27, 56
ASTMS (Association of
    Supervisory, Technical and
    Managerial Staff) 28
Atkinson, J. 60
'Aubry' laws (1998/2000) 230
Auerbach, S. 86
austerity measures 36, 96
Australia 198
    compulsory arbitration 291
    Congress of Trade Unions 200
authoritarianism 165, 166
    opportunity to relieve tensions
    associated with 284
autonomy 53, 54, 55, 56, 116, 240,
    284
    failure of initiative designed to
    give 243
    may foster exclusion 141
    political 103
    potential threat to 201
    responsible 170
    TQM and 241
    wage bargaining 35

B & Q 118
Bach, S. 215, 217, 218
backache 259

BAE Systems 252
Bailey, R. 217
Bain, G. 30
Bain, P. 260
Bairstow, S. 118, 139
Baker, Kathleen 153
balance of power 10
    capital and labour 60, 72, 271
    unequal 7
Baldry, C. 260
ballots 103, 109, 191, 274
    in-house, controversial 152
    postal 84, 111, 273
    secret 84, 273
banking sector 40, 52
bar workers 285
Barber, Brendan 295
Barclays Bank 190, 192, 193, 194
bargaining 39–40, 102
    centralized 97
    cross-border networks 100
    distributive 287
    equality 137–8
    industry-level 291
    integrative 287
    local 215, 217
    national 215, 216
    productivity 21
    shop-floor 27
    single-employer 40
    unregulated 21
    see also collective bargaining;
    multi-employer bargaining
bargaining power:
    enhanced 20
    growth of 38
    latent 288
    weakened 288
barriers 165, 292
    economic 63, 64, 94, 100
    language 189
    political 100
    women's progress 123
Bassett, P. 163
Batstone, E. 27
Bay of Cadiz 282
Bayliss, F. 219
Beaumont, P. 41, 68, 150
Belgium 96

Bell, Daniel 54
Bell, M. 131
Benefits Agency 215, 261
Benelux countries 91
'benevolent autocracy' 166
Berlusconi, Silvio 272
Bertelli, Ann 153
best practice 68, 240
Beynon, Huw 11, 30, 52, 53,
    57, 59, 60, 258, 259, 260,
    262, 284
Birmingham City Council 283
black workers 118, 136, 137,
    138, 140
Blair, Tony 91, 103, 104, 192, 222,
    232
Blue Book 21
Blyton, P. 38, 281, 282
BMW 70
boards of directors 42, 220
Body Shop 152, 184
Boeing 72, 282
Bolivia 271
Bolton Committee of Enquiry on
    Small Firms (1971) 165
bonuses:
    failure to be awarded 211
    generous 220
Boraston, I. 27
Borders 152
Borg Warner 193
Boston, S. 135
Bourneville 22, 148
Boxall, P. 240
Boyd, C. 259
Bradley, H. 62, 117, 118, 119, 122,
    140, 256, 261
Brandt, Willy 92
Branine, M. 118
Brannen, P. 43
Brazil 72, 79
breach of discipline 246
breaking of machinery 282
Bridgford, J. 93
British Airways 118, 259
    mass absenteeism 284
British Involvement and
    Participation Association
    191
Broderick, J. 281
Brown, D. 164
Brown, W. 37, 40, 151, 194, 222,
    289
'brute facts of power' 4
Bryson, A. 185
BSkyB 152

BT (British Telecom) 66, 133, 212
Buchan, Will 196, 197
budget deficits 96, 272
building industry 38
bullying procedures 293
Burchell, B. 252, 261
Burchill, F. 217
Burnham committee (1919) 39,
    217
'burn-out' 284
bus operations 188
business closures 252

cabin crew 170, 259
CAC (Central Arbitration
    Committee) 151
Cadbury's confectionery
    plant 22, 148
call centres 56, 200, 260,
    262, 278
    intense and relentless pace of
        work 284
    jobs threatened by transfer of
        operations 66
    turnover rate 284
Cambodia 71, 74, 77
campaigns 74, 76, 77, 78
    'in-your-face' 199
    'winnable' issues 200
    working time 227
Canada 64, 78
capital 10
    demands of 32
    enhanced mobility of 62
    industrial 71
    labour and 30, 31, 52, 60, 72,
        271
    owners of 10
capitalism 31
    accommodating 102
    development of 3, 33
    differences in way organized
        across countries 67
    exploitative conditions of wage
        labour under 24
    feature of development of 62
    flexible 255
    long-term viability of 31, 36
    nature of the market economy
        172
    neo-liberal 255, 256
    transformation in the
        organization of 55
    understanding role of the state
        under 31
car boot sales 281

car manufacturers 69, 150
    see also BMW; Ford; General
        Motors; Honda; Nissan;
        Rolls-Royce
car parts 275
care workers 255
Caribbean 118, 136
Carley, M. 188
cash compensation 251
cash registers 68
casualized jobs 89
catering staff 277
Cavite free-trade zone 73–4
CBI (Confederation of British
    Industry) 92, 130, 233
CEEP (European Centre of
    Enterprises with Public
    Participation and of
    Enterprises of General
    Economic Interest) 92
CEF (College Employers' Forum)
    216
Central America 199
    see Guatemala; Honduras;
        Mexico
Central Restaurant Group 171
chalet attendants 224–5
Chamberlain, N. 37
Chang Kai 272
Charles, N. 136
Charter of the Fundamental
    Rights of the European Union
    (2000) 95
cheap labour 66, 136
    cost savings generated by 65, 71,
        79, 80, 93
    migrant workers 62
    need for, on a massive scale 272
    popular locations for 71
chemicals industry 149
Chibebe, Wellington 32
Chichester 70
child labour 74, 77
    abolition of 75, 76
childcare 138, 139, 285
China 66
    economic reforms designed to
        create capitalist market
        economy 272
    extremely low labour costs 71
    migrant workers 62
    production of female sanitary
        products 72
    suppression of independent
        trade unionism 32
    tiny wages 73

chocolate works 164, 239–40, 245
CIPD (Chartered Institute of
Personnel and Development)
283
Citibank 239
city academies 218
Civil Service 215, 256, 261
Clack, G. 227
Clark, J. 241
class:
diminution as a source of social
identity 180
getting rid of old legacies 192
class consciousness 10, 28
class rule 31
Claydon, T. 149
cleaning staff 277
Clegg, H. 6, 8, 41, 162, 164
Clinton, Bill 77, 78
closed shop:
influential factor contributing to
decline of 22
'post-entry' 22
prohibited 84
undermining of 86
clothing industry 135, 166, 221,
284
coal mining industry 25, 26, 85,
253, 279
decline of 52
strike activity 270
Coca-Cola 64
Cockburn, C. 124, 127, 137
cocklepickers 62
codes of conduct 74, 76, 77
codes of practice 220
codetermination 183
coercion:
consent and 31, 171
crude 166
coercive approach 34, 160
coercive comparisons 68, 70
coercive power 86
Cohen, R. 71
Cold War divisions 78
Colgan, F. 140, 141
collective agreements 7, 19, 221,
289
industry-level 183
path-breaking 21
collective bargaining 40–1, 87, 94,
229
appropriate topics for 138
awards and 291
centralized systems of 64, 90,
220, 221

contraction/diminution of
208–11, 214, 219, 220
decision to facilitate greater
coordination of 99
declined 10
distinction between
consultation and 43
dwindling extent of 11
embraced 18
employment regulations
governing 65
employment rights more
effectively secured
through 35
encouraging the extension
of 290
European-level, genuine 100
evolution and development
of 38–9
first major studies of 8
formal separation from
participation rights 183
'free' 33, 34
functions and evolution of 17
goals secured by 9–10
greater onus on 25
hostility towards 153
important feature of the process
287
industry-by-industry 221
managerial prerogative and 33
multi-employer level 183
national machinery 157
nature of 37–8
operated to detriment of women
and black workers 137
outcome of 7
priorities 135
public sector 39, 215
reform of 290
right to 75, 76, 95
special role accorded to 9
way of challenging 212
weak or decentralized 63
willingness to incorporate
equality demands within 137
collectivism:
eroded 180
way of undermining 214
collectivist approach 291
college lecturers 216, 259, 262,
280
Colling, T. 137, 164
collusion 233
Colombia 32
commercialization pressures 276

Commission for Equality and
Human Rights 129
commitment 155, 158, 172, 240,
243
absence of, among employers
99
enhancing 9, 238
high 69, 159, 160, 161, 173
improved 41
scepticism about genuineness
of 74
shared 191
work, performance and 9
common law 33
Common Market 91
'common rule' 25
communications 61, 238–40
good 193
improvements in 66
open, transparent and rigorous
system of 184
poor 164
communications industry 97
community networks 199
Community trade union 201
company councils 185, 186
compensation culture 294, 295
compensation payments 251, 275
competition 65, 261
destructive 19
foreign 225
global, pressures of 62
international 26
unfair 221
competitive advantage 56, 156,
238
key source of 170
quality as a source of 240
working time as a tool for 231
competitive pressures 51, 57, 60,
61, 65, 229, 231, 271
greater 258–9
increasing 209
intense 172, 259
more sustained, companies
exposed to 255
competitive tendering 256
competitiveness 75, 86
attempts to increase 256
challenged 26
damaged 34, 93
enhanced 63, 84, 88, 251, 259
improvements in 35, 90, 96, 259
maintaining 5
major constraint on 84
obstacles to 87

competitiveness (*cont.*):
  potential threat to 88
  source of 87, 89
  stimulating 63
  sustaining 88
compliance 212
  efforts to secure 170
  means of enforcing 241
compositional approach 180,
    181
compositional effect 208
compromise 290
  negotiated 287
compulsory redundancy 253,
    254
'compulsory unionism' 90
computer programmers 56
computerization 260
conciliation 289
  state-supported 290
  see also ACAS
conditions of employment 59, 127
  decisions that affect 41
  good, flexible workers who
    benefit from 56
  greater privileges in 116
  harmonization of 116
  significant worsening of 65
  terms and 6, 24, 25, 37, 38, 116,
    129, 132, 218, 253, 256
  union membership as 22
  worse in a new job 256
conflict 26, 267-98
  armed, desire to eliminate
    possibility of 92
  class 10
  contained 37, 38, 43
  ideological 109
  institutionalizing 37, 38
  joint regulation contains 10
  largely caused by external
    agitators 8
  major 109
  political 109
  potential for 5, 9, 56
  potential manifestation of 227
  reduced emphasis placed on 155
  rendered increasingly
    archaic 55
  unions characterized by 107
  unwarranted emphasis on 11
  see also industrial conflict
conflict avoidance 35
conflict of interest 110, 172
  absence of 9
conflict resolution 10, 39

Conley, H. 255
consent 31, 171, 173
  control and 243
conservatism 136
  constraints on activities that
    encourage 110
  political 102
Conservative party/government
    (UK) 34, 88, 89, 90, 93
  collective bargaining
    discouraged by 208, 215
  deregulationary public policy
    approach 128, 224
  dislike of multi-employer
    bargaining 210
  flexible working and 57
  hostile political environment
    under 104, 290
  neo-liberal policy approach
    favoured by 94
  opt-out from EU social chapter
    188
  policies that stimulated the role
    and authority of managers in
    the public sector 157
  pre-hearing reviews (1980s) 294
  public policy under 84-7
  self-employment supported by
    53
  self-regulation encouraged by
    220
  shaken by industrial action in
    NHS 216-17
  trade unions and 87, 102-3, 107,
    110-12, 149, 152, 156, 178, 181,
    185, 273, 274
  wages councils abolished by 221
construction industry 53
consultation:
  information and 184, 185, 191
  joint 43-5, 184
  redundancy 93, 254
consultation rights 183, 186-7
consumer goods 26
contracting out 261
contracts 273
  breach of 280
  employment relationship as
    ongoing series of 5
  fixed-term 58, 59, 98, 132
  flexible 216
  indeterminate 4
  notion of 3, 4
  one-sided 54
  open-ended 4
  short-term 53

standardization of 164
  temporary 255
control 4, 6, 20, 55
  bureaucratic 170
  collective 284
  consent and 243
  craft 24
  direct 170
  finance-based forms of 172
  financial 172
  freelance contractors 53
  managers need to exercise 170
  need to exercise 160, 173
  novel techniques in attempt to
    exercise 170
  self-employed workers 54
  sharing 10
  see also managerial control
convergence 63, 64, 68, 87
  growth of 99
  Maastricht criteria 96
  rendering the process sluggish
    100
cooperation 9, 56, 167, 170, 173
  active, expecting 241
  conflict and 5
  economic 91, 92
  trust and 192, 261
Corby, S. 289
core employees 58, 60
corporatism 35, 36, 96
corrective approach 248
'cost minimization' approach 169
cost savings 26, 64
  generated by cheap labour 65,
    71, 79, 80, 93
Costain 53
costs 53, 54
  cutting 172, 261
  legal 274
  means of taking out 259
  recouping 225
  severance payments 251
  sparing organization from 59
  reducing 60, 73, 259
  see also labour costs
cotton industry 24, 25, 26, 107
Council of Ministers (EU) 92,
    93, 187
country-of-origin effect 64,
    66-7, 68
courts 273
craft societies 38
craft-workers 24, 25
Cranfield School of
    Management 191

CRE (Commission for Racial
Equality) 127, 129, 130
creativity 241
crimes 32
Crouch, C. 84, 96
Crown Prosecution Service 130
Cully, M. 159, 167, 184, 229, 239,
249, 255, 258, 280
culture change 212
Cunningham, R. 123
currency 96
see also EMU; Euro
customary practices 7, 25, 225
customer complaints 242
customer enquiries 56
customer relations 282
customer service operations 66,
157, 260
better 118
degrading and debasing feature
of 171
sabotage behaviour 283
CWU (Communication Workers'
Union) 66, 109, 200
Czech Republic 64, 100

Danford, A. 192, 242, 252, 260,
274
D'Art, D. 212
Davies, P. 11, 36
Davis, E. 291
deaf people 200
decentralization 215
decision-making 6, 103
biased 124
collective 85
complexity and elitist bias of
100
devolution of 157, 215
EC/EU 93, 100
employee participation in 93
gender perspective should
inform 131
involvement in 238
management must share 9
nation-states 62
operational, devolution of 215
pressure to enhance shareholder
value dominated 68
strategic business 191
trade union 107, 108, 137, 138,
139, 140
worker influence over 240
also managerial decision-
making; organizational
decision-making

defence-related firms 253
de-industrialization 52
Delaney, L. 123
Delbridge, R. 239, 247
Delors, Jacques 93, 97
Delta Airlines 170
demand:
accommodating 44
aligning the workforce to meet
changes in 60
anticipated 57
emergence of less predictable
patterns of 55
fluctuations in 254
greater work effort 258
labour, decline in 72
major fluctuations in 259
rude customers 283
unpredictable 55
demand management 84, 89, 90
democracy, *see* union democracy
demonstrations 199, 272, 277
illegal 32
demotion 249
deregulated labour markets 57, 62,
65, 70, 86, 90, 105
desirability of 87
economic competitiveness
contingent upon 91
emphasis on the importance of
106
flexible 63, 88
necessary component of
competitive economy 112
neo-liberal capitalist preference
for 256
NMW policy a marked contrast
with policies 224
social dislocation created by 89
destruction 282
developing countries:
effect of MNCs on jobs and
employment relations 71
favourable trading rights 77
jobs affected in 73
MNC investment in 81
presence of trade unions
increases labour costs in 75
pressure on suppliers in 73
pressured to liberalize markets
63
relatively little economic benefit
from globalization 74
sweatshop conditions endured
by workers in 73
Dicken, P. 62

Dickens, L. 87, 88, 123, 128, 137,
138, 292
Dickens, R. 224
Dickson, T. 163
'dignity' 201
directives 92, 95, 98, 118
equal treatment/equality 128,
130
fixed-term work 132
information and consultation
rights 183, 186–7
obligation/need to comply with
93, 128, 188
parental leave 129, 131
part-time workers 129
working time 88, 94, 185, 227,
231
Disability Discrimination Act
(1995) 128
disabled people 118, 121, 128, 130
disadvantage 117–20, 126, 131,
133
gender 135
immigrant workers 199
part-time workers who
experience 130
race-based 136
readiness of individuals to
submit complaints 132
reducing 121
structural causes of 129
tools for challenging 122
disciplinary procedures 159, 167,
245, 246–7, 249
appropriate 244
mandatory 'minimum' 245
threat of action 260
discipline 7, 242, 244–50
'industrial' 102
tighter managerial control of
243
disclosure 220
discontent 213
simmering 278
underlying 276
discrimination 7, 276
age 118, 130, 223
direct 127
disability 118, 130
formal denunciations of 136
gender 164
indirect 127
lesbian and gay workers 118
potential claims 138
race 35, 118, 122
religious belief 130

discrimination (*cont.*):
sex 35, 93, 130, 295
tools for challenging 122
unfair 122
unlawful 127
workplace, elimination of 75
disguised employment 54
disguised redundancy 252
disinvestment 65
dismissal of employees 35, 247,
248, 252, 274
collective 250
consultation ought to
encompass ways of
avoiding 254
desire to make it easier for
employers 251
lawful 275
summary 245
see also unfair dismissal
disposable workforce 255
dispute resolution 287–95
interventions designed to
help 27
procedures for 19
see also industrial
action/disputes
disruption 8, 9, 20
mitigating 18
potential for 10, 150
distress 262
divergence 64
diversity 120, 231
managing 124–6
representing, in trade unions
139–42
division of labour:
narrow 27
sexual 135
see also NIDL
docks 25, 253, 284
domestic circumstances 53
'dominant paradigm' 10
donations 104
Donnelly, M. 253
Donovan, *see* Royal Commission
Doogan, K. 256
Douglas, Roger 90
downsizing 261
downward communications 239,
240
DRC (Disability Rights
Commission) 130
Druker, J. 209, 214
DTI (Department of Trade and
Industry) 133, 187

due process 247
Dundon, T. 167, 277
Dunleavy, P. 31, 36
dyestuffs 284
Dynamex Friction 275

earnings:
collective bargaining continues
to influence 208
inflationary increases in 20
irregularity of 59
supplementing 21
Earnshaw, J. 247
easyJet 259
EC (European Community) 93–4
ECA (Electrical Contractors'
Association) 209
ECB (European Central Bank) 96
ECJ (European Court of Justice)
92, 185, 232
economic boom 26
economic change 55
economic depression 39
'economic dominance' effect 66
economic growth 36
means of stimulating 63
tremendous 76
economic instability 35
economic integration 93
economic policy 34
economic stability 35
education 28, 216, 218, 258
changes to the delivery of 56
Edwards, P. 4, 32, 36, 68, 221,
223, 226, 244, 245, 246, 247,
248, 249, 254, 258, 284, 286
Edwards, T. 66, 67, 69
EEC (European Economic
Community) 91, 92
obligations of membership 128
obstacle to development of
social and employment
policy 93
EEF (Engineering Employers'
Federation) 19
efficiency savings 251, 259
effort 242
greater, means of extracting
260
incentive to reduce 21
judgements of 257
marked increase in intensity of
258
maximum 5
pressure to increase 259
productive 4, 257

EIFs (European Industry
Federations) 92
EIRO (European Industrial
Relations Observatory) 295
electrical contracting industry
209
electrical goods 26
electricity-generating plants 85
electronics assembly 201
electronics goods 72
email 55
Emergency Powers Act (1920) 34
Employee Councils 185, 186
see also EWCs
employee involvement 17
participation and 41–5, 238–44
Employers for Work-life Balance
Forum 133
employers' associations 183, 209,
216, 246
attempts to bargain with unions
by means of 20
decline of multi-employer
bargaining through 22
growth and development of 23
incorporating into state policy-
making processes 35
rationale for formation of 41
rise and fall of 18–19
Employment Act:
(1990) 22, 86
(2002) 88, 130, 131, 245, 246
employment agencies 59, 62, 252
employment conditions, *see*
conditions of employment
employment opportunities 71
employment protection 65
employment regulations:
national-level, MNC ability to
subvert 65
relaxation of 65
weaker 65
employment relations 51–82
conflict and 267–98
elements of 17–47
employment relationship and
3–5
experiencing 237–65
in a global economy 61–81
managing 147–75
politics of 83–114
social divisions and 115–44
stability and predictability in
209
state policy and 84–91
studies of 8–11

Employment Relations Act:
  New Zealand (1991) 90
  UK (1999) 87, 129, 150
employment relationship 3–7
  end of 52–4
  management of 37
employment rights:
  individual, more extensive
    system of 88
  interventions ostensibly
    designed to improve 89
  limited improvements in 105
  major expansion in scope of 87
  more effectively secured through
    collective bargaining 35
  most radical and far-reaching
    reform of 219
  regulations governing 65
  self-employed workers do not
    benefit from 54
  slight improvements in 78
  statutory 33
  undermined 73
Employment Service (UK) 213
employment tribunals 245, 249,
  275, 276, 292
empowerment 240, 241, 242–3
EMU (Economic and Monetary
  Union) 95–7
engine drivers 282
engineering industry 20, 25, 27,
  65, 92, 284
  light 26
  national agreement (1898) 38
  shop stewards 40
  multi-employer bargaining
    214–15
engineering unions 228
England 216, 275
  eastern 62
  north-east 26, 52, 178, 242
  south-east 26
  south-west 252
  see also Lancashire; Leeds;
    London; Manchester;
    Merseyside; Midlands;
    Nottinghamshire;
    Portsmouth; Southampton;
    Swindon; Yorkshire
entrepreneurs 33
EOC (Equal Opportunities
  Commission) 127, 129, 130
EPZs (export processing zones) 72,
  74, 75, 77, 79
  anti-union repression in 73
equal opportunities 120, 121–4

desirability of 127
indefensible neglect of 136
liberal 125
equal pay legislation 128
equality 91, 93, 118
  business benefits of 122
  employer-led initiatives 122–3
  gender 136
  initiatives 124
  mainstreaming 131
  managing 120–7
  public policy and legislation
    127–9
  race 130
  trade unions and 135–7
  voluntary initiatives to promote
    132
equality action 131, 132
equality bargaining 137–8
Erickson, C. 277
Esso 21, 172
ethnicity/ethnic minorities 118,
  137
  female workers 166
ethnocentric management style
  67
ETI (Ethical Trading Initiative) 76
ETUC (European Trade Union
  Confederation) 92, 98, 99
EU (European Union) 77
  employment legislation 30
  enlargement (2004) 100
  equality action 131
  gender perspective should
    inform all decision-making
    131
  impetus for reform generated by
    legislation 130
  implementation of legislation
    186–7
  influence on employment
    relations 91
  institutions 92
  legal regulation of working time
    231
  legislation and growth of non-
    union forms 185
  longest average working week in
    228
  pressure on Italy to reduce
    budget deficit 272
  social dimension 77, 78, 92, 93,
    94–5, 96, 97, 100
  wage inequality 219
  working time 229, 230
  see also directives; social chapter

EU Constitutional Treaty
  (2004) 95
Euro (single currency) 96
European Commission 92, 93, 94,
  95, 97, 98, 99, 231, 233
  action programmes to improve
    labour market position of
    women 131
  former president of 272
  social partners rely heavily on
    100
European Metalworkers'
  Federation 92
European Parliament 92, 233
Eurotunnel call centre 186
EWCs (European Works Councils)
  98, 100, 184, 188–90
Ewing, K. 274
executives 220
  under-representation of women
    119
expertise 22, 24
exploitation 10, 31
  migrant workers 62
  potential 24, 171
exports 71, 73
  eroded markets 26
  see also EPZs

factories 24, 26, 74
  food-processing 62, 243
  'world-market' 71
Fair Wages Resolutions (1891) 221
fake/mock customers 170
family responsibilities 122, 123,
  129, 131
family-friendly policies 88, 129,
  130, 131, 133
  improved access to
    arrangements 138
  working practices 195
fashion industry 76
fast-food industry 64, 65, 153, 189,
  285
fat-cat pay 220
fatigue 259
Fawley oil refinery 21, 23,
  149, 172
FBI (US Federal Bureau of
  Investigation) 282
FBU (Fire Brigades Union) 105,
  106, 276
FDI (foreign direct investment)
  61–2
  promoting greater levels of 74
federations of employers 18

feedback 159
  potential effects 70
Felstead, A. 54, 55
female translators 53, 54
feminism 137
Fenley, A. 244
Ferner, A. 64, 66, 67, 68, 69, 70, 96
fiddles 281–2, 285, 286
financial services 52, 56, 149, 252,
  259, 260
  global institutions 271
  markets 61
  short-termist system 67
Finland 188
First World War (1914–18) 43
  union growth during 25
FLA (US Fair Labor Association) 76
Flanders, A. 8, 10, 20, 21, 23, 36,
  37, 41, 101, 230, 231
flexibility 63, 116, 117, 156, 233
  encouraging and reinforcing
    155
  enhanced 64, 251
  greater, employers impelled to
    pursue 258–9
  labour 172
  management 218, 242
  pay 212
  removal of wages councils 221
flexible employment/working
  arrangements 58, 59, 131, 133
  patterns 52, 57
  rapid growth in extent of 60
  trend towards 180
'flexible firm' model 58, 60
flexible specialization 55–6
flirting 171
food industry 150
  manufacturing 201
  processing 26, 62
  production 55
  retail sector 40
footwear industry 38
Ford 67, 72
  Halewood 11, 254
Forde, C. 59
Fordism 55
foreign subsidiaries 64, 65–6, 69
  ability to secure compliance
    of 68
  MNC capacity to diffuse
    employment relations
    practices to 67
  vanguard practices in 70
formality 167
Forth, J. 185

forward diffusion 65–6, 67, 69
Fosh, P. 107
Foster, D. 261
Fox, A. 4, 8, 9, 41, 168, 171
France 67, 91, 96, 271
  statutory minimum wage 221
  working time 229, 230
franchise arrangements 54
Fraser, J. 53
fraternal arrangements 166
free markets 31, 90
'free production zones' 72
free trade 63
  promoting 74
  workers in poor countries
    benefit from prosperity
    generated by 73
  see also NAFTA
Freedland, M. 11, 36
freedom of association 75
  negated 274
freedom of contract 4
freelance contractors 52, 53–4
Frenkel, S. 27
Friction Dynamics 275
friendly benefits 25
fringe benefits 117
  reasonably generous 169
frontier of control 5
frozen food factory 243
frustration 286
Fryer, R. 251
full employment 20, 26, 27, 40, 89
  economic policy dominated by
    pursuit of 90
  explicit abandonment of 84
  principal goal of economic
    policy 34
Fuller, L. 282
further education colleges 215,
  216, 252, 259, 262, 276

Gall, G. 10, 184, 269, 271
Gallie, D. 57, 59, 239, 258, 260
Gamble, Andrew 86
gangmasters 62
Gap 74
Garnier, Jean-Pierre 220
Garrahan, P. 242
gas industry 25, 133
GCHQ (Government
  Communications
  Headquarters) 87
gender 131
  disadvantage 119, 120, 135
  discrimination 164

divisions 118
equality 122, 136
inequality 135
pay gap 119, 120, 128
General Motors 64
general secretaries 110
general strikes 26, 272
Gennard, J. 162
Germany 63, 67, 91, 93, 96
  eastern 64
  engineering unions 228
  industry-by-industry collective
    bargaining 221
  MNCs operating in Britain 68,
    69, 70
  works councils 183
Giddens, Anthony 89
girls 196
Glasgow 42, 260
Glaxo-SmithKline 220
global dominance effect 67–8
global integration effect 68, 69
global markets 240
globalization 61–71, 89, 271
  neo-liberal economic
    restructuring associated with
    255
Glover, I. 118
GMB Union 105, 201
go-slows 280
goals:
  assumption that employers and
    employees share 8
  common 9, 168
  HRM policy 154
  managerially-determined 212
  policy 35
  secured by collective bargaining
    9–10
  strategic 214
  unions characterized by conflict
    over 107
Goldstein, J. 108
Gold, M. 53
Gollan, P. 186
Goodman, J. 247, 292
Goodrich, C. 5
Gospel, H. 21, 23, 185, 209
Goss, D. 165, 166, 232
Gouldner, Alvin 245
Gourlay, S. 162, 163
GPMU (Graphical Paper and Media
  Union) 152, 201
Gramsci, Antonio 31
Gratton, L. 158, 237
Gray, A. 223

Gray, J. 62
Green, F. 228, 229, 258
Green Parties 105, 272
Greene, A.-M. 122, 124, 125, 135
greenfield sites 212
Greenock 163
grievances 159, 167, 185, 268,
    288, 294
  expressing 280
  individual, take on a collective
    dimension 277
  numerous, source of 276
  one of the few ways of
    expressing 285
  resolution of 287
  vast range of 278
Griffin, J. 268
Grimshaw, D. 68, 75, 218
Gross Domestic Product 96
gross misconduct 245
group-based team briefings 159
Growth and Stability Pact (1996) 96
GSP (Generalized System of
    Preferences) regimes 77
Guardian, The 62, 125, 220, 283
Guatemala 73, 77
Guest, D. 154, 155, 193, 237
Gunnigle, P. 212

hairdressing 221
Hakim, C. 119
Hall, M. 87, 88, 94, 184, 185, 187,
    188, 254
Hall, P. 63
harassment 293
  sexual 245
'hard' HRM 156, 157
Harris, L. 171, 283
Harrison, E. 147
Hart, David 85
Hayek, Friedrich von 86
HCAs (healthcare assistants) 218
Head, J. 9
health 254
  damaged 259
  psychological 256
health and safety 35, 73, 94, 185,
    231, 232
health services 56, 216, 293
Healy, G. 122
Heath, Edward 84
Heery, E. 107, 138, 200, 202, 212,
    213, 256
Heinz 67
Held, D. 62, 65
Hendy, J. 274

Herod, A. 11
Hewitt, Patricia 66
Hewlett-Packard 160-1, 172, 239
Heyes, J. 223, 231, 284
high-tech industries 149
Hill, S. 241
Hirst, P. 62
HM Treasury 133, 215, 261
Hobsbawm, E. 26
Hochschild, A. 170
Hoggett, P. 261
holiday entitlement 117, 228
homeworkers 54, 55
Honda 152
Honduras 73
horizontal segregation 119
hospital trusts 261, 277
hospitality industry 52, 133, 221,
    225, 276, 282
  NMW and 224
  sabotage 283
  turnover levels 285
host-country effect 68-70
hotel industry, *see* hospitality
    industry
hours of work:
  children 31, 228, 231
  excessive 122, 123, 134, 233
  flexible 133
  long 71
  minimum hours off 259
  nineteenth-century laws
    restricting 31
  proposals to increase 26
  teaching 216
  unsocial 284
  women 31, 122, 123, 228, 229,
    231
House of Commons Employment
    Committee (1994) 8-9
Howard, John 291
HRM (human resource
    management) 244, 249
  effective, pursuit of 214
  emergence of 11
  employment relations and
    154-62
  implications of managerial
    interventions 237
  major best practice
    interventions 240
  rise of 170
  sophisticated approaches 9,
    162-5, 167, 169, 238
  work intensification in airline
    industry and 259

HSBC (Hong Kong and Shanghai
    Banking Corporation) 66, 220
  mass occupation of branch 277
Hudson, M. 241, 252, 260
human rights 76
Human Rights Watch 32
Hungary 100
Hyman, J. 133
Hyman, R. 5, 8, 20, 24, 25, 31, 35,
    36, 89, 96, 99, 101, 109, 110,
    131, 183, 188, 196, 268, 279

IBM 64, 74, 163, 164, 169
ICFTU (International
    Confederation of Free Trade
    Unions) 32, 73
ideology 6
  anti-union 73, 86
  complementary 33
  conservative 10
  labourism as 102
  neo-liberal 86, 87
  political opportunism and 86
ill-health 283, 284
illicit activities 281
ILO (International Labour
    Organization) 74-5, 274
imbalance of power 5, 23, 30
  helping to ameliorate, between
    capital and labour 31
IMF (International Monetary
    Fund) 36, 63
immigrants 136, 199-200
immunities 273
incentive-based payment systems
    211
incentives 230
  effort reduction 21
  location 72
  MNC 65
income 4
  additional, needed 233
  negative impact on 231
  working-class 63
incomes policies 35
  development of 34, 36
  imposition of 36
  voluntary 34
'incorporation' process 216
independence 53
India 66
individualism:
  emphasis on 163
  espoused belief in 208
  market 33
  rise of 180

individualization:
  pay 214
  substantive 164
Indonesia 71, 74, 79, 221
industrial action/disputes 28
  bitter 149, 216
  Conservative government
    shaken by 216–17
  damaging 184
  disruptive 150
  effective form of 284
  high-profile 273
  key 216
  legislation restricting 84, 86
  major error contributing to 20
  national recognition agreements
    secured as a result of 38
  small-scale, often short 40
  successfully used to reduce the
    working week 228
  wave of (1978–79) 36
  see also strikes
industrial conflict 10
  extent and dimensions of 271
  forms of 279–86
  help to stifle 291
  high level of 20
  institutionalized 38
  major, across Europe 96
  managers could effectively
    contain 27
  means of defusing 44
  non-strike manifestations of
    278
  understanding 277, 278
industrial relations 289
  cooperative 190
  promoting the improvement
    of 290
  sophisticated system of 163
  state modernization of 230
  undermining 212
industrial tribunals 293–5
  see also employment tribunals
industrial unrest:
  considerable 271
  growing 43
  major 25
  significant instances of 8
  sustained 34
  widespread 272
industrialization 20, 227
  sustained and rapid 24
inequality 116–20, 126, 138
  gender 118, 131, 135
  pay 72, 91, 93, 219–26

reducing 121
  structural causes of 129
inflation 224
  concern to reduce 84
  higher 86
  means of reducing 35
  restrictive policy regime to
    prevent 96
informality 167
information and consultation
  arrangements 184, 185, 191
information flows:
  informal 70
  managers to employees 239
information technology 55
  developments in 260
  improvements in 66, 72
  innovations in 61
  widespread use of 56
injuries at work 284
Inland Revenue 213
innovation 56, 69, 70, 241
  conditions for 172
  high-profile instances of 214
  information technology 61
  institutional 93
  management-inspired 214
  managerial 20–3
  marked absence of 231
  opportunities opened up for 161
  particularly evident in large
    MNCs 133
  relevant 240
  stifled 230
  technological 56, 261
  twentieth-century history of 67
insecurity 74
  redundancy and 250–7
Institute of Directors 220
institutionalization:
  absence 283
  industrial conflict 287
  tipping 171
intensification of work 257–62
interest groups 30, 103
  supranational 97
interim labour injunctions 273
internal market 93
international labour standards
    71–81
internationalization 64
internet 55, 56
interventionist approach 21
intimidation 74, 164
investment 64, 72
  inward 65

  MNC decisions about 65
  popular locations 71
  price to be paid for attracting 73
  see also FDI
involvement 158, 159
  see also employee involvement
Ireland 212, 219
  statutory minimum wage 221
iron 52, 201
ISTC (Iron and Steel Trades
    Confederation) 201
Italy 91, 96
  general strikes 272

Jackson, Ken 106, 111
Jacobi, O. 183
Japan 69, 239, 247, 277, 290
Jarrow 26
JCCs (joint consultation
    committees) 43
jealousies 213
Jefferys, S. 230
Jewson, N. 55, 124
JIB (Joint Industry Board) 209
JICs (Joint Industry Councils)
    38–9, 43
job creation 294
job cuts 259
job evaluation techniques 22
job insecurity 59, 254–6
job losses 72, 220
  avoiding 68
  consequences for livelihoods 256
  cooperation essential to prevent
    271
  customer services 66
  financial payments to
    compensate for 250
  manufacturing 86, 181
  prospect of 256
  significant numbers of 252
  threat of 250
job opportunities 71, 73, 230
  absence of 53
  advertising 118
  few(er) 75, 118
job protection 62, 63
job regulation 6, 8
  study of institutions of 9
job satisfaction 241, 243
  low 164
job security 251, 255
  damage to 272
  greater 116
  guaranteed 159
  threats to 187

job-sharing arrangements 122, 133
job tenure 255, 256
job titles 260
joint proceeds 284
joint regulation 7, 11, 38
  contains conflict 10
  employers' associations role in 19
  undermining 212
Jones, Jack 102
Jordan, B. 30, 31
Joseph Rowntree Foundation 258
JPCs (joint production committees) 43
judicial interference 34
'juridification' 35
'Justice for Janitors' campaign 199, 200, 277

Kampfner, J. 105
Kay, J. 90
Keller, B. 99, 183
Kelly, J. 31, 36, 138, 196, 277
Kenya 73
Kessler, I. 212, 214
Kessler, S. 219, 290
key markets 72
Keynesian methods 84, 89, 90
Kirton, G. 122, 124, 125, 135, 140
Klein, Naomi 72, 73–4
'knocking' practice 284
knowledge workers 52
  occupational change and rise of 54–7
Kodak 67
Korczynski, M. 242
Kuhn, J. 37
Kwik Fit 152

Labor government (New Zealand) 90
labour:
  capital and 30, 31, 52, 60, 72, 271
  changing pattern of use 53
  compulsory 75
  cross-border mobility 91
  decision to shed 252
  demand for 72
  dissatisfaction with conditions of 285
  dual function of 172
  forced 75
  interests of 31
  international standards 71–81
  managed more efficiently 52, 60
  manual 55, 56
  maximum return possible for 5
  migrant 62
  non-standard 57
  paternalist approaches to management of 248
  sexual, potentially exploitative 171
  special nature as a commodity 4
  state must react to concerns of 32
  see also cheap labour; child labour; also under following headings prefixed 'labour'
labour costs 63, 65, 71
  cuts in 172, 251
  helping to keep down 171
  lower 93
  need to keep under control 172
  presence of trade unions increases 75
  substantially reduced 72
labour force:
  female participation in 119
  traditional, size of 57
  young, turnover among 285
labour-intensive activities 261
labour laws 65, 76
  exemption from 72
  interpreted in ways that benefited employers 33
  systematic violation of 73
  transgressed 78
labour market 167
  action programmes to improve position of women 131
  assumption about 56
  changes in 219
  conditions 166
  disadvantaged position in 199
  external 8
  flexible 57–60, 88
  necessary precondition for 86
  notable feature of 59
  rough end of 198
  significantly damaging prospects 222
  support for reforms 89
  tight/tightening 20, 224
  weakening of institutions of regulation 221
  younger entrants to 53
  see also deregulated labour markets
Labour party/government (UK) 34, 35, 84, 91
  Age Diversity in Employment (1999) 118
  attempt to challenge links between unions and 85
  concessions on WTR 232, 233
  desirability of building partnerships 195
  desirability of reconciling work and family life 127
  employer-led efforts in promoting equality at work 132
  employment relations and 87–90
  flexible working and 57
  general election manifesto (1992) 222
  landslide victory (1997) 104
  most radical and far-reaching reform of employment rights 219
  neo-liberal policy approach favoured by 94
  opposition to proposed EU directive 187
  opt-out from EU social chapter reversed by 188
  pre-hearing review process 294
  public policy, equality and 129–32
  self-regulation encouraged by 220
  strong advocate of partnership approach 192
  trade unions and 101–6, 151, 179, 180, 182, 273, 274, 275, 276
  transfer of jobs to India 66
labour power:
  latent 4, 14, 51, 227
  potential 4, 257
labour rights:
  abuses 73, 74
  violation of 32
labour supply 20
  economy-wide, improving 251
labour unrest, see industrial unrest
labour utilization 258
  efficient 21
  more effective 155
  perceived under-utilization 21
  strategic approach to 58

labourism:
  politics of 101–2, 106
  return to the tradition of 103
laissez-faire 33
Lancashire cotton industry 24,
  107
language barriers 189
Lansbury, R. 291
large-scale enterprises 6, 28
Lashley, C. 242
Latin America 200
Lawrence, Stephen 130
lay-offs 254
Leadbeater, C. 55
Leading Edge organizations 158,
  239
learning:
  classroom-based 200
  opportunities 195
Ledwith, S. 140, 141
Leeds 59
left-wing politics:
  challenges 102, 104
  electoral competition between
    right-wing and 109
  governments 89, 90
Legal and General 190
Legge, K. 156, 159, 161
Leidner, R. 285
leisure 52
Leopold, J. 103
lesbians and gays 118, 139, 141
Lewis, P. 251
Lewis, R. 290
Lewis, S. 134
Li Qi 272
liberal approach 139
liberal market approach 67
liberal-pluralist approaches 30,
  109, 111
  two fundamental problems with
    31
liberalization 63, 77
Liff, S. 123, 124, 125
LIFO ('last-in, first-out') criterion
  250
Lipton, Sir Thomas 196, 197
living standards 71
  improvements in 81
  maintained 28
  policies that challenge 272
  potential to increase/raise 74, 76
  protecting 78
  relative decline in 36
  worldwide improvements in 79
Lloyd, C. 185, 186

Lloyds TSB 66, 133
Loach, Ken 199
local authorities 39, 59, 255
  removal of colleges from control
    of 288
  single-employer bargaining
    restricted to small number of
    40
location decisions 72
London 26, 196
  Covent Garden 201
  Docklands 197
  weighting allowances 280
  see also TELCO
London Metropolitan University
  280
lone parents 129, 131
long-term employment 255
Lord, A. 123
Los Angeles 199
low pay 39, 55, 89, 135, 171,
  219–26
  public attention drawn to 277
loyalty 9, 169, 172
LPC (Low Pay Commission) 222,
  223
Lucas, R. 9, 221
Ludlum, S. 11, 104
Lupton, T. 281

Maastricht Treaty (1993) 94, 95,
  96, 98
McBride, A. 140, 142
McDonalds 65, 153, 189, 282
Machin, S. 219, 220
'macho management' approach
  149
McIlroy, J. 87, 103, 104, 108, 110,
  274
McIntosh, I. 281
McIvor, A. 23
McKay, S. 130, 184
McKee, L. 132
McKersie, R. 287
Maclean, C. 132
McLoughlin, I. 162, 163
Macpherson inquiry (1999) 130
magazine publishing 149
mainstreaming 131
Major, John 231
'making-out' process 281
Malaysia 66
'management by stress' 242
management style 168, 169
  authoritarian 243
  ethnocentric 67

  non-union firms 169–70
  open 163
  typologies of 170–2
management techniques:
  associated with NPM 261
  new 109, 261
  scientific 20, 26
  sophisticated, progressive 158
managerial authority 166
  unilateral exercise of 276
managerial control 20, 21, 186
  attempt to introduce more
    sophisticated and rigorous
    systems of 26
  augmenting 212
  discipline used as a means of
    attempting to enforce 249
  enhanced 261
  extent of 6, 38, 54, 56
  limits of 167
  means of extending 242
  opportunities to challenge 170
  posing little challenge to 284
  significant 184
  stricter imposition of 242
  tighter 243
  tipping as a source of 171
managerial decision-making 184,
  186, 188
  no opportunity to challenge
    189
  trade unions role in influencing
    7
managerial 'flying squads' 153
managerial function 6, 157
managerial initiative 21, 42
managerial power 188–9
managerial prerogative 6, 19, 27,
  45
  combination of collective
    bargaining and 33
  employers found it hard to
    maintain 20
  enhancing 150, 195, 212
  exercise of 24, 41, 244, 290
  extended 245
  limits to 168, 170
  redundancy process 251, 254
  rendered legitimate 8
  scope of 170, 173, 174
  small firms 167
  strengthening of 253, 274
  sustaining 170
  upholding 9, 18, 240, 243
managerial relations 4
managerial weakness 20

Manchester (Trafford Park) 197
Mandelson, Peter 103
Manila 74
Manning, A. 224
manual workers 55, 56–7, 119, 230
  holiday entitlement 117
  means of keeping ahead of 28
  skilled 252
  status divide between
    non-manual and 116
manufacturing industry 27
  agro-chemicals and dyestuffs
    284
  car components 193, 274
  computer-controlled machinery
    in 55
  erosion of 52
  export-oriented 272
  global sourcing strategies 73
  growth of 26
  importance of finance-based
    forms of control 172
  job losses in 86, 181
  low-cost locations 71–2
  male-dominated 137, 180
  popularity of overtime bans 280
  sabotage sometimes thought to
    be specific to 282
  single-employer bargaining
    common in 40
maquiladora sector 72, 78
Marchington, M. 22, 41, 43, 44–5,
  147, 238, 241
Marco Aledo, M. 282
'Margam Way' 193
Marginson, P. 97, 188
market economies 172
  capitalist 272
  competitive, desirability of 89
  coordinated 63, 67
  liberal 63, 67
  managing employment relations
    in 172–3
market forces 84, 86, 89
  job insecurity and 256
market integration 91, 92
  impetus for 95
  means of facilitating 96
  pressures of 99–100
  vehicle for promotion of 94
market testing 256
Marks, A. 194, 195
Marks and Spencer 76, 164, 169
Marlow, S. 166, 167
Mars, G. 281
Marsh, D. 103

Martin, A. 93, 94, 96
Martin, G. 68
Martin, R. 108, 111
Marx, Karl 2, 31
Marxism 10, 31, 36
Mason, D. 124
Massachusetts 153
'master and servant' legislation 33
maternity leave 88, 127, 129
  extended provision 130
Mauthner, N. 132
Mazda 72
media industry 97
mediation 289, 292
mergers and acquisitions 64
Merseyside 254
Mexico 64, 72, 78, 199
MFGB (Miners' Federation of
  Great Britain) 25
Michels, Robert 110
Michigan 64
Microsoft 64
Midlands (West/East) 166, 167
midwives 216
migration:
  black workers 136
  globalization and 62
Miliband, R. 36
militancy 18, 43, 111
  contained 23, 38, 44
  growing 21
  moderating 44
  mutual concern to purge 209
military-style management 74
milk distribution 54
Millward, M. 185
Milton Keynes 152
'Ministeel' 169
Minneapolis 153
Mitterrand, François 230
MNCs (multinational companies)
  61–81, 94, 95, 116
  ability to redirect investment 93
  anti-union tactics adopted by
    154
  cross-border arrangements for
    employee information and
    consultation in 184
  enhanced scope enjoyed by 100
  inherently precarious nature of
    jobs 74
  innovation particularly evident
    in 133
  institution whose policies are
    favourable to 94
  Japanese 290

opportunities to dilute the
  scope of EWCs 189
mobilization theory 275–8
'model employer' tradition 39
modernization 192
  obstacles to 20
  state 230
money supply 26, 84
Moody, K. 63, 64, 72, 79
morale 256
  fiddles help to sustain 282
  low(er) 172, 261
  potential to erode 213
Morecambe Bay 62
Morris, Bill 275
Moss, B. 100
MSFU (Manufacturing, Science
  and Finance Union) 139–40,
  192, 201
Mugabe, Robert 32
Mukherjee, N. 122
Müller-Jentsch, W. 183
multi-employer bargaining 19,
  20, 39, 65, 214
  almost complete disappearance
    of 208
  declining incidence of 22
  dwindling importance 210
  eschewed 67
  influence eroded 40
  national 209, 218
  public sector 215–18
multinationals, *see* MNCs
Mumford, K. 290
Munro, A. 138, 179
murder 32, 130
Murdoch, Rupert 149
'mutual gains enterprise' 192, 193

NAALC (North American
  Agreement on Labor
  Cooperation) 78
NAFTA (North American Free
  Trade Agreement) 77, 78
nation-states 62, 100
  economic capacities of 92
  extent to which they can
    regulate their own economies
    and labour markets 89
  liberalization of trade relations
    between 63
  uniformity in employment
    relations systems across 63
National Administrative
  Offices 78
national agreements 210

'national business system'
    concept 67
national differences of interest
    189
National Federation of Women
    Workers 135
National Group on
    Homeworking 55
National Insurance
    contributions 54
national newspapers 212
National Policy Forum 104
NatWest 188
NCB (National Coal Board) 85
NEC (National Executive
    Committee) 104
NEDC (National Economic
    Development Council) 34–5
negotiations 5, 19, 246, 257, 287–8
    centralized 18
    end-product of 30
neo-corporatism 35
neo-liberalism 31, 63, 64, 84–7, 89,
    94, 255, 256
    assault on trade unionism 181
    countries sympathetic to 100
    employment relations and 90
    implementation of policies 271
Netherlands 96, 229
new economy 52–61
new industries 26
New Labour 104
new right 31, 86, 89
new technology 55, 56, 219
    minimum wage appears to have
        caused firms to invest in 225
New Zealand 90, 198–9
News International 149
newspaper publishing 273
NHS (UK National Health Service)
    39, 122, 192, 195, 214, 218
    ancillary staff 179
    creation of trust hospitals (1991)
        215
NIDL (New International Division
    of Labour) 71, 72
Nike 74, 76, 77
Nippon CTV 247, 277
Nissan 69, 150
NMW (UK National Minimum
    Wage) 55, 88, 129, 179
    failure of employers to pay 293
    failure to comply with 184
    pay inequality, low pay and
        219–26
Nolan, J. 262

Nolan, P. 56, 57, 58
non-compliance 73
    sanctions for 4
non-manual labour 28, 116
non-standard workers 57, 58, 255
non-union firms 191, 239–40,
    245, 247, 276
    employee representation
        183–90
    management style 169–70
    sophisticated HRM and 162–5
Noon, M. 281, 282
norms:
    absence 283
    established, erosion of 60
    international labour 88
    masculine 136
North Wales 275
Norwich Union 66
NOTA ('Not on the Agenda') group
    109
Nottinghamshire 85
NPM (new public management)
    157, 261
NUM (National Union of
    Mineworkers) 85
nurses 216–17, 218, 261
NUT (National Union of Teachers)
    39

objectives 22, 155, 156, 158
    company, employees well
        informed about 239
    HRM 214
    managerial 282, 286
    realization of 172, 184
    shared 9
obligations 4, 75
    contractual enforcing 3
    international 274
    likely 4
    reciprocal 54
    statutory 6
occupational change 54–7, 117
O'Connell Davison, J. 54
OECD (Organization for Economic
    Cooperation and
    Development) 221
offences 244, 245
office cleaning industry 199
off-the-job training 159
Ogbonna, E. 171, 283
oil industry 21, 23, 133, 149, 172
older workers 118
    redundant 252, 254
O'Leary, B. 31, 36

oligarchy 110
Oliver, N. 69
opportunism 86, 281
Opportunity 2000 (Opportunity
    Now) 122
organizational decision-making
    192
    influence over 193, 194, 279
Organizing Works initiative 201
Ortega, B. 153
output 211, 229
    short-term improvements in
        262
over-capacity problems 259
overseas companies 64
overtime 229, 231, 233, 262
    bans on 279, 280
    excessive 21
    lucrative opportunities 284
    rewarded with doughnut and
        pen 74
    systematic 230
    unpaid 231
    voluntary, refusal to undertake
        280
Oxenbridge, S. 194, 199
Oxfam 76, 79
Oxfam study/report (2004) 55, 73

Panasonic 188, 189
parental leave 129–30
Parker, P. 22
part-time jobs 52, 57, 200
    agency workers 252
    comparisons with full-time
        workers 130
    high number of 228
    poorly remunerated 119
    rights of workers 98
    rise in number of 180
    women the overwhelming
        majority holding 58, 229
participation 17, 184, 188
    cycles of 44
    extensive 69
    involvement and 41–5, 238–44
    proposals to enhance 93
    under-represented groups 140
    women in trade unions 136
partnership agreements 169,
    190–6
'passive acquiescence' 166
paternalism 166
paternity leave 88, 130
pay determination 208–19
pay freeze 186

pay review bodies 216, 217
Payne, J. 195
Peccei, R. 193
Peck, J. 11
peer pressure 242
penalties 245, 249
  financial 254
pension contributions 54
performance:
  boosting 192
  building 156
  concern about 259
  criteria for measuring 125
  desire to improve 184
  detailed comparisons of
    subsidiaries 68
  detrimental effect on 20
  directors' pay-offs should be
    based on 220
  disputes detrimental to 40
  enhanced pressures 261
  expectations about standards
    of 4
  financial 158, 160, 172
  HRM and 158–61
  improvements in 18, 160, 21,
    238, 240, 256, 262
  individual targets 213
  monitoring 260
  pay systems linked to 155
  points awards based on 253
  relationship between work,
    commitment and 9
  short-term 124, 158
  standards of 242
  targets used intensively in
    public sector 261
  tighter managerial control of
    243
  undermined 208
  worst of any rich state 90
performance-based approaches
  208
  see also PRP
performance management systems
  260
personality tests 159
personnel management 157
  historical weakness of 20
personnel policies 22
personnel techniques 172
PFI (Private Finance Initiative) 105
pharmaceutical companies 212,
  220
Philippines 73
physical force 30

pickets 85, 275, 277
piece-rates 281
Pierson, C. 30, 31, 36
Piore, M. 55
Pirelli 241
pit closure 85
Pizza Express 184, 185
Plaid Cymru 105
pluralist approach 168
pluralist frame of reference 8, 9,
    10, 11, 20, 21, 27
POA (Prison Officers' Association)
    289
Poland 100
Polanyi, K. 4
police forces 25, 127
  military-style tactics 85
politics 72, 83–114
Poole, M. 43
Portsmouth 72
Portugal 188, 221
post-Fordism 55
'post-industrialism' 54
Post Office 119
poverty 74
  women entrenched in 73
power relations 68
power struggle 288
Poynter, G. 56, 260
premium payments 21
pressure groups 128
Price, R. 28, 30, 116, 117
printing industry 22, 38, 97, 201,
    214
prison sentences 32
prison service, *see* POA
private property interests 33
privatization 63, 90, 212, 271
problem-solving experience 241
Proctor and Gamble 72
Prodi, Romano 272
product market environment 167
production:
  cheaper sources of 74
  closely monitored by buyers 73
  craft 24
  efficient 171
  excessive hourly targets 73
  high-quality goods and services
    240
  large-scale enterprises 24
  mass 26–7, 55, 67
  new and more intensive
    techniques 24
  ownership of, and control over 10
  peer pressure to fulfil quotas 242

reason used for suspending 254
re-locating 64
stopped by strikes 272
wartime 43
productivity 68, 160
  attempts to increase 256
  improvements in 76
  means of enhancing 172
  opportunities detrimental to 21
  way of boosting 225
productivity agreements 21–2
professional occupations 56
professionalism 22
profitability 6, 261
  improving 62
  maximized 67
property rights 251, 273
  enforcing 3
proportionality 140
prosperity 71, 75
  potential for 73
protectionism 78
  blatant 77
PRP (performance-related pay)
    211–13, 214, 261
Prudential 66
psychology 9
public expenditure 96
public limited companies 220
public policy 84–7, 90, 127–35
public relations 77
public sector 52
  absenteeism prevalent in 283
  budget limitations/cuts 57, 259
  collective bargaining in 39
  discontent voiced by workers
    in 36
  employers in more than twenty
    countries 92
  employment relations in 19, 40
  implementation of
    Whitleyism 39
  low pay for women 39
  management of employment
    relations 157
  multi-employer bargaining in
    215–18
  new jobs 182
  PRP schemes 212, 213
  race equality 130
  restructuring 56, 215, 256, 261
  temporary staff 60
  wage moderation 96
  white-collar workers 28
  work intensification 258, 260,
    261

publishing industry 53, 201
Puma 76
punctuality 247
punishment 249
fear of/threat of 248
Purcell, J. 150, 168, 169, 212, 240

QMV (qualified majority voting)
93, 94, 98, 187
quality 241
need to prioritize 240
service 260
quality circles 159, 240
initial failure of 239
quality management, *see* TQM
quasi-revolutionary conditions 25
Quintanilla, J. 68
quitting 284–5, 286

Race for Equality 122
Race Relations Act:
(1976) 127
(2000) 130
'race to the bottom' 71–4, 79
racism 136
radical approach 10, 11, 139, 140
Radiven, N. 221
railways 25, 188
dispute 282
platform staff 258
Rainnie, A. 165, 166
Ram, M. 166, 167, 171
Ramsay, H. 44, 194
rationalization 22, 97
initiatives 252, 270
recession 26, 186, 252
reciprocity 3
recruitment 201
and selection 159
redundancy 92, 93, 185, 259
insecurity and 250–7
redundancy payments 35
disputes over 293
Redundancy Payments Act (1965)
251
Reebok 76
re-employment 252, 293
Rees, T. 136
refuse collectors 281
Regini, M. 96
religious belief 130
relocation 66, 72, 282
re-negotiation 246, 257
repression 31, 32, 34, 73, 74, 86
'Respect at Work Zone' 201
restaurants 171, 184, 242

restraint of trade 33
restructuring 22, 28, 97, 123, 156,
251, 276
and closure 194
intense 192
labour market 256
neo-liberal 63, 255
organizational, health service
and local government 178
plant closures and job cuts
associated with 42
public sector 56, 215, 256, 261
retailing 40, 52, 73, 118, 164, 169,
197
codes of conduct 77
ethical 152
multi-employer bargaining
214–15
NMW and 224
retirement 118
reverse diffusion 69–70
reward 214
Rewards for Failure (government
discussion paper 2003) 220
Richards, W. 122
Richardson, M. 192, 252, 260
Rigby, M. 282
right-wing politics 86
critics of tribunal system 295
electoral competition between
left-wing and 109
government 272
risks 53
RMT (Rail Maritime and
Transport) union 105, 106,
249
roadblocks 85
Roberts, G. 227
Robinson, P. 58, 255
Rollinson, D. 167, 247, 249, 277
Rolls-Royce 70
Ross, G. 93, 96
Roy, D. 281
Royal Commission on Trade
Unions and Employers'
Associations (1965–8) 20, 37,
40, 293
Royal Dockyards 39
Royal Mail 109, 169, 269, 276
Royal & SunAlliance 220
Royle, T. 148, 189, 282
Rubery, J. 68, 75, 221, 223, 226
rude customers 283
rules 245–6
breaches of 244, 248
can be interpreted flexibly 249

disciplinary 247
rules-based approach 6, 7
Rutherford, S. 122
Ryanair 152, 259

Sabel, C. 55
sabotage 282–3
relatively minor 285
safety standards 259
see also health and safety
Sainsbury's 188
salaries 220, 276
sales and marketing 56
Salmon, J. 256
Samuel, R. 24
sanctions 4, 77, 244, 245, 246
capacity of employers to impose
274
disciplinary 248, 249
satellite television 152
Scandinavia 220
Scanio, Alfonso Pecorao 272
Scargill, Arthur 85
Schlosser, Eric 153
Scholarios, D. 253
schools 215, 218
schoolteachers 39, 216, 217
effective work-to-rules 280
newly qualified 255
temporary teaching assignments
58
scientific management techniques
20, 26
scientific, professional, and
quasi-professional workers
28, 117
Scotland 68, 105, 163
defence-related firms 253
miners 85
oil and gas industry 133
spirits industry 195
see also Glasgow; Greenock; SSP
Scott, A. 18, 164, 239–40, 243, 245,
246
Scott, W. 279
Scullion, H. 284
SEA (Single European Act 1987)
93, 97
Seattle (WTO meeting 1999) 77,
78, 271
Second World War (1939–45) 39,
43
strikes forbidden 34
trade union membership
during 26
Security Service (MI5) 85

segregation 118, 119, 120, 126, 128, 130
  difficult to break down 136
  helping to reinforce patterns of 135
  long-established patterns of 123
SEIU (Service Employees International Union) 199
self-control 241
self-discipline 248, 249
self-employed people 52, 53–4, 209
  absence of paid holidays and other benefits 59
self-interest 171
semi-skilled workers 25
Sennett, Richard 255
service sector 56, 137, 170
  businesses open for longer periods 231
  employee sabotage in 283
  long-standing jobs 57
  part-time jobs 52, 119
  women in 52, 180
severance payments 251
  enhanced 254
Sex Discrimination Act (1975) 127
sexism 139, 140
sexual orientation 118, 121, 130
Shackleton, J. 294, 295
share options 220
shared interests 9
shareholder value 67, 68, 259
shareholders 261
  ever-faster returns for 255
  maximizing returns to 6
shift patterns 259
shipbuilding industry 26, 38
  decline of 52
shipyard workers 282
shirking 212
shop stewards 42, 178–9, 194–5
  development of structures 30
  engineering industry 40
  growing influence/significance of 22, 26
  role of 22, 27
short-haul routes 259
short-term staff 59
sick pay 25
sickness absence 283
Siemens 68
'Silver Book' agreement 216
Simms, M. 200
Simpson, Derek 106, 111, 219
Singapore 71

'single channel' model 183
single currency 100
Single European Market (1993) 93
single-channel system 185
Sisson, K. 40, 41, 97, 150, 155, 172, 214, 215, 227, 229, 231, 238
skilled workers 24
Slater, G. 56, 58
slogans 272
small- and medium-sized employers 53, 92, 133, 165–7
Smith, V. 282
Smith (W H) 76, 239
Social Action Programme (EEC 1974) 92, 93
social change 180
social chapter (EU) 88, 91, 93–4, 129, 130
  opt-out from 188, 232, 233
social contract 35
social democracy 34, 89
social dialogue 97–8
  weaknesses of 99
social divisions 115–44
social dumping 93
social inclusion 89
social justice 75, 121, 122, 138
social pacts 96
social partners 87–8, 92, 97, 98
  cross-national understandings within and between 99
  reliance on European Commission for support 100
social services 283
Socialist Labour Party 104
socialists 101, 25
  development of political project 10
'soft' HRM 156, 157, 158
software engineers 56
solidarity 228
  collective 28
  impeded 78
Soskice, D. 63
South Korea 72, 76, 79, 271
South Wales 26, 85, 193, 274
  miners 85
  unemployment 52
Southampton 21
Southern California 199
Soviet bloc (former) 61, 100
Spain 64, 68, 221, 282
specialist skills 60
spirits industry 195
sportswear 76

SSP (Scottish Socialist Party) 104, 105
Stagecoach 188
standard of living, see living standards
standardized products 26–7, 68
Stanworth, C. & J. 53
staple industries 52
state intervention 18, 28, 33, 34–6, 290
  avoiding 128
  classic social democracy characterized by emphasis on 89
  designed to repress the trade unions 86
  treated as fundamental threat to liberties 31
state ownership 44
state policy 84–91
state role 30–2
status divide 116–17
statutory minimum wage, see NMW
steelmaking industry 25, 201, 253
  decline of 52
  strike activity 270
Steuer, M. 162
Stewart, P. 242, 252, 260
Stiglitz, J. 63, 74
Stirling, J. 93
Storey, J. 6, 150, 172, 238
Strange, S. 62
stress 258, 259, 261, 262, 294
strikes 26, 73, 135, 150
  and employment relations 268–78
  legislation restricting 86
  major 253
  miners (1984–5) 85
  organizing, without breaching common law 33
  readiness to use 25
  restricted 31
  right to take action 95
  troops as breakers of 34
  undermining 19, 31
structural adjustment programmes 271
sub-contracting arrangements 58, 73
  increased preference for 53
  internal 24
'substitutionist' approaches 152
Suff, R. 193
Summers, J. 133

Sunderland 242
supermarkets 73, 191, 194, 241, 281
supervisory abuses 74
supply-side factors 258
'suppressionist' approaches 152
supranational regulation 99–101
Sussex 70
sweatshop labour 73, 74, 77, 166
Sweden 65, 188
'sweetheart' deals 150
Swindon 152
SWT (South West Trains) 249
SWU (Service Workers' Union) 198–9
systems-based approach 5

Taiwan 71
targets 73, 213, 260
    intensively used in public sector 261
Tarmac 53
task-based participation 240
Taylor, A. 11, 104
Taylor, B. 272
Taylor, P. 118, 194, 260
teaching unions 39
Teague, P. 78, 92, 95, 99
Teamsters union 153
teamworking 109, 159, 240, 261
    benefits of 241
    critical interpretations of 242
    increased use of 155
    viable 243
technical assistance 75
technological change 54, 55, 56
TELCO (The East London Communities' Organization) 277
telecommunications 260
    opening up of markets 99
teleworking arrangements 98
Telford 59
temporary staff 52, 57, 58, 60, 285
    irregularity of earnings 59
terms of employment 7
    previous, do not count 60
    see also conditions of employment
Terry, M. 30, 184, 185, 187, 196
Tesco 76, 169, 191, 192, 194, 215
textiles industry 72, 221, 223
TGI Fridays 242
TGWU (Transport and General Workers' Union) 22, 62, 102, 110, 184, 197

'Link Up' strategy 197
recruitment drive among restaurants 201
strike action 275
Thames Water 210
Thatcher, Margaret 22, 85, 93
third parties 289
'third way' concept 89
Thompson, A. 41
Thompson, G. 62
threats 153
    and intimidation 74
tipping 171
'totting' practice 281
TQM (Total Quality Management) 240–1
Trade Union Act (1984) 103, 111
trade unions 5, 7, 8, 10, 35, 36, 75, 90
    balance of power between employers and 10
    black activists 122
    bodies that represent interests of 92
    campaigns against sweatshop labour 74
    challenging 148–54
    cooperative relationships with 69
    decline of 11, 25–6, 161, 178, 179–82
    desire to challenge collective power of 85
    development of 17, 23–30
    discipline and the victimization of 249
    equality agenda and 135–7
    hostility towards 9, 33, 68, 153, 156, 181, 197, 273
    internal democracy 85
    interventions favourable to 87
    lesbian and gay members 139, 141
    managing with 18–23
    membership and power eroded 52
    moderate 33, 290
    opposition to 67
    organizing 196–202
    partnership approach with 192
    policies to undermine 31, 72–3
    politics of 83
    powerful 220
    powerless 63
    recruitment 159, 197–8, 201
    reduction in influence of 261

    reform of 76, 84
    representation of workers' interests 178–9
    representing diversity in 139–42
    repression of 31, 32, 34, 73, 74, 86
    resisting 9, 10, 68
    right to join/organize in 73, 76
    role threatened 63
    treated as criminal conspiracies 33
    violence towards 32
    weakened 60, 62, 84
    women in 135–42
    see also AEEU; Amicus; Community; CWU; ETUC; FBU; GMB; GPMU; ICFTU; ISTC; MFGB; MSFU; NUM; NUT; POA; RMT; SEIU; SWU; Teamsters; TGWU; TUC; UDM; Unifi; Unison; USDAW; Workers' Union; ZCTU; also under various headings, e.g. closed shop; collective bargaining; industrial action; partnership agreements; shop stewards; union democracy
training 200
    certified 209
    education and 28
    relevant skills 222
    wide-ranging and sophisticated methods 170
transfer of jobs 66
translation services 53, 54
transnational corporations 64
transparency 193, 220
transport industry 25, 99, 273
Treaty of European Union (1993), see Maastricht
Treaty of Rome (1957) 91
tripartism 84, 87
trust 192, 261
    erosion of 294
    lack of 289
Tsogas, G. 77
TUC (Trades Union Congress) 34, 35, 55, 76, 151, 232, 233, 295
    better access to government ministers 87
    increasing influence of 26, 28
    Migrant Workers report (2003) 62
    'New Unionism' project 198
    opposed efforts to combat race-based disadvantage 136

Organizing Academy (1998) 200, 201
Partners for Progress conference (2000) 192
recruitment drives 197
role of 28, 29
Tucker, Greg 249
Turnbull, P. 38, 251, 252, 253
Turner, H. 107, 227
Turner, T. 212
turnover 225
high levels of 284, 285
Tüselmann, H.-J. 70

UDM (Union of Democratic Mineworkers) 85
UEAPME (European Association of Craft, Small and Medium-Sized Enterprises) 92
uncertainty 254, 294
understandings:
cross-national 99
day-to-day 246
informal 7
Undy, R. 86, 87, 111, 273
unelectability 102
unemployment 25, 96, 230, 254, 256
disabled people especially prone to 118
effect on union membership 181
high 52, 53
increasing 86, 181, 182
low 6
mass 26
unfair dismissal 244, 275, 276, 293
average award for 295
protection from 246
UNICE (Union of Industrial and Employers' Confederations of Europe) 92, 97, 98
Unifi (union) 193
uniform-wearing 54, 242
unilateral regulation 25
union democracy 107–12, 140
Unison 105, 138, 140, 142, 195, 277
unitary perspective 8, 9, 10, 11, 21, 155
unitary style 168
United Biscuits 188
United Distillers 192, 194
United States 63, 76, 159
competing more effectively with 92

cooperative management-union relationships 192
diminution of manufacturing employment 282
dominance in global economy 67
effects of minimum wages 222
fast-food industry 285
favourable to neo-liberal policy imperatives 64
growing non-union sector 163
HRM 158
immigrant workers 199–200
major organizations relocated 72
managing diversity approach 124
Organizing Institute 200
retailer codes of conduct 77
union-building approach 198
union-busting approaches 152, 153
see also NAALC; NAFTA
University of Warwick 105
unofficial strikes 268, 269, 273, 274
unpaid leave of absence 249
unscientific management 20
unscrupulous employers 76
unskilled workers 25, 72
unsocial hours 231
Upchurch, M. 192
Upper Clyde Shipbuilders 42
upward communications 239, 240
USDAW (Union of Shop, Distributive and Allied Trades) 191, 197
utilities companies 241, 242

value for money 157
vandalism 282
'vanguard' unions 201
Varul, M. 69, 70
vehicle components 193
verbal warnings 245
vertical segregation 119, 126
victimization 249
violence 32
Virdee, S. 136
Virgin Atlantic 152
voluntarism 290
employment relations and 32–4
eroded 35
voluntary agreements 95, 98, 151, 152, 187

voluntary redundancy programmes 253, 254
vulnerability 255

Waddington, J. 88, 106, 181
wage differentials 224
wage drift 20, 21
wage labour 3
exploitative conditions of 24, 286
obscuring the realities of 57
wage premiums 219
wage restraint 271
opposition to 102
union support for 36
voluntary 35
wage-work bargain 5, 6, 7, 83, 170, 207, 257, 269
actions that alter terms of 254, 281, 282, 284
employers enjoy considerable freedom to juggle terms of 225
wages:
below subsistence 74
downward pressure on 76
flexibility over 63
inflationary increases 10, 20
kept in check 72
living 76
loss of 271
low(er) 21, 63, 66, 71, 76, 282
market relations determine 4
migrant workers 62
minimum 73, 89; see also NMW
moderate demands 25
poverty 74
promise of 4
proposals to cut 26
pushing up to well above NMW rate 224
time lost deducted from 196–7
unfair competition arising from undercutting of 221
unpaid 272
upward pressure on 34
wages councils 221
waiting staff 242
Wales 105, 216, 276
see also North Wales; Plaid Cymru; South Wales
Walker, A. 118
Wal-Mart 73, 153
Walton, R. 287
Walton, Sam 153
war effort 34, 39

Ward, K. 123
warnings 245
'Washington Consensus' 63
Washington state 282
Wass, V. 251, 252, 253
water industry 210
'waves of interest' approach 45
Webb, J. 126
Webb, S. and B. 23, 25
Weber, Max 30
Wedderburn, D. 86
Weiss, L. 95
welfare state dismantling 90
well-being 256, 284
well-qualified professionals 255
Welsh Assembly 104
WERS (Workplace Employment
    Relations Survey 1998) 19,
    121, 159, 160, 165, 167, 210,
    217, 229, 231, 238, 242, 249,
    255, 258
West Germany 91
White, G. 214, 217
white-collar workers 116, 241
    holiday entitlement 117
    rise of unionism 28
Whitley inquiry (1917) 38, 39, 40,
    43
Whitston, C. 246, 248, 258
Whyman, P. 96
wildcat strikes 269
Wilkinson, A. 10, 11, 41, 241
Wilkinson, B. 69
Williams, S. 193, 288
Willman, P. 185
Wills, J. 11, 189, 193, 194
Winchester, D. 215, 218
'winter of discontent' (1978–9) 36,
    102
women:
    disadvantaged 120, 138
    exclusion of 136
    factory jobs 26
    job opportunities 73
    job tenure 255
    labour market
        prospects/position of 88, 131
    largely female workforce 72

low-paid 39, 55, 136, 220
over-representation in
    lower-grade occupations 119
part-time jobs 52, 58
pay equality between men and
    91, 93
professional, large financial
    settlements 295
public sector 39
relatively well-off 122
role of 117
routine jobs 55, 56
service sector jobs 52, 180
trade union activity 135–42
under-representation in
    executive and managerial
    roles 119
working hours 31, 122, 123, 228,
    229, 231
    see also discrimination; gender;
        segregation
Wood, J. 289
Wood, S. 55, 57, 159
'Work and Parents Taskforce' 131
Work Foundation 133
work-ins 42
work-life balance 129, 132–4
work-study techniques 228
work-to-rules 279, 280
workers' rights 32
Workers' Union 196, 197
'workforce agreement' concept
    185
working class 10, 28, 63
    pressure for reform working time
        228
working conditions:
    basic, harmonized 117
    better 73
    collective action to improve 277
    decline in 56
    determination to resist major
        encroachments on 276
    downward pressure on 74, 76
    erosion of 271
    exploitative 55
    fair and just, right to 95
    flexibility over 63

improvements in 74, 79
poor 55, 71, 73, 135, 196,
    277
potentially damaging changes to
    269
resisting managerial challenges
    to 284
sweatshop 73, 74
unpleasant 284
    see also conditions of
        employment
working practices 69, 160, 243
    customary 25
    established, erosion of 60
    family-friendly 195
    new, easing the introduction of
        192
working time 88, 94, 117
    developments in pay and
        207–36
    proposed reductions in 186
    regulation 99
    see also hours of work
workloads, see intensification of
    work
works councils 183
    see also EWCs
workshops 24
world markets 67, 71, 72
Wray, D. 9
Wrench, J. 136
written warnings 245
WTO (World Trade Organization)
    63
    Seattle meeting (1999) 77, 78,
        271
WTR (Working Time Regulations,
    UK 1998) 227, 232–3

Yao Fuxin 32
Yorkshire miners 85
young(er) workers 200
    NMW rates for 222–3
    response to dissatisfaction in
        fast-food industry 285

ZCTU (Zimbabwe Congress of
    Trade Unions) 32